Managing a
Global
Workforce

Managing a Global Workforce

Challenges and Opportunities in International Human Resource Management

Second Edition

Charles M. Vance and **Yongsun Paik**

M.E.Sharpe
Armonk, New York
London, England

Library of Congress Cataloging-in-Publication Data

Vance, Charles, 1952–
Managing a global workforce : challenges and opportunities in international human resource
management / by Charles M. Vance and Yongsun Paik.—2nd ed.
    p. cm.
Includes bibliographical references and index.
ISBN 978–0–7656–2349–2 (pbk. : alk. paper)
    1. International business enterprises—Personnel management. 2. Personnel management.
I. Paik, Yongsun, 1956– II. Title.

HF5549.5.E45V36 2010
658.3—dc22   2010018822

Printed in the United States of America

The paper used in this publication meets the minimum requirements of
American National Standard for Information Sciences
Permanence of Paper for Printed Library Materials,
ANSI Z 39.48-1984.

CW (p)   10   9   8   7   6   5   4   3   2   1

Contents

Preface

As this second edition goes to press we note signs that the global recession triggered by the credit crisis originating in the United States in late 2007 is abating. The integrated world economy driven by globalization has witnessed a sharp contraction in trade, investment, and jobs. Some critics who sarcastically watched this global economic meltdown have popularized a new term, "deglobalization." Contrary to their expectation, however, East Asian economies hit hardest by the recent global recession due to their high dependence on exports have quickly rebounded. Most Latin American economies also are recovering thanks to a gradual increase in commodity prices and the adoption of more prudent and sophisticated monetary and fiscal policies. In the midst of unpredictable world economic fluctuations, organizations are learning two simple yet challenging lessons: globalization is irreversible, and organizations must remain vigilant and ready to adjust to the ever-changing business environment. Indeed, in China and beyond, many business leaders consider the current business environments to be in a state of crisis. But as a Chinese word for crisis (*weiji*) carries with it the double meanings of both "threat" and "opportunity," organizations large and small throughout the world may find that the effective management of their workforce can serve to seize opportunities that will propel them ahead within the globally competitive arena.

In this second edition we have made some significant changes and improvements to reflect recent developments. We have followed helpful feedback from past adopters of our first edition, including relevant considerations in nearly every chapter for managing a global workforce during a serious global economic crisis. Although we are seeing signs of significant economic improvement, we believe this second edition now is more pertinent to a broader range of economic conditions.

The recent global recession has caused a paradigm shift in offshore outsourcing and immigration. MNCs are now deliberately using outsourcing to transform their business processes rather than simply to lower costs. India, the world's number one destination of outsourcing, also is quickly learning to outsource its businesses to other countries. In addition, we discuss the implications of a decline in immigration, both domestic and international, for the global economy. Furthermore, globalization is no longer driven solely by companies in developed countries. MNCs from the important BRIC emerging economies (Brazil, Russia, India, and China) are expanding their influence on the global market through increased trade and foreign direct investment. These new developments mean that the war for talent has intensified. Whether companies conduct business in developing or developed countries, there is a growing scarcity of skilled managers and workers alike. This is exactly why the human resources function (practiced by both managers and human resource professionals) has become ever more important for recruiting, retaining, and developing workers at all levels, as well as a cadre of global managers who can perform their best anywhere, anytime. Within this global context, we note many difficult and vexing workforce-related challenges, such as those faced in Europe driven by pressures for greater economic flexibility. These challenges are forcefully illustrated by recent demonstrations and violence in France in protest against new employment laws that favor business staffing flexibility and promote long-term increased employment at the short-term expense of younger workers. We also have added new opening chapter scenarios and end-of-chapter short case studies. These provide additional opportunities for stimulating class discussions that are pertinent to current chapter topics.

In our many years of teaching executive, graduate, and undergraduate programs and courses related to global workforce issues, we have felt the need to emphasize the critical role of the human resource function in achieving organizational objectives. In addition, we have recognized that managers and leaders have a central responsibility in supporting and implementing this human resource function, with the professional assistance of human resource professionals and specialists. However, we have not been satisfied with existing texts on international human resources that seem directed more at human resource specialists rather than the more generalist managers and senior decision makers in charge of strategy formulation and implementation. Existing texts also focus primarily on the challenges and needs of expatriates of the multinational firm's home country and neglect host country and third country nationals, as if the expatriates were the only members of the global workforce that mattered. In addition, employees involved in a firm's contracted and outsourced work largely have been left out of the picture. We therefore have written this text to provide a more complete and comprehensive picture of the challenges and opportunities that arise in managing an organization's total global workforce. Addressed in this book are not only traditional micro human resource issues such as staffing, compensation, and performance appraisal, but also macro human resource issues such as immigration and offshore outsourcing, which carry important implications for global human resource planning.

We have many people to thank; people who have contributed much to the development of this text, including our past students with whom we have shared the development of new insights related to the continually evolving and expanding arena of international human resource management. We are especially grateful to editor Harry Briggs of M.E. Sharpe, whose ongoing professional guidance, great patience, and encouragement have been essential to the successful completion of this text and second edition. We are particularly indebted to Irene Chow of the Chinese University of Hong Kong, Sully Taylor of Portland State University, and Mark Mendenhall of the

University of Tennessee at Chattanooga for their earlier helpful feedback and guidance on our work. Besides these talented colleagues, our work also has greatly benefited from numerous academics and practitioners in the field throughout the world with whom we have interacted over the years at professional meetings and through other professional communications, and under whose influence we continue to learn.

We also express thanks to our past MBA research assistants, including Alexis Young, Anthony Markovich, and Marcella Perez, who were of great help with literature and manuscript reviews, data collection, and refinement details.

Although we are very pleased with the result of our second edition, we acknowledge our human limitations and possible errors in our attempt to provide a comprehensive, useful picture of current issues and important practices in international human resource management. We also know how quickly this picture can change. We therefore invite those who use this text—students, instructors, and practitioners alike—to give us feedback, whether confirmatory or corrective, and share insights, thus joining with us in a collegial effort to better understand the current and developing challenges and opportunities in managing a global workforce.

Charles M. Vance (cvance@lmu.edu) and
Yongsun Paik (yspaik@lmu.edu)
Los Angeles

Managing a
Global
Workforce

1 Introduction and Overview

ATTRACTING FACTORY WORKERS IN CHINA

Who would guess that there could be a shortage of factory workers in China, the world's most populous country? But after decades of abundant cheap labor willing to put up with long hours and uncomfortable working conditions, the Pearl River Delta—southern China's manufacturing heartland, which produces a large share of the world's shoes, clothing, and electronics—is facing labor shortages estimated at 2 million under the level of demand. Workforces in other regions are also in short supply. As a result, more Chinese manufacturers are paying much closer attention to something they rarely did before: keeping their low-wage workers happy and attracting new ones.

This labor shortage is partly due to the nation's increased prosperity, which is leading to the rapid growth of rival, higher-paying manufacturing facilities in other regions of China, often drawing from the heretofore plentiful labor supply in southern China. To add to the challenge, the government's increase in agricultural subsidies, along with increases in grain sale prices and the cost of living in urban areas, make leaving the urban factory and returning to the farm a more attractive proposition.

The labor shortage in coastal cities is also unexpected, given China's population of more than 1.3 billion, high levels of unemployment, and surplus rural labor officially estimated at 150 million. Some optimistic economists believe that this is a short-term problem that will soon be resolved as rural migrant workers become informed about the rising labor demand. However, others believe that the shortage is more deeply rooted, resulting from rising skill requirements and slower labor force growth due to China's strict population control policies.

To compete for the limited supply of qualified workers, some manufacturers are building facilities with previously unheard of amenities such as swimming pools, dormitories with television access, libraries, gymnasiums, and even churches. Manufacturers that have started locating inland to take advantage of pay scales that are about 40 percent lower than on the coast face much higher start-up costs, particularly in providing attractive facilities to make up for the loss of urban attractions. Apache II

Footwear Ltd., which makes sneakers for Adidas-Salomon AG, relocated to Qingyuan, a town two hours' drive north of Guangzhou and about 300 kilometers northwest of Hong Kong. Qingyuan is known for its scenic mountain views and tasty, free-range chicken. Apache is building a $25 million compound that will include housing for married workers, a church, a school, a mall, and a sports hall. Already workers are using the new kindergarten and a well-stocked supermarket. "It's not just about pay, it's about lifestyle," says Apache Chief Executive Steve Chen. "We're building a community so people will stay."

Ngai Lik Industrial Holdings Limited, also in Qingyuan, is facing problems recruiting workers to work at its plant, which makes CD players for Walmart, despite delights such as a pool table, a fully equipped karaoke room, and dancing on weekends. Hopeful manager Nelson Chiu explains that "nobody knows about this place yet," while a bright red job advertisement banner hangs outside the factory with the words, "JOB OPENINGS FOR GREAT NUMBER OF WOMEN WORKERS."[1]

INTRODUCTION

So much for the image of China as the great source of virtually limitless, readily available cheap labor. At present, the cost of labor in China might be much lower than in economically developed countries, although the gap is rapidly decreasing. Yet the manufacturers from countries who are planning to expand into China are facing ever-changing and increasing challenges in attracting an adequate supply of qualified human resources. But the human resource (HR) challenge in China is certainly not limited to the manufacturing sector. In addition to its manufacturing presence in China, which helps the company deliver the low-cost part of its slogan, "Save money. Live better," Walmart is steadily increasing its store network and piloting a convenience store format. Walmart is being joined by Canada's Metro, Dutch retailer SPAR, French giant Carrefour, and many others. Despite the recent global economic crisis, these companies are spurred on by the easing of the Chinese government's restrictions (for example, joint venture requirements, definitions of what can be sold and where, and so on) and the allure of China's consumer market, the fastest-growing market in the world. With the easing of restrictions, financial service firms are also trying to enter the China market and tap into that country's burgeoning wealth. China's infrastructure development remains a significant opportunity for foreign firms. Multinational construction firms are also landing opportunities, including building malls in China to address increasing consumer spending interests. Alongside China, India has a hopeful future in the global market arena fueled by more supportive government policies and the twin growth engines of manufacturing and services. Yet the critical development of its infrastructure is seriously hobbled by the dearth of skilled workers within its more than 1.1 billion population.[2] All of these areas related to growth and new business development have significant challenges associated with the acquisition, deployment, and management of labor.

For those managers and business decision makers throughout the world who are interested and engaged in doing business beyond their own country's borders, exciting opportunities and significant challenges are arising rapidly with the growing influence of globalization.[3] In fact, as a result of increasing globalization, even those business professionals and companies who wish to remain within their national boundaries and not venture abroad are facing new opportunities and ever more daunting business challenges. The "abroad" is coming to them in droves in the form of foreign competition, foreign technology and other products, foreign suppliers, foreign customers, foreign business partners, and foreign labor (both legal and undocumented). In fact, this foreign labor is increasingly available both in many domestic labor markets and abroad through offshore outsourcing. So whether you go abroad or stay at home, you are in the global marketplace. As Jack Welch, the notable former chief executive officer of General Electric, is often quoted as saying, "Organizations must either globalize or they die."[4]

Critical to the success of all organizations, both for-profit and not-for-profit, in our increasingly global marketplace is the ability to plan for, attract, develop, and retain capable and committed employees, whether this human talent is found at home or abroad.[5] This ability in workforce talent management should not be restricted to those individuals who specialize in human resources, but should be a top priority for every executive, manager, and business professional. Each should see him- or herself as a human resource practitioner (as opposed to a human resource professional or specialist)—dealing with people issues in daily business practice and having a strong interest in attracting and retaining capable and committed employees for the long-term success of the company. As we will examine in this text, components of a successful talent management in organizations worldwide have been found to include (1) workforce analytics and planning; (2) employee role and competency design; (3) employee recruitment, selection, and onboarding (i.e., managing the entry process); (4) talent deployment and redeployment; (5) recognition, rewards, and engagement; (6) performance management; (7) learning and training; (8) individual career mapping; (9) leadership development; and (10) succession planning. And we are not speaking here only of ethical or humanitarian considerations about managing people in the global workplace. Organizations that use these critical talent management practices have outperformed other organizations across four standard financial metrics: return on assets, return on equity, net profit margin, and earnings before interest.[6]

This top priority on human talent is not misplaced or exaggerated: Many studies—domestic and international—continue to identify the human factor within organizations and in strategic alliances as the greatest source of sustainable competitive advantage.[7] People (whether your own or those obtained through outside sources such as a temp agency) are essential for the effective implementation of company plans and strategies—both in carrying out the work and in providing input and feedback on how strategy implementation can best proceed. It also is becoming increasingly apparent with recent developments in knowledge management that employees at all levels and worldwide company locations can provide valuable input on important external opportunities and threats, essential for effective strategy formulation and adjustment.[8] But the challenge of managing human resources effectively to achieve organizational strategic objectives only increases in scope and complexity with the introduction of multiple cultures, differing national practices and regulations, and physical distances involved with global commerce.

GLOBAL MARKET CONTEXT

Company leaders endeavor to manage their organizations within a growing global market context, with rapidly changing social, political, economic, and technological forces. Within this global context, leaders face the need to carry out their work activities through the efforts of their own home country employees as well as their foreign employees, agents, organization partners, and suppliers. As organizational boundaries become more permeable and less distinct with new work relationships and collaborative agreements (such as strategic alliances, international joint ventures, and outsourced services), and with corresponding new, more flexible workforce arrangements (for example, part-time and temporary employees and contracted labor services), the perception of what constitutes an organization's workforce must also be adjusted. Thus, this changing workforce, which is essential for achieving organizational goals and objectives, is becoming more global, diverse, flexible, multisourced, and complex in nature. This world scenario presents vastly different opportunities and demands and increasingly difficult challenges than were even faced at the end of the twentieth century.

With this global context in mind, we must emphasize the importance of balancing attention on the local context in global workforce management, because key factors influencing the effective management of human resources can differ dramatically from one local context to another.[9] Figure 1.1 provides a broad picture of the many different external global and local contextual factors that may influence key internal company factors, which in turn determine global workforce management. Even such broad issues as global efforts to reduce poverty, debilitating national debt, illiteracy, hunger, social conflict and warfare, and sickness are relevant here because they affect the overall context within which multinational corporations (MNCs) may operate and expand. We now examine each of these important external and internal factors, which often interact and are closely interrelated, to gain a clearer picture of the broad context for managing a global workforce.

EXTERNAL FACTORS INFLUENCING GLOBAL WORKFORCE MANAGEMENT

Figure 1.1 indicates several important factors external to a firm that managers should consider as they plan and make decisions affecting their global workforce. These factors may bear greater influence at different times, and some represent more local influences warranting customization whereas others represent much more general and global influences.

Economy

Just as local, national, regional, and global economic strength can greatly influence business activity, economic conditions can greatly affect workforce decisions for carrying out business activity. For example, where an economy is perceived as weak, company growth plans may be put on hold, a hiring freeze instituted, and the use of temporary employees emphasized. Where regions differ in their economic favorability, MNCs shift their business activity focus to gain the greatest benefit for the company,

Figure 1.1 **Factors Influencing Global Workforce Management**

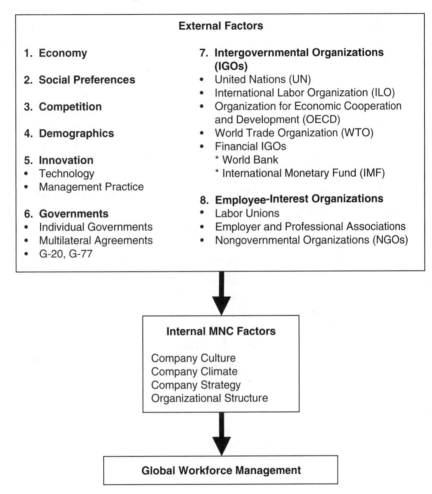

thus placing differing workforce demands in different regions. Exchange rates across the financial markets of the global economy can affect human resource arrangements to a significant degree. For example, when China decided in 2005 to allow its yuan currency to float slightly upward against the U.S. dollar, the average cost for U.S. MNCs of outsourcing to China suddenly increased (from $12.08 to $12.33 per hour).[10] An economic crisis, such as the Asian financial crisis of the mid-1990s, can trigger broadscale workforce downsizing, compensation reductions, and other employee-related cost savings to protect business solvency.[11]

Social Preferences

This factor is made up of the broad set of beliefs, values, norms, customs, attitudes, and expectations held by groups, communities, and societies. Culture, which represents a major consideration of social preferences with a profound, pervasive influence on international business and global workforce management, will be examined in detail in Chapter 2 and referred to throughout this book. Social preferences are also greatly influenced by today's communications technologies, such as the Internet, which increase widespread awareness of new issues, opportunities, and social models, rapidly changing traditional norms and expectations. Social preferences may change over time, such as the growing sentiment in many countries against smoking in public areas, which may in turn influence government action toward new laws and regulations. These preferences also may be influenced by other factors, such as government legislation and court rulings against workplace discrimination, which has resulted in changed public expectations about gender representation in the workplace, especially in Western countries. For example, the current use of the gender-neutral term *flight attendant* rather than the feminine term *stewardess* commonly used in the past was greatly influenced in the United States by a federal court ruling that female gender is not a legitimate or bona fide occupational qualification for effectively providing airline hospitality service. The court made this ruling despite evidence of contrary popular opinion, which in turn led to a shift in social expectations. Globally there also is an increasing movement in corporate social responsibility (CSR)—greater awareness of the need for socially responsible corporate behavior toward the environment, communities hosting MNC operations, and employees associated with MNC business. This increased global awareness, with the resulting pressure to preserve global reputation and public image, in many cases is raising expectations for the standard behavior and reporting that companies must meet to be accepted as viable participants in the global marketplace.[12]

Competition

Global competition to increase market share and profitability by increasing the number of satisfied customers at lower costs is a primary driver of globalization. Companies that are reluctant to compete risk bankruptcy. With greater accessibility to cheaper labor markets, companies are motivated to move their operations, which affects workforce relations and employment in both home country and host country environments. With the support of advancing information and communication technologies, companies are able to gain efficiencies by consolidating and moving, through offshore outsourcing, many operations to less expensive labor markets. A company's human resources also represent a primary source of competitive advantage through such key contributions as workforce innovation and human capability. Companies compete for quality human resources and are able to successfully attract and retain human talent through their workforce management practices.

Demographics

As we will examine in detail in Chapter 3, labor force *demographics,* or general labor characteristics such as age, gender, ethnicity, and skill base, can influence the nature of challenges and practices of workforce management. For example, in many industrialized countries an aging labor force must be replaced to meet work demand, which causes many governments to loosen immigration restrictions and allow more people of different cultures and ethnicities into their labor force, thus introducing new diversity challenges into the workplace. The labor skill base also is a critical area of demographics that MNCs carefully consider when planning for opening operations in other countries. Although a low local wage rate can be an attractive factor in foreign direct investment (FDI) considerations, such an advantage may not compensate for a labor force lacking in basic skills, which will require significant training costs and time to get operations up to an acceptable level.

Innovation

Our world is changing continuously, posing an ongoing challenge for organizations to monitor and anticipate changes and adjust appropriately to survive and compete successfully. Innovations that improve organizational performance often usher in major changes worldwide that affect workforce management. Two particular forms of innovation that we will examine here involve management practice and technological innovation.

Management Practice. Throughout the world, new developments and innovations in management practice, from action-learning training methods to zero-based human resource forecasting, can potentially affect people in the workplace. The sending abroad or "offshoring" of back-office operations, whether in-house or outsourced services, to foreign worksites is a management practice innovation that is especially pertinent to global workforce management. Outsourcing itself represents an important innovation in management practice that allows companies to focus on their core competencies while partnering on-site or on a distance basis with other firms that provide a service that they do best, thus introducing particular challenges in workforce management across company borders. As with any successful adoption of innovation, effective workforce learning and adjustment to change are needed to overcome natural resistance.

Organizations can pick up new ideas and innovations for improving workforce management practice in a number of ways, including attending professional conferences and meetings where information is disseminated formally through professional presentations and informally through networking, and keeping up with professional publications and online newsletters. A first-generation Iranian-American executive who runs a successful packaging business in the United States once commented to us that the primary reason he maintains about 25 percent of his business abroad is to force him to travel to various parts of the world, which exposes him to new ideas that he can adopt to improve his business. It is critical for organizations and managers to use different means to regularly scan their external environment for sources of potentially useful innovations and proven "best practices" of other companies, which, if appropriate, can be adopted and spread company-wide through effective internal knowledge-management processes.

Organizations also can tap into current ideas and innovations in the external environment by engaging consulting organizations to diagnose problems, provide solutions, and help implement programs that have been proven effective in other firms. A wide variety of consulting firms, both large and small, helps disseminate innovations for improving workforce management practice. Some firms, such as Towers Watson, may provide general human resource consulting services, whereas others, such as ORC Worldwide, specialize in workforce compensation at all levels.

Technological Innovation. One of the most visible external factors affecting global workforce management today is technological innovation. When companies adopt a technical innovation—even a simple upgrade in computer software—workforce training is needed. On a much broader scale, we see that technological innovation is bringing greatly increased efficiencies to work processes and reducing the number of workers needed to achieve the same level of productivity. In fact, as will be discussed in Chapter 3, more jobs worldwide have been lost in the manufacturing sector due to technological innovation in work operations than to any other factor. In addition, innovations in the information and communication technologies have facilitated the ability of companies to "offshore" many back-office and call center services.

Governments

Besides their membership in intergovernmental organizations, governments individually and collectively (through bilateral and multilateral agreements and regular meetings) have a central role in regulating economic activity and can exert tremendous influence on workforce management practices. We now examine these individual and collective forms of government influence.

Individual Governments. A key purpose of government is to secure and protect the well-being of its citizens, including their economic livelihood. Thus, governments typically are active forces in facilitating economic health, which leads to increased employment opportunity for the national labor force. In the global marketplace, governments are increasingly active in improving national infrastructures, investing in education and labor force skill development, and negotiating tax arrangements to successfully attract MNCs that provide new jobs through their foreign direct investment. Governments also have a responsibility to monitor labor practices to protect the rights of workers, as well as those seeking employment, and to ensure safe working conditions. This ongoing employee protection and specification of workforce management policy is achieved through the establishment of government agencies, laws, and regulations that prescribe and enforce acceptable company behavior.

Besides compliance to employment laws and regulations, individual governments also may exert less direct forms of influence to encourage responsible workforce management within their borders. Examples include the appointment of a minister for corporate social responsibility within the U.K. Department for Trade and Industry and France's legal requirement for companies to include social and environmental impact in their annual reports. As with social preferences, government employment laws and regulations can differ dramatically from one country to another. For example, the job opening announcement ending the opening scenario of this chapter, "JOB OPENINGS FOR GREAT NUMBER OF WOMEN WORKERS," would be legally prohibited in several developed countries that consider gender an irrelevant factor in most employment decisions. Therefore, managers should review local and national laws and regulations to ensure legality in making workforce management decisions.

Multilateral Agreements. Beyond the influence of a single government, two or more governments commonly form agreements and treaties that serve to promote cross-border commerce and economic development for all governments involved. For example, the North American Free Trade Agreement (NAFTA), the Association of South East Asian Nations (ASEAN) Free Trade Area (AFTA), and Mercado Común del Sur (MERCOSUR), (abbreviation for Southern common market, involving Argentina, Brazil, Uruguay, and Paraguay, as well as other South American countries, as associate members) all represent multilateral agreements that have increased trade across borders with accompanying workforce implications. These treaties and agreements often stipulate workforce standards and requirements that each country must uphold. However, a common criticism of these agreements is that they specify that only present labor laws of each country be upheld and fail to require adherence to the higher standards of the United Nations (UN) or International Labor Organization (ILO).[13]

The most integrated multilateral agreement between governments is the European Union (EU), with an extensive governing and regulatory structure affecting organizations in all EU current and prospective member countries as well as companies doing business within this huge economic bloc. Thus, the EU has a powerful impact on global business practice. The establishment of the EU and its labor mobility provisions has resulted in a major increase in labor migration across national borders, creating much greater challenges in managing diversity than experienced in the past, as well as bringing into developed countries of the EU an increasing supply of highly motivated labor from less-developed economies and generating a downward pressure on local wages. To signal EU priorities and keep focused attention on important social issues associated with business, the European Commission (the driving force and executive branch of the EU) designated 2005 as the year of corporate social responsibility in EU countries.[14]

In light of its continued growth, anticipated future expansion, and lack of previous consolidated policy guidelines, the EU's Charter of Fundamental Rights was solemnly proclaimed in Nice in December 2000. The fifty-four–clause charter sets out in a single text, for the first time in EU history, the whole range of civil, political, economic, and social rights of EU citizens and all persons residing in the EU, as well as a significant set of explicit guidelines affecting workforce and employment practice (see Figure 1.2 for a sampling of workforce-related rights from the EU Charter). These rights are based on the fundamental rights and freedoms recognized by previous EU documents and constitutional traditions of EU member countries, including the Council of Europe's Social Charter and the Community Charter of Fundamental Social Rights of Workers.[15]

Although individual member states continue to carry out specific employment policy

Figure 1.2   **Sample of Worker Protection Guidelines from the European Union's Charter of Fundamental Rights**

- No one shall be held in slavery or servitude.
- No one shall be required to perform forced or compulsory labor.
- Trafficking in human beings is prohibited.
- Everyone has the right to education and to have access to vocational and continuing training.
- Nationals of third countries who are authorized to work in the territories of the Member States are entitled to working conditions equivalent to those of citizens of the Union.
- Any discrimination based on any ground such as sex, race, color, ethnic or social origin, genetic features, language, religion or belief, political or any other opinion, nationality, disability, age, or sexual orientation shall be prohibited.
- Equality between men and women must be ensured in all areas, including employment, work, and pay.
- The Union recognizes and respects the right of persons with disabilities to benefit from measures designed to ensure their independence, social and occupational integration, and participation in the life of the Community.
- Workers and employers have the right to negotiate and conclude collective agreements at the appropriate levels and, in cases of conflicts of interest, to take collective action to defend their interests, including strike action.
- Every worker has the right to protection against unjustified dismissal, in accordance with Community law and national laws and practices.
- Every worker has the right to working conditions that respect his or her health, safety, and dignity.
- Every worker has the right to limitation of maximum working hours, to daily and weekly rest periods, and to an annual period of paid leave.
- The employment of children is prohibited. The minimum age of admission to employment may not be lower than the minimum school-leaving age. Young people admitted to work must have working conditions appropriate to their age and be protected against economic exploitation and any work likely to harm their safety, health, or physical, mental, moral, or social development or to interfere with their education.
- Everyone shall have the right to protection from dismissal for a reason connected with maternity, and the right to paid maternity leave and to parental leave following the birth or adoption of a child.

and can follow their own employment regulations where they satisfy EU guidelines, the EU Charter of Fundamental Rights provides a common focus on employment rights. And although the EU Charter is only a political declaration, it is likely to have legal effects, as the EU's European Court of Justice will take it into account in its decisions. The EU has passed numerous specific directives and regulations for protecting worker rights and well-being that are now centrally reinforced and reconfirmed by the EU Charter of Fundamental Rights. A good illustration of EU influence on changing and improving workforce protective rights was the review of employment policies and practices in Estonia, a country striving to eventually join the EU (achieved in 2004) after complying with EU requirements. In an EU report that reviewed Estonian social policy progress toward future EU accession, the EU called on Estonia to increase the unemployment benefit, to extend the right to strike to the public sector, and to put an end to the potential exploitation of children by family firms.[16]

The G-20, G-77. Besides forming long-term agreements and treaties involving cross-border commerce, governments meet regularly on an informal basis to discuss common pressing issues that can have major implications for global workforce management. The Group of Twenty (G-20) Finance Ministers and Central Bank Governors was

Figure 1.3 **Country Members of the Group of 20 (Represented by Finance Ministers and Central Bank Governors)**

- Argentina
- Australia
- Brazil
- Canada
- China
- France
- Germany
- India
- Indonesia
- Italy
- Japan
- Mexico
- Russia
- Saudi Arabia
- South Africa
- South Korea
- Turkey
- United Kingdom
- USA
- European Union

established in 1999 to bring together important industrialized and developing economies to discuss key issues in the global economy. It eclipsed the global stature of the Group of 7 (G-7) leading industrialized national governments with the realization in the recent global economic crisis that a much broader representation of developed and emerging markets was needed to effectively steer the world economy.[17] To facilitate G-20 cooperation, the managing director of the International Monetary Fund (IMF) and the president of the World Bank and their assistants also participate in G-20 meetings on an ex-officio basis. The G-20 therefore convenes important industrial and emerging-market countries from all regions of the world (refer to G-20 members in Figure 1.3). Altogether, G-20 countries (including the EU as the twentieth member) represent about 90 percent of global gross national product and 80 percent of world trade, as well as two-thirds of the world's population.

There is also growing solidarity among countries represented on the poorer end of the economic spectrum, as evidenced by regular meetings of the Group of 77. Established in 1964 by seventy-seven developing countries at the end of the first session of the United Nations Conference on Trade and Development in Geneva, the membership of the G-77 has increased to 130 countries. However, the original name has been retained because of its historic significance. As the largest coalition of developing countries in the UN, the G-77 provides the means for the developing world to articulate and promote its collective economic interests, foster economic and technical cooperation among developing countries, and enhance its joint negotiating capacity on major international economic issues. For example, a major concern among developing countries is the growth of increasing labor and environmental restrictions and standards affecting foreign direct investment, which they identify as greatly slowing and decreasing the amount of country investment that would help build the economy and provide much-needed jobs.

Intergovernmental Organizations

Beyond governmental meetings and agreements, much more in-depth, ongoing transnational governmental and administrative activities and supportive structures are provided by the formation of intergovernmental organizations. An intergovernmental organization, or IGO, is an institution made up of the governments of member states that have joined together to cooperate on common goals. An IGO usually has a formal, permanent structure with various organs to accomplish its tasks.

United Nations. The UN, with its 192 general assembly members, is the largest, most comprehensive IGO and global forum in the external environment of global workforce management. A multitude of agencies and initiatives of the UN carry out its global priorities of peace and security, economic and social development, human rights, humanitarian affairs, and international law. In addition to the workings of its agency specifically dedicated to international labor issues (the ILO), the UN has a high-profile influence on global workforce management through its Global Compact, officially launched in 2000. The UN Global Compact is a list of ten universal principles in the areas of human rights, labor, the environment, and anticorruption (refer to Figure 1.4). The Global Compact is completely voluntary and does not monitor, enforce, or measure the behavior or actions of companies relative to the compact. Rather, the Global Compact relies on a joint effort involving public accountability and transparency, companies with enlightened corporate social responsibility, labor representatives, and nonprofit citizen organizations (for example, nongovernmental organizations, or NGOs) to promote adoption of the principles upon which the compact is based. To facilitate the global acceptance and utilization of these principles, the administrative function of the Global Compact offers policy dialogue meetings, training, country/regional support networks, and sponsored implementation and test projects.[18]

International Labor Organization (ILO). With a primary focus on the global labor force, the ILO is the specialized agency of the UN that seeks the promotion of social justice and internationally recognized human and labor rights. The ILO was founded in 1919 at the end of World War I through the tripartite participation of governments, employers, and employee unions during the initial planning of the ill-fated League of Nations. It became the first specialized agency of the UN in 1946. The ILO formulates and monitors international standards in basic labor rights across a broad spectrum for its 178 member countries. Within the UN system, the ILO maintains its unique tripartite structure with workers and employers participating as equal partners with governments and provides training and advisory services to all parties in such areas as vocational training and rehabilitation, employment policy, labor and industrial relations, management development, social security, labor statistics, and occupational safety and health.

In 1998, in an effort to build considerable global influence among member governments and employer and worker organizations to counter serious workforce challenges associated with globalization, the ILO adopted the Declaration on Fundamental Prin-

Figure 1.4 **United Nations Global Compact**

Human Rights
- Principle 1: Businesses should support and respect the protection of internationally proclaimed human rights; and
- Principle 2: make sure that they are not complicit in human rights abuses.

Labor Standards
- Principle 3: Businesses should uphold the freedom of association and the effective recognition of the right to collective bargaining;
- Principle 4: the elimination of all forms of forced and compulsory labor;
- Principle 5: the effective abolition of child labor; and
- Principle 6: the elimination of discrimination in respect of employment and occupation.

Environment
- Principle 7: Businesses should support a precautionary approach to environmental challenges;
- Principle 8: undertake initiatives to promote greater environmental responsibility; and
- Principle 9: encourage the development and diffusion of environmentally friendly technologies.

Anti-Corruption
- Principle 10: Businesses should work against all forms of corruption, including extortion and bribery.

Source: U.N. Global Compact Web site (www.unglobalcompact.org) (accessed June 7, 2010).

ciples and Rights at Work.[19] The Declaration, expected to be upheld and reinforced by ILO member countries, covers four major areas:

1. Freedom of association and the right to collective bargaining
2. The elimination of forced and compulsory labor
3. The abolition of child labor
4. The elimination of discrimination in the workplace

Organization for Economic Cooperation and Development (OECD). The OECD, which was created as an economic counterpart to North Atlantic Treaty Organization (NATO), grew out of efforts in 1947, supported by the United States and Canada, to coordinate the reconstruction of Europe after World War II. Since then its mission has been to help governments achieve sustainable economic growth and employment and rising standards of living in member countries, thus contributing to the development of the world economy. Based in Paris, the OECD is a main proponent of economic globalization and an active overseer of associated economic, social, environmental, and governance challenges. Its thirty member countries are demonstrably committed to a market economy and a pluralistic democracy. These countries produce 60 percent of the world's goods and services and are home to almost 90 percent of foreign direct investment flows and to 97 out of the top 100 MNCs. The OECD shares expertise and views on topics of mutual concern with more than 100 countries worldwide, from Brazil, China, and Russia to the least developed countries in Africa. For more than forty years the OECD has been one of the world's largest and most reliable sources of comparable statistical, economic, and social data.

In 1976 the OECD set forth its *Guidelines for Multinational Enterprises,* covering a wide range of corporate responsibility issues, including employment and industrial relations, environment, information disclosure, competition, financing, taxation, and science and technology. These guidelines represent a multilaterally endorsed and comprehensive code of conduct recommended by governments to MNCs. The guidelines have been revised periodically, and although not legally binding, many members of the OECD reportedly refer to them when drafting national legislation on corporate behavior. For example, the Netherlands links financial support plans for large companies to compliance with the OECD guidelines. Recently revised OECD guidelines call for support for core labor standards promoted by the ILO's Declaration on Fundamental Principles and Rights at Work (for example, the right of employees to be represented by trade unions of their choice and to bargain collectively, nondiscrimination, and the elimination of child labor and forced labor) and expand workforce management concerns to also involve employees of suppliers as well as executive bribery and corruption. As another illustration of OECD influence, South Korea is one OECD member that has come under OECD official censure and imposed measures for change due to its failure to live up to promises made in its membership application to reduce labor union restrictions. The revised guidelines also provide stronger implementation procedures through the creation within countries of so-called National Contact Points for working with governments and companies to promote the guidelines, handle inquiries, and help to resolve issues that arise.[20]

World Trade Organization (WTO). The World Trade Organization is the only global intergovernmental organization dealing with the rules of trade between nations, which involves tariff and trade barrier reductions and the resolution of international trade disputes. At its heart are the WTO agreements, negotiated and signed by the bulk of the world's trading nations and ratified in their parliaments. The WTO has currently 153 members, accounting for more than 97 percent of world trade. Decisions are made by the entire membership, typically by consensus. The WTO's goals are to regulate and help facilitate a smooth, fair, and predictable conduct of global business among producers of goods and services, exporters, and importers.

An ongoing debate has existed about whether the WTO should maintain its relatively conservative stance or use sanctions and regulations to ensure the protection of core labor and broader human rights among trading partners, such as those advocated by the ILO. Unions in developed countries, motivated to preserve local jobs by restricting work operation relocation and foreign direct investment in developing countries, are particularly vocal in support of the WTO requiring developing countries to adhere to high labor standards. Governments of developing countries generally are against a WTO immediate requirement of higher labor standards, which they believe serve as a cost barrier to increased FDI, a significant source of new tax revenue and jobs. Those taking the perspective of developing nations such as the Philippines and Malaysia argue that the WTO's inclusion of new labor standards contributes to denying developing countries the benefits from their current comparative advantage in labor-intensive products, and ultimately slows the process of development and industrialization in poor countries, robbing them of the potential gains of trade liberalization.[21]

Financial IGOs. The two major global institutions that focus on financial issues attendant to challenges and needs of globalization are the World Bank and the IMF. Both are dedicated to reducing world poverty and raising the economic health and stability of developing countries. The IMF, supported by its 186 country members, has a more narrow financial focus, working to promote international monetary cooperation, exchange stability, and orderly exchange arrangements. With particular regard to the needs of developing countries, the IMF provides advice and technical services to restructure debt and revise fiscal and economic regulatory policy toward greater national investment in infrastructure, education, and other internal factors leading to economic growth and employment. Frequently the IMF is criticized by labor and other employee interest groups when its fiscal policy advice and debt restructuring prescriptions conflict with local labor practices, such as in IMF recommendations to loosen restrictive labor laws that are believed to impede new business development and FDI.[22]

The World Bank, an agency of the UN, has a much broader scope than the IMF, working directly and in partnership with member governments, agencies, and nonprofit organizations such as World Vision and CARE to support programs and projects to counter illiteracy, disease, child and family abuse, corruption and fraud, and other maladies associated with poverty in developing countries. The World Bank provides loans, policy advice, technical assistance, and knowledge-sharing services to low- and middle-income countries to reduce poverty and improve living standards, as well as advisement on labor market development.[23] The Bank promotes growth to create jobs and to empower poor people to take advantage of economic growth opportunities. One of the world's largest sources of development assistance, the World Bank is composed of five subagencies, all owned by its 184 member countries and whose activities include providing interest-free loans and credit for project and program support, private sector investment, investment risk insurance, and dispute resolution assistance. The World Bank also works closely with the IMF, particularly, as noted, in overseeing deliberations of the G-20, and requires joint membership in the IMF.

IGO Impact. There has been criticism of the voluntary nature of IGOs' various declarations, guidelines, conventions, and measures because of their general lack of enforceability. For example, although China is a member of the ILO and is supposedly obligated to follow the Declaration on Fundamental Principles and Rights at Work, including the "freedom of association and the effective recognition of the right to collective bargaining," it still currently violates this core right of the Declaration by banning the formation of independent labor unions that could engage in collective bargaining on the workers' behalf.[24] Nevertheless, the UN Global Compact, OECD *Guidelines,* and ILO Declarations serve as clear, consistent standards for all member countries to work toward. For example, the active efforts of the OECD directed at reducing corporate corruption in the global marketplace through close company interaction and conference hosting has resulted in measurable improvement of company behavior in this arena. And although there continue to be difficult challenges associated with social support and labor protection in China with its ongoing immense economic transformation, significant improvements have been identified since

China's accession to the WTO and agreement to observe membership requirements of that world body.[25]

There also is evidence that the encouragement of voluntary norms and codes of conduct can bring about a significant shift in corporate behavior to maintain a positive corporate image and reputation, and to encourage the formation of self-managing internal company values and ethical codes for doing business. In addition, there likely will continue to be greater diligence in fully adopting and enforcing these rights and principles and other conventions and recommendations that are placed in high profile when they are reinforced by other global entities, and especially when made contingent to funding, loan, and trade approvals by the World Bank, IMF, and the WTO.[26] For example, in 1999, the United States, with WTO facilitation, signed a three-year trade pact granting up to 14 percent annual increases in the U.S. quota of garment imports from Cambodia if businesses in that country met the ILO's core labor standards. Although the process led to strikes and angered some employers, the Cambodian government made inspections mandatory for any garment factory desiring to export to the United States. There also is a strong expectation that the WTO eventually will act, for the purpose of increasing world trade and business operation efficiencies, to harmonize the many different forms of labor rights and protections under a common set of standards required of companies operating in all WTO member governments and their trading partners. As stated by ILO Director-General Juan Somavia, "The global economy needs a floor of core labor standards. . . . It could be five years, but labor rules are going to be there."[27]

Employee-Interest Organizations

Many nonprofit organizations are dedicated to protecting and promoting the interests of workers and improving workforce management practice. These organizations of diverse purposes and sizes are found at local, national, regional, and global levels. They continue to interact with governments, intergovernmental organizations (e.g., the UN and World Bank), and companies and help shape public opinion and social preferences to exert powerful influence on how people are managed in the world marketplace. Major forms of these employee-interest organizations include labor or trade unions, employer and professional associations, and NGOs.

Labor Unions. Technically, a labor or trade union is a group of workers that acts collectively to address common concerns or issues associated with an employment arrangement. However, we are treating unions here as external factors that influence global workforce management because they are typically structured as separate entities, external to firms that legally represent employees and often collectively comprise their membership across many organizations. Unions can vary dramatically in purpose and structure from one country to another, with some being organized by industry (for example, the United Kingdom's National Union of Rail, Maritime and Transport Workers), others by profession, trade, or functional area (for example, Australia's Queensland Nurses' Union), and yet others with an emphasis on broader social and political issues. In some countries unions have a close, collaborative relationship

Global Workforce Challenge 1.1
**Advancing Global Workforce
Professional Practice Through SHRM**

Founded in 1948 under the name of American Society for Personnel Administration (ASPA), the Society for Human Resource Management (SHRM) is the world's largest association devoted to human resource (HR) management. Representing more than 200,000 individual members in more than 550 affiliated chapters located in more than 100 countries, the Society's mission is to serve the information and skill needs of HR professionals by providing the most essential and comprehensive resources available through conferences, workshops, professional certification, a membership directory for making valuable contacts throughout the world, placement services, speaker and consultant referral, and publications. In addition to being an influential voice, SHRM's mission is to advance the HR profession to ensure that HR is recognized as an essential partner in developing and executing organizational strategy. SHRM's Global HR newsletter is published twice per month and mirrors this online community's focus on international HR management issues as well as development in global employment laws and best practices. SHRM also provides specific professional development and certification for HR professionals with international and cross-border responsibilities through its Global Learning System comprehensive test preparation and reference tool, and its Global Professional in Human Resources certification exam.

Source: Adapted from information available at www.shrm.org (accessed May 10, 2010).

with local business and government agencies, while in other countries, particularly in emerging markets, unions may contribute to a very adversarial and stormy industrial relations climate characterized by frequent work stoppages, strikes, and even violence.[28] Although unions generally have primary influence on workforce issues at local and national levels and are beginning to make advancements toward global solidarity, they still lag far behind the global reach of MNCs. Because unions have a key role in ongoing employee relations in many organizations, they will be examined in much more detail in Chapter 11.

Employer and Professional Associations. Employer associations focus primarily on the interests of their member companies, yet activities also indirectly involve the interests of employees. Like trade unions, employer associations are often recognized as legal entities, particularly where their role involves the regulation of relations between employers and unionized employees. And like employee trade unions, employer associations can vary greatly in size and may be structured by industry, such as the United Kingdom's Retail Motor Industry Federation, or functional specialization, such the Employers Group of Southern California, which specializes in human resource management needs of small- and medium-size firms. One of the largest employer associations is the Union of Industrial and Employers' Confederations of Europe (UNICE), which describes itself as "the voice of business in Europe," with membership made up of thirty-four business federations from twenty-seven European countries.[29]

Traditionally, the principal role of an employer association has been to represent its members during multiemployer collective bargaining with recognized trade unions. Although multiemployer bargaining continues in some industries, employer associations now place much greater emphasis on providing advisory services and training in several aspects of workforce management. For example, the sales professionals from manufacturing and distribution firms participate in a week-long Qualified Safety Sales Professional course covering fundamentals in risk management, safety engineering, and workers' compensation, co-sponsored by the International Safety Equipment Association and the Safety Equipment Distributors Association.[30] These organizations also are particularly active in lobbying and trying to influence government and world body laws and measures in ways that are favorable to or at least minimally restrictive for employer firm members, including those related to workforce management.

Professional associations address the practical knowledge and career needs of working professionals who likely would not be organized in a union. These non-profit organizations, often with global membership, have focuses ranging from very general and functional, such as the Society for Human Resource Management, to much more specific, such as the International Association for Human Resource Information Management. Like employer associations, professional associations primarily emphasize the improvement of organizational performance. They are very active in disseminating innovation and knowledge, including that related to global workforce management, through such means as conferences, workshops, publications, and online discussion groups, for improving workplace performance (for example, refer to Global Workforce Challenge 1.1 for more detailed information about SHRM, a leading professional association for global human resource professionals).

Nongovernmental Organizations (NGOs). Perhaps the strongest force today to moderate the great global influence of MNCs is the combined impact of NGOs, which have exploded upon the national and global scene in ever-increasing numbers over the past thirty years. This dramatic NGO presence has been facilitated by global changes in prosperity, education levels, freedom, mobility, increased transparency of markets, and advances in information and communications technologies, coupled with a growing awareness of governments' inability or unwillingness to safeguard against negative developments incident to globalization. NGO influence in various forms is responsible for major changes in corporate behavior and policy as well as greatly increased government scrutiny and reform activity. MNCs are increasingly confronted by a range of international agreements on operational standards and codes of conduct, including those related to workforce management issues, driven by strong collective, network-leveraged NGO pressure for both standard/code development and implementation.[31]

There are literally millions of these independent, nonpartisan, nonprofit advocacy and human services groups worldwide, from very small entities to much larger organizations such as Human Rights Watch, Amnesty International, World Vision, and

CARE. Collectively, NGOs constitute a significant source of employment, such as the Catholic charity Caritas, which runs kindergartens, hospitals, special homes, and care facilities. Caritas is the second largest single employer in Germany. Sometimes referred to as social entrepreneurship or citizen groups, NGOs can be religious based or nonsectarian, and their missions, generally related to social, humanitarian, and environmental concerns, differ greatly. NGOs may have a global focus with a central headquarters and offices in many countries, or they may have a local, community, or national focus. They may be characterized as more vocal and high-profile *advocacy* groups, applying intense public pressure through the mass media on governments and corporations, or they may be more *operational* in nature, assisting in implementation projects and activities in line with their mission through partnerships with governments, corporations, and other NGOs. Many NGOs sponsor both advocacy and operational activities.[32]

Based on high-profile media coverage of major economic meetings, NGOs may be perceived more commonly as vehement activist adversaries of MNCs and of weak or corrupt governments that collude with MNCs. However, a growing trend for entrepreneurial NGOs is to "fill in the cracks" or exploit niche opportunities in social and environmental protection services that are not addressed by governments and MNCs. Many of the largest NGOs have working relationships and even official associative status with IGOs such as the UN or World Bank. In fact, NGOs are increasingly active partners with MNCs, governments, and IGOs in monitoring, diagnosing, and serving these needs. MNCs often see major advantages that NGOs provide in assisting with the implementation of corporate commitments to social responsibility, including the following:[33]

- Local knowledge base, because NGOs tend to work closely with grassroots movements
- Local network and community connections
- Credibility, given the NGOs' altruistic mission and purpose
- Past and existing partnerships with governments

In some cases an MNC may use the operational expertise of NGOs in carrying out its own plans, such as with independent, impartial safety inspections at company-owned and outsourced manufacturing facilities around the world. Local and international NGOs may provide particularly valuable assistance in building bridges and initiating collaborative dialogue and relations with local business leaders, union leaders, and government officials, especially for FDI planning and implementation in emerging markets that often are characterized by adversarial and stormy industrial relations climates.[34] Or NGOs themselves may approach MNCs to gain corporate, financial, and other resource commitment and sponsorship to support the NGOs' goals, which again may enhance the MNCs' reputation in social responsibility. Operational NGOs may also provide direct assistance with company workforce management needs, such as with Mission Australia, a nondenominational Christian organization providing employment training and placement services for disadvantaged and homeless individuals. Another example is MAYA (Movement for Alternatives and Youth Awareness), a Bangalore-based NGO that launched LabourNet, a multi-industry job placement

---

Global Workforce Professional Profile 1.1
NGO Professional Lucy Kanu: Making a Difference in the World

As a former manager of small- and medium-size business development at a prominent nonprofit organization, Lucy Kanu had worked with poor women throughout Nigeria. She could not help noticing the success disparity between the self-assured women in the semi-urban areas and the women from poorer communities. In 2003, Kanu founded Idea Builders after she identified disadvantaged women and young people who were motivated but struggling to balance reality with the promised possibilities of a better life. Idea Builders continues to grow and add to its programs and is gaining international recognition as a stand-out Nigerian-based NGO.

In 2007, after a rigorous search and selection process, Idea Builders was recognized by the Ashoka Foundation as a leading NGO operating in Nigeria. Kanu as executive director was awarded an Ashoka fellowship for innovation in poverty reduction through the work that Idea Builders has performed in rural communities throughout Nigeria. Ashoka's announcement of Kanu's award noted, "Lucy is leading a new approach to community development. By maximizing local ideas and capacity, creatively engaging partners, and ensuring replication, she is ensuring sustainability and scale for income generation projects."

Ashoka fellows are recognized leaders in social entrepreneurship and present innovative solutions to societal problems. Ashoka is an international organization that is committed to supporting bold new ideas and to recognizing that compassion, creativity, and collaboration can be tremendous forces for change. Ashoka operates in more than sixty countries around the globe in every area of human need.

Source: Idea Builders Web site,www.IdeaBuilders.org.ng.

---

network for the informal sector working poor. According to MAYA's director, J.P. Solomon, "informal labor constitutes 90 percent of the workforce, and we intend to provide a framework for them to interact with the market in a mutually beneficial manner."[35] On a broader scale, NGOs led by passionate social entrepreneurs have been very impressive with their initiative, resource mobilization, and persistence in networking and collaborating to provide educational, health and safety, housing, and other community development services that greatly enhance the local social and labor infrastructure within which MNCs may recruit workers and operate successfully. For example, since the 1980s, NGOs in cooperative networks have assisted Mexican *colonias,* or poor, marginalized communities along the U.S.–Mexico border, in developing the community and providing basic services for local workers. [36]

INTERNAL COMPANY FACTORS INFLUENCING GLOBAL WORKFORCE MANAGEMENT

In addition to the previously examined factors in the external global environment, important factors within a company can have a major influence on workforce management. The combination of these internal factors often has a greater influence on company operations in general and workforce management in particular than the important external factors that we have previously examined. They can also help distinguish a company from others in the same environment. Major internal factors that we examine briefly here are company culture, climate, strategy, and structure.

Company Culture

An organization's culture represents the overall prevailing set of assumptions, attitudes, beliefs, norms, priorities, and values within the organization. It is greatly influenced by founding leaders and the collective common history of its members. For example, Teva Pharmaceuticals is a rapidly growing multinational firm based in Israel with foreign operations in Europe and North America. Its top management is made up of Israelis with common early experience in Israel's military, so it is no wonder that the culture can be characterized as informal, aggressive, fast paced, and "commando-like."[37] The culture of an organization is communicated explicitly (for example, through employee handbooks, written messages, and executive speeches) and implicitly (for example, through behavior modeled by leaders, informal communications such as the "grapevine," and reward/punishment contingencies) to indicate which behaviors are desired and which are unacceptable. Thus, culture can have a powerful influence on behavior expressed by organizational members and tends to orient and educate new organizational members naturally. Because of its pervasive and often unconscious nature, organizational culture is very difficult to change, typically requiring considerable time and comprehensive planning for altering company behavior and practice, especially focusing on a thorough redesign of company rewards (both formal and informal). Some organization cultures, like national cultures, can be very "tight," or homogeneous, with little variation in style and preference of acceptable behavior; other cultures, such as those in MNCs with extremely decentralized operations that share only a common name—and perhaps not even that—can be very loose, or have several subcultures.[38]

With its pervasive influence, organizational culture has a major impact on managerial thinking patterns and philosophy and is expressed behaviorally through general management style, strategy, company policy and behavioral prescriptions, and actual practices. For example, an MNC's ethnocentric culture at headquarters tends to perpetuate its own leadership homogeneity, with major developmental opportunities and leadership promotions being reserved for those of the same nationality as the current leadership. Although national culture is emphasized more in this text due to the focus on global workforce management, the importance of the influence of corporate culture should not be underestimated. In fact, several researchers and practitioners believe that corporate culture can have a greater influence and unifying effect on MNC behavior and performance than national culture, as will be examined in Chapters 7, 9, and 10, dealing with global workforce training, performance management, and compensation, respectively.[39]

Company Climate

Unlike the very entrenched, enduring nature of company culture, company *climate* refers to the overall present level of satisfaction of a workforce. Climate can change quickly, such as with an announcement of necessary downsizing of employees and no pay increases for the coming year. Despite its potentially quick-changing nature, workforce climate can have a major impact on employee retention as well as such key company performance measures as productivity, profitability, and customer satisfaction. Because workforce preferences can differ dramatically from country to country, management should not assume that the same workforce practices and rewards will yield a high level of worker satisfaction across all operations. Instead, they must continually obtain worker feedback to assess local levels of satisfaction and customize local workforce management practices to optimize satisfaction within each operation.[40]

Strategy and Structure

A company's strategy is the overall approach it takes to help it compete in the global marketplace. A recurring message in this book is the importance of aligning workforce management practices and particular human resource functions (for example, training and compensation) to company strategy. Effective workforce management is key to successful company strategy implementation. For example, critical employee adjustment and socialization issues with company growth strategies involve cross-border alliances, including mergers and acquisitions. And a global cost-saving strategy involving offshore outsourcing of manufacturing and basic administrative operations has major implications for workers in both the home country and in planned foreign or host country operations.[41]

Strategic management may involve an identification of core company values, followed by an alignment of company policies, activities, and programs that are consistent with those values. An increasingly common value, especially among larger MNCs, is the recognition of accountability to stakeholders of the MNC, including employees, consumers, governments, and even external entities such as IGOs and NGOs that request equitable treatment and protection of employees. Thus, the protection of human rights and workplace health and safety is increasingly emerging as an important internal value among many MNCs, which then implement consonant practices across their global workplaces (both company owned and outsourced). In fact, many recognize their adherence to high workforce standards as a source of competitive advantage through improved stakeholder relationships and global company reputation for social responsibility.[42]

An organization's structure is characterized by how it is organized, both physically and administratively. This structure greatly determines how employees perform their work. Smaller firms tend to have less formal structures, where people regularly interact in a way to attend to problems and resolve them in a timely fashion. However, in larger organizations where such interactions are less predictable due to distance or the sheer number of employees, a more formal structure with regular meetings

---

Global Workforce Challenge 1.2
Globalization's Race to the Top

A common nightmare of globalization features poor people working in unsafe conditions to produce goods for consumers in the West. It is part of what critics call a "race to the bottom," where MNCs compete in seeking out places where labor is cheap and safety, health, and environmental laws are weak. Yes, MNCs roam the globe in search of low-cost labor, but many of them export health and safety standards when they open factories in the developing world, while others monitor and ensure acceptable behavior by suppliers to protect their corporate image and adhere to espoused values.

After protest groups rattled Nike in the 1990s, exposing the deplorable working conditions under which some of its high-priced goods were made, Nike began monitoring its suppliers to try to ensure that workers are safe and that their basic rights are protected. Nike's 2004 Corporate Responsibility Report details its extensive—and expensive—efforts. The company now employs more than ninety people in twenty-one countries to enforce a code of conduct that covers safety, child labor, overtime pay, and human rights. It carried out more than 1,300 inspections and audits during 2004 and contracted with the Fair Labor Association, an independent nonprofit agency, to perform unannounced audits of 5 percent of its plants.

When Western MNCs build their own plants in the developing world, they bring along U.S. and EU health and safety standards. Intel, for instance, employs nearly 20,000 people at assembly and testing facilities in Costa Rica, China, Malaysia, and the Philippines that look much like its facilities in Silicon Valley. "It's tough at first to import that Intel safety culture and our attention to environmental detail," says Dave Stangis, Intel's director of corporate responsibility. "But over time, it starts to spread." DuPont goes a step further: It has a unit called Safety Resources, which has built a business of consulting with industrial companies in China, India, and other places that want to improve their health and safety records.

Does globalization represent a "race to the bottom," as has frequently been asserted? Maybe not. In fact, well-known Western firms are scrambling to protect their public image by complying and even taking impressive leads in following and enforcing standards posed by the EU, ILO, UN, OECD, and other entities lobbying for workforce protection. And these rising standards are spreading in step with rising social expectations. This continual, nearly competitive push to optimize company image and reputation in corporate social responsibility may actually constitute a "race to the top."

Sources: Adapted from C. Thauer, "Corporate Social Responsibility: A Race to the Bottom or a Race to the Top?" Presented at the ISA-ABRI Joint International Meeting, Pontifical Catholic University, Rio de Janeiro, Brazil (July 22, 2009); M. Gunther, "Cops of the Global Village," *Fortune* 151(13) (2005): 158–62.

---

and reporting procedures may be more productive. Companies with very centralized structures exert significant controls from central headquarters, decreasing the level of autonomy and decision-making responsibility at foreign operations. Very decentralized structures, on the other hand, often yield significant decision-making responsibility to local managers in foreign operations. Because of the major impact of company strategy and structure on workforce management, we will examine both topics in more detail in Chapter 4.

KEY PERSPECTIVES IN GLOBAL WORKFORCE MANAGEMENT

The purpose of this book is to help current and future managers and human resource professionals of all organizations—large and small, profit and nonprofit—recognize and understand the critical human resource issues underlying the broad global challenges that they face. This book is intended to help managers and human resource professionals enhance their competence in making effective human resource–related decisions to better cope with competitive global business challenges and opportunities. This book contains particular areas of emphasis that reflect our own direct experience and understanding as well as our professional and personal values that greatly influence our work. We will now briefly examine the areas of emphasis that are fundamental to this book.

GLOBAL PERSPECTIVE

In this text we specifically refer to global strategy as operating with one global market in mind, emphasizing standardization across countries and centralized control from headquarters in managing the business. However, we also more generally consider *global* to involve managing the firm with a broad perspective, combining both international and domestic dimensions. From the title *Managing a Global Workforce* and throughout the book, our use of *global* simply refers to the management of a firm's human resources wherever they may be located in the world—both in locations abroad and in the home country of company headquarters. This broad use of the term *global* is appropriate not only for large multinational enterprises that have operations throughout the world, such as GE, Michelin, and Siemens, but also for smaller firms with few operations abroad, or even for business professionals who fully intend to focus on their own country's domestic market. For smaller companies planning to initiate or expand operations abroad, the entire world provides a useful context without unnecessary restriction. In addition, even for those not intending to do business abroad, global business forces (for example, global competition, products, vendors, and immigrant labor) are coming to them in increasing numbers and varieties.

When we use the term *international* we are generally referring to issues abroad and away from the national or domestic market of a firm's headquarters, whereas when we use the term *global,* we are considering both contexts in managing the entire enterprise. Although what we cover in this book certainly is pertinent to nonprofit organizations and other forms of enterprise management and ownership, we generally take a corporate business enterprise perspective and refer to the multinational corporation, or MNC. Also, although the term *multinational* often refers to an enterprise with 50 percent or more of its business conducted or derived away from the home country domestic market, we use the term broadly, and *MNC* will have relevance to firms with operations in only one or a few other countries.

INCLUSIVE VIEW OF WORKFORCE

This book focuses on managing the entire workforce, wherever they may be located in the world, to carry out international business objectives effectively. However, past and even much of the current literature on international human resource management seems to be stuck in a time warp, with little emphasis on the organization's employees who do not have citizenship in the home country of company headquarters or who are contingent workers and not technically employed within the organization on a regular basis.

Many businesses in developed countries seem to have not progressed very far from the ethnocentric model of imperialism. The businesses focus predominantly on the headquarters–home-country expatriate working abroad and returning (repatriation), along with accompanying family member adjustment. However, nonexpatriate employees working for the company in foreign operations typically are left out of the picture completely or are given only a brief mention at best. Concepts of preparing employees to work abroad and building global leadership skills and global perspectives are too often reserved only for the home country workforce. Nevertheless, this ethnocentric focus will continue to change as more enlightened and less ethnocentric organizations perceive that human talent does not recognize national borders, citizenship, or ethnic distinctions, and these firms increasingly demonstrate competitive advantage through the effective management of a truly global workforce.

The existing international literature on human resource management contains little mention of the growing global contingent workforce at all employment levels (including temporary employees, consultants, and other workers fulfilling contracted and outsourced services) that increasingly is called on to accomplish company work demands in more efficient and flexible ways. The international business arena is experiencing more blurred workforce boundaries associated with increasing uses of these contingent workers as well as those involved with various strategic alliances and joint ventures.[43] Yet successful MNCs still need to maintain an active influence on (if not manage directly) the workforce in those new organization structures and working relationships. Especially in such areas as quality control, corporate governance, and social responsibility, MNCs must consider all employees involved in their primary and secondary business practices. With the increasingly vigilant and watchful eyes of worldwide consumers and other global stakeholders, MNCs are finding that they cannot separate their products and services from those workers who produce and provide them, even when this work is contracted out.

HUMAN RESOURCES AND GLOBAL BUSINESS ETHICS

Supporting the effort in this book of increased workforce inclusiveness described in the previous section is a guiding sense of international business ethics. We deeply agree with the fundamental values of a particular global enterprise, the Society of Jesus, better known as the Order of Jesuits, within the Catholic Church, which includes the development of the whole individual, social justice, and service of others as part of its educational institutional efforts throughout the world. We agree with

Donaldson's ethical framework of social contract theory, which states that any society has the right to expect that profit-generating organizations within its national borders will enhance the general interests of consumers, employees, and other stakeholders within the society.[44] With particular regard to the management of a total and inclusive global workforce, we believe that there are key moral responsibilities that institutions acquire, including the following:[45]

1. Assist all employees, regardless of national origin and location, in the successful execution of their assignments.
2. Avoid the semblance of discriminatory treatment.
3. Encourage full status of foreign employees and their host countries into the global economy.
4. Foster personal enlightenment and self-enrichment of all employees.
5. Help all employees develop useful, marketable skills.
6. Contribute to the development of a greater, more functional national labor skills base in countries that host MNC international operations.
7. Encourage a long-term focus on creating an enduring value for a maximum number of stakeholders, rather than short-term and shortsighted profit for only a few.

In addition, the human resource function is increasingly placed in the role of the "conscience" of the organization and has an important responsibility of creating and monitoring an organizational culture and overall internal environment that supports and encourages ethical behavior, including the previously listed moral responsibilities.[46] This role extends from the corporate boardroom in establishing guidelines for corporate governance, especially those affecting the behavior and compensation of managers and executives, to all levels of the organization with the development of comprehensive policies and practices that encourage productive and ethical behavior and discourage and decisively correct unacceptable and unethical behavior.[47] For example, to counter the incidence of dishonesty and fraud, which typically follows the presence of such essential elements as incentive, opportunity, rationalization, and capability, the human resource function can draw upon several of its key specializations including job design (to thwart opportunity); reward, compensation, and disciplinary systems (to provide a sense of fairness and equity as well as a clear and adequate disincentive to committing fraud and other undesirable behaviors); and training (to build internal values and thought processes that support values of honesty and integrity).[48] This significant role of human resources in international business ethics is particularly challenging because of its increased scope across national borders with vastly different legal systems and regulations, cultures, and social expectations.

GLOBALIZATION AND SOCIAL IMPERATIVES

We are unashamed supporters of globalization. We believe that the worldwide sharing of ideas through open global trade and other forms of cooperative interaction leads to greater advancement in innovation in all areas of human endeavor, which ultimately can benefit humanity (for a powerful illustration, consider Case 1.1 at the end of this chapter). On an individual level we frequently note and have experienced firsthand how involvement in international business and education (which also is a business in a broader sense) frequently results in new insights leading to business process and productivity improvements as well as personal growth and development.

On a macroeconomic level we agree with many others that unrestricted and open markets, with transparent and equitable market transactions and distribution, ultimately lead to prosperity for poorer and richer countries involved in free trade.[49] Supachai Panitchpakdi, director general of the WTO, emphasized this point when he claimed that what would be better in the long run than the generous worldwide offer of immediate aid for the countries and people devastated by the 2004 tsunami in Southeast Asia is greater access to world markets for their agricultural and manufactured products. Although the short term is extremely important, we often neglect the longer-term perspective. He noted, "Greater access to markets in both developed and emerging developing country markets, as well as reform to their own trade regimes, would be a powerful contribution to economic recovery in the region."[50]

Robert Reich, former U.S. Secretary of Labor, offered the following as important reasons for support by developed countries (the United States in particular) of a liberalized free trade policy, even when it may result in job displacement in the developed countries:

> We should stop pining after the days when millions of Americans stood along assembly lines and continuously bolted, fit, soldered, or clamped what went by. Those days are over. And stop blaming poor nations whose workers get very low wages. Of course their wages are low; these nations are poor. They can become more prosperous only by exporting to rich nations. When America blocks their exports by erecting tariffs and subsidizing our domestic industries, we prevent them from doing better. Helping poorer nations become more prosperous is not only in the interest of humanity but also politically wise because it lessens global instability.[51]

Thus, globalization can result in greater prosperity for those countries involved in unfettered world trade and in greater humanitarian support for less developed countries in the interest of humanity—the primary focus of our charitable programs of providing international aid. There is evidence, for example, that increased openness to trade, and especially involving direct FDI by organizations committed to corporate social responsibility, can contribute to the decrease of economic discrimination, forced labor, and child labor.[52] We believe that increased global economic development also can result in a safer and more stable world political environment—a goal ever more on our minds since the events of September 11, 2001. In fact, it has been cogently demonstrated that the same conditions that foster and support corruption in international business also allow for the development and spread of terrorism.[53] Increased globalization that brings with it significant foreign direct investment and the accompanying standards of full disclosure and transparency of financial transactions will not only help reduce corruption, which in the past has prevented the full humanitarian benefits of free trade to accrue to the people, but will also foster a more open environment that counters the development and spread of terrorism. Nevertheless, the long-range macroeconomic benefits of globalization and free trade for all countries involved cannot move quickly enough to avoid and assuage the pain and stress of work and labor migration, job displacement, and threats to labor safety and health. National governments, intergovernmental organizations, NGOs, and MNCs should work closely together and on an ongoing basis to secure and protect fundamental human and labor rights, provide appropriate labor standards, and support those displaced with necessary social assistance and, where possible, retraining for new job placement. MNCs have the opportunity before them to take a proactive lead as positive change agents.[54]

Furthermore, we believe that it is in the long-term economic interest of MNCs, individually and collectively, to invest in the ongoing care and development of the labor force of the countries where operations are located.[55] Those in the local labor force represent future consumers of MNC products and services as well as potential entrants into the MNC's local workforce. And where organizations are increasingly competing for worldwide talent, especially for staffing present and future key leadership positions for planning and implementing global business initiatives, it makes little sense to restrict the leadership gene pool to only the home country of MNC headquarters.

ONGOING CHALLENGE OF CONVERGENCE VERSUS DIVERGENCE

We are witnessing a significant convergence of economic, technological, political, and social practices around the world, from instant communications facilitated by the Internet and global cell phones to cigarette-free workplaces, restaurants, and even entire countries. More specifically, in international management and human resources we are seeing an increased sharing and adoption worldwide of recognized best practices that contribute to global competitive advantage. Where possible, we advocate the adoption and use of best practices and general principles of effective human resource management. We examine many of these in this book where such convergence is warranted, such as in the systematic processes of training design and performance management. However, we are very mindful of the limitations of "universal" perspectives in management and of the pervasive impact of cultural differences, particularly involving the implementation of company plans and objectives, which require local customization and adjustment from a divergence perspective. We therefore maintain due respect for each perspective throughout this book.

BOOK OVERVIEW

Consistent with the "challenges and opportunities" theme from the title, each chapter of this book presents important *challenges* that organizations face today as well as useful ideas and best practices–tested approaches for addressing those challenges, representing important *opportunities* for action. Following each chapter is a list of pertinent Web sites that provide immediate and more detailed information, resources, and useful contact information for specific professional assistance related to the general topic of the chapter.

In Chapter 2 we examine the concept of culture and its powerful, pervasive, and persistent influences on all forms of human behavior, including multicultural activities involved in international business. We also consider two frequently cited cultural models and their managerial implications. In Chapter 3 we consider major changes and developing trends in the global labor market along with their significant implications for multinational firms. These trends include the phenomenon of globalization and its causes, the impact of major technological advancements, changes in global labor force demographics and the influence of migration that are adding increasing diversity to our global workforces, the emergence of contingent workers as a significant component of the labor force, and the impact of the increased use of offshore sourcing as an alternative to domestic production.

In Chapter 4 we examine both the strategic roles of human resource management on global organizational performance and the impact of MNCs' competitive strategy and organizational structure on international human resource management practice. We also present a new strategy process paradigm for enhancing human resource management's contribution to competitive advantage in the global marketplace. Chapter 5 analyzes the important role of HR planning in effectively carrying out an MNC's strategic plans through the people factor as well as in preparing the organization throughout its worldwide operations for optimal long-term productivity in utilizing human resources. Important considerations for HR planning include the determination of work demand and labor supply based on strategic objectives, external environment scanning, work organization and job design, and analysis of important sources of labor supply, considering both contingent and regular employee sources. In addition, long-term HR planning issues examined in Chapter 5 include forecasting labor supply trends and opportunities, building global capability, and succession planning.

Chapter 6 focuses on global staffing for filling immediate work demand through the processes of recruitment and selection. This chapter first examines important general factors that influence global staffing in MNCs and then considers more specific approaches, tools, and important considerations for recruiting and for selecting viable candidates from both internal and external sources. In Chapter 7 we first examine the strategic role and key contributions of training and then consider fundamental concepts and principles for guiding important global training and development activities. We also consider the critical imperatives of training and development for the global workforce, including building global competencies and workforce alignment, as well as particular considerations for expatriate training, with a special focus on training for female expatriates and host country national employees.

Chapter 8 examines important issues and practices associated with managing traditional long-term international assignments successfully, including predeparture planning and preparation, on-site management for effective adjustment and ongoing support, and repatriation. Also considered are issues that may be unique to women expatriates and third country nationals in their expatriate assignments as well as host country national *inpatriates,* who are assigned to relocate and work at MNC headquarters in the home country. In addition, we examine practices and challenges associated with rapidly increasing forms of short-term international assignments, including work as a "virtual" expatriate with international teams and with global virtual teams, as well important considerations surrounding frequent travel.

Chapter 9 examines the important performance management process within a global work environment and considers challenges and ideas for continual work performance enhancement in multicultural contexts through regular feedback mechanisms and accurate performance appraisal practices. In Chapter 10 we examine challenges in managing compensation and rewards across national borders involving significantly differing cultural and economic conditions while maintaining internal and external equity and perceptions of fairness. This chapter also provides successful approaches for providing appropriate incentives to attract potential expatriates and inpatriates for foreign assignments and describes cost adjustments to avoid material loss due to the foreign assignment. Finally, Chapter 11 provides an analysis of current pressing issues in global employee relations, including forced labor, child labor, and critical health and safety concerns. This chapter also discusses particular roles and practices of MNCs and labor unions in global employee relations.

Following each chapter summary, as with this introductory chapter, are questions for personal reflection and possible class discussion about the chapter's opening real-world scenario in global workforce management. The information presented in each chapter is aimed at increasing understanding and providing helpful tools for analyzing and addressing the challenges and issues presented in the opening scenario. These questions are followed by two brief cases for additional analysis and discussion pertinent to the chapter. Following the questions is a list of useful resource Web sites pertinent to major topics of the chapter. In most instances considerable information is available at those sites, but for some sites a registration or membership fee is required for full resource access.

SUMMARY

The HR function, pertinent to both large MNCs and to small and medium-size firms everywhere, is critical for the successful operation of global business. Key activities within the HR function include HR planning, staffing, training compensation, performance management, and managing employee relations, all of which are made more challenging on a global scale due to the myriad cultural and national differences in foreign operations. These important activities involved in global workforce management are greatly influenced by several factors both in the external environment and within the internal environment of the firm.

QUESTIONS FOR OPENING SCENARIO ANALYSIS

1. What major forces are causing changes in the supply of labor to meet work demand in southern China's manufacturing heartland? Are these forces unique to the situation depicted in the opening scene?
2. How are these changes leading to new challenges in the basic human resource management functional areas of recruitment, compensation, and employee relations?

3. Based on the opening scene, why is it important for managers involved in international business to continually monitor challenges and opportunities facing their organizations?
4. Would the ending job advertisement fit the legal and social expectations of your country? What are implications of such an advertisement for managing a global workforce?

CASE 1.1. THE UNITED NATIONS OF BANANAS

Much has changed in Datu Paglas, Philippines, a secluded town on the island of Mindanao that exemplified the chaos that engulfs the Muslim areas of the southern Philippines. Until recently, rice and cornfields sat fallow as many of the area's farmers headed into the hills to join a separatist army, the Moro Islamic Liberation Front (MILF). Many were being gunned down in blood feuds with rival political clans, and kidnapping syndicates sprang up as some locals decided to trade in humans rather than crops. The island's economic prospects were extremely dim.

Today, everyone from the Philippine government to the World Bank is holding up Datu Paglas as one of the Muslim south's rare economic success stories. Hundreds of MILF fighters have laid down their arms and returned to the banana plantations and rice paddies to work and live in greater security. A mini-mall and development bank have opened, and foreign and Philippine entrepreneurs are trekking into Mindanao's jungles to build factories, such as a new Korean-financed plastics plant. Over 450 years of Spanish and American military rule and conflict could not yield such positive results. How did this transformation at Datu Paglas occur? It took leadership, multiple-stakeholder cooperation and goodwill, and the opportunities of globalization.

The highly respected town mayor, Mr. Ibrahim Paglas (for whose family the town is named), was eager to halt the area's senseless violence and deaths, including the assassination of several of his close relatives. He brokered peace with the warring clans and used his cultural and political influence to curb crime and violence. Knowing that an enduring peace could come only with economic prosperity, he also brokered a very attractive deal with wary investors from Saudi Arabia, Italy, and the MNC Chiquita Brands International, to develop a banana plantation in the fertile countryside. The resulting local company, La Frutera, Inc., is the largest foreign-investment project in the Philippines' Muslim autonomous region.

Perhaps the most unlikely figure at La Frutera is Yaal Pecker, an Israeli who grew up on a kibbutz, or communal farm, near the Sea of Galilee. During his service in the Israeli military in the 1980s, Mr. Pecker fought Muslim militants in Lebanon. He went on to become an agricultural specialist with the Israeli firm, Plastro International, which was brought on board by La Frutera's foreign investors for its strong reputation in irrigation technology. Any potential tension between the Israelis and the Saudi investors was outweighed by the desire for the Israeli company's expertise. Israeli company participation also needed approval from the highest levels of the MILF command. One day Mr. Paglas hiked through the jungle with an Israeli representative to meet with the MILF chairman, who was also Paglas's uncle. The MILF chairman asked if the Israelis were helping his people, and Paglas assured him they were. That was it—the MILF commander declared that the Israelis were welcome. As operations developed, Mr. Pecker and six of his Israeli colleagues worked hand in hand with former MILF guerrillas who tend the fields, oversee fumigation, and provide security. Both sides see themselves as members of similar agricultural cultures and overlook religious and political cultural differences. "They're farmers, just like me," the gruff Mr. Pecker says. "What's the big deal?"

La Frutera's fruit is in heavy demand in Japan, China, and the Middle East. Its business now is filtering through the rest of Mindanao's small economy. Mr. Paglas has set up trucking, security, and gas station companies to serve the plantations. They provide jobs to local residents, while the town's new bank offers loans to other aspiring entrepreneurs. "My life is much better since I left the MILF," says Rocky Daud, twenty-four, a former MILF field commander in the jungles of Mindanao and now a member of La Frutera's 2,000-person workforce. Today he makes what is considered locally a decent paycheck and can afford appliances and other goods from the newly opened mini-mall. "I don't want to go back to the hills," he says. Abbie Paus, who now oversees forty-five men in La Frutera's fields, was a fighter for most of his forty years, roaming the area's green hills and occasionally ambushing Philippine army patrols and bandits. "I can now send my children to school," he says.

Mr. Paglas's ability to unite Muslims, Jews, and Christians in a Southeast Asian region gripped by sectarian and ethnic conflict has opened the eyes of leaders from cities as far away as Tehran and Jerusalem. The vastly improved situation at Datu Paglas is aided by Mr. Paglas's unquestioned authority as a Muslim chieftain. In fact, the national government received his assistance in securing the successful release of three employees of a Chinese oil company who were kidnapped by a local gang. Even after stepping down as mayor, Mr. Paglas still has the last word in enforcing security arrangements and settling disputes. As he explains, "I tell people that if they have guns near my plantation, I'll kill them."

QUESTIONS FOR CASE ANALYSIS AND DISCUSSION

1. What message does this case send to those who categorically deny any value from globalization?
2. What conditions and factors are necessary to bring about the positive outcomes of globalization? In particular, what human factors are critical?
3. What social and human aspects surrounding Datu Paglas have changed with globalization (for example, movement toward global cultural convergence), and what aspects remain very much the same (for example, persistence of a cultural divergence effect)?

CASE 1.2. MNC COLLABORATION IN SOCIAL RESPONSIBILITY

Although several high-profile MNCs such as Nike and Gap now work regularly with labor rights groups to monitor and correct worker abuses in their vast global networks of supplier factories, still only about 100 U.S. and European MNCs are involved. According to some sources, the vast majority of Western companies haven't followed suit even after a decade of activism on the issue. Likely the most troubling absence has been that of large retailers such as Walmart and Target, which increasingly control pricing power in overseas manufacturing. The persistent downward pressure posed by this pricing power in turn dictates how much money factories can spend on improving labor conditions.

But now with a new major collaborative project, Nike, Patagonia, Gap, and five other companies have joined forces with six leading antisweatshop groups to devise a single set of labor standards with a common factory-inspection system. The goal of this project, known as the Joint Initiative on Corporate Accountability and Workers' Rights, is to replace today's overlapping hodgepodge of approaches with something that is easier and cheaper to use—and that might gain acceptance by more companies. After two years of discussion, the parties quietly signed an agreement in April 2005 to run a pilot project in several dozen Turkish factories that produce garments and other products for the eight companies. If it works, the thirty-month experiment would create the first commonly accepted global labor standards as well as a way to adhere to them. Essentially, this arrangement would provide a private-sector counterpart to the ILO principles that most countries have long endorsed but rarely enforced. The rights groups hope that the Walmarts of the world will ultimately sign on, finding it easier to join in than to try to explain why they can't embrace such a commonly accepted standard.

This collaborative experiment will try to address in a common-supplier market the problem of an MNC working with one supplier to establish appropriate worker safety and rights standards and then dropping that supplier in favor of a cheaper supplier—which, however, likely lacks the same level of worker protections. The desired outcome is that common workforce guidelines will keep companies from undercutting one another on labor standards as they search for the cheapest supplier. However, there is still a long way to go in resolving contentious details associated with the project—often the greatest conflict is found among the rights groups involved—and it may well take the full thirty months of the project to sort out everything. A recently resolved controversy has been the acceptance to disclose supplier companies, often withheld in the past on the claim of proprietary information. There are also ongoing questions about the methodology of inspections. One existing model has very strict codes, but participating companies can choose which of their factories will be inspected and thus easily sidestep plants that are likely to show problems. Another approach has weaker codes but much stricter monitoring and no input from member companies on which plants are to be inspected. However, this approach audits only about 5 percent of a company's entire factory list each year. The most contentious detail to unravel is likely over wages, where there is an effort to adopt the idea of companies guaranteeing a "living wage" standard of pay rather than a local country's minimum wage, which may greatly lag behind the ability to support a reasonable living standard.

QUESTIONS FOR CASE ANALYSIS AND DISCUSSION

1. Given current differences held by MNCs on worker rights and safety codes, how could the acceptance of a common standard be attractive to many MNCs that have core values of social responsibility?

2. What are the potential advantages of a collaborative model as presented here over existing efforts by the ILO, the OECD, and the United Nations to gain the acceptance and observance of worker codes?

3. What are important other sources of world stakeholder support that would be helpful in expanding and successfully implementing a global program as described here?

RECOMMENDED WEB SITE RESOURCES

Society for Human Resource Management (http://shrm.org). World's largest association devoted to HR management. Represents more than 190,000 individual members worldwide and serves the information needs of HR professionals by providing comprehensive resources through conferences, membership-directory networking, and publications. More than 500 affiliated chapters in more than 100 countries.

Human Resource Management International Digest (http://miranda.emeraldinsight.com, then click Journal Title and search for Human Resource Management International Digest). Publishes concepts, applications, commentary, and research for understanding general HR trends and ideas around the world. Features experienced appraisal and reviews of current thinking on HR management that has been published in the top 400 management journals. Also provides current news about employment law and valuable HR Web sites and books.

Towers Watson (www.towerswatson.com). Global HR consulting firm providing a rich source of current knowledge for managing human resources on a global scale through current announcements and news briefs, research documents and reports, and magazines and newsletters.

NGO Café (www.gdrc.org/ngo/ncafe-f.html). Meeting place for NGOs to discuss, debate, and disseminate information on their work, strategies, and results. NGOs searching for partners can also list their requests here.

AusAID (www.ausaid.gov.au/ngos/default.cfm), Charity Village (www.charityvillage.com). Links to Australian, U.K., and Canadian international NGOs.

NOTES

1. Adapted from "International: Executive Pay Needs Realignment," *Oxford Analytica Daily Brief* (April 2009): 1; M. Fong, "A Chinese Puzzle: Surprising Shortage of Workers Forces Factories to Add Perks; Pressure on Pay—and Prices," *Wall Street Journal,* August 16, 2004.

2. A. Batson, "World News: China's Labor Market Sees Surge in Demand," *Wall Street Journal,* November 13, 2009; R. Joshi, "Ready for Recovery: How Much You Gain from the Recovery Will Depend on Two Things: The Strength and Shape of the Revival and Your Company's Deeds During the Downturn," *Business Today* (November 2009), ABI/INFORM Global; E. Bellman and J. Range, "Shortage of Laborers Plagues India," *Wall Street Journal,* May 1, 2009; D. Lee, "China Draws in Foreign Retailers," *Los Angeles Times,* January 1, 2005.

3. M. Steers and L. Nardon, *Managing in the Global Economy* (Armonk, NY: M.E. Sharpe, 2006).

4. S. Hicks, "Successful Global Training," *Training & Development* 54 (2000): 95.

5. V. Vaiman and C.M. Vance, eds., *Smart Talent Management: Building Knowledge Capital for Competitive Advantage* (Northhampton, MA: Edward Elgar Publishing, 2007), 195–216.

6. B. Leisy and N.S. Rajan, "Tackling Global Talent Management," *Workspan* 52 (3) (2009): 40–45.

7. S. Singh, "Globalization Puts Focus on HR," *Canadian HR Reporter* 18 (11) (2005): 1–2; A. Taylor, "An Operations Perspective on Strategic Alliance Success Factors: An Exploratory Study of Alliance

Managers in the Software Industry," *International Journal of Operations & Production Management* 25 (5/6) (2005): 469–90; C.R. Greer, *Strategic Human Resource Management: A General Managerial Approach,* 2nd ed. (Upper Saddle River, NJ: Prentice Hall, 2001); H.P. Conn and G.S. Yip, "Global Transfer of Critical Capabilities," *Business Horizons* 40 (1) (1997): 22–31.

8. T. Felin, T.R. Zenger, and J. Tomsik, "The Knowledge Economy: Emerging Organizational Forms, Missing Microfoundations, and Key Considerations for Managing Human Capital," *Human Resource Management* 48 (4) (2009): 555–70; Y. Paik, C.M. Vance, J. Gale, and C.A. McGrath, "Improving Global Knowledge Management Through Inclusion of Host Country Workforce Input," in K.J. O'Sullivan, ed., *Strategic Knowledge Management in Multinational Organizations* (Hershey, PA: Information Science Reference, 2007), 167–82; C.M. Vance and Y. Paik, "Forms of Host Country National Learning for Enhanced MNC Absorptive Capacity," *Journal of Managerial Psychology* 20 (7) (2005): 590–606.

9. I.H. Chow, J. Huang, and S. Liu, "Strategic HRM in China: Configurations and Competitive Advantage," *Human Resource Management* 47 (4) (2008): 687–706; C.F. Fey and H.J. Park, "Institutional Theory and MNC Subsidiary HRM Practices: Evidence from a Three-Country Study," *Journal of International Business Studies* 38 (3) (2007): 430–47; I.H. Chow, "The Impact of Institutional Context on Human Resource Management in Three Chinese Societies," *Employee Relations* 26 (6) (2004): 626–42.

10. E.S. Browning, "Yuan Move Might Stir Big Ripples," *Wall Street Journal,* July 25, 2005.

11. G. Lee and A. Teo, "Organizational Restructuring: Impact on Trust and Work Satisfaction," *Asia Pacific Journal of Management* 22 (1) (2005): 23–39; P.J. Carswell, "The Financial Impact of Organisational Downsizing Practices—The New Zealand Experience," *Asia Pacific Journal of Management* 22 (1) (2005): 41–63.

12. A. Muller and A. Kolk, "Extrinsic and Intrinsic Drivers of Corporate Social Performance: Evidence from Foreign and Domestic Firms in Mexico," *Journal of Management Studies* 47 (1) (2010): 1–26; J. Tan, "Institutional Structure and Firm Social Performance in Transitional Economies: Evidence of Multinational Corporations in China," *Journal of Business Ethics* 86 (2009): 171–89; J.P. Carpenter, "Endogenous Social Preferences," *Review of Radical Political Economies* 37 (1) (2005): 63; N.K. Balasubramanian, D. Kimber, and F. Siemensma, "Emerging Opportunities or Traditions Reinforced? An Analysis of the Attitudes towards CSR, and Trends of Thinking about CSR in India," *Journal of Corporate Citizenship* 17 (2005): 79–92; P. Thompson and Z. Zakaria, "Corporate Social Responsibility Reporting in Malaysia: Progress and Prospects," *Journal of Corporate Citizenship* 13 (Spring 2004): 125–36.

13. Human Rights Watch, "CAFTA's Weak Labor Rights Protections: Why the Present Accord Should be Opposed" (March 2004), http://hrw.org/english/docs/2004/03/09/usint8099.htm.

14. W. Luetkenhorst, "Corporate Social Responsibility and the Development Agenda: The Case for Actively Involving Small and Medium Enterprises," *Intereconomics* 39 (3) (2004): 157–66.

15. D. Ryland, "The Charter of Fundamental Rights of the European Union: Pandora's Box or Panacea?" *Managerial Law* 45 (4–6) (2003): 145–74; J. Kenner, *EU Employment Law: From Rome to Amsterdam and Beyond* (Oxford, UK: Hart, 2002); L. Funk, "A Legally Binding EU Charter of Fundamental Rights?" *Intereconomics* 37 (5) (2002): 253–62; also refer to details of the charter at www.europarl.eu.int/charter/.

16. "Estonia Struggles to Comply with European Social Charter," *Asia Africa Intelligence Wire,* October 15, 2004.

17. "G7 in the Sidelines: The Grouping Needs to Make an Informal Contribution," *Financial Times,* October 5, 2009.

18. H. Runhaar and H. Lafferty, "Governing Corporate Social Responsibility: An Assessment of the Contribution of the UN Global Compact to CSR Strategies in the Telecommunications Industry," *Journal of Business Ethics* 84 (4) (2009): 479–95; A. Rasche, "Toward a Model to Compare and Analyze Accountability Standards: The Case of the UN Global Compact," *Corporate Social Responsibility and Environmental Management* 16 (4): 192–205.

19. R. Montgomery and G. Maggio, "Fostering Labor Rights in Developing Countries: An Investors' Approach to Managing Labor Issues," *Journal of Business Ethics* 87 (Supplement 1) (2009): 199–219; L. Akin, "Working Conditions of the Child Worker in Turkish Labour Law," *Employee Responsibilities and Rights Journal* 21 (1) (2009): 53–67; B. Boockmann and R. Vaubel, "The Theory of Raising Rivals' Costs and Evidence from the International Labour Organisation," *The World Economy* 32 (6) (2009): 862–87.

20. A. Gurría, "Setting the Standards and Building Confidence: Organisation for Economic Cooperation and Development," *The OECD Observer* 273 (2009): 3; S. Altschuller and A. Lehr, "Corporate Social Responsibility," *The International Lawyer* 43 (2) (2009): 577–88; International Labor Organization. "OECD Updates Guidelines for Multinationals with Link to ILO Standards," (Fall 2000), http://www.us.ilo.org/archive/ilofocus/2000/fall/0008focus_9.cfm.

21. B. Konstantinov, "Human Rights and the WTO: Are They Really Oil and Water? *Journal of World Trade* 43 (2) (2009): 317–338; J. Rollo and L.A. Winters, "Subsidiarity and Governance Challenges for the WTO: Environmental and Labour Standards," *World Economy* 23 (4) (2000): 561–76; R.T. Luib, "Malaysia to Be Hurt if Labor Standards Used by WTO," *Business World,* August 14, 2000.

22. E. Mekay, "Labor: Unions Say IMF Bids Croatia Cut Worker Rights," *Global Information Network,* February 5, 2003; B. Edwards, "IMF and World Bank to Labor Unions: Drop Dead," *Report on the Americas* 34 (4) (2001): 4–5; V. Lloyd and R. Weissman, "Against the Workers: How IMF and World Bank Policies Undermine Labor Power and Rights," *Multinational Monitor* 22 (9) (2001): 7–11.

23. "Qatar: Planning Council and World Bank Set Phase Two of the Labour Market Strategy's National Action Plan in Motion," *Tribune Business News,* February 12, 2009.

24. P. Alston, "'Core Labour Standards' and the Transformation of the International Labour Rights Regime," *European Journal of International Law* 15 (3) (2004): 457–522; M. Gonzalez and C.V. Martinez, "Fostering Corporate Social Responsibility through Public Initiative: From the EU to the Spanish Case," *Journal of Business Ethics* 55 (3) (2004): 275; T.D. Merchant, "Recognizing ILO Rights to Organize and Bargain Collectively: Grease in China's Transition to a Socialist Market Economy," *Case Western Reserve Journal of International Law* 36 (1) (2004): 223–53.

25. O.F. Williams, "The UN Global Compact: The Challenge and the Promise," *Business Ethics Quarterly* 14 (4) (2005): 755–74; Y. Zhu and M. Warner, "Changing Chinese Employment Relations Since WTO Accession," *Personnel Review* 34 (3) (2005): 354–70; F. Zhai and Z. Wang, "WTO Accession: Rural Labor Migration and Urban Unemployment in China," *Urban Studies* 39 (12) (2002): 2199–217.

26. J. LaDou, "World Trade Organization, ILO Conventions, and Workers' Compensation," *International Journal of Occupational and Environmental Health* 11 (2) (2005): 210–11; Anonymous, "Bribery: Does the OECD Convention Work?" *OECD Observer* (December 2004–January 2005): 20–21; C. MacKenzie, "Moral Sanctions: Ethical Norms as a Solution to Corporate Governance Problems," *Journal of Corporate Citizenship* (Autumn 2004): 49–61; K.K. Herrmann, "Corporate Social Responsibility and Sustainable Development: The European Union Initiative as a Case Study," *Indiana Journal of Global Legal Studies* 11 (2) (2004): 205–32; K.A. Elliott and R.B. Freeman, *Can Labor Standards Improve Under Globalization?* (Washington, DC: Institute for International Economics, 2003).

27. A. Bernstein, "Do-It-Yourself Labor Standards: While the WTO Dickers, Companies Are Writing the Rules," *Business Week,* November 19, 2001; J. Rollo and L.A. Winters, "Subsidiarity and Governance Challenges for the WTO: Environmental and Labor Standards," *World Economy* 23 (4) (2000): 561–76.

28. C. Reade and M.R. McKenna, "Seeding the Clouds for Industrial Relations Climate Change in Emerging Economies," *Thunderbird International Business Review* 51 (2) (2009): 125–41.

29. S. Silvia and W. Schroeder, "Why Are German Employers Associations Declining? Arguments and Evidence," *Comparative Political Studies* 40 (12) (2007): 1433–459; P. Lewis, A. Thornhill, and M. Saunders, *Employee Relations: Understanding the Employment Relationship* (New York: Prentice-Hall/Financial Times, 2003).

30. A. Lutes, "Keeping an Eye on Safety," *Industrial Distribution* 94 (4) (2005): 18.

31. V.S. Chand, "Beyond Nongovernmental Development Action into Social Entrepreneurship," *The Journal of Entrepreneurship* 18 (2) (2009): 139–66; J.P. Doh and T.R. Guay, "Globalization and Corporate Social Responsibility: How Non-Governmental Organizations Influence Labor and Environmental Codes of Conduct," *Management International Review* 44 (2) (2004): 7–29; D. Bornstein, *How to Change the World: Social Entrepreneurs and the Power of New Ideas* (New York: Oxford University Press, 2004); J.P. Doh and H. Teegen, "Nongovernmental Organizations as Institutional Actors in International Business: Theory and Implications," *International Business Review* 11 (2002): 665–84.

32. D. Arenas, J. Lozano, and L. Albareda, L. "The Role of NGOs in CSR: Mutual Perceptions Among Stakeholders," *Journal of Business Ethics* 88 (1) (2009); 175–97; T. Guay, J.P. Doh, and G. Sinclair, "Non-Governmental Organizations, Shareholder Activism, and Socially Responsible Investments: Ethical, Strategic, and Governance Implications," *Journal of Business Ethics* 52 (1) (2004): 125–39; "Non-Governmental Organizations and Business: Living with the Enemy," *Economist,* August 9, 2003; P. van Tuijl, "NGOs and Human Rights: Sources of Justice and Democracy," *Journal of International Affairs* 52 (2) (1999): 493–512; L. Gordenker and T. Weiss, *NGOs, the UN, and Global Governance* (Boulder, CO: Lynne Rienner, 1996).

33. B. Castleman, B. Allen, S. Barca, S.R. Bohme, et al. "Code of Sustainable Practice in Occupational and Environmental Health and Safety for Corporations," *International Journal of Occupational and Environmental Health* 14 (3) (2008): 234–5; C.J. Choi, P. Cheng, J. Kim, and T.I. Eldomiaty, "Dual Responsibilities of NGOs: Market and Institutional Responsibilities and Ethics," *Journal of Corporate Citizenship* 17 (Spring 2005): 26–29; H. Teegen, J.P. Doh, and S. Vachani, "The Importance of Nongovernmental Organizations (NGOs) in Global Governance and Value Creation: An International Business Research Agenda," *Journal of International Business Studies* 35 (6) (2004): 463–83.

34. Reade and McKenna, "Seeding the Clouds."

35. "NGO Unveils Initiative for Informal Laborers," *Businessline,* June 9, 2004; R. Phillips, "Australian NGOs: Current Experiences of Corporate Citizenship," *Journal of Corporate Citizenship* 17 (Spring 2005): 21–25.

36. A. Donelson, "The Role of NGOs and NGO Networks in Meeting the Needs of U.S. Colonias," *Community Development Journal* 39 (4) (2004): 332–44.

37. L. Claus, "Strategic Global HR at Teva Pharmaceuticals," *Thunderbird International Business Review* 48 (6) (2006): 891–905; Y.L. Doz and M. Dalsace, *Teva Pharmaceuticals: Global Integration* (Fontainebleau: INSEAD case study, 2002).

38. B.J. Punnett, *International Perspectives on Organizational Behavior and Human Resource Management,* 2d ed. (Armonk, NY: M.E. Sharpe, 2009); E.A. Schein, *Organizational Culture and Leadership,* 2d ed. (San Francisco: Jossey-Bass, 1997); P.J. Frost, L.F. Moore, M.R. Louis, C.C. Lundberg, and J. Martin, *Organizational Culture* (Newbury Park, CA: Sage, 1985).

39. J. Gapper, "Corporate Culture Shock Is a Big Deal," *Financial Times* (London), July 31, 2008: 9; T. Kell and G.T. Carrott, "Culture Matters Most," *Harvard Business Review* 83 (5) (2005): 22–23; M. Booe, "Sales Force at Mary Kay China Embraces the American Way," *Workforce Management* 84 (4) (2005): 24–26; R. Lunnan, J.E. Lervik, L.E. Traavik, S.M. Nilsen, R.P. Amdam, and B.W. Hennestad, "Cultural Counterpoints: Global Transfer of Management Practices across Nations and MNC Subcultures," *Academy of Management Executive* 19 (2) (2005): 77–80.

40. D.J. Terry and N.L. Jimmieson, "A Stress and Coping Approach to Organisational Change: Evidence from Three Field Studies," *Australian Psychologist* 38 (2) (2003): 92–101; S. Benton, "A Four-Point Plan for Creating a Healthy Workplace Climate," *Canadian HR Reporter* 14 (7) (2001): G9; M. Buckingham and C. Coffman, *First, Break All the Rules: What the World's Greatest Managers Do Differently* (New York: Simon & Schuster, 1999).

41. G.K. Stahl and M.E. Mendenhall, *Managing Culture and Human Resources in Mergers and Acquisitions* (Palo Alto, CA: Stanford University Press, 2005); B. Leavy, "Outsourcing Strategies: Opportunities and Risks," *Strategy and Leadership* 32 (6) (2004): 20–25; R.S. Schuler, S.E. Jackson, and Y. Luo, *Managing Human Resources in Cross-Border Alliances* (New York: Routledge, 2003).

42. M. Kaptein, "Business Codes of Multinational Firms: What Do They Say?" *Journal of Business Ethics* 50 (1) (2004): 13–31; A. Bernstein, "Do-It-Yourself Labor Standards: While the WTO Dickers, Companies Are Writing the Rules," *Business Week,* November 19, 2001.

43. E. Dütschke and S. Boerner, "Flexible Employment as a Unidirectional Career? Results from Field Experiments," *Management Revue* 20 (1) (2009): 15–33; A. Taylor, "An Operations Perspective on Strategic Alliance Success Factors: An Exploratory Study of Alliance Managers in the Software Industry," *International Journal of Operations & Production Management* 25 (5/6) (2005): 469–90; P. Morosini, *Managing Cultural Differences: Effective Strategy and Execution across Cultures in Global Corporate Alliances* (London: Elsevier Science and Technology, 1998).

44. T. Donaldson, *Ethics of International Business* (New York: Oxford University Press, 1989).

45. C.M. Vance and E.S. Paderon, "An Ethical Argument for Host Country Workforce Training and Development in the Expatriate Management Assignment," *Journal of Business Ethics* 12 (1993): 635–41; see also M. Velasquez, D.J. Moberg, and G.F. Cavanaugh, "Organizational Statesmanship and Dirty Politics: Ethical Guidelines for Organizational Politicians," *Organizational Dynamics* (Autumn 1983): 65–80.

46. M.R. Vickers, "Business Ethics and the HR Role: Past, Present, and Future," *HR Planning* 28 (1) (2005): 26–32; J. Rossheim, "Human Resources Is Tapped to Address New Compliance Complexities," *Workforce Management* 83 (7) (2004): 74–76; J. Sullivan, "Could HR Have Saved Enron?" *Canadian HR Reporter* 17 (15) (2004): 23.

47. E. Krell, "How to Conduct an Ethics Audit," *HRMagazine,* 55(4) (2010): 48–51; C. Caldwell, "Proactive HR in the Metamorphosis of Corporate Governance," *China Staff* 10 (1) (2003): 11–17.

48. D.T. Wolfe and D.R. Harmanson, "The Fraud Diamond: Considering the Four Elements of Fraud," *CPA Journal* 74 (12) (2004): 38–41.

49. J. Bhagwati, *In Defense of Globalization* (Oxford: Oxford University Press, 2004).

50. S. Panitchpakdi, "Aid Is Good; Trade Is Better," *Wall Street Journal,* January 17, 2005, A14.

51. R. Reich, "Nice Work if You Can Get it," *Wall Street Journal,* December 26, 2003.

52. U. Iram and A. Fatima, "International Trade, Foreign Direct Investment and the Phenomenon of Child Labor; The Case of Pakistan," *International Journal of Social Economics* 35 (11) (2008): 809–22; E. Neumayer and I. de Soysa, "Globalisation, Women's Economic Rights and Forced Labour," *The World Economy* 30 (10) (2007): 1510–35.

53. Q. Li, "Does Democracy Promote or Reduce Transnational Terrorist Incidents?" *Journal of Conflict Resolution* 49 (2) (2005): 278–97; K. Thachuk, "Corruption and International Security," *SAIS Review* 25 (1) (2005): 143–52.

54. B.F. Bobo, *Rich Country, Poor Country: The Multinational as Change Agent* (Westport, CT: Praeger, 2005); A. Otieno, "Studying the Millennium Development Goals," *UN Chronicle* 41 (4) (2005): 53; F. Haralabos, J. Masson, and V. Klenha, "Improving Opportunities for Adult Learning in the Acceding and Candidate Countries of Central and Eastern Europe," *European Journal of Education* 39 (1) (2004): 9–30; A.K. Ghose, *Jobs and Incomes in a Globalizing World* (Geneva: International Labour Office, 2003).

55. M. Marquardt and N. O'Berger, "The Future: Globalization and New Roles for HRD," *Advances in Developing Human Resources* 5 (3) (2003): 283–95.

2 Cultural Foundations of International Human Resource Management

THE FAILURE OF ROVER IN BULGARIA

Rover, the British subsidiary of automobile manufacturer BMW, was very interested in entering the Eastern European market with its Maestro model. After some initial failed partnership attempts, Rover finally entered a joint venture (named Rodacar AD) in 1995 with a private Bulgarian company, The Daru Group, with a manufacturing facility at the Black Sea port of Varna. Rover knew that partnering with this local company could provide low-cost access to existing manufacturing facilities in an economically unstable environment. The partnership made sense since The Daru Group owned Daru Car, the official BMW dealer in Bulgaria, and it was also a major shareholder of two local financial institutions. But the joint venture failed after only eight months, which may be attributed to simple bad luck due to the tragic death in an auto accident of a key Rover executive. The facts in the business plan seemed to indicate that Rover's joint venture plan for entering the Bulgarian market was very sensible. Yet a closer examination of the cultural underpinnings can be very enlightening.

The Bulgarian economic ideology is heavily influenced by Marxism and its socialist tradition, and it was common practice for government bureaucrats to proactively take benefits for themselves and allied companies while using the state as protection. Overlooking this prevailing political ideology, Rover did not take adequate care to legally protect its interests and secure valuable offers that the company had been promised by Bulgarian government officials, such as a significant exemption from taxes and customs duties as well as a major government purchase of Maestro cars. But the Bulgarian government didn't make good on their early promises. The British company also lacked essential knowledge of the idiosyncrasies of Bulgarian social culture. The British tend to base actions on established rules, while Bulgarians emphasize relationships. In Bulgaria, personal contacts, rather than impersonal rules, are of vital importance to the success of a deal. Relationships are also very important in making staffing decisions, whereas the British focus more in merit in employee selection decisions. The British also expect their business agreements to be enforceable and followed strictly, while the Bulgarians value business agreements more as a starting point and believe that they can always be modified as the circumstances change. Bulgaria also is considered a high-context culture, where the surrounding context and circumstances are critical in communication and understanding. The United Kingdom is regarded as a low-context culture, where pretty much "what you see is what you get." The British tend to be more direct and explicit, while the Bulgarians tend to be more indirect, circuitous, and often vague in their communications. Without a clearer understanding of these culturally based foundations, Rover's plan for a successful joint venture was doomed to fail from the start.

Apart from the argument with Bulgarian government officials over what was or was not promised (although the public record supports Rover's view), Rover's managers became furious when the Bulgarian government gave major local auto competitors, Skoda of the Czech Republic and Lada of Russia, preferential treatment in a special exemption from certain import duties and a much larger order of cars for the government fleet. This development made clear that relationships really matter most in Bulgaria. Upon Rover's eventual announced decision to pull out of the joint venture, Bulgaria's deputy prime minister, Rumen Gechev, said that the Maestro cars were not competitive with newer models and that Rover's marketing strategy was faulty. Asked about these comments, Rover corporate spokesman Vincent Hammersley said, "Mr. Gechev was not saying those things at the opening of the factory last year." Obviously, before entering into such a cooperative agreement, the British should have learned much more about the political ideological nature and the values and norms of the Bulgarian culture.[1]

INTRODUCTION

A society's culture is represented by its collective pattern of prevailing norms, beliefs, values, and basic assumptions governing thought processes and subsequent behavior. The opening scenario illustrates how understanding different cultures is critical to achieving successful joint ventures in international business. Without proper knowledge of the different cultures involved, an international joint venture company will not be able to achieve its targeted goal by streamlining existing operations. Instead, it will experience wasteful confusion and debilitating, destructive conflict. And far beyond international joint ventures, these potential negative outcomes can take place in many other business situations—at home or abroad—where cross-cultural interactions are not supported by cultural awareness training and proactive planning.

Culture is central to the effective management of a global workforce. As rather cynically yet accurately stated by Geert Hofstede, one of the pioneers of the study of national cultures throughout the world, "Culture is more often a source of conflict than of synergy. Cultural differences are a nuisance at best and often a disaster." Our sensitivity to possible cross-cultural differences is critical to avoiding such nuisance and disaster. National culture can have a pervasive, powerful influence in organizations. (The importance of its influence on various aspects of global workforce management is noted throughout this book.) In this chapter, we discuss the concept of culture and its role in managing people across borders. We also introduce two frequently cited cultural models and their managerial implications.

UNDERSTANDING CULTURE

Culture affects and governs all facets of life by influencing the values, attitudes, and behaviors of a society. An individual is affected and engrained with his or her cultural society of origin. As a pervasive influence in a society, culture is a learned phenomenon, beginning at birth, and is often unconscious and deeply integrated with one's understanding of the world.[2] Culture can be examined in various ways, including as observable artifacts and behaviors (such as food, dress, and dance), deep cognitive structures (beliefs and values, the way group members tend to process information), or both. Culture has both behavioral and cognitive components. "Culture is defined as the socially transmitted behavior patterns, norms, beliefs and values of a given community."[3] People from the same community use the elements of their culture to interpret their surroundings and guide their interactions with other persons. Furthermore, culture is a phenomenon derived from an interaction of psychological and social factors as individuals internalize messages about rules, beliefs, values, preferences, and expectations from the social environment. Avruch notes, "Culture is a derivative of individual experience, something learned or created by individuals themselves or passed on to them socially by contemporaries or ancestors."[4] Similarly, Hall defines culture as "a pattern of behavior transmitted to members of a group from previous generations of the same group."[5]

It should be noted that culture is not just a national phenomenon. The preceding definition of culture involving common experience and deeply held values and beliefs shared among members of a community also can extend to "communities" at different levels, such as at the personal level (e.g., retired persons or people with common life experiences such as disabilities); work groups; public and private organizations; professional associations and other social networks; strategic alliances; and even supranational units such as the European Union, the IMF, and Amnesty International.[6] People sharing similar working conditions and job tasks, such as in information systems networking, also can develop similar beliefs and priorities that influence their behavior by virtue of their common work experience. Closer to the concept of national culture are regional and local cultures, especially important for countries—geographically large and small—having significant social and ethnic diversity, where there may be quite different subcultures from one region and location of a country to another.

The concept of culture also can extend to individual organizations, as human communities, which, through common experience over time, develop their own distinct set of values, norms, priorities, and beliefs (i.e., "the way we do things in our organization.") In fact, many MNCs strive to develop a common cultural identity of the organization that transcends the traditional influence of national culture.[7] Hofstede distinguishes between organizational culture and national or ethnic group culture in terms of level of conscious awareness, where organizational culture involves more of an employee's mindful identification with certain beliefs, values, and priorities commonly held within an organization. On the other hand, national or ethnic group culture—to which we are exposed from birth—is much more implicit and even unconscious, involving our basic assumptions about the world and ways to understand

and interpret our daily experiences.[8] Both can coexist in today's global organizations, in some cases more easily than in others. Such dual presence is illustrated by Chinese retail managers working for the French MNC Carrefour in Beijing, who consciously accept the company's espoused values of being committed, caring, and positive, yet still feel strangely uncomfortable with Carrefour's overall competitive strategy of being the preferred retailer wherever it operates, preferring instead a sense of harmonious coexistence with local competition. The understanding of national culture, organizational culture, and local culture is particularly relevant to our study of global workforce management, and these different cultural contexts are examined throughout this book. However, in this chapter we focus primarily on general characteristics of national culture.

Culture encompasses information and assumptions that allow us to interpret each other's statements, actions, and intentions. For example, when people from different cultures begin to interact, they often lack a "common pool of information and assumptions."[9] Typical approaches to international management attempt to promote awareness of and sensitivity to national and ethnic culture to enhance one's ability to avoid misunderstanding and to better understand and predict the behavior of people from other cultures. And in many cases the study of culture is very helpful to guide the modification of one's own behavior to better fit in with predominant cultural expectations, that is "when in Rome, do as the Romans do." With particular regard to managing a global workforce, the more familiar one is with the cultural values and norms of a country, the more likely one can best interact with, understand, and manage its people.

We would like to make an important note here about the distinction between general cultural patterns and stereotypes. When we learn about general cultural characteristics and differences between cultures, we are merely dealing with general patterns. We must remember that there can be considerable variation within cultures, and we must not expect every individual to behave in a manner consistent with general cultural characteristics in every situation. Also, even though a general cultural characteristic may be accurate for individuals in most situations, they are also able to adapt their behaviors to the needs of a particular situation. Although there is value in learning about general cultural characteristics and tendencies to help guide our comprehension of otherwise puzzling or even offensive behaviors we encounter, we also must be careful not to form rigid perceptions and fall into the mistake of simply relying on stereotypes. Group stereotypes, which can be positive or negative, are based on the assumption that all individuals in a certain group have the same characteristics. Decisions based on stereotypes risk being inaccurate, not to mention unfair, when individuals at the focus of the decisions do not conform to the stereotype, as may often be the case. Although general cultural patterns may be useful, especially in first learning and gaining insights about a given culture, these patterns must be challenged and refined continually. Challenging these cultural assumptions is particularly important due to a persistent fallacy held by many of national culture homogeneity, where intracountry cultural diversity can actually be as great as intercountry diversity. In addition, cultures are not stable but evolve, albeit slowly, over time, and these potential changes should be taken into consideration.[10] And ultimately, to be effective in managing human resources at home and abroad, we must get to know, manage, and assess employees on an individual level.

CULTURAL DISTANCE

One of the first reactions that we have in traveling abroad for the first time is the differences in signs, written and spoken language, rules and norms, and accepted practices. The collective degree of these differences or overall "foreignness" that we notice refers to the *cultural distance* between our culture and that of the country we are visiting. Due to the somewhat similar cultural history and background between Canada and Australia, we would consider these countries as having relatively small cultural distance, whereas the cultural distance between Canada and Japan would be large. The cultural distance between two countries is often considered in plans for international business expansions, with the assumption that business expansion into another country where the cultural distance gap is large would require greater adjustment effort and expense than when the gap is small. The initial adjustment expense in overcoming challenges and conflict from significantly different culturally based perspectives, communications, and practices may be great with large cultural distance, such as in the acquisition of a foreign operation. However, this expense can be greatly offset by significant performance gains and long-term profitability when the impeding effects of cultural distance can be overcome, resulting in a new organization with greatly expanded cross-cultural understanding and broader and more versatile capability.[11]

Where cultural distance is great between an MNC's home country and host country, the MNC is often motivated, especially at the early stages with minimal experience in a new location, to send a home country expatriate to maximize company strategic control and implementation of company objectives amid the divergent cultural forces of the host country environment.[12] The degree of cultural distance also should be taken into consideration in preparing and training individuals for international assignments, where more careful planning and predeparture training to support foreign adjustment might be necessary where cultural distance is great. However, it should be noted that this cultural distance or degree of adjustment challenge is often not symmetrical or experienced the same way in opposite directions, especially where one individual moves from a village in a developing country such as the Philippines to live in Zurich, Switzerland, and another individual moves from Zurich to live in less comfortable circumstances in the Philippines.[13]

TIGHT VERSUS LOOSE CULTURE

Cultures may differ from one another not only in their physical and behavioral manifestations, but also in how persistent and pervasive they are. In some "tight culture" societies there is virtually complete agreement in terms of what constitutes acceptable behavior for a given situation, whereas in "loose cultures" there may be much greater expression of, and tolerance for, diversity. A tight culture, such as Thailand, tends to have greater uniformity and agreement due to greater ethnic and religious homogeneity than

Figure 2.1   **Globalization and Its Impacts on Culture**

Economic Imperatives	Impacts on Culture	Strategic Implications
Globalization	Convergence	Global Integration
Localization	Divergence	Local Responsiveness
Glocalization	Crossvergence	Balance between Global Integration and Local Responsiveness

what is found in a looser culture, such as the United Kingdom.[14] Tight cultures, such as Korea and Japan, also tend to resist the loss of original cultural identity. In addition, tight cultures tend to resist close inner-circle acceptance of those from foreign cultures, as long-time *gaijin* or foreigners in Japan often report subtle and not-so-subtle experiences of exclusion. In general, as a country becomes more exposed to and influenced by other cultures, its predominant culture tends to become less tight and loosens its restrictions on individuals, thus resulting in a more individualistic society where people feel at liberty to express themselves in different ways.[15]

GLOBALIZATION AND CULTURAL CONVERGENCE

One of the main characteristics of culture is that it is not static. Culture continually evolves. Accordingly, given the prominent role of globalization in this book, we would like to present different views about how global and regional economic integration have affected and will most likely continue to affect the different dimensions of culture that we have examined. Figure 2.1 summarizes the impact of different economic imperatives on culture.

As discussed earlier, globalization refers to an increasing integration of markets as well as production processes across borders. Rapid innovations of technology and decreased trade and investment barriers have made it possible for firms to launch and market their products simultaneously to many different countries. As a result, globalization has encouraged cultural homogeneity and diffusion. For example, Music Television, more commonly known as MTV, has created a truly global market through the use and expansion of new technologies, various media venues, and cultural sensitivity. MTV believes that there is a world pop culture and sensibility among twelve- to thirty-four-year-olds who have viewpoints, attitudes, and consumer habits that have been shaped by the last twenty-five years of technology. MTV is a perfect example of a global brand because its message is spread internationally and accepted by teens worldwide.

We found that globalization contributed to convergence of work values that various religions advocate in their own way. A recent study by Parboteeah and colleagues provides strong evidence that all forms of religion are related to important work outcomes.[16] This carries a very important message for MNCs that often have to manage diverse group of people with differing religious beliefs. Traditionally, religions have been considered a source of conflict that impedes the effective management of people across different cultures. Research results, however, imply that MNCs from a country with predominantly Christian background can achieve business success in Islamic and/or Buddhist countries and vice versa. As such, cultural convergence implies that as nations become industrialized, they experience a significant change in values and adopt behaviors that embrace free-market capitalism.[17]

This supposition suggests that through the imperatives of industrialization and economic development, the value systems of managers become increasingly similar. For example, traditionally collectivistic developing countries will take on more individualistic work values.[18] Therefore, cultural convergence, driven by the rapid spread of technology, enables MNCs to apply relatively identical general business and specific HR management practices across countries. There is growing evidence of a convergence effect in international business and management practices, especially with regard to strategic planning.[19] Von Glinow and colleagues found some significant converging trends in international HR management practices across cultures, arguing that these universal best practices can enhance a firm's capability and may well contribute to sustainable competitive advantage.[20] Such a view manifests a universalist orientation that calls for a unified approach to different country circumstances.[21]

For example, hiring practices in different countries are undergoing major changes due to the globalization of modern industries. In spite of prevailing cross-national differences, the trend toward convergence seems to be irresistible. In a comparative study of personnel selection practices in thirteen countries, two selection criteria were found as the most commonly used recruiting practices across countries: (1) evidence of the person's ability to perform the technical requirements of the job and (2) impressions gained from a personal interview.[22]

Despite this claim toward HR management practice convergence, a striking similarity in hiring practices was found among U.S., Australian, and Canadian firms due to their common Anglo cultural roots. Likewise, East Asian countries such as Japan, Korea, and Taiwan demonstrated a remarkable similarity due to their historical and cultural ties. Similarly, Drost and colleagues reported that although they did not find any universal training and development practices, significant similarities were detected within each specific region of Asia, Mexico and Latin America, and North America.[23] The common practices found within these clusters are believed to be influenced by cultural values and industry trends. This similarity suggests that the impact of cultural differences still prevails in HR management practices despite the convergence effect driven by global integration.

LOCALIZATION AND CULTURAL DIVERGENCE

Despite the global and regional integration of national economies, cultural differences still remain strong, just as blood is thicker than water. As Holton introduced cultural polarization as an opposite concept to cultural homogenization, global integration may not always result in cultural conformity and convergence.[24] Managers still recognize the need to adapt management practices to the local environment. As Hofstede argues, for example, the cultural emphasis upon individualism that is so prevailing in Western society is often not so effective in Eastern society where collectivism is more valued. It is interesting to note that Japanese management approaches were praised when the Japanese economy was prosperous, and many American companies were encouraged to adopt the HR management approaches of Japanese companies. For example, Ouchi's Theory Z attributed the success of Japanese companies in the 1970s mainly to their unique HR management practices and recommended that American companies adopt their management approaches.[25] Conversely, when the Japanese economy was in a deep recession and the U.S. economy was in a boom in the 1990s, Japanese companies were encouraged to adopt American management approaches focusing on individual achievement and a more flexible labor market. The pendulum has begun to swing back as the U.S. media expresses concern over lost confidence in corporate America, and many Japanese executives have renewed support of the values of Japanese-style management.[26] American companies are now learning the hard way that many of the systems designed to nurture excellence in the 1990s actually fostered corruption and bad performance. This is particularly true in the aftermath of the credit crisis in America in late 2007; U.S. corporate governance is in question.

Refuting the convergence claim, Pucik states that the HR function is seen as an obstacle to globalization because of the ethnocentric and parochial HR systems that are designed only for an MNC's home country and are ill-fitting elsewhere.[27] For example, in a ten-country comparative study of compensation, culture was found to exert a significant impact on employee preference for specific compensation practices.[28] Cultural divergence is particularly prominent in recent works that challenge the universality of traditional U.S.-based principles of HR management.[29] We found strong support for the divergence perspective in different cross-cultural studies on HR management practices, performance appraisal in particular. These results are noteworthy because they demonstrate significant differences among Chinese culture-based countries that have often been regarded as culturally homogenous: Hong Kong, Taiwan, and Singapore. These findings imply that there are limits to the idea of a "common" culture, particularly based on common ethnicity, with sharp differences between some Asian countries and even within societies strongly influenced by neo-Confucianism.[30]

Similarly, based on other research we concluded that attempts at transferring generally accepted or "universal" management concepts to Russia that do not take into account the cultural values of Russian managers would likely have little chance of success.[31] We found significant differences between U.S. and Russian managers in perceptions about management style that would be expected and reinforced by employees, particularly related to leadership functions. Though our research indicates that assuming direct transferability of American and "universal" management techniques is erroneous, it does not mean that countries cannot learn from each other. On the contrary, benchmarking business approaches that work in other countries is one of the most effective ways of getting new ideas in the area of management and organization.

GLOCALIZATION AND CULTURAL CROSSVERGENCE

Convergence and divergence perspectives represent polar extremes. As most firms struggle to find the optimal trade-off between globalization and localization, sometimes called glocalization, perhaps the reality is closer to a more balanced or middle-ground view called crossvergence, or hybridization (i.e., the intermixing of cultural systems between different countries).[32] The concept of hybridization contends that cultures are shaped and reshaped through interactions with other cultures in which people consciously or unconsciously insert new meanings into their own cultural understanding.[33] Basically, crossvergence theorists argue that as the global economy grows and features increasingly meaningful interactions, countries will influence one another economically as well as culturally. According to this perspective, since a certain operational system (e.g., the Japanese just-in-time system) is embedded in a specific culture, it needs to be reinterpreted and recontextualized when it is introduced into to a different country.[34] Similarly, when expatriate managers introduce a new leadership style in managing a host country workforce, they cannot simply impose it onto them, but rather should carefully modify it in a cultural context that is meaningful to local employees. For example, a form of hybrid HR management pattern is emerging in foreign-invested Western enterprises in China, with significant differences between the HR management practices of the traditional Chinese unit and MNC's Western home country practices, and mediated by local institutional differences.[35]

Jackson argues that two potentially opposing loci of human values exist.[36] Traditionally, Anglo-Saxon countries such as the United States, the United Kingdom, and Australia have long practiced instrumentalism, which considers human resources mainly as a means to an end, emphasizing individual competence of employees to make the best use of these human resources through a calculated, utilitarian exchange between employers and employees. Just as time needs to be managed in the most efficient manner, people also need to be managed efficiently. In stark contrast, Eastern countries such as Japan and Korea traditionally value human beings in their own right; that is, they view people as an end in themselves and show interest in developing the maximum potential of employees. From their perspective, people are not seen as a short-term disposable resource, but as a long-term integral part of the organization. Jackson found that as the global economy increases the interaction between countries and results in the crossfertilization of HR management systems, Anglo-Saxon countries are softening their instrumental approaches, with a resulting greater interest in longer-term human development and investment. Likewise, a commitment to the humanistic approach in East Asian countries tends to weaken by the introduction of Western instrumental approaches. Such a crossvergence trend is particularly visible in economies that experience a rapid transformation of their society as the interface of Western and Eastern cultures intensifies. Although there may be dominating influences from stronger and more successful economies, such as the United States, that compel transitional and emerging countries to adopt counterculture solutions, crossvergence has given rise to successful hybrid management systems.[37]

To summarize, crossvergence means that different management approaches are expected to converge in the middle. Globalization of the world economy has made it possible for countries to learn from one another and studying and benchmarking business approaches that work in other countries is an effective way to get new potentially valuable ideas.[38] Interest is increasing in combining indigenous and Western cultures in the practice and development of international business. This crossvergence trend is particularly true of the transitional economies of the former Soviet bloc, China, and other developing nations.

Figure 2.2   **Hofstede's Cultural Dimensions and Their Managerial Implications**

Cultural Dimensions	Interpretations	Managerial Implications
Uncertainty Avoidance	Rigidity vs. Flexibility	Formal vs. Informal Procedures
Power Distance	Equality vs. Inequality	Centralized vs. Decentralized Decision Making
Individualism vs. Collectivism	Self vs. Group	Individual vs. Group Rewards
Masculinity vs. Femininity	Material Success vs. Concern for Others	Competition vs. Cooperation
Confucian Dynamism	Virtue vs. Truth	Long-term vs. Short-term Orientation

Source: Adapted from G. Hofstede, *Cultures and Organizations: Software of the Mind* (New York: McGraw Hill, 1997).

MAJOR MODELS OF NATIONAL CULTURE

Culture represents a system of values and norms that are shared among a group of people and that, taken together, constitute a design for living.[39] Although values are abstract ideas and convictions about what people believe, norms are prescribed behaviors that are acceptable in a specific society. Both values and norms are influenced by many factors such as religion, language, social structures, education, and so on. Values are more difficult to learn than norms because they are not easily observable. Yet, it is essential for business managers to study values in order to understand the reasons and motivations behind specific behaviors and cultural norms. The following section introduces two commonly used models of culture and their managerial implications. In addition, the results of the GLOBE study are explained, a recent major research project on national culture.

HOFSTEDE'S CULTURAL DIMENSIONS AND MANAGERIAL IMPLICATIONS

Geert Hofstede defined national culture as the set of collective beliefs and values that distinguish people of one nationality from those of another.[40] His original comprehensive study, which he conducted while working at IBM as a psychologist, involved more than 100,000 individuals from fifty countries and three regions. In the study, Hofstede identified four important dimensions in national culture. The validity and reliability of these four cultural variables have been tested and found to be very strong in subsequent studies.[41] Later he added another cultural dimension, so-called Confucian dynamism, which captures the difference between a long-term and short-term orientation.[42] Figure 2.2 summarizes Hofstede's cultural dimensions along with their managerial implications.

Uncertainty Avoidance

This Hofstede dimension refers to the extent to which people feel comfortable when they are exposed to an ambiguous or uncertain situation. People in a low uncertainty avoidance society are more willing to take risks and appreciate flexibility and informality in the workplace. In contrast, people in a high uncertainty avoidance society tend to be risk averse and favor rigid and formal decision-making processes in the workplace. Under high uncertainty avoidance, security is a strong motivator relative to achievement or self-fulfillment, and order and predictability are paramount. Rules are important and must be obeyed to avoid chaos. Communication is direct and unequivocal to avoid confusion. Often this directness in high uncertainty avoidance countries such as Germany is mistaken for rudeness, when in reality it is an effort to ensure the clarity of a message of rule observance to preserve order. It is no surprise that Germany is a world leader in precision engineering and manufacturing.

The perceived difference in tolerating uncertain situations has several important implications at both the macro and micro levels. First, at the macro level, the acceptance of uncertainty is essential for innovation because it requires a tolerance for risk and change. Technological innovation is critical for economic growth and enhanced competitiveness in the global market. However, the development of technology or innovation itself is a risky adventure because it requires a long-term resource commitment. The U.S. culture of low uncertainty avoidance and tolerance for risk and change has often been mentioned as a main source of the country's technological leadership in the world.[43] Conversely, people who are culturally inclined to avoid the risks and uncertainties of life tend to think that developing a new technology from the ground up may be too risky.[44] In cultures where individuals are reluctant to accept a certain amount of uncertainty and risk, a relentless attempt to develop new technology may end up only depleting their limited national resources. Accordingly, high uncertainty avoidance countries tend to represent a less favorable environment for technology development than low uncertainty avoidance countries.

Second, at the micro or organizational level, in high uncertainty avoidance societies numerous formal internal rules and regulations exist to control the work process of employees. Roles must be specified and instructions detailed. In low uncertainty avoidance societies, managers are allowed to exercise more latitude and discretion in their decision making rather than relying on rigid internal rules and regulations.

Power Distance

Power distance refers to the extent to which people have an equal distribution of power. In a large power distance culture, power is concentrated at the top in the hands of relatively few people whereas people at the bottom are subject to decisions and instructions given by superiors. Conversely, in a small power distance culture, power is equally distributed among the members of the society. It is important to note that the particular predominant perspective on power distance is held and reinforced by most members of the society. Even in high power distance countries such as Mexico and India, both those in positions of power and authority and those at the lowest organizational levels accept without question the wide gap in power and authority with accompanying status, privileges, and wealth. Lower-level employees often feel uncomfortable with expatriate managers from moderate to lower power distance countries (such as the United States) who may attempt to establish more participative and egalitarian management practices.

Managers in high power distance societies tend to believe in giving subordinates detailed instructions with little room for interpretation. Subordinates are supposed to respect the authority and superiority of upper management. Thus, the "mechanistic characteristics" of high power distance cultures, such as inequality among the members in the society, lack of free communication across different levels of the hierarchy, and centralized control, can stifle employee creativity and new ideas. Multilevel hierarchies effectively widen the social gap between superiors and subordinates. Such structures tend to stifle the innovation process and send clear messages to employees not to operate outside their domain.[45] Quinn argued that policies that foster inequality among the members of an organization impede innovation.[46] Standardized organizational procedures and rigid centralized control have been found to hinder the flexibility needed for innovation.

In contrast, "organic characteristics," such as lack of hierarchical authority and less centralization, tend to promote employee interaction, lateral communication, and less emphasis on the rules. Nondirective, hands-off monitoring systems have often been implemented to allow the creativity and exploration necessary for successful innovation.[47] Hauser argued that the technical and social complexities of innovative projects demand extensive communication.[48] Unstructured, freewheeling, multidirectional communication across levels of an organizational hierarchy will facilitate innovation. Conversely, people in high power distance cultures rarely partake in informal communication between different levels of hierarchy. A lack of informal communication in high power distance cultures can impede the free flow of necessary information and the constructive communication needed for innovation.

Individualism versus Collectivism

Individualism means that people seek and protect their own interests over the common goal of the society and their role in the society. In an individualistic culture, people are comfortable with having the authority to make a decision based on what the individual thinks is best. In a collectivistic culture, people tend to belong to groups or collectives and look after each other in exchange for loyalty. Two major elements in Hofstede's concept of individualism include autonomy and variety.

In individualistic societies, employees are provided with a great deal of personal freedom and autonomy. First, many researchers believe that freedom and independence are essential for effective research and development (R&D) and innovation.[49] IBM's main theme, "how to build individuality into firms in the interest of innovation," reflects the same view. However, collective cultures do not usually allow the same amount of freedom and independence necessary for organizational members to think creatively and, thereby, fail to cultivate an environment that fosters an innovative spirit.

Another element in a collective culture that discourages innovation is the reluctance to accept variety and diversity in society. Innovation means doing things differently. Variety in an organization must be sufficient to foster experimentation, learning, adaptation, pursuit of new roads, and generation of opportunities. Promoting and maintaining multiple perspectives are essential to the innovative process. As discussed earlier related to the concept of "tight cultures," collective cultures put a great deal of pressure on their members to conform without their being aware of it. The overwhelming and unconscious pressure for conformity and uniformity in collective cultures does not cultivate an environment for diversity and provides less room for people to deviate from established norms, thus impeding the innovation process.

As we examine in Chapter 9, the cultural influence of individualism versus collectivism also can influence employee performance evaluation policies and practices. While an individualistic culture tends to emphasize individual merit or achievement, a collectivistic culture measures contributions to teamwork and group achievement. It is also believed that people in a collectivistic culture such as Japan are willing to show a higher level of loyalty to their organization compared to people in an individualistic culture such as the United States, where the general sentiment holds job mobility for personal career advancement as more important than organizational loyalty.

Masculinity versus Femininity

Hofstede believes that the masculine dimension is very closely related to the concept of achievement motivation introduced by McClelland and Winter.[50] A masculine culture is basically a performance-driven society where rewards and recognition for performance are the primary motivational factors for achievement. In masculine cultures some major innovations are simply the outcome of financial rewards, prestige, and a sense of accomplishment. In masculine societies, people are supposed to be competitive, ambitious, assertive, and willing to take risks in order to achieve their goals. This type of culture tends to give the utmost respect and admiration to the successful achiever who fulfills his or her ambition and demonstrates assertiveness and willingness to take risks in order to achieve goals. Top management positions are usually filled with men who tend to display dominant and assertive characteristics, which tend to be discouraged among women by societal gender norms. Expressing this behavior, men are perceived in a positive light (assertive), whereas women are seen in a negative light (aggressive).

On the other hand, in feminine cultures people tend to emphasize the quality of the "whole" life rather than money, success, and social status, which are easier to quantify. They are willing to reach out to the underprivileged and share their wealth with them. Accordingly, the pursuit of sustained economic development, keeping the balance between industrialization and environmental preservation, is considered more valuable than simple gross national product (GNP) growth. Overall, organizations with a feminine culture are not as competitive as those with a masculine culture, because the former places higher priority on concern for others and little distinction is made between men and women in the same position. Scandinavian countries have long been considered feminine cultures. It is no surprise that they tend to be world leaders in personal taxation to support social security and support needs.

Confucian Dynamism

This dimension was added later to Hofstede's original research findings. Using a different survey instrument called the Chinese Value Survey, Hofstede and

Global Workforce Challenge 2.1
China and the Cross-Cultural Training Imperative

The Chinese have a saying that "he who knows two cultures lives two lives." This is an apt expression to keep in mind as we continue to integrate with China as a central player in the global marketplace. Greater cross-cultural understanding and sensitivity will continue to be in high demand on the part of all participants. Although convergence in broad economic and strategic practices will continue, deep-seated differences will still exist between Western and Eastern management styles and specific practices involved in implementing economic policy and company strategy. There are fundamental differences in personal worldviews, including those regarding the role of family, government, religion, age, and so on, and the impact of family and educational environment on individual development is huge. It would be fanciful to assume that all Chinese managers who receive Western-style management training will be immediately transformed and behave like Western managers. Cross-cultural training programs for Western professionals working in China should have a set of personality traits identified as most suitable for the proposed cultural environment, and trainees should be screened for at least potential promise in those traits. Besides these specific traits and associated, supportive behaviors, cross-cultural training should also concentrate on general skills in cross-cultural adaptability and ability to observe and read cultural differences, which are so essential at the critical early stages of preliminary negotiations and cross-cultural encounters.

Cross-cultural issues are further challenged by internal cultural disparities that have nothing to do with East-West differences. For example, in China there are considerable disparities between entrepreneurs from peasant stock, who have suddenly flourished with China's ascent in embracing the global market economy, and the more established technocrats with a college education who are dominant in the fields of engineering and natural sciences. In addition, there are major differences between Western national cultures, based on different basic value systems, which can add complexity and potential confusion in multiple-party transactions in China.

Three key priorities for guiding cross-cultural training efforts to help bridge the cross-cultural divide and support future successful business operations in China and with Chinese partners worldwide follow:

• *Sense of Belonging.* It will be important to transcend national differences and focus on common work goals and objectives, including having a clear understanding of mutual benefits gained through collaboration and interdependence. A Chinese manager working for a British firm in Sweden, despite the multiple national cultures, will still feel part of the company team. For Western managers, training on the Chinese concept of *guanxi,* or relationships in a network of contacts linked by varying degrees of mutual obligation, can help lead to greater influence within and between organizations, with less of a sense of isolation and working in a vacuum.

• *Moral Foundation Commonalities.* Similarities in religion and basic moral principles between East and West can outweigh differences. Common ground can

(continued)

Global Workforce Challenge 2.1 (continued)

be found in the need for harmony created by a set of moral rules and the need for a conscience to guide the individual and elements of mutual obligation. By emphasizing these common moral foundation needs, cross-cultural training help develop a common bond for the organizational relationship.

   • *Language.* Differences in language can create different ways of looking at the world. The Chinese language is descriptive in its written form. In the West, the tendency is toward greater precision in defining meanings. In cross-cultural settings, this precision can limit conceptual thought flexibility. Training also should be customized to be aware of where language problems might occur. In Poland, former U.S. President Jimmy Carter apparently once said that he "desired the Poles carnally." Language difficulties might come from poor translation or an error in the choice of an idiomatic phrase. More seriously, language might be a source of failure to communicate an important concept or conceptual process. Training can be very beneficial in nonverbal communications and intuition, involving the use of a much broader set of information cues in the communication process.

Sources: Adapted from A.D. Wright, "Respect Cultural Differences When Training, Experts Say," *HR Magazine* 54 (12) (2009): 19–20; "Adopting a Cultured Approach to Training," *Training Strategies for Tomorrow* 16 (6) (2002): 4–6.

Bond identified a new cultural dimension, "long-term versus short-term orientation," which strongly reflects Confucianism, a cultural backbone of East Asian countries.[51] Long-term orientation captures the following elements: adaptation of tradition to the modern context, high savings ratio driven by thrift, patience and perseverance toward slow results, and concern with respecting the demand of virtue. They claimed that these characteristics, unique to people in East Asian countries such as Japan, Korea, and China, explained the cultural ethos strongly associated with the region's remarkable economic growth in the 1970s and 1980s. On the other hand, a short-term orientation contains the following aspects: respect for traditions, lower savings rate, quick-results orientation, and concern with possessing the truth.

Hofstede emphasized that this particular cultural dimension was missing in his original study and was relevant only to countries in East Asia. Confucian dynamism may reflect a society's search for virtue rather than truth, truth being driven by religious ethics in Western countries. Along with the different proclivity toward uncertainty avoidance, short-term versus long-term orientation also has been identified as a main source of conflict resulting in decreased performance in international joint ventures (IJVs).[52] In IJVs that involve considerable cross-cultural interaction and where managers' perceptions about time orientation differ significantly (for example, in one IJV partner the focus is on short-term gains whereas the other partner emphasizes the long term), effectiveness in implementing strategy and achieving strategic performance goals can be greatly diminished.

Figure 2.3 **Trompenaars and Hampden-Turner's Cultural Dimensions and Their Managerial Implications**

Cultural Dimensions	Interpretations	Managerial Implications
Universalism vs. Particularism	Rules vs. Relationships	One Principle vs. Many Different Ways of Conducting Business
Specific vs. Diffuse Cultures	Range of Involvement in Public vs. Private Space	Distinction and Size Difference between Public and Personal Life
Achievement vs. Ascription Cultures	How Status Is Accorded	Merit-based Performance vs. Respect for Elders and Titles
Individualism vs. Communitarianism	Individual vs. Group	Personal Responsibility vs. Group Consensus
Emotional vs. Neutral Culture	Range of Feelings Expressed	Animated Expression vs. Self-control
Time Orientation	Monochronic vs. Polychronic	Keeping Schedules vs. Flexibility
Orientation to Nature	Human Being's Mastery Over vs. Subjugation to Nature	Internal Control vs. External Control

Source: Adapted from F. Trompenaars and C. Hampden-Turner, *Riding the Waves of Culture: Understanding Cultural Diversity in Global Business* (New York: McGraw-Hill, 1997).

Hofstede's research has received several criticisms. First, the research may have been culturally bound because his research team, composed of Europeans and Americans, may have unintentionally influenced the analysis of the answers by their Western perspective. Second, as mentioned already regarding regional and local subcultures, many countries have more than one culture. For example, the United States has multiple regional and local subcultures, because the country consists of various ethnic groups and regional traditions, with a strong emphasis on local autonomy and individual states' rights. Therefore, it may be presumptuous to generalize a certain country's culture. Most important, his findings may have lost explanatory power over the years because culture is not static and changes over time, albeit slowly. Despite these criticisms, Hofstede's research still remains a seminal work and many scholars continue to apply his model to their cross-cultural studies in various disciplines, including international business and management.

TROMPENAARS AND HAMPDEN-TURNER'S SEVEN CULTURAL DIMENSIONS

Other scholars also have explored cultural dimensions that underlie the patterns of behaviors and logical reasoning in different countries and have offered additional perspectives. Adopting Parsons's five relational orientations as their starting point, Trompenaars and Hampden-Turner identified seven important cultural dimensions.[53] They viewed culture mainly as the way in which a group of people solves problems and reconciles dilemmas. Figure 2.3 summarizes their cultural dimensions along with their managerial implications.

Universalism versus Particularism

Universalism is a belief that there exists only a single management principle that should be applied to all situations. People from universalistic cultures tend to believe that their way of doing business or managing people is the universal one and the best way and should be adopted by all other countries. For example, U.S. culture contains strong characteristics of universalism and represents the mentality of American people toward the world. Hampden-Turner argues, "However strange and disquieting it may seem to a foreigner, it is no mere coincidence that the championship of the American 'national pastime' is known as the World Series."[54] Likewise, the Los Angeles Lakers are called "World Champions," despite the fact that no teams from other countries compete in the National Basketball Association Championship series. These examples illustrate the mind-set of many Americans that the United States is indeed the world. Euro Disney's struggle with the startup of a new theme park in Paris was due largely to an indifferent assumption of top Disney management that whatever works at home would also work in other countries. They believed that their management approach represented the successful model that should be replicated wherever they set up a new theme park.[55]

Conversely, particularistic cultures highlight the peculiarity and distinctiveness of a country's culture that is different from those of other countries. Both at the country and individual levels, the emphasis is on building long-term relationships and being sensitive and responsive to the unique circumstances surrounding that relationship. Japan has been considered a country with strong particularism. Due to the physical insularity of the country, Japan has developed many idiosyncrasies of its own culture such as greater emphasis on teamwork and excluding foreigners. Unlike people in a universalistic culture, people in a particularistic culture assume that local circumstances determine the way of doing business in different countries. Much of Japan's world economic success in entering into and then dominating new world markets has been the result of its ability to be sensitive to local market conditions and customer needs. And just as Japanese companies believe that they should alter their way of conducting business according to the host country culture, they expect that foreign companies in Japan should adapt their business practices to local business environments.

People from universalistic cultures flourished in earlier years when global product standardization and mass production was in vogue, but they faced great challenges and immediate need to adapt when world consumers began to demand customization to individual needs and tastes. Those from universalistic cultures also tend to believe in absolute justice and truth and extend great resources to their protection. It is no surprise that the United States leads the world in the number of lawyers per capita. Those high in universalism take moral principles very seriously because they recognize the existence of a unified approach to business. In contrast, people in particularistic cultures tend to interpret justice or moral convictions in a more flexible manner, depending on the local and current circumstances. For example, Chinese cultures tend to focus more on building long-term relationships in a protracted negotiation and tend to prefer more vague contracts that allow greater flexibility should conditions change. Given a change in circumstances, they might even try to renegotiate an agreement after the contract has been signed and agreed on by all parties. It is not difficult to predict that organizations from universalistic and particularistic cultures could experience misunderstandings and conflict when they conduct business together.

Specific versus Diffuse Cultures

This cultural dimension concerns perceptions regarding private versus public space and how each is handled. In specific cultures, people clearly separate public space from private space. Furthermore, in specific cultures the size of public space is larger relative to private or personal space and is greatly compartmentalized. In other words, people in a specific culture tend to be very friendly and willing to open their public space to other people with whom they do not have an acquaintance and admit them into a segregated compartment with a limited personal commitment.

In diffuse cultures, the distinction between private and public spaces is rather unclear and blurry. Everything is related, and business is just another form of social interaction.[56] Business relationships are expected to be enduring and spill over into personal relationships and vice versa. Specific cultures tend to compartmentalize public and private life into separate roles, where one role does not influence another. For example, one can be a mother, tax accountant, and volunteer officer in a local service organization without these roles affecting one another. However, in a diffuse culture, roles tend to extend beyond their official boundaries, such as a teacher being especially respected and revered in other public and private settings unrelated to teaching. It is no wonder that diffuse cultures tend to have greater difficulty with role confusion.

Furthermore, for diffuse cultures the size of public space is almost equal to that of private space. Therefore, in diffuse cultures, people tend to reserve even their public space (for example, professional work situations) for those with whom they are familiar, because accepting the entry of unknown people could also mean the uncomfortable opening of their private space. Accordingly, when one conducts business in a diffuse culture such as Japan, one should expect that having the best price or quality is not enough, and that the in-group versus the out-group distinction is crucial because people tend not to trust outsiders. This is why establishing a long-term relationship is critical to business success in a diffuse culture, which often is the case in an emerging market where one takes advantage of strong familial and personal relationship ties to reduce business transaction cost due to the absence of reliable legal and social institutions.[57] With particular regard to managing a global workforce, specific cultures tend to reflect a predominant use of personal merit as the primary criterion for guiding such important HR decisions as employee staffing, compensation, and discipline without prejudice. However, this approach tends to be very alien to diffuse cultures that favor members of one's family or social community.

Achievement versus Ascription Cultures

Achievement cultures value personal competency and an outcome resulting from individual hard work. What matters most in an achievement culture is an objective track record of individual accomplishment. Therefore, an individualistic culture also tends to be associated with achievement culture. In contrast, an ascription culture means that people are conferred a certain status based on specific characteristics such as title or position, age, and profession. People in an ascription culture value personal connections and family background more than the individual's qualifications. They expect those in authority to act in accordance with the roles ascribed to them by fate or a divine power; actual performance and results are less important. Appearance accorded by title and status is more important than substance driven by individual qualification.

This concept corresponds to high-context versus low-context cultures as defined by Hall, particularly regarding interpersonal communications.[58] In low-context countries, communication relies more heavily on the literal meaning of the words used—as with the achievement orientation, words are judged by their own merit. Meanings of written and spoken communication are more direct and explicit. In high-context cultures, much more of the context surrounding or related to the written or spoken communication is involved in conveying the message, including timing and physical surroundings. Also, factors such as the social status of the communicators and the nature of their relationship are considered important parts of a message. The meaning of everything said in high-context communication has to be interpreted in the context of the observable surroundings and social relationship between the individuals. To people from high-context cultures, the bluntness and directness of low-context communication styles, with undue consideration of the relationship or other contextual conditions, can seem insulting or rude.

In an ascription culture, a high-trust relationship is based on membership of a common family, province, or class of graduates. These represent preexisting relationships. In China interpersonal ties among people are known as *guanxi*.[59] In *guanxi* relationships, the ethical basis of purchasing decisions is traditionally the set of obligations that arise from a specific relationship rather than from a set of universal principles such as quality and price, which are usually highly valued in achievement cultures. Therefore, it is not uncommon for managers in ascription cultures to favor friends or relatives when recruiting new employees over people who may possess higher qualifications but do not have any preexisting relationships.

Individualism versus Communitarianism

Individualism refers to the culture that emphasizes the interests of self or of his/her own immediate family. In contrast, communitarianism, a synonym for *collectivism* as used by Hofstede, emphasizes group (for example, a team of employees) interests before individual interests and seeking group consensus in decision making. However, the Hofstede and Trompenaars/Hampden-Turner research findings were not identical regarding countries identified as either individualist or communitarian cultures.

Affective versus Neutral Culture

People in affective or emotional cultures are not hesitant to reveal their innermost feelings whereas people in neutral cultures tend to control their emotions carefully and maintain their composure. For example, the Japanese are known to be difficult to read, while Koreans and Americans express their feelings in public freely.[60] People

Global Workforce Professional Profile 2.1
Dr. Norihito Furuya: Global Cross-Cultural Awareness Consultant

Dr. Norihito (Nori) Furuya is CEO and cofounder of the IGB (Institute of Global Business) Network, a management and organization consulting collaboration committed to developing high-performing global organizations, teams, and individuals. Furuya has been involved in cross-cultural and other forms of global business education and consulting for nearly forty years. He has lived and worked in the United States, the United Kingdom, Kuwait, and Bahrain, with approximately ten years abroad from his native Japan in expatriate assignments. His past and current clients are Fortune 500 and medium-size companies that are focused on developing key competencies in managers to support their global operational effectiveness. Besides his executive administrative responsibilities with the IGB Network, Furuya also currently is working in the areas of global management development and transnational cultural management as a consultant, trainer, and coach with the Kozai Group, Inc. In this work he actively assists companies in assessing and developing the global skills and competencies of their managerial cadre through the Kozai Group's Global Competencies Inventory, its Intercultural Effectiveness Scale, and customized training programs based on the inventory assessment results.

A particularly notable professional experience that tested Furuya's cross-cultural expertise came when he was living and working in Kuwait as director of the Middle East headquarters of a large Japanese MNC. In his position Furuya worked in budget management, HR, and managed other administrative responsibilities for the regional offices and contracted agencies located in more than fifteen countries from Libya to India. He often faced frustrating challenges in sudden changes and delays greatly influenced by the prevailing Arab cultural characteristic with minimal orientation to time. His firm also was responsible for the safety and security of Japanese expatriates—the most established expatriate population in the Middle East—and their families living in the region. His skills in diplomacy and cross-cultural sensitivity were especially tested while working in Bahrain, when Iraqi troops invaded Kuwait in early August 1990, and all expatriates and their families were moved to Baghdad. Although the family members were released in a few days and flown back to Japan, the expatriate managers were taken as hostages into Iraqi military bases and held for over six months, during which time Furuya diligently worked as a liaison officer with the Japanese ambassador to secure their release.

Another important experience came in working with senior Japanese executives in the United States on legal problems related to allegations of lax attention to sexual harassment at lower levels of the organization. The Japanese firm with operations in the United States provided several measures to increase sensitivity to and prevent sexual harassment. However, when sexual harassment claims actually were raised, Japanese management, motivated more by a culturally based tendency to protect the organization and "hide the shame," performed inadequate investigations of the claims and engaged in legally costly efforts to block government inquiry. Through his ongoing training and coaching efforts, Furuya was able to help Japanese management develop HR practices and procedures with greater transparency and honesty that would have much better success in the U.S. business environment.

in neutral cultures may consider the behaviors of people from affective cultures immature; people from affective cultures may view the stoic behaviors of people from neutral cultures as insincere and deceiving. This perception may cause problems during cross-cultural negotiations between managers from affective and neutral cultures.

Time Orientation

People across cultures may deal with the concept of time in a different manner. Time orientation contains two different connotations. First, the time dimension is related to how people actually use time. A monochronic, or sequential approach to time means that people use time in a linear way. Time is perceived as being a tangible asset almost like money. For example, people in a monochronic culture such as the United States or Germany, tend to think that time is money; it should be saved and spent in the most efficient manner possible. In this type of culture, punctuality is a virtue, and people must always keep schedules. At the same time, they tend to make a clear distinction between work and pleasure. People may be relaxed only during their leisure time, while they concentrate on assigned tasks only during working hours. In contrast, a polychronic, or a synchronous, approach to time suggests that people use time in a circular way. People in polychronic cultures such as France and Italy tend to have a more flexible view about time and can handle multiple agendas at one time. Furthermore, they consider that maintaining human relations is more important than keeping schedules. Accordingly, they do not clearly separate their work from pleasure and do not mind mixing them.

Another time-related difference concerns people's orientation to past, present, and future. This orientation points to whether people are likely to see the future as an extension of the past. Some cultures place greater emphasis on tradition and precedence and interpret the future in the context of what happened in the past. Cultures that emphasize the present seem to live for the moment, insisting on an immediate return on investment, whether it is time, capital, or effort. Finally, and related to the previously discussed long-term orientation of Confucian dynamism, some cultures tend to view the future as more important than the past and are willing to sacrifice the present for a better future in terms of saving money or foregoing immediate pleasure and satisfaction.

Orientation to Nature

This cultural dimension concerns how people in a society orient themselves to nature. First, people might think that human beings are supposed to dominate nature. Second, some people believe that they need to live in harmony with nature. A third and final orientation toward nature is a sense of subjugation to nature. In other words, human beings cannot and should not master nature because a supreme being or supernatural force is supposed to govern individual fate and destiny. In general, people in future-oriented cultures tend to believe that they can improve their situations and even influence nature as a result of their own actions and ideas. In contrast, people in past-oriented cultures do not believe that individual actions and ideas can change

Figure 2.4 **GLOBE's Cultural Dimensions and Their Managerial Implications**

Cultural Dimensions	Interpretations	Managerial Implications
Uncertainty Avoidance	Rigidity vs. Flexibility	Risk-taking vs. Risk-averse
Power Distance	Equality vs. Inequality	Authoritarian vs. Democratic Decision Making
Institutional Collectivism	Individual vs. Group	Independence vs. Interdependence
In-group Collectivism	In-group vs. Out-group Distinction	Organization Loyalty vs. Mobility
Gender Egalitarian	Male and Female Role Differences	Equal Opportunity vs. Discrimination
Assertiveness	Self-confidence vs. Agreeableness	Internal vs. External Locus of Control
Future Orientation	Determinism vs. Optimism	Status Quo vs. Change
Performance Orientation	Results vs. People	Meritocracy vs. Connection
Humane Orientation	Self-Interest vs. Concern for Others	Profits vs. Social Responsibility

Source: Adapted from House et al. (eds), *Culture, Leadership, and Organizations: The GlOBE Study of 62 Societies* (Thousand Oaks, CA: Sage Publications, 2004).

the will of a supreme being who is supposed to decree what will happen in the future. Therefore, they are more inclined to accept whatever fate life deals them. As will be discussed in Chapter 9, a sense of personal responsibility and accomplishment in the workplace may be difficult for employees in these fatalistic cultures, dampening the meaning and personal incentive impact of pay-for-performance reward systems and results-based negative performance evaluations.

THE GLOBE (GLOBAL LEADERSHIP AND ORGANIZATIONAL BEHAVIOR EFFECTIVENESS) STUDY

The GLOBE research project represents the most recent, comprehensive study on culture and its impact on leadership. Using middle level managers from 951 organizations in 62 countries, a team of 170 scholars from around the world worked together and identified nine cultural and six leadership dimensions.[61] This chapter limits the discussion to cultural dimensions and Figure 2.4 summarizes these dimensions along with their managerial implications.

To overcome criticism against Hofstede's research, the primary goal of the GLOBE research project was to advance empirically based theories to explain how cultural distinctiveness across countries influences leadership effectiveness from a global manager's perspective. Yet the results are very similar to Hofstede's. Six out of nine cultural dimensions that the GLOBE study found useful in distinguishing one culture from another replicate Hofstede's findings: uncertainty avoidance, power distance, societal collectivism, in-group collectivism, gender egalitarianism, and assertiveness orientation.

Hostede's concept of collectivism was separated into two categories: institutional collectivism and in-group collectivism. Whereas institutional collectivism (Collectivism I) measures how organizational and societal institutional practices encourage and reward the collective distribution of resources or collective actions (such as with the strong societal commitment to social services in the Scandina-

Global Workforce Challenge 2.2
Business School Update:
Cross-Cultural Competencies

U.S. business schools have traditionally found great success with their MBA programs, with students flocking to them from all over the world. However, there has been a trend in falling applications and sliding enrollments. Although some claim that the MBA has become overpriced, others believe that the problem is much more serious. The market may be telling the business schools that what you get in an MBA may not be what you need for success in the twenty-first century. More and more corporations prefer to train their own managers in-house, but not just because of rising costs—they also want to be sure that their employees acquire skills and values that business schools fall short in delivering.

For many business schools, the speed of change in the global economy and in corporate culture may be making part of their curriculum obsolete. Outsourcing to India and China, the rise of customer power, the spread of broadband, and other huge developments are changing not only the economic context in which companies operate but also the way companies operate. CEOs of global corporations are demanding that their people be able to manage innovation teams, global supply chains, strategic design, and the consumer experience. But most business school curricula still focus on analytical courses—accounting, marketing, and finance. Today, companies increasingly need softer people skills: observing consumers (including those from different cultures); collaborating with teams (including virtual teams arrangements); conceiving new products and services; and, perhaps most important, working across cultures with Chinese, Germans, Indians, Italians, Russians, Koreans, Japanese, and so on, and a large number of suppliers and partners from an increasing number of countries. Cross-cultural competencies are a top priority for business school instruction if the schools aim to be responsive to the needs of globally competitive organizations in the twenty-first century.

Sources: Adapted from S. Jain, "Enhancing International Business Education Through Restructuring Business Schools," *Journal of Teaching in International Business,* 20 (1) (2009): 4–34; "Business Schools for the 21st Century," *Business Week,* April 18, 2005, 112.

vian countries), in-group collectivism (Collectivism II) refers to how individuals express pride in and loyalty to family or organization, and value family bonding or organizational cohesiveness. Similar to Hofstede's masculinity versus femininity dimension, the GLOBE study advances gender egalitarianism versus assertiveness orientation. A feminine culture reflects more equal representation of gender roles and less assertiveness or more cooperation in social relationships. In contrast, a masculine culture corresponds to different gender roles and more assertiveness; a society values aggressiveness and confrontation or competition in social relationship to achieve one's goal.

The other three cultural dimensions that the GLOBE study discovered are future orientation, performance orientation, and humane orientation. Future orientation refers to the degree to which individuals in organizations or societies engage in future-oriented behaviors such as planning or investing in the future. Future-oriented societies tend to take more time in making decisions and value deliberate and systematic planning. Performance orientation is defined as the extent to which individuals or societies encourage and reward group members for performance improvement and excellence. This dimension is similar to Trompenaar's achievement versus ascription cultures in that while a high performance orientation culture stresses an individual's continuous improvement through training and development, a low performance orientation culture tends to emphasize family connections and social background rather than individual accomplishment. Finally, the humane orientation measures how individuals in organizations and societies encourage and reward individuals for being fair, altruistic, generous, and caring. In a high humane-oriented society people tend to show sympathy and support for the underprivileged, while in a low humane-oriented society people value self-enhancement and independence along with power and material success. As such, this cultural dimension shares the similar attributes of Hofstede's masculinity and femininity dimension. To conclude, the GLOBE study basically corroborates and integrates the findings from the previous seminal cultural studies by Hofestede and Trompenaars.

FINAL CAVEATS ON CULTURE AND GLOBAL WORKFORCE MANAGEMENT

Whatever position one may take among the various cultural orientations discussed in this chapter, it is hard to deny the fact that cultural differences still exist across borders. It is probably true that we tend to overemphasize cultural differences, suggesting a distinctive approach to conducting businesses in each country. As many consultants and even academics commonly suggest a ready-made formula, such as a "dos and don'ts" list for correctly handling cultural differences, people are easily trapped in the pitfall of hypersensitivity, in which they tend to over-rate or exaggerate the influences of cultural differences. Markóczy illustrates this point vividly with the comment, "When we view behavior from someone of our own culture, we treat it in a rather mundane manner, but when we view the identical behavior from someone of another culture, we attribute deep cultural explanations."[62]

More often than not, we tend to search for an easy answer based on nationality whenever different behaviors are shown among people from different cultural backgrounds. However, as mentioned earlier, stereotypes regarding national culture may not always be accurate and should be exercised with great caution. For example, in diffuse cultures such as Japan and China, a prevailing norm is that developing personal relationships comes first, before business. It is thought that the primary goal of Western negotiators is to secure a contract, and of Asians, particularly the Japanese and Chinese, is to develop a relationship. However, Salacuse found that the "preference for a relationship was not as pronounced among the Chinese (54.5 percent) as one might have expected from the literature, and the Japanese (45 percent) appeared almost evenly divided on the question as did the Americans (46 percent)."[63] As we accumulate more information about an individual, people need to find answers to different behaviors from the particular individual rather than from the individual's nationality. Therefore, it is imperative that when you sense a cultural distinction, look first for a mundane, ordinary explanation before attributing the cause to deep cultural differences.[64]

Individuals also differ in the internalizations of what their national culture means and do not always act in accordance with generalizations regarding their national culture.[65] Although people from the same culture probably tend to demonstrate similar actions and behaviors under specific circumstances, it would be naive to assume that all people from a certain culture will follow the same pattern of behaviors. Not all actors, even in ostensibly the same social group or institution, necessarily carry the same array of multiple cultures (cultures are socially distributed); nor for any given actor is the psychological or motivational salience of a given subculture the same as for any, or all, other actors (cultures are psychologically distributed).[66]

Individuals have different affiliations and experiences, which socially distributes culture differently. Differences in the psychological distribution of culture are so significant that "for two individuals even the same cultural representations (resulting, for instance, from a completely shared sociological placement) can be differentially internalized."[67]

Cai and Fink, who focus on the individualist-collectivity dichotomy, investigated the notion that individuals do not always act in accordance with theories or generalizations about their cultures. Using individuals as the unit of analysis rather than measuring individualism-collectivism by national culture, their findings contradict prior assumptions often made about cultural differences. Contrary to previous generalizations about cultural impacts on conflict-resolving modes, Cai and Fink found that individual actors from individualist cultures were more likely than collectivists to prefer the avoiding style. Furthermore, the two groups did not differ in their use of the dominating or competitive conflict style.[68] Hence, it seems unlikely that culture-based approaches to negotiation are highly predictive of what will happen in an actual negotiation interaction involving individuals from different national cultures. Another study even challenges the conventional wisdom that Americans are very individualistic. Bond and colleagues found that Americans are not as individualistic as Hofstede's study has suggested.[69] Similarly, Americans received moderately high scores on egalitarian commitment.[70]

The level of a country's industrial development, its cultural values, and the degree and nature of its cultural interactions may all play a part in the nature of its HRM practices and their appropriateness to the economic and cultural context within which they operate. We close this chapter by suggesting that though we should be sensitive to cultural differences, we should also appreciate the commonalities of our human family and be careful not to overestimate the impact of cultural differences. One must be aware of the possibility of cultural differences and what they might be, but one must also use this awareness cautiously and not overgeneralize and lose sight of the individual, which should be the primary focus for making accurate and fair HR decisions. To end this chapter with this appreciation for diversity within the likely much greater commonality of our human family, consider this moving account of world traveler Jeff Greenwald:

> A turning point in my travel life occurred August 11, 1999, in the central Iranian town of Isfahan. A handful of Americans had been allowed into the country to witness the total eclipse of the sun. As the eclipse began—it would take more than an hour to reach totality—I walked alone to Isfahan's vast Imam Khomeini Square: An American among 50,000 Iranians. . . . There were Iranians of all ages and descriptions: solemn mullahs, picnicking families, and groups of students. Nearly everyone was wearing eye protectors and gazing open-mouthed at the moon-bitten sun. The place was filled with European and Arabian media. Suddenly there was an uproar: A raucous anti-U.S. demonstration erupted nearby. American flags were set ablaze, and fists pounded the air. The European news teams rushed in for better camera angles. At the same time, something even more unexpected happened. Dozens of Iranians—middle-aged couples, Muslim clerics, schoolchildren—rose to their feet and formed a protective circle around me. A child took hold of my finger; a young man placed his hand on my shoulder. An older man, wearing a black turban and thick beard, leaned toward me. "You see those people?" He pointed toward the demonstrators. "They should get a job." This startling encounter, in a place so full of apprehensions, set my worldview on its ear. I was reminded that a single humane encounter can erase years of mistrust and preconceptions. Travelers who take a few steps off the beaten path find that the most exotic locales are not alien. They're the homes of people much like ourselves, who have hopes and fears we would find familiar.[71]

SUMMARY

Understanding cultural differences is critical to success in international business, because there are roles played by culture in global workforce management. We have examined basic concepts for understanding culture, as well as different views about how global and regional economic integration have affected and will continue to affect different dimensions of culture, including convergence, divergence, and crossvergence. We also have examined several important dimensions for gaining insights and understanding about the cultures of employees that staff our organizations domestically and abroad. Notwithstanding the importance of recognizing cultural differences, we caution against developing inflexible cultural stereotypes and exaggerating the influence of cultural differences.

QUESTIONS FOR OPENING SCENARIO ANALYSIS

1. Consider Hofstede's quote mentioned earlier: "Culture is more often a source of conflict than of synergy. Cultural differences are a nuisance at best and often a disaster." How was this quote applicable to the opening scenario concerning the international joint venture between Rover and Daru Group?
2. From your reading of this chapter, what are the major fundamental differences between British and Bulgarian cultures, and how were these differences manifested in the respective companies' practices and behaviors?
3. What lessons can you take from this chapter's opening scenario for your planning of international joint ventures?

CASE 2.1. CROSS-CULTURAL ASSESSMENT OVER A CUP OF COFFEE

Livia Markóczy is a consultant working in the United Kingdom. She conducted a study of organizations in Hungary with a diverse group of managers from different countries. One of the companies she visited was Tungsram, a GE-owned lighting company in Budapest, Hungary. As she conducted interviews with the American expatriate managers there, she had the distinct feeling that Americans did not know how to treat their guests. After each meeting with an American, she walked away with a feeling that somehow she was not welcome. In reflecting on why she found the Americans rude, she noticed that all of the Hungarians had offered her coffee, whereas only one of the Americans did so. She immediately started to speculate that the Americans had a more "get down to business" attitude, while the Hungarians were more interested in spending time getting to know each other. Unlike the Americans, the Hungarians seemed to be more people oriented and relationship oriented.

Upon further reflection, Livia asked herself how she arrived at such a cultural diagnosis. Perhaps her speculation was correct, but maybe there were other reasons for the American managers' behavior—reasons unrelated to deep cultural differences. Could it perhaps be that the Americans drink less coffee than Hungarians? Or maybe Americans drink coffee at certain times of the day? Indeed, she had met one American who offered her coffee at 8:30 A.M. It could be that offering coffee to office visitors is just an arbitrary aspect of Hungarian culture. Or perhaps Americans generally don't enjoy the way coffee is made in Hungary.

Livia's deep, culturally significant explanation of American impersonal, business-only nature and lack of hospitality was the one that came to mind instinctively after her initial experiences. But once she forced herself to look for mundane alternative explanations, they seemed at least as plausible as the deep cultural one. Although she could not rule out the possibility of a fundamental difference in mind-sets, she definitely learned that first she should explore the mundane possibilities behind behavioral differences before passing final judgment.

Source: Adapted from "Us and Them," *Across the Board* (February 1998): 44–48.

QUESTIONS FOR CASE ANALYSIS AND DISCUSSION

1. Why do you think people tend to exaggerate cultural differences?
2. What are the most effective ways to deal with either real or imaginary cultural differences?
3. Do you have any similar experiences that indicate we should be very cautious in interpreting and generalizing cross-cultural differences?

CASE 2.2. CULTURE CONFLICT SOUTH OF THE BORDER, DOWN MEXICO WAY

Jim Sanders, a distribution manager for a U.S. kitchen appliance manufacturer, has recently been assigned to work in Guadalajara, Mexico, at the regional manufacturing and distributions operation. His boss, regional manager Carlos Puente, also located in Guadalajara, is Mexican, as are most of his peers and all of his subordinates. Jim has been in Guadalajara for only a few months but already has major concerns. He remembers that upon his arrival he was very excited and optimistic about his working opportunity in Mexico, feeling like he could have taken on the world and won. Now Jim wonders if he can have any success at all.

Jim came to Mexico feeling confident that the management style that brought him so much success in the United States would propel him to similar high performance in Mexico. He was a problem solver and loved to dive in and attack problems openly and directly. Also, based on his past success with work groups in the United States, he reasoned that by involving all Mexican sales staff in the process of determining how to best sell their kitchen appliances, the company could attain double-digit growth easily. Certainly the local sales staff would be in the best position to know how to grow the business in their respective sales districts.

Therefore, in the first meeting with his sales staff, rather than telling them what he thought needed to be done, he posed the question to the group for open discussion. Only then did Jim realize how quiet his Mexican employees could be. After some time, Jim felt he needed to jump-start the discussion and tossed out his idea of using more billboard advertising. The group suddenly came alive and enthusiastically supported the idea as a fine one. Then the deafening silence returned once more. This process repeated itself a few more times until Jim decided to terminate the meeting, and he slunk away to his office in frustration. How unfortunate he felt to be stuck in this assignment with a bunch of lazy employees with no initiative, or who were incompetent and unable to make useful suggestions, or both!

But Jim's employees were not his only worry. His boss, Carlos, seemed to be cold and brusque with him lately—certainly not the warm, hospitable person he remembered from their first interactions. Maybe this change in Carlos's demeanor began a few weeks ago at a regional management team meeting, where Jim teased (out of actual feelings of frustration in not getting started on time) other Mexican managers for arriving ten to fifteen minutes late. Or perhaps he was correct in sensing a bit of tension in that meeting, conducted by Carlos as the senior manager, when Jim brought up several ideas for improving the various functional areas (including those not directly in his own team) of the regional operations in Mexico—ideas that he knew worked well in the United States. Despite making what he thought were insightful suggestions time after time in subsequent meetings, Jim's relationship with his boss seemed to grow colder.

Jim began fearing the company's Mexican operations were doomed due to failure in a culture where indolence, incompetence, and bureaucracy prevailed. But as he monitored actual performance of the operation, he was amazed that this part of the company was showing strong profits and growth. Jim thought that perhaps there was something wrong with him, and that he was not cut out for an international assignment after all. Jim saw his two- or three-year assignment in Mexico stretching before him as an eternity of potential failure. Worse yet, he wondered how his impending failure with this important international assignment might damage his future opportunities with the firm.

Source: Adapted from D. Rutherford, "Who's in Charge?" *Business Mexico* 15 (2) (2005): 36–37.

QUESTIONS FOR CASE ANALYSIS AND DISCUSSION

1. What particular dimension or dimensions of culture seem to be most central to the problems that Jim is experiencing?
2. What are possible causes of Jim's ineffectiveness in leading his sales team? What are sources of Jim's deteriorating relationship with his boss, Carlos?
3. In a coaching meeting with Jim, what insights would you share with him about cross-cultural differences that might be at the root of his problems? How should Jim behave differently to help improve his present difficulties at work?

RECOMMENDED WEB SITE RESOURCES

Cultural Profiles Project (www.settlement.org/cp/english). A rich source of information about country cultures and backgrounds from the Canadian office of Citizenship and Immigration, providing a useful picture of immigrants entering the labor force.

Executive Planet (www.executiveplanet.com). A comprehensive guide to business culture and etiquette in forty-four countries, including general cultural background and information on making appointments, business dress, conversation, gift giving and entertaining, negotiations, and general public behavior.

Hofstede's Country Profiles (www.geert-hofstede.com). A comprehensive national culture profile analysis and interpretation of Hofstede's five cultural dimensions for fifty-six countries provided by ITIM International, a global consulting firm on national and organizational culture. Useful business etiquette advice is also provided for thirty-one countries.

International Business Etiquette and Manners (www.cyborlink.com). Information on practical cultural and behavioral characteristics of thirty countries and geographic regions, including insightful information from Hofstede's cultural dimensions. Includes an interactive capability for posing specific questions for expert assistance, as well as references for each country and region for obtaining additional individual information resources.

The World Factbook (www.cia.gov/cia/publications/factbook) and Country Background Notes (www.state.gov/r/pa/ei/bgn). U.S. government sources that provide a considerable depth of information about countries, including people, economy, government, communications, and transnational issues, and from which general cultural characteristics may be inferred.

NOTES

1. Adapted from D. Elenkov and T. Fileva, "Anatomy of Business Failure: Accepting the 'Bad Luck' Explanation vs Proactively Learning in International Business," *Cross-Cultural Management: An International Journal* 13 (2) (2006): 132–41.

2. G.J. Hofstede, "Research on Cultures: How to Use It in Training," *European Journal of Cross-Cultural Competence and Management* 1 (1) (2009): 14–21.

3. J.W. Salacuse, "Ten Ways That Culture Affects Negotiating Style: Some Survey Results," *Negotiation Journal* 14 (1998): 222.

4. K. Avruch, *Culture and Conflict Resolution* (Washington, DC: United States Institute of Peace, 1998), 5.

5. E. Hall, *Beyond Culture* (Garden City, NY: Doubleday/Anchor, 1976).

6. G. Fink and W. Mayrhofer, "Cross-Cultural Competence and Management: Setting the Stage," *European Journal of Cross-Cultural Competence and Management* 1 (1) (2009): 42–65; J. Gapper, "Corporate Culture Shock Is a Big Deal," *Financial Times* (London), July 31, 2008: 9.

7. D.R. Briscoe, R.S. Schuler, and L. Claus, *International Human Resource Management: Policies and Practices for Multinational Enterprises,* 3d ed. (London: Routledge, 2009).

8. Hofstede, "Research on Cultures: How to Use It in Training."

9. Salacuse, "Ten Ways That Culture Affects Negotiating Style."

10. R.L. Tung, "The Cross-Cultural Research Imperative: The Need to Balance Cross-National and Intra-National Diversity," *Journal of International Business Studies* 39 (1) (2008): 41–46.

11. T.H. Reus and B.T. Lamont, "The Double-Edged Sword of Cultural Distance in International Acquisitions," *Journal of International Business Studies* 40 (8) (2009): 1298–1316.

12. S. Colakoglu and P. Caligiuri, "Cultural Distance, Expatriate Staffing and Subsidiary Performance: The Case of US Subsidiaries of Multinational Corporations," *International Journal of Human Resource Management* 19 (2) (2008): 223–39.

13. J. Selmer, R.K. Chiu, and O. Shenkar. "Cultural Distance Asymmetry in Expatriate Adjustment," *Cross Cultural Management* 14 (2) (2007): 150–60.

14. D.C. Thomas and K. Inkson, *Cultural Intelligence: Living and Working Globally,* 2d ed. (San Francisco: Berrett-Koehler Publishers, 2009).

15. R.S. Parker, D.L. Haytko, and C.M. Hermans, "Individualism and Collectivism: Reconsidering Old Assumptions," *Journal of International Business Research* 8 (1) (2009): 127–39.

16. K. P. Parboteeah, Y. Paik, and J. Cullen. "Religious Groups and Work Values: A Focus on Buddhism, Christianity, Hinduism and Islam," *International Journal of Cross Cultural Management,* 9 (1) (2009): 51–67.

17. R.T. Pascale and M.A. Maguire, "Comparison of Selected Work Factors in Japan and the United States," *Human Relations* 33 (1930): 433–55.

18. D. Dunphy, "Convergence/Divergence: A Temporal View of the Japanese Enterprise and Its Management," *Academy of Management Review* 12 (1987): 445–59.

19. P. Sparrow, R. Schuler, and S. Jackson, "Convergence or Divergence: Human Resource Practice and Policies for Competitive Advantage Worldwide," *International Journal of Human Resource Management* 5 (2) (1994): 267–99.

20. M.A. Von Glinow, E. Drost, and M. Teagarden, "Converging on IHRM Best Practices: Lessons Learned from a Globally Distributed Consortium on the Theory and Practice," *Human Resource Management* 41 (1) 2002: 123–40.

21. K.J. Sweetman, "Doing Business in Japan: Does It Pay to Act Local?" *Harvard Business Review* (September/October 1996): 13.

22. Y.P. Huo, H.J. Huang, and N.K. Napier, "Divergence or Convergence: A Cross-National Comparison of Personnel Selection Practices," *Human Resource Management* 41 (1) (2002): 31–44.

23. E. Drost, C. Frayne, K. Lowe, and M. Geringer, "Benchmarking Training and Development Practices: A Multi-Country Comparative Analysis," *Human Resource Management* 41 (1) (2002): 67–85.

24. R. Holton, "Globalization's Cultural Consequences," *The Annals of the American Academy* (July 2000): 140–51.

25. W. Ouchi, *Theory Z: How American Business Can Meet the Japanese Challenges* (Reading, MA: Addison-Wesley, 1981).

26. M. Pudelko, M. "The End of Japanese-Style Management?" *Long Range Planning,* 42(4) (2009): 439–62.

27. V. Pucik, "Human Resources in the Future: An Obstacle or a Champion of Globalization," *Human Resource Management* 36 (1) (1997): 163–67.

28. K.B. Lowe, J. Milliman, H. De Cieri, and P.J. Dowling, "International Compensation Practices: A Ten-Country Comparative Analysis," *Human Resource Management* 41 (1) (2002): 45–66.

29. Y.S. Paik, C. Vance, and D. Stage, "The Extent of Divergence in Human Resource Practice across the Chinese National Cultures: Hong Kong, Taiwan, and Singapore," *Human Resource Management Journal* 6 (2) (1996): 20–31.

30. C. Rowley, *Human Resource Management in the Asia Pacific Region* (London: Frank Cass and Company, 1998).

31. Y. Paik, C. Vance, A. Zhuplev, and D. Stage, "US-Russian Cooperative Business Involvement: An Analysis of Potential Cross-Cultural Management Style Fit," *Journal of International Management* 3 (4) (1997): 351–73.

32. D. Ralston, D. Holt, R.H. Terspstra, and Kai-Cheng Yu, "The Impact of National Culture and Economic Ideology on Managerial Work Values: A Study of the United States, Russia, Japan, and China," *Journal of International Business Studies* 28 (1) (1997): 177–207.

33. B. Shimoni and H. Bergmann, "Managing in a Changing World: From Multiculturalism to Hybridization—The Production of Hybrid Management Cultures in Israel, Thailand, and Mexico," *Academy of Management Perspectives* 20 (3) (2006): 76–89.; P. Werbner and T. Modood, eds., *Debating Cultural Hybridity: Multi-cultural Identities and the Politics of Anti-racism* (London: Zed Books, 1996).

34. M.Y. Brannen, J.K. Liker and W.M. Fruin, "Recontextualization and Factory-to-Factory Knowledge Transfer from Japan to the U.S.: The Case of NSK." In K.J. Liker, M.W. Fruin, and S.P. Adler, eds., *Remade in America: Transplanting and Transforming Japanese Management Systems* (New York: Oxford University Press, 1999).

35. J. Morris, B. Wilkinson, and J. Gamble, "Strategic International Human Resource Management or the 'Bottom Line'? The Cases of Electronics and Garments Commodity Chains in China, *International Journal of Human Resource Management* 20 (2) (2009): 348–71; F.L. Cooke, *HRM, Work & Employment in China* (London: Routledge, 2005); J. Benson, P. Debroux, M. Yuasa, and Y. Zhu, "Flexibility and Labour Management: Chinese Manufacturing Enterprises in the 1990s," *International Journal of Human Resource Management* 11 (2) (2000): 183–96.

36. T. Jackson, *International HRM: A Cross-Cultural Approach* (London: Sage, 2002).

37. T. Jackson, "The Management of People across Cultures: Valuing People Differently," *Human Resource Management* 41 (4) (2002): 455–75.

38. Paik et al., "US-Russian Cooperative Business Involvement."

39. G. Hofstede, *Culture's Consequences: International Differences in Work-Related Values* (Beverly Hills, CA: Sage, 1984), 21.

40. G. Hofstede and M. Bond, "Hofstede's Cultural Dimensions: An Independent Validation Using Rokeah's Value Survey," *Journal of Cross-Cultural Psychology* 15 (1984): 417–33.

41. M. Hoppe, "A Replication of Hofstede's Measures" (unpublished doctoral dissertation, University of North Carolina, Chapel Hill, 1990).

42. G. Hofstede and M.H. Bond, "The Confucius Connection: From Cultural Roots to Economic Growth," *Organizational Dynamics* 16 (4) (Spring 1988): 5–21.

43. H. Park and Y.S. Paik, "Impact of National Culture on Transfer of Technology: Demand Side Analysis," *Journal of Global Business* (Spring 2002): 49–58.

44. S. Shane, "Cultural Influences on National Rates of Innovation," *Journal of Business Venturing* 8 (1) (1993): 59–73.

45. I. Botero and L. Van Dyne, "Employee Voice Behavior: Interactive Effects of LMX and Power Distance in the United States and Colombia," *Management Communication Quarterly* 23 (1): 84–104; P. Evans, A. Farquhar, and O. Landreth, *Human Resource Management in International Firms, Change, Globalization, Innovation* (New York: St. Martin's Press, 1990).

46. J. Quinn, "Managing Innovation: Controlled Chaos," *Harvard Business Review* 58 (1985): 134–42.

47. J. Galbraith, "Designing the Innovating Organization," *Organizational Dynamics* (Winter 1982): 5–25.

48. M. Hauser, *Developing an Innovative Organizational Culture: Dimensions, Instruments and a Change Process* (San Francisco: Jossey-Bass/Pfeiffer, 1998).

49. B. Kedia, R.T. Keller, and S.D. Julian, "Dimensions of National Culture and the Productivity of R&D Units," *Journal of High Technology Management Research* 3 (1) (1992): 1–18.

50. D.C. McClelland and D.G. Winter, *Motivating Economic Achievement* (New York: Free Press, 1969).

51. Hofstede and Bond, "Hofstede's Cultural Dimensions."

52. H.G. Barkema and F. Vermeulen, "What Differences in the Cultural Backgrounds of Partners Are Detrimental for International Joint Ventures," *Journal of International Business Studies* 28 (1997): 845–64.

53. F. Trompenaars and C. Hampden-Turner, *Riding the Waves of Culture: Understanding Diversity in Global Business,* 2d ed. (New York: McGraw-Hill, 1998).

54. C. Hampden-Turner, "The Boundaries of Business: The Cross-Cultural Quagmire," *Harvard Business Review* (September/October 1991): 94.

55. R.J. Barnet and J. Cavanagh, *Global Dreams: Imperial Corporations and New World Order* (New York: Touchstone, 1994).

56. J. Scarborough, *The Origins of Cultural Differences and Their Impact on Management* (Westport, CT: Quorum Books, 1998).

57. S. Li and S.D. Maurer, "Managing in a Relation-Based Environment: A Teaching Agenda for International Business," In J. McIntyre and I. Alon, eds., *Business and Management Education in China* (Singapore: World Scientific Publishing Co. Inc., 2005), 47–66.

58. Hall, *Beyond Culture.*

59. L. Yadong, "Guanxi Principle, Philosophies and Implications," *Human Systems Management* 16 (1997): 43–51.

60. M. Tung, "Handshakes across the Sea: Cross-Cultural Negotiating for Business Success," *Organizational Dynamics* 19 (3) (Winter 1991): 30–40.

61. R. House et al., eds., *Culture, Leadership, and Organizations: The GLOBE Study of 62 Societies* (Thousand Oaks, CA: Sage, 2004).

62. L. Markóczy, "Us and Them," *Across the Board* 35 (2) (1998): 44–48.

63. Salacuse, "Ten Ways That Culture Affects Negotiating Style," 226.

64. Markóczy, "Us and Them," 44–48.

65. D.A. Cai and E.L. Fink, "Conflict Style Differences between Individualists and Collectivists," *Communication Monographs* 69 (2002): 67–87.

66. K. Avruch, *Culture and Conflict Resolution* (Washington, DC: United States Institute for Peace, 1998), 60.

67. Ibid, 19.

68. Cai and Fink, "Conflict Style Differences between Individualists and Collectivists."

69. M.H. Bond, P.P. Fu, and S.F. Pasa, "A Declaration of Independence for Editing an International Journal of Cross-Cultural Management," *International Journal of Cross-Cultural Management* 1 (1) (2001): 24–30.

70. P.B. Smith, S. Dugan, and F. Trompenaars, "National Culture and Values of Organizational Employees: A Dimensional Analysis across 43 Nations," *Journal of Cross-Cultural Psychology* 27 (2) (1996): 231–64.

71. J. Greenwald, "12 Tips for Bridging the Cultural Divide," *Los Angeles Times,* January 23, 2005.

3 Changes and Challenges in the Global Labor Market

BRAZILIAN COMMUNITY IN CHINA ENJOYS THE BENEFITS OF GLOBALIZATION

Dongguan, a city of some 7 million people situated about 56 miles (90 kilometers) north of Hong Kong, is China's footwear capital, exporting 600 million pairs of shoes per year. It is rather unexpected that we would find here a thriving community of Brazilians, estimated to number three thousand, who mostly work in the footwear industry. These Brazilians trace their roots to southern Brazil, which was the center of the shoe export business until the early 1990s. At that time, a reduction in Brazil's trade barriers, an appreciating currency, and pressure from cheap Chinese labor caused the exports to decline. The surviving firms moved north, to the parts of Brazil where labor costs were cheaper. Chinese firms continued to undermine the Brazilian producers at the lower end of the market thanks to an abundance of cheap labor, but they lacked the knowledge and craftsmanship needed to make fancier shoes. This encouraged a slow migration of skilled Brazilian shoemakers, some with advanced training in tanning, to seek business in China with Chinese companies. Ricardo Correa is the owner of Paramont Asia, which sold more than 35 million pairs of ladies' shoes in 2007. Influenced by the combination of price pressures in Brazil and a shortage of skills in China, Correa migrated to China in 1995. His firm now takes design specifications for shoes from its customers and then manages product development and quality control in factories in China. Most of the manufactured shoes are then exported to America. Of Paramont's eight hundred employees, one hundred are Brazilian, and day-to-day business is conducted in English.

Brazilians in other professions have followed the shoe specialists to offer support services such as running restaurants or teaching Portuguese to the children of shoemakers. Dongguan's Brazilian community is now China's largest, twice the size of Shanghai's and almost the triple the size of that in Beijing. Brazil's foreign affairs ministry plans to open a consulate in the nearby provincial capital of Guangzhou to better serve the Brazilian citizens. In the past two Brazilian presidential elections, a polling station was set up in Dongguan. Brazilians appreciate the lower crime rate in China and the fact that they can earn higher salaries than local workers or Brazilian counterparts back home. "The more I go back to Brazil the more I like China," says Ari Filipini, a Brazilian worker at Paramont. But the march of globalization never ends; it is now applying pressure on Dongguan's factories to cut costs. Some shoemakers are closing down factories and moving further inland or to other Asian countries where labor rates are cheaper. The Brazilians moved once before, and they can always move again.[1]

INTRODUCTION

The opening scenario illustrates how people are actively seeking job opportunities in our global economy despite language and cultural barriers. With more open borders and cheaper and supportive transportation and telecommunications, the global economy makes it easier for people to move from one country to another, seeking better jobs and a higher standard of living. At the same time, it has led to ethnic and cultural tension and conflict within a country where immigrants are not viewed positively as new labor force entrants contributing to economic growth and widespread prosperity.

It is in this broad context that this chapter examines major changing trends, often complex and interrelated, in the global labor market along with their implications for governments and multinational firms. First, we examine the concept of globalization and its causes, along with important consequences associated with global workforce management. Second, we examine how technological advancements are contributing to significant changes in world business. Third, we discuss changes in global labor force demographics and the influence of migration, which is adding increasing diversity to global workforces. Fourth, we discuss the emergence of contingent workers as a significant component of the labor force. Fifth, we analyze the impact of the increased use of offshore sourcing as an alternative to domestic production. Finally, the chapter concludes with a discussion of the implications of these trends for managers and HR professionals.

GLOBALIZATION

Globalization is all about "competing with everyone from everywhere for everything."[2] Globalization involves a shift toward a more integrated and interdependent world economy. It is the expansion of interrelated economic and social activities beyond national borders and toward more world-encompassing dimensions. The continued dismantling of both trade and investment barriers allows for the creation of integrated markets and production processes.

From the demand side, integration of markets means that globalization enables consumers to purchase lower-priced goods and services, spurs economic growth, increases income, and creates new jobs. Globalization also has increased purchasing power and enhanced standards of living without risking high inflation. From the supply side, the so-called global assembly line created though the integration of production processes across borders forces manufacturers to drastically reduce costs for the services and goods they offer. MNCs are aggressively seeking location advantages for cost savings that exist anywhere in the world. Globalization has enabled nations to specialize in industries where they have comparative advantages based on the favorable mix of skills and resources unique to their countries. Furthermore, globalization has brought about increased productivity as a result of the spread of technology and competitive pressures for continual innovation on a worldwide basis.

Despite these benefits, critics of globalization have argued that although it has provided expanded business opportunities to MNCs, many workers in either developed or developing countries have not gained much from the globalization of markets and production.[3] According to this claim, globalization has destroyed manufacturing jobs in wealthy, developed countries. As evident in the United States, many manufacturing jobs have packed up and left, in search of lower wages and decreased problems with labor unions. The result of this exodus has been the elimination of thousands of manufacturing jobs in the United States and other developed countries that are experiencing the same phenomenon. In turn, the wage levels of unskilled workers in these affected nations start to decline. As unskilled workers lose their higher-paying manufacturing jobs and cannot transfer what they know into other positions of employment, they are forced to take lower-paying unskilled jobs elsewhere to survive.

Another negative effect in the push for globalization is the propensity for companies to move to countries with fewer labor and environmental regulations. This trend occurs because stringent labor laws and environmental restrictions can increase the costs of goods and services, resulting in reduced profits and competitiveness. In doing so, many MNCs are allegedly taking advantage of unskilled and unprotected workers in developing countries.

While the first wave of globalization was led by firms in developed countries such as the United States and Japan, firms from emerging market economies such as China and India have increasingly become major players and participants in the global economy. Some critics of capitalism have pointed out that the recent meltdown in the global economy triggered by the credit crisis has reversed the global integration of the movement of goods and capital as demonstrated by the sharp decrease in world trade and FDI. However, it is interesting to note that the largest emerging markets, such as China and India, are doing less badly relative to more developed East Asian economies such as Singapore and Taiwan.[4] In fact, it is Asia's emerging economies that have played a leading role in leading the way out of the global recession begun in late 2007.[5]

The process of globalization has engendered two important phenomena: international migration and outsourcing. On one hand, globalization has opened up new job opportunities to young skilled workers, resulting in a so-called brain drain of a talented group of people through an acceleration of international migration from developing to developed countries. On the other hand, globalization has provided increased employment opportunities in both low- and high-skilled jobs in developing countries as companies from developed countries increasingly resort to offshore outsourcing.

TECHNOLOGICAL ADVANCEMENTS

We continue to witness an ongoing introduction of awesome technological innovations at a mind-boggling pace of change in which they are adopted and integrated within our professional and personal lives. These relentless technological advances are spurred on by a global entrepreneurial spirit paired with the desire for increased efficiency and productivity, heightened by increasing global competitive forces. Technological advancements continue to have a profound effect on how work is designed and conducted, including at the traditional workplace and through virtual working arrangements. The rapid pace of change with technological innovations requires a workforce that can rapidly adapt, through effective training systems, to exploit new opportunities presented by these innovations.

However, there are increasing concerns about the misuse of new technologies in the workplace, which jeopardizes not only organization productivity but also workplace and public safety. This includes employees' careless personal practices including e-mailing, Web surfing, texting, and accessing the proliferating forms of social networking media.[6] In addition, these continuous technological advancements provide increased speed, with attendant expectations of quick response time, which contributes to an increasingly stressful work environment that also extends into one's personal life with ever-present handheld devices that maintain continuous contact with work.[7] On the other hand, when managed effectively technological advancements also permit greater work flexibility than ever before, which can lead to a satisfying and valuable work/life balance.[8]

The acceleration of globalization is greatly attributable to these advances in technology, which have not only improved the worldwide capacity for timely and detailed communications, coordination, and process integration, but also have increased the rate of "creative destruction," as noted by Joseph Schumpeter a number of decades ago. Creative destruction is the continuous scrapping of old technologies to make way for the new. It is inevitable in this competitive global business environment that old procedures, jobs, and industries will die and new ones will be created to replace them. Yet workers being replaced by this creative destruction process naturally grow to resent globalization and feel that the gains from globalization disproportionately benefit the large corporations or the countries with the lowest labor costs such as China and India. These displaced workers become enraged at MNCs that are perceived only as valuing the efficiencies of the marketplace, and they demand protection for their jobs from politicians who promise to defend their rights.

This continued priority of MNCs on greater efficiency and cost reduction, facilitated by technological advancement, is why increasing numbers of workers in developed countries such as the United States, Germany, and Japan tend to blame domestic job loss on outsourcing to India, China, and other low-wage countries. Yet such a competitive drive for increased efficiencies through utilizing technological advancements is also a major source of work restructuring and resulting job loss in emerging economies such as China and India. It is not outsourcing, but rather the drive for productivity gains through applied technological innovations that is the real culprit behind job loss and the failure to quickly return to previous employment levels in an economic rebound—and this is a worldwide phenomenon.[9]

CHANGES IN LABOR FORCE DEMOGRAPHICS AND MIGRATION

The past few decades have noted significant changes in worldwide external labor market and internal workforce demographics. Many of these changes toward greater

Global Workforce Challenge 3.1
Western Europe and Globalization

A major effect of globalization, with its greater accessibility to cheaper labor markets, is the increasing movement of MNCs to countries where lower labor costs provide a competitive advantage. A number of MNCs are cutting jobs more heavily in Western Europe than in other regions. Household appliance maker Electrolux AB of Sweden is evaluating twenty-seven factories for possible closure as part of a strategy to shift the focus of its production from high-wage Western Europe to countries with cheaper costs, especially Mexico and some in Eastern Europe. Carmaker General Motors is shedding 12,000 employees in Europe, including nearly a third of its 32,000-strong German workforce.

"There's clearly a geographical trend," says Julian Callow, chief economist at Barclays Capital in London. "The basic message is that globalization has a lot further to run, and in that reshaping, Europe is increasingly being bypassed." Part of the reason in this shift is labor costs, including wages, high payroll taxes, and strict labor laws that impose costly working practices. On this front, European industry is at a greater disadvantage than the United States in competing with new manufacturing powerhouses such as China. Electrolux, for example, is scaling down production in Western Europe to keep up with both its existing rivals that already have moved production to low-wage countries and its new competitors from China.

"It's purely driven by consumers," says Electrolux spokesman Jacob Broberg, "because consumers are not willing to pay extra for a product that's produced in a specific country." Buyers of household goods look at the price and the brand. In addition to European operations, a smaller number of plants in the United States and Australia could be closed. As with several other firms, IBM is centralizing administrative tasks, which don't have to be located near the customer, in a smaller number of global centers, mostly in the United States, Central Europe, China, and India, rather than in Western Europe where labor costs are the highest. The United States has also lost jobs to lower-wage countries, particularly in the manufacturing sector, but its relatively flexible labor and capital markets have helped the economy shift from manufacturing to services. However, in Western Europe, stricter labor laws and more powerful unions, as well as heavy regulation favoring established monopolies that make it difficult for new entrants in the service sector, have made labor flexibility and transition much more difficult to achieve.

Source: Adapted from M. Walker, "Western Europe's Labor Woes: In Globalization Era, Multinationals Flee for More Flexible Areas," *Wall Street Journal,* August 1, 2005, A7.

diversity have been due to changes in migration patterns with increased transportation opportunities and more open national borders to support world trade and replace decreases in local populations. There also are continuing changes in domestic migration patterns that are important for MNCs to understand as they plan for an adequate supply of qualified employees to staff their host country operations.

Figure 3.1 **World Population, 2007**

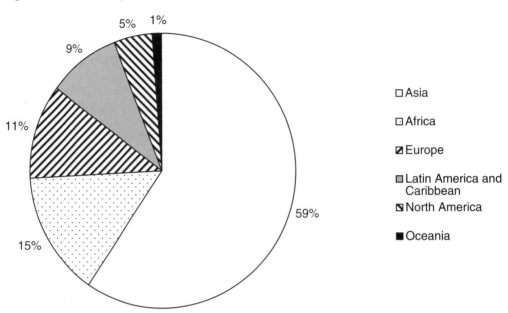

Source: Population Division, Department of Economic and Social Affairs of the United Nations Secretariat (2007).

GENERAL CHANGES IN WORLD DEMOGRAPHICS

As of November 2009, the world's population was estimated by the UN Census Bureau to be 6.8 billion, with 5.5 billion (or 81 percent of the world's total population) living in less developed regions. Current UN population projects estimate that by 2050 the world's population will increase to nearly 9.2 billion, 2.4 billion more than in 2009, and an increase equivalent to the combined current populations of China and India.[10] As indicated in Figure 3.1, Asia is currently the most populous region in the world, making up roughly 60 percent of the world's population. China ranks as the largest country in terms of population, with more than 1.3 billion people. India is close behind (and expected to pass China) with a population of over 1.1 billion, followed by the United States and Indonesia.

The UN projects a slight modification of the world's population distribution in 2050, with most regions remaining relatively unchanged. Some notable changes include a 4 percent decline in Europe's population that will likely be replaced by a 7 percent increase in Africa's population, boosting this latter region to a 21 percent share of the world's population.[11] A solution for Europe would be to import more than 100 million new immigrants. France alone would need to import some five hundred thousand immigrants a year—five times more than the country currently absorbs.

As the populations of industrialized nations age, the transfer to elderly dependence from child dependence will be more pronounced. Today, in developed countries, for every retired person only 4.5 people are active in the labor force. As the number of

Global Workforce Challenge 3.2
Filling Growing Labor Shortages with Older Workers

Four years ago, Kato Manufacturing Co. of Nakatsugawa, Japan, faced a problem that much of Japanese industry will come up against: a lack of working-age people for its factories. With Japan's birthrate declining rapidly for decades, the pool of young workers was shrinking, and those who grew up in this small town in central Japan were fleeing to look for jobs in the cities. To cope, this small metal-parts maker tried out a source of labor it had never considered before: the elderly. And with an invitation, the elderly came running. When Kato placed inserts in the local paper inviting "keen people over 60" to apply, the company was flooded with one hundred candidates, even though the jobs were for weekends.

Kato Manufacturing is dealing with a problem that is beginning to sweep the world—an aging population combined with a shrinking labor force. The problem is unprecedented in modern times, and its most predictable effect would be to sap economic growth: If a country's labor force declines and higher production per worker doesn't make up for this drop, its economy will shrink. Though Japan is running into this difficult challenge first, other nations are going to have to deal with it soon as well. In Japan, more than 20 percent of the population is over sixty-five years old, up from 10 percent just twenty-five years ago. Italy and Germany are in about the same situation. The United States is better off, not slated to reach that proportion until 2036, because of its higher birthrate and immigration rate (both legal and illegal), but it still is struggling to figure out how to finance social security in a grayer future. Even China, the most populous nation with its one-child policy, is beginning to age rapidly, with the elderly making up 22.7 percent of the population by 2050, up from only 6.9 percent in 2005.

But unlike the United States, Japan is reluctant to rely on large-scale immigration to bolster the labor force. Instead, it is trying another strategy: enticing the elderly to work longer before receiving retirement benefits, effectively dealing with old age by making it start later. In fact, the Japanese government is encouraging older workers through a phased plan of making retirement benefits available later and later, moving from the recent age sixty to age sixty-five by 2025. This older-worker trend might sound like a move that goes against worldwide trends. Western Europeans, for example, have been retiring earlier over the past twenty-five years, encouraged by governments that thought the move would ease chronic unemployment.

But if Japan succeeds in using the elderly to solve its looming labor shortage, it could provide a new policy model for other nations. There are some hopeful signs. Many Japanese workers are enthusiastic about working longer, even though the official retirement age remains a relatively young sixty. The International Labour Organization says 71 percent of Japanese men ages sixty to sixty-four work, mostly in post-retirement jobs. That compares with 57 percent of American men and just 17 percent of French men in the same age group. With the invitation of older people back to the workforce, especially for manufacturing jobs, companies are showing concern for the increased burden on older workers by redesigning jobs and adapting machines to relieve the strain on aging joints.

Japan's declining labor force comes from two trends linked with economic develop-

(continued)

Global Workforce Challenge 3.2 (continued)

ment. Better diet and health care have helped raise Japan's average life expectancy at birth to eighty-two, the highest in the world. At the same time, women in Japan are having fewer and fewer children—an average of 1.28 each, compared with 2.04 in the United States—so there are fewer people available to join the labor force. These trends are also rippling elsewhere in the world. Italy and Spain, for example, have fertility rates roughly the same as Japan's, and South Korea's rate recently plunged even lower to 1.19. Russia's population is also declining at a significant rate. Younger populations in developing countries such as Brazil and India give their economies a demographic advantage—but only a temporary one, because the same birthrate and life-expectancy trends are taking hold there amid growing prosperity.

Sources: Adapted from W. Zinke, *Utilizing Older Workers for Competitive Advantage. The New Human Resources Frontier* (Boulder, CO: Center for Productive Longevity, 2009); S. Moffett, "Senior Moment: Fast-Aging Japan Keeps Its Elders on the Job Longer," *Wall Street Journal,* June 15, 2005, A1, A8.

people over age sixty-five increases in developed countries, the labor force will decrease. This trend means that the smaller younger generation will need to support a large number of elders, placing significant pressure on such areas as health care and retirement social services. Italy is feeling the pinch now, and Japan will soon follow. It has been estimated that, mostly due to mortality and a low birthrate, Italy's population will fall by 13 percent between 1990 and 2030, and the population of Japan will be reduced by 4 percent during the same time period. While the elderly population in developed countries has increased significantly, most developing countries' young population is in the higher proportion. Two-thirds of the world's two billion young people live in developing countries.

INTERNATIONAL MIGRATION

As previously suggested, a solution to the dramatic demographic change of decreasing national population in developed countries is to allow more migration between developed and developing countries—just as the United States has done, along with Canada, Germany, Italy, and the United Kingdom. But such immigration is not without its challenges. We now examine important issues and trends associated with international migration, including arguments for and against it and policy implications for government officials.

Scotland, which has one of Europe's lowest birthrates, is seeking ways of boosting immigration to tackle chronically low economic growth rates. There is a growing need to attract more economically active young men and women from England and overseas as a fundamental means of stimulating economic growth. However, if more young people move to developed countries from developing countries, this condition might pose direct economic implications because the latter will fall further behind the rest of the world.

Figure 3.2 **A Comparison of Countries by Three Criteria of Immigration**

Rank	Attractiveness to Migrants	Accessibility to Migrants	Need for Migrants
1	United States	Australia	Japan
2	United Kingdom	Canada	Italy
3	Australia	Singapore	Portugal
4	Norway	New Zealand	Finland
5	France	Israel	Czech Republic

Source: "With Millions on the Move, This Guide Maps the Routes to Prosperity," *Wall Street Journal,* September 19, 2008, A18.

As the opening case vividly illustrates, globalization, with its increased information and communications access, has made people aware of conditions and opportunities abroad. Although the recent global financial crisis temporarily slowed down the rapid pace of international migration, that pace is returning and will continue to accelerate as long as people see opportunities in other parts of the world. Such migration is changing the cultural foundation of most developed nations. For example, 10 million immigrants will enter the United States in the next decade. More than three hundred thousand people from the Korean peninsula live in Los Angeles. In Dade County, Florida, there are 123 nationalities in the school system. Europe is going through similar demographic changes with increased immigration. Germany has changed its citizen laws to make it easier for Turkish immigrants to become citizens. In Brussels, 50 percent of the children are born to Muslim mothers. Because culture is the foundation of any polity, political consensus will increasingly fragment as more people from different cultural backgrounds live within the same political jurisdiction.[12]

However, according to a study commissioned by the Economic Intelligence Unit and Western Union, not all international immigrants are moving from poor to rich countries; nearly half are moving from developing countries to other developing countries. This study provides a measure of opportunity for people leaving their homelands and moving to countries that might adopt them. About 200 million people worldwide live outside their country of origin, compared with 75 million people just four decades ago.[13] As Figure 3.2 shows, the United States remains the world's most attractive country for immigrants. But it ranks seventh in accessibility, a criterion influenced by such factors as ease of hiring foreign nationals and government immigration policy. Former British colonies such as Australia, Canada, Singapore, and New Zealand rank among the highest in accessibility. In terms of need for immigrants, Japan turns out to be the country that most needs immigrants, followed by countries in Western Europe.

Challenges facing global HR planning do not have to be directed at foreign countries. In the interest of helping their domestic business sectors access an adequate supply of qualified labor to meet work demand, several countries have changed their immigration laws. Countries such as Japan and Switzerland, in facing the challenge of overemployment where the domestic labor supply is insufficient to fill the needs of the domestic work demand, have periodically relaxed their work visa and immigration requirements to allow the entrance and temporary legal work status of workers from less-developed countries. In the 1960s, to supply its domestic heavy manufacturing work demand, Germany encouraged a major influx of Turkish employees. German Turks now constitute the largest minority group in Germany. In the United States, immigration laws have changed significantly from mere emphasis upon U.S. family relations for granting citizenship and work visas to placing a premium on technical skills and professional contribution to the U.S. labor force. Many people expect that the United States will introduce a more lenient immigration policy under the Obama administration. But it still remains to be seen if the U.S. government will launch a new open-door policy on a large scale. After years of growth, even illegal immigration to the United States from Mexico and Central America temporarily decreased substantially.[14] This reduction was likely due to the recent global economic recession, which also triggered massive unemployment in the United States.

Arguments for Immigrant Workers

Five major countries officially welcome international migrants as permanent residents: the United States, Canada, Austria, Israel, and New Zealand. Collectively, these countries accept 1.2 million immigrants a year.[15] About eight hundred thousand immigrants each year are officially admitted to the United States. Former Federal Reserve Chairman Alan Greenspan commented in testimony before the U.S. Congress, "I've always argued that this country has benefited immensely from the fact that we draw people from all over the world." The leading students and brightest scholars are from China or Taiwan or practically anywhere on earth. In many respects the United States considers the world as its talent pool. The growth of the U.S. high-tech industry has been fueled by a steady flow of highly educated immigrants and foreign students.

According to the U.S. Bureau of Labor Statistics, the share of immigrants in the U.S. labor force is expected to increase from its current 13 percent to about 20 percent by 2030.[16] Asia, home to 60 percent of the world's population, is a major source of immigrants for North America and Europe. Asians represent about a third of the total immigrants to the United States, and more than half come from Latin America.

Immigrants can bring many benefits to their newly adopted countries. First, because immigrant workers are usually cheaper to employ than native workers in developed countries, employers often prefer to hire them to remain cost competitive. Second, immigrants are willing to do jobs that natives spurn. For example, in South Korea, local laborers would not want to perform the so-called 3-D jobs: dirty, dangerous, and difficult. Thus, the country has become increasingly dependent on an imported labor force for these areas. Third, immigrants are also increasing the tax income base for the government to help cover the staggering financial claims of the growing number of retired people in developed countries. Finally, a vibrant immigrant economy might help revive a stagnant local economy.

Immigrants often have the same personal characteristics as entrepreneurs. They are by nature risk-takers, and are more likely to be self-employed than natives. These immigrant entrepreneurs are making a significant contribution to economic growth and innovation, keeping firms and national economies globally competitive. A 2007 study by the Center for an Urban Future examined immigrant small business entrepreneurs in four cities across the United States. The study concluded that immigrant entrepreneurs have emerged as key engines of growth for cities.[17] A 2006 study by Duke University and the University of California at Berkeley indicates that the founders of 25 percent of engineering and science companies included at least one immigrant. Nationwide, these immigrant-founded companies produced $52 billion in sales and employed 450,000 workers in 2005.[18]

Thus, it is no longer only in lower-end jobs where immigrants replace natives. In Japan, the United States, and Canada large numbers of immigrants are filling such disciplines as engineering, mathematics, medicine, and virtually all aspects of computer systems work. Also, the needs of an aging population will create an enormous opportunity for caregiver careers such as licensed practical nurses, physicians' assistants, and physical therapists.[19] These new developments support the view that developed countries cannot afford not to have immigration to supply an adequate number of the labor force to meet these job demands.

Nevertheless, there are significant and serious challenges and consequences related to immigration at societal, organizational, and individual levels. A major issue is the acculturation of the new immigrant entrants into the new society and workforce. But there are challenges even when immigrants embrace common basic ideals and values of the new society. For example, a professional Filipino immigrant husband and wife working in Los Angeles recently remarked on their adjustment difficulty, based on their early cultural foundations of high power distance and collectivism, in working for a younger manager or boss or working individually on major projects rather than as a supportive team. These fundamental, persisting cross-cultural differences should be acknowledged for supporting effective immigrant employee adjustment and utilization. We now examine serious issues and challenges in current arguments against the growing trend of immigrant workers.

Arguments against Immigrant Workers

Not all people view immigration as a solution to the current economic and social problems in developed countries. Immigrants might not be welcome if large parts of a country's native population feel threatened not only because the immigrants take away jobs from local people but also because they become a source of social unrest and ethnic strife. In the United States, despite the benefits immigrants bring to the economy, they are increasingly seen as liabilities, not assets. Security rather than economic issues are forming an anti-immigrant national consciousness. The ease with which terrorists can cross borders raises the question to many Americans, "Why are we being forced to open our borders so that these people can enter?" To ensure domestic security, the U.S. government put a moratorium on student visas after it was discovered that a large number of the 9/11 terrorists entered the county by those means. However, foreign students on F1 visas contribute $12.3 billion to the U.S. economy annually. Many security reforms will have potentially adverse effects on the free flow of goods, capital, and people from which the U.S. economy has benefited.

Anti-immigration sentiment is even more conspicuous in Europe. Many residents in Europe link immigration to rising crime rates, deteriorating discipline in schools, and white flight from the cities. In addition, immigrants have much higher unemployment rates than native-born workers. In contrast to the United States, Europe's immigrants come in large groups from a few countries. This trend makes assimilation difficult with the other naturalized Europeans because the immigrant communities are large enough for newcomers to remain segregated within their own groups. European countries admit large groups of immigrants from other cultures whose customs are difficult to assimilate and who cannot speak the language of their new home. Many of these new immigrants come from Arabic countries that have a history of conflict with Western states.

The recent resurgence of anti-Semitic attacks in Western Europe, as well as attacks on those who criticize or parody (such as with published cartoons) various beliefs or practices of some Muslim groups, have intensified these feelings. Traditional European xenophobia intensifies the problem of assimilation, jeopardizing the use of tools to deal with the inevitable problem of immigration. Concerns expressed by European leaders about Turkey's entry into the European Union can be understood in this context. On the surface, European politicians insist that their reservations are based on standards of democracy and human rights and on controlling immigration and terrorism. In reality, however, many fear that this strong reluctance is based on a fear that Turkey's inclusion, while leading to increased trade with the Muslim world, would facilitate the entrance of Muslim terrorists into Europe.[20]

Even the governments in the booming Gulf Arab states are becoming increasingly anxious about the erosion of their national cultures as their growing economies invite ever-larger numbers of foreign workers. The problem is most clearly evident in the United Arab Emirates, where expatriates account for more than 90 percent of the private sector labor force.[21] Riding on the coattails of anti-immigration sentiment, a report titled "Immigration, Labor Markets and Integration," released by France's national planning commission, Commissariat Général du Plan, contends that there is no demographic issue that justifies the encouragement of mass immigration in the coming years. "Immigration will resolve neither the problem of an aging population nor the foreseeable deficits of our pension system," says François Héran, chairman of the study group that produced the report. This view certainly challenges the conventional wisdom that low European birthrates will require massive immigration to maintain population levels in the future. The following is an excerpt from the report:

> Working immigrants are concentrated at the bottom of the ladder. They are twice as likely to be unemployed as the national average, and twice as likely to have no vocational qualifications. They are three times more likely to remain in jobs earning the minimum wage, without promotion. Manual and semi-skilled workers account for only 25 percent of the French labor force, but 48.5 percent of all manual workers are immigrants.

The Plan's team stresses that, according to their survey, immigrants to France largely do not provide the kinds of skills that the French economy will need in the future, and that the relatively low economic performance of immigrants suggests that they are unlikely to be net contributors to the welfare and pension system. The new wave of Muslim immigrants into France has not come from occupied territories, and their population is rapidly expanding. Approximately 5 to 7 million Muslims are said to now be living in France, or twice the number reported to be living in neighboring Germany. Muslims are expected to account for 29 percent of the total population within the next decade.[22]

Opponents to immigration argue that although the economic benefits are marginal, the costs are great: Immigration leads to massive overcrowding, traffic congestion, and overstretched public services; exacerbates the housing crisis; imports poverty, crime, and public health problems such as AIDS and tuberculosis; increases social tension; and creates enclave communities. More important, dependence on immigrants discourages companies from adopting family-friendly practices, training the unskilled, and retaining older workers. The British government policy of using nurses from developing countries means it needn't improve pay and conditions to ensure that British nurses want to stay. Dependence on cheap Indian information technology (IT) experts meant U.S. firms stopped training their own people. Unskilled immigration encourages us to be a low-wage, low-productivity economy rather than a high-wage, high-productivity one. Unskilled immigration depresses unskilled wages and increases inequality. Immigration prompts a massive transfer of wealth from those who compete with immigrants to those who employ immigrants, deepening the unequal distribution of income in favor of rich over poor.

Negative impacts of immigration are not limited to the receiving countries. Immigration is also often disastrous for sending countries. The more that developed countries attract skilled migrants, the more they are stripping developing countries of the people they need most to achieve economic development. Ghana has one of the best free university systems in Africa, but it is being undermined because a third of Ghana's graduates leave the country. Jamaica's education system is collapsing because Western developed countries have enticed away many of its teachers. Health systems in Africa are undermined by the West's poaching of their doctors and nurses. Brain drain of highly educated people from developing countries makes the future prospect of these countries only gloomier.

Despite its considerable anti-immigration rhetoric, research funded by the European Union found no direct cause-and-effect link between crime, unemployment, and immigration, dealing a huge blow to ultranationalist and racist parties throughout Europe. A report released by the EU Commission contends that regulated immigration is vital for the EU's future, because shortages of labor could result without it. The report points to evidence that immigrants do not cause the underground "black market" economy, but rather such an informal economy encourages migration, both in Southern and Northern Europe. The EU-funded report made it clear that attempts in Germany to stem illegal entry failed to curb the informal economy. The presence of a black market economy might act as a "magnet" for poorer immigrants, encouraging them to stay in Europe once they were involved in such an environment.

On a brighter note, referring to ethnic diasporas such as overseas Chinese and Indians, Tung argues that brain "circulation" replaces the traditional concept of brain drain versus brain gain because of the growing mobility of human talent across borders.[23] This increasing phenomenon involves people who move back and forth between their country of origin and the adopted country to take advantage of career and new venture opportunities in both countries, resulting in an overall increase in benefits for both countries.[24] Recent related research analyzes the formation of transnational technical communities (TTCs), or groups of immigrants active in both home- and host-country technical networks, who collectively are effecting significant flows of venture capital investments to their original home country.[25] Despite this trend, it is still a challenge for these emerging economies to attract skilled and highly educated people to sustain economic growth.[26]

Immigration Policy Implications for Government Officials

International migration is a global challenge for the twenty-first century. As discussed earlier, immigration has both positive and negative impacts on importing countries. Therefore, it is critical for a government to set up an immigration policy that can maximize the net gain of immigration through imported skilled human resources, and thereby enhance its global competitiveness. MNCs can have a significant influence on the development of socially responsible immigration policy that also achieves this net gain.

Immigration experts argue that the success of integrating foreigners into a society is based on access to the job market. Societies that are more integrated seem to offer more opportunities for immigrants. Segregation among different races and ethnic groups has disproportionate and adverse effects on schools and home ownership rates. Recent riots in France illustrate the division between France's big cities and their poor suburbs, and frustrations simmering in housing projects to the north and northeast of Paris, which are heavily populated by North African and Muslim immigrants and their French-born children who struggle with high unemployment, crime, and poverty.[27]

Furthermore, residential segregation has grave consequences for minority employment and minority business-ownership rates. Substantial differences exist between the United States and Europe in their approach to handling immigrant workers. "In the [United States] the worst thing that an immigrant can do is be on any form of public assistance—the expectation is that immigrants come here to work and enter the labor market," says Susan Martin, director of the Institute for the Study of International Migration at Georgetown University. "In Europe, the worst thing an immigrant can do is being in the labor market."[28]

The first priority of a government should be to bring immigrants into the labor market. Language barriers, discrimination, lack of skills, and poor educational levels contribute to the many reasons why immigrants are disproportionately jobless in Europe. It is increasingly claimed that Europe is too generous with its welfare and too restrictive with its jobs. Furthermore, many jobs in Europe are simply not open to foreigners. For example, in France, more than fifty professions are closed to non-EU citizens. Partly because of rules like this and other red tape, there is a paradox in Europe's single market: Although official unemployment rates are high, many labor shortages exist. For immigrants specifically, the oft-repeated mantra of the European Union—free movement of people—might be an illusion. An immigrant in Belgium, for instance, might receive Belgian working papers, but the document is not valid in any other EU country unless he or she has EU citizenship. "European governments think about migration in negative terms—why people move and the problems it causes," said Andrew Geddes of the University of Liverpool. "Immigration is seen in almost wholly negative terms, as a drain, as a burden, as a cause of social problems." It is not difficult to understand how costly such restrictive immigration policies in Europe might be in competing for a skillful labor force in the global market.

In addition to more integrative immigration policies, expansion in trade between the sending country and the receiving country can also help reduce unwanted migration. Foreign direct investments (FDIs) increase jobs and trade and control migration in the long term, but they might increase migration in the short term. When, for example, MNCs make investments in developing countries, in the early stages they either send managers and other professionals to help operate the business or allow the entry of migrants from neighboring countries to work in FDI-created factories.[29]

DOMESTIC MIGRATION

People move not only across borders but also within a country, greatly affecting local labor conditions and characteristics that MNCs consider for their global business planning. For example, William Frey indicated that 70 percent of the U.S. foreign-born population, most of them Hispanic, live in "melting pot" states such as California and New York, which makes the labor force in those states more racially and ethnically diverse. On the other hand, internal migrants born in the United States are more likely to relocate into "new sunbelt" areas such as Nevada and Arizona.[30]

Most immigrants to the United States have clustered in ten states where 30 percent of the population resides. In these melting pot states, the white population has declined to 50 percent—lower than the other forty states. For the first time in a century, California's foreign-born population is greater than its out-of-state-born population. Immigrants dominate lower-level occupations and those requiring less-skilled workers. At the upper end of the spectrum, long-term residents tend to seize managerial and professional jobs.

Another important continuing trend is migration from rural to urban areas. According to UN estimates, by 2025 the urban population is expected to exceed the rural population by 1.3 billion people. For example, despite restrictions and economic penalties associated with migration, as well as a temporary slowdown due to the recent global economic crisis, more young people in rural China are moving to cities and to coastal provinces such as Guangdong and Fujian. Similarly, in Mexico the younger generation continues to leave rural areas for cities along the U.S./Mexico border, looking for jobs and a higher standard of living. However, the recent global financial crisis demonstrated a serious reversal of this trend, triggering the return of those urban workers as their jobs disappeared. In China, after years of the contribution of these migrant workers to the country's phenomenal economic growth, upon returning home with the recent economic crisis they presented a potential source of unrest as social systems in the rural areas grew more strained.[31]

EMERGENCE OF THE CONTINGENT WORKFORCE

Another important trend in the global labor market is the continued increase in the contingent workforce—the workers whose jobs are dependent or contingent upon present work demand (more specific HR utilization issues will be examined later in Chapter 5 on global HR planning). It has been estimated that about 90 percent of U.S. employers use temporary workers.[32] Permanent workers typically have full-time, long-term jobs and also enjoy benefits such as pensions, health insurance, and vacation time. However, these benefits are usually not available to temporary workers. Use of contingent workers has been referred to as "just-in-time staffing," a term derived from the Japanese just-in-time system of automobile production.[33] The United States is not alone in its increasing reliance on contingent workers. Large Japanese firms have long used them to buffer their core employees from unemployment caused by economic fluctuations. Furthermore, the use of contingent workers is increasing in Canada, Mexico, and Europe, especially in the Netherlands, Great Britain, Spain, Sweden, and France.[34]

USE OF CONTINGENT WORKERS

Estimates of the size of the global contingent workforce vary widely, partly because of the differing ways in which contingent workers are defined. Some estimates before the recent economic downturn placed the number of contingent workers in some locations as high as 35 percent.[35] No matter how accurate statistics might be, the general consensus is that contingent workers are a large and important component of the global workforce. Some observers even predict that the temporary workforce will grow faster than the permanent one for years to come. Although the temporary workforce as a whole has grown significantly, the most rapid growth in recent years has been in professional, technical, and managerial workers. The dramatic increase in the demand for temporary professional and technical workers has led to the formation of specialized temporary employment companies, many of which are integrated globally.

A survey of more than four hundred vice presidents and human resource management directors throughout North America by the Olsten Corporation, a large staffing services company, revealed that almost a third of the companies were using contingent professional staff for a variety of departments, including marketing, human resources, and other functional areas. In particular, there has been explosive growth in the use of temporary professionals in the high-tech area—highly educated workers skilled in new technologies. High-tech companies, such as Microsoft and Silicon Graphics International as well as telecommunications giants AT&T and Nortel are relying more and more on temporary staff to work as computer systems analysts, computer programmers, engineers, and technical writers. Peter Allan has identified major forces that encourage a continued role for the contingent workforce to play in modern economies.[36] We now examine several of these major forces.

Increasing Interdependence of the Global Economy

As has been especially evident with the recent global financial crisis, our global economy has significant interdependence of national economies across borders. What affects business and employment in one country or geographical region can have major repercussions in other parts of the world. Accordingly, businesses need to be vigilant

Global Workforce Professional Profile 3.1
Wendy Marsh: Navigating the Global Sea of Competitive Market Change

"The global business environment is constantly changing and at a faster pace. We often are halfway through implementing one strategy when we find we need to change it," says Wendy Marsh, a director of International Strategic Change at a large international retail organization. The global retail industry in general is facing significant market change with increasing competition from global competitors and increased price-point pressure on products from mass-market or value channel organizations such as Walmart in the United States and Tesco in the United Kingdom. To meet this global challenge requiring greater agility and local market responsiveness, Marsh supports her organization's decentralization strategy of in-market teams at regional headquarter locations with operational and product development functions co-located. The previous model had centralized production development in North America for any location. According to Marsh, this new blend of creative skills joining management at local retail operations achieves much greater flexibility and a more collaborative culture, which will result in product being more localized and better placed in each market.

To help build these new capabilities, the organization is sending experienced expatriates from North America on short-term assignments to foreign operations to work closely with local managers and new hires in the creative functions to transfer working knowledge—a more effective approach for transferring tacit knowledge and experience than formal training. To cope with ongoing change, Marsh believes that employees at all levels need to be more flexible and adaptive to changes—whether in the priorities of daily work or large-scale shifts in strategy based on the macroeconomic environment. Marsh asserts, "I really think that flexibility is a key competency of the future." Workforce flexibility is becoming an increasingly important goal in guiding staffing and promotion decisions as well as training activities.

A major challenge that Marsh faces in the global arena is what she calls the "tyranny of the time zones," where she often works with offices in Europe, North America, and Asia. "With strategic planning meetings, it's hard to get everyone involved at the same time. We often hold a morning teleconference meeting with Europe and an afternoon meeting with Asia, but it is very hard to have complete consistency in the flow of knowledge and strategic ideas in these very interactive meetings." To help build consistency, besides these regular meetings, the knowledge flow is supplemented by written communication channels, an international intranet site, and frequent personal foreign site visits.

Marsh received a bachelor's of science degree from Bowling Green State University and a Ph.D. in Industrial/Organizational Psychology from Pennsylvania State University. One phone call found her in London working with a European human resources team on efforts to build the capability of leading others through transformation as well as moving from a technical and transactional model to one that is more strategic and flexible. "I love the fascinating challenge in my regular work with people of a variety of country cultures," says Marsh. "Some cultures manage change better than others. How I work with people from other cultures to successfully achieve the same objectives can be very different."

and be ready to respond quickly to sudden, unexpected, or unforeseen changes in faraway places. The use of a contingent workforce provides employers with flexibility to meet sudden fluctuation in demand arising in the global marketplace. Companies with large numbers of permanent, full-time employees may find it difficult to reduce their staff quickly, particularly because of the pain such reduction would inflict on their people. To meet such challenges effectively, companies are inclined to maintain a lean workforce of core employees and have a body of contingent workers who can be more readily cut back as the need arises.

Competitive Pressures

The need for a global market presence intensifies the competitive pressures on firms to maintain or increase productivity at least partly by cutting variable and fixed labor costs. Using a contingent workforce better serves these goals than maintaining a large pool of permanent workers. Temporary workers are typically paid less and have fewer benefits than regular workers, and they are recruited, hired, and trained by temporary staffing firms. Also, they might work harder if they are trying to become permanent employees.

Virtual Companies

Small companies might not be willing, or might be unable, to handle functions such as recruiting and selecting workers, benefits and payroll, workers' compensation, and unemployment insurance claims. They might also be reluctant to employ a permanent workforce to handle these activities, so they outsource these functions to temporary staffing firms that provide these services for a fee. Such an arrangement benefits firms not only in saving the fixed costs of a permanent workforce but also in the reduced expenses derived from economies of scale accrued to an outsourced firm that provides the same service to multiple firms.

Technological Innovation

New industries have developed rapidly in this information age. The dot-com fad, although proving to be a bubble that swept the whole world entering the twenty-first century, illustrates how quickly and easily one can create new businesses. In order to keep up with ever-changing technologies, firms need to employ highly trained and skilled workers who are highly valued. However, employers might not always have the needed talent on board or the human or financial resources to develop it. The contingent workforce can be used to accommodate such needs. Independent contractors or consultants can be brought in as technical experts for important projects, such as new product development and the design and installation of complex new information systems.[37]

Changing Relationship between Employers and Employees

The longstanding implicit social contract between employers and employees seems to have come to an end in recent years, even in countries like Japan where employees are offered a lifetime employment system. Instead of enjoying lifetime employment, employees now assume responsibility for developing knowledge and skills that will enable them to market themselves to other employers. Continued company downsizing to remain competitive makes it difficult for employers to make long-term commitments to employees while employees in turn are not expected to show their loyalty to the employers.

Many governments are relaxing or eliminating strong job-protection rules, making it extremely difficult and costly for employers to lay off full-time workers during a business slowdown. Although it is still difficult for Japanese companies to lay off employees, South Korea has introduced new labor laws that legally allow companies to lay off workers. In many European countries, Spain in particular, the number of temporary and part-time jobs has increased dramatically over the past two decades, partly because some governments have actively encouraged the use of contingent workers to combat unemployment.[38]

In addition to changes in the social contract between employers and employees, far-reaching changes in employee needs, expectations, and lifestyles have come to alter relations in the workplace. Increases in the number of working mothers and the rise of dual-career families have led to demands for flexible working arrangements to strike a balance between family responsibilities and jobs. Population aging also contributes to an increased number of contingent workers, because the contingent workers need more flexibility to care for their elders as well as their children. Temporary work with its flexible working schedule is also being seen as a way of life for some professional, technical, managerial, and executive people.

OFFSHORE SOURCING

Although immigrant workers represent one solution to the declining number in developed countries' workforce, offshore sourcing is another option that can achieve the same objective by utilizing the overseas workforce without physical transfer of workers. The phenomenon of offshore sourcing of MNC work, whether to company-owned and managed foreign subsidiaries or to other contracted (i.e., outsourced) operations, has become increasingly popular among MNCs because it allows them to produce goods at lower costs in developing countries. However, just as an influx of immigrant workers can pose an economic threat to the home country labor force, so can offshore sourcing present a threatening picture with the movement of work abroad that would otherwise support local employment. Consider this excerpt from a *BusinessWeek* cover story that raised concerns about sending upscale jobs abroad, such as chip design, engineering, basic research, and even financial analysis:

> All kinds of knowledge work can be done almost anywhere. "You will see an explosion of work going anywhere," says Forrester Research, Inc., analyst John C. McCarthy. He goes so far as to predict at least 3.3 million white-collar jobs and $136 billion in wages will shift from the United States to low-cost countries by 2015. Europe is joining the trend, too. British banks like HSBC Securities, Inc., have huge back offices in China and India; French companies are using call centers in Mauritius; and German multinationals from Siemens to roller-bearings maker INA-Schaeffler are hiring in Russia, the Baltics, and Eastern Europe.[39]

Figure 3.3   **Number of U.S. Jobs Moving Offshore***

	2005	2010	2015
Life Sciences	3,700	14,000	37,000
Legal	14,000	35,000	75,000
Art, Design	6,000	14,000	30,000
Management	37,000	118,000	288,000
Business Operations	61,000	162,000	348,000
Computer	109,000	277,000	473,000
Architecture	32,000	83,000	184,000
Sales	29,000	97,000	227,000
Office Support	295,000	791,000	1,700,000
Total	586,700	1,591,000	3,362,000

*To low-wage countries such as India, China, Mexico, and the Philippines.

Because Japan has skill and labor shortages, it also has started to contract out product manufacturing to Taiwan, Korea, and other neighboring countries. The dramatic global growth in offshore job sourcing, whether through internal company workforce development abroad or outsourced labor arrangements, is reflected in the U.S. job movement forecast in Figure 3.3, with an estimated increase between 2005 and 2015 of nearly 473 percent in total U.S. jobs moved abroad.

The rise of a globally integrated economy has been beneficial to developing countries. However, it is not yet clear how this new wave of globalization will affect the labor force of developed economies. For example, in the 1990s, the United States had to import hundreds of thousands of immigrants to ease engineering shortages. For decades, immigrant Asian engineers in the U.S. labs of Texas Instruments, IBM, and Intel have played an important role in American technology breakthroughs. The difference now is that Indian and Chinese engineers are managing R&D teams in their home countries. Sending routine service and engineering tasks to nations with a surplus of educated workers can redeploy the U.S. labor force and capital to higher-value industries and cutting-edge R&D. However, the opposite scenario is equally plausible. Displaced workers at home due to outsourcing might have to unwillingly accept lower salaries in return for corporate efficiency. This displacement will pose serious socioeconomic issues if foreign countries increasingly specialize in high-skilled areas where the United States has a comparative advantage.

Just as the recent financial crisis has adversely affected international as well as domestic immigration, it also has dampened offshore sourcing activity. To illustrate, the number of offshore outsourcing deals that global financial services firms signed were reduced by almost one-third in 2008 compared to 2007.[40] Many banks put discussions about offshore outsourcing contracts on hold or just canceled them altogether. However, some predict a more positive scenario, estimating that cost-saving spurred by the financial crisis will result in a major resurgence in financial service offshore outsourcing over the next several years following the crisis.[41] There are strong arguments for developed countries not to restrict offshore outsourcing, pointing to actual job development and economic benefit within those countries. For example, according to Bureau of Economic Analysis (BEA) data, in 2008 U.S. exports of services were

$550 billion and imports were $405 billion, resulting in a $145 billion surplus. These figures indicate that the United States continues to have a competitive advantage in high-value, high-skilled services, which is supported by the lower-cost offshore outsourcing of certain business processes. Restricting offshore outsourcing would backfire because it would increase costs for U.S. companies, since U.S. services outsourced abroad represent significant savings for U.S. goods and services exports.[42]

Offshore outsourcing increases MNCs' strategic flexibility by either contracting their manufacturing processes outside the home country or by forming joint ventures. The development of a dynamic organizational network through contracting and joint ventures enables firms to maximize the specialized competence of individual operations and to use human resources more effectively that would otherwise have to be accumulated, allocated, and maintained by a single organization. This development means a company's global competitiveness will increase due to its ability to perform a certain value-creation activity in a country where it can be produced most efficiently. In other words, companies are learning to capitalize on global talent pools to introduce new products and services to market sooner and at lower costs. Many executives in developed countries now believe that offshore sourcing can transform their businesses, resulting in corporate growth through the better use of their own skilled domestic workforce, and even resulting in local domestic job creation, not just the exploitation of cheap wages abroad.[43] However, offshore sourcing also has drawbacks. Due to the nature of some jobs, offshoring may be impractical, such as work requiring frequent face-to-face interaction with customers. Where work is outsourced offshore (rather than sourced abroad to facilities directly operated by the MNC), it increases dependence on independent operators for assurance of the quality of components and finished products. Given the increasing recognition of the value of strategic factors such as durability and quality rather than simple cost savings, offshore sourcing might not be a viable option in the long run. Increasing dependence on independent suppliers can lead to companies' losing sight of emerging technologies and thereby design and manufacturing abilities. Furthermore, not all value-added functions are amenable to offshore sourcing. With this realization, major firms like Caterpillar and GE now are engaging in a trend called *onshoring* or *reshoring* by bringing some of their manufacturing operations back to their home country for benefits of closer home market proximity, including reduced shipping costs and logistics complexity (and also often encouraged by home government tax incentives).[44]

In addition, distinct cross-cultural risk factors can have a critical impact on the success of an offshore outsourcing relationship. Not only can corporate cultural differences between the client organization and the vendor influence the performance of offshore outsourcing, but differences in national cultures may affect every area of business relationships, systems, processes, and work interactions.[45] Furthermore, the cross-cultural risk of services placed offshore also can be great when significant interaction is required between customers of the MNC's home country and employees in the offshore location who differ culturally, including in nuances of communication style and language expression. Not only can these cultural differences interfere with perceptions of quality customer service, such as with offshore call centers where language and other cultural differences can contribute to miscommunication and frustration, but the perceived offshoring of such home country jobs can also lead to a diminished image of the MNC in the customer's eyes.

GLOBAL WORKFORCE MANAGEMENT CHALLENGES

In this ever-changing business environment, how do firms manage the major changes and challenges in the global labor market effectively? The global economy requires firms to transform themselves into global companies that are able to compete with anybody, anywhere, anytime. This imperative means that companies must excel in a number of dimensions that create a new level of competitive advantages. "Whether MNCs rely on imported workers or on a foreign workforce, human capital is by far the most important source of competitive advantage in the global economy," asserts Nobel laureate Professor Gary Becker of the University of Chicago. Countries are competing with each other for a scarce and valuable human resource in much the same way they competed for gold or oil previously. Frank Smith, vice president of global organizational development and training at Wyeth-Ayerst Pharmaceuticals, said, "A big payoff of globalization is the capacity to gather the best talent from anywhere to work on your biggest problems. The war over talent will get worse, not better." The decreasing number of people in developed countries between the ages of thirty-five and forty-five will not only create greater competition for viable workers but also increase the difficulty of succession planning. These changes will present several challenges for managers and HR professionals.

First, as we will examine further in Chapter 5, managers and HR professionals need to develop the ability to collect relevant information about the talent pool of people around the world to effectively use an offshore sourcing strategy or to import temporary workers from abroad. In other words, companies should ensure that strategies for movement and utilization of people and work are in place to attract, retain and cultivate global human capital. To attain this goal, global HR strategies need to be tightly integrated with business strategies. Unfortunately, many countries have extended their privacy laws to prevent cross-border personnel data flows. This legal obstruction creates tremendous problems for global HR planning and control, which might hamper or completely stall a company's important operations.

Second, faced with an aging global population and contingent workforce, companies that handle the upcoming demographic change skillfully will be able to reward workers more generously and still earn a higher shareholder return. The effective management of a global workforce composed of both continuing and contingent employees requires special attention to issues of equity and fairness. This requirement means that managers and HR professionals need to devise appropriate compensation and benefits schemes for their workers.

Third, companies should be able to manage and leverage the differences and similarities in the diversity of national and business cultures, and managers should learn how to collaborate with foreign partners to minimize culture clash. For example, cultural differences can present problems with outsourcing business in developing countries. Without a proper understanding of a host country's culture, employees might not be evaluated and assigned tasks based on their job skills. In a recent Gartner, Inc., survey of nine hundred U.S. companies that outsource IT work offshore, a majority complained of communication difficulty.[46] Foreign language proficiency, communication skills, and knowledge of foreign culture are valued highly in international business. There is growing recognition that a positive relationship exists between cross-cultural communications and effective teamwork and productivity.

Fourth, managers and HR professionals should follow government immigration policies closely and influence the shaping of these policies as deemed necessary. An MNC's active and socially responsible involvement in its home country's immigration and other labor policy formation is important, ultimately because government policies either reinforce or hinder the competitiveness of a country's firms and economy. For effective strategic planning, managers also need to be familiar with some domains in developing countries where either foreign direct investments or outsourcing is prohibited.

SUMMARY

In this chapter we have examined major trends in the global labor market along with their implications for governments and firms. These trends include changes in world demographics, impacts of immigration on developed countries, the emergence and influence of contingent workers as a significant component of the labor force, and the positive and negative impact of the increased use of offshore sourcing as an alternative to domestic production and operations. Finally, we discussed important implications of these trends for HR managers.

QUESTIONS FOR OPENING SCENARIO ANALYSIS

1. Why did the Brazilian shoemakers move to China?
2. How is this situation with the Brazilian firms consistent with the global trend of migration and movement of labor across national boundaries? How does it differ?
3. Do you anticipate any potential social tensions between Chinese and Brazilians resulting from the cross-border migration? If so, what could be their cause?

CASE 3.1. INDIA IS SENDING JOBS ABROAD

One of the constants of the global economy has been companies moving their tasks and jobs to India. But rising wages, demand for workers who speak languages other than English, and competition from countries looking to emulate India's success as a back office—such as China, Morocco, and Mexico—are challenging that model. Many executives acknowledge that globalization will increasingly spread a company's jobs around the globe. The future of offshore sourcing is "to take the work from any part of the world and do it in any other part of the world." To beat emerging rivals offering lower prices and geographic advantage, Indian companies are hiring workers and opening offices in other developing countries, before their clients do. In May 2008, Tata Consultancy Service, which already had five thousand workers in Brazil, Chile, and

Uruguay, announced the opening of a new back office in Guadalajara, Mexico. Wipro, another Indian technology services company, has outsourcing offices in Canada, China, Portugal, Romania, and Saudi Arabia, among other locations. And last month, Wipro said it was opening a software development center in Atlanta that would hire five hundred programmers in three years. The company was even considering additional hubs in Idaho and Virginia to take advantage of American "states that are less developed."

Infosys, another Indian outsourcing giant, is trying to become a global matchmaker for outsourcing: any time a company wants work done somewhere else, even just down the street, Infosys wants to get the call. To achieve this goal, it recently opened offices in the Philippines, Thailand, and Poland. In each outsourcing hub, local employees work with minimal supervision from Indian managers. Infosys says its outsourcing experience in India has taught it to carve up a project, allocate each part to suitable workers, double-check quality, and then export a final, reassembled product to clients. The company argues it can replicate its Indian back offices in other countries and develop Chinese, Mexican, or Czech employees to be more productive than local outsourcing companies could make them.

Some analysts compare such an offshore outsourcing strategy to the Japanese penetration of the U.S. auto market in the 1970s. Just as the Japanese learned to make cars in America without Japanese workers, Indian vendors are learning to outsource abroad without Indians. In one project, an American bank wanted a computer system to handle a loan program for Hispanic customers. The system had to work in Spanish. It also had to take into account variables particular to Hispanic clients: many, for example, remit money to families abroad, which can affect their bank balances. The bank thought a Mexican team would be the best for this task due to the language proficiency and cultural familiarity. But instead of going to a Mexican vendor, or to an American vendor with Mexican operations, the bank retained three dozen engineers at Infosys, which had recently opened shop in Monterrey, Mexico. Such is the new offshore outsourcing: a company in the United States hires an Indian vendor headquartered seven thousand miles away to supply it with Mexican engineers working 150 miles south of the U.S. border.

Source: Adapted from Anand Giridharadas, "Outsourcing Works, So India Is Exporting Jobs," *The New York Times,* September 25, 2007: A1.

Questions for Case Analysis and Discussion

1. From this case, how would you describe this new wave of offshore outsourcing?
2. Why did Indian outsourcing companies have to change their strategy?
3. What kinds of challenges do you anticipate that Indian companies will face in implementing this new outsourcing strategy?

Case 3.2. Europe: The New Destination for Latino Workers

The enduring U.S. dilemma of immigration from Mexico and other Latin American countries has begun to shift across the Atlantic to Europe. Europe's population of legal and illegal Latinos has surged in the past decade, especially since the 9/11 terrorist attacks, which made the U.S. borders more difficult to maneuver. The Latino immigrants, reaching half the number now in the United States, are pushed to leave their countries due to poverty at home and pulled by demand for workers overseas. Their movement is facilitated by more porous European borders as well as forged documents.

Latinos represent the fastest-growing immigrant community in Italy, Switzerland, Spain, and Britain. Tiny Switzerland, formerly a trilingual society of German, French, and Italian, now has about 1 million residents who speak Spanish, including long-term guest workers from Spain and new arrivals from Latin America. Spanish is about to pass Italian as the country's third-most-spoken language, after German and French. That Europe, not the United States, has become the primary destination for millions of immigrants, including those from Latin American countries, says much about globalization's shifting tides as well as the way economic integration and security issues play out on either side of the Atlantic. Until recently, the European Union granted open access to Latin Americans arriving as tourists. A united Europe offers Latin Americans who land anywhere in the European Union an open door to labor markets in the twenty-five member states and even to countries not part of the European Union.

Spain is the most popular portal for Latin immigrants. Its population of legal Ecuadorian immigrants has surged from just seven thousand in 1999 to more than two hundred thousand—and at least that many illegal immigrants as well. Besides the linguistic similarities, Spain for years granted a special status to Latin Americans because of its strong ties with the region. Spanish citizenship can be available after twenty-four months of residency. There is also a burgeoning black market in Spanish birth certificates and passports. Since 1996, Spain has been among the fastest-growing economies in Europe with its strong tourism and construction sectors attracting many foreign job seekers.

Madrid's leading newspaper, *El Pais,* reported that 550,000 Latin Americans entered Spain as tourists in 2002 but only 86,000 left. How many stay in Spain or move on to other European countries is unknown. "Planes come in every day from South America with 350 passengers, and leave with 150," says Silvestre Romero, the chief inspector at Madrid's Barajas International Airport. "We know they're not tourists." Jose Quhizhpe, a thirty-five-year-old laborer arriving from Quito, Ecuador, with his six children in tow, says he is visiting his wife, who has found work as a domestic in Bilbao in northern Spain. The children are on vacation, he explains. "Maybe we'll stay here for their school," he says, as he lines up the family before an immigration inspector. As many as fifteen flights arrive daily in Madrid from Latin America's major cities, and only a few travelers are turned back each day, usually Peruvian and Colombian men with counterfeit passports.

Europe's governments are trying to curtail the influx of illegal immigrants, adding new regulations every year to restrict entry as well as the movements of those apparently looking for work. Two years ago the European Union adopted a common visa policy, and it soon will begin requiring airlines to inform immigration officials of tourists who fail to use their return tickets. But efforts to control the wave of illegal immigrants come up against economic and cultural forces that foster it. Many Europeans are happy to employ the new immigrants because they tend to work for less money than previous generations of transient laborers. Particularly in Spain, the cost of integrating these largely Catholic, Spanish-speaking immigrants is much lower than integrating those from Africa and the Middle East. The trend also serves the diverging demographics. These young men and women, among the first of their families to finish high school, are often the frustrated job seekers of Latin American countries that are unable to sustain enough growth to absorb the millions entering the labor force each year. With its graying labor force, Europe is facing a shortage of labor, especially those catering to the old and infirm. More Swiss mothers are entering the labor force, and they need extra help at home with jobs such as cleaning and babysitting, which attract mainly women. These Latinas have an advantage over Muslim women, whose husbands and fathers reportedly discourage their wives and daughters from working in a stranger's house. As a sign of resistance, Swiss employers have been known to instruct their maids to dye their dark hair blond to avoid detection.

Source: Adapted from J. Millman and C. Vitzthum, "Europe Becomes New Destination for Latino Workers," *Wall Street Journal,* September 12, 2003: A1, A7.

QUESTIONS FOR CASE ANALYSIS AND DISCUSSION

1. What are possible implications of this trend in Latino migration for HR planning in businesses in Europe?
2. What are possible sources of workplace conflict that might arise as Latinos enter the mainstream labor force in larger numbers?
3. What are particular practices and activities that European managers and HR professionals can engage in to take advantage of this migration trend for Latinos in Europe?

RECOMMENDED WEB SITE RESOURCES

International Labour Migration (www.ilo.org/public/english/protection/migrant). Provided by the International Labour Organization, offering research and data about the increasing international migration issue, including current dynamics of international labor migration, globalization, and regional integration and the benefits of international labor migration.

International Labour Organization (www.ilo.org). Besides migration, the ILO also provides considerable information and reports accessible from this home Web site related to labor market conditions, including labor statistics and changing demographics information.

International Monetary Fund (www.imf.org). Current world demographics and labor force trends can be noted in research sponsored and reported by the IMF. Simply enter "world demographics" or "labor force trends" in the search field at the top of the home page. For example, an entry of "world demographics" yielded the informative chapter 3 of the IMF World Economic Outlook (WEO) September 2004 report, "How will demographic change affect the global economy?"

The Outsourcing Times (www.blogsource.org). A rich source of basic information about offshore outsourcing as well as current research and announcements of current global developments related to managerial, economic, and political concerns.

Work on International Migration (go to www.oecd.org/maintopic and then click International Migration). Based on continued monitoring of migration movements and policies in member countries of the Organization for Economic Cooperation and Development (OECD) and outside the OECD area, provides an in-depth analysis of the economic and social aspects of migration, including the role of migration in alleviating labor shortages; links between migration, demography, and economic growth; and the fiscal impact of migration.

NOTES

1. Adapted from "Business: Footloose Capitalism; Brazilians in China," *Economist,* September 13, 2008.

2. H. Sirkin, J. Hemerling, and A. Bhattacharya, *Competing with Everyone from Everywhere for Everything* (New York: Boston Consulting Group Inc., 2008).

3. D. Bacon, "Globalization: Two Faces, Both Ugly," *Dollars and Sense* (March/April 2000): 18–20.

4. "Turning Their Backs on the World," *Economist,* February 21, 2009.

5. "An Astonishing Rebound," *Economist,* August 15, 2009.

6. J.T. Arnold, "Twittering and Facebooking While They Work," *HR Magazine* 54 (12) (2009): 53–55; R. Connell, "Another Red-Light Probe for Metrolink," *Los Angeles Times,* December 2, 2009; J. Mathews, "Northwest Pilots Appeal License Revocation," *Aviation Daily* 378 (27) (2009): 6; C. Borchert, "Killing Time Electronically," *Canadian Underwriter* 75 (6) (2008): 66–67; M. Segalla, "An International Study of Dysfunctional E-Mail Usage and Attitudes Among Managers" *International Journal of Human Resources Development and Management* 5 (4) (2005): 425–36.

7. D. Lauter, "French Experience Rise in Job Stress Beyond Usual Grumbling," *Los Angeles Times,* November 1, 2009.

8. Anonymous, "Flexible Hours in the Ranks," *HRMagazine: SHRM's 2010 HR Trend Book* (January 2010): 16–17; M. Laff, "Teams that Stay, While on the Go," *Training and Development* 63 (7) (2009): 18–19.

9. "The Price of Efficiency," *Business Week,* March 22, 2004.

10. United Nations, Department of Economic and Social Affairs, Population Division, Population Facts, 2010, available at http://www.un.org/esa/population/.

11. Ibid.

12. Vital Speeches of the Day, "What the Future Holds," *Vital Speeches of the Day,* March 1, 1999, 313–16.

13. "With Millions on the Move, This Guide Maps the Routes to Prosperity," *Wall Street Journal,* September 19, 2008.

14. "Latest Immigration Wave: Retreat," *Wall Street Journal,* October 2, 2008.

15. P. Martin and J. Widgren, "International Migration: Facing the Challenge," *Population Bulletin* 57 (1) (2002): 3–39.

16. G. Epstein, "New Melting Pot," *Barron's* 82 (2) (2002): 17–19.

17. Center for an Urban Future, "A World of Opportunity" (February 2007) www.nycfuture.org.

18. V. Wadhwa, A.L. Saxenion, B. Rissing, and G. Gereffi, "America's New Immigrant Entrepreneurs, Part I" (January 4, 2007). Duke Science, Technology and Innovation Paper No. 23, http://ssrn.com/abstract=990152.

19. "280 Philippine Nurses, Caregivers to Arrive in Japan Sun" *Jiji Press English News Service,* May 8, 2009; L. Longtin, L. Mahoney, and W. Press, "A Foreign Recruitment Success Story," *Nursing Management,* 40(10) (2009): 12–15.

20. Epstein, "New Melting Pot."

21. "Gulf Arab States Are Fretting at the Rising Number of Foreign Workers," *Economist,* September 3, 2008.

22. M. McDonald, "The French Identity Crisis," *Commentary* 129 (5) (2010): 47–49; Think & Ask Non-Profit News, "Immigrants Work in the States, Riot in France" (November 2005), thinkandask.com.

23. R.L. Tung, "Brain Circulation, Diaspora, and International Competitiveness," *European Journal of Management,* 26 (5) (2008): 298–304.

24. E. Chacko, "From Brain Drain to Brain Gain: Reverse Migration to Bangalore and Hyderabad, India's Globalizing High Tech Cities," *GeoJournal* 68 (2–3) (2007): 131–40.

25. R. Madhavan and A. Iriyama, "Understanding Global Flows of Venture Capital: Human Networks as the 'Carrier Wave' of Globalization," *Journal of International Business Studies* 40 (8) (2009): 1241–59.

26. "Wanted: Skilled Workers for a Growing Economy in Brazil," *New York Times,* July 2, 2008.

27. Think & Ask, "Immigrants Work in the States," http://www.thinkandask.com/2005/111205french.html.

28. *Turkish Daily News,* March 15, 2003.

29. "Foreign Workers Face Turning Tide; Backlash in Europe," *International Herald Tribune,* December 25, 2002.

30. Martin and Widgren, "International Migration."

31. "China Fears Restive Migrants as Jobs Disappear in Cities," *Wall Street Journal,* December 2, 2008.

32. A. Von Hippel, C.S.L. Mangum, D.B. Greenberger, R.L. Heneman, and J.D. Skoglind, "Can Organization and Employees Both Win?" *Academy of Management Executive* (February 1997): 93–104.

33. U.S. Bureau of Labor Statistics, "Report on the American Workforce" (Washington, DC: U.S. Department of Labor, 1999).

34. R. Theler Carter, "Eurotemping," *HR Magazine* (1999): 122–28.

35. K. Barker and K. Christensen, *Contingent Work* (Ithaca, NY: Cornell University Press, 1998).

36. P. Allan, "The Contingent Workforce, Challenges and New Directions," *American Business Review* (June 2002): 103–10.

37. S.F. Matusik and C.W.L. Hite, "The Utilization of Contingent Work, Knowledge Creation and Competitive Advantage," *Academy of Management Review* (October 1998): 680–97.

38. E.L. Andrews, "Only Employment for Many in Europe Is Part-Time Work," *New York Times,* September 1, 1997.

39. "Is Your Job Next?" *Business Week,* February 3, 2003.

40. "How the Financial Crisis Will Affect the Outsourcing Industry," *Economist,* October 9, 2008.

41. "Outsourcing Shops Feel the Street's Pain," *Business Week,* October 13, 2008.

42. "The Future of Outsourcing," *Business Week,* January 30, 2006.

43. "U.S. Services Providers Continue to Dominate Sourcing Market," *Coalition of Service Industries* (April 14, 2004).

44. K. Maher and B. Tita, "Caterpillar Joins 'Onshoring' Trend," *Wall Street Journal,* March 12, 2010.

45. K. Schomer, "Cross-cultural Risk Factors in Offshore Outsourcing," Change Management Consulting and Training, 2006, http://www.cmct.net/articlepdfs/CMCT_article_risk_factors.pdf.

46. Ibid.

4 The Key Role of International HRM in Successful MNC Strategy

HOW DO MNCs COMPETE IN EMERGING MARKETS?

IBM's global strategy has evolved in three different stages. Its first stage was consistent with the nineteenth-century "international model," with firms based in their home country and selling goods through overseas sales offices. Then stage two followed in the form of the classic multinational firm in which the parent company creates a small replica of its headquarters in different countries around the world. Now as the company views important emerging markets such as China and Brazil, which are critical to its continued growth, IBM is redesigning its strategy to a globally integrated transnational model, moving people and jobs anywhere in the world, based on the optimal conditions of labor skills, competitive labor cost, and overall business environment. While the attraction to these emerging markets was originally for cheap labor, now IBM looks at foreign markets as opportunities for obtaining high skills and high value. Winning the "war for talent" is a pressing issue for IBM and other MNCs as there are extremely high turnover rates in emerging markets. IBM believes that its global presence gives it an edge in recruitment and retention over local competitors.

The most attractive potential customer in developing countries is the government, because of the infrastructure development boom that spans everything from mobile phone networks to roads, airports, energy, and water supply. In drawing up plans for the economic development, governments rely on the reputation of MNCs in assisting their countries. As these projects require substantial spending, companies such as Cisco and GE have recently started establishing long-term problem-solving relationships with governments instead of offering specific products and services. And rather than simply delivering the same old products and services to target the emerging mass consumer market in these developing countries, MNCs are re-engineering their business models to be cost-effective and to effectively compete with local firms.

How can these MNCs successfully implement their strategic shift? HR management is the key to their success. The expatriate managers now deployed by MNCs in emerging markets are generally of a much higher caliber than the "young bucks or retirement-posting

Figure 4.1   **Three Different HR-Related Areas of MNCs' Capabilities for Enhancing Performance**

1. Strategic capabilities
   a. Fully exploiting worldwide capabilities
   b. Acting on changing globalization drivers
   c. Making moves against competitors around the world

2. Organizational capabilities
   a. Development and leadership training: Developing talent and leadership for innovation and renewal
   b. Knowledge transfer: Leveraging global capabilities effectively
   c. Organizational structure for optimal global performance

3. Managing process capabilities
   a. Nurturing global management talent
   b. Transferring best practices
   c. Stimulating transfer of critical capabilities

types" they used to send. The MNCs' management advantage is based more on training and experience of running a large business than on exposure to other countries. In fact, most MNCs are reducing their use of expatriates, and the smaller number of expatriates that they do send are expected to train local managers as their successors. Among the challenges facing MNCs are the lack of emerging market experience in their senior ranks and retaining capable local managers. The latter can be difficult as local companies often try to poach qualified managers who have been trained by the MNC.[1]

INTRODUCTION

Changes in the contemporary global economy highlight many of the emerging challenges facing HR management. It is not an exaggeration to say that the international success of most companies will be determined largely by how well HR issues are handled. Figure 4.1 identifies three different and critical HR-related areas of MNCs' capabilities for enhancing performance in their global operation. These critical areas include vital activities for deriving competitive advantage such as nurturing global management talent, encouraging knowledge transfer, developing leadership talent for innovation and renewal, and transferring best practices and capabilities.[2] Most important, HR management has redefined its role to become much a more important factor in the strategic development of the business. Therefore, in this chapter we examine the strategic roles of HR management on global organizational performance and the impact of MNCs' competitive strategy and organizational structure on international HR management practice. Then we will present a new paradigm for enhancing HR management's contribution to competitive advantage in the global marketplace.

KNOWLEDGE TRANSFER

According to one survey, top managers believe that the effectiveness of transferring human knowledge, expertise, and critical capabilities is the most important factor for transferring an MNC's performance. HR management has become the key means of transferring a firm's critical capabilities.[3]

As the opening case illustrates, one of the key developing areas for HR management is the globalization of business, which requires the sourcing of the right people to fill overseas postings, the effective management of their staff during their assignment and subsequent postings, and their eventual repatriation with greater expertise to share. International assignments are increasingly considered a mechanism for vital transfer of knowledge and capabilities needed for success.[4]

There are two major classes of knowledge: *explicit* and *tacit*.[5] Explicit knowledge can be codified (that is, expressed in words and numbers) and easily communicated and shared in the form of hard data, manuals, codified procedures, or universal principles. Contrary to explicit knowledge, tacit, or implicit, knowledge is not easily visible and expressible, making it difficult to share or communicate with others. More specifically, tacit knowledge consists of the "know-how" or learned skills that result from personal experience, that is, learning by doing. In other words, tacit knowledge has to do with an employee's "practical expertise" rather than information that can be derived from books or manuals.[6] Although MNCs have effectively leveraged advances in technology to collect, store, and communicate explicit knowledge through the use of global databases, the effective widespread management of tacit knowledge remains largely elusive.[7]

Much of the knowledge transferred between the units of an MNC is not explicit but implicit or tacit. This tacit knowledge is embedded in the individual experience and skills of the organization's members and is revealed only through its application. Given that tacit knowledge cannot be codified or explained in manuals, a company needs to rely on personnel transfer for knowledge dissemination. Unfortunately, few MNCs recognize the importance of HR management practices that promote the sharing of tacit knowledge throughout the entire organization.

GLOBAL LEADERSHIP TRAINING AND DEVELOPMENT

In order to transfer knowledge or critical capabilities across borders effectively, managers need to develop not only an in-depth knowledge in specific functional areas but also an ability to effectively communicate with people who have different cultural values and norms. As one of the top managers of a U.S. MNC remarked, "My top globalization issue is people development and building a learning organization." These companies are trying to find a way to manage the free flow of talent and necessary skills around the world with the objective of building a competence-based organization. Globalization implies accepting that cultural diversity in management composition and management style contributes to the competitive advantage of the global company. To develop and manage a global organization implies developing and managing people who can think, lead, and act from a global perspective, and who possess a global mind-set as well as global skills. Developing managers with a global mind-set is the most critical factor in creating a truly global organization.

Managers with a cosmopolitan mind-set understand intuitively that different cultural norms have value and meaning to those who practice them. Differences in behavioral patterns and social norms that create cultural distance may impede and complicate not only interpersonal relations between managers from different cultural backgrounds but also the contexts of decision making as established within the MNC.[8] This is because people with different cultural backgrounds have different "frames of reference."[9] A frame of reference refers to a set of patterned meanings or the collective mental programming that is shared by a specific group of people. Thus, frames of reference determine and regulate whether or not particular ends, as well as the means to those ends, would be acceptable. They further dictate appropriate behavior by stipulating positive and negative sanctions for what is expected (or forbidden) behavior within each specific setting. Moreover, positive and negative sanctions are often communicated through a variety of nonverbal means, such as facial expressions, body postures, or hand gestures.

Difficulties in understanding behavioral characteristics and in properly interpreting various verbal and nonverbal signals pose great challenges to managers as they are exposed to a new and different environment. Global leaders are those who overcome these challenges by understanding ways to influence the actions and beliefs of others. "Three distinct sets of competence or characteristics were identified in previous research: cultural savvy, unwavering character, and dual perspective."[10] An executive cannot develop a global perspective on business or become comfortable with foreign cultures by staying at headquarters or taking short business trips abroad. Indeed, the most effective way to fundamentally change how people think about doing business globally is by having them work abroad.

STRATEGIC CONTROL NEEDS

Another important reason why international HR management has taken on more strategic importance involves its potential contribution in controlling and coordinating subsidiaries, and in achieving and maintaining the appropriate strategic positioning of the organization.[11] As global competition continues to intensify, it becomes increasingly important for MNCs to maintain control over their international operations.[12] Broadly defined, *strategic control* refers to an MNC's ability to ensure that its various operating units around the world act in accordance with its overall policy in a systematic, coordinated, and consistent manner. Such a task often represents a challenge for MNCs because their global strategies or policies may not necessarily coincide with local units' customary practices or profit-maximizing strategies.[13]

MNCs have relied primarily on the conventional means of output-based control such as financial, quality, and personnel performance measures. However, researchers recognize the limitation of output-based control when cultural distance is substantial between the home country of an MNC parent and the host country of its subsidiary.[14] As an alternative to formal, output-based control, therefore, less formal control structures, such as cultural and behavioral control, have received increased attention as meaningful mechanisms through which the MNC's control needs may be satisfied. The transfer of company human resources—managers and professionals in particular—between the units of an MNC has become a major vehicle for exercising behavioral control and instilling a consistent corporate culture and strategy throughout the entire organization.

Specifically, the use of expatriate personnel has been recognized as an important control mechanism to monitor and evaluate the activities and behaviors within the foreign operation or subsidiary. Studies related to company control through expatriates sent from company headquarters generally suggest that the assignment of the expatriates increases an MNC's control over its overseas units by influencing the goals and values of subsidiary managers to reflect those desired by the parent company.

COMPETITIVE STRATEGIES OF MULTINATIONAL CORPORATIONS

When faced with the many challenges of expanding and conducting business abroad, MNCs may adopt wide-ranging options of business strategy and structure to build distinct organizational capability. Four major strategy types used by MNCs to overcome these challenges and compete on an international and global scale are global cost leadership, multidomestic, transnational, and regional. As we will see, each of these fundamental strategies has important roles and practices in the management of global human resources.

The fundamental challenge for MNCs is to establish a system that will effectively accommodate the two conflicting needs of globalization and localization. The task does not concern the simple dichotomous question of centralized or decentralized organization or decision-making structure. Nor is it to decide whether or what functions should be globalized or localized. Rather, the task involves creating a system that will concurrently be centralized enough for global integration and coordination and decentralized enough for local responsiveness.[15] In other words, MNCs should be not only cost competitive but also capable of delivering products that satisfy the needs and preferences of local customers, which often differ from one country or region to another. However, the relative emphasis on these two imperatives varies according to the industry's characteristics. For example, Michelin's tire business tends to be very successful worldwide with relatively little required localization or customization to meet local preferences and tastes. However, even the nearly omnipresent global icon McDonald's has found a need to adjust to local preferences, such as focusing on lamb and chicken instead of beef in India, and offering mayonnaise instead of ketchup in Germany (you can get ketchup with your fries but usually for a small fee—unheard of in the United States).

GLOBAL COST-LEADERSHIP STRATEGY

The fast-changing global business environment, driven by the globalization of markets and the acceleration of products and technology life cycles), necessitates that MNCs develop a global strategy. A global strategy is noted when a firm's competitive position in one country is significantly influenced by its position in other countries. A firm integrates its activities worldwide to capture and benefit from linkages and synergies among countries, thereby gaining a competitive advantage. In firms that pursue a global strategy, the higher levels of coordination and interdependence required between foreign affiliates and parent company operations require that the company be globally integrated. MNCs attempt to realize cost-saving efficiencies and economies of scale and scope by integrating and coordinating operations around the world and by developing highly standardized products and marketing approaches.[16]

MULTIDOMESTIC STRATEGY

Cross-national diversity likely impedes organizational effectiveness for firms employing a global strategy. With different national and regional laws and cultures, attempts to use a standard promotional message or product can be very problematic. For example, in a breakfast cereal television advertisement, Kellogg's showed children eating the product, mentioned the cereal's vitamin enrichment, and used the company slogan, "The best to you each morning." Regulators in Germany considered the slogan to be an unfounded health claim that had to be removed. The part claiming the value of the extra vitamins was deemed by regulators in the Netherlands as having questionable support, and the same commercial was cancelled in France, which does not allow children to endorse products. The child endorsement problem was overcome in Austria, where very small adult actors were substituted for the children.

To a great extent, consumers continue to demand locally differentiated products reflecting substantial divergence in standards, tastes, and perceived needs, even across countries within a regional bloc, such as the European Union, that purports to be integrated and one large market. Consequently, attempts to implement standardized policies and operational procedures worldwide across all international operating units may completely disregard the special needs of individual subsidiaries, including the different regulations in the nations in which they are located.[17] As a result, with declining local market interest, as well as local regulatory obstructions and even fines, the overall performance of the organization might decrease. To deal with these differences effectively, MNCs can adopt a multidomestic strategy that emphasizes local responsiveness.

When local differences are substantial, the firm's strategies often must be adapted to meet the particular conditions of each local market. The extent and direction of the adaptation may differ significantly from one local market to another, such as from the French-speaking western side of Switzerland to the German-speaking central and eastern side to the Italian-speaking southern region. Coca-Cola's strategy of "think local, act local" represents a multidomestic approach. For example, they are developing a pear-flavored drink for Turkey and a new berry-flavored Fanta in Germany. Coke is trying to adapt to the local tastes rather than just pushing classic Coca-Cola. Thus, under such conditions, regional and/or country managers in each area are provided with substantial autonomy to adapt the strategies of the home country product divisions to fit the specificity of the local situations.

TRANSNATIONAL STRATEGY

Recent changes in the global marketplace suggest that MNCs can sacrifice neither global integration or local responsiveness. Competitive pressures in an increasing number of industries indicate that firms pursue globalization and localization simultaneously. Recent developments in information and communication technology have enhanced the global integration of economic activities as large MNCs attempt to increase economic efficiencies by utilizing the most cost-effective inputs and by marketing their outputs from and to various places around the globe.

Concurrently, the same technological development has also served to intensify competition in each local market. Countries are vastly different from one another in terms of political, legal, economic, and sociocultural environments. Consumer tastes and preferences of one country differ significantly from others, and many countries are also highly diverse in terms of religion, ethnic groups, language, and income levels. This distinctiveness creates mounting pressure on MNCs to provide locally appropriate products and services. Success in local markets, therefore, requires that MNCs be locally responsive. A good example can be found in the case of clothing and packaged food.

Firms adopt a transnational strategy to meet the seemingly conflicting challenges of high pressures for both cost reductions and local responsiveness. Transnational strategy emphasizes global learning, that is, the flow of skills and product offerings should flow not only from headquarters to the foreign subsidiary but also from the foreign subsidiary to headquarters. The subsidiaries under a transnational strategy have greater autonomy than those under a global strategy, yet they are not as independent as those under a multidomestic strategy. The transnational strategy seeks to conduct a network of activities with multiple headquarters spread across borders; with these multiple key decision centers the company optimizes both global efficiency and local responsiveness.

REGIONAL STRATEGY

Although a transnational strategy typically is considered the most ideal, in reality it is not always easy to achieve the optimal balance between global integration and local responsiveness. As an alternative to balancing the trade-off between global strategy and multidomestic strategy, many MNCs have employed a so-called regional strategy.[18] Furthermore, the rise of regional trading blocs, such as the European Union and the NAFTA, has led MNCs to reassess the anticipated rise of globalization and has facilitated the utilization of a regional strategy. Some scholars even argue that global strategy has not come true.[19] Focusing on the idiosyncrasies of each separate economic region, regional strategy represents a compromise between multidomestic and global strategy.

STRUCTURING FOR OPTIMAL GLOBAL PERFORMANCE

As indicated in Figure 4.1, another strategic organizational capability to maximize an MNC's performance concerns the design of an appropriate organizational structure. Introducing the right type of organizational structure in accordance with competitive strategy is critical in securing MNC competitiveness. We now examine important forms of organizational structure for global business: global product division, global area division, global transnational division, and regional headquarters.

GLOBAL PRODUCT DIVISION STRUCTURE

When benefits from global integration are significant and local differences are minor, firms establish a global product division structure. Under this structure all functional activities tend to be controlled by a product group. Because product managers at headquarters make product decisions for the global market, input from overseas local subsidiaries is often discouraged. Local managers under this structure are usually

---

Global Workforce Challenge 4.1
Cross-Border Mergers for Growth and Transformation

Corporate mergers present big challenges and many fail, but especially those between companies from different nations, with different legal systems, customers, investors, and national cultures, which are notoriously risky. There are often significant biases and negative attitudes to overcome. In one study, German executives said they regarded Polish managers with whom they worked as corrupt and lazy. Pat Russo, former CEO of Alcatel-Lucent, was mocked for failing to speak French fluently, although she worked in Paris. Yet more firms, from developed and emerging economies, are learning to make cross-border mergers work. Culture does, of course, matter. "Every CEO who has been through a cross-border merger says he knew culture was going to matter but did not realize how much," says Caroline Firstbrook, head of strategy for consulting industry leader Accenture in Europe. Certainly, national differences persist. Western managers in Japanese companies learn the value placed on formality and harmony. British executives have just acquired the U.S. habit of short lunch breaks without alcohol, only to find that Spanish executives like to thrash things out over an unhurried meal. But company cultures often differ for other reasons besides national background. Some companies are freewheeling and allow their business units autonomy, while others are rigid and bureaucratic. In Alcatel-Lucent's case, to confuse matters, the French company was laid-back and the U.S. company much more direct and assertive.

What seem like national tensions are often corporate ones in disguise. Big banks built through cross-border mergers, such as Deutsche Bank and UBS, are prone to tussles among "the Germans" and "the Brits" or "the Swiss" and "the Americans." But these fights really are less about nationality than about company attitudes toward risk taking. In addition, cross-border mergers face higher barriers to success because companies in different countries must operate differently. Legal systems and traditions vary widely. U.S. companies accustomed to dismissing employees rapidly are sometimes baffled by French labor law that impedes quick dismissal.

Yet many companies in Europe, North America, Asia, and Latin America make mergers work. General Electric is a practiced acquirer, and so are Cemex of Mexico and ArcelorMittal, the steel group giant with origins from Spain, France, and Luxemburg. Nippon Sheet Glass of Japan has appointed Stuart Chambers of Pilkington, the UK company it bought in 2006, as chief executive. These successful global leaders seek cross-border mergers to broaden their cultures. These companies regard cross-border mergers not as an unfortunate necessity to gain market access but as a means of transforming themselves. They take on the merger challenge because they believe they will gain more from doing that than by remaining insular.

Source: Adapted from J. Gapper, "Mergers Can Bring Opportunities as well as Obstacles," *The Irish Times.com,* August 4, 2008.

---

involved only in the local administrative, legal, and financial affairs of the company. Accordingly, local autonomy is very limited, and the local subsidiaries are treated as cost centers as opposed to profit centers. Existing studies generally indicate that firms in global industries (in which the benefits of global integration are large and local differences are small) will adopt a global product division structure.

GLOBAL AREA DIVISION STRUCTURE

A global area division structure is adopted when local adaptation of the firm's products and services is critical to its business success. When local differences are substantial, the firm's strategies often must be adapted to meet the particular conditions of each local market. Furthermore, the extent and direction of the adaptation might differ significantly from one local market to another. Thus, under such conditions, firms establish a global area division structure; regional and/or country managers in each area are provided with substantial autonomy to adapt the strategies of the home country product divisions to fit the specificity of the local situations. Firms in multidomestic industries (in which local differences are substantial and the benefits of global integration are small) are usually expected to establish a global area division structure.

GLOBAL TRANSNATIONAL DIVISION STRUCTURE

To meet the growing challenge for both global integration and local responsiveness, a transnational or matrix division organizational structure has been suggested.[20] The four critical elements of the transnational structure are (1) both local managers overseas and headquarters managers at home share a global perspective; (2) the relationship between the two is balanced without one dominating the other; (3) there exists a frequent and extensive two-way flow of ideas, information, resources, and personnel between the two locations; and (4) significant linkages are established across the various operating units and with headquarters.

The idealized form of a transnational structure seems to share the important characteristics of a matrix organizational structure in which local subsidiaries report to both area and product managers.[21] As such, some researchers indicate that MNCs should be viewed as networks of horizontal decision making, where local subsidiaries and headquarters are positioned at a horizontal rather than a hierarchical level. It would then be reasonable to expect that the transnational structure may also be exposed to potential problems of conflict and confusion frequently associated with the matrix structure, under which both product divisions and the area divisions have authority over the local units. Frequent communications and coordination between product and area divisions are essential to ensure alignment. Otherwise, when the goals of the two divisions are inconsistent, the resulting confusion and conflict may lead to suboptimal performance.[22]

REGIONAL HEADQUARTERS STRUCTURE

As an alternative to the matrix structure, MNCs have adopted a regional headquarters (RHQs) structure. This design represents an organizational form intended to overcome the potential tension between headquarters' pull for global efficiency and local operating units' push for national effectiveness.[23] Logically, a regional strategy goes hand in hand with RHQs. Major competitors in the global consumer electronics industry have adopted the RHQ structure, including Matsushita, Toshiba, Sony, Samsung, and Thompson. This trend is not surprising because the global consumer electronics industry represents one of the most serious cases in which a balance of globalization and localization is vital for success.

Under this structure, RHQs are established in major geographical areas. Typically, MNCs have created three RHQs in response to the emergence of the Triad Phenomenon of the global economy: North America, Europe, and Asia. Depending on their products and strategies, some MNCs have established additional RHQs in other areas, such as Samsung's Chinese RHQ and Matsushita's Latin American RHQ. In attempts to fully implement its "cross-border management mentality," Coca-Cola also manages its operating divisions through the use of RHQs. Each individual foreign subsidiary is responsible for reporting back to its respective RHQ.

The advantages of the RHQ structure could include economies of scale in regional strategic planning, effective utilization of globally trained human resources, efficient exchange of information, management of interdependence between and among headquarters and local units, and improved control and coordination of business activities. Capitalizing on these advantages, the RHQs may serve as a critical balance between headquarters at home and local operating units and thereby help an MNC to attain the ultimate transnational goal of concurrent globalization and localization. Operational goals and directions, determined through extensive collaboration between product divisions and the RHQs, are typically provided to the local units in a clearer fashion under the RHQ structure than under the matrix structure.

LINKING HUMAN RESOURCE MANAGEMENT PRACTICES TO COMPETITIVE STRATEGY AND ORGANIZATIONAL STRUCTURE

What are the implications of these distinctive competitive strategies and organizational structures for HR management practices? HR policies and practices are influenced by the company's structure and strategy, which in turn must be responsive to the demands of the surrounding institutional and cultural environments.[24] So how can firms effectively align their HR management practices, policies, and overall approaches with these competitive strategies and organizational structures to maximize performance? The contingency model shown in Figure 4.2 suggests the fit between each strategy and structure and corresponding human resource approach or orientation.

ETHNOCENTRIC ORIENTATION

Organizations with a global strategy along with a global product division structure are usually required to maintain a higher level of control at headquarters so that they ensure effective coordination and integration among different overseas units. It is plausible that local host country managers at a foreign affiliate may not always act in accordance with the goals of an entire MNC—they may seek the economic interests of the affiliate before those of headquarters.[25] Thus, when imperatives for global integration and coordination are high, conflicts between headquarters and foreign affiliates are likely to be pronounced. To overcome the problem of this potential goal misalignment, MNCs follow an ethnocentric orientation by placing the authority and major decision-making functions in the hands of corporate headquarters (or their

Figure 4.2 **Organizational Fit among Strategy, Structure, and Human Resource Management Approach**

Competitive Strategy	Organizational Structure	HRM Orientation
Global	Global Product Division	Ethnocentric
Multidomestic	Global Area Division	Polycentric
Transnational	Global Matrix Division	Geocentric
Regional	Regional Headquarters	Regiocentric

expatriate extensions abroad), rather than in the hands of the foreign subsidiaries. Under ethnocentrism it is believed that the home country headquarters' way of doing business is superior or at least preferable to any approach followed outside the home country.

To ensure that the headquarters home country's way is followed, the ethnocentric orientation typically relies heavily on home country expatriate assignments to foreign operations. Expatriate managers sent from headquarters, in general, enhance an MNC's control of overseas subsidiaries and reduce the MNC's reliance on the rigid, distant, bureaucratic control mechanisms that have become less suitable to meet the local diversity and complexity of the global operations of MNCs. The use of expatriates not only prevents the leaking of important information, thereby protecting technological know-how, but also facilitates the transfer of a company's core competencies to overseas subsidiaries through local workforce interactions.

The existing literature recognizes several other advantages of staffing foreign subsidiaries with expatriates from the home country rather than local host country nationals. Compared to their locally hired counterparts, headquarters home country expatriates are generally believed to have a better understanding of overall corporate priorities, an easier acceptance of headquarters-determined rules, and a greater commitment to overall corporate goals. The expatriates' familiarity with the corporate culture and the control system of headquarters results in more effective communication and coordination.[26] Expatriates are effective in replicating existing organizational practices and operating procedures of headquarters in their assigned local units. Furthermore, the transfer of managers from headquarters to the foreign subsidiaries facilitates the creation of an information network consistent with the corporate culture.[27] This advantage occurs because headquarters' home country expatriates can learn functional behaviors congruent with corporate goals more easily than local managers, because the expatriates are more likely to understand the corporate culture and strategy. More details of expatriate staffing, including significant potential risks and disadvantages, are examined in Chapter 6.

POLYCENTRIC ORIENTATION

Under a multidomestic strategy that focuses on individual local markets rather than the global market, MNCs must maximize local responsiveness. For these MNCs, achieving and maintaining a high intensity of integration across their entire foreign operation is less important. Rather, to more effectively track and respond to market-specific needs, decision making is decentralized and foreign affiliates are granted much greater autonomy.[28] When MNCs try to implement a multidomestic strategy, an ethnocentric orientation may lead to cultural myopia, or an overall failure of a firm to understand host country differences that may require different approaches to marketing and management. To adequately address this concern, a polycentric orientation can be utilized to require people from the host country to manage the foreign organization. This type of HR management practice is based on cultural particularism, as discussed in Chapter 2, which involves sensitivity to the distinctiveness and idiosyncrasies of different countries. Native host country managers are familiar with the intricacies of the local culture and possess a network of established contacts in the area. In contrast to expatriates, these local managers possess a high degree of local environmental competence but typically a low degree of internal company functional competence. A polycentric orientation, through the employment of host country nationals, eliminates language barriers and avoids adjustment problems faced by expatriate managers and their families.

MNCs can capitalize on the environmental competency of host country candidates to ensure efficient operations in the foreign country. The underdeveloped functional competency of these candidates can be improved with extensive functional training at company headquarters, which can increase their understanding and acceptance of organizational culture and strategy while providing specific technical training. Overall, a polycentric orientation is a relatively inexpensive alternative for companies that want to expand globally but lack sufficient skill in upper management positions compared to an ethnocentric orientation.

Despite the benefits of customizing HR management practices to local needs by using local managers, a polycentric orientation has some drawbacks. The lack of global cohesion and uniformity between the various global units may make the strategic shifts difficult to implement. In order for a polycentric orientation to be successful, companies need to require a strict adherence to certain corporate standards. A polycentric approach also prevents both host country and parent company nationals from gaining experience outside their respective countries. Isolation can also grow due to language barriers, national loyalties, and cultural differences, particularly when considering the relationship between the various levels of management within the subsidiary and corporate headquarters.

GEOCENTRIC ORIENTATION

A geocentric orientation is aimed at solving the problems associated with an ethnocentric as well as a polycentric orientation. Unlike the previous two approaches, this orientation lies on the assumption that the most qualified and well-trained candidates are sought to occupy important management positions within both corporate headquarters and international corporations, regardless of nationality. Such a staffing approach for an MNC is attractive in companies with an interdependent organizational structure, thus relying heavily on cross-border collaboration between headquarters and overseas subsidiaries as well as among overseas subsidiaries themselves. It eliminates a hierarchy of influence and facilitates the creation of a truly international company that identifies with the interests of both the parent and host countries by allowing the development of the best people, for the best positions, regardless of location. Therefore, firms following a transnational strategy and matrix division structure are likely to adopt the geocentric orientation.

A geocentric orientation leads to a strong unified corporate culture and an informal management network because people no longer feel bound by cultural ties and national loyalties. The transfer of core competence is facilitated because an increased number of people are taught the techniques that make the company successful, further contributing to global success. Ideally, organizations should maintain a cadre of cosmopolitan managers who possess a high degree of both functional and environmental competence. In reality, cosmopolitan candidates may be nonexistent or scarce, leaving firms no choice but to select either expatriates or host country nationals and to provide them with training to improve their functional or environmental areas of weakness.

REGIOCENTRIC ORIENTATION

Rather than attempting to hire nationals from a specific country, a regiocentric orientation expands the candidate pool by seeking people from within a specific region. The regiocentric approach is appealing because it allows and promotes the interaction between executives transferred to RHQs from subsidiaries in the region and multinational home country nationals posted to the RHQs. This approach can also be beneficial to the MNCs that continue to experience shortages in well-trained global managers.[29] By assigning these home country nationals to the RHQs, the MNCs can expect to capture more concentrated and effective utilization of scarce human resources than by separately assigning them to local units in a smaller number.

When multinational home country expatriates are assigned to RHQs, in most cases these managers are first groomed in various business divisions at home. During this period, they not only develop their professional knowledge but also are socialized into the company, creating social networks and cultivating relationships with their peers. Some of them would then be assigned to various local host country units and RHQs. Upon completion of overseas assignments, these expatriates would return to the product divisions for which they used to work. As a result of this job rotation, managers at different locations and levels, for example, RHQs, product divisions, or local units, often become members of informal information networks based on these established relationships. Such information networks form a critical basis and common alignment through which a significant amount of control and coordination may be achieved. Though speculative, this network development outcome may be a reason why Japanese MNCs consistently are reported to use a higher proportion of expatriate managers in their overseas units than their American or European counterparts. By supplementing formal communication channels with such informal ones, MNCs can achieve the concurrent goals of globalization and localization.

INCREASED ROLE OF HRM IN CROSS-BORDER STRATEGIC ALLIANCES AND MERGERS AND ACQUISITIONS

Cross-border strategic alliances and mergers and acquisitions (M&As) are becoming more prevalent strategies and structural choices as MNCs face increasing competition in the global marketplace. Strategic alliances are inter-firm cooperative agreements aimed at achieving strategic objectives and competitive advantage for the alliance partners.[30] The simplest form of strategic alliance is a contractual arrangement, such as agreement over licensing, marketing, promotion and distribution, development and service. The most complex form of strategic alliance is a joint venture, involving the long-term creation of a separate legal entity (generally a corporation, limited liability company, or partnership) through which the business of the alliance is conducted. Strategic alliances can be particularly advantageous in dealing with high environmental uncertainty and rapidly changing technological innovation, allowing companies to focus on their core competencies while sharing the total risk of a new venture with another party. However, the practical day-to-day operations of the alliance must be in alignment with its common goals and agreed-upon objectives from the alliance formation. As strategic alliances are based on interfirm relationships with shared objectives and resource control, they are more susceptible to opportunistic behaviors of individual partners and conflicts that are difficult to correlate with quantitative objective measurements. Furthermore, it is challenging to measure the risks and consequences associated with asymmetric partner learning and benefits, unsatisfactory cooperation, and clandestine partner conduct. Consequently, the role of HR management is critical to successfully plan and manage alliances with people who are equipped with appropriate skills and competencies, including cross-cultural knowledge. In some cases alliances can lead to a more permanent form of partner resource combination when partners merge or one is acquired by another to form a single legal entity.

Although the recent global credit crisis reduced the number of cross-border M&As, MNCs are increasingly adopting M&As as a growth strategy. A cross-border M&A is the preferred entry mode for MNCs into new markets because it provides them with a high level of control while eliminating many of the performance and relational risks traditionally associated with strategic alliances.[31] Unfortunately, it has been reported that 83 percent of M&A transactions fail to deliver shareholder value, and 53 percent actually destroy value.[32] This is a staggering figure and indicates that M&As do not result in a successful growth strategy as often as is expected. MNCs fail to adapt their strategies to the host country environment, including national cultural differences, resulting in unprofitable acquisitions. Furthermore, difficulties experienced by an acquiring firm in managing its acquired firm may be directly related to fundamental differences in the priorities and values held by their organizational cultures.

Whatever the causes of the disappointing outcomes of an M&A might be, typically MNCs have overlooked the role of HR management in creating a successful integration.[33] HR policies and practices are key to a successful M&A, and the lack of attention to HR management, particularly in the early stages, can be disastrous. Unfortunately, HR managers usually do not get involved until the announcement of the M&A deal.[34] For a successful M&A, HR management should be involved in overall strategy development, target examination, preparation of pre-deal contracts, due diligence, integration planning, and employee communication within each company.[35] The significance of blending corporate cultures and retaining key employees is not visible on financial statements. To ensure a successful integration, early planning of

---

Global Work Force Challenge 4.2
Building Leadership during Good Times and Bad

According to a study conducted by Hewitt Associates, IBM and Procter & Gamble head the 2009 list of global top companies for leaders. Other firms on the global top 10 list are General Mills, McKinsey, India's ICICI Bank, McDonald's, GE, Greece's Titan Cement, China Mobile Communications, and India's Hindustan Unilever. One distinguishing characteristic that sets these companies apart—in good times and in bad—is a continuing strong commitment to building leadership capability within their organizations. "Strong leadership is a critical element in helping global companies successfully compete, yet many organizations lack the know-how and infrastructure for creating a robust pipeline of leaders for future success. Simply put, they lack the discipline of building leaders," said Robert Gandossy, global practice leader of leadership consulting at Hewitt. He continued, "Our research and experience tell us that while leadership talent is in short supply around the world, the global top companies for leaders are still able to groom a near-constant supply of world-class leaders . . . year after year and regardless of economic conditions. This capability gives them a unique advantage over their competitors and will poise them to emerge stronger—and more quickly—out of the economic downturn."

Hewitt finds that leadership development at these organizations is an institutionalized practice and mind-set, with the development plans clearly tied to business results. Companies in Asia, the fastest-growing region in the world, realize that they need strong leadership talent to drive growth. They recognize that next-generation leaders are receiving accelerated and customized development opportunities as a result of the growing complexity and scale of the market. As the top companies in Asia-Pacific continue to assess and strategize the challenges of a new economy, their creativity and determination to develop effective leaders will position them well for both short- and long-term success. "The top companies for leaders in Asia-Pacific do three things exceptionally well," said Mano Ramakrishnan, a project manager for Hewitt's leadership study. "First, they place great focus on assessing and selecting their leaders. In particular they are very clear about the type of leaders they need to drive business success. Second, they accelerate leadership development by emphasizing experiential learning and customized development programs. Third, they recognize the importance of building a leadership brand," he said. "In particular, many top companies emphasize corporate social responsibility as a key aspect of their leadership brand. They understand that many top talent want more than success at their organizations-they also want to positively impact their greater community."

Source: Adapted from *The Nation* (Thailand, MultiMedia.com, Business Section), November 30, 2009.

---

a seamless integration is very important. This important work can range from planning massive changes for two very different cultures to small changes for two similar cultures. Investors are generally skeptical about mergers where the cultures, reflected in the styles of the top management teams, are perceived to be incompatible, while they are supportive of mergers where the cultures appear to be compatible.[36]

Other important HR management strategies to ensure a successful M&A integration include effective communication, deliberate retention schemes, and effective methods for adjusting to labor regulations in a host country. The current global financial crisis makes the HR due diligence process even more imperative as acquired companies are likely to bring more baggage and risk to the M&A. Target companies may attempt to cover up company HR problems in an effort to appear more marketable to potential buyers. HR due diligence may also pose more challenges as the acquiring company must assess whether financial weaknesses in the acquired company are due to the sluggish economy, which will disappear when the economy picks up again, or if they are the result of genuine workforce problems (e.g., low morale, critical skill deficits) that would remain even after an economic recovery. Accordingly, the contribution of HR management is critical to appropriately address all these issues.

PARADIGM SHIFT OF INTERNATIONAL HUMAN RESOURCE MANAGEMENT FROM CONTINGENCY MODEL TO PROCESS DEVELOPMENT

In the past, international HR management has played a reactive or a supplementary role in supporting an MNC's competitive strategy and organizational structure. Increasingly now and in the future, the strategic role of HR management needs to be proactive in influencing the optimal competitive strategy and designing an appropriate structure. The traditional focus on structure as a means of control and coordination has been seen as inadequate to deliver the corporate "glue" for global organizations. A shift has taken place in the international management literature from a "fit" between strategy and structure to an emphasis on active value-adding processes that optimize environmental responsiveness and competitive advantage, such as developing global leadership competencies and supporting the transfer of knowledge and best practices.[37] We now focus on these critical processes, which facilitate the development of organizations that are capable of meeting challenges of both global integration and local responsiveness.

DEVELOPING GLOBAL LEADERSHIP COMPETENCIES

One of the critical roles of HR management is to help develop managers with effective leadership competencies for working with people across countries. Being an effective global leader requires a combination of three competency clusters: business acumen, relationship management, and personal effectiveness.[38] While no one would deny the fact that understanding a different culture is critical in managing people with different values and norms, culture-specific leadership not only tends to overemphasize the role of culture but also limits leaders in their effectiveness to a specific country. Even Hofstede admits that culture is often inappropriately applied in research settings because too often there is little theoretical justification for expecting cultural differences and no model to identify what differences should be expected.[39] Furthermore, conflicting evidence exists on whether a host country workforce (HCW) would prefer a leadership style adapted to the host country or not. Selmer reported that Hong Kong Chinese middle managers preferred the American style to the style

---

Global Workforce Professional Profile 4.1
Mr. Nobuhiro Tanaka,
Corporate Representative at Toshiba Corporation

Mr. Nobuhiro Tanaka has been working at Toshiba, one of the oldest and largest consumer electronic appliance companies in Japan, for more than thirty years. He joined the company after graduating from Keio University in Tokyo, one of the most prestigious universities in Japan. He has held many different positions since he joined the company, including sales manager and senior vice president of the international division. Mr. Tanaka is now a corporate representative appointed by corporate top management in the role of representing Toshiba Corporation in Europe. His job is to help top management with strategic decision making by providing a critical regional perspective about Toshiba's businesses. Specifically, he analyzes the competitiveness of each in-house company in Europe and advises corporate top management of necessary strategic changes. Each in-house company functions independently, doing business globally, and is responsible for its own business results. For example, Digital Media Network Company is in charge of advanced audio and video products such as color TVs and DVD players. Tanaka is one of four corporate representatives among the high-ranked executives assigned to assist the in-house company's business and support subsidiaries in the region through their respective regional headquarters (RHQs).

Toshiba recently redesigned its global organizational structure, including the roles of RHQs, to enhance its global competitiveness by assigning different yet complementary roles to corporate-level and company-level RHQs. Whereas the former is responsible mainly for integrating and coordinating intercompany activities from a strategic perspective, the latter takes care of operational integration as well as local responsiveness in a specific region. By removing the operational function from corporate RHQs, each in-house company has more autonomy in mobilizing necessary business resources and developing an appropriate business approach to fit their own business environments. This new, two-tiered RHQ arrangement aims at more effectively meeting the challenge of balancing global integration and local responsiveness. As a corporate representative, Tanaka serves as a consultant providing his expertise and experiences in resolving the conflicting interests of individual companies to optimize profits for the whole group. He believes that his extensive experiences in international assignments at the earlier stage of his career broadened his perspective about global business and enable him to perform his job successfully.

---

of the local bosses.[40] Conversely, Suutari argued in his study of comparative leadership in European contexts that due to identified cross-cultural differences, expatriates typically pointed out that they had to adjust their leadership style in order to lead an HCW successfully.[41] Thus, the outcome of using different types of leadership styles in cross-cultural environments is not always accurate or easy to predict. In addition, it is costly and time-consuming to develop managers who are capable of leading different HCWs in each and every market. This type of leadership may only have been effective in supporting a multidomestic strategy designed to respond to individual markets where consumers continue to demand locally differentiated products and services, and reflecting substantial divergence in standards, tastes, and perceived needs.

The emergence of a global market where consumers now demand relatively similar products and services requires a different style of leadership. To effectively implement a transnational strategy that combines global integration and local responsiveness, managers cannot simply concentrate on working with the HCW in a specific market, but also should learn how to communicate effectively with people of cultural diversity and should develop global strategic skills. The significance and complexity of these challenges requires new cross-cultural leadership competencies that involve equally complex thinking and problem-solving skills. The GLOBE study described in Chapter 2 identified universally desirable leadership attributes and behavior, such as motivating, dynamic, honest, and decisive. Global leaders should be able to demonstrate inspiration and integrity to their subordinates, and to make intuitive decisions and dynamic approaches in the face of uncertainty.[42] Consequently, as we will examine in Chapter 7, MNCs need to develop a new cadre of leadership that is capable of more effectively handling the complexity and intricacies of a global business environment, as well as more sensitivity to the perceptions and expectations of members of the local HCW in their respective host country business environment.

ENCOURAGING THE TRANSFER OF KNOWLEDGE AND BEST PRACTICES

It is almost mandatory that MNCs shift managers from one location to another to transfer best practices. Otherwise the MNC will lose out on a vital knowledge resource within the organization—the individual and tacit know-how of its employees. Most of what an employee knows is located in this "soft side." Unfortunately, many companies are not adequately harnessing the more personalized form of internal knowledge. For example, there is evidence that East Asian culture does not foster formal knowledge sharing to the extent that Western organizations do, as in the case of the global consulting firm Accenture, based in the United States.[43] Because of East Asian culture's view of knowledge and existing language differences, knowledge contributions within Accenture remain severely biased toward the American offices, thus exposing a serious "knowing-doing" gap problem. Despite Accenture's extreme emphasis on its one global database system called the Knowledge Xchange (KX), person-to-person contact and personal networks are more important in conducting business and sharing knowledge and know-how in high-context countries such as those in East Asia. This emphasis reflects those cultures' traditional focus on interactive relationships, social cohesion, and a team-oriented mentality. A more personalized system facilitates the flow of tacit knowledge with greater ease than a codification-based one, such as Accenture's KX system. A major problem arises from the fact that although Accenture pursues a global competitive strategy driven by high cost pressure, it rarely sends expatriates to run its overseas subsidiaries, using many local managers instead. Consequently, managers from the United States are denied any opportunity to work with local managers and to more informally, through interactive relationships, learn about best practices originating in the overseas subsidiaries. Therefore, these potentially valuable best practices often fail to find their way into the U.S.-dominated official KX system and are not disseminated throughout the various units of the global firm.

MNCs need a top-down initiative to establish and legitimize the role of transferring core competencies within the organization. Yet one of the main problems many MNCs face is the inability to disseminate throughout the organization existing knowledge held within various units, as well as preserve this knowledge within the MNC's collective organizational memory. This problem is caused, as illustrated in the earlier discussion of Accenture, primarily by a company's failure to enable its employees to share and contribute their knowledge, both explicit and tacit. To share important knowledge among different units of the MNC, it is critical to establish an organizational structure and corporate culture that facilitate the active exchange of best practices. Effective MNCs that value and invest in HR are able to facilitate skill acquisition, learning, and accumulation of intangible knowledge assets. The HR function can play a vital role in identifying each manager's skills and knowledge and encouraging their dissemination to appropriate locations throughout the organization.

MNCs also must establish appropriate rewards to encourage knowledge acquisition and effective transfer, such as a monetary bonus and recognition approach that rewards new idea generation and sharing. And since typically "you don't get what you don't measure," if knowledge sharing is a missing or minor part of employee performance evaluations, there will be inadequate incentive to encourage knowledge-sharing contributions. More targeted compensation and performance evaluation methods will motivate employees to take knowledge sharing seriously and encourage better and more thorough contributions to the transfer of best practices. It is the responsibility of HR management to establish such compensation and reward systems that produce a global learning environment conducive to knowledge sharing across borders.

SUMMARY

International HR can have several forms of strategic influence on an organization's ability to compete in the global marketplace. In turn, particular strategies and structures that MNCs choose tend to have an impact on international HR management practices. We have examined a contingency model to understand how different international HR management approaches may be selected to support the effective implementation of distinctive competitive strategies and organizational structures. We also have examined an important paradigm shift from the more traditional contingency model to a focus on critical HR management processes that help address the dual challenge of global integration and local responsiveness.

QUESTIONS FOR OPENING SCENARIO ANALYSIS

1. How would you describe IBM's new global competitive strategy?
2. How can IBM effectively modify its international HR management strategy as the company moves away from its traditional international model to become a "globally integrated enterprise?"
3. How is effective recruitment, selection, training, development, and retention critical to IBM's strategy for success in emerging markets?

Case 4.1. Is Accenture's Global Face Really a Facade?

Multinational consulting firms offer additional value to their clients by leveraging knowledge gained by their subsidiaries around the world. Accenture is considered one of the most successful companies in the consulting industry, a field in which knowledge has always been the primary asset. Accenture's entire knowledge management model is based on one global database system called the Knowledge Xchange (KX). The KX houses approximately seven thousand individual databases. Its primary purpose is to store explicit knowledge—client deliverables, presentations, methodologies, best practices, and other document forms—that can be accessed by its employees through its global network using the company's intranet. Thus, as the single most important tool for knowledge creation and transfer at Accenture, the entire KX system is highly standardized and, thereby, cost efficient. The KX is absolutely imperative to a consultant's daily work. It is not uncommon for a system user to access knowledge on more than ten different databases on the KX every day.

The KX was initially established to link Accenture's entire global network, pulling expertise and knowledge from around the world into one collective system and uniting the entire organization. Ironically, however, the explicit knowledge-based, standardized nature of Accenture's management system contributes to a growing knowledge gap across this MNC. Specifically, Accenture's codification-based knowledge management strategy, "one global firm" corporate philosophy, and hierarchical organizational structure all significantly hinder its ability to convert the knowledge of its individual employees around the world into the working knowledge of the collective organization.

Accenture does not recognize that this corporate philosophy has the countereffect of creating a culture in which its East Asian offices are actually being alienated. There is a unilateral flow of knowledge from the United States to East Asia. Very little in the KX actually originates in East Asia. It is almost as if Accenture does not value the knowledge created in its East Asian offices. Obviously, national culture plays a significant role in producing this gap and in hindering employees in East Asia from contributing their knowledge. East Asian culture is typically a high-context society, with informal dealings and person-to-person communication constituting a large part of business culture. Consequently, those in East Asia seem to be less willing to share their knowledge with coworkers with whom they are not in direct personal contact. Also, within the Accenture East Asian offices, global databases are not viewed as strictly the one and only vehicle for knowledge preservation. Furthermore, the language barrier makes it extremely difficult for East Asians to write the English abstracts that must accompany their KX contributions, which makes time a significant factor as well.

The rigidity of the KX and the standardization of its practices and work processes have not only discouraged Accenture's East Asian employees from making KX contributions but also unintentionally prevented them from knowledge sharing and conducting business based on personal relationships, which is how they traditionally prefer to work. Accenture's pervasive corporate culture has completely nullified the

East Asian cultural approach to working. The resulting gap is increasingly turning the MNC from "one global firm" to "one American firm" that limits a potentially strategic and competitive advantage in effective human knowledge and expertise sharing on a global scale. In effect, the idea of "one global firm" is a facade.

QUESTIONS FOR CASE ANALYSIS AND DISCUSSION

1. What are the key characteristics of Accenture's global knowledge management strategy?
2. Why does Accenture's global knowledge management strategy fail to utilize potentially valuable knowledge generated in East Asia?
3. What are key roles that managers could play to improve the current global knowledge management strategy at Accenture?

CASE 4.2. FOREIGN BUYOUTS HEIGHTEN TENSIONS IN GERMANY

German companies, both foreign- and German-owned, are laying off well-paid German workers and opening factories in places like Poland and China. Profits at some companies have improved, and the German stock market has risen significantly (80 percent between 2003 and 2005), and has seen a strong rebound after the recent global economic crisis. But the layoffs have added to unemployment and heightened popular suspicion of business executives' self-serving motives in Germany. Many Germans blame their high unemployment and economic sluggishness on business owners and managers pursuing profit at the expense of the German dream of a more humane capitalism. Beyond Germany, hostility against free markets has swept much of Western Europe, contributing to increasing conflict over EU policy and governance, which has been criticized as promoting unfettered American-style capitalism that undermines Europe's important social protections.

Germans are getting particularly angry at the midsize, traditionally family-owned businesses, known as the *Mittelstand,* which employ 70 percent of the labor force. These employers historically have had a stronger commitment to their German workers than bigger corporations affected by the stock market. But now the *Mittelstand* is changing as well, partly as a result of acquisitions by foreign firms. Private equity investors, mainly from the United States and the United Kingdom, often borrow heavily to acquire these German companies, with the goal of significant earnings by later taking them public. These outsiders have acquired a growing portfolio of more than 5,500 German companies since the late 1990s. Many of these deals have led to operations moving to low-wage Eastern Europe and Asia.

One tendency contributing to changes of ownership and strategy in the *Mittelstand* is the waning interest of the descendants of entrepreneurs who founded many of the family businesses. In 1999, Charles Grohe, chairman of Grohe Water Technology AG, which manufactures high-quality faucets and showers adorning upscale hotels and residences around the world, sold the company to British investors and retired to Switzerland. These British investors loaded themselves with debt to make the acquisition and failed to effect structural changes leading to profitability, especially to overcome debt interest payments and German taxes. Then in 2004, they sold Grohe to U.S. and Swiss investors who planned, with the help of consulting firm McKinsey & Co., to cut 3,000 of Grohe's 4,300 jobs in Germany and make or outsource 80 percent of their products in China, Poland, Thailand, and other low-cost countries.

The German media quickly learned of the Grohe developments and made the company a public example of how foreign investment firms are harming German interests. Grohe workers staged noisy demonstrations, and Germany's powerful engineering union, IG Metall, took up the case. Amid this intense negative publicity, Grohe's management announced concessions: Only 1,233 German jobs would be replaced by expanding company facilities to lower-cost countries, including Thailand and Portugal. But David Haines, the new CEO of Grohe and a British marketing expert with experience at Coca-Cola and telecommunications giant Vodafone, was adamant that Grohe has to move more production to cheap-labor countries or risk losing market share to rivals who have already done so. Grohe says its average worker in Germany costs 51,000 euros a year, including benefits and administrative expenses, whereas workers in Portugal cost a third as much and workers in Thailand a tenth as much.

Source: Adapted from M. Walker, "Among Germans, Foreign Buyouts Heighten Angst," *Wall Street Journal,* June 30, 2005: A1–A2.

QUESTIONS FOR CASE ANALYSIS AND DISCUSSION

1. What social and cultural issues are presenting challenges to successful acquisitions of German firms by foreign companies?
2. Besides attention to internal issues, why must cross-border acquisitions also pay close attention to government policy and broader labor market issues?
3. What recommendations do you have for the foreign owners and management of newly acquired firms like Grohe to help them successfully ride the conflicts and challenges attending needed economic transformations in high social welfare countries like Germany?

RECOMMENDED WEB SITE RESOURCES

Mercer Human Resource Consulting (www.mercerhr.com). With more than 13,000 employees in some 145 cities and 41 countries and territories, this consulting firm specializes in human resource strategy development and implementation to meet organization needs.

Towers Watson (http://www.towerswatson.com/). Global consulting firm specializing in employee benefits, rewards, and overall talent management and strategies.

Worldwide Consulting Group (www.worldwideconsulting.com). Provides strategic planning information and consulting services for multinational companies in such areas as foreign employment law, company formation, international mergers and acquisitions, international employee benefits, transnational and multicountry employee compensation, international and domestic organizational development, expatriate programs, international employee relations, and global HR programs.

NOTES

1. "Rich-World Multinationals Strike Back," *Economist,* September, 18, 2008.

2. H. Conn and G. Yip, "Global Transfer of Critical Capabilities," *Business Horizons* (January/February 1997): 22–31.

3. Ibid.

4. M. Downes and A.S. Thomas, "Knowledge Transfer through Expatriation: The U-curve Approach to Overseas Staffing," *Journal of Managerial Issues,* 12 (2002): 131–49; S. Bender and A. Fish, "The Transfer of Knowledge and the Retention of Expertise: The Continuing Need for Global Assignments," *Journal of Knowledge Management,* 4 (2000): 125–37.

5. I. Nonaka and N. Takeuchi, *The Knowledge-Creating Company* (New York: Oxford University Press, 1995).

6. I. Nonaka and N. Konno, "The Concept of 'Ba': Building a Foundation for Knowledge Creation," *California Management Review* 40 (3) (1998): 40–54.

7. J. Preffer and R. Sutton, *The Knowing-Doing Gap: How Smart Companies Turn Knowledge into Action* (Boston: Harvard Business School Publishing, 1999).

8. G. McEvoy and B. Parker, "Expatriate Adjustment: Causes and Consequences," in *Expatriate Management: New Ideas for International Business,* ed. J. Selmer (Westport, CT: Quorum Books, 1995): 97–114.

9. R. Lachman, A. Nedd, and B. Hining, "Analyzing Cross-National Management and Organizations: A Theoretical Framework," *Management Science* 40 (1) (1994): 40–55.

10. J.S. Black, A. Morrison, and H.B. Gregersen, *Global Explorers: The Next Generation of Leaders* (New York: Routledge, 1999).

11. H. Harris and L. Holden, "Between Autonomy and Control: Expatriate Managers and Strategies," *IHRM in SMES* 43 (1) (2001): 77–100.

12. R. Vernon, L. Wells, and S. Rangan, *The Manager in the International Economy,* 7th ed. (Upper Saddle River, NJ: Prentice-Hall, 1996).

13. G. Hedlund, "A Model of Knowledge Management and the N-Form Corporation," *Strategic Management Journal* 15 (1994): 73–90.

14. L. Gomez-Meija and L. Palich, "Cultural Diversity and the Performance of Multinational Firms," *Journal of International Business Studies* 28 (2) (1997): 309–35; R. Hamilton and R. Kashlak, "National Influences on Multinational Control System Selection," *Management International Review* 39 (2) (1999): 167–89.

15. C. Bartlett and S. Ghoshal, "Organizing for Worldwide Effectiveness: The Transnational Solution," *California Management Review* 31 (1) (1989): 54–74.

16. J. De la Torre, Y. Doz, and T. Devinney, *Managing the Global Corporation: Case Studies in Strategy and Management* (New York: McGraw-Hill, 2000).

17. N. Adler and S. Bartholomew, "Managing Globally Competent People," *Academy of Management Executive* 6 (3) (1992): 52–65.

18. A. Morrison, D. Ricks, and K. Roth, "Globalization versus Regionalization: Which Way for the Multinational?" *Organizational Dynamics* 19 (3) (1991): 17–29.

19. A. Rugman, *The End of Globalization: Why Global Strategy Is a Myth & How to Profit from the Realities of Regional Markets* (New York: AMACOM, 2001).

20. Bartlett and Ghoshal, "Organizing for Worldwide Effectiveness," 54–75.

21. C. Bartlett and S. Ghoshal, "Matrix Management: Not a Structure, a Frame of Mind," *Harvard Business Review* 68 (4) (1992): 138–45.

22. C. Prahalad and Y. Doz, *The Multinational Mission* (New York: Free Press, 1988).

23. D. Sullivan, "Organization in American MNCs: The Perspective of the European Regional Headquarters," *Management International Review* 32 (1992): 237–50.

24. R.S. Schuler, P.S. Budhwar, and G. W. Florkowski, "International Human Resource Management: Review and Critique," *International Journal of Management Reviews,* 4 (1) (2002): 41–70.

25. I. Björkman, W. Barner-Rasmussen, and L. Li, "Managing Knowledge Transfer in MNCs: The Impact of Headquarters Control Mechanisms," *Journal of International Business Studies,* 35 (5) (2004): 443–55; D. Tan and J.T. Mahoney, "Explaining the Utilization of Managerial Expatriates from the Perspectives of Resource-based View, Agency, and Transaction-costs Theories." *Advances in International Management,* 15 (2004): 179–205.

26. H. Scullion, "Staffing Policies and Strategic Control in British Multinationals," *International Studies of Management and Organization* 24 (3) (1994): 541–54.

27. Bartlett and Ghoshal, "Organizing for Worldwide Effectiveness," 54–74.

28. I. Tarique, R. Schuler, and Y. Gong, "A Model of Multinational Enterprise Subsidiary Staffing Composition," *International Journal of Human Resource Management,* 17 (2) (2006): 207–24; R.A. Belderbos and M.G. Heijltjes, "The Determinants of Expatriate Staffing by Japanese Multinationals in Asia: Control, Learning and Vertical Business Groups." *Journal of International Business Studies,* 36 (3) (2005): 341–54.

29. P. Vanderbroeck, "Long-Term Human Resource Development in Multinational Organizations," *Sloan Management Review* 34 (1) (1992): 95–99.

30. H.D. Hopkins, "Cross-Border Mergers and Acquisitions: Do Strategy or Post-Merger Integration Matter?" *International Management Review* 4 (1) (2008): 5–7.

31. Y. Paik, "Risk Management of Strategic Alliances and Acquisitions between Western MNCs and Companies in Central Europe," *Thunderbird International Business Review* 47 (4) (2005): 489–511; T.K. Das and B.S. Teng, "Trust, Control, and Risk in Strategic Alliances: An Integrated Framework." *Organizational Studies,* 21 (2) (2001): 251–83.

32. KPMG, *Unlocking Shareholder Value: The Keys to Success* (London: KPMG, 1999).

33. Hopkins, "Cross-Border Mergers and Acquisitions"; A. DeNisi and S.J. Shin, "Psychological Communication Interventions in Mergers and Acquisitions," in *Mergers and Acquisitions: Managing Culture and Human Resources,* G.K. Sthal and M. E. Mendenhall, eds. (Stanford: Stanford University Press); J.E. Bryson, "Managing HRM Risk in a Merger," *Employee Relations* 25 (1) (2003): 14–30.

34. R. Aguilera and J. Dencker, "The Role of Human Resource Management in Cross-border Mergers and Acquisitions," *International Journal of Human Resource Management,* 15 (8) (2004): 1355–70; S. Wells, "HR's Efforts to Integrate Compensation Strategies and Practices Are a Key Component of Successful Mergers and Acquisitions," *HR Magazine* 49 (5) (2004): 66–73.

35. M.N. Clemente and D.S. Greenspan, *Empowering Human Resource in the Merger and Acquisition Process.* (Glen Rock, NJ: Clemente, Greenspan & Co., Inc., 1999).

36. S. Chatterjee, M. Lubatkin, D. Schweiger, and Y. Weber, "Cultural Differences and Shareholder Value in Related Mergers: Linking Equity and Human Capital," *Strategic Management Journal,* 13 (3) (1992): 319–34.

37. S. Kobrin, "Is There a Relationship between Geocentric Mind-Set and Multinational Strategy?" *Journal of International Business Studies* 25 (3) (1994): 493–511.

38. T. Brake, *The Global Leader: Critical Factors for Creating the World Class Organization* (Chicago: Irwin Professional Publishing, 1997).

39. G. Hofstede, "A Case for Comparing Apples with Oranges—International Differences in Values," *International Journal of Comparative Sociology* 39 (1) (1998): 16–31.

40. J. Selmer, "Expatriate or Local Boss? HCN Subordinates' Preferences in Leadership Behaviour," *International Journal of Human Resource Management,* 7 (1996): 165–78.

41. V. Suutari, "Variation in the Leadership Behaviour of Western European Managers: Finnish Expatriates' Experiences," *International Journal of Human Resource Management* 7 (3) (1996): 677–707.

42. R. House et al., eds., *Culture, Leadership, and Organizations: The GLOBE Study of 62 Societies* (Thousand Oaks, CA: Sage, 2004).

43. Y. Paik and D. Choi, "The Shortcomings of a Standardized Global Knowledge Management System: The Case Study of Accenture," *Academy of Management Executive* 19 (2) (2005): 81–84.

5 | Global Human Resource Planning

"WHO ARE OUR EMPLOYEES, ANYWAY?"

"We are treated like animals," Sudaryanti, a 23-year-old garment worker from a Gap factory in Indonesia, said through an interpreter. "We are abused if we do not work the way the supervisor wants." Sudaryanti—who, like many Indonesians, uses only one name—was in the United States with several other Indonesian workers to raise awareness of poor labor conditions in factories used by San Francisco-based Gap, Inc. These garment workers from Indonesia are appealing to consumers in the United States to boycott Gap products to protest labor conditions at factories in Southeast Asia, Africa, and Latin America. Charging that many of the Gap-contracted factories are sweatshops, the workers said conditions were inhumane.

In a twenty-four-page study on working conditions in Gap factories, the Union of Needletrades, Industrial and Textile Employees (UNITE) accused Gap of poor health and safety conditions in their contracted factories. While Gap does pay minimum wage in most of the countries where it hires factories, it is still hard for most workers to make ends meet, said Ginny Coughlin, the director of UNITE's Global Justice for Garment Workers Campaign. Some workers in the company's Lesotho factories, for example, earn about thirty cents an hour.

The report also alleged union-busting activities by management and, in some instances, corporal punishment to force laborers to meet quotas. UNITE's study cited alleged abuses at Gap factories in Cambodia, Lesotho, Indonesia, Bangladesh, El Salvador, and Mexico. A spokeswoman for Gap said the factories were not owned by Gap but were independently contracted by Gap and other companies.[1] It is true that the employees in UNITE's study were technically not employees of Gap. But the resulting global outcry, damaging to company reputation and image, continued to hold Gap accountable and rejected what was perceived as a superficial distinction. From this and similar experiences, it is clear that in their effective HR planning, organizations today need to broaden their definition of who their employees really are.

INTRODUCTION

HR planning provides the essential link between MNC strategy and people—those who make strategy work—including outsourced workers like those in the opening scenario. For success in the global business arena, HR planning should be part of the strategic management process, in terms of strategy formulation and implementation. Critical involvement of global HR planning in the strategy formulation process includes scanning the environment for opportunities and threats and taking an inventory and assessment of the organization's current human resources.[2] Without an internal assessment of the organization's human capability, strategic plans can be laid that, at least for the present and near future, are far too ambitious and unrealistic. This can lead to wasted time and resources when reality crashes down on attempts to implement the strategy. HR decision making cannot be an afterthought; it must be an integral part of the international business strategy formulation process, ideally involving HR professionals as key members on the strategic planning team.[3]

Global HR planning should be responsive to both the short-term and long-term needs and plans of the organization and its worldwide operations. For example, if a company's goals in a particular international business venture are only exploratory or temporary in nature, it would most likely make sense to seek a short-term or temporary labor supply to meet the corresponding uncertain or temporary work demand. Or where an organization is expecting to capitalize on a long-term future growth opportunity in a particular foreign market, such as China or South America, it should include in its global HR plan specific considerations about efforts in local employee recruitment, training, and succession planning to ensure the long-term availability of an effective supply of managers and business professionals to lead this eventual international expansion activity. Thus, whether the scope for global HR planning is for the near future or for the much longer term, it should link with company strategic planning to develop policies, plans, programs, and activities that provide the human talent to help carry out and achieve those strategic plans.

Unfortunately, much of the literature fails to include global HR planning as the critical nexus between strategic planning and specific HR practices, such as in the area of employee selection and staffing, where we often see an immediate move into a discussion about how to effectively select and prepare expatriates for foreign assignments. In this particular case there is a premature assumption that an expatriate is the appropriate form of human talent to fill foreign work demand before adequate thought is taken about the strategic objectives and the characteristics of the particular work demand—and home country expatriates are not always the most cost-effective supply of human talent. In fact, they often represent the most expensive! The lack of HR planning for linking HR practices to the strategic goals and objectives of the firm make the organization vulnerable to the fads and popular practices of the day, which typically address business goals and needs in only a superficial, noncustomized way. Before staffing and other detailed action plans are made, there should be thoughtful consideration, as part of careful global HR planning, about the nature of the present and future work demand and potentially viable sources of labor supply—wherever they may be, both in the short term and long term—that serve to achieve the strategic objectives of the firm.

In this chapter we examine the important role of HR planning in carrying out an MNC's strategic plans effectively through the people factor as well as in preparing the organization throughout its worldwide operations for optimal long-term productivity in utilizing human resources. Important considerations for the HR planning function include the determination of work demand and labor supply based on strategic objectives, external environment scanning, work organization and job design, and analysis of important sources of labor supply. In addition, we will examine long-term HR planning issues including forecasting labor supply trends and opportunities, building global capability, and succession planning strategies.

FROM STRATEGY TO DECISIONS ABOUT WORK DEMAND AND LABOR SUPPLY

Once international business strategies are determined, specific cost-effective (that is, highly effective at minimal expense) implementation or action plans must be considered. Global HR planning plays a central role in this implementation phase in determining both *what* kinds of human work and tasks need to be carried out and *who* will do this work. The *what* component in this HR involvement may be considered part of *work demand;* it leads directly to decisions regarding work organization and design, such as breaking down larger business performance plans and goals into specific coordinated and integrated tasks, responsibilities, and jobs for people to perform. The *who* component of global HR planning for strategy implementation comprises many different kinds of decisions related to the *supply* of appropriate human resources or labor with specific skills to address the identified work demand.

It is important to keep in mind, as suggested in Figure 5.1, that actual work demand identified in global HR planning should be driven by and based on the company's international business strategies and plans, and that considerations about labor supply should in turn be based on the nature of the immediately identified (short-term) and forecasted (long-term) work demand. In effective global HR planning there should be a logical flow from strategy to work demand to labor supply, with each step consistent with and responsive to the previous step. For example, a business expansion strategy from Chicago to Argentina should not, at least primarily, involve work assignments (that is, work demand) that investigate European markets, or seek to be implemented solely by Chicago headquarters employees (labor supply) that are completely ignorant of Spanish. Nor should assignments be undertaken involving multinational virtual teams unless there is a clear connection with company strategy as well as a solid indication that a team design is a viable way to address work demand.

Company strategy can be directed both at what the company *desires to do* (for example, increase production inventories, expand and customize products or services for a new foreign market, or increase market share in a particular economic region) and what the company *desires to become,* such as in terms of internal strategic capability and competence.[4] We will examine these latter, rather longer-term internal-developmental company objectives later in this chapter. But considerations about company work translated from short-term and longer-term strategic objectives as well as decisions

Figure 5.1 **Global HR Planning**

regarding human resources that will enable the company to meet work demand should not be made without a careful scanning and assessment of the external environment, which can greatly influence those work demand and labor supply decisions. We now briefly examine critical factors in the external environment that should be monitored on an ongoing basis as part of a thorough, effective HR planning effort.

EXTERNAL ENVIRONMENTAL SCANNING

Business leaders today must continually scan the environment and maintain awareness of changing and developing challenges—presented by threats and opportunities—to successfully carrying out business plans and competing in our global marketplace. With its close interface with strategic planning, HR planning personnel should also continuously scan the environment for the array of complex, interrelated challenges that present themselves.[5] The major overarching current trends, influences, and developments discussed earlier, including globalization, contingent work arrangements, technological advancements, changing demographics, and national culture, must be monitored regularly in terms of their implications for new work demand and the ability to meet that demand through human labor or automation. Other important external challenges pertinent to global HR planning that should be assessed on an ongoing basis include labor market conditions and characteristics, opportunities and restrictions presented by foreign governments and other organizations concerned with labor interests, global competition, cross-national cooperation and conflict, and the impact of broad economic forces and market changes on labor supply cost-effectiveness.

LABOR MARKET CONDITIONS AND CHARACTERISTICS

One of the primary engines driving our increasing globalization is the opportunity presented by increased demand for manufactured goods to satisfy an ever-increasing world consumer appetite. The opportunity is especially attractive with the burgeoning growth in the sourcing of the manufacturing operations for these goods to countries such as China, Vietnam, Romania, Malaysia, India, Brazil, Portugal, Mexico, and Thailand representing attractive labor markets where the labor supply is plentiful, of an adequate skill level, and relatively inexpensive compared with the labor supply in more developed countries. In fact, some countries with a relatively low-cost labor force also hold a comparative advantage in terms of technical skills, such as India and the countries of Central and Eastern Europe, which are attracting considerable high-tech work demand, in addition to back-office administrative services, to be filled by their low-cost but highly skilled computer programmers and engineers.[6] Inevitably, market forces of supply and demand come into play in global HR planning. As more firms source their work to a foreign country with an attractive, heretofore low-cost labor force, there is increasing competition for a limited labor supply, which then eventually drives up the cost of labor for the MNC, as has recently been reported regarding labor characteristics in southern coastal regions of China.[7]

Within the increasing globalization movement, HR planning should include a careful and ongoing scanning of various national labor markets to identify particular opportunities or potential problems related to the supply of labor to support ongoing MNC strategic objectives. Scanning of global labor markets might consider current levels of adult literacy and technical skills among the present labor force. As with the earlier example, the United Kingdom is significantly behind France and Germany in the number and proportion of the national labor force achieving craft-level qualifications in engineering and technology, suggesting that plans for expanding heavy R&D and high-tech business activities into the European Union might favor Germany or France where the global labor force would be more capable of supporting these more demanding and knowledge-intensive business activities.[8] Of course, in cases where MNCs open operations in host countries that have a plentiful labor supply for low-skilled jobs but lack a sufficient supply to meet higher skilled and technical work demand, they should maintain flexibility and mobility to provide the needed higher skilled labor through expatriate assignments from the home country. Or they might seek such higher skilled labor from a third country, such as with the common employment by Western MNCs of engineers and other high-tech professionals from India in Middle Eastern and other developing countries.

GOVERNMENTS AND OTHER LABOR INTEREST ORGANIZATIONS

Inevitable threats to the rapid expansion of globalization fostered by the low cost of labor in developing countries arise both from home as well as abroad in those host countries where the sourced operations are located. A company in its home country can feel strong social pressure in terms of patriotism and national solidarity to not move jobs (work demand) to other countries, which would result in the immediate loss of jobs and an increase in national unemployment—the latter often more of a fear than reality.[9] This protectionist fervor has escalated in the United States in the heat of state and national politics with legislation efforts aimed at curbing U.S. company offshore outsourcing by removing associated tax incentives.[10] Governments and influential unions supported by those governments can also impede or completely prohibit certain kinds of work, such as those related to key industries and national security, from being sourced to other countries.

In their negotiations with MNCs for initial or renewed foreign direct investment within their borders, host country governments also can require, for optimal FDI spillover of knowledge and skills, that MNCs staff their local operations with targeted levels of host country supervisors and managers (with appropriate training provided). Or they may place joint venture requirements to encourage sharing of expertise.[11] Of course, MNCs that hold a much more inclusive perspective of their global human resources beyond those located within the headquarters country borders will recognize host country employee leadership development and higher-level staffing as an opportunity to continue to pursue the strategic goal of building a truly global workforce.

Governments in host country low-cost labor markets are becoming very competitive in providing MNCs with attractive incentives in the form of tax breaks and exemptions from certain costly labor regulations in exchange for foreign direct investment.[12] Yet they also can begin to exact increasing costs for the access to and use of its labor supply in the form of higher taxes and the passage and enforcement of more costly and restrictive labor laws. These foreign governments also can require significant company payments to address the social costs of employee job displacement when the MNC determines to close operations in that country and move to another country with more favorable labor and other operational costs.[13] In addition, local labor unions—and, increasingly, international and local NGOs and other international bodies that monitor labor concerns (for example, the United Nation's International Labour Organization)—can place great pressure on MNCs to improve HR policies and practices related to labor standards, job security, equal opportunity, compensation and benefits, and skill development.[14] Of course, many MNCs will readily bear the costs of developing host country workers to build internal talent and increase efficiencies as well as gain a favorable reputation within the host country as a job provider and contributor to the local economy. And in the longer term these developing host economies, with a positive history with the MNC, represent a growing and amiable consumer market.[15]

GLOBAL COMPETITION

Companies compete both at home and abroad to attract and retain customers by attempting to consistently deliver high-quality products and services at lower costs. Organizations also compete for the human talent itself that drives competitive advantage. Essential to an organization's ability to succeed in the increasingly competitive global arena—whether or not an organization even ventures abroad—is its ability to attract and deploy a motivated, innovative, team-oriented, cooperative, responsive, flexible, and competent workforce at all levels. This ability has been central to Toyota's growth and success in building a reputation for high quality and reliability, and for Southwest Airlines' ongoing profitability (despite pre- and post-9/11 industry distress) and leading performance in important customer service measures.[16] Therefore, a critical function of HR planning is to continuously watch the competition and scan the environment for best practices in employee recruitment, selection, placement, work design, training and development, compensation, change and performance management, and other HR management practices that contribute to a world-class, high-performance workforce.

CROSS-NATIONAL COOPERATION AND CONFLICT

Several different regional and multinational trade treaties and agreements among various countries have important HR planning implications related to business conducted with and within participating countries. Such treaties and agreements include the Organization for Economic Cooperation and Development or OECD (composed of most of the countries of Western Europe plus North America, South Korea, Japan, and Australia), the North American Free Trade Agreement (Canada, the United States, and Mexico), and the Association of South East Asian Nations (Indonesia, the Philippines, Thailand, Singapore, Malaysia, Vietnam, Laos, Cambodia, Brunei, and Myanmar). The most formalized and integrated of these treaties is the European Union (with twenty-seven members and three candidate members as of May 2010), which has adopted a common constitution and, at least for most of its members, a common currency (the euro).[17]

Important HR planning implications of these agreements include joint venture formation and appropriate staffing to promote treaty country partnerships, standardization and harmonization of acceptable HR practices, formation and staffing of regional headquarters and HR functions corresponding to treaty member geographic arrangements, movement of workforce operations across participating national borders to take advantage of operational efficiencies, and appropriate cross-cultural awareness skill development for those involved with treaty country interactions.[18] In addition, managers and decision makers must be aware of important current and changing guidelines and even detailed requirements that these multiple-country agreements can have related to professional licensing, union representation, benefits, training, work standards, and worker rights.[19]

Economic studies on new market development as a result of the formation of the regional trade blocs of the European Union and NAFTA have demonstrated impressive increases in work demand and associated labor supply utilization for participating countries. In fact, some U.S. manufacturing companies have been able to survive and become even more competitive because of NAFTA, which provided a cheaper supply of labor for lower-end manufacturing requirements, while they retained and even expanded their higher-end manufacturing and design operations in the United States. However, at times treaty arrangements may also provide a threat and lead to particular cost advantages favoring companies headquartered in treaty member countries, where the overall cost of business can become increasingly expensive so as to outweigh the low cost of labor. Such has been the case for several Japanese and Korean MNCs along the U.S. border in Mexico that have pulled out and relocated their increasingly expensive Mexican maquiladora operations due to their new less-favorable status and now costly tariffs and other requirements as companies representing nonmember countries of NAFTA.

Aside from various forms of global cooperation, serious forms of conflict within and between countries, including localized and global terrorism, can have important implications for the human side of business and must be attended to as part of HR planning. Ongoing trade wars and skirmishes between countries can present obstacles for foreign business development in those countries, including those associated with HR staffing and utilization. More serious cross-country conflicts, such as that between Pakistan and India, can also thwart regional business stability and business development efforts affecting HR planning. Internal country instability and violence, such as guerrilla and civil warfare or a coup d'état, can have a debilitating impact on company plans. For example, Fidel Castro's overthrow of the Batista regime in 1959 and the Ayatollah Khomeini's takeover of Iran in 1978 had a crippling effect on their respective countries' foreign direct investment and associated international labor activity. In fact, both situations featured a significant emigration of labor to safer and more viable political havens, such as the United States and Western Europe. And social and political unrest in such countries as Colombia, Ecuador, China, and Russia has created a demand for extra surveillance, security, and protective services, such as in the oil industry where foreign executive bodyguard services are in great demand.[20]

JOB DESIGN FOR MEETING GLOBAL STRATEGY WORK DEMAND

Once work demand that directly addresses the implementation of company strategy and business objectives has been identified, decisions are needed regarding work organization and design, involving breaking down larger business performance plans and goals into specific coordinated and integrated tasks, responsibilities, and jobs for people to perform. The work responsibilities and tasks, as well as the qualifications or requirements necessary to perform them (for example, knowledge, skills, and abilities), are considered in detail through a process called job analysis.[21] The job analysis process forms the basis upon which key employment decisions related to recruitment, selection, training, performance appraisal, and compensation are made.[22] Major methods of job analysis include incumbent employee observation, interviews, questionnaires, or keeping a diary or log; when jobs are new, expert input by experienced managers or other professionals often can be useful.[23] The process of job analysis typically results in the development of a document known as a job description, listing the duties and responsibilities, working conditions, supervision or reporting arrangements, and knowledge and skills required to perform the job effectively. This document should be reviewed regularly and discussed with employees and revised if necessary to ensure that work performance expectations are clearly understood.

We now will examine some major factors influencing global work design. We also will consider major forms of international working arrangements, including work assignment accommodations, which are utilized for implementing international business strategic goals and objectives. The roles and contributions of these factors and general work arrangements should be considered as part of overall HR planning on a global scale and should be considered broadly to include all MNC employees, whether they come from the home country or abroad.

PRIMARY FACTORS INFLUENCING GLOBAL WORK DESIGN

Given an identified work demand in some foreign environment, several potentially critical factors must be considered in the design of work that meets that work demand. These factors include cultural adaptation considerations, regulatory influence on work design, labor market skill levels, available technology and infrastructure, and personal accommodation needs.

Cultural Adaptation Considerations in Work Design

As in so many other areas involving detailed workplace implementation in international business, local cultural characteristics must be considered in the effective design of work. Although general tasks and responsibilities for similar jobs can be identified from central corporate headquarters, their specific working conditions and arrangements in their foreign location should be carefully examined to ensure a good fit with local cultural norms and expectations. For example, in cultures characterized by high power distance (such as the Philippines, Mexico, and Venezuela), reporting relationships are expected to be more formal and distant, whereas in cultures with lower power distance (such as Austria, Israel, and Denmark), these relationships are generally more comfortably experienced as informal and with closer and open interaction.[24] In one study we compared the perceptions of Mexican, U.S., and Indonesian lower-level manufacturing employees about what they regarded as appropriate and inappropriate supervisory behaviors and found that these employees differed significantly across national cultures. U.S. and Indonesian employees differed from Mexican employees, for example, in placing a premium on a supervisor's honesty and identifying such supervisory behaviors as "disciplines and criticizes in public" and "flaunts power" as having a particularly negative impact on worker performance. These findings support the reputed high level of power distance in Mexican culture, with the tendency to ascribe to Mexican managers and supervisors the privilege, based on their position of power, of choosing whether to be honest and follow through on past promises, or to flaunt position power or criticize in public. This study demonstrated that a common set of supervisory behaviors that could be prescribed from MNC headquarters would not likely fit the differing expectations and preferences of subordinate employees in those different counties but would need to be customized to fit the local culture.[25]

National and local cultures may differ in the extent that they emphasize personal or group structures in their personal and work activities—those preferring individual structures being high on individualism while those preferring group or team structures being high in collectivism. The most individualistic countries include the United States and other English-speaking countries, whereas the most collectivist countries include Venezuela, Colombia, and Pakistan.[26] Employees in Japan's highly collectivistic culture have been known to identify their job affiliation with a particular company in a very personal way, such as, "I *belong to* Kentucky Fried Chicken of Japan."[27] Thus, in highly collectivistic countries it may be more appropriate in certain work situations to design jobs as part of a highly interactive and interdependent team, where working space itself is designed to be common and open (for example, no separating offices or cubicles) to encourage optimal team interaction. However, such a physical work design can prove disturbing to those accustomed to more privacy, as was found in a study of U.S. interns working in Japan who were very uncomfortable with the open, exposed office and laboratory workspaces.[28]

Regulatory Influence on Work Design

Different governments might have specific restrictions about how work is organized and carried out. In particular, they may specify how work is organized for breaks for rest and even prayer time (such as in some Islamic regimes) or how many hours a day a business can remain open (for example, in Germany until 1998, most stores were not allowed to remain open past 6 P.M.). Governments also might specify how

Global Workforce Challenge 5.1
Today's Workplace Is All aTwitter!

Matt Blalock knew something wasn't right. Over a few months' time, he'd watched the productivity of a talented staff member at his small Web-based retail business decline markedly. But he wasn't sure why, until a little investigation revealed the reason: The employee was spending as much as 85 percent of the work day on social networking and media sites such as Twitter, Facebook, and AIM Express. That person no longer works for Blalock, nor do many otherwise talented workers who have been fired from over 25 percent of firms responding to a recent survey. Many employers are leery of social media use in the workplace because they fear abuse similar to what Blalock experienced. Other concerns include information technology security and loss of corporate message control. But the trend has gotten too big to ignore. The use of social media started as fringe alternative behavior, says Jonathan Pyle, vice president of consulting services at ThinkHR Corp., an HR consultancy based in Pleasanton, California. "Now it's part of business and life."

It is certain that the social media phenomenon isn't going away anytime soon. To avoid problems, employers need to set clear boundaries that depend on factors such as the corporate culture, the work environment, and the industry, among other things. Many companies have URL-filtering programs to block access to Web sites with inappropriate workplace content, such as pornography and gambling. It may be tempting to add social media Web sites to the list, but experts caution against it. Blocking may contribute to an uncomfortable climate of distrust. In addition, it eliminates, or severely limits, the opportunity for employees to use social media justifiably to achieve business goals. Plus, thanks to Web-enabled mobile devices, blocking access from the company server doesn't offer ironclad guarantees. Social media have become so ubiquitous that experts say every company should have a policy on acceptable use. "Even if you're not currently using social media tools for business reasons, you still should put together policy about employees' personal use," says Nancy Flynn, executive director of the Columbus, Ohio-based ePolicy Institute and author of *The e-Policy Handbook* (AMACOM, 2001).

In addition, experts recommend having a brief policy statement outlining corporate philosophy on social media. The policy statement should specify sites or tools encompassed by the policy, who is permitted to use them and for what purposes, restrictions on usage (e.g., only during lunch and break times for personal use), and the consequences of infractions. As with all new policies, employees should sign an acknowledgment of receipt and assert that they understand the policy when it is introduced. And due to the ever-changing nature of social media, acceptable-use policies should be reviewed and updated at least on an annual basis. At Millward Brown, a market research and brand-consulting firm with seventy-seven offices around the world, usage policies are reviewed annually by a committee of IT and HR representatives. In addition, the server forces each user to re-acknowledge understanding of the policy every sixty days. But policy alone is not enough. "If you simply put together this policy and pass it out, you're

(continued)

Global Workforce Challenge 5.1 (continued)

going to have some resentful employees," says Flynn. "If you combine training with policy, most employees will then comply, but it's hard to expect compliance from employees who are operating in the dark." As part of effective training, be sure to explain the "whys" behind the policy, and, wherever possible, use examples of appropriate and inappropriate use.

Source: Adapted from J.T. Arnold, "Twittering and Facebooking While They Work," *HR Magazine* 54 (12) (2009): 53–55.

many hours a week employees can work and give very tight restrictions on the availability of overtime work arrangements. Governments might also differ in regard to whether they either have or enforce regulations on the design of work that ensures employee safety.

Labor Market Skill Levels

Depending on the levels of skills and knowledge available in the labor force, jobs can be designed with more or less technical complexity or requiring more or less careful supervision (also part of the work design). Where a labor force possesses a high level of knowledge and skills, jobs can be designed to include higher levels of complexity and technology, with more tasks than might be appropriate in an area where the labor force is less educated. And where fewer tasks are involved for each job a greater number of employees might be required to satisfy the work demand. One U.S. multinational toy manufacturer found that its plant in Tijuana, Mexico, was able to design work with enough complexity and integration with technology to manufacture products there in three days. In China, where the local labor was abundant and much cheaper but did not, at that time, have the level of labor force skills to support work with such technical complexity, its operation took three weeks to produce the same products.

Available Technology and Infrastructure

Work design must also take into account such factors as the availability and development of technology in the local area of business operations as well as the surrounding infrastructure supporting business. Where technology is unavailable, work must be designed in a more simplified form, which, as in the previously mentioned China example, often results in the need for many more employees to handle simple tasks. Appropriate technology might be available, but it may be useless if it lacks the needed supportive infrastructure (for example, available and affordable electricity, computer support systems, communications, transportation, and so on).

As new technologies are developed and utilized throughout the world to improve efficiencies and productivity, human work is constantly being redesigned to effectively interface with new technology. The field of sociotechnical systems seeks to optimize this interaction in work design between new technologies and the human dimension leading to improved productivity and workforce satisfaction.[29] Along with the productivity boon associated with these technological innovations, current challenges with the introduction of new technologies into the design of work include potential threats to proprietary information security, managing an increasingly virtual workforce that is able to work remotely, and dealing with serious amounts of wasted time and distractions during work hours due to personal use of the Internet, texting, and various popular social networking media programs.[30]

Significant work redesign also becomes needed around previous human-driven tasks that are now automated, and requiring higher employee skills for managing automated operations. In many cases complete jobs are being automated or even eliminated entirely through technological innovation and work process redesign. Although some consider economic downturns as the primary reason for layoffs and unemployment, over the long term the greatest cause for job loss worldwide, especially in the manufacturing sector, is increased efficiency and automation from technological innovation.[31]

Personal Accommodation Needs

In addition to the need to accommodate the design of jobs to fit the cultural and skill level requirements of employees, individual employees may have unique circumstances that might influence the design of their work, especially where current technologies are available to support a more flexible accommodation. For example, where long commutes are required, longer but fewer work days might be arranged,[32] and/ or work may be designed on a "telework" basis that can be performed independently at home or at some other more convenient remote location with regular communications with the traditional office or worksite via telephone, fax, or the Internet (such as via simple Skype videoconference or e-mail and Web site upload and download). There is evidence that more flexible and mobile telework is associated with significant workplace benefits, including higher productivity and top talent retention. As reflected in Figure 5.2, aside from France, there appears to be a general trend toward strong acceptance in several developed economies of this work design innovation supporting greater flexibility.[33] The Netherlands leads the world in the rapid increase in telework, involving 18 percent of the workforce.[34] In fact, it is estimated that more than 137 million workers worldwide engage in telework on at least a part-time basis. Survey results strongly suggest that employees worldwide desire to have more opportunities for telework and that their top priority is to obtain increased flexibility to control their own working time to provide better balance with personal life demands and interests.[35]

MAJOR FORMS OF INTERNATIONAL WORK ARRANGEMENTS

Besides traditional domestic full-workday arrangements at the company worksite (and these traditional workdays can differ dramatically around the world, such as in

Figure 5.2 **Percent of Employees in Each Country Stating Lack of Company Permission to Work from Home**

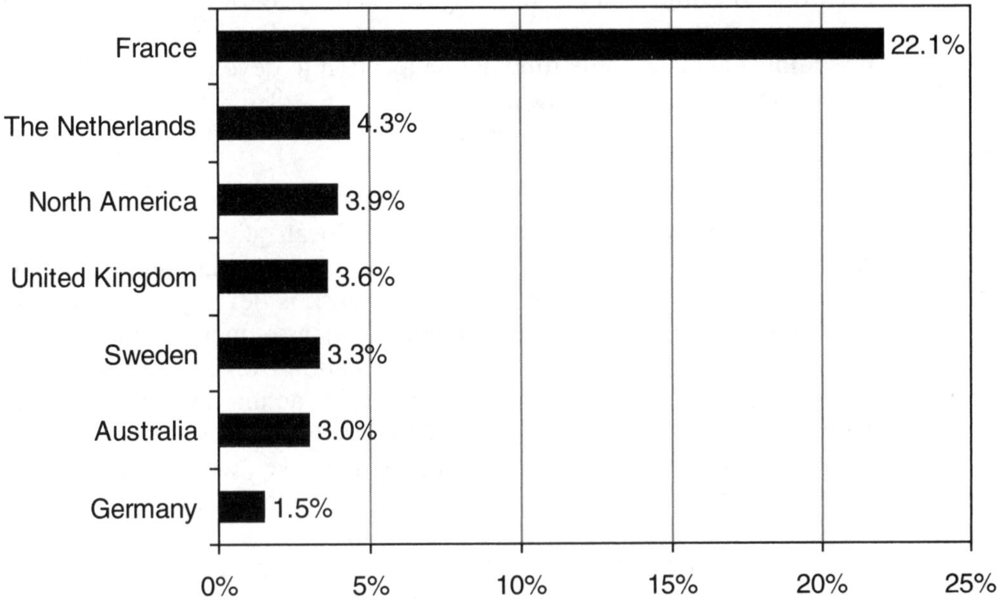

Latin countries that often take an early afternoon extended lunch and rest period and then return to work until much later in the evening, such as 8 P.M. or 9 P.M.), various forms of working arrangements might be made to fit the global work demand needs of the organization and its employees. Common forms of these international work arrangements include extensive travel, short-term foreign assignments, expatriate assignments, inpatriate assignments, virtual expatriate assignments, and multinational virtual teams.

Extensive Travel

Some kinds of regional sales and management jobs require almost constant travel to various business locations in a country or economic region. These kinds of jobs may require regular and frequent customer contact, active coordination of various geographically dispersed business partners, or ongoing supervision that cannot be replaced completely by virtual contacts. Extensive travel work arrangements are often part of an early and developing phase of business development and might eventually result, as business becomes more established and predictable, in more permanent assignments at the worksites to where the previous travel had been targeted. They can also be part of a regional assignment, such as with an executive who works at regional headquarters in Brussels but travels considerably during the week to other operations in Western Europe and returns home to a Paris suburb on weekends. Besides the added travel expense, extensive travel can grow very burdensome and tiring for the traveler as well as severely interfere with the traveling employee's personal life. One single American woman in Vienna, whose regional work in business development in the health care industry involved extensive travel, commented to us that although her work constituted an exciting growth experience for her, she felt that the tremendous amount of travel required of her greatly interfered with her personal life in not providing adequate stable time in one location to develop personal and meaningful relationships outside of work.

Short-Term Foreign Assignments

With increasing priorities for cost savings and localization of talent, short-term foreign work assignments, or sometimes called *secondments,* ranging from a few months to a year, are on the rise.[36] Where sufficient work is developed in a foreign location, employees might be sent there temporarily, such as on a two-month assignment, or for multiple work periods at the foreign location over an extended length of time. Short-duration foreign assignments can provide an interesting break, challenge, and professional development opportunity for employees who have worked in the same domestic location for a long period of time. However, when the assignments become more frequent and require more time at the foreign location than back at the home workplace, their attractiveness can begin to diminish significantly—again with growing operational costs perceived by the organization and personal life-balance costs as perceived by the employee. Frequently we have noted that foreign short-term work assignments, particularly to the same foreign worksite, lead to extended or expatriate work assignments for two to five years and more at the foreign location. One American expatriate working for Intel Corporation in Rome remarked to us that after nearly a year of spending one week at home after working the rest of each month in Rome on what originally had been foreseen as a short-term work assignment, he finally made a request and was allowed to move his family to Rome and convert to an extended expatriate assignment.

Expatriate Assignments

Traditionally organizations, particularly in earlier stages of their business expansion abroad, have sent managers as expatriates from their home country locations—often company headquarters—for three years or longer. The demand for their services has been based primarily on the need to fill a critical skills gap by transferring operating knowledge and techniques and general managerial skills held by the expatriate to the distant subsidiary, thereby allowing the MNC to more directly provide coordination and controls to ensure that the foreign subsidiary is performing up to MNC expectations and consistent with MNC strategy. The expatriate assignment represents an important boundary-spanning function between the MNC and the host country business environment.[37] In the course of filling this assignment there typically is a transfer of knowledge and skills from the expatriate to members of the local workforce, whether formally through training efforts or informally through the expatriate's behavior modeling and daily work interactions with local employees. Much of the focus of this knowledge transfer has been on the cognitive domain in the form of specific, concrete knowledge about procedures, techniques, and methods for accomplishing tasks. In addition, there are likely other valuable forms of learning transfer in the "emotional intelligence" or affective domain such as with productive attitudes and values as well as higher-level thinking, team building, and problem-solving skills. For example, David Cheung, who has worked in different financial management capacities since 1994 in Motorola (China) Electronics Ltd., and is currently the CFO for Otis China in Tianjin, noted the following regarding his experience with American expatriates, including interns that were abroad primarily for their own experience and development:

> In my opinion, expatriates have played an important role in China's progress, in teaching the Chinese technical knowledge as well as problem-solving and managerial skills. Our American managers here usually bring in a sense of "you can do it" spirit. They usually are more outgoing, friendly, treating everyone as equal, and are more able to lead a team and get people motivated to improve and bring about changes. I have often had foreign interns in my organizations. Very often, they are people full of energy, ideas, enthusiasm, and great motivation, which had a positive impact on my organizations by their good example. The Americans are usually not shy about things even when they don't know the subject well. They have the confidence to learn and to try. This is what many of the local Chinese employees need to learn.[38]

This immediate purpose of filling a critical skills gap with accompanying knowledge/skill transfer for optimal MNC control appears to be the most common assignment objective for expatriates.[39] Two additional major purposes for sending expatriates abroad include supporting individual learning and global competency development for future company leadership as well as organization development of the host operation and MNC as a whole.[40] Vladimir Pucik has differentiated between demand-driven foreign site work and learning-driven international assignments, where companies increasingly recognize that cross-border mobility afforded by expatriate assignments represents a valuable learning tool and opportunity for the expatriate.[41] Gary Oddou has identified two types of expatriates: those assigned to go abroad to fix a problem and those identified as "high potentials" for the firm who are assigned abroad to build global business competencies.[42] Particular purposes of organization development served by expatriate assignments have been described as effecting global workforce socialization to common values and priorities, widespread global orientation and core competency development, and development of informal networks.[43] More recent work on the expatriate assignment's potential contributions to organization development has expanded the focus to include organizational learning and effective global knowledge management, where expatriates, upon returning to MNC headquarters (regional or global), potentially serve as important sources of knowledge and learning for the organization about foreign markets.[44]

Despite the previously listed beneficial purposes of the expatriate assignment, some significant disadvantages should be considered before automatically structuring work to be fulfilled through expatriate job designs. First, expatriate assignments can be very expensive. The maintenance costs of expatriates in a host country range from three to ten times the cost of domestic employees with similar responsibilities.[45] Second, the frequency of premature terminations of expatriate assignments or failure to achieve the assignment goals are reported at disturbing levels.[46] One U.S. study showed that nearly one-third of expatriates who remained in their positions did not perform to the level of expectation of their superiors back at headquarters.[47] Third, an over-reliance on the use of expatriates for management and leadership responsibilities in foreign operations can lead to limited development of other members of the MNC workforce not coming from MNC headquarters, contributing to an overall underutilized and underdeveloped global talent pool.[48] Fourth, the long-term exclusive use of expatriates for managing foreign operations, rather than qualified host country nationals with differing viewpoints and backgrounds, can significantly diminish the breadth of experience-based perspectives and knowledge about foreign markets that can be returned to MNC headquarters, limiting the MNC's ability to innovate and compete on a global scale due to its narrow, ethnocentric frame of reference.[49] Finally, the decision to send an expatriate on an assignment to maximize operational control, particularly due to the host country's high cultural distance from the MNC home country, may be ill-founded. One recent study found that a higher ratio of MNC home country expatriates is related to lower subsidiary performance, particularly in cases where cultural distance is high, thus presenting a greater challenge to the expatriate.[50]

Inpatriate Assignments

A work assignment featuring the transfer of foreign managers from their host country operation locations to global or regional headquarters on a semipermanent or permanent basis is known as inpatriation.[51] A major purpose of this kind of work assignment is to increase the foreign inpatriate manager's understanding of company strategy, culture, and critical operations and practices. And upon return to the host country in a position of leadership, this now more broadly experienced manager can exert greater control on the foreign operation consistent with MNC headquarters.[52] And just as expatriates have traditionally been MNC agents of knowledge and skill transfer to employees in the host operations, the returned inpatriate manager can serve as a knowledge transfer agent in a similar fashion—and perhaps with greater credibility as someone originating from the host country workforce. Inpatriate managers, through their active involvement at MNC headquarters, can also serve to infuse knowledge of the corresponding host country market throughout the global organization as well as provide a means to enrich the MNC management team by adding a multicultural perspective to global strategy development.[53]

Inpatriation assignments are likely more appropriate for organizations of intermediate and advanced levels of internationalization whose host country employees have significant experience with the company and that possess adequate capital resources to support such a long-term HR investment. There may be other limitations and costs as well—many of which are similar to the challenges of cross-cultural adjustment, premature assignment termination, and assignment failure to meet goals and objectives.[54] Also, where great benefit can be achieved through the infusion of broader and multicultural perspectives within MNC management at company headquarters, this value can be effectively achieved only if significant cross-cultural awareness and diversity training efforts and deep-seated, often stressful organizational culture changes are made to prepare the MNC to be receptive to these new perspectives and supportive of the new inpatriate participants on the MNC management team.[55]

Virtual Expatriate Assignments

Considering the high costs associated with expatriate assignments, and with more managers and executives preferring not to uproot themselves and their families for foreign assignments, companies are increasingly using assignments that combine short travel trips with virtual interaction through telephone and cyberspace. In these arrangements, virtual expatriates are traveling to the foreign operations for a short period of time for direct interaction with local employees and managers and then continuing with follow-up direction, coordination, and supervision on a distance basis through telephone and other electronic forms of interactive communication including e-mail, video teleconferencing, the Internet, and company-controlled intranet sites—all considered forms of telework.[56] The virtual arrangement allows executives to take an assignment without subjecting them and their families to the culture shock of a move abroad. These arrangements also expose the employee to valuable developmental global management issues, while still permitting closer touch with the home office.

According to a PricewaterhouseCoopers survey of 270 organizations in twenty-four European countries employing 65,000 expatriates, there has been a significant increase in this practice, with about two-thirds of the companies employing virtual expats, up from 43 percent in 1997.[57] More than 80 percent of the companies surveyed reported employees had turned down assignments because of dual-career problems or family issues. Another major reason that executives are balking at overseas assignments was identified as the career risk of being far away from headquarters where key budgeting decisions and informal power and politics maneuvering are played out. One Scottish-born executive who is in charge of the Middle East and Pakistan for GlaxoSmithKline is not based in the Middle East but instead at the drug maker's London headquarters. But other than for personal convenience, he indicated being based in London improved his ability to garner limited company resources for his team, as in this statement: "My role is to get resources for my team, and being based at headquarters helps me lobby for them."[58] Despite their growing use in MNCs, virtual expatriate assignments will not completely replace expatriate assignments because the latter work arrangement still potentially holds a huge face-to-face advantage in solving problems in a timely fashion as they arise, especially in building trusting and open communication relationships necessary for effective team performance—a potential limitation of the virtual assignment. Indeed, as one Australian executive for a U.S. multinational in Sydney whimsically remarked to us, "Virtual expats are often called 'seagull' executives who every now and then suddenly swoop in, drop their 'business' on their foreign team, and then fly back to headquarters."

Global Virtual Teams

The globalization of business and the growing competitive trend of leaner and flatter organizations using the best organizational talent available in the MNC, no matter where in the world that talent is located, have combined with new information and communications technologies leading to the formation and continued growth of complete or partial working arrangements known as global or multinational virtual teams.[59] Global virtual teams have been described in different ways, with the virtual aspect of the team ranging from occasional to total reliance on communication technologies as the medium for team interaction. But their work has three design components in common: (1) responsible for formulating and/or implementing decisions that are important to their organization's global strategy, (2) use a substantial amount of communications technology to support group member interactions, and (3) comprise members working and living in different countries. Most are knowledge-based teams formed to improve organizational processes, develop new products, or satisfy complex customer problems.[60] A distinct advantage of global virtual teams, especially those spread longitudinally around the world, is the ability to perform work asynchronously, helping global organizations bridge different time zones effectively and enabling teams to be productive over more than one work period. In addition, dispersed members' proximity to different customers, markets, practices, perspectives, and resources in their local contexts can enhance flexibility and innovation capability, thus increasing the ability of the team to balance local awareness with a broader, strategic perspective of the united global MNC team.[61]

Although there seems to be great potential in the use of global virtual teams, there are several basic sociotechnical challenges in making them work effectively. These challenges include managing conflict—a natural by-product of working groups—over differing cultural backgrounds and with much greater distances and delayed or asynchronous periods of interaction. Synchronous interaction in groups is a more orderly process wherein verbal and nonverbal cues help regulate the flow of conversation, facilitate turn taking in discussion, provide immediate feedback, and convey subtle meanings. In lean, asynchronous communication typically found in multinational virtual teams, especially those stretching across Asian, European, and American time zones, the conveyance of cues is hindered, feedback is delayed, and interruptions or long pauses in communication often occur.[62] As will be discussed later in Chapter 8 on managing international assignments, global virtual teams must find workable solutions for overcoming the obstacle of asynchronous communications and for temporally coordinating their interactions and flows of information associated with work schedules and deadlines, developing trust, aligning the pace of efforts among group members, and agreeing on the time spent on particular tasks.[63]

SOURCES OF GLOBAL LABOR SUPPLY FOR MEETING WORK DEMAND

Once work demand has been identified and human jobs (as opposed to automated or robot-delivered work) have been designed into specific tasks and responsibilities, various sources of labor can be considered to fill this work demand. These sources of labor may be regular or standard employees or employees that are often classified as nonstandard or contingent.

REGULAR OR STANDARD EMPLOYEES

Regular or standard employees have been better known in the past as "full-time" or "permanent" employees. However, these terms have been dropped largely due to the presence of other employee groups (such as "temps," or temporary employees) who also put in full working hours per day or week (that is, full time). And especially in litigious environments such as the United States, companies are avoiding the use of language such as "permanent," which can be interpreted by employees and the courts as a guarantee of employment that would interfere with company flexibility in utilizing needed restructuring or downsizing through employee layoffs. Regular or standard employees often are considered full members of the organization and generally are recipients of full benefits typically provided by the organization. These employees often are considered to be at the core of the organization's employment picture, where other "noncore" employees serve as layers beyond the core that provide work as needed and as afforded by the organization. As has been practiced by large Japanese firms for many years, the noncore employees serve as a protective buffer for their core employee counterparts, and these nonstandard employees tend to be the first ones to lose their jobs or to have their working hours diminished in tight financial times.[64]

Before looking at nonstandard or contingent employees, we first will consider three major groups of regular employees as sources of labor in global HR planning: parent country nationals, host country nationals, and third country nationals. We also will examine their relative strengths and limitations as we consider their roles in ongoing global MNC operations.

Parent Country Nationals (PCNs)

PCNs are citizens, or at least legal residents, of the "home country" of the parent company or the country where the primary company headquarters is located. PCNs are also sometimes called "parent *company* nationals," rather than parent *country* nationals, perhaps to avoid a possible patronizing offense (which we have noted firsthand in the past) that people might take with this term, especially when they are from former colonies of a parent country (such as Australia versus the United Kingdom). Although in most uses of the term PCNs are presently employed by the MNC, they also could be members of the larger national labor force where the MNC is headquartered.

A particular strength of a PCN as a labor source, especially one that comes from a managerial or executive level within the MNC and has significant experience with the MNC at company headquarters, is typically his or her understanding of the company culture, priorities, and strategy and what it takes to be successful within the MNC. In addition, the experienced PCN is likely well networked within the MNC and has a good understanding of the key decision makers and power brokers within the organization. Company familiarity and connections are essential for effective MNC control, coordination, and integration of activities across the MNC,[65] as well as for competing for and obtaining needed company resources to support current project goals and activities. Employees who are recruited from within the national labor force where the MNC is headquartered likely share the same language and might also share similar national cultural characteristics that influence business behavior and decision making. However, particular limitations of PCNs include a possible lack of familiarity with and difficulty in personally adjusting to a foreign business location of the MNC. Related to this lack of foreign-site adaptability is the possible inability to adjust headquarters policies and practices to fit the local job and business requirements of the foreign business operation.

Host Country Nationals (HCNs)

HCNs are citizens or residents of a country that "hosts," or provides local property and facilities, for MNC operations abroad. As a labor source, HCN employees can come from the ranks of existing MNC employees in the host country operation, such as in the case of an employee from within the local foreign operation promoted to a management position or an inpatriate assignment. HCN employees can also come from outside the firm and from within the surrounding host country national labor force. An obvious advantage of HCNs as a source of labor is their ready availability in the local environment. Compared with less-experienced PCNs, HCNs also tend to possess greater familiarity with the local culture, common business practices, and economic conditions. Due to this local familiarity, HCN managers may actually provide a greater degree of strategic control in business formulation and implementation than PCNs. This greater knowledge possessed by HCN managers for controlling local operations, along with their generally lower costs and degree of assignment risk involved, help explain why we see increasing trends by MNCs in selecting HCN top leadership for their foreign operations.[66] However, HCNs may at least initially lack a clear understanding of the predominant national and organizational culture of MNC headquarters, or its business priorities, accepted and expected business practices, and strategic mind-set.[67] HCNs might not share a common language with PCNs, thus potentially posing a serious challenge to effective communications and business interactions.

Third Country Nationals (TCNs)

When staffing a foreign operation in a host country, new employees could be citizens or residents of a different third country apart from the parent or host country.[68] TCNs can represent a useful alternative labor source for filling work demand where the focus is on obtaining the most cost-effective labor, regardless of what country the employee comes from. This staffing approach often follows an overall regiocentric strategy, where regional employees are assigned as TCNs to nearby host country operations. For example, MNCs within the European Union increasingly are responding to opportunities presented by European integration by reclassifying intra-European assignments as a domestic job transfer that follows local pay structures than a traditional international relocation, which often incurs an array of costly benefits and compensation measures such as housing allowances, cost-of-living differentials, and hardship premiums.[69]However, significant disadvantages to the use of TCNs include their possible lack of understanding of the local HCN culture and difficulties with local public sentiment and governmental obstruction where TCNs are perceived as taking away jobs from local HCNs. In addition, TCNs, like HCNs, may have language difficulty in communicating effectively with PCNs and MNC headquarters, and they may not have a clear understanding of MNC strategic priorities, accepted business practices, and organizational culture.

CONTINGENT OR NONSTANDARD WORKFORCE

Contingent or nonstandard employees are those who work on a flexible basis as needed or contingent to an organization's work demand and have neither an explicit nor implicit contract for continuing employment.[70] Despite temporary cutbacks due to the recent global economic crisis, these "as needed" employees, in their many different forms, represent a rapidly growing source of labor for flexibly filling seasonal and changing global work demand and serving to increase overall world employment, not just to fill in for layoffs and lost jobs.[71] Estimates of the size of the contingent workforce vary, mostly because of the differing ways in which contingent or nonstandard employees are defined. Some estimates have described contingent workers reaching as high as 30–50 percent of the U.S. workforce in the near future.[72] But the United States is not alone nor even in the lead in its significant reliance on contingent workers. As noted earlier, large Japanese firms have long used contingent workers to buffer their core employees from unemployment. Furthermore, the use of contingent workers is increasing in Canada, Australia, Mexico, and Europe, especially in the Netherlands, Great Britain, Spain, Sweden, and France.[73] An international study estimated an average of approximately 25 percent of the world labor force is in "casual" nonstandard or contingent employment.[74] This dramatic growth in demand for more flexible contingent workers has fueled the development of the worldwide temporary employment industry led by global firms such as Adecco (see Profile 5.2), Randstad, Kelly Services, and Manpower.

Although national culture and economic structure can have a major influence on the extent of use of contingent employees, such as in Spain where changes to part-time working arrangements are preferred over layoffs, it is clear that contingent workers are a large and important component of the global workforce.[75] Several labor forecasters predict that the contingent or nonstandard workforce will grow faster than the standard one for years to come.[76]

Reasons for Major Growth of the Contingent Labor Sector

The phenomenal worldwide growth of the contingent labor sector has been promoted by various interests, including companies, governments, and workers themselves. We now will examine major reasons for this significant growth.

Promoting Company Flexibility. To meet increasing global competitive demand, contingent employees are used on an economical "as needed" basis, allowing the company to relatively easily adjust up or down the number of workers employed and

---

Global Workforce Professional Profile 5.2
The Adecco Group

The Adecco Group, a Fortune Global 500 company based in Zurich, Switzerland, has over 28,000 employees and 5,700 offices in more than 60 countries and territories around the world. Formed in 1996 from the merger of founding firms Adia and Ecco, Adecco recognizes that there is a growing demand for both flexibility and skills on the part of the global workforce, and offers a wide variety of services, connecting more than 500,000 colleagues (placed workers) with over 100,000 company clients every day. These services fall into broad categories related to general and professional employee staffing: temporary employment, permanent placement, outsourcing, consulting, and outplacement. Here is a personal account giving a flavor of Adecco's professional activities:

> Stanislav Jacel, 47, is a Polish master electrician. He worked for 30 years in Poland and built up his own company, but wanted a better life for his family and started looking for work abroad. He heard about Adecco and the opportunities for skilled workers. This soon led to a placement in Norway. Says Jacel, "Since my apprentice days at sea, I'd fancied living in Scandinavia. When Adecco suggested a move to Norway, it was a dream come true. They paid for a language course and within months I was working at an electrical and electronics supplier on behalf of Adecco Norway. The versatility of the work, requiring different skills, has made me a better electrician. I also supervise and organize less senior colleagues from Poland, which is both challenging and satisfying."

Free movement of labor in much of Europe offers valuable flexibility in labor sourcing to address acute skill shortages faced by countries and employers. Adecco connects qualified people with attractive career opportunities, and coaches and trains candidates, creating flexible workforces that can be deployed where they are needed most. From Adecco's stated vision and mission:

> We inspire individuals and organizations to work more effectively and efficiently, and create greater choice in the domain of work, for the benefit of all concerned. As the world's leading provider of HR solutions—a business that has a positive impact on millions of people every year—we are conscious of our global role.

Source: Adapted from the Adecco Group Web site, www.adecco.com.

---

their working hours based on the existing work demand and economic conditions, and thus not have to pay for excess labor supply when work demand slackens. Although generally first to be cut during economic difficulty, an increase in the use of contingent employees among employers who want to test the new economic waters before hiring more regular employees, represent an important harbinger of more favorable economic conditions ahead.[77]

Supply Factors. In some cultures a large sector of the labor may be available to work only on a part-time basis, such as where women are expected to attend to most of the childcare and other household management responsibilities.[78] In several countries we also have noted that senior citizens, with increased health and longevity, may return from complete retirement to the workplace on a part-time basis to generate extra income and provide additional variety in their lives.

Screening Function. Temporary employees and their part-time employee counterparts who are working a smaller number of hours allow for management to sample their work performance before making a long-term commitment for more regular employment. Such an approach also gives the potential new regular employee a chance to really get to know the organization. Thus, this probationary process may enhance the effectiveness of new standard-employee staffing decisions.[79]

Technological Change. Significant changes in technology often lead to (a) outsourcing or reassigning work outside of the company to those specializing in new technology expertise, (b) automation of work and robotics that typically reduce the number of needed employees as well as change the nature of the work, and (c) rapid changes that demand flexibility and diminish the need for long-term employment commitments— all of which lead to a greater demand for contingent employment arrangements.[80]

Employment Legislation and Deregulation. Some forms of employment legislation on behalf of "full-time" or regular employees, such as what many regard as very generous employment benefits for regular employees in Scandinavian countries, might therefore create an economic motive for companies to increase their use of part-time and other nonstandard employees. Also, through deregulation, companies might become freer to utilize more flexibility in their staffing practices, where part-time, temporary, and other contingent staffing arrangements typically play a dominant role.[81]

In many European countries, temporary and part-time jobs have increased significantly in number. In fact, they have become the most important source of new jobs, partly because some governments have actively encouraged the use of nonstandard employees to reduce unemployment. This trend is likely to continue as governments, in their political interest, strive to promote economic growth and to increase employment levels.[82]

Worldwide Growth in Numbers of Small Businesses. Many forces have contributed to the global increase in the number of small businesses, including the increase in corporate outsourcing of functions, corporate downsizing, and the lure of being one's own boss. Unwilling or unable to handle specialized business functions peripheral to the small company's core competency (for example, security, payroll, marketing research, and staffing) and reluctant to employ a permanent workforce to handle these activities, many small businesses outsource these services for a fee to consultants, contractors, and special service vendors. In this way the small employer is not weighted down by the fixed costs of regular employees because the arrangement with the vendor firm can be terminated at the end of the contract period.[83]

Changes in Employer-Employee Relationships and Expectations. The long-standing psychological contract between employers and employees of lifelong employment and job security is greatly diminishing worldwide. Downsizing, such as following privatization (where excess employees were previously carried by state-owned enterprises), due to workforce redundancies after mergers and acquisitions, as a result of technological integration and productivity improvements, or simply due to companies worldwide trying to lower employment costs in the face of global competition, has led to an increased sense of employees being their own free agents and not committed on a long-term basis to a single employer. Many employees who have left their employers have become independent contractors, marketing the knowledge and skills they acquired working for their previous employer. By obtaining new work on a contingent basis, they also can add to their stock of knowledge and skills, thereby enhancing their employability.

Changes in Employee Personal-Life Needs and Lifestyle Preferences. In addition to changes in the psychological contract between employers and employees, major changes in employee needs, expectations, and lifestyles have come to alter work arrangements in the workplace. The dramatic increase, especially in developed countries, in the number of working mothers and the rise of the two-career family have led to the demands for flexible working arrangements provided by contingent employment. Employees with responsibilities for the care of children or aging parents, or both, often secure contingent employment because of the flexibility in hours and days worked.

Temporary work, traditionally reserved for the lower employee ranks, is also increasingly being seen as a way of life for some professional, technical, managerial, and executive employees. They enjoy the greater variety of temporary projects and assignments and prefer to work on a contingent basis because they gain a sense of freedom by not having to make a commitment to remain long-term with one employer. Other employees prefer flexibility in the number of hours and days worked, providing them the freedom to pursue other interests.

Major Forms of Contingent or Nonstandard Employees

Contingent or nonstandard employees, whether domestic or international, are clearly important to an organization, yet they often are overlooked or are inadequately considered as an important part of organizational performance and productivity. The following are major forms of contingent employees found in the global labor force that should be part of a company's global HR planning process.

Part-Time Employees. While short-term excess work demand is likely most often addressed by regular employees through overtime, part-time employees (typically working fewer hours than in a country's normal workweek on an ongoing basis) represent the most common source of the growing contingent labor force to meet excess work demand.[84] Both regular employees working overtime and part-time employees who have worked with the organization on an ongoing basis avoid recruitment and training costs of other contingent employees in meeting excess work demand. The eligibility of part-timers for company benefits depends on various factors, including the number of hours worked and the terms of the company's benefits plans. As mentioned earlier, the global part-time workforce continues to be dominated numerically by women. However, due to continuing changes in traditional work arrangements underlying standard employment (where men were traditionally predominant), the rate of growth of part-time employment tends to be higher for men than women. In fact, one study found that the growth rate of part-time employment is much higher for men in every country of the European Union.[85]

Temporary Employees. Temporary employees represent another major source of contingent workers hired to help companies meet global work demand, although many countries differ in the degree to which this "free agent" class of employees is acceptable. American businesses continue to lobby for changes in legislation, which currently limits the number of visas for foreign workers who want to work temporarily in the United States.[86] The demand for temporary workers in Europe and Asia has also grown. The temporary help industry in Europe today is about 50 percent larger than that in the United States. Across Europe, companies have hired temporary workers in large numbers to create a flexible labor force that can adjust to economic cycles.[87]

Although they originally were used to fill skill shortages, such as when a regular employee was ill, or assist with the completion of projects having a finite duration, temporary employees are increasingly being used by companies to supplement the regular workforce on an ongoing basis, with the size of this group of employees ebbing and flowing, depending on the workload and health of the economy, and providing a protective buffer of stability for regular employees.[88] In addition, contrary to the common image of temporary employees as low-level administrative workers, temporary employees increasingly are found in higher managerial and professional positions.[89] These employees are often supplied by temporary services agencies, which retain the employees on their payroll, or may be in-house company employees—sometimes called "floaters," who are on the company's payroll but typically not eligible for full company benefits.

Paralleling the rise of the global company has been the globalization of temporary help firms that are major suppliers of temporary workers. To continue to provide temporary employees to their clients that are operating or expanding internationally, temporary staffing companies have also been expanding beyond their borders by opening foreign offices or by acquiring temporary-help firms in other countries.[90]

Employee Leasing. The use of employment leasing by MNCs has increased significantly, as indicated in studies with Japanese and European executives.[91] Under an employee-leasing arrangement a company might transfer all employees, a large part of the employees, or sometimes only the employees of a separate facility or site to the payroll of an employee-leasing firm or Professional Employer Organization (PEO) in an explicit joint-employment relationship. The PEO then leases the workers back to the client company and administers the payroll and benefits, maintains personnel records, and performs most of the functions handled by an HR department. Besides saving the company on HR operational costs, depending on the countries involved employee-leasing arrangements can also provide positive MNC tax benefits as well as tax benefits for international professional employees. As one PEO's slogan asserts, "We take care of your people so you can take care of your business." However, serious problems can arise when companies fail to include people as a central part of their business planning—and it may be hard to lease back loyalty and commitment that previously provided a source of competitive advantage.

Contracted Services. Specialized tasks, usually of a nonrecurring nature and generally requiring a high level of independence, professional judgment, discretion, and skill are frequently performed on a contract basis by individuals, such as consultants, or groups of professionals from special professional services firms. These professionals often travel or work on projects far from their homes and may have multiyear or indefinite assignments, as is the case with an American consultant and professional acquaintance of ours working for the government of the United Arab Emirates in Abu Dhabi on the design and construction of their national airport.

Bechtel has found a significant improvement in its global projects through employing contracted services. For example, for their copper and gold mines in Chile, they used to do all the engineering, design, and equipment purchase in the United States and then send their own construction people to work with employees in Chile to build a plant. Now Bechtel typically does the conceptual engineering in the United States and hires contracted Chilean mechanical and electrical engineers, who are more familiar with local conditions, to do all the detail engineering in Chile.[92]

Outsourced Services. When a company contracts with an external organization to provide the ongoing, full managerial responsibility over a specific function, we move into the domain of outsourced services—whether onsite, domestic, or offshore. As in the opening scenario, Gap and many other U.S.-based manufacturers, in seeking labor-cost savings to successfully compete in the global marketplace, outsource the manufacturing of many of their products on a long-term contract basis to firms in developing countries. But as mentioned previously, such offshore outsourcing is not limited to lower-skill work processes. Many multinationals are outsourcing their high-tech design functions offshore to countries such as India where skills are high yet labor costs are still low.[93] Outsourcing higher skill but nonessential or noncore back-office operations (like payroll and accounting) to countries such as India can reduce operating costs while simultaneously providing a foothold in an important emerging market. GE Capital Corporation, which moved its development and back-office operation to India as early as 1997, now employs 2,000 people in its Indian office.[94] In fact, such increasing long-term offshore outsourcing arrangements of higher skilled functions has caused a rise in parent country concerns for the loss of national skill dominance and capability, previously held in the parent country by the MNCs who are growing increasingly dependent on their outsourced contractors.[95]

Despite what might appear to be very attractive cost savings initially, companies should conduct careful HR planning prior to outsourcing to identify possible hidden costs and difficulties that have caused some firms to reverse their offshore outsourcing decisions.[96] Thorough HR planning allows companies to carefully address issues

---

Global Workforce Challenge 5.2
Not Every Job Can Be Successfully Moved Abroad

When sales of their security software slowed in 2001, ValiCert, Inc., began laying off engineers in Silicon Valley to "offshore" employment and hire replacements in India for a fraction of the labor cost. ValiCert expected to save millions annually while cranking out new online security software for banks, insurers, and government agencies. There were optimistic predictions that the company would cut its U.S. budget in half and hire twice as many people in India, and colleagues would swap work across the globe every twelve hours, putting more people on tasks to complete them sooner. But that is not what actually happened.

The Indian engineers, who knew little about ValiCert's software or how it was used, omitted features that U.S. customers considered standard. The software had to be rewritten in Silicon Valley, delaying its release by months. U.S. programmers, accustomed to quick chats over cubicle walls, spent months writing detailed instructions for tasks assigned overseas, delaying new products. Fear and distrust thrived as ValiCert's finances deteriorated, and coworkers, fourteen time zones apart, exchanged curt e-mails. Due to its floundering, a key project that had been offshored to employees in India was brought back to the United States, a move that irritated some Indian employees.

Shifting work to India eventually did help cut ValiCert's engineering costs by 30 percent, keeping the company and its major products alive—and saving sixty-five positions that remained in the United States. But the company still experienced a difficult period of instability and doubt and recovered only after its executives significantly refined the company's global division of labor. The successful formula that emerged was to assign the India team bigger projects rather than tasks requiring continual interaction with U.S. counterparts. The crucial creative job of crafting new products and features stayed in Silicon Valley. In the end, exporting some jobs ultimately led to adding a small but important number of new, higher-level positions in the United States. One of these new hires was Brent Haines, a software architect charged largely with coordinating the work of the U.S. and India teams. This responsibility often means exchanging e-mail from home with engineers in India between 11 P.M. and 3 A.M. California time, as Mr. Haines reviews programming code and suggests changes. Such collaboration requires extensive planning, he says, "something very unnatural to people in software."

Sources: Adapted from G. Cornell, "Offshoring Work is a Quick Fix Laden with Many Pitfalls," *NJBIZ* 22 (42) (2009): 17; S. Thurm, "Lesson in India: Not Every Job Translates Overseas," *Wall Street Journal,* March 3, 2004: A1, A10.

---

such as skill and language requirements, regulatory and political environment of the potential offshore location, cultural compatibility, alternative talent pools, workforce training requirements, and especially work design requirements.[97] For example, in his analysis of success factors in outsourcing offshore service jobs, David Wagner suggests that jobs with high information intensity (supported by reliable and efficient digital platforms) as well as low need for physical presence are the primary candidates for offshore outsourcing. However, even with minimal physical presence, virtual presence is still necessary in maintaining a productive working relationship with an offshore outsourced vendor. Cultural differences related to power distance and active versus passive working attitude can greatly affect relationship quality and offshore outsourcing success, and should not be ignored. It has been recommended that to effectively manage offshore outsourcing relationships, clear role definitions and procedures should be provided, along with strong leadership and active attention to culture, either by adapting to the client's or vendor's national culture.[98]

MNC Concerns Regarding Contingent Employees

The contingent workforce represents a major source of labor that MNCs should consider carefully in their plans for filling work demand. In some less-developed countries MNCs may actually gain greater social and political approval by employing more host country employees on a part-time basis than fewer employees on a full-time or more standard basis. However, particularly in more developed economies, a heavy reliance on nonstandard employees may bear a price related to reduced job satisfaction and a climate of job insecurity among standard or regular employees.[99] In the United States and Europe, where the percent of the contingent workforce is on the rise, the number of persons highly satisfied with employment terms and conditions has fallen significantly and is lower in those countries such as Spain where nonstandard employment is most frequent. And where employee job satisfaction is low, organizations might suffer a reduction in workforce loyalty, commitment, and subsequent reduced productivity.[100]

With regard to employee work that is completely outsourced, organizations can suffer significant problems when they now consider that these employees working for outsourcing service firms are no longer their concern and responsibility. With the outsourcing arrangement comes a severing of *direct* control of employee work quality. Decreased worker commitment, loyalty, and competence can occur, which ultimately compromises productivity. For example, a major worry that managers have with their outsourced call centers that often cross international borders is that those employees' lack of commitment and identification with the company product or service may spill over into the quality of customer interaction, with comments such as, "Yes, I know what you mean . . . I don't like the product either," or "I'm not exactly sure . . . I don't really work for this company." There is also an ongoing concern about customer perceptions of company products or services provided by offshore employees, whether they are outsourced or actually employed by the MNC. To help build company quality image and brand loyalty with customers, which might appear compromised by low-cost offshore arrangements, many organizations are increasingly hesitant to disclose their ties to offshore workers. For example, although in the past we have inquired at the end of a successful call center service interaction about the workplace country location of the service employee and learned that he or she was in India or the Philippines, we received the following official response to the same inquiry from an employee working at a call center for a large financial services firm: "I'm very sorry, but for security purposes we are not allowed to disclose that information."

Despite lacking direct control and the presence of distinct, formal organizational boundaries, many organizations still deem the outsourced employees who design and manufacture their company products and provide company services as worthy of their

Global Workforce Professional Profile 5.1
**Christopher North: Linking Successful HR Planning with
Social Responsibility and Human Development**

"We have a very significant interest in the immediate and long-term needs of the greater community here in Tijuana, as well as larger Mexico," says Christopher North, vice president and general manager of Aerodesign de Mexico, part of C&D Zodiac, Inc., of the United States and Zodiac, S.A., of France. Aerodesign's 430 employees in its two buildings in Tijuana, near the California, U.S.–Mexico border, design and manufacture commercial aircraft interiors (such as seats, overhead bins, and lavatories) for major aircraft manufacturers such as Airbus and Boeing. North's personal commitment to the local community is evidenced by the nonprofit organization he and his wife, Julianne, founded. Build a Miracle builds homes and provides educational opportunity in impoverished areas of Tijuana. North adds, "And our interest in the community is further reflected at Aerodesign in programs focused on employee education and training and in creative benefits programs such as housing subsidies."

North's interests in social issues in Mexico go back more than twenty years when he was an undergraduate at Loyola Marymount University in Los Angeles, where he and his wife started a student service group organizing monthly trips to orphanages and communities in northern Mexico. Part of that effort included raising over $100,000 to purchase land and build a trade school at a boy's home in Tecate, Mexico, which they ran hands-on after graduating and during the first six months of their marriage. From this experience, North saw firsthand a need to make up for the country's educational system that, due to extreme poverty and administrative obstacles, was failing to prepare youths for a future competitive labor market. After the completion of his MBA at UCLA in 1991, North founded Aerodesign along with the owners of industry leader C&D Aerospace. North translated the needs he had perceived in the nonprofit sector into HR policies, such as the following:

- Educational expense reimbursement program for school-aged children of employees
- Technical training and English language instruction
- An on-site adult education school offering primary and secondary education to employees
- Up to US$2,000 in building materials or cash as a home down-payment subsidy

"We never say no to anyone asking to take an English or technical course," says North. However, this commitment to education and skill development, for both employees and their family members, is not without significant benefit to the company. North adds, "With greater competence in English, our Mexican managers don't have to depend on me and other bilingual executives as they interact with English-speaking customers and suppliers." This development is

(continued)

Global Workforce Professional Profile 5.1 (continued)

especially important at Aerodesign because the company has no foreign-born employees besides North himself. "World Class Quality, Mexican Pride" adorns the wall above the main production area and embodies, among other things, the idea that there is no limit to how high local talent can rise at Aerodesign. North further claims that a focus on training and the resultant ability of the company to support fully integrated finished product manufacturing with engineering support have insulated the company against competition from other low-cost labor regions such as the Far East. Productivity and experience become more important than the impulse to move abroad in search of labor for under a dollar per hour.

The result of proactive HR policies such as those at Aerodesign in the long term is a stronger Mexican labor force; in the short term the company enjoys increased workforce commitment and loyalty, directly translating into productivity and employee retention. In fact, turnover at Aerodesign averages less than 12 percent annually, while other Tijuana manufacturing facilities commonly experience turnover above 100 percent per year. North has developed a strategy for dealing with both turnover and lack of formal education: "One key to manufacturing success in Mexico, whether the issue is high turnover, the lack of experienced personnel, or both, is the identification and development of a core team, an A-list of individuals at all levels that can successfully move from one project or department to another and infuse the organization's unique culture, competency, and spirit into new programs. Within this group, future leaders and managers are groomed—there are success stories that motivate others to excel."

Low turnover increases the reliability and certainty of a capable workforce that is available to meet work demand—critical to effective human resource planning and achievement of business objectives. Besides education, provision of building materials, and down-payment assistance, North has initiated other practices to build employee loyalty and retention, such as a subsidized lunch program and payment of the employee portion of the social security tax. All of these benefits are provided by the company under programs that are income tax free to the employees. "While many companies provide a lunch program or transportation subsidies, very few are aware of the existence of our other benefits programs, which by being tax free to the employees, increase their take-home pay and leverage our payroll expenditure to its maximum potential." A final benefit of creating a desirable place to work is the decrease in recruitment costs as internal employee referrals become the primary means of finding new employees. According to North, because turnover has so many causes, there is no single remedy, and only a multifaceted approach to the creation of a desirable workplace will minimize its impact. He does make it a point to debunk one myth about turnover in the border region. North explains, "One of the common misconceptions is that employees who come from the south to work here only do so for a brief stay until they can find a way to get across the U.S. border. This is simply not the case. The majority who come here to work for our company and other manufacturing facilities are much more likely to stay here or return to the south than to cross the border."

ongoing consideration, retaining various practices and procedures in the outsourcing agreement to ensure the high quality of employee performance. For example, this consideration is at the root of intensive training provided for internationally sourced call center workers on American culture, slang, and communication styles. And Japanese auto manufacturers, with their concern for consistent high quality, have long provided quality-improvement training for the employees of their outsourced U.S. auto parts suppliers—not simply assuming that the outsourced organization will take care of this important area of employee management.[101]

As the opening case of this chapter illustrated, organizations can also suffer significant costs in image and public relations—both at home and abroad—when they outsource employment services and, with this cost-savings strategy, also divorce a sense of social responsibility to the outsourced employees, who nevertheless are still associated with the company's product. Levi Strauss & Co., long noted for being an employer of choice and having a strong commitment to social responsibility, appears to have a strong sense of their global employees—both internal and external—worthy of their HR planning and consideration. In 1991, Levi Strauss made basic worker rights a public priority by becoming the first multinational company to establish a comprehensive code of conduct, known as "Terms of Engagement," designed to serve as a guide in the selection of countries and foreign business partners (that is, contractors and subcontractors who manufacture or finish Levi products and suppliers who provide the material) that follows workplace standards and business practices consistent with the company's employee treatment values and policies. A team of internal inspectors audits facilities for compliance with the Terms of Engagement both before and after Levi Strauss enters into a business relationship. Their inspectors currently monitor compliance at approximately six hundred cutting, sewing, and finishing contractors in more than sixty countries.[102]

HR PLANNING FOR THE LONG TERM

Besides regularly scanning the environment for threats and opportunities in the external labor supply related to meeting immediate and short-term work demand for carrying out MNC objectives, HR planning should also study external trends and conditions pertinent to the firm's long-term survival and competitiveness. In addition, MNCs should look internally for the long term to consider the MNC's organizational culture and core capabilities that it desires to build across its global workforce in the coming years as well as plan for the future managers and leaders who will successfully direct the MNC.

COUNTRY LABOR FORECASTING

Environmental scanning should consider such longer-range factors as national birthrate statistics, health conditions and mortality, the nature and quality of educational systems within a country, and changing demographic trends in workforce participation to gain a clearer picture of the nature of the global labor force available for supplying long-term future work demand (that is, for the next five or ten years).[103] For example, several developed countries in Europe and Asia are reporting a significant decrease in birth rates, presenting a challenging economic future with a larger percentage of older workers and retirees and fewer younger workers, placing increasing demands on health care and retirement benefits.[104] In particular, Russia's demographic profile has several serious implications for the country's economic future pertinent to HR planning. According to one study, in the absence of large-scale immigration, Russia with its low birth rate will not have the labor resources to sustain high economic growth rates. In addition, poor health conditions and mortality will affect the quality of the workforce and make it all the more difficult to sustain the productivity improvements needed for desired growth in support of continued economic transition.[105] Related to national education trends, it has been reported that the United Kingdom is among the lowest in participation rate in advanced secondary education in countries of the European Union and lags considerably behind Germany, France, and the Netherlands in the extent of post-school training that young people receive while same-aged cohorts pursue higher education.[106] Pertinent to MNCs in their long-range planning for international work sourcing, this information suggests that in the years ahead the labor market in the United Kingdom might have less of a local labor force capability for meeting the work demand of high-tech and knowledge-based jobs.

HR Planning for Global Capability

Global HR planning should keep in mind what it wants to become in the long run related to organization capability—including shared organizational core competencies and culture and workforce alignment or shared mind-set—and plan its HR activities and policies accordingly.[107] For example, Royal Dutch/Shell desired to develop a "multicultural multinational" organization, where the senior management team at its London headquarters would become more globally competent in its long-range and top-level decision making. Therefore, to achieve this strategic objective it used global HR planning to develop specific policies and practices in international workforce staffing and development that resulted in thirty-eight countries being represented among its London senior management team.[108]

International firms large and small also should carefully plan their selection, training, performance management, and remuneration practices to support the acquisition of common core priorities and competencies that promote alignment and coordination across national boundaries.[109] This increased alignment and coordination in turn can contribute to faster, consistent, high-quality responsiveness to customer needs around the globe. For example, the great global success of McDonald's has been based largely on the company's ability to quickly transfer to foreign entrepreneurs the overall capability of managing the entire complex McDonald's business system in a consistent manner, yet with sensitivity to local market conditions. In addition, the development of an MNC culture characterized by common values, beliefs, priorities, and identification with the company also creates a deep and enduring structural mechanism within the MNC to informally teach, influence, and reinforce desirable behavior throughout the MNC.

Companies that have as a major strategic objective to develop greater company-wide global leadership capability have been encouraged to increase, through global HR planning, their number of young managers involved in extended foreign assignment experiences (including inpatriation). Here the expatriate is sent abroad more for the purpose of individual professional development (and collectively over time, organizational development) than for accomplishing more traditional business goals abroad.[110] Furthermore, an expatriate assignment should be considered as only a part of the employee's experience with the organization; longer-range HR planning should consider expatriate return (repatriation), placement, and ongoing career development. In fact, some companies have created positions in charge of global talent management, where a professional or team is responsible for setting up systems to identify potential leaders, track careers company-wide, provide and structure a variety of international experiences, and monitor assignment performance for future planning.[111] Some MNCs also actively promote internal MNC sharing and dissemination of new knowledge and experience gained from foreign assignments for enhancing global orientation, alignment, and leadership capability.[112]

GLOBAL SUCCESSION PLANNING

Global succession planning concerns the careful selection of talented employees for calculated grooming and eventual replacement of senior managers who leave the MNC because of retirement, reassignment, or for other reasons. Effective succession planning aims for minimal disruption and confusion arising from such leadership changes, with a view to implementing company strategy and achieving organizational goals in a smooth and continuous manner. There is strong evidence that companies with a predetermined, formal succession plan for their senior managerial assignments, including two levels below the top, enjoy a higher return on investment than those without such a plan.[113] These succession plans include detailed developmental strategies and activities for their managers to make the plans work. According to Robert Gandossy, global practice leader of leadership consulting at Hewitt Associates, the most effective global companies for the long term are " . . . able to groom a near-constant supply of world-class leaders . . . year after year and regardless of economic conditions." He believes that this internal developmental capability to support succession plans gives these firms a unique competitive advantage.[114] MNCs should engage in careful global succession planning to reduce chance and uncertainty about the availability of senior executive leadership talent for future company guidance. In some companies, succession planning is integrated into a twice-yearly people-review process. Global succession planning first involves making a projection of future needs for senior managers within the firm. Then there is a careful selection from pools of promising manager candidates throughout the MNC to find those best suited to fill higher-level management positions. Finally, a flexible plan is formulated to ensure that these potential successors develop the core competencies needed to advance the strategic interests of the organization. To further develop this plan, management and human resources should work collaboratively with the identified, interested high-potential individuals to design six-month, one-year, and three-year development activities—with regular opportunities for feedback and reassessment—

involving such activities as formal training, international virtual teams, short-term foreign assignments, and extended foreign assignments.[115]

SUMMARY

Global HR planning provides a vital link between MNC strategy and the implementation of strategy through the human factor. Global HR planning should scan the environment for both immediate and longer-term threats and opportunities as they influence the supply of labor and human talent to meet immediate and anticipated long-term work demand. This critical function also should carefully examine appropriate approaches for organizing and designing work and working arrangements to meet company objectives as well as carefully consider sources of talent—both internal and external—for filling work demand. Finally, HR planning should look internally to design and coordinate various HR activities that build long-range capability to ensure MNC survival and competitiveness.

QUESTIONS FOR OPENING SCENARIO ANALYSIS

1. What changes in global work supply have taken place that contributed to the situation of Gap and its global workforce?
2. What are possible forces that might contribute to an MNC's lack of a sense of responsibility toward workers in different parts of the world who produce its products or deliver its services? In fact, what external forces can even interfere with this sense of responsibility?
3. Is this opening scenario dealing only with a global phenomenon? Can you think of local work outsourcing arrangements (such as within a university campus boundaries) where there is a clear gap between the nature of treatment and benefits of an organization's regular employees and nearby outsourced or contracted workers who also supply needed labor to meet the organization's work demand?

CASE 5.1. HR PLANNING FOR EXECUTIVE-LEVEL GENDER DIVERSITY

It isn't easy for a woman to gain top-level positions in large MNCs, even in our "modern" age. This added difficulty for women reaching the executive suite should be a major concern for HR planning, which aims at providing a capable workforce to meet future work challenges and demands. Gender-based obstacles end up greatly limiting the talent pool for the company's future leadership and leads to less insightful executive teams that lack a diversity of perspectives and experiences that match a more evenly gendered, lower-level employee and customer profile. It is especially hard for women to get to the top in a firm that is in a masculine line of business, but Fran Keeth is a major exception. Fran holds both global and regional positions with Shell. At the global level she is executive vice president chemicals and at the regional level she is president and CEO of Shell Chemical LP, the U.S. arm of Shell Chemicals Ltd., based in London. Fran is the first woman to hold such lofty leadership in the chemicals industry.

Fran earned a bachelor's degree in accounting and then went on for an MBA and a law degree, all from the University of Houston in Texas. She started her career in Houston in 1970, at Shell Oil Company, a subsidiary of a Royal Dutch/Shell, where she worked first as a secretary while studying at the same time. Fran held many different positions in Shell Oil Company. She worked in the finance and tax departments with increasing responsibility, and in 1991, she became a general manager of Product Finance. After twenty-two years with the company, in 1992, she was sent to London as a deputy controller, area coordinator for the East Australasia regions, and oil products finance manager. She left Shell in 1996 and worked for Mobil as their worldwide controller. But one year later she returned to Shell and started to work in Shell Chemicals as global executive vice president of finance and business systems. This position led her to the position of president and CEO of Shell Chemicals in 2001, and finally to executive vice president chemicals in 2005.

Her resume seems to be quite typical, but Fran has said the fact that she is a woman made it more difficult for her to advance in the company. She experienced the unique social challenges of being a woman, such as being told to leave the conference room during a planning meeting, because the matter was "discussed only with managers," the speaker assuming that as a woman she could not possibly be a manager. Fran says that one reason for women having difficulties is that it is often assumed that women are not interested in international assignments and that they would not like to travel because of their family. She believes that this reluctance on a woman's part can be the case in some situations, but it should not be an automatic assumption. A distinct advantage for Fran was her career path that was almost completely in finance, which is seen more as a core function of the whole business rather than more support and secondary functions of sales and marketing where women often reside and remain.

One of Fran's main objectives now is to make it easier for women to develop their careers and to gain more responsibilities in her company. By 2015, the company aims to have more than 25 percent of its executive positions held by women. In 2001, the figure for women in such positions in Shell Chemicals was 11 percent. She also has created workshops for managers to gain a better understanding of the stereotypes that are common when it comes to women in higher positions. The result she hopes to see is a change in the traditional way of thinking. "The new career-advancement system will be no less based on merit than it had been when a man was in charge," Fran says. Instead, she predicts that Shell will have a broader talent pool and an environment where women will have better chances to succeed. She adds, "They will be able to put more energy into their work; they won't have to spend their time trying to fit in."

QUESTIONS FOR CASE ANALYSIS AND DISCUSSION

1. Why would you say an MNC in its HR planning should be interested in gaining a greater representation of women employees across its various employee levels, including the top leadership ranks?

2. What are particular obstacles that women might face in gaining higher positions of responsibility in their organizations? Would you consider some industries and specialties less conducive to increased women leadership?

3. What would you recommend for Fran Keeth to assist her in HR planning to achieve greater women representation among top management?

CASE 5.2. A GOOGLE SEARCH—FOR TALENT

As a leader in innovation, Google also is breaking tradition in its strategies for ensuring the availability of top human talent to meet work demand. On a sunny spring day in Bangalore, India's info-tech hub, a group of engineers and math majors, all in their twenties, hunch over terminals at an Internet café. This event is the Google India Code Jam, a contest to find the most brilliant coder in South and Southeast Asia. Participants are competing in writing some difficult code for a first prize of US $6,900 and a coveted job offer from Google, Inc., to work at one of its R&D centers. The contestants begin at 10:30 A.M., emerging exhausted three hours later. "It's been incredibly difficult and awesome," says Nitin Gupta, a computer science undergrad at the Indian Institute of Technology at Bombay.

Google has staged Code Jams in the United States, but this is its first such event in Asia, and there is an incredibly large response. Some fourteen thousand hopeful aspirants registered from all over South and Southeast Asia for the first round in February. The top fifty from that event were selected for the finals in Bangalore: thirty-nine from India, eight from Singapore, and three from Indonesia. "It's a dog-eat-dog world," says Robert Hughes, president of TopCoder, Inc., the Connecticut testing company that runs the Code Jams for Google. "Wherever the best talent is, Google wants them." With this highly publicized event, Google now has a new pool of Asian talent to choose from. According to Krishna Bharat, head of Google's India R&D center, all the finalists will be offered jobs—and Google needs them for its new but understaffed Indian center.

Google has faced a difficult staffing challenge due to fierce talent recruitment in IT, where engineering students are assured a job a year before they graduate. Adding to this challenge is Google's exacting hiring standards that surpass those of most other employers. But the Code Jam serves as a useful shortcut through its usual staffing process, where applicants usually go through seven stages that can last months and at the end are likely to get rejected due to Google's extremely high standards. But Google has found that much of this screen is done through the Code Jam approach, resulting in a final pool of viable candidates.

Source: Adapted from J. Puliyenthuruthel, "How Google Searches—For Talent," *Business Week,* April 11, 2005: 52.

QUESTIONS FOR CASE ANALYSIS AND DISCUSSION

1. How does the Code Jam method improve on more traditional HR planning approaches to ensure timely availability of appropriate talent to meet work demand?

2. How is Google's Code Jam effort consistent with an overall geocentric or regiocentric staffing approach?
3. Besides the rapid generation of viable candidates, what are other possible benefits to Google of this highly publicized Code Jam event in South and Southeast Asia?

RECOMMENDED WEB SITE RESOURCES

Hewitt Associates (http://www.hewitt.com). A global human resources outsourcing and consulting firm delivering a complete range of integrated services to help companies manage their total HR and employee costs, enhance HR services, and improve their workforces.

Human Resource Planning Society (www.hrps.org). A global association and network of senior HR executives, consultants, and university faculty and researchers.

RHR International (www.rhrinternational.com). Provides information and consulting services related to succession planning, high-potential employee development, and overall talent management.

NOTES

1. I. Stewart, "Workers Call for Holiday Gap Boycott," *Associated Press State and Local Wire,* November 28, 2002, available at: http://www.organicconsumers.org/clothes/120202_sweatshop.cfm.

2. C.R. Greer, *Strategic Human Resource Management: A General Managerial Approach,* 2d ed. (Upper Saddle River, NJ: Prentice-Hall, 2001); H. DeCieri and P.J. Dowling, "Strategic Human Resource Management in Multinational Enterprises: Theoretical and Empirical Developments," *Research in Personnel and Human Resources Management* 4 (1999): 305–27; L.K. Stroh and P.M. Caligiuri, "Strategic Human Resources: A New Source for Competitive Advantage in the Global Arena," *International Journal of Human Resource Management* 9 (1998): 1–17; M. Festing, "International Human Resource Management Strategies in Multinational Corporations: Theoretical Assumptions and Empirical Evidence from German Firms," *Management International Review* 37 (1997): 43–63; S. Taylor, S. Beechler, and N. Napier, "Towards an Integrative Model of Strategic International Human Resource Management," *Academy of Management Review* 21 (1996): 959–85; P.M. Caligiuri and L.K. Stroh, "Multinational Corporate Management Strategies and International Human Resource Practices: Bringing IHRM to the Bottom Line," *International Journal of Human Resource Management* 6 (1995): 494–507.

3. B.E. Becker, M.A. Huselid, and D. Ulrich, *The HR Scorecard: Linking People, Strategy, and Performance* (Boston: Harvard Business School Publishing, 2001); R.S. Schuler, S.E. Jackson, and J. Storey, "HRM and Its Link with Strategic Management," in *Human Resource Management: A Critical Text,* ed. J. Storey (London: International Thomson, 2000): 115–32.

4. D. Ulrich and N. Smallwood, "Capitalizing on Capabilities," *Harvard Business Review* 82 (6) (2004): 119–27; H.P. Conn and G.S. Yip, "Global Transfer of Critical Capabilities," *Business Horizons* 40 (1) (1997): 22–31.

5. C.R. Greer, *Strategic Human Resource Management.*

6. "The New Global Shift," *BusinessWeek Online,* February 3, 2004, www.businessweek.com/magazine/content/03_05/b3818001.htm; W. Underhill, "Estonia: Hack Heaven; Eastern Europe's Whiz Kids Make Good," *Newsweek,* July 26, 2004; N. Spiro, "Central Europe's Investment Drive," *Global Finance* 18 (4) (2004): 24–27.

7. M. Fong, "A Chinese Puzzle: Surprising Shortage of Workers Forces Factories to Add Perks: Pressure on Pay—and Prices," *Wall Street Journal,* August 16, 2004.

8. C. Hendry, *Human Resource Strategies for International Growth* (London: Routledge, 1994).

9. Americans' fears of "the great sucking sound," created by the large departure of American jobs heading south into Mexico due to the passage of the North America Free Trade Agreement, seem at least on a national level to have been ill-founded, with various reports indicating a restructuring of job types (for example, lower-skilled jobs increasing in Mexico), with a net gain of jobs and trade for the United States, Mexico, and Canada due to NAFTA. For example, refer to G. Mohar, K. Fanning, E. Chelini, and S. Tanger, "A Silent Integration," *Business Mexico* 15 (3) (2005): 46–47; M. Heller, "Trade Statistics Show NAFTA Benefits Canadian Exports to U.S.," *Knight Ridder Tribute Business News,* December 11, 2004; K. Cook, "NAFTA: A Clear Success for U.S. and Mexican Textile and Cotton Trade," *AgExporter* 16 (1): 22–23.

10. D.T. Griswold, "Outsource, Outsource, and Outsource Some More," *National Review* 56 (8) (2004): 36–38; S. Hirsh, "Economy Moves to Front of Presidential Campaign," *Knight Ridder Tribune Business News,* August 15, 2004.

11. B.S. Javorcik, "Does Foreign Direct Investment Increase the Productivity of Domestic Firms? In Search of Spillovers through Backward Linkages," *American Economic Review* 94 (3) (2004): 605–27.

12. M. Hart-Landsberg and P. Burkett, "Contradictions of China's Transformation: International," *Monthly Review* 56 (3) (2004): 81; A. Wong and K. Tan, "2004 Malaysian Budget: Building on Success, Investing for the Future," *Journal of International Taxation* 15 (2) (2004): 43–45; T.C. Choe, "Romania Set to Strengthen Economic Fundamentals and Outlook," *Business Times* 22 (December 2003); J. Ermisch and W. Huff, "Hypergrowth in an East Asian NIC: Public Policy and Capital Accumulation in Singapore," *World Development* 27 (1) (1999): 21–38.

13. International Labour Organization, *Termination of Employment Digest: A Legislative Review* (Geneva: International Labour Office, 2000), available at www.ilo.org; C. Evans-Klock et al., "Worker Retrenchment: Preventive and Remedial Measures," *International Labour Review* 138 (1) (1999): 47–66.

14. D.R. Briscoe and R.S. Schuler, *International Human Resource Management,* 2d ed. (London: Routledge, 2004): 140–41; Z. Ye, "Migrant Women Negotiate Foreign Investment in Southern Chinese Factories," *Signs* 29 (2) (2004): 540–43; B. Edwards, "Selling Free Trade in Central America," *NACLA Report on the Americas* 37 (5) (2004): 8–9; T. Guay, J.P. Doh, G. Sinclair, "Non-Governmental Organizations, Shareholder Activism, and Socially Responsible Investments: Ethical, Strategic, and Governance Implications," *Journal of Business Ethics* 52 (1) (2004): 125–39; K.J. Min, "Labour Pains," *Far Eastern Economic Review* 166 (2)7 (2003): 19; J.P. Doh and H. Teegen, *Globalization and NGOs: Transforming Business, Governments, and Society* (Westport, CT: Praeger, 2003).

15. K.E. Meyer, "Perspectives on Multinational Enterprises in Emerging Economies," *Journal of International Business Studies* 35 (4) (2004): 259–76; S.S. Makki and A. Somwaru, "Impact of Foreign Direct Investment and Trade on Economic Growth: Evidence from Developing Countries," *Journal of Agricultural Economics* 86 (3) (2004): 795–801.

16. A. Taylor, "Toyota's Secret Weapon," *Fortune* 150 (4) (2004): 60–64; C. Couch, "Riding the Lean Tornado," *Manufacturing Engineering* 132 (6) (2004): 14–15; J.B. Treece, "How Toyota Threw Out the Old to Start Anew," *Automotive News* 78 (6098) (2004): 30D–31D; D.R. Stewart, "Southwest Airlines Reports 52nd Straight Profitable Quarter," *Knight Ridder Tribune Business News,* April 16, 2004; L. Tanner, "Corporate University Approach Taking Hold," *Dallas Business Journal* 26 (51) (2003): 31.

17. A. Staab, *The European Union Explained: Institutions, Actors, Global Impact* (Bloomington, IN: Indiana University Press, 2008); Refer to "The EU at a Glance," available at http://europa.eu/abc/european_countries/index_en.htm.

18. L. Claus, "Similarities and Differences in Human Resource Management in the European Union," *Thunderbird International Business Review* 45 (6) (2003): 729; C. Martin and I. Sanz, "Real Convergence and European Integration: The Experience of the Less Developed EU Members," *Empirica* 30 (3) (2003): 205; T. Glover, "BT Benefits as European Companies Move Back Offices to Low-Cost Countries," *Knight Ridder Tribune Business News,* June 15, 2003.

19. C. Costello, ed., *Fundamental Social Rights: Current European Legal Protection and the Challenge of the EU Charter on Fundamental Rights* (East Kilbride, Scotland: Kilbride Books, 2001); R. Nielsen, and E. Szyszczak, eds., *The Social Dimension of the European Union* (Copenhagen: Copenhagen Business School Press, 1997); L. Senden, "Anti-Discrimination Law and the European Union,"

Common Market Law Review 41 (1) (2004): 278–82; G. Chivers, "EC Could Ban Working over the 48-Hour Week," *Computer Weekly,* February 24, 2004; OECD, *Codes of Corporate Conduct: An Inventory* (Paris: OECD, 1998); B. Birmingham, "Social Security and Pension Arrangements for Workers Posted Abroad and Their Employers," *Pensions: An International Journal* 8 (2) (2003): 109–26; P. Hofheinz, "European Battle Is Taking Shape over Temp Work-EU Ministers Will Take Up a Proposal to Expand Rights of Short-Term Labor," *Wall Street Journal,* October 3, 2002.

20. "Asia: Muscle for Hire; China," *Economist,* January 10, 2004; M. Kiriakova, "Terrorist Attacks: A Protective Service Guide for Executives, Body Guards, and Policemen," *Law Enforcement News* 28 (576) (2002): S13; J. Gray, "Strongarm Tactics: Every CEO Needs a Bodyguard, a True Symbol of Status," *Canadian Business* 73 (10) (2000): 69; D.J. Schemo, "U.S. Companies Operate in Colombia, but Very Carefully," *New York Times,* November 6, 1998; N. Banerjee, "BP Amoco Discovers Risks of Doing Business in Russia," *Journal Record,* August 17, 1999, 1.

21. G. Dessler, *Human Resource Management,* 9th ed. (Upper Saddle River, NJ: Prentice-Hall International Editions, 2003).

22. W.F. Cascio, *Managing Human Resources: Productivity, Quality of Work Life, Profits,* 6th ed. (New York: McGraw-Hill/Irwin, 2003).

23. W. Mondy and R. Noe, *Human Resource Management,* 9th ed. (Upper Saddle River, NJ: Prentice-Hall, 2005).

24. G. Hofstede, *Culture's Consequences: International Differences in Work-Related Values* (Newbury Park, CA: Sage, 1980).

25. C.M. Vance and Y. Paik, "One Size Fits All in Expatriate Pre-Departure Training? Comparing the Host Country Voices of Mexican, Indonesian and U.S. Workers," *Journal of Management Development* 21 (7) (2002): 557–71.

26. H.C. Triandis, "Vertical and Horizontal Individualism and Collectivism: Theory and Research Implications for International Comparative Management," in *Advances in International Comparative Management,* ed. J.L.C. Cheng et al. (Stamford, CT: JAI Press, 1998): 7–35.

27. J. Nathan, *The Colonel Comes to Japan* (New York: Learning Corp. of America, 1981).

28. T. Masumoto, "Learning to 'Do Time' in Japan: A Study of US Interns in Japanese Organizations," *International Journal of Cross Cultural Management* 4 (1) (2004): 19–37.

29. J. Olivella, L. Cuatrecasas, and N. Gavilan, "Work Organisation Practices for Lean Production," *Journal of Manufacturing Technology Management* 19 (7) (2008): 798–811; G. Liu, R. Shah, and R.G. Schroeder, "Linking Work Design to Mass Customization: A Sociotechnical Systems Perspective," *Decision Sciences* 37 (4)(2006): 519–45.

30. "Former Employees a Growing IT Security Threat," *PR Newswire,* November 10, 2009; J. Mulki, F. Bardhi, F. Lassk, and J. Nanavaty-Dahl, "Set Up Remote Workers to Thrive," *Sloan Management Review* 51 (1) (2009): 63–69; J.T. Arnold, "Twittering and Facebooking While They Work," *HR Magazine* 54 (12) (2009): 53–55.

31. R. Reich, "The Jobs Picture Still Looks Bleak," *Wall Street Journal,* April 12, 2010; "The Price of Efficiency; Stop Blaming Outsourcing. The Drive for Productivity Gains Is the Real Culprit behind Anemic Job Growth," *BusinessWeek,* March 22, 2004; S.J. Glain, "Economists Say 'Offshoring' Overblown as a Problem," *Knight Ridder Tribune Business* (March 13, 2004): 1.

32. "The New World of Work: Flexibility Is the Watchword," *Business Week,* January 20, 2000); M. Conlin, "9 to 5 Isn't Working Anymore," *Business Week,* September 20, 1999; W.F. Cascio, "Managing a Virtual Workplace," *Academy of Management Review* 14 (3) (2000): 81–90.

33. M. Laff, "Teams that Stay, While on the Go," *Training and Development* 63 (7) (2009): 18–19.

34. Danish Board of Technology, "Teknologi-Radet," *Conclusions from a Conference on Teleworking* (convened by the Danish Board of Technology, Copenhagen May 2–5, 1997), www.tekno.dk/eng/piblicat/teleworks/htm.

35. Laff, "Teams that Stay, While on the Go," 18–19; Society for Human Resource Management "The New Workforce: Generation Y," *Workplace Visions* 2 (2001): 1–7.

36. J.A. Hauser, "The Dollars and Sense of International Assignments," *Workspan* 47 (2) (2004):

30–35; L. Shotwell, "The American Council on International Personnel: Facilitating the Movement of International Personnel," *Migration World Magazine* 30 (3) (2002): 35–36; "Business: Nasty, Brutish and Short," *Economist* (December 16, 2000): 70–71.

37. K. Johnson and L. Duxbury, "The View from the Field: A Case Study of the Expatriate Boundary-Spanning Role," *Journal of World Business,* 45 (1) (2010): 29–40.

38. Personal e-mail from David Cheung, Chief Financial Officer, Otis Elevator (China) Investment Co., Ltd., Tianjin, People's Republic of China, August 16, 2004.

39. Windham International, *Global Relocation Trends 1999 Survey Report, May 1999.* This survey was based on responses of 264 major U.S. MNCs, with input from approximately 75,000 expatriates, www.gmacglobalrelocation.com/WhitePapers/whtpprs.pdf.

40. M.E. Mendenhall, H.B. Gregersen, and J.S. Black, *Globalizing People through International Assignments* (New York: Addison-Wesley, 1999); D.A. Ondrack, "International Human Resources Management in European and North American Firms," *International Studies of Management and Organization* 9 (1985): 6–32; A. Edstrom and J.R. Galbraith, "Transfer of Managers as a Coordination and Control Strategy in Multinational Organizations," *Administrative Science Quarterly* 22 (1977): 248–63.

41. V. Pucik, "Globalization and Human Resource Management," in *Globalizing Management: Creating and Leading the Competitive Organization,* ed. V. Pucik, N.M. Tichy, and C.K. Barnett (New York: Wiley, 1992): 61–81.

42. G.R. Oddou, "Managing Your Expatriates: What the Successful Firms Do," *HR Planning* 14 (4) (1991): 301–8.

43. H.P. Conn and G.S. Yip, "Global Transfer of Critical Capabilities," *Business Horizons* 40 (1) (1997): 22–31; D. Ondrack, "International Transfers of Managers in North American and European MNCs," *Journal of International Business Studies* 16 (3) (1985): 1–19; A. Jaeger, "Contrasting Control Modes in the Multinational Corporation: Theory, Practice, and Implications," *International Studies of Management and Organization* 12 (1) (1982): 59–82.

44. S. Wang, T.W. Tong, G. Chen, and H. Kim, "Expatriate Utilization and Foreign Direct Investment Performance: The Mediating Role of Knowledge Transfer," *Journal of Management* 35 (5) (2009): 1181–1206; J.B. Hocking, M.E. Brown, and A.-W. Harzing, "Balancing Global and Local Strategic Contexts: Expatriate Knowledge Transfer, Applications and Learning Within a Transnational Organization," *Human Resource Management* 46 (4) (2007): 513–33; M. Downes and A.S. Thomas, "Knowledge Transfer through Expatriation: The U-Curve Approach to Overseas Staffing," *Journal of Managerial Issues* 12 (2002): 131–49; A. Bird, "International Assignments and Careers as Repositories of Knowledge," in *Developing Global Business Leaders: Policies, Processes, and Innovations,* ed. M.E. Mendenhall, T.M. Kuhlmann, and G.K. Stahl (Westport, CT: Quorum Books, 2001): 19–36.

45. "Expatriate Adjustment and Performance: An Analysis of Interviews with American Expatriate Business Managers and Executives," ExpatRepat Services, Inc. (2000), www.expat-repat.com/research_report.htm.

46. H. Lee, "Factors that Influence Expatriate Failure: An Interview Study," *International Journal of Management* 24 (3) (2007): 403–13; V. Suutari and C. Brewster, "Repatriation: Evidence from a Longitudinal Study of Careers and Empirical Expectations among Finish Repatriates," *International Journal of Human Resource Management* 14 (7) (2003): 1132–51; J.S. Black and H.B. Gregersen, "The Right Way to Manage Expats," *Harvard Business Review* 77 (March/April, 1999): 52–63.

47. Windham International, *Global Relocation Trends 1999 Survey Report* (New York, 1999).

48. B.S. Reiche, "The Effect of International Staffing Practices On Subsidiary Staff Retention in Multinational Corporations," *International Journal of Human Resource Management* 18 (4) (2007): 523–36; C.M. Vance and E.S. Paderon, "An Ethical Argument for Host Country Workforce Training and Development in the Expatriate Management Assignment," *Journal of Business Ethics* 12 (8) (1993): 635–41.

49. Y. Fang, G. Jiang, S. Makino, and P. Beamish, "Multinational Firm Knowledge, Use of Expatriates, and Foreign Subsidiary Performance," *The Journal of Management Studies,* 47 (1) (2010): 27–54; M. Harvey, M.M. Novicevic, M.R. Buckley, and H. Fung, "Reducing Inpatriate Managers' 'Liability of Foreignness' by Addressing Stigmatization and Stereotype Threats," *Journal of World Business*

40 (3) (2005): 267–80; M. Harvey and M. Novicevic, "The Influence of Inpatriation Practices on the Strategic Orientation of a Global Organization," *International Journal of Management* 17 (3) (2000): 362–71.

50. S. Colakuglu and P. Caligiuri, "Cultural Distance, Expatriate Staffing and Subsidiary Performance: The Case of US Subsidiaries of Multinational Corporations," *International Journal of Human Resource Management* 19 (2) (2008): 223–29.

51. B.S. Reiche, "The Inpatriate Experience in Multinational Corporations: An Exploratory Case Study in Germany," *International Journal of Human Resource Management* 17 (9) (2006): 1572–90; M. Harvey, M. Novicevic, and C. Speier, "Strategic Global Human Resource Management: The Role of Inpatriate Managers," *Human Resource Management Review* 10 (2) (2000): 153–75; M. Harvey, D. Ralston, and N. Napier, "International Relocation of Inpatriate Managers: Assessing and Facilitating Acceptance in the Headquarters' Organization," *International Journal of Intercultural Relations* 24 (6) (2000): 825–46.

52. C.M. Vance and Y. Paik, "Toward a Taxonomy of Host Country National Learning Process Involvement in Multinational Learning Organizations" (paper presented at the Annual Meeting of the Academy of Management, Washington, DC, August 2001); Harvey and Novicevic, "The Influence of Inpatriation Practices on the Strategic Orientation of a Global Organization," 362–71; M.G. Harvey, M.F. Price, C. Speir, and M.M. Novicevic, "The Role of Inpatriates in a Globalization Strategy and Challenges Associated with the Inpatriation Process," *HR Planning* 22 (1) (1999): 38–50.

53. C.M. Vance and E.A. Ensher, "The Voice of the Host Country Workforce: A Key Source for Improving the Effectiveness of Expatriate Training and Performance," *International Journal of Intercultural Relations* 26 (2002): 447–61; J. Martinez and J. Quelch, "Country Managers: The Next Generation," *International Marketing Review* 13 (3) (1996): 709–34; J. Quelch, "The New Country Manager," *McKinsey Quarterly* 4 (1992): 155–65; C. Bartlett and S. Ghoshal, "What Is a Global Manager?" *Harvard Business Review* 70 (1992): 124–32.

54. M. Harvey and M.R. Buckley, "Managing Inpatriates: Building a Global Core Competency," *Journal of World Business* 32 (1) (1997): 35–52.

55. Harvey, Ralston, and Napier, "International Relocation of Inpatriate Managers," 825–46.

56. J.M. Nilles, *Managing Telework: Strategies for Managing the Virtual Workforce* (New York: John Wiley and Sons, 1998); P.F. Jackson and J.M. Van der Wielen, eds., *Teleworking: International Perspectives: From Telecommuting to the Virtual Organization* (London: Routledge, 1998).

57. A.M. Greene, "A Virtual Reality?" *CA Magazine* 134 (1) (2001): 10.

58. J. Flynn, "E-Mail, Cellphones and Frequent-Flier Miles Let 'Virtual' Expats Work Abroad, but Live at Home," *Wall Street Journal,* October 25, 1999.

59. T.R. Kayworth and D.E. Leidner, "Leadership Effectiveness in Global Virtual Teams," *Journal of Management Information Systems* 18 (2001): 7–40; B.L. Kirkman, B. Rosen, C.B. Gibson, P.E. Tesluk, and S.O. McPherson, "Five Challenges to Virtual Team Success: Lessons from Sabre, Inc.," *Academy of Management Executive* 16 (3) (2002): 67–79.

60. S.A. Furst, M. Reeves, B. Rosen, and R.S. Blackburn, "Managing the Life Cycle of Virtual Teams," *Academy of Management Executive* 18 (2) (2004): 6–20; B.L. Kirkman, B. Rosen, P.E. Tesluk, and C.B. Gibson, "The Impact of Team Empowerment on Virtual Team Performance: The Moderating Role of Face-to-Face Interaction," *Academy of Management Journal* 47 (2): 175–92; E. Kelley, "Keys to Effective Virtual Global Teams," *Academy of Management Executive* 15 (2) (2001): 132–33; M.K. Ahuja and J.E. Galvin, "Socialization in Virtual Groups," *Journal of Management* 29 (2001): 1–25; M.L Maznevski and K.M. Chudoba, "Bridging Space Over Time: Global Virtual-Team Dynamics and Effectiveness," *Organization Science* 11 (2000): 473–92.

61. C. Saunders, C.V. Slyke, and D.R. Vogel, "My Time or Yours? Managing Time Visions in Global Virtual Teams," *Academy of Management Executive* 18 (1) (2004): 19–31; J.C. Gluesing, T.C. Alcordo, M.L. Baba et al., "The Development of Global Virtual Teams," in *Virtual Teams That Work: Creating Conditions for Virtual Team Effectiveness,* ed. C.B. Gibson and S.G. Cohen (San Francisco: Jossey-Bass, 2003): 353–80; M.L. Maznevski and N.A. Athanassiou, "Designing the Knowledge-Management

Infrastructure for Virtual Teams: Building and Using Social Networks and Social Capital," in *Virtual Teams That Work:* 196–213.

62. M. Montoya-Weiss, A.P. Massey, and M. Song, "Getting It Together: Temporal Coordination and Conflict Management in Global Virtual Teams," *Academy of Management Journal* 44 (6) (2001): 1251–63.

63. B. Williamson, "Managing at a Distance," *Business Week,* July 27, 2009; A. Overholt, "Virtually There?" *Fast Company* 56 (March 2002): 108–14; R. Ocker, S. Hiltz, M. Turoff, and J. Fjermestad, "The Effects of Distributed Group Support and Process Structuring on Software Requirements Development Teams: Results on Creativity and Quality," *Journal of Management Information Systems* 12 (3) (1995–96): 127–53.

64. J. Wernau, "Temp-Work Rise a Ray of Hope in Jobs Picture: October Increase Could Presage Gain in Permanent Jobs," *Tribune Business News* (November 7, 2009); R. Blumenthal, "Bring on the Temps," *Barron's,* 89 (11) (2009): 15; S. Strom, "In Japan, a Shift in the Culture by Freelancers," *New York Times,* November 16, 2000.

65. S.J. Kobrin, "Expatriate Reduction and Strategic Control in American Multinational Corporations," *Human Resource Management* 27 (2) (1998): 63–76.

66. R.A. Belderbos and M.G. Heijltjes, "The Determinants of Expatriate Staffing by Japanese Multinationals in Asia: Control, Learning and Vertical Business Groups," *Journal of International Business Studies,* 36 (3) (2005): 341–54; J.A. Volkmar, "Context and Control in Foreign Subsidiaries: Making a Case for the Host Country National Manager," *Journal of Leadership & Organizational Studies* 10 (1) (2003): 93–105.

67. Conn and Yip, "Global Transfer of Critical Capabilities," 22–31.

68. C. Reynolds, "Strategic Employment of Third Country Nationals," *HR Planning* 20 (1) (1997): 33–39.

69. "Travelling More Lightly: Staffing Globalisation," *The Economist* June 22, 2006; PricewaterhouseCoopers, *International Assignments: European Policy and Practice* (Europe: PricewaterhouseCoopers 1997–98).

70. Thomas C. Greble, "A Leading Role for HR in Alternative Staffing," *HR Magazine* 42 (February 1997): 99–104.

71. Laff, "Teams that Stay, While on the Go," (2009); Anonymous, "Where are Contract Workers Filling Talent Gaps?" *HR Focus,* 86 (3) (2009): 10–11; M. Smith, C. Fagen, and J. Rubery, "Where and Why Is Part-Time Work Growing in Europe?" in *Part-Time Prospects: An International Comparison of Part-Time Work in Europe, North America, and the Pacific Rim,* ed. J. O'Reilly and C. Fagan (New York: Routledge, 1998): 35–56.

72. I. Speizer, "An On-Demand Workforce," *Workforce Management* 88 (11) (2009): 45–49.

73. Laff, "Teams that Stay, While on the Go"; M. Gunderson, "Contingent and Informal Sector Workers in North America," *Perspectives on Work* 5 (1) (2001): 27–29; S. Strom, "In Japan, a Shift in the Culture by Freelancers," *New York Times,* November 16, 2000; E.L. Andrews, "Sweden, the Welfare State, Basks in a New Prosperity," *New York Times,* October 8, 1999, A1; H. Cooper and T. Kamm, "Loosening Up: Much of Europe Eases Its Rigid Labor Laws, and Temps Proliferate," *Wall Street Journal,* June 4, 1998; S. Strom, "Japan's New 'Temp' Workers," *New York Times,* June 17, 1998, C1; E.L. Andrews, "Only Employment for Many in Europe Is Part-Time Work," *New York Times,* September 1, 1997.

74. J. Mangan, *Workers without Traditional Employment: An International Study of Non-Standard Work* (Northampton, MA: Edward Elgar, 2000).

75. B. Pfau-Effinger, "Culture or Structure as Explanations for Differences in Part-Time Work in Germany, Finland, and the Netherlands," in *Part-Time Prospects: An International Comparison of Part-Time Work in Europe, North America, and the Pacific Rim,* ed. J. O'Reilly and C. Fagan (New York: Routledge, 1998): 177–98.

76. I. Speizer, "An On-Demand Workforce," *Workforce Management* 88 (11) (2009): 45–49; P. Allan, "The Contingent Workforce: Challenges and New Directions," *American Business Review* 20 (2002): 2, 103–10; B.J. Feder, "Bigger Roles for Suppliers of Temporary Workers," *New York Times,* April 1, 1995, 37.

77. J. Schramm, "For Now, Avoiding Ties That Bind," *HR Magazine* 54 (11) (2009): 84; J. Sullivan, "A Flexible Force," *Workforce Management* 87 (12) (2008): 58.

78. J. Romeyn, "Flexible Working Time: Part-Time and Casual Employment," Industrial Relations Research Monograph 1, University of New South Wales, June 1992.

79. F.D. Blau, M.A. Ferber, and A.E. Winkler, *The Economics of Women, Men and Work,* 3d ed. (Upper Saddle River, NJ: Prentice-Hall, 1998).

80. "The New World of Work: Flexibility Is the Watchword," *BusinessWeek,* January 10, 2000; also M. Conlin, "9 to 5 Isn't Working Anymore," *BusinessWeek,* September 20, 1999; U.S. Department of Labor, "Workers on Flexible and Shift Schedules in 1998," in *Labor Force Statistics from the Current Population Survey* (1999).

81. C. Cousins, "Changing Regulatory Frameworks and Non-Standard Employment: A Comparison of Germany, Spain, Sweden, and the UK," in *Global Trends in Flexible Labour,* ed. A. Felstead and N. Jewson (London: Macmillan, 1999): 100–20; B. Burchell, S. Deakin, and S. Honey, *The Employment Status of Individuals in Non-Standard Employment* (Cambridge, UK: ESRC Center for Business Research and Department of Trade and Industry, 1999).

82. E.L. Andrews, "Only Employment for Many in Europe Is Part-Time Work," *New York Times,* September 1, 1997, A1.

83. M. Trottman, "Employer Firms See Burgeoning Market," *Wall Street Journal,* June 24, 1998.

84. Mondy and Noe, *Human Resource Management.*

85. Smith, Fagen, and Rubery, "Where and Why Is Part-Time Work Growing in Europe?" 35–56.

86. J. Laabs, "Global Temps Fill the Workforce Void," *Workforce* (October 1998): 60–68.

87. H. Tan and C. Tan, "Temporary Employees in Singapore: What Drives Them?" *Journal of Psychology* 136 (1) (2002): 83–102.

88. Blumenthal, "Bring on the Temps"; Strom, "In Japan, a Shift in the Culture by Freelancers."

89. Anonymous, "Physician Temps," *Trustee,* 62 (5) (2009): 5; Anonymous, "Where are Contract Workers Filling Talent Gaps? (2009).

90. R.L. Rose and M. Dubois, "Temporary Help Firms Start New Game: Going Global," *Wall Street Journal,* June 5, 1996.

91. R.S. Belous, "Coming to Terms with the Rise of the Contingent Workforce," in *The Human Resource Management Handbook,* ed. D. Lewin, J.B. Mitchell, and M.A. Zaidi (Stamford, CT: JAI Press, 1997): Part 11, 3–19.

92. C.M. Solomon, "Moving Jobs to Offshore Markets: Why It's Done and How It Works," *Workforce,* 78 (7) (1999): 50–55.

93. "Business: America's Pain, India's Gain: Outsourcing," *Economist,* January 11, 2003.

94. V. Mehta, "Outsourcing to India," *Mortgage Banking* 62 (12) (2002): 76–84.

95. "Offshore Outsourcing and America's Competitive Edge: Losing Out in the High Technology R and D and Services Sectors." White paper prepared by the Office of U.S. Senator Joseph I. Lieberman (May 11, 2004), available at http://lieberman.senate.gov/newsroom/whitepapers/Offshoring.pdf.

96. S. Thurm, "Lessons in India: Not Every Job Translates Overseas," *Wall Street Journal,* March 3, 2004.

97. D. Chadee and R. Raman, "International Outsourcing of Information Technology Services: Review and Future Directions," *International Marketing Review* 26 (4/5) (2009): 411–438.

98. D. Wagner, "Success Factors in Outsourcing Service Jobs," *Sloan Management Review.* 48 (1) (2006): 7.

99. N. de Cuyper, B. Sora, H. de Witte, A. Caballer, and J.M. Peiró, "Organizations' Use of Temporary Employment and a Climate of Job Insecurity Among Belgian and Spanish Permanent Workers," *Economic and Industrial Democracy* 30 (4) (2009): 564–591; Mangan, *Workers Without Traditional Employment.*

100. M. Buckingham and C. Coffman, *First, Break All the Rules: What the World's Greatest Managers Do Differently* (New York: Simon & Schuster, 1999).

101. D. Streitfeld, "A Crash Course on Irate Calls," *Los Angeles Times,* August 2, 2004; T. Nishiguchi, *Strategic Industrial Sourcing: The Japanese Advantage* (Oxford: Oxford University Press, 1994).

102. G.A. Smith, "A Trade Policy That Works for Everyone: Why It Matters and What It Will Take," United Nations Association Forum: Globalization with a Human Face: New Groundrules for a New Era (San Francisco, October 12, 1999), available at www.globalgroundrules.org/ILOGSmith.htm.

103. K. Bock and T. Dieter, "Education and Employment in Germany: Changing Chances and Risks for Youth," *Education Economics* 6 (1) (1998): 71–92; S.P. Ellis, "Anticipating Employers' Skills Needs: The Case for Intervention," *International Journal of Manpower* 24 (1) (2003): 83–97; K.C. Krishnadas, "Applications Engineering Gains Ground in India," *Electronic Engineering Times,* December 8, 2003; E. Clifton, "Population: Rich Nations Get Richer, and The Poor Get . . . Babies," *Global Information Network,* August 20, 2004; E. Olson, "Women Called Mideast's Untapped Resource," *New York Times,* September 17, 2003; B. Yang, D. Zhang, and M. Zhang, "National Human Resource Development in the People's Republic of China," *Advances in Developing Human Resources* 6 (3) (2004): 297.

104. R. McDougall, *Europe's Baby Bust* 24 (5) (2004): 43–44; R. Johnson, "Economic Policy Implications of World Demographic Change," *Economic Review: Federal Reserve Bank of Kansas City* 89 (1) (2004): 39–64.

105. "Russia Economy: Demographic Profile," *EIU ViewsWire,* July 15, 2004.

106. Hendry, *Human Resource Strategies for International Growth.*

107. Ulrich and Smallwood, "Capitalizing on Capabilities," J. Nahapiet and S. Ghoshal, "Social Capital, Intellectual Capital, and the Organizational Advantage," *Academy of Management Review* 23 (2) (1998): 242–66.

108. "The Discreet Charm of the Multicultural Multinational," *Economist,* July 30, 1994.

109. H. Etemad, "Internationalization of Small and Medium-sized Enterprises: A Grounded Theoretical Framework and an Overview," *Canadian Journal of Administrative Sciences* 21 (1) (2004): 1–21; Conn and Yip, "Global Transfer of Critical Capabilities," 22–31.

110. Harvey and Novicevic, "The Influence of Inpatriation Practices on the Strategic Orientation of a Global Organization," 362–71; M.G. Harvey and M.R. Buckley, "Managing Inpatriates: Building a Global Core Competency," *Journal of World Business* 32 (1): 35–52; J.S. Black and H.B. Gregersen, "The Right Way to Manage Expats," *Harvard Business Review* (March/April 1999) 77: 52–63.

111. R. Freedman, "Creating Global Leaders," 189 (2003): 20; M.E. Mendenhall, T.M. Kuhlmann, and G.K. Stahl, eds., *Developing Global Business Leaders: Policies, Processes, and Innovations* (Westport, CT: Quorum Books, 2001).

112. "Colgate-Palmolive Database Captures Cultural Awareness: Expatriate Knowledge Put to Good Use," *Human Resource Management International Digest* 11 (6) (2003): 19.

113. T. Huang, "Succession Management Systems and Human Resource Outcomes," *International Journal of Manpower* 22 (7/8) (2001): 736–47; J.W. Walker, "Perspectives: Do We Need Succession Planning Anymore?" *HR Planning* 21 (3) (1998): 9–11; P. Wallum, "A Broader View of Succession Planning," *Personnel Management* 25 (9) (1993): 42–45; A. Carretta, "Career and Succession Planning," in *Competency Based Human Resource Management,* ed. A. Mitrani, M. Dalziel, and D. Fitt (London: Kogan Page, 1992).

114. "The Nation" (Thailand, MultiMedia.com, Business Section), November 30, 2009.

115. R.A. Stringer and R.S. Cheloha, "The Power of a Development Plan," *HR Planning* 26 (4) (2003): 10–17; T. Huang, "Succession Management Systems and Human Resource Outcomes," *International Journal of Manpower* 22 (7/8) (2001): 736–47.

6 Global Staffing

GLOBAL STAFFING AT THE ROYAL DUTCH/SHELL GROUP

Shell People Services handles all of the hiring for professional-level employees within the Royal Dutch/Shell Group of companies, with joint headquarters in the United Kingdom and the Netherlands and spanning over 145 countries. The Shell Group employs more than 119,000 people globally in its energy and petrochemical business of exploring, developing, producing, purchasing, transporting, and marketing crude oil and natural gas, as well as generating electricity and providing energy efficiency advice.

Shell People Services provides only English-based tools and practices in its staffing services, as English is the global language of all professional employees within the Shell Group. Shell has put a great deal of effort into creating a strong recruiting function. To aid in global recruiting, Shell uses SAP, an inter-enterprise software application that provides a common database and a common workflow process. Shell provides all potential candidates with global information about Shell and uses its company Web site as a global posting board for opportunities across the globe. Shell also provides some general information to potential candidates around the world, such as job descriptions, whether specific positions require global travel, the initial location of positions, and how each position fits within Shell.

Shell also uses a global system to select administrative, clerical, and technician positions as well as globally standardized structured interview protocols for every job group they hire (such as engineering, business science, and technology). However, due to the need for technology to be flexible to support different countries' legal issues, Shell has not pushed for a global platform for a standardized recruiting system but adapts technologies on a national and regional basis. One form of increasing standardization across several countries is mandated legal protection for job candidates in the staffing process, such as avoiding employment discrimination. Over time, through the influence of work councils, unions, and government regulations, countries are implementing laws that may look different but have similar intent. Shell has found that managers in nonlitigious countries often do not fully appreciate the rigor needed to ensure local compliance; therefore, the company actively provides training to increase awareness of local legal requirements and practices to avoid legal problems.

In creating global staffing systems, Shell also faces issues of how to assess competencies on a global basis. Shell's goal is to understand what each competency means across cultures and to devise assessment methods that will allow the company to capture those culture-specific behaviors. Shell uses a global assessment center for assisting with candidate selection and has standard training for all assessors who administer the assessment center. To ensure the success of the assessment center, Shell allows for local accommodation due to compliance and cultural factors. In addition, Shell tries to ensure that candidates are not assessed differently because of cultural differences between those participating in the assessments or interviews. For example, Shell would want to ensure that an assessor from a gregarious culture does not rate a candidate from a more reserved culture as inadequate simply due to cultural differences.

Shell's emphasis has been to hire locals within each of their operating units, but this practice has come under pressure due to the increasing number of global candidates. The company has found it challenging to remain loyal to local hiring practices, yet at the same time utilize the talent that it is able to attract worldwide.[1]

INTRODUCTION

The global race for securing human talent is becoming an increasingly evident competitive reality. The effective staffing of organizations is a critical imperative in good and bad economic times, such as during the recent global economic crisis, when smart organizations can attract strong talent at lower costs and prepare for gaining a head start when the economy begins to heat up.[2] Once, through careful HR planning, work demand for achieving long- and short-term performance objectives has been identified and designed into jobs with specific goals and tasks to accomplish and the decision has been made against outsourcing particular work responsibilities, the focus shifts to the professional activity of *staffing*. As illustrated in the opening scenario with the Royal Dutch/Shell Group, staffing involves actively filling those jobs in a timely fashion with appropriately qualified individuals from inside or outside the MNC, wherever they may be found in the relevant recruitment area (in some cases worldwide) and consistent with the MNC's strategy. The ability to attract qualified workers and keep the workplace adequately staffed is tied closely to careful assessments through HR planning of external labor market conditions and government actions as well as the effectiveness of the organization's overall reward system to attract and retain workers—whose interests and preferences are ever-shifting—relative to competing employers.

Staffing does not involve only bringing new people into the organization. From a broader perspective, staffing encompasses the many activities related to moving employees into, throughout, and out of an organization in the pursuit of satisfying work demand and meeting organizational objectives.[3] Staffing also considers how to best *retain* desirable employees—to prevent them from moving out of the organization prematurely. Hence, staffing can involve such employee deployment and movement decisions and activities as recruitment, selection, transfers, promotions, layoffs, firing, and retirement as well as influence the total compensation package and reward system to provide optimal attraction to the company and reason to remain.

Although the terms *recruitment* and *selection* often are used synonymously, they are distinct and different processes. Recruitment involves considering both internal and external sources to produce viable candidates to fill a given work demand, whereas selection involves gathering appropriate information and deciding from among those candidates who to choose to fill the work demand.[4] In this chapter we limit our focus on global staffing to filling *immediate* work demand through the processes of recruitment and selection; for existing internal employees, staffing generally pertains to transfers and/or promotions. We first examine important general factors that influence global staffing in MNCs; then we consider more specific approaches, tools, and important considerations for recruiting and for selecting viable candidates. In Chapter 8, dealing with managing international assignments, we will examine the special staffing activity involving transfer of an employee upon the completion of a foreign assignment back to his or her own country—a process known as *repatriation.*

GENERAL FACTORS AFFECTING GLOBAL STAFFING

As with all other HR management decisions and practices, global staffing should be linked to the overall strategy and objectives of the multinational enterprise. These strategies and objectives are of course influenced by and set within the context of the overall global business environment.[5] Thus, employee recruitment and selection decisions comprising the process of immediate staffing to meet work demands are influenced by such important general factors as the firm's business strategy, stage of international development, specific foreign market experience, host government restrictions and incentives, host country sociocultural restrictions, and plans for individual and organization development. There also can be various situational factors such as economic trends and conditions, the nature and duration of the international work itself, MNC resources available for staffing, and availability of willing and able candidates. We now will examine each of these factors as they relate to staffing decisions.

MNC BUSINESS STRATEGY

The *primary* focus of a firm's human resources agenda throughout all of its processes and activities should be the optimal support and reinforcement of company strategy, in efforts and activities involving both strategy formulation and implementation.[6] The staffing function itself, preceded by careful global HR planning, has a potentially huge impact on strategic management. This impact is especially made through the recruitment and selection of key MNC leaders who have a major influence in formulating MNC strategy, and through the selection and placement of middle managers throughout the MNC who have a vital role in implementing and carrying out the strategic direction of the firm. As previously discussed with regard to global HR planning, staffing should seek to fit and reinforce the strategic direction and priorities of the MNC.

For example, where MNCs place strong priorities on centralized decision making and high integration of global operations, we often see the use of PCN expatriates to optimize control in achieving these priorities.[7] Or where an MNC desires to follow a strategic alliance strategy of focusing on its core competencies and reducing labor costs, the staffing function will likely employ outsourcing to support this strategy, such as through increasing the outsourcing of noncore back-office operations, or even resort to a broader level of external partner selection in complementary alliances, typically noted in international joint ventures.[8] We now examine in greater depth important implications for the staffing function held by the ethnocentric, polycentric, regiocentric, and geocentric strategic orientations introduced in Chapter 4. In addition, we examine important staffing issues and practices for success with the general alternative foreign entry mode strategy of international joint ventures.

Ethnocentric Approach

Staffing that is consistent with an ethnocentric approach is typically characterized by all or most key positions at a foreign operation being filled by parent country nationals (PCNs). As mentioned earlier regarding stages of company internationalization, PCNs are often utilized in earlier stages of internationalization to optimize control for the purpose of transmitting company culture and instituting and implementing company procedures and methods.[9] Or for much more experienced MNCs, the company might desire to retain a heavy use of PCNs for managing foreign operations due to the perceived lack of qualified local home country national (HCN) talent.[10] This need for strategic control can be magnified by greater operational challenges posed by cultural distance or by nature of industry, particularly where product complexity and/or product safety concerns are high.[11] However, reflecting their greater "in-group," more ethnocentric, orientation, there is evidence that many Asian firms, especially those with larger foreign operations and with higher ownership ratios, tend to staff the senior management positions in their foreign operations with their own PCNs.[12]

As in all international HR decisions, MNCs electing to follow an ethnocentric staffing approach should keep in mind several potential disadvantages and costs.[13] First, expatriates represent a considerable direct cost for the MNC compared to HCN and typically third-country national (TCN) managers. Many estimates of the cost of expatriates run from three to as much as five times the expatriate's normal salary.[14] In addition, the adjustment process of expatriates to their host country surroundings, as well as of the HCNs to the new expatriate, often takes considerable time. This adjustment period, or "learning curve," itself represents a time span of costly suboptimal performance and a chance for costs to be greatly expanded by mistakes and poor decisions. There also can be significant costs associated with the often-overlooked adjustment of the HCNs to the new PCN. One of the authors noted this reality in a recent visit to a Japanese electronics manufacturing plant in Tijuana that continues to follow an ethnocentric staffing approach for the plant's upper management. The plant's Mexican HR director mentioned that each change in Japanese senior management every four or five years resulted in a less productive adjustment period for the employees as they got to know the new managers and featured some added stress and anxiety with the need for the locals to prove themselves again to new superiors.

As an additional potential disadvantage, an ethnocentric staffing approach limits the promotional and developmental opportunities of HCNs, which might lead to their increased dissatisfaction and related costs of lower productivity and increased turnover. Also, due to PCN compensation typically being based on home country rates and often increased by inducement premiums and allowances, there may be a significant pay gap with HCNs whose compensation is based at a lower local rate, potentially causing additional dissatisfaction due to perceptions of inequity.[15] These potential sources of HCN dissatisfaction are likely linked to the generally negative attitudes toward PCNs found by Hailey[16] when he examined the attitudes and perceptions toward their expatriate colleagues of local managers working for multinational companies in Singapore. He found that many of the local managers were openly resentful of expatriates and often considered them technically unqualified, unable or unwilling to accommodate to the local culture, and representative of a "colonial mentality" of the parent company.

Polycentric Approach

As previously described in Chapter 4, under a polycentric strategic orientation, each major foreign subsidiary is usually somewhat independent and is typically managed by a local HCN who is very familiar with the competitive demands of the local market. Some major advantages of the staffing of foreign operation management with HCNs consistent with this approach include a strong familiarity of operation management with local social norms and customs, language fluency, costs that are typically less than an expatriate assignment, and no foreign adjustment problems for an employee and any accompanying family members. And despite being a multinational corporation with headquarters in some distant country, the heavy use of HCNs from top management down in the operation can win the support and confidence of the local government and people who see the operation as benefiting their citizens.

A powerful example of this advantage of significant HCN staffing occurred in the United States when anti-France fervor was growing after France continued to block a U.S.-backed measure at the UN Security Council on disarming Iraq. The U.S. state of South Carolina, well known for its protectionist and ultrapatriotic stance toward American manufacturing, took up a resolution calling for a boycott of French products, which passed overwhelmingly in its state house of representatives. But before the measure was taken up in the state senate, it was dropped when lawmakers realized that many of the Michelin tires of France-based Group Michelin SA that are sold in the United States are actually made in factories in South Carolina, which provide many jobs for Americans from senior management on down.[17]

A major disadvantage of a polycentric staffing policy may be the lack of effective flow of information and productive interaction between MNC headquarters and the foreign subsidiary due to language and cultural differences as well as the growth of unfavorable "us versus them" stereotypes caused by a lack of local meaningful interaction and common experience between PCNs and HCNs. Additional disadvantages can include the lack of international professional skill enhancement and career development opportunities for HCNs who remain in their host country operations,[18] as well as suboptimal sharing of valuable knowledge and information and cross-cultural understanding that can be enhanced through HCN inpatriate assignments at MNC headquarters.[19] Furthermore, with severely restricted international management opportunities in foreign subsidiary operations, PCN managers and executives might also miss valuable global competency development opportunities, which can ultimately lead to lower effectiveness on the part of the MNC headquarters strategic management team.[20]

Regiocentric Approach

Under a regiocentric strategic approach we often see a predominance of HCN staffing at the local subsidiary, however, with an increased movement of senior HCN managers to head up operations in other countries of the economic region, such as a French national to a Spanish operation of IBM in Madrid. In these cases we also often see PCNs represented at regional headquarters, which provides opportunities for cross-cultural interaction beyond what is found in the polycentric approach. The former HCN managers themselves (now considered TCNs) with these cross-border assignments also gain useful albeit less culturally distant international career experience; however, they are still generally limited to this regional level with little chance of promotion to the top management strategic team back at parent company headquarters. As with the polycentric approach that risks developing multiple independent national units with few common links and identification with MNC headquarters, a regiocentric staffing policy can contribute to regional "kingdoms" that have a less-than-optimal exchange of knowledge and resources among themselves or with MNC headquarters.

Geocentric Approach

As mentioned in Chapter 4, MNC staffing policy driven by a geocentric strategic orientation considers and selects the best talent for important jobs throughout the world operations of the MNC, regardless of nationality.[21] This staffing policy works well especially within industries whose products or services involve minimal cultural differentiation such as in the high-tech electronics or automotive industry.[22]

Several significant advantages with staffing under the geocentric approach include increased global leadership development opportunities for HCNs who were heretofore held back, especially by ethnocentric and polycentric staffing policies; increased opportunity for cross-cultural learning and knowledge sharing throughout the firm, with meaningful cross-border interactions; greater opportunity for developing a common MNC identity and mind-set; and a more widespread development of key global competencies throughout the MNC leading to a distinct competitive advantage in human capital.[23] Nevertheless, a geocentric staffing policy may be restricted in cases where local governments require certain levels of HCN professional and managerial presence in their host country operations or place significant documentation and qualification requirements for hiring foreign nationals. A geocentric staffing policy may also prove prohibitively expensive to implement fully due to compensation adjustment needs and relocation expenses. Furthermore, as mentioned earlier, staffing decisions might also have a major objective of skill development for the selected employee, whose skills for the assignment are acceptable but certainly do not represent the greatest talent available within the MNC—thus overruling a purely geocentric approach.

International Joint Ventures

Where international joint venture (IJV) strategies are implemented, staffing decisions are essential to the success of the operation and often have implications and relate to issues around potential cross-cultural conflict, control, and temporary versus permanent (that is, one-way) staffing assignments. Figure 6.1 lists critical questions about IJV staffing decisions to address once the number of employees and skill needs have been determined through careful HR planning. Due to its important position as a major strategic mode of entry into foreign markets,[24] we will now carefully examine IJV staffing issues and practices in more detail.

One staffing question facing IJVs is how to staff these operations in a manner that minimizes costly cross-cultural conflict. Alliance strategies such as domestic joint ventures are difficult enough to pull off with any degree of success without adding the additional potentially exacerbating IJV element of national culture differences. But although cross-cultural differences can lead to disruptive and wasteful conflict in IJVs, an analysis of high-performing IJVs with multinational management teams indicates that cultural diversity does not necessarily lead to poor performance. In fact, there is evidence that this diversity might even contribute to a competitive advantage by providing a broader range of perspectives for managing the IJV within such complex economic and cultural systems.[25] Salk and Brannen suggest that negative outcomes of cultural differences among IJV employees (including within the IJV management team) can be minimized and even avoided where staffing decisions focus more on expertise and interpersonal skills in filling IJV management responsibilities and less on the ability to exert traditional power and control.[26]

In the early days of Corning's long-term IJV with Samsung in a manufacturing operation in South Korea, Corning as the senior partner desired to have daily operational control and therefore staffed the South Korean operations with a management team of American expatriates.[27] Both partners soon found, however, that the close involvement of Corning managers at this operational level led to significant inefficiencies and delays due to language and cultural differences. A major step forward for improvement then took place when both sides agreed to staff the IJV management with Korean managers transferred from Samsung, retaining, however, one Corning executive to serve primarily in an IJV coordinating role with Corning headquarters. This new staffing arrangement, with Corning releasing significant direct control and Samsung Korean managers primarily in charge of the local South Korean daily operations, also led to an increased feeling of mutual trust and respect between the two IJV partners, which contributed to further productive interactions and learning between the two IJV partners.

Figure 6.1 **Critical Staffing Decisions for International Joint Ventures**

- Which partner is to have primary control of staffing the IJV management? Of staffing IJV lower-level employees? How will senior employee selection decisions be made?
- Who is responsible for forecasting ongoing IJV staffing needs?
- Who will have which specific IJV recruitment responsibilities?
- What preference in IJV management staffing is there for temporary versus permanent job assignment with the IJV?
- How much cross-cultural diversity is desired in the IJV management team? What positions should be filled by each IJV parent company?
- For whom do the employees work? For one of the partners, or for the separate IJV?
- To what degree and for what positions must there be agreement on staffing among IJV partners? How will disagreements regarding staffing be resolved?

Another challenge of control through IJV staffing was illustrated by an American beer manufacturer that began an IJV with a junior beverage manufacturing partner in South Korea that was considered to have a good sense of the local South Korean target market. The American partner desired to retain direct control in key local operational decisions and hired a local Korean manager (not from the Korean partner) from the local labor force in Seoul to head up the IJV operations. The American company didn't want to place someone at the head who came from the Korean junior partner firm because they were concerned that this person would sense an allegiance to the junior partner and make decisions primarily according to the Korean partner's interests and perspectives—even contrary to the wishes of the American senior partner. However, the American partner soon found that this South Korean national at the head of the South Korean IJV operation was still greatly influenced by the local culture and predominant local ways of thinking and continually made decisions according to the often-conflicting wishes of the junior South Korean partner. Increasingly we note that to retain active and direct control of foreign IJV operations and still have leaders who are very familiar with the local market, many MNCs now hire local talent and train them in company strategy, culture, and procedures for a significant period, either locally in the host country or as inpatriates at MNC headquarters, then place these prepared host country managers in key leadership positions back in the local host country IJV.[28]

Useful research has been conducted on leadership staffing of the two primary foreign entry mode strategies, wholly owned subsidiaries and IJVs, with temporary PCNs versus more permanent local HCNs.[29] The findings suggest that the new foreign venture leaders' development of trust and organizational commitment are greatest, regardless of whether PCNs and HCNs are used, when the wholly owned subsidiary entry mode is employed, primarily due to the organization's long-term commitment to the success of the venture, where the IJV is often perceived as only a tentative or experimental venture. This research supports a general trend for IJV staffing on the value, where possible, of creating a sense of permanence or long-term personal stake in the success of IJV assignments. Where foreign partner PCNs are used, they should expect to remain with the IJV without a clear expectation of return to the parent company, or that their future career with the parent organization is directly dependent on their success with the IJV. Or they might be used more for the purpose of developing future IJV leadership talent and serving as a temporary source of knowledge transfer and for filling critical technical knowledge gaps.[30]

Due to the potentially greater disruptive impact of an international assignment on personal lives and professional careers, the foreign partner might experience greater difficulties than the host country local partner in finding willing and capable leaders for IJV assignment,[31] thus again favoring the HCN for IJV leadership selection. However, where foreign partner PCN staffing of IJV leadership is perceived as essential, such as when HCNs lack technical knowledge and managerial expertise needed for successful IJV strategy implementation, these difficulties facing foreign partner PCN staffing can be surmounted by a clear demonstration by top management of their commitment to the success of the IJV and the PCNs assigned there. For example, when Procter & Gamble recognized an immense long-term market development opportunity and entered China in the 1980s, government restrictions made IJVs the only entry mode option, but the Chinese partners clearly did not have adequate managerial and technical talent to meet IJV staffing needs. To attract top talent within Procter & Gamble to staff these new IJVs, Procter & Gamble's top management, including the CEO himself, were actively involved in the recruitment, selection, ongoing support, and repatriation of those assigned to the IJVs. This clear demonstration by top management of its long-term commitment to the success of its market development strategy in China *and* to the welfare of the PCNs themselves was essential to the successful staffing of the IJVs with highly qualified PCNs.[32]

STAGE OF INTERNATIONAL DEVELOPMENT

Several studies have supported a general concept of progression of businesses through various stages of international development, or "internationalization," beginning with export activity and progressing through the development of foreign sales offices, licensing agreements and foreign direct investment with manufacturing facilities, international division formation, multinational status, and finally integrated global enterprise.[33] However, firms of all sizes differ greatly in the pace of their evolution toward increased internationalization, and some bypass stages through acquisitions and joint ventures. Some new ventures that are "born global" even begin with a primary focus on the global marketplace, skipping the earlier traditional forms of internationalization.[34]

Staffing decisions at each of these stages of internationalization can differ significantly due to the unique work demands of each stage. At the simple export stage a firm is likely interested in obtaining the contracted services of an export agent and eventually a sales firm or independent sales representatives to promote product distribution. For example, firms interested in starting up cost-saving manufacturing operations across the U.S.–Mexico border frequently contract with local experienced firms that provide "shelter operation services" that assist with the procurement of these Mexican border facilities as well as the subcontracted staffing and day-to-day management of Mexican assembly workers.[35]

At the more advanced level of the multinational enterprise, firms are often greatly interested in transferring company knowledge and technical expertise to foreign wholly owned subsidiaries, as well as coordinating with headquarters and controlling foreign operations to ensure consistency with parent company policies and procedures.[36] MNCs frequently accomplish these knowledge transfer and control purposes through expatriate PCNs assigned to these operations.[37] Finally, at the stage of integrated global enterprise the firm has a large assortment of internal talent to consider for staffing its domestic and global operations. Following the geocentric approach described earlier, the MNC at this stage recruits and selects internal talent based on a determination of the best talent available and representing the highest return on staffing investment, regardless of national boundaries. Often at this stage we see now experienced HCNs replacing PCNs in managing foreign operations. External and nonstandard or contingent sources of employees are also frequently considered at this level, again depending on the nature of the particular work demand and the comparative advantage of these sources.

SPECIFIC FOREIGN MARKET EXPERIENCE

As in the very early stages of internationalization, multinational firms that have little experience with a specific foreign market are likely to staff these new foreign operations to a significant degree with local management that is very familiar with the specific market. This staff may be local HCN managers who have been instrumental in the planning for this new market entry, or TCNs, perhaps from a neighboring country, who have considerable experience and expertise with the local market. Although PCNs might be involved to ensure proper communication and coordination with company headquarters, local HCNs or experienced TCNs can more effectively address initial critical decisions faced by the new foreign operation, including the complete staffing of this operation most likely with HCN employees. In some cases, especially where the firm is reluctant to hire an experienced HCN or TCN from outside the MNC on a long-term basis, this experienced manager might be hired on a short-term (for example, three years) or full-time consultancy basis until the firm has had enough time to develop internal talent for effectively managing the foreign operation.

HOST GOVERNMENT RESTRICTIONS AND INCENTIVES

Host governments, in following their traditional safeguarding responsibility on behalf of their working citizens, often require MNCs to demonstrate that HCNs are not available to fill certain managerial or technical professional positions before they grant entry visas and work permits to PCNs and TCNs selected by the MNC. With regard to labor available to staff lower-level employment positions, Western European governments and their political movements are actively moving to restrict and reduce the number of foreign asylum seekers and immigrants, who often are perceived as low-wage threats to existing national employment opportunities.[38] Often new business development abroad can be significantly delayed due to governments blocking work permits for expatriates selected for heading up this new international work. Or, because a work permit is granted generally only for an expatriate and not for an accompanying spouse or partner, expatriates might be reluctant or even refuse to accept a foreign assignment

Global Workforce Professional Profile 6.1
Valery Polyakov: Leading Professional Recruiting Services across Russia

"Up until now, there has been a popular myth in Russia that recruiting companies help people find new jobs. In reality this is not so. Our task is to find required personnel for companies, or weed out along the way the majority of contenders striving to fill the vacancies," explains Valery Polyakov, founder and president of Metropolis Personnel Group (MPG), the largest Russian network of recruiting agencies. MPG incorporates recruiting companies from fifty-three cities in Russia and Ukraine, from the Pacific in the Far East to the Baltic Sea in Europe. Polyakov adds, "In 1989 when we began, almost all of the economy in the USSR was under state control. The private sector was just emerging and services in personnel recruiting were completely new. And managers in state-controlled companies were often surprised when they learned that we wanted to receive payment for searching and finding their required personnel."

In 1996, the Association of Personnel Search consultants was established and Polyakov became its vice president. Now, the realization of the need to pay for recruiting services is no longer a surprise to anybody. The situation in Russia is completely different, although the state has retained control over the defense industry, railway transport, and some of the largest enterprises in the oil and gas sector. The majority of Russian companies are publicly or privately held entities, and many of them have become clients of recruiting organizations. In 2008 there were more than two thousand professional service companies, out of which six hundred were based in Moscow. Russian recruiting and executive search companies now successfully compete with the largest global companies such as Adecco, Kelly Services, and Korn/Ferry. "Professional recruiting service businesses play a great positive role in the economic development of our country and its integration in the world economy," explains Polyakov. "Searching for the best personnel for the best companies, we optimize personnel resources across the nation. The best executives and professionals are given the opportunity to work where their talent has the most effective application."

Polyakov graduated from Moscow State University and obtained his PhD in economics. Prior to 1989 he was a department chief in a large R&D center in the defense sector, and taught part-time at Moscow State Technological University as well as the Russian Academy of Economics. Going into business, Polyakov remained highly interested in teaching, and now often participates in recruitment training sessions in Russia and Ukraine. Polyakov also is well known as an author of books and several hundred articles about careers in human resources and general management. Polyakov remarks, "We professional recruiters know better the obstacles and the ways to overcome them in the process of finding a good job. When I write books or articles, and when I give interviews for newspapers, radio, or television I use my experience to help people explore methods and techniques of self-marketing in the labor market." Russian journalists sometimes jokingly call him the grandfather of Russian recruiting. Polyakov has the right to this title as the well-known professional and founder of the first recruiting company in Russia.

Source: Provided by Dr. Anatoly Zhuplev of Loyola Marymount University, Los Angeles, California.

without an accompanying spouse or partner who also desires employment. However, many governments have begun to change their laws or quota restrictions related to employment-related immigration to better meet their local economic development demands, especially for higher-skill jobs, thus facilitating international transfers and cross-border staffing.[39] This significant change in immigration practice in support of national economic growth was seen in the United States during the dramatic growth of the Internet dot-com industry with a quota increase for the H-1B work visa.[40]

Governments and NGOs also might place demands or lobby for staffing requirements for MNCs that are making foreign direct investment, especially in developing countries, such as specifying that certain numbers of HCNs be hired and at particular levels.[41] These requirements might also stipulate what minimal percentage of supervisor and management level positions must be staffed by HCNs at a future date, giving the MNC some time to develop this managerial expertise among the HCNs. Governments can also provide significant tax, tariff, local labor force training, and other incentives to encourage MNCs' foreign direct investments, leading to significant HCN staffing.[42] For example, China, with its entry into the WTO, is making a major commitment to attract FDI to increase levels of regional and national employment through providing tax and other financial incentives to foreign MNCs as well as investing in infrastructure improvements and basic skill enhancement for a labor force that presents a very attractive low wage rate.[43]

SOCIOCULTURAL CONSIDERATIONS

There are often important social and cultural considerations affecting staffing decisions. Two of these considerations are general social norms and, more specifically, women in international staffing.

General Social Norms

Segalla and his colleagues have suggested the importance of symbolic as well as more traditional functional considerations in making international staffing decisions, where culture may have an important influence on staffing policy.[44] Although the consideration of such factors as gender, age, consanguinity (that is, family ties), or previous friendships might seem irrelevant and even unethical and illegal in some cultures where the primary focus is a candidate's technical ability to perform a job,[45] such factors may be expedient in other cultures. For example, placing a younger HCN over an older one could be problematic in some cultures that accord special respect and privilege to older members of society. Related to expatriate staffing, Selmer and colleagues recently found that the age of expatriates assigned to operations in Greater China had a positive association with expatriate managerial performance, providing support to the presumption that the age of business expatriates matters in a Chinese cultural context. Practical implications include introducing age among other selection criteria, training older expatriates how to exploit their age advantage, or at least providing support against age discrimination in expatriate selection for work in Greater China.[46] And although frequently discouraged in Western developed countries, nepotism (that is, hiring immediate and extended family members) may prove to be a very useful staffing approach in different cultural contexts, such as in Asia and the Middle East.[47] Therefore, due to the reality of the influence of social expectations and cultural preferences in the workplace, these factors should at least be acknowledged and considered where appropriate when making staffing decisions.

Women and International Staffing

Despite national laws and policies that might prevail at company headquarters prohibiting discrimination against women in the workplace, cultural norms and expectations widely held in other countries, such as some Islamic and Asian societies and in some areas of Latin America, might need to be considered when making staffing-assignment decisions about women in those countries, especially involving work and supervisory interactions with men.[48] We are not suggesting that a company's commitment to equal opportunity as a core value must be compromised when doing business abroad. Rather, we contend that an awareness of local expectations regarding women in the workplace can serve as a warning about where conflict and dissatisfaction might arise and where possible open communication, sharing of company values and clear behavioral expectations, and training interventions might be useful to help avoid conflict and unnecessary difficulty, including wasteful litigation. And in some cases it might be determined that it is just not worth the effort and difficulty in trying to force gender diversity into a line of male machine operators at a manufacturing plant in the Philippines or into an all-female section of toy-parts assembly in a maquiladora plant near the U.S. border in Mexico—especially where no opposite gender candidates show an interest.

Nevertheless, women have been relatively untapped as a source of human talent in the international business arena, and notably for women expatriates, constituting a form of "expatriate glass ceiling."[49] But the key to international business success will be the ability to mobilize and utilize human resource talent to the fullest extent in formulating and implementing new global business strategies. This imperative is particularly challenging because the number of skilled, educated workers in many labor markets, particularly in developed countries, is decreasing at the same time as the demand for them is increasing.[50] Therefore, where possible, MNCs can benefit greatly by broadening their employment sources and not limiting their pool of talent by improperly excluding particular groups of employees due to personal characteristics that are irrelevant to job performance, such as gender.[51] To illustrate, one Western bank, when it was attempting to enter the Japanese market several years ago, was quite concerned about its ability to compete locally for top-quality talent. However, this Western bank found that the heavy local Japanese cultural preference for male university graduates gave it a distinct advantage over Japanese banks with a relatively open field in recruiting and hiring top *female* graduates.

One particularly persistent bias against women in international business concerns women in U.S. and other Western MNCs serving as expatriates. There has been an increase in the number of women being sent on foreign assignments, to approximately 20 percent. Yet women still lag significantly behind their male MNC expatriate counterparts, although they constitute close to 50 percent of the middle management ranks from which expatriates are usually recruited.[52] Not only does this suboptimal utilization of the labor force represent a significant threat for MNCs in meeting growing demand for international talent but it also points to fewer opportunities for professional skill and career development for women. And with an increasing premium being placed on previous foreign business experience in considering employees for advancement and executive promotion,[53] individuals who are unfairly denied these important career-enhancing foreign business opportunities might begin to seek legal redress at an increasing rate.

Some of the most powerful obstructing factors that have influence in the early selection phase of expatriate assignments appear to involve unfavorable perceptions from management at headquarters regarding interest among women in obtaining foreign work experience as well as general concerns about female candidates' success potential in foreign assignments. A common misperception held by predominantly male managers who may provide input on or directly make expatriate assignment decisions is that women have less interest than men in obtaining international work experience in the form of an expatriate assignment. Although there is evidence that family factors may represent a greater obstacle for women than for men in accepting an expatriate assignment, the assumption of women's lack of interest is unfounded and both unproductively and unfairly restricts this staffing talent pool.[54] Nevertheless, due to this common misperception, women may be less likely to be considered for foreign assignments unless they are assertive in making their interest in international work experience clearly known by management.

Other major reasons given by managers for selecting men over women for foreign expatriate assignments typically have fallen into the category of business necessity—to avoid costly failure and to promote and optimize the competitive viability of business operations abroad.[55] However, it is rather perplexing to hear these arguments when a majority of women on expatriate assignments allegedly claim that their international assignments were successful, even in such countries as Japan and Korea where male managers seem to almost completely dominate business circles.[56] In fact, many field studies identify distinct advantages of women expatriates over their male counterparts.[57] Mounting evidence suggests that women may actually adapt better than men in cross-cultural business situations.[58] Steinberg noted that a major benefit of being a woman in overseas business is high visibility.[59] When competing for the attention of a foreign executive in obtaining a desired business deal, a sole female sales representative will have the advantage of being remembered among the otherwise homogeneous male sales representative competition. Researchers examining a reportedly high success rate of Western female expatriates have concluded that these women are not necessarily subject to the same traditional gender-based restrictions in local business interactions and involvement as are their HCN sisters.[60] It has even been suggested that females also may benefit from a positive self-fulfilling prophesy or halo effect held by the foreign businesspersons who expect that the female expatriate is extremely capable and talented because she was able to overcome all of the gender-biased obstacles that were presumed to be placed in her way back home.[61] Field studies also have pointed to women's advantage in social skills, which are of great value in building trusting relationships with employees and customers in the international marketplace, including good listening skills, a less direct and confrontational communication approach, and emphasis on cooperation over competition. In fact, Varma and colleagues found that Indian HCNs preferred American female expatriates as co-workers significantly more than American male expatriates, likely due to the women's less aggressive, more supportive style.[62] To further examine an apparent unfounded bias against women serving in expatriate assignments, we compared the perceptions of American managers in the United States, who had potential input on foreign assignment selection decisions, with the perceptions of managers and businesspersons in foreign environments of Germany, South Korea, and Mexico on several measures regarding the viability of American women serving in expatriate assignments. We found that overall the American managers held a less positive view regarding American women's potential for success in the foreign business environment than those representing actual international business environments. In subsequent research we found quite disconcerting evidence that Western graduate business education might actually be contributing to strengthening and reinforcing this bias, where young entering male students reflected less of a bias against women expatriates than their upper-level and MBA male student counterparts.[63] These results only add to previous studies and voices of women in the international workplace who suggest that the biggest obstacle faced by women for international business career success was not in their foreign business environments. Rather, the biggest obstacle existed back in their own corporate headquarters where closed, informal selection procedures for international assignments and unfounded negative perceptions about the probability of female expatriate assignment success often discouraged managers from seriously considering female candidates for a foreign assignment.[64]

To effectively recruit and increase the number of women in expatriate positions, companies should consider the following ideas:

- Provide awareness training countering the bias to relevant managers involved in possible expatriate selection, emphasizing that many women actually would welcome an international assignment, and that the dual management career challenges are similar to what would be faced with male expatriates.
- Create a system for identifying and keeping track of employees willing to take foreign assignments, with a concerted effort to include potential female candidates in this database. This approach helps to organize and formalize the career planning and expatriate selection process, making it less random and prone to bias.
- Use successful female expatriates to encourage and recruit other women, providing seminars and encouraging networking interactions and mentoring relationships to talk about the pros and cons of foreign assignments and plan for upcoming opportunities.
- Be flexible about timing, providing a reasonable deadline for deciding whether to accept an assignment and being flexible about the starting date to accommodate possible child-care responsibilities that tend to fall more frequently on the mother.
- Provide employment assistance where possible for an accompanying male spouse,

who might be feeling greater stress as a "trailing spouse" in the couple's new foreign experience.[65]

PLANS FOR INDIVIDUAL AND ORGANIZATIONAL DEVELOPMENT

As mentioned in Chapter 6, on HR planning, immediate staffing decisions can also be influenced by longer-range goals and objectives of the firm related to individual employee development or the development of the organization's capability as a whole. Caligiuri and Harvey and their colleagues have discussed the value of staffing PCNs in expatriate assignments and HCNs in inpatriate assignments for enhancing their individual global competencies,[66] which when continued over time can collectively contribute to greater organizational capability and global competitiveness.[67] The selection of HCNs for inpatriate assignments also has been recommended as a reverse knowledge-transfer strategy for building greater capability at company headquarters in considering diverse perspectives and meeting the demands of global diversity as well as enhancing the capability of the MNC's strategic management team in making decisions that reflect the realities of the host country business environment.[68] Finally, the benefits of the selection of HCNs for inpatriate assignments and PCNs for expatriate assignments have been examined relative to their respective contributions to organizational learning and development through global knowledge management.[69]

SITUATIONAL FACTORS INFLUENCING STAFFING DECISIONS

Some fairly obvious but still important situational determinants of international staffing decisions include the nature and duration of the task or work assignment itself, the financial resources of the MNC available for staffing, the availability of qualified and willing candidates, and economic trends and conditions. A task of immediate need that requires a high level of specialized expertise in computer systems design or strong foreign language fluency would direct the staffing efforts to only those candidates possessing the requisite skills. And if the work need is only for a perceived short duration, such as the completion of a special project or seasonal workload or to handle an unusual, immediate emergency, staffing would most likely consider contingent labor sources such as temporary employees or consultants or internally in the form of a temporary assignment or an ad hoc work team.

Staffing needs often influence an MNC's selection decision for the location of foreign direct investment, where there increasingly is a preference, due to greater dependence upon advanced technologies in operations, for countries that can offer labor with relative higher levels of literacy, skills, and discipline rather than merely the lowest wages.[70] Where qualified talent is not available internally and the international firm lacks the financial resources or inclination to hire on a regular full-time basis someone to fill the work demand, staffing might consider a less expensive contingent labor source or, where time is not a critical factor, develop the requisite skills within the firm through targeted employee training. In a host country work situation, often PCN and TCN employees are recruited and selected simply due to the present lack of qualified employees within the host country labor force. And, of course the availability of not only qualified but also *willing* candidates is also in some situations a critical factor, such as with work that carries with it significant danger and personal risk, as noted with Bechtel's and Halliburton's efforts to staff workers for projects to help rebuild Iraq[71] or oil production companies in Colombia and Ecuador that repeatedly have been besieged by terrorism and kidnappings.[72]

Finally, the state and health of regional, national, and global economies can have a significant influence on staffing activity. For example, the East Asian financial meltdown of 1997 quickly spread from Thailand to other neighboring countries, greatly depressing economic health and plans for new business development, and in turn greatly reducing staffing levels and plans for filling previously perceived work demand.[73] Also, staffing plans within the tourism industry were indefinitely postponed or cancelled completely by the global impact of 9/11 in 2001 and the subsequent SARS outbreak in 2003.[74]

In the remainder of this chapter we will go beyond general staffing issues to examine special considerations and methods for international recruitment and selection. The level of sophistication in the practice of international recruitment and selection is still relatively rudimentary, and these existing practices often are not very rational and objective.[75] Nevertheless, the ideas presented here based on current research and leading practice should be weighed carefully for their potential to contribute to international business success.

GLOBAL RECRUITMENT OF HUMAN RESOURCES

As mentioned earlier, HR recruitment involves finding and encouraging qualified individuals to apply for a job opening. Particularly important areas to consider include the geographic scope of recruitment and whether internal versus external candidates should be sought.

GEOGRAPHIC SCOPE OF RECRUITMENT

The geographic scope of sources considered for locating qualified potential job candidates might be worldwide when the company is following a geocentric approach and is searching for top talent regardless of national pedigree.[76] And more out of necessity, a broad scope can be followed when particular professional skills are highly sought after but are in short supply, such as to fill critical national nurse shortages.[77] Or the geographic scope might be relatively narrow, such as when recruiting for executive-level employees, found mostly at or near company headquarters, needed for new foreign operations that lack an MNC's proprietary knowledge and expertise, and especially subject to an ethnocentric staffing orientation. Although the low costs of Web-based recruiting have allowed the geographic area for recruitment to increase dramatically,[78] other costs and restrictions related to the overall staffing effort, such as candidate travel for interviews and dealing with difficult country visa and immigration policies, might lead to minimizing the geographic recruitment area as long as it is likely to produce a reasonable supply of qualified candidates for a job opening.

INTERNAL VERSUS EXTERNAL CANDIDATES

Another important consideration in planning for recruitment is whether to search for candidates beyond entry level from sources inside or outside of the organization. Of course, in the early phases of staffing for a new wholly owned subsidiary in a foreign host country, most of the staffing at lower and middle levels would likely result from external recruitment sources located locally within the host country. Nevertheless, many MNCs, including Merck, 3M, and IBM, encourage an internal recruitment "promotion from within" policy where possible, in the home country and abroad, in hiring for job openings at all levels beyond entry level.[79] They follow this preference for internal recruitment due to the following advantages of this approach:

1. Where effective human resource information systems (HRIS) are in use, qualified candidates are easier to identify and contact, representing significant savings in time and financial resources.
2. With an effective HRIS, the work performance background and developmental progress of potential candidates are readily available to enhance selection decision validity.
3. Promotion from within can have a significant boost on employee morale and motivation, increasing retention and productivity, both for the promoted candidate and for employees who see such an internal staffing practice as holding promise for their own career advancement within the firm.[80]
4. Reduction in training and socialization time and costs are very possible because existing employees are likely to be much more aware of the unique organizational culture, priorities, procedures, and overall business practices than is a newcomer.[81]

The fourth advantage is particularly important for traditional expatriate assignments where the expatriate is expected to carry considerable company knowledge to the host country operation to maintain foreign operation control in alignment with the MNCs goals and strategic objectives.[82] Also particularly pertinent to expatriate assignments, Harvey and Novicevic have added the following additional advantages to the list:

5. Internal candidates are frequently easier to persuade into taking an assignment abroad.
6. With their social knowledge of the company's culture, internal candidates are familiar with the value of international career paths within the organization.
7. Because they have an internal track record (see point 2), internal candidates are more likely to be trusted in the organization and, therefore, generate confidence in their ability to extend needed headquarters control to the global operations.[83]

On the other hand, recruiting new employees from the outside may provide the following benefits:

1. Bring fresh new ideas and viewpoints into the organization.
2. Reduce training costs where technically trained employees are recruited.
3. Provide additional greatly needed human resources, especially in times of growth, without overusing and overburdening existing internal staff.
4. Provide greater objectivity and flexibility in making critical decisions, without a history of past commitments, relationships, and expectations that can impede needed change.[84]

Nevertheless, especially with regard to filling expatriate assignment needs, an emphasis on the utilization of external expatriate candidates is problematic. This concern is due to the lack of verifiable information on the external candidates' past experience, typically higher recruitment costs when they are coming from the home country labor market, little knowledge and experience regarding company culture and strategy, and lack of history with MNC headquarters to develop trust and ongoing support.[85]

GLOBAL RECRUITMENT METHODS—INTERNAL

Where internal candidates are sought for the reasons mentioned in the previous section, organizations can use formal and informal means to search for potential employees inside the MNC who have interest and possess appropriate skills for a particular foreign assignment. The primary internal methods that we consider here include job posting, skills inventories, and internal network referrals.

Job Posting

Company newsletters, bulletins, and computerized intranet in-house communication systems can carry announcements of job openings for a foreign assignment or can be used in a foreign operation to support a local "promotion-from-within" policy. These internal company announcements about job openings can include information about the nature of the position and major qualifications required as well as how to apply or "bid" for this job opportunity. In many cases the company might want to target these internal communications according to its overall purposes and objectives. For example, it wouldn't make much sense for a large MNC to fill a general company newsletter—received by company employees around the globe—with information about supervisory opportunities in a facility in the Philippines, especially if the company's purpose is to develop and promote local talent in the Philippines.

Skills Inventories

Many organizations have developed useful databases and inventories on both local and global levels that facilitate an internal search for employees with interest and requisite skills to fill an international assignment.[86] For example, a Belgian firm with existing operations in Spain, Chile, and Argentina might desire to open a new facility in Mexico, headed by a manager with significant company experience, technical capability, and strong Spanish language fluency. By keeping a current skills inventory of its worldwide employees and entering into this database search specifications about such important factors as years of experience, nature of technical skills, and degree of Spanish fluency desired, the MNC might be able to readily identify and make plans for how to attract potential candidates with the desired attributes for this foreign assignment.

Internal Network Referrals

Organizations typically use informal communications as a means to "spread the word" and identify possible internal candidates for promotion or transfer assignment. Through their contacts throughout the organization, managers often are able to learn of qualified individuals who have previously expressed an interest in the type of job opening available. The manager then can contact these individuals directly. Several expatriates currently serving on foreign assignment have identified this informal networking means of internal recruitment, often through their own manager to whom they had previously expressed an interest, as the primary way they were informed of an international assignment opportunity.[87] For this informal approach to effectively work there must be an open sharing of career interest information, such as through the ongoing performance management process between manager and employee, as we will examine in Chapter 9.

GLOBAL RECRUITMENT METHODS—EXTERNAL

Particularly when recruiting to fill entry-level positions or when internal talent is not available or desirable to fill other job opportunities, various external recruitment methods can be employed. We will now briefly examine several of these methods including advertising, employee referrals, field recruiting, internships, Internet and related software, and professional recruitment firms.

Advertising

Direct advertising to the external public can reach a large number of potential applicants in a number of ways, from a simple "Help Wanted" sign in a shop window to a transnational search involving multiple forms of media. In a recent trip to Tijuana, Mexico, we even noted a van driving through the city with a loudspeaker blaring out an appeal for people to come apply for work at a nearby factory. Plamex, the very successful Mexican subsidiary in Tijuana for Plantronics Corporation (a leading manufacturer of lightweight communications headsets based in Santa Cruz, California), has found good recruitment success with a subtle advertisement strategy. In its approach, Plamex provides professional business cards for each employee at every level. It has found that when its employees pay holiday visits to family members farther south in Mexico, from where most of Tijuana's labor supply originates, the employees leave their business cards with friends, inevitably leading to new recruits for the company. Regardless of the method or medium, it should fit the local culture and regulatory

Global Workforce Challenge 6.1
In Staffing, Should Nepotism Always Be Avoided?

For many, nepotism is synonymous with corruption. For example, politicians accused Nicolas Sarkozy of nepotism after the French president's twenty-three-year-old son said he was a candidate for head of a public agency that runs Paris's financial district, La Defense. Business nepotism is commonly condemned with the claim that it favors relatives over those who may have more talent. It therefore rewards the incompetent, harms efficiency, reduces social mobility, and perpetuates class barriers. But this common perception about nepotism is not accurate in business today, and a broad trend in family member hiring and succession is becoming more and more apparent as family enterprise continues to explode globally.

A recent survey by the Raymond Institute for Family Business places the number of family-run businesses in the United States at over 24 million and finds that they are posting higher revenues despite a slower economy—up 50 percent since 1997. Family businesses are also slower to lay off employees in difficult economic times, plan better for the future, and provide more opportunities for women than nonfamily businesses. And a study in *The Journal of Finance* finds that family-run businesses are 5 percent to 6 percent more profitable and tend to be valued 10 percent higher by the stock market than their non–family-run counterparts.

Though they may be reluctant to admit it, many companies prefer to hire the relatives of existing employees. In addition, most people do in fact find jobs through kin-based networks. Motorola, a company that has been family run for three generations, promotes family involvement through a summer camp program for employees' children. Before they are allowed to join the ranks, successful companies often require family members to earn advanced degrees in business or other related fields, or spend at least five years working for another firm—especially a competitor where different perspectives can be brought to the company. Other companies put family members through a rigorous apprenticeship program designed to discourage all but the truly committed.

Contrary to the assumption that nepotism in hiring is always and everywhere bad and something to be avoided, the record of many businesses in the United States and abroad tells a different story. What we are seeing is essentially a return to the entrepreneurial family model that has always been the heart of the capitalist system.

Sources: Adapted from L. Grensing-Pophal, "All in the Family," *HR Magazine* 52 (9) (2007): 66, 68–70; A. Bellow, *In Praise of Nepotism* (New York: Doubleday, 2003).

conditions. In the opening scenario of Chapter 1, the banner advertisement outside a Chinese factory that reads, "JOB OPENINGS FOR GREAT NUMBER OF WOMEN WORKERS," may be acceptable in the hinterlands of China but would quickly run afoul of antidiscrimination law in the United States, as would German expectations that job candidate resumes include birth dates. Advertisements also should be directed at reaching the intended audience. Too broad an advertisement approach might attract unqualified candidates and create an extra load on the selection process, whereas too narrow an approach might miss qualified candidates who could bring great value to the organization.

Employee Referrals

Many companies have found the employee-referral approach to be very useful in attracting competent and committed employees—especially small- to medium-size operations that might not have the demand or budget to justify professional recruitment agencies. In many companies and operations around the world, 25 percent to 30 percent of the new hires come from employee referrals. And Mike Weston, CEO of LogicaCMG Offshore Services, believes this percentage is growing.[88]

Under an employee-referral approach employees typically are provided a financial reward and/or gift for referring a candidate who is eventually hired. In some successful cases employees have even brought in groups of friends with whom they had worked in previous companies.[89] The employee-referral approach tends to be very effective in attracting qualified and loyal new employees similar to their successful internal company employees who have referred them. Gautam Sinha, CEO of TVA Infotech, a Bangalore-based IT recruitment firm, believes that employee referrals are successful because employees are generally well equipped to sell the company to their friends and acquaintances. These current employees also tend to have a clear idea of the required skill sets and requirements for success with the company. In addition, the newly recruited employee, through informal orientation already provided by the person making the referral, tends to know what to expect from the job and the company, thus decreasing the likelihood of early departure due to unfulfilled expectations.[90]

However, this similarity has a downside in terms of developing workforce diversity, because employees naturally tend to refer friends and people from their social circles who are similar to themselves.[91] In fact, in some countries, such as the United States, an overreliance on the referral approach can lead to accusations of discrimination and costly litigation when it can be shown that this approach tends to give some ethnic group an advantage over others (that is, the predominant employee ethnic group generally referring candidates of the same ethnicity).[92]

A particular class of employee referral involves hiring not only friends who are recommended by valued employees but their family members as well. This practice of hiring family members, sometimes referred to as nepotism, is often banned and associated with corrupt business practices.[93] Nevertheless, this practice may be highly preferred and valued in different cultural contexts, such as in Asia and the Middle East.[94] And where careful control is placed on hiring those who are truly qualified for a job, nepotism can be very helpful in recruiting several highly committed employees in a timely manner and at a very low cost, resulting in high workforce stability and continuity.[95]

Field Recruiting

Many companies actively send professional internal recruiters out into the external environment in field recruiting activities, such as to domestic or international college career centers, company- or government-sponsored outplacement service centers, school- or local government-sponsored career fairs, or meetings of professional associations—all places where potential candidates might seek employment opportunities. An engineering firm in Munich, Germany, for example, might send a recruitment team (for example, including a professional recruiter and an engineer) to a job fair in eastern Germany sponsored by a local municipal government to meet with potential engineering candidates who have been laid off due to plant closures and corporate restructuring.

Internships

Companies are increasingly working closely with domestic and international university programs to develop internship arrangements where students may work on a part-time basis during a school year or full-time during a summer prior to graduation. This working arrangement, whether in exchange for pay, academic credit, or both, can provide valuable experiential learning and resume-building experience for the student.[96] And as a recruitment tool, appealing internships can be successful in attracting very capable students whom managers can assess further for organizational fit and potential before making hiring decisions. Especially for potential future international assignments, international internships also serve as a valuable trial test of an individual's ability to adapt and adjust to a foreign work environment. Those who want to return for regular employment to a foreign location where they in the past had significant internship experience are already self-screened and would be returning with their eyes wide open and likely not pose the adjustment risk and productivity toll of those without work and living experience in that region. However, internships might not be appropriate when employees need to be hired fairly quickly. In addition, when performed effectively internships tend to require considerable company time in planning and supervision.[97]

The Internet and Related Software

There has been tremendous growth in the use of the Internet as an external recruitment tool. As evidence, Internet usage for recruiting purposes in Global 500 companies increased from 29 percent in 1998 to 88 percent in 2001.[98] With increasing widespread availability and usefulness of the Internet and e-mail for resume and applicant data collection, as well as availability of integrated software tools for automated applicant data scanning and analysis for screening purposes, companies are finding that the use of these new technologies is significantly reducing both the cost and time needed to fill many positions. The Internet is also able to improve on traditional advertising by targeting specialized Web sites and electronic newsletters and bulletin boards to more effectively reach particular groups of interest (such as expatriate newsletters and relocation services). In addition, through effectively designed Web sites, companies can develop realistic job and working environment previews for potential candidates who can use this information to determine their degree of interest for a particular job opportunity—and in many cases screen themselves out in a very cost-effective fashion.

Despite its strengths, the use of e-recruitment has potential drawbacks, as outlined by Sparrow:

- Attracts too many applicants to process effectively and in a timely manner, creating an excessive workload and possibly hurting the company's image.
- Presents a challenge when the recruiting company is not well known in new foreign markets.
- Attracts questionable data of highly variable quality; offers a lack of quality control in getting a response from truly interested targeted groups.
- Contains an inherent discrimination against other qualified candidates due to mostly male candidates applying from a small range of countries.[99]

Notwithstanding these shortcomings of the Internet and related software, there doubtless will continue to be significant growth in new cost-effective technological applications for improving external recruitment. As with other advancements in best practices, managers should regularly monitor these e-technology advances for adoption where deemed appropriate for improving company recruitment efforts.

Professional Recruitment Firms

There is a rapidly growing worldwide industry for firms that perform various forms of assistance in "sourcing," or providing labor to fit company employment needs.[100] These service providers can range from agencies that provide "temps" or employees that work for the company for a limited period, to executive search firms, such as Korn/Ferry International based in Los Angeles, which assist only with the external recruitment of senior executives. Up to 50 percent of executive searches now cross international borders, and thus the ability of executive search firms to offer an integrated service with cross-border capability is a competitive edge.[101] There is a growing trend among smaller search firms to use global partnerships, allowing a much wider geographical sourcing of candidates, whereas larger firms are going public and opening offices in large metropolitan areas around the world.

A fairly new and developing segment of the professional recruitment services industry is often called "temp-to-hire," led by global firms such as Adecco (headquartered in Switzerland), Randstad (the Netherlands), and Kelly Services (United States). Many professional recruitment services firms, large and small, provide employees from entry to middle management and even professional levels initially on a temporary basis, but afterwards these employees may be hired by the company on a regular employment basis when future work demand and employee fit warrant such a decision. In fact, even when future work demand is certain, companies are increasingly using such temp-to-hire firms to recruit employees on a temporary basis and then carefully watching these workers as a probationary test prior to making regular-hire decisions.

GLOBAL SELECTION OF HUMAN RESOURCES

The selection decision of which job candidates to accept and which to reject can have powerful implications for future business success. At the executive level, the selection decision determines what kind of leadership is going to guide the organization and shape its future. We first will briefly examine general principles of selection that increase the likelihood that an employment decision will benefit the organization and encourage you to seek additional specialized sources of information on the general practice of selection. We then will discuss important considerations and methods of selection pertaining particularly to international assignments.

GENERAL PRINCIPLES AND PRACTICES OF EMPLOYEE SELECTION

Triangulation

This term literally means to measure something from three different angles to achieve an accurate assessment. Many human resource selection techniques and tools are available to provide information about a candidate for making a selection decision—whether or not to hire. And each measure used to assess a candidate generally has particular strengths and limitations. The more kinds of measures used provides a field of data, and the areas of agreement or convergence of the data from these measures tend to provide much more accuracy in predicting the future success of a candidate than data provided by a single measure or assessment. When only one approach or measure is used, the quality of that decision will be vulnerable to the limitations of that particular measure. To illustrate, there reportedly was once a company president who desired to surround himself with brilliant employees and decided to use a standard IQ test alone to select all new employees. In time the president found that he had indeed hired a large number of intellectually superior employees. However, he regrettably noted that company performance and productivity had deteriorated considerably due to internal conflicts and poor coordination of effort—his individually brilliant employees didn't know how to work together as a team. Clearly, additional and varied selection measures would have been helpful.

Focus on Job Relevance

The actual requirements of a job should guide all selection activities and decisions, and the results of the various assessments of a job candidate should be judged against those relevant job requirements. We recently noted in a newspaper in Argentina that the qualifications requested in a job announcement for a secretary included such characteristics as "young woman" and "attractive." Although an employer might personally desire a particular gender and attractiveness in a candidate, those characteristics in themselves will be inadequate in getting the required work done. Of course, local mores may prescribe particular characteristics such as those related to age and gender, and in these cases a fit with local cultural expectations might represent an important job qualification. Nevertheless, to increase the likelihood of making effective selection decisions in hiring the best talent—and in some countries, to also avoid costly litigation due to claims of unfair treatment and discrimination related to age, gender, ethnic background, and so forth—a general rule to follow would be to ensure that all selection methods and decisions are clearly job-related.

In some cases a strict focus on job-relatedness and a candidate's ability to perform the actual requirements of a job can result in the hiring of candidates who otherwise might not even be seriously considered. For example, in the United States the Americans with Disabilities Act requires that employers make reasonable accommodations for hiring people with disabilities who, with accommodation, would qualify for a job opening. Employers are now not allowed to simply rule out a candidate with a disability without consideration of possible accommodation. And as part of the selection process, managers are strongly encouraged to not refer directly to the disability but to ask the candidate to demonstrate or explain how, with a reasonable accommodation, he or she would perform the critical responsibilities of the job. We have met several managers who have indicated that if they had not been directed by these legal guidelines when considering candidates with disabilities, they would have simply dismissed many of these candidates, assuming that they would be unable to perform the job. But when forced to allow the candidates to *demonstrate their ability to perform relevant job requirements,* these managers were repeatedly amazed at how wrong their assumptions proved to be, resulting in the hiring of very valuable employees for the company. They clearly learned how their faulty assumptions and negative expectations regarding people with disabilities were much greater and limiting than the actual disability.

Investment in Developing Interviewing Skills

The employment interview is generally the most frequently used method for employee selection, yet in the hands of untrained managers and supervisors, it often has one of the lowest validity rates in predicting the future company success of a job candidate.[102] Therefore, to increase the accuracy of this widely used and potentially valuable selection method, organizations should invest in training on interviewing skills for their managers and supervisors and other employees involved in the selection process. Such training should cover different interviewing approaches and when they can be most effectively used, practices for conducting an effective interview, and what to avoid in an interviewing situation (for example, interviewer domination, asking of questions unrelated to the job, and premature judgments of the candidate).

An important focus of this training should be on the behavioral interview technique, which is becoming a primary and highly successful interviewing tool for many organizations. Based on the strong evidence that past behavior is the best predictor of future behavior,[103] this approach requires the candidate to describe specific experiences in the past in which he or she demonstrated an important job-related behavior. Situational interviews can also be effective, which require the candidate to describe how he or she would solve a particular problem relevant to the job. For both behavioral and situational interview approaches, the interviewer should carefully prepare beforehand by examining the critical behaviors needed for the job and developing behaviorally based questions that elicit a picture of how the candidate performed those behaviors in the past or how he or she would perform those behaviors in a particular situation relevant to the job.

Influence of Culture on Selection Measures

In carrying out employee selection on a global scale a careful consideration should be made regarding the possible influence of cultural differences in affecting the results and conclusions of selection tests and other methods and measures for assessing candidate fit and qualifications. For example, in some Western cultures nonverbal behavior, such as a firm handshake and considerable eye contact, exhibited by a job candidate in an initial interview might convey the impression that the candidate is confident, enthusiastic, and forthright, whereas a weak handshake and evasive, minimal eye contact might convey to the Western interviewer the impression of insecurity, low self-esteem, or even untrustworthiness and intent to withhold truth. However, in many Asian cultures the latter behavior by an interviewee would be considered very appropriate, with direct eye contact held to a minimum as a sign of respect for the interviewer.

Assessment centers are generally seen as one of the most robust and valid selection techniques. But their often culture-bound assumptions about "appropriate" candidate behavior in one country might not effectively translate elsewhere. For example, British Airways experienced difficulty in applying its standard approach in recruiting Japanese candidates for its Graduate General Manager Program. The candidates found it difficult to take the lead in group exercises or to use the word "I." But with some modification in exercise design and cross-cultural sensitivity training, candidates were able to demonstrate in their own culturally comfortable ways the relevant competencies targeted for assessment.[104]

Differential effects of culture are particularly problematic in the use of personality tests. The subtle interaction between language and culture make it hard to discern if test results are due to national cultural differences or individual candidate characteristics. For example, the personality assessment questionnaire item, "I work hard," although meaningful to British managers, is associated with the much less desirable concept of "toil" for French managers.[105] Consistent with the principle of triangulation, for overcoming potentially misleading effects of cultural differences it is preferable to use multiple selection methods and not to place too much weight on one approach.[106]

SELECTING EMPLOYEES FOR FOREIGN ASSIGNMENTS

The cost of making a poor selection decision can be great, especially so when it involves a foreign assignment. In the final section of this chapter we will examine key considerations and important methods for effectively selecting employees for foreign assignment. Although we will present this information in terms of expatriate selection, in many cases these considerations and methods are applicable across international employee categories of PCN, TCN, and HCN.

Focus on the Most Important Criteria for Success

Related to the previously mentioned important general practice of focusing all selection efforts on job relevance, the most important criteria for achieving success with the international assignment should be considered carefully. And the most important selection criteria depend on the nature of the international assignment. An extended assignment that will feature considerable interaction with a foreign workforce whose culture is very different from that of the expatriate (for example, one with high cultural distance) might point to important selection criteria such as a candidate's local language fluency, ability to adjust, and ability to relate in a sensitive way with other cultures. However, these abilities might not be as important in a much shorter assignment to a foreign operation representing little cultural distance (for example, from Southern Germany to Austria) or involving predominant interaction with PCNs and little HCN interaction.

The primary criterion for selecting employees for a foreign assignment traditionally has been "demonstrated technical competence"—again based on the notion that past behavior is a strong predictor of future performance. However, the major flaw with that reasoning is that the past technical competence likely took place in a domestic work environment without the significant number of uncertainties, unfamiliar conditions, and differing cultural variables contained in the intended new foreign work environment. Selection criteria are now changing to a wider range of skills and personality characteristics, such as interpersonal and relationship-building skills, personal intent and motivation for obtaining international work experience, cross-cultural sensitivity, adaptability, tolerance for ambiguity, and overall inquisitiveness—all deemed appropriate for expatriates filling the critical boundary-spanning role between the MNC and the foreign work environment.[107] In particular, because the ability to adjust to the foreign environment—both on the part of the expatriate and especially any accompanying spouse and family members—appears to have as great or even greater determination in foreign assignment success than the expatriate's technical competence,[108] the assessment of this adjustment ability should likely be given significant weight in the overall selection decision.

Methods for Selecting Employees for a Foreign Assignment

Three major approaches are used, often in combination, for selecting employees for a foreign assignment: (1) a psychometric approach for predicting international management competencies, (2) an experiential approach, and (3) an overall clinical risk assessment approach. We now briefly examine each of these major approaches.

Psychometric Approach. This general approach using personality tests argues that there are identifiable competencies associated with foreign assignment success and that the accurate measurement of these competencies can be used to identify and predict effective performers in international assignments. As with domestic selection measures, many MNCs develop their own customized competency measures. For example, the Society for Worldwide Interbank Financial Telecommunication measures thirty critical success factors, one of which of primary importance is "international mind-set."[109]

However, significant challenges facing these assessments based on a psychomet-

Global Workforce Challenge 6.2
**The Increasing Attractiveness of
Older Expatriates**

In a global environment where companies have less money for country club memberships and other traditional expatriate perks, older workers are an increasingly attractive option because their relative mobility, immersion in corporate culture, and experience make them the cheapest option to get an operation up and running—including in developing countries. For instance, sending an older worker abroad usually means avoiding international school tuition for children, which in China can cost as much as $26,000 per child per year. When it comes to pioneering expatriate employees for new operations in developing countries, we find that a surprising number are older people. China in particular is attracting people who would be thinking about retirement if they were back home in the United States or Europe, but who are now in hot demand in a nation long on laborers but short on leaders—and a nation especially noted for its respect for elders. Ford Motor Company over the years has resorted to its pool of retired U.S., German, British, and Australian auto workers when it needed something done right on the operations side of the China business.

When sixty-one-year-old Gene Allison was looking around Greenville, South Carolina, for a way to cap off a long manufacturing career, he struck upon an idea to move to China. He jumped on plans by his company, Rockwell Automation, Inc., to build a plant in Shanghai, encouraged by his wife who always had a fascination with Asia. He worked for four years setting up the facility and more recently has shifted to keeping tabs on machinists and providing local coaching and advisement at factories run by local suppliers in China. "I think I'll be here the rest of my career—which might be only one or two more years," Allison says. Unlike old-timers, younger workers in U.S. plants often haven't been exposed to the lower-tech manufacturing methods that still power much Chinese industry. In addition, in their later career stage, older expatriates are likely more interested in developing and mentoring others. Mr. Allison is comfortable, nearing the end of his career, providing a valuable contribution by grooming a team of Chinese quality-control experts to take his place when he finally retires.

Sources: Adapted from J. Selmer, J. Lauring, and F. Yunxia, "Age and Expatriate Job Performance in Greater China," *Cross Cultural Management* 16 (2) (2009): 131–48; J.T. Areddy, "Older Workers from US Take Jobs in China," *Wall Street Journal,* June 22, 2004: B1, B6.

ric approach include their difficulty in measuring predictive success and reliability due to the questionable quality of data from the greatly variable and diverse foreign work environments. They also may tend to be too cumbersome in the international staffing setting where more concern may be placed on simply finding willing internal candidates for foreign assignments. Thus, many MNCs may decide not to emphasize the use of psychometric testing for expatriate selection purposes. This inclination is reflected in the following experienced advice to other international HR professionals by Michael Schmidt of Human Resource Consulting:

I don't think that psychometric testing is required prior to sending people abroad. Nor is it established HR practice, to the best of my knowledge. . . . Personally, after twenty-five years of HR experience in managing international transfers and having been transferred from Germany to the United States myself, I am unconvinced that any single personality trait can be identified that either helps or hinders an employee's (or their family members') transferability across country and culture borders.[110]

Experiential Approach. There are three main forms of this second approach, which emphasizes the expatriate candidate's direct experience with many of the realities of the future assignment. These forms differ primarily in their level of time perspective and expense. The first approach, which utilizes an *assessment center technique* (including in-basket exercises, relevant job assignments, and work simulation), places the candidate in various relevant situations and with common and critical tasks that he or she likely would face in the foreign assignment. Therefore, the assessment and comparison of competing candidates' performance on these job-related tasks would tend to have a high degree of validity.

The second form of experiential approach, which requires more time and expense, is a *foreign site preview visit,* or familiarization trip. Here the candidate and her/his spouse and even children may be invited to visit the actual area of the proposed foreign assignment to experience it firsthand. It is of great importance that this brief visit be planned and made as realistic as possible to provide an accurate preview rather than merely an enticing tourist-oriented experience in a foreign and exotic location. This foreign site familiarization trip can be very effective in providing a realistic picture to ensure that the candidate makes an informed decision as well as helping prepare the expatriate—intellectually and emotionally—for the foreign assignment, fostering enhanced adjustment. Nevertheless, it can represent a significant time investment and expense, as indicated by Martin Asdorian of LAMA Associates, Inc., "It can be a big bucks item. To fill a position in Port-of-Spain, Trinidad, I once had to send four candidates with their spouses before I got one willing to take the job."[111]

A third form of the experiential approach for expatriate selection, *developing an internal international cadre or talent pool,* requires significant HR planning and a much longer time perspective than the other forms. This method relies on the MNC's long-range investment in building within its managerial ranks international competencies through foreign work experience. Where a significant number of managers are involved in international developmental assignments of relatively short duration in their early careers, the MNC is able to build up a talent pool of experienced potential candidates for longer-range expatriate assignments. And the quality of the candidates' performance during their early experience can be used as a sound basis for predicting their likelihood of future success in the extended expatriate assignment.

As part of its long-range effort to identify and develop an internal supply of international leadership to meet the demands of future international business growth, Cadbury Schweppes annually has sent sixteen managers through an international assignment as part of its accelerated development program, generating relevant data about each individual's intercultural adaptability and potential for success in extended foreign assignments.[112] This method requiring long-range planning and coordination is recommended by international HR consultant Michael Schmidt, who asserts, "The best indicator for future success in international assignments is past success in international assignments. So you may want to build and maintain an international mobile cadre of managers and professionals in your organization. Short- or medium-term assignments (six to twelve months) at an early stage of a person's career may be part of your HR strategy as well—call it real-life testing."[113]

Clinical Risk Assessment Approach. This third approach investigates candidate competencies and ability to adjust to the demands of the foreign assignment in addition to other factors affecting success beyond the expatriate, including the adaptability of the accompanying partner, dual-career difficulties, the nature of supporting structure in the foreign assignment, cultural distance and technical difficulty of the assignment, and accountabilities and responsibilities.[114] Through this comprehensive assessment, candidates who present an overall picture of greatest potential with minimal risk might be the best choice for a foreign assignment.

SUMMARY

Important general factors that influence global staffing at all employee levels include company business strategy, company stage of international development, specific foreign market experience, host government restrictions and incentives, sociocultural considerations, plans for individual and organization development, and situational factors. Important areas of consideration for global recruitment include the geographic scope of recruitment and whether internal versus external candidates should be sought. Managers should consider several alternative recruitment methods to ensure that they are able to attract an optimal number of qualified candidates at a reasonable cost.

General guiding principles and practices for global selection include triangulation, maintaining a focus on job relevance, investing in building interviewing skills among supervisors, and being aware and controlling for the potentially distorting influence of cross-cultural differences. When selecting employees for foreign assignments, MNCs might consider psychometric, experiential, and clinical risk assessment approaches. Finally, to increase the likelihood of foreign assignment success, MNCs should more broadly consider other candidate characteristics besides technical competence, including interpersonal skills, personal intent and motivation for obtaining international work experience, cross-cultural sensitivity, adaptability, tolerance for ambiguity, overall inquisitiveness, and the viability of a positive experience for accompanying family members.

QUESTIONS FOR OPENING SCENARIO ANALYSIS

1. Based on what you have learned from this chapter, how would you critique the Shell People Services staffing function? Particular strengths? Any weaknesses or potential limitations?
2. What are various methods used by Shell People Services to maximize its ability to have a global reach for talent yet fit local workplace conditions?
3. How is the Shell Group using its global staffing function to contribute to overall competitive advantage?

CASE 6.1. MNC STAFFING PRACTICES AND LOCAL ANTIDISCRIMINATION LAWS

The U.S. legal landscape is full of lawsuits by minorities and women claiming discrimination at the hands of whites and men. And in recent years there also have been lots of claims by whites claiming "reverse discrimination" against preferential treatment with affirmative action. But the case against Marubeni America, the New York subsidiary of a big Japanese trading company, involves a different sort of alleged prejudice—a U.S.-based foreign-owned company discriminating against people who fall outside of their ethnic group or national origin. This pattern of discrimination is a growing concern due to the increasing presence of MNCs in the United States. Though the Marubeni case isn't unprecedented, the e-mails and other evidence cited in this case offer a rare inside look into the employment practices of an MNC operating in a host country where local law conflicts with employment practice.

The plaintiffs in this case—two Caucasian executives—accused the local subsidiary, general manager, chief financial officer, and head of human resources of discriminating against Americans, non-Asian minorities, and women. The suit alleges that non-Asians are promoted less frequently and paid less than Asians. The two-hundred-worker company has no African Americans or females and just one Hispanic among its 121 top officers and managers, the suit says, and just three African-American lower-level employees. The suit also claims that weekly meetings were conducted in Japanese, effectively excluding non-Japanese-speaking employees, and that some executives frequently used racial and ethnic slurs. The suit was brought by Kevin Long, a senior HR employee, and Ludvic Presto, the company's top internal auditor, both of whom were placed on paid administrative leave—a move their lawyers claim was retaliation for complaining about discrimination. The two men are asking for a minimum of $4 million each in severance payments, plus pension and other benefits, and $55 million in damages and legal costs. Two current female HR workers also filed similar complaints with the U.S. Equal Employment Opportunity Commission.

Although Marubeni strongly contests the validity of these claims about discrimination, damning e-mail records suggest otherwise. Mr. Long received the following e-mail from Yuji Takikawa, a vice president of the U.S. company's textile unit, requesting help hiring a salesperson: "I want a person who has aggressiveness, high IQ. We prefer male and 25 to 30 years old. Asian, like Chinese, Japanese, of course American or others is fine. As you know, in case of American guy, once reach high income, all of a sudden stop working. This is my feeling." On another occasion, an executive wrote in an e-mail to Mr. Long that two other top company officials had discussed replacing a pregnant employee because they were worried "about her unstable situation after the delivery." Mr. Long replied that their grounds for wanting to replace the woman, who had been with the company for fifteen years, were "inappropriate and considered pregnancy discrimination in this country." The head of human resources of the local operation, in a farewell e-mail upon retirement, wrote that the company's outside lawyers had "done a masterful job" at protecting the company from litigation from groups that he described using racial slurs.

Marubeni isn't the first Japanese-owned U.S.-based company accused of national-origin discrimination. In 1980, thirteen female American secretaries sued Sumitomo Shoji America, Inc., alleging it hired only male Japanese nationals for management jobs. The company claimed it was immune from the suit based on a 1953 treaty with the United States that gave both countries' corporations limited immunity from each other's employment discrimination laws so they could make sure that only their own citizens held targeted positions in operations based in the other country. But the U.S. Supreme Court rejected this argument, ruling that all foreign-owned subsidiaries in the United States are subject to U.S. employment laws. Sumitomo agreed in a settlement to pay more than $2.6 million to current and former employees and to accelerate efforts to recruit and promote qualified women.

Source: Adapted from K. Scannell, "Lawsuit Charges US Unit of Japanese Company with Bias," *Wall Street Journal,* January 20, 2005: B1, B2.

QUESTIONS FOR CASE ANALYSIS AND DISCUSSION

1. What message does this case have for MNCs as they plan and carry out staffing and other workforce management activities in their foreign host operations?
2. What evidence does this case provide that local management was guilty of unfair discrimination according to U.S. labor laws?
3. Do you believe that the behavior of local Marubeni managers would be acceptable in other counties where it is not specifically prohibited by local labor laws?
4. Besides avoiding legal costs, can you think of any other reasons to avoid discriminatory behavior when making staffing decisions in global workforce management?

CASE 6.2. LOCAL STAFFING FOR GLOBAL BUSINESS OUTSOURCING SUCCESS

Wipro Technologies of Bangalore, India, was having trouble persuading German companies to outsource offshore their chip and software design work to Wipro—until the company hired Walter Ortmueller. The German engineer talks, looks, and thinks like the Indian outsourcer's prospective clients, and that puts him in a better position than his Indian bosses to overcome common local fears about sending high-tech production and back-office operations halfway around the world to workers who speak a different language. Using a middleman "from the same country generates automatic trust," says Mr. Ortmueller, whose twenty years of contacts in the industry now help him scout and win clients for Wipro. The company had only two technology-design customers when it found Mr. Ortmueller in March 2003, and a year later had ten, most of which it attributes to having a center in Germany staffed with German engineers.

Outsourcing is finally beginning to crack the European market, once a staffing strategy was added of using a heavy sprinkling of local representatives from the same cultural background as the target clients. "Local presence was a must for the customers" in Europe, says Sangita Singh, Wipro's chief marketing officer. European businesses "want to be sure that their voice can be heard within a large organization that doesn't have its center of operations in Europe," she says. Using locals also provides "the cultural and linguistic ties that make the clients smile and helps us build stronger relationships," Ms. Singh adds. Mr. Ortmueller understands, for example, that German businesspeople would rather take a direct and unambiguous "no" response for an answer than receive a delayed response. Germans, he says, also are not as open to bargaining as Indian or U.S. companies are. "If they don't like the price, they say 'thanks' and call the next provider," he says.

Offshore outsourcing is growing dramatically in Europe, although still behind the U.S. pace due to European labor laws that make relocating jobs through offshore outsourcing a long and costly process. To avoid layoffs, many European companies outsource only work and projects that require new hiring. But European businesspersons also are generally more reluctant than Americans to take risks or try out new ideas, Indian outsourcers say. But local hires like Mr. Ortmueller help clients overcome this reluctance. "Without a local partner, our clients would simply not do outsourcing. We bridge the distance between different geographies that can generate a lot of misunderstandings," says Ortmueller. When Mr. Debjit Chaudhuri first came to Germany in 1999 to open an outsourcing office for India's Infosys Technologies, Ltd., a Bangalore-based consulting and IT services firm, German companies "didn't know what I was talking about," he says. "You need to build confidence, trying to keep it as German as possible, while giving you the benefits of outsourcing."

Mr. Chaudhuri's office hires Germans for their knowledge of the country's laws and regulations as well as its markets. It also tends to use locals for face-to-face interactions with German customers to bridge language and cultural differences. Wipro has similar client-development centers in Sweden, Britain, the Netherlands, and Finland and puts the same emphasis on using locals in each country. The company also has sales offices in eight countries in Europe, and for each the marketing team is about 90 percent locals, Ms. Singh says, compared with only 30 percent in the U.S. sales offices. She adds that in the United States, where language and cultural differences are less of an issue, the sales staff "could all be Indian."

Source: Adapted from A. Campoy, "Think Locally: Indian Outsourcing Companies Have Finally Begun to Crack the European Market," *Wall Street Journal,* September 27, 2004: R8.

QUESTIONS FOR CASE ANALYSIS AND DISCUSSION

1. Usually hiring locals is associated with a general multidomestic or polycentric overall strategic approach to international business. Is this the case with Wipro Technologies of Bangalore, India?

2. How does Wipro's and other similar companies' local staffing approach in Europe support company strategy and help achieve competitive advantage?

3. Why is this local staffing approach to support outsourcing client development

so important in Europe compared to the United States? Is this approach necessary in all global operations? What added costs might be associated with this local staffing approach?

RECOMMENDED WEB SITE RESOURCES

Diversity Directory MindExchange.com (www.mindexchange.com/europe.htm). Extensive list of European firms providing staffing, recruitment, and employment advertising services.

The International Association of Corporate & Professional Recruitment (www.iacpr.org). An international group of senior-level corporate human resource and recruitment executives, retained executive-search professionals, human capital consultants, and academics committed to the recruitment and success of executive leadership.

International Executive Search Federation (www.iesf.com). An international group of senior-level corporate human resource and recruitment executives, retained executive-search professionals, human capital consultants, and academics committed to the recruitment and success of executive leadership.

Manpower (www.manpower.com). A world leader in the employment services industry, offering a continuum of services in permanent, temporary, and contract recruitment; employee assessment; and career transition management. With 4,300 offices in sixty-seven countries and territories, the largest market is France, followed by the United States and United Kingdom. In 2003, there were 25,000 staff employees worldwide and 2.3 million people placed on temporary and contract assignments in 2003.

Robert Half International (www.rhi.com). World's largest specialized staffing services firm with more than 325 offices in North America, Europe, Australia, and New Zealand.

Selection Research International (www.sri-2000.com). An international group of corporate psychologists and management consultants specializing in providing organizations research-based guidance, assessment tools, and other resources for global staff assessment and selection.

NOTES

1. Adapted from D. Wiechmann, A.M. Ryan, and M. Hemingway, "Designing and Implementing Global Staffing Systems: Part I—Leaders in Global Staffing," *Human Resource Management* 42 (1) (2003): 71–83.

2. A.Y. Lewin, S. Massini, and C. Peeters, "Why Are Companies Offshoring Innovation? The Emerging Global Race for Talent," *Journal of International Business Studies* 40 (6) (2009): 901–925; E. Gordon, "The Global Talent Crisis," *The Futurist,* 43 (5) (2009): 34–39; J. McGregor, "Keeping Talent in the Fold," *Business Week,* November 3, 2008.

3. C. Fombrun, N.M. Tichy, and M.A. Devanna, *Strategic Human Resource Management* (New York: Wiley, 1984).

4. W.L. French, *Human Resources Management,* 5th ed. (Boston: Houghton-Mifflin, 2003).

5. A. Bird and S. Beechler, "The Link between Business Strategy and International Human Resource Management Practices," in *Readings and Cases in International Human Resource Management,* ed. M. Mendenhall and G. Oddou (New York: South-Western College, 2000): 70–80; R.S. Schuler, "Strategic Human Resources Management: Linking the People with the Strategic Needs of the Business," *Organizational Dynamics* 21 (1) (1992): 18–32.

6. Ibid.; C.R. Greer, *Strategic Human Resource Management: A General Managerial Approach,* 2d ed. (Upper Saddle River, NJ: Prentice-Hall, 2001).

7. N. Ando, D.K. Rhee, and N.K. Park, "Parent Country Nationals or Local Nationals for Executive Positions in Foreign Affiliates: An Empirical Study of Japanese Affiliates in Korea," *Asia Pacific Journal of Management* 25 (1) (2008): 113–34.

8. P. Evans, V. Pucik, and J. Barsoux, *The Global Challenge: Frameworks for International Human Resource Management* (New York: McGraw-Hill/Irwin, 2002); V. Mehta, "Outsourcing to India," *Mortgage Banking* 62 (12) (2002): 76–84; C.K. Prahalad and G. Hamel, "The Core Competence of the Corporation," *Harvard Business Review* 68 (May/June 1990): 79–91; J.B. Quinn and F.G. Hilmer, "Strategic Outsourcing," *Sloan Management Review* 35 (4) (1994): 43–55.

9. K. Monks, H. Scullion, and J. Creaner, "HRM in International Firms: Evidence from Ireland," *Personnel Review* 30 (5/6) (2001): 536–53; H.V. Perlmutter, "The Tortuous Evolution of the Multinational Corporation," *Columbia Journal of World Business* 4 (1) (1969): 9–18; D.A. Heenan and H.V. Perlmutter, *Multinational Organization Development* (Reading, MA: Addison-Wesley, 1979).

10. H. Deresky, *International Management: Managing across Borders and Cultures* (New York: Harper Collins College, 1993).

11. S. Colakoglu and P. Caligiuri, "Cultural Distance, Expatriate Staffing and Subsidiary Performance: The Case of U.S. Subsidiaries of Multinational Corporations," *International Journal of Human Resource Management* 19 (2) (2008): 223–39; A.W. Harzing, *Managing the Multinationals: An International Study of Control Mechanisms* (Cheltenham, UK: Edward Elgar, 1999).

12. R. Bebenroth, D. Li, and T. Sekiguchi, "Executive Staffing Practice Patterns in Foreign MNC Affiliates Based in Japan," *Asian Business & Management* 7 (3) (2008): 381–403.

13. A. Hain-Cole, "Expatriate Talent Market Trends," *Benefits & Compensation International* 39 (7) (2010): 24; Y. McNulty, H. De Cieri, and K. Hutchings, "Do global firms measure expatriate return on investment? An empirical examination of measures, barriers and variables influencing global staffing practices. *The International Journal of Human Resource Management* 20 (6) (2009): 1309–26; W.V. Poe, "The Expatriate: Employers and Employees Alike Should Consider Financial Implications of Overseas Assignments," *St. Louis Commerce Magazine* (March 2001), www.stlcommercemagazine. com/archives/March2001/accounting.html.

14. Poe, "The Expatriate"; Black and Gregersen, "The Right Way to Manage Expats."

15. S.M. Toh and A.S. Denisi, "Host Country National Reactions to Expatriate Pay Policies: A Model and Implications," *Academy of Management Review* 28 (4) (2003): 606–21.

16. J. Hailey, "The Expatriate Myth: Cross-Cultural Perceptions of Expatriate Managers," *International Executive* 38 (1) (1996): 255–71.

17. G.R. Simpson, "Multinational Firms Take Steps to Avert Boycotts over War," *Wall Street Journal,* April 4, 2003.

18. C.M. Vance and Y. Paik, "Where Do American Women Face Their Biggest Obstacle to Expatriate Career Success? Back in Their Own Backyard," Special Issue on Women in Management: Cross-Cultural Research, *Cross-Cultural Management: An International Journal* 8 (3/4) (2001): 98–116.

19. Y. Paik, C.M. Vance, J. Gale, and C.A. McGrath, "Improving Global Knowledge Management Through Inclusion of Host Country Workforce Input," in *Strategic Knowledge Management in Multinational Organizations,* ed. K.J. O'Sullivan (Hershey, PA: Information Science Reference, 2007): 167–82; Harvey et al., "The Role of Inpatriates in a Globalization Strategy and Challenges Associated with the Inpatriation Process," http//www.entrepreneur.com/tradejournals/article/546575821./htm/, accessed June 17, 2010.

20. M.A. Carpenter, W.G. Sanders, and H.G. Gregersen, "Bundling Human Capital with Organizational Context: The Impact of International Assignment Experience on Multinational Firm Performance and CEO Pay," *Academy of Management Journal* 44 (3) (2001): 493–511.

21. A.Y. Lewin, S. Massini, and C. Peeters, "Why are Companies Offshoring Innovation? The Emerging Global Race for Talent," *Journal of International Business Studies* 40 (6) (2009): 901–25.

22. Ibid.

23. N. Noorderhaven and A. Harzing, "Knowledge-Sharing and Social Interaction Within MNEs," *Journal of International Business Studies* 40 (5) (2009): 719–41; M.E. Mendenhall, T.M. Kuhlmann, and G.K. Stahl, eds., *Developing Global Business Leaders: Policies, Processes, and Innovations* (Westport, CT: Quorum Books, 2001): 1–16; S.J. Perkins, *Internationalization: The People Dimension* (London: Kogan Page, 1997).

24. R.S. Schuler, S.E. Jackson, and Y. Luo, *Managing Human Resources in Cross-Border Alliances* (London: Routledge, 2004).

25. N. Boyacigiller and N.J. Adler, "The Parochial Dinosaur: The Organizational Sciences in a Global Context," *Academy of Management Review* 16 (1991): 1–32.

26. J.E. Salk and M.Y. Brannen, "National Culture, Networks, and Individual Influence in a Multi-national Management Team," *Academy of Management Journal* 43 (2) (2000): 191–202.

27. Harvard Business School, *Forging the International Partnership* (Boulder, CO: David Grubin Productions, Inc., 1995).

28. Evans et al., *The Global Challenge: Frameworks for International Human Resource Management* (New York: McGraw-Hill, 2002); M. Harvey, C. Speier, and M. Novicevic, "A Theory-Based Framework for Strategic Global Human Resource Staffing Policies and Practices," *International Journal of Human Resource Management* 12 (6) (2001): 898–915; Harvey et al., "The Role of Inpatriates in a Globalization Strategy and Challenges Associated with the Inpatriation Process."

29. H. Park, M. Gowan, and S. Hwang, "Impact of National Origin and Entry Mode on Trust and Organizational Commitment," *Multinational Business Review* 10 (2) (2002): 52–61.

30. Konopacke, Werner, and Neupert, "Entry Mode Strategy and Performance"; J.P. Killing, "How to Make a Global Joint Venture Work," *Harvard Business Review* (May/June 1982): 120–27.

31. R.L. Tung, "Career Issues in International Assignments," *Academy of Management Executive* 2 (3) (1988): 241–44.

32. Evans et al., *The Global Challenge.*

33. O. Moen and P. Servais, "Born Global or Gradual Global? Examining the Export Behavior of Small and Medium-Sized Enterprises," *Journal of International Marketing* 10 (3) (2002): 49–72; B.M. Oviatt and P.P. McDougall, "Toward a Theory of International New Ventures," *Journal of International Business Studies* 25 (1) (1994): 45–64; J. Johanson and J.-E. Vahlne, "The Mechanism of Internation-alization," *International Marketing Review* 7 (4) (1990): 11–24.

34. Moen and Servais, "Born Global or Gradual Global?"

35. M. Celestino, "Manufacturing in Mexico," *World Trade* 12 (7) (1999): 36–42; D. Eaton, "Taking Shelter," *Business Mexico* 9 (4) (1999): 22–23.

36. Evans et al., *The Global Challenge.*

37. Y. Fang, G. Jiang, S. Makino, and P. Beamish, "Multinational Firm Knowledge, Use of Expatri-ates, and Foreign Subsidiary Performance," *The Journal of Management Studies,* 47 (1) (2010): 27–54; I. Björkman, W. Barner-Rasmussen, and L. Li, "Managing Knowledge Transfer in MNCs: The Impact of Headquarters Control Mechanisms," *Journal of International Business Studies* 35 (5) (2004): 443–55.

38. J. Sheehan, "What Troubles Europe?" *Commonweal* 137(8) (2010): 16–18; D. Murphey, "Reflec-tions on the Revolution in Europe: Immigration, Islam, and the West," *The Journal of Social, Political, and Economic Studies* 35(1) (2010): 109–115.

39. "Business: Bridging Europe's Skills Gap," *Economist,* March 31, 2001; R. Konrad, "Foreign Techies Move In," *Fortune* 144 (10) (2002): 30.

40. L. Wayne, "Workers, and Bosses, in a Visa Maze," *New York Times,* April 29, 2001.

41. T.H. Moran, *Beyond Sweatshops: Foreign Direct Investment and Globalization in Developing Nations* (Washington, DC: Brookings Institution Press, 2002); A. Walter, "Do They Really Rule the World?" *New Political Economy* 3 (2) (1998): 288–92; S. Lall, *Competitiveness, Technology and Skills* (Cheltenham, UK: Edward Elgar, 2001).

42. S. Lall, *Competitiveness, Technology and Skills*; S. Lall, *Attracting Foreign Investment: New Trends, Sources and Policies* (London: Commonwealth Secretariat, Economic Affairs Division, 1997).

43. S. Song, "Policy Issues of China's Urban Unemployment," *Contemporary Economic Policy* 21 (2) (2003): 258–69; K.H. Zhang, "What Attracts Foreign Multinational Morporations to China?" *Contemporary Economic Policy* 19 (3) (2001): 336–46.

44. M. Segalla, A. Sauquet, and C. Turati, "Symbolic vs. Functional Recruitment: Cultural Influences on Employee Recruitment Policy?" *European Management Journal* 19 (1) (2001): 32–43.

45. R.I. Gopalkrishnan, "International Exchanges as the Basis for Conceptualizing Ethics in International Business," *Journal of Business Ethics* 31 (1) (2001): 3–24; T. Donaldson, "Values in Tension: Ethics Away from Home," *Harvard Business Review* 74 (5) (1996): 48–62.

46. J. Selmer, J. Lauring, and F. Yunxia, "Age and Expatriate Job Performance in Greater China," *Cross Cultural Management* 16 (2) (2009): 131–48.

47. V. Brand and A. Slater, "Using a Qualitative Approach to Gain Insights into the Business Ethics Experiences of Australian Managers in China," *Journal of Business Ethics* 45 (3) (2003): 167; K.M. Al-Aiban and J.L. Pearce, "The Influence of Values on Management Practices," *International Studies of Management and Organization* 23 (3) (1993): 35–52.

48. C.L. Owen, R.F. Scherer, M.Z. Sincoff, and M. Cordano, "Perceptions of Women as Managers in Chile and the United States," *Mid-American Journal of Business* 18 (2) (2003): 43–50; C.L. Owen and R.F. Scherer, "Doing Business in Latin America: Managing Cultural Differences in Perceptions of Female Expatriates," *SAM Advanced Management Journal* 67 (2) (2002): 37–41; S. Paternostro, *In the Land of God and Man: A Latin Woman's Journey* (New York: Plume, 1998); N. Gaouette, "Voices from behind Her Veil: Women in Conservative Islam Societies Talk about Their Lives, and How the West Perceives Them," *Christian Science Monitor,* www.csmonitor.com/2001/1219/pls3-wogi.html.

49. G.S. Insch, N. McIntyre, and N.K. Napier, "The Expatriate Glass Ceiling: The Second Layer of Glass" *Journal of Business Ethics* 81 (1) (2008): 19–28; Y. Paik and C.M. Vance, "Evidence of Back-Home Selection Bias Against U.S. Female Expatriates," *Women in Management Review* 17 (2) (2002): 68–79; O. Culpan and G.H. Wright, "Women Abroad: Getting the Best Results from Women Managers," *International Journal of Human Resource Management* 13 (2002): 784–801.

50. P. Vanderbroeck, "Long-Term Human Resource Development in Multinational Organizations," *Sloan Management Review* 34 (1) (1992): 95–99.

51. A.B. Fisher, "When Will Women Get to the Top?" *Fortune,* September 21, 1992, 44–56.

52. Y. Altman and S. Shortland, "Women and International Assignments: Taking Stock—a 25-Year Review," *Human Resource Management* 47 (2) (2008): 199–216; "Expatriate Activity Growth Continues," *Area Development Site and Facility Planning* 38 (6) (2003): 16.

53. "Labor Letter Section," *Wall Street Journal,* March 22, 1994; J.S. Lublin, "Taking Steps Can Cut Risk of Rocky Return from Overseas Stint," *Wall Street Journal,* August 25, 1993.

54. P. Tharenou, "Disruptive Decisions to Leave Home: Gender and Family Differences in Expatriation Choices," *Organizational Behavior and Human Decision Processes* 105 (2) (2008): 183–200; L. Stroh, A. Varma, and S.J. Valy-Durbin, "Why Are Women Left at Home: Are They Unwilling to Go on International Assignments?" *Journal of World Business* 35 (3) (2000): 241–55.

55. M. Linehan, "Women International Managers: The European Experience," *Cross Cultural Management* 8 (3/4) (2001): 68–84; Stroh et al., "Why Are Women Left at Home"; N.J. Adler, "Women Managers in a Global Economy," *HR Magazine* 38 (9) (1993): 52–55; D.N. Izraeli, M. Banal, and Y. Zeira, "Women Executives in MNC Subsidiaries," *California Management Review* 23 (1) (1980): 53–63.

56. N. Napier and S. Taylor, *Western Women Working in Japan* (Westport, CT: Quorum Books, 1996); C. Steinberg, "Working Women Have Their Work Cut Out for Them Overseas," *World Trade* 9 (2) (1996): 22–25; R.I. Westwood and S.M. Leung, "The Female Expatriate Manager Experience: Coping with Gender and Culture," *International Studies of Management and Organization* 24 (3) (1994): 64–85; N.J. Adler, "Women Managers in a Global Economy," *Training and Development* 48 (4) (1994): 30–36.

57. Altman and Shortland, "Women and International Assignments"; A.B. Fisher, "Overseas, US Businesswomen May Have the Edge," *Fortune,* (September 28, 1998: 30–34; Steinberg, "Working Women Have Their Work Cut Out for Them Overseas"; N.J. Adler and D.N. Izraeli, *Competitive Frontiers—Women Managers in a Global Economy* (Cambridge, MA: Blackwell, 1994).

58. Altman and Shortland, "Women and International Assignments"; J. Selmer and A.S.M. Leung, "Expatriate Career Intentions of Women on Foreign Assignments and Their Adjustment," *Journal of Managerial Psychology* 18 (3) (2003): 244–58.

59. Steinberg, "Working Women Have Their Work Cut Out for Them Overseas."

60. Paik and Vance, "Evidence of Back-Home Selection Bias Against U.S. Female Expatriates"; W. Kirk and R. Maddox, "International Management: The New Frontier for Women," *Personnel* 65 (3) (1988): 46–49.

61. N.J. Adler, "Competitive Frontiers: Women Managing across Borders," *Journal of Management Development* 13 (2) (1996): 24–41; Adler, "Women Managers in a Global Economy."

62. A. Varma, S.M. Toh, and P. Budhwar, "A New Perspective on the Female Expatriate Experience: The Role of Host Country National Categorization," *Journal of World Business* 41 (2) (2006): 112–20.

63. C.M. Vance, Y. Paik, and J. White, "Tracking Bias Against the Selection of Female Expatriates: Implications and Opportunities for Business Education," *Thunderbird International Business Review* 48 (6) (2006): 823–42.

64. H. Harris, "Think International Manager, Think Male: Why Are Women Not Selected for International Management Assignments?" *Thunderbird International Business Review* 44 (2) (2002): 175–203.

65. Insch, McIntyre, and Napier, "The Expatriate Glass Ceiling"; K. Tyler, "Don't Fence Her In," *HR Magazine* 46 (3) (2001): 69–77.

66. P. Caligiuri, "Global Competence: What Is It, and Can It Be Developed through Global Assignments?" *HR Planning* 24 (3) (2001): 27–35; Harvey et al., "The Role of Inpatriates in a Globalization Strategy and Challenges Associated with the Inpatriation Process."

67. Mendenhall et al., *Developing Global Business Leaders: Policies, Processes, and Innovations.*

68. Vance and Paik, "Where Do American Women Face Their Biggest Obstacle to Expatriate Career Success?"; Harvey et al., "The Role of Inpatriates in a Globalization Strategy and Challenges Associated with the Inpatriation Process."

69. Vance et al., "Including the Voice of the Host Country Workforce"; M. Downes and A.S. Thomas, "Knowledge Transfer through Expatriation: The U-Curve Approach to Overseas Staffing," *Journal of Managerial Issues* 12 (2) (2000): 131–49; M. Downes and A.S. Thomas, "Managing Overseas Assignments to Build Organizational Knowledge," *HR Planning* 22 (4) (1999): 33–48; S. Bender and A. Fish, "The Transfer of Knowledge and the Retention of Expertise: The Continuing Need for Global Assignments," *Journal of Knowledge Management* 4 (2) (2000): 125–37; Carpenter et al., "Bundling Human Capital with Organizational Context"; K. Kamoche, "Knowledge Creation and Learning in International HRM," *International Journal of Human Resource Management* 8 (3) (1997): 213–25.

70. Lall, *Competitiveness, Technology and Skills*; D. Spar, "Foreign Investment and Human Rights," *Challenge* (January/February 1999): 55–80.

71. M. Vesely, "Jobs for the Boys," *Middle East* 334 (March 2003): 52–55.

72. J. Ryder, "Kidnap and Ransom: A Clear and Present Danger," *Financial Executive* 18 (9) (2002): 20.

73. K. Philbeam, "The East Asian Financial Crisis: Getting to the Heart of the Issues," *Managerial Finance* 27 (1) (2001): 111–33.

74. K. Evans, "U.S. News: Travel Spending Sinks Sharply—Tourism Industry's First Decline Since 9/11 Attacks Prompts Deep Discounts," *Wall Street Journal,* March 20, 2009; C. Prystay, "The SARS Outbreak: SARS Squeezes Asia's Travel Sector—Industry Study Says Virus May Cost Economies Billions of Dollars, Millions of Jobs," *Wall Street Journal,* May 16, 2003.

75. P.R. Sparrow, "International Recruitment, Selection and Assessment," in *The Global Manager: Creating the Seamless Organization,* ed. P. Joynt and B. Morton (London: IPD House, 1999): 87–114; H. Harris and C. Brewster, "The Coffee Machine System: How International Selection Really Works," *International Journal of Human Resource Management* 10 (3) (1999): 488–500.

76. Lewin, Massini, and Peeters, "Why Are Companies Offshoring Innovation?"

77. "Recruiter Responds to Severe U.S. Nurse Shortage," *Health and Medicine Week* (April 28, 2003): 37.

78. E.A. Ensher, T.R. Nielson, and E. Grant-Vallone, "Tales from the Hiring Line: Effects of the Internet and Technology on HR Processes," *Organizational Dynamics* 31 (3) (Winter 2002): 224–44.

79. Greer, *Strategic Human Resource Management: A General Managerial Approach.*

80. W. Chan, "External Recruitment versus Internal Promotion," *Journal of Labor Economics* 14 (4) (1996): 555–70.

81. C.D. Fisher, L.F. Schoenfeldt, and J.B. Shaw, *Human Resource Management,* 5th ed. (Boston: Houghton-Mifflin, 2003).

82. A. Edstrom and J. Galbraith, "Transfer of Managers as a Coordination and Control Strategy in Multinational Firms," *Administrative Science Quarterly* 22 (2) (1977): 248–63.

83. M. Harvey and M. Novicevic, "Selecting Expatriates for Increasingly Complex Global Assignments," *Career Development International* 6 (2) (2001): 69–86.

84. Fisher, Schoenfeldt, and Shaw, *Human Resource Management.*

85. Harvey and Novicevic, "Selecting Expatriates for Increasingly Complex Global Assignments."

86. For example, see "Software Solves Problem of Global Succession Planning at Friesland Foods," *Human Resource Management International Digest* 15 (6) (2007): 21–23.

87. C.M. Vance, "The Personal Quest for Building Global Competence: A Taxonomy of Self-Initiating Career Path Strategies for Gaining Business Experience Abroad," *Journal of World Business* 40 (4) (2005): 374–85.

88. A. Prayag, "Employee Referrals Popular among HR Managers," *Businessline* (July 6, 2004): 1.

89. J. T. Arnold, "Employee Referrals at a Keystroke," *HRMagazine,* 51(10) (2006): 82–88.

90. Prayag, "Employee Referrals Popular among HR Managers."

91. K. Taylor, "British Employers Can Cut Costs by Hiring via Worker Referrals," *Knight Ridder Tribune Business News* (July 4, 2004): 1.

92. T. Petersen and I. Saporta, "The Opportunity Structure for Discrimination," *American Journal of Sociology* 109 (4) (2004): 852–902; W. Thomas, "Mitigating Barriers to Black Employment through Affirmative Action Regulations: A Case Study," *Review of Black Political Economy* 27 (3) (Winter 2000): 81–102; M. Carroll, M. Marchington, J. Earnshaw, and S. Taylor, "Recruitment in Small Firms: Processes, Methods and Problems," *Employee Relations* 21 (3) (1999): 236–50.

93. A.G. Wirth, "Asian Update," *Canadian Shareowner* 11 (5) (1998): 24–25.

94. Brand and Slater, "Using a Qualitative Approach to Gain Insights into the Business Ethics Experiences of Australian Managers in China"; Al-Aiban and Pearce, "The Influence of Values on Management Practices."

95. B.P. Sunoo, "Nepotism—Problem or Solution?" *Workforce* 77 (6) (1998): 17.

96. C.M. Vance and Y. Paik, "AmCham-Based International Internships: A Cost-Effective Distance Field Learning Model for Improving MBA International Business Education," in *New Visions of Graduate Management Education: Research in Management Education and Development* (Vol. 6) ed. C. Wankel and R. DeFillippi (Greenwich, CT: Information Age Publishing, 2006): 283–305; S. Howard, "Internship Opening Doors to the Real World," *Resource* 10 (2) (2003): S4–S5; J. Stewart and V. Knowles, "Mentoring in Undergraduate Business Management Programs," *Journal of European Industrial Training* 27 (2–4) (2003): 147–59.

97. M.E. Scott, "Internships Add Value to College Recruitment," *Personnel Journal* (April 1992): 59–63.

98. Ensher et al., "Tales from the Hiring Line."

99. Sparrow, "International Recruitment, Selection and Assessment."

100. N. Theodore and J. Peck, "The Temporary Staffing Industry: Growth Imperatives and Limits to Contingency," *Economic Geography* 78 (4) (2002): 463–93.

101. Sparrow, "International Recruitment, Selection and Assessment."

102. R.W. Mondy, R.M. Noe, and S.R. Premeaux, *Human Resource Management,* 8th ed. (Upper Saddle River, NJ: Prentice-Hall, 2002); M. Moody, "Ready Aim Hire," *Director* 52 (July 1999): 50.

103. J. Kennedy, "What to Do When Job Applicants Tell Tales of Invented Lives," *Training* 36 (October 1999): 110.

104. Sparrow, "International Recruitment, Selection and Assessment."

105. R. Feltham, C. Lewis, P. Anderson, and D. Hughes, "Psychometrics: Cultural Impediments to Global Recruitment and People Development," British Psychological Society Test User Conference, 1998.

106. Sparrow, "International Recruitment, Selection and Assessment."

107. K. Johnson and L. Duxbury, "The View from the Field: A Case Study of the Expatriate Boundary-Spanning Role," *Journal of World Business* 45 (1) (2010): 29–40; Selmer and Leung, "Expatriate Career Intentions of Women on Foreign Assignments and Their Adjustment"; J.S. Black, A. Morrison, and H.B. Gregersen, *Global Explorers: The Next Generation of Leaders* (New York: Routledge, 1999).

108. H. Lee, "Factors that Influence Expatriate Failure: An Interview Study," *International Journal of Management* 24 (3) (2007): 403–13; J. Selmer, "Adjustment of Third-Country National Expatriates in China," in *The Future of Chinese Management,* ed. M. Warner (London: Frank Cass, 2003); C. Brewster, *The Management of Expatriates* (London: Kogan Page, 1991).

109. Sparrow, "International Recruitment, Selection and Assessment."

110. M. Schmidt, posted January 12, 2003 on International HR listserv (international-hr@lists.lyris.net), sponsored by Expat Forum, www.expatforum.com.

111. M. Asdorian, Jr., posted January 11, 2003 on International HR listserv (international-hr@lists.lyris.net), sponsored by Expat Forum, www.expatforum.com.

112. Sparrow, "International Recruitment, Selection and Assessment."

113. Schmidt, international-hr@lists.lyris.net.

114. Sparrow, "International Recruitment, Selection and Assessment."

7 Global Workforce Training and Development

MOTOROLA UNIVERSITY

Motorola considers education to be an employee right as well as a responsibility. Every Motorola employee, regardless of nationality or location, must complete at least forty hours of training a year. This educational requirement usually takes place through Motorola University, which is probably the best known and most widely benchmarked corporate university in the world. Motorola University is a worldwide system of business training divided into four regions: Europe, the Middle East and Africa, the Americas, and the Asia-Pacific. Each region has a director and a team of training design and delivery experts at various sites in twenty countries. Each regional delivery center directs customer interfaces, delivers programs and services (including Six Sigma and other business training for external customer organizations), and provides consulting for customers on performance improvement and organizational learning.

The university's activities vary according to regional needs. Nevertheless, there is a common global mind-set among the university staff, which helps to ensure that each Motorola University employee can provide or locate a solution to any training problem in the organization. The company's updated computer system enables its PCs to be networked globally. Like the growing number of corporate universities worldwide, Motorola University is shifting its focus from developing employees' general skills to meeting imminent business needs. Among the university's priorities are to develop leadership and management in the global market and build the power of the Motorola brand. The company must create more than two hundred new businesses a year in order to maintain planned growth in the years ahead, and is actively and systematically using company-wide training to reach this performance goal. The university has its own evaluation team to determine whether a particular training course meets its objectives and how the course can be improved. Motorola believes that its strong commitment to company-wide employee education pays off, and has documented U.S. $17 billion in savings from worldwide internal application of its Six Sigma training.[1]

INTRODUCTION

Although training might be considered by some organizations as a wasted expense of time and resources and something to be minimized or outsourced where possible, many MNCs such as Motorola, as shown in the opening case, are investing heavily in training due to their appreciation for its clear impact on gaining competitive advantage in the international arena. As once stated by Andrew Grove, one of the founders of Intel, "Training is quite simply one of the highest leverage activities a manager can perform."[2] Whether the manager is directly involved in providing training for his or her staff or is planning the training agenda for an entire operation to be implemented by other managers or training professionals, an awareness of important issues and potential valuable contributions of training for various members of the global workforce is essential for achieving long-range effectiveness and even company survival. On a broader scale, as organizations globalize, dedicated training efforts, such as through the formation of centralized corporate universities, can help firms to spread a common culture and values and drive change simultaneously across the whole organization. Even in a severe economic downturn such as with the recent global economic crisis, training represents a valuable investment for retaining good employees, keeping them involved in productive activities, and building leadership and other talent assets to prepare companies to spring forward with the eventual economic rebound.[3]

Although learning is a natural and automatic occurrence in the workplace as individuals are motivated to adapt to and master their surroundings, the professional training function is directed at bringing about desired learning in as reliable, timely, and economical a manner as possible. The field of training and development, also known as human resource development (HRD), involves all of the purposeful activities directed at learning that contribute to desired change in individual, group, and organizational behavior.[4] In fact, in this field, which has its roots in behavioral psychology, learning is equated with *measurable behavior change*—the "bottom line" emphasis and priority of organizational performance objectives. Activities of HRD can include *immediate* learning goals such as workforce mastering of a new technology that is being disseminated throughout a MNC, as well as *long-range* learning goals, such as developing a larger, stable supply of global leaders throughout the MNC. Although the terms *training* and *development* are used interchangeably in this book, training typically corresponds to efforts designed to address immediate learning needs within an organization, whereas development typically corresponds to efforts aimed at meeting longer-range learning objectives and is commonly reserved for middle managers and higher executives within the MNC.[5]

To provide a greater understanding and appreciation of the role of training and development for successfully competing in today's global marketplace, this chapter first will examine the strategic role and key contributions of training and then consider fundamental concepts and principles for guiding important global training and development activities. We finally will examine critical imperatives of training and development for the global workforce, including building global competencies and workforce alignment, and particular considerations for HCN and expatriate training, including a special focus on training for female expatriates.

STRATEGIC ROLE OF TRAINING AND DEVELOPMENT IN THE GLOBAL MARKETPLACE

Training plays a central role in the effective *implementation* of organizational strategy and merits thoughtful planning and investment of company resources. An MNC might formulate a brilliant strategy, but it will go nowhere without effective execution and implementation, particularly by means of the current and high-quality mastery of knowledge and competencies as well as solid commitment to the priorities and direction of the organization. We now examine five specific ways in which training can assist organizations in gaining a competitive advantage in our global marketplace.

QUALITY AND CUSTOMER SATISFACTION

Various studies have identified "reliability" as a primary if not *the* most important standard that customers use in evaluating the quality of a product or service.[6] This high premium on reliability is consistent with the total quality, Six Sigma, and ISO 9000 movements, which place a priority on using training to help employees achieve *consistent* quality performance, thus reducing the *variability* of performance from a high-quality standard.[7] And a reduction in variability or variation from a defined standard of performance is essentially the same as increasing the reliability of performance at that desired standard. Therefore, in this way training provides an important contribution to the achievement of customer satisfaction.

DECREASING COSTS

A major strategy for competitive success is satisfying customer needs at lower costs than other firms are able to achieve—thus allowing the use of cost savings to develop new lines of business or service for better satisfying customers, or especially to reduce costs for the customer for products or services. Through effective training, as mentioned earlier, a company can reduce "rejects" and unacceptable performance that yields undesirable results. And because these rejects represent undesirable costs to the organization, their reduction and even elimination through effective training (for example, "zero defects," in total quality language) represent important cost savings.

An additional means of lowering costs is the reduction of wasted time that could be put to more productive use. Training is important for reducing the "learning curve," or time it takes for an employee to achieve an acceptable level of performance mastery. Thus, a shortened learning curve means less time is spent on less productive, suboptimal performance with its associated higher costs of mistakes and necessary higher degree of supervision, representing clear cost savings for the organization. In our global economy, where turbulence and change are increasingly common features of doing business, the agility, or ability of an organization to learn and adapt to needed change swiftly—as presented in the form of threats or opportunities—achieved through effective training and acquisition of new knowledge and skills represents a huge source of cost savings.[8]

The *inability* to adapt and change rapidly also means the potential costly loss of business to competition that can adapt and meet changing customer demand more quickly. Although not as universal and prominent a criterion as reliability, timeliness also has been strongly linked to customer satisfaction.[9] Training again comes into play here by promoting the ability, through rapid skill and process mastery, to reduce the time required to deliver a satisfying product or service to a customer. If your product is of similar price and quality as that of the competition, but yours is consistently available sooner upon the customer's order due to your well-trained, competent workforce, your business will likely lead the competition.

ORGANIZATIONAL LEARNING AND KNOWLEDGE MANAGEMENT

We increasingly are noting the strategic role of organizational learning and knowledge management as companies compete globally.[10] In their research on thirty-five major MNCs from North America, Europe, and the Asia-Pacific region, Conn and Yip found that MNC effectiveness in transferring critical capabilities was by far the most important factor affecting success of a foreign venture.[11] As mentioned in Chapter 4, related to knowledge transfer, knowledge held by individuals can be in the form of *tacit knowledge,* or capability possessed by an individual based on his or her overall level of experience and expertise. Typically this tacit knowledge is not consciously reflected upon, but simply drawn on as work tasks demand. This knowledge often is shared through teamworking arrangements in which the less-experienced employee can observe the actions and decision-making behavior of the more expert employee. Training professionals also can observe these experts to capture their tacit forms of expertise and convert this tacit knowledge into more explicit knowledge and training objectives to be disseminated systematically throughout the firm. Company-wide training plays a major two-part role here through (1) its involvement in the identification of knowledge and competency needs for addressing performance problems and requirements and (2) subsequent systematic diffusion and transfer of knowledge and skills throughout the organization.[12] Collective individual learning and knowledge acquisition resulting from training and various formal and informal forms of experience sharing may result in productive organizational learning, or changes in MNC culture, policies, and commonly accepted practices. Collaborative efforts, including joint ventures, may be engaged in to provide a valuable exchange and sharing of ideas, knowledge, and experience.[13] However, this sharing and dissemination of new knowledge and competencies will proceed only in a haphazard, unpredictable manner unless systematic practices of training are adopted.

GLOBAL ALIGNMENT

Various training activities and related efforts can be used to help build internal employee alignment, or a common mind-set, throughout the MNC that brings control and consistency to offset the unavoidable uncertainty and rapid change within the environments of global business.[14] Beyond this common mind-set, training also can build a common commitment and sense of values to guide decisions; shared attitudes provide additional stability and support for unity of action. This alignment is particularly crucial as MNCs continue to expand into foreign markets through mergers and acquisitions with foreign organizations whose employees unavoidably possess different priorities, values, and ways of thinking, with typically greater differences corresponding to greater cultural distance.[15]

BUILDING GLOBAL TALENT

An increasing priority for MNCs is the development of high-potential employees, from wherever they are found in the global organization, into effective managers and leaders who are able to think and compete effectively on a global scale. This development of needed talent to meet the firm's present and future international business needs cannot be left to happenstance. Training can serve a vital function for helping global professionals and leaders reliably and effectively develop general international competencies (for example, international adjustment skills) that are crucial for their present and future success. Training also is an essential tool for developing specific knowledge and skills that meet unique international assignment demands (such as foreign language ability and knowledge of local laws pertinent to a particular international assignment).[16]

FUNDAMENTAL CONCEPTS AND PRINCIPLES FOR GUIDING GLOBAL TRAINING AND DEVELOPMENT

Several basic concepts and principles can help guide decisions regarding employee training and development at home and abroad. We will now examine some of them, particularly as they apply in the international context. Many of these important fundamental concepts and principles for effective practice are discussed in more detail in texts specializing in training and development,[17] but managers should have a general understanding of them as they consider the learning and development needs of their global workforce.

DOMAINS OF LEARNING

As might be expected, most training is aimed at increasing knowledge, awareness, and understanding—all relating to the *cognitive domain* of learning and involving intellectual and rational thinking processes. Two other domains of learning are also important and have different considerations in the learning process: the affective and psychomotor domains.[18]

The *affective domain* deals with emotions, feelings, values, beliefs, attitudes, and expectations—all often combined into the general category of motivation.[19] In some cases employees might actually have the skills or knowledge to perform effectively, but they lack sufficient commitment or desire to perform in an expected fashion. The changing of attitudes, commitment, or desire to perform effectively pertains to learning in the affective domain and tends to require much more active participant interaction, involvement, and sharing of feelings in the learning process

Global Workforce Challenge 7.1
Toyota's Training Investment in India's Future

Harish, age seventeen, who comes from a family that lives below the poverty line of US$177 in annual income, was a good student but had no particular ambition. Then his schoolteacher alerted him to an advertisement by Toyota in the local paper. The automaker was inviting applications from seventeen-year-old poor and needy students for factory training. It offered free board, lodging, and education, plus a monthly stipend of US$38. There were five thousand applicants, and Harish was one of sixty-four boys from the southern state of Karnataka who was selected by Toyota Tech, Toyota's new training institute, the first outside of Japan. Harish now wants to be an automotive engineer. "I am so happy and can't believe," says Harish in his broken English about how his life and dreams have changed. They certainly have. His mother and grandmother earn 65 cents daily as farm laborers, a brother is a bus cleaner, and a sister is training to be a nurse. But Harish is determined to change his life, thanks to Toyota. In the three months he has been at the Toyota Tech, he has saved $8 to give to his mother. "I want to make her proud," he says, outlining his determination to excel in his three-year course and bag the $180 and $230 fellowships for hardworking students.

Toyota has spent US$5.6 million to set up the institute, which has a faculty of twenty-one permanent, on-contract, and part-time employees. Toyota emphasizes that it makes good business sense to operate the center in India. The country's automobile market is among the fastest growing in the world at 1.5 million cars sold annually, a figure that is expected to soon double. "For us to manufacture more cars, we must have good people. The institute is such a step toward that," says Toyota India Managing Director Atsushi Toyoshima. Like most Indian and global auto players, Toyota, which has been selling its cars in India for over a decade, is also expanding its business in Karnataka. But expansion requires talent, and India is woefully short of such specialized technical talent and education. There are about 4,500 state-run technical institutes littered across India. But at a time when manufacturing in India is booming, these institutes are considered obsolete.

The students are taught by Toyota's best Indian engineers and technicians, who spend time in Japan for specialized training. The coursework is based on Toyota's Japanese parent institute's curriculum, but adapted to India for students who have lived quite modest, unexposed lives. In addition to technical training, the students take self-improvement courses such as yoga and English, and have lessons on personal grooming, cleanliness, and discipline. Toyota plans to employ the students after completing their three-year training, although they have the option of leaving the company and working elsewhere—no bonded servitude here. "It is a corporate social responsibility initiative for us," says the school's principal, Mr. Somanath, previously the head of a nearby training institute. But Toyota also wants to make its investment pay off. When the boys go on vacation, Toyota encourages them to go home in their institute uniforms, which is bound to impress the locals. Harish's experience shows the strategy is working. When he was home, he was bombarded with questions from his friends. He beamed proudly, "I have suddenly gained respect in my society."

Source: Adapted from N. Nandini Lakshman, "Toyota Trains India Teens," *BusinessWeek.com,* January 23, 2008.

than is typically the case for learning in the cognitive domain. Examples in the affective domain include predeparture training efforts directed at helping expatriates and family members to overcome concerns about a new foreign assignment or to reduce and eliminate prejudice against a host country workforce with whom the expatriates will be working. Even when the objectives of training lie primarily in the cognitive domain, there still should be careful consideration of the affective domain for how the training will attract and maintain interest, appear meaningful and relevant, provide positive expectations and confidence, and serve as an overall satisfying experience, especially with immediate feedback indicating successful mastery of the new skills or knowledge.[20]

A third domain of learning, the *psychomotor domain,* often relates to the acquisition of new physical skills, such as typing, correct enunciation of previously unfamiliar and difficult vocal sounds in a new foreign language, or becoming accustomed to driving on the opposite side of the road (for example, switching from driving in Germany to driving in Japan).[21] Here we have a combination of the "psyche," or intellect, and motor coordination. However, this domain also pertains to the learning of information in the cognitive domain but at a very deep level. A fairly common characteristic of this domain of learning is that mastery tends to require significant practice, typically to the level of unconscious, rote, or near-automatic performance—often referred to as overlearning.[22] For example, although to a great extent falling in the cognitive domain, learning to speak fluently in a new language involves the psychomotor domain, where an individual does not have to stop to conjugate a verb or organize the appropriate string of foreign words to effectively express an opinion—the language flows forth automatically. Many tasks require an individual to perform in the midst of significant distractions and stressful conditions where, although a conscious focus might be lacking, the person is still able to perform flawlessly due to the unconscious or automatic nature of this deep level of learning.

LEVELS OF LEARNING

Within the cognitive domain are various levels of learning, and they should be differentiated depending on the nature of the desired performance of the employee.[23] The levels of learning acronym, "CASE," shown in Figure 7.1, provides a simple distinction regarding these levels with their increasing depth and cognitive complexity. The most shallow level, at "C," involves the basic comprehension of a message, rule, or principle. "A," at the next level, involves the ability to analyze a problem situation and break it up into an effective examination of the most important parts of the situation. "S" involves the ability to synthesize or reassemble the parts to form a clear total picture or diagnosis of a solution or set of alternative solutions to the problem. "E," at the deepest level of learning, pertains to evaluating the most appropriate action to take based on existing objectives or determining the decision that would yield the greatest value. Effective managerial decision making resides at this deepest level of learning in the cognitive domain and is often equated with wisdom gained through lessons learned from direct experience or vicariously through case study or relevant models.[24]

Figure 7.1 **CASE Model on Levels of Learning in the Cognitive Domain**

Level of
Complexity

Low

C = Comprehend a message, rule, or principle.

A = Analyze a problem situation and break it up for an effective examination of the most important parts of the situation.

S = Synthesize or reassemble the parts of the problem situation to form a clear total picture or diagnosis of a solution or set of alternative solutions to the problem.

High

E = Evaluate the most appropriate action to take or the decision that would yield the greatest value.

PRINCIPLES OF ADULT LEARNING

Although many principles of learning apply to both adults and children, particular needs for adults for optimizing successful training in organizations include the following:[25]

1. *Familiarity:* Relating the new training to the participants' previous experience or what they already know.
2. *Pragmatic or Problem-Centered:* Meaningful in addressing relevant problems or fulfilling real needs as perceived by the participants.
3. *Personal Influence and Control:* The participants perceive that they have self-direction, influence, and control in the learning process, with active involvement and frequent meaningful interaction with the trainer and fellow participants.
4. *Values of Mutual Trust and Respect, Openness, and Honesty:* All involved in the training have something to share and contribute and are worthy of respect and trust. This respect and trust are based on expectations of openness and honesty in all of the interactions of the training—between trainer and participants and among all participants.

SENSITIVITY TO CROSS-CULTURAL DIFFERENCES

As with all other practices of international HR management, general training concepts and principles should be implemented with sensitivity to possible effects of cultural differences.[26] Notwithstanding the previously mentioned general adult learning priorities of openness and participant control in the learning process, trainees in many countries typically bring with them years of experience in formal education where instructors are supreme and not to be questioned. Americans who conduct training in Western Europe and Asia often experience hesitancy on the part of participants to assert personal control and become actively involved, most likely due to the fairly passive learning and authoritarian instructor roles with which they are familiar and to which they have grown accustomed.

This tendency to avoid asserting personal control in the learning process also will likely be high in cultures with high power distance, where the trainer's leadership status and role of authority should not be questioned or challenged. In one study we noted this tendency based on the perceptions of host country managers in Hong Kong, Indonesia, Malaysia, the Philippines, and Thailand.[27] However, notwithstanding this particular similarity among these Pacific Rim countries, we also found significant differences among the countries on other dimensions related to accepted conduct and management of training, such as degree of trainer supervision, frequency of feedback, use of extrinsic rewards and controls, and opportunities for interaction. We concluded that managers planning workforce training should *not* simply assume (1) significant homogeneity or similarity among Pacific Rim countries and (2) that principles guiding the management of training in their own home country would also likely be appropriate for their local employees in other countries.

SYSTEMS APPROACH

To ensure that training is used effectively and has the desired impact on employee and organizational performance, training and development efforts should be guided by a systems approach. Although there are several models and versions of this systems approach, they generally tend to follow a similar *systematic,* scientifically based procedure that thoughtfully takes into account many different parts, or *systems,* that are relevant to the training and work performance situation.[28] Figure 7.2 features six basic phases of a systems approach to training and development. We will now briefly discuss each phase separately.

Phase 1: Conduct Needs Assessment

This first phase of training needs assessment is extremely important for, first of all, determining whether a training need actually exists rather than simply following a desire to employ a current workplace fad.[29] Rather than a lack of knowledge and skills, it has been our experience that suboptimal employee performance is often due to poor communication, poor job design and work procedures, or a reward system with disincentives to performance and inadequate incentives (both financial and nonfinancial), or a combination of these. Even when it has been determined that training is warranted for supplying new knowledge and skills, a careful needs assessment is important for ensuring that training is designed and implemented cost-effectively (that is, achieving objectives at minimal cost in time and resources) as well as sup-

Figure 7.2 **Systems Approach for Training and Development**

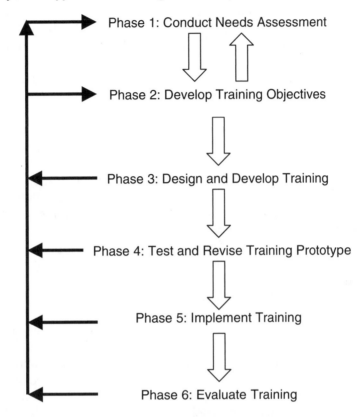

ported and reinforced by work design and supervision, the reward system (formal and informal), and the overall workplace environment.

A thorough training needs assessment examines training needs at the organizational level, the job or work operations level, and the individual level.[30] Examined at the *organizational level* are factors such as organizational performance objectives, available resources, and possible supportive changes from the organizational culture and reward system. At the *work operations level* the nature of the particular performance to be mastered is carefully examined and the training content for supplying new knowledge or skills to enable this desired performance is considered. In cases of an existing performance problem or desire to improve performance, this analysis might also examine the causes of the performance problem, including particular behaviors contributing to the problem that should be avoided in the future. In addition, the prevailing conditions in which the work is to be performed (for example, job design, supervision and other potential sources of support and reinforcement, or possible obstacles impeding performance) are studied. This examination of the level of work operations should include input from as many different sources as possible of those involved in the particular work performance, including those directly performing the work, previous holders of the job, supervisors, customers, and subordinates. For example, input from members of a host country workforce having experience with past expatriates can be very useful for enhancing the validity of expatriate training by identifying what specific behaviors expatriates should avoid and what they should engage in to optimize their success in the expatriate assignment.[31]

Finally, at the *individual level* the particular needs or characteristics of the trainee or trainees are carefully considered. Besides the level of familiarity with the training material, particularly relevant to global business at this level are personal factors such as trainee language skills, technical and basic skills, and cultural influences. For example, in their analysis of possible country sites for foreign direct investment in Central and Eastern Europe, MNCs in the high-tech industry have looked favorably on the Czech Republic due to that country's high levels of literacy and skills in computer technology within the labor force compared to other countries of the region. Thus, in anticipating future training needs for their host country operations, these MNCs would consider the individual characteristics of the Czech Republic's workforce as very positive due to their familiarity with high-tech applications and lack of the need to provide considerable basic skills and remedial training.

Phase 2: Develop Training Objectives

Based on the preceding needs assessment, detailed training objectives are developed that identify what specific behaviors the *intended* trainees (keeping in mind their particular needs and characteristics) are supposed to be able to perform as a result of the training as well as the expected conditions in which the behavior is to be performed. These objectives are very important in providing guidance for each of the subsequent phases of the systems approach to training—with each phase being carried out with close attention to the specifications of the objectives. The responsiveness of each subsequent phase to fitting the particular training objectives should be assessed at the end of each phase.

Phase 3: Design and Develop Training

The training is now designed and prepared based on the training objectives, including such decisions as selection of training method or combination of methods or how the training will be provided or delivered, including selection of possible trainers and the sequence of training material presented. Plans also should be made here for possibly adjusting or redesigning the work environment to ensure that the soon-to-be-acquired knowledge and skills are actually supported and reinforced. For example, besides providing effective technical skills training at MNC headquarters for HCNs visiting from various foreign operations, there should be a plan to ensure that the appropriate equipment and tools are ready and available back at the foreign operations for the HCN trainees' use after the training—otherwise the newfound skills might rapidly begin to atrophy ("If you don't *use* it, you *lose* it").

A cardinal rule guiding the selection of training methods is that the most *cost-effective* method or combination of methods to use *depends upon the training objec-*

tives. Generally, experiential methods (for example, practice, role playing, international travel, and work experience with a foreign culture) are very effective training methods. And if it is desirable for trainees to be able to *demonstrate* appropriate behavior for a given situation, they ideally should have the opportunity to *practice* the skill-based behavior until they are able to demonstrate their mastery at the end of the training. But experiential training approaches also tend to require much more expense and time—which might not be available—and are often much less predictable than more passive, less intensive training approaches, such as readings, computer-assisted media, or brief live presentations. Ultimately the particular needs of the training situation, reflected in the training objectives, should dictate the methods used to effectively achieve the objectives at the lowest possible cost.

Phase 4: Test and Revise Training Prototype

Once the training plans are set and appropriate materials are developed, there ideally should be a trial test of the training to make sure that it is on target and leads to achievement of the training objectives. In every training program there are inevitably unexpected "bugs" in the program that should be eliminated for achieving optimal training effectiveness. Where possible, a small group of those representing the intended audience or the recipients of the training should receive the training on a test basis prior to its widespread usage. Or there should be at least some kind of review by those representing the perspective of the intended recipients to increase the likelihood that the training is on target. For example, in preparing for the training of lower-level HCNs in a foreign operation, besides giving earlier input as part of the needs assessment process, HCN supervisors or managers could be very helpful in reviewing the intended training plans prior to actual implementation—especially in helping to avoid confusion or culturally based insults or offending messages.[32] As a more concrete illustration, we once prepared a leadership training session for executives from the People's Republic of China (PRC). One of the assigned readings for this training included a very brief but positive reference to the Dalai Lama, generally a very unpopular figure within the PRC due to his advocacy of the liberation of Tibet from the PRC. Not wanting to cause a politically charged distraction from our intended training objectives, we were grateful that those reviewing and translating our materials into Mandarin spotted this potential problem and respectfully suggested that we might want to delete the reference to the Dalai Lama.

Phase 5: Implement Training

The training plan is now fully implemented, with careful attention to ensure that the training is being implemented according to the plan.

Phase 6: Evaluate Training

Finally, the training is evaluated in terms of its effectiveness in achieving the training objectives—the objectives themselves guiding this evaluation process (represented in

Figure 7.2 by the dark arrow flow from Phase 6 to Phase 2). For example, as a result of the cross-cultural awareness training, are the PCNs able to describe particular general behavioral characteristics of the workforce of a host country firm that they have just acquired? Or beyond their ability to merely describe, are they also able to demonstrate appropriate behavior for a given cross-cultural situation in which conflict might be involved? As mentioned earlier, the training objectives should specify what the trainees should be able to do as a result of the training, and the evaluation should assess whether this behavioral learning objective has been achieved.

The trainees might be able to demonstrate mastery of the new knowledge or skills, even in specific applications months later, back in the workplace. However, in an effective training evaluation there also should be an assessment of whether the newly acquired knowledge and skills actually result in improved performance and organizational productivity. Thus, the evaluation also should examine the original work and organizational productivity needs to determine if the training actually results in work performance improvement (represented in Figure 7.2 by the continuing arrow flow from Phase 6 back to Phase 1). When this evaluation demonstrates that performance needs still have not been met, there should be a reexamination of the training objectives to determine if and where they might not have fully captured the needs based on the original needs assessment (represented in Figure 7.2 by the reverse arrow from Phase 2 back to Phase 1). Of course, it is possible that the original training objectives were correct at the time, but changes might have occurred in the organization or work environment requiring a revision in the training objectives and the total training effort provided. For example, due to rapid changes in technology, this final evaluation phase often points to the need to revise the existing training objectives, which were previously accurate and appropriate, and therefore also the subsequent training effort based on these objectives.

TRAINING TRANSFER

Ultimately a successful training effort should result in individual performance improvement leading to enhanced individual and organizational productivity. Effective learning and mastery of new skills and knowledge are futile unless there is a positive transfer of this learning back into the workplace. To encourage effective positive transfer of the training there are several things that managers can do before, during, and after the training effort takes place.[33]

Before the training effort takes place, there should be clear commitment obtained from accepted leaders and top management for the training.[34] The accepted leaders and top managers of the organization typically have a powerful influence on what behavior is perceived as appropriate and valued and what behavior should be avoided in the organization. Therefore, these leaders and top managers should clearly demonstrate their approval and acceptance of the behavior that is the focus of the training—and they can do this through adequate budget allocation for the training, supportive public statements, and even participating in the training themselves. Where the accepted leaders are not necessarily the top managers, such as in a foreign operation led by PCNs yet having other very respected and influential HCNs among the workforce,

---

Global Workforce Professional Profile 7.1
Johanna Hassan Hollowich: Global Training Consultant

Johanna Hassan Hollowich is the founder and president of Potencium Limited, an international training and consulting company with clients throughout Asia/Pacific, Europe, and the Americas. Founded in 2001, Potencium specializes in providing consultancy and training services in the fields of virtual teams, global collaboration, leadership, communication skills, and professional development. Potencium provides customized in-house and online learning programs to meet the unique needs of each client. Hollowich has more than twenty-five years of consulting experience. She has a master's degree in Adult Learning and Education from London's City University, with a focus on training intervention techniques, group dynamics, mentoring, and management development. Prior to forming Potencium, Johanna was a senior consultant for Canning International UK (a cross-cultural consultancy) and Rostrum Pharmaceutical Training, a division of MDS Pharma Services UK (a major international clinical research organization).

Hollowich advises companies in more than twenty countries on how to develop in their employees the essential skills required for today's competitive global marketplace. She has successfully facilitated international business solutions that include presenting more than five hundred training programs and designing a variety of online e-learning courses. For her worldwide client base Johanna utilizes experienced multilingual intercultural associates from countries around the world including China, France, Germany, India, Italy, Mexico, Russia, and Singapore. Some of her clients include Boeing (Russia, U.S.); General Motors (Australia, Canada, India, Mexico, U.S.); Kuopio University (Finland); Northrup Grumman (U.S.); Novartis (Japan, Switzerland, UK, U.S.); Novo Nordisk (Denmark, Singapore); Walt Disney (France, UK, U.S.); and Yahoo! (U.S.). Hollowich has built a strong reputation as an international consultant and is known for her innovative and motivational style of training. A native of England, Hollowich has offices in London and Los Angeles, and knows only too well the challenges of working globally and remotely.

---

their clear support for the program should also be obtained ahead of time. In addition, there should be clear support for the new behaviors being taught within the local organizational culture—represented by the predominant beliefs, values, norms, and priorities of the local workforce. Without this local organizational cultural support, any newly acquired behaviors will be discouraged and soon extinguished. In some cases there will need to be a preceding, or at least concurrent, effort to change the organizational culture to effectively support the desired new skills and behaviors that are targeted in the training. A careful review and possible revision of pertinent company policies, procedures, and workplace conditions should also take place beforehand to ensure that any obstruction that might be posed to the utilization of the new skills is removed. Finally, as part of the needs assessment process, it should be determined beforehand approximately when the targeted skills would be used at work and then schedule this "just-in-time" training so that new skills can be applied as soon as possible to avoid skill loss due to lack of use.[35]

During the training one of the most important measures to ensure positive transfer to the workplace is the use of practice, preferably in as close a simulation as possible of the real working situation in which the targeted skills would be used. Because on-the-job training takes place in the actual workplace, this approach when conducted with effective coaching and supervision tends to have optimal positive learning transfer. Away from the workplace, experiential exercises and role playing can be particularly effective methods for combining practice with realism to enhance positive transfer.

Following training an effort should be made by the supervisors of those trained to encourage the use of the new skills to ensure their retention. Thus, managers and supervisors should be very much aware of and involved in the employee's new skill-acquisition process and plan work accordingly. In addition, there should be functional integration of other human resource activities, such as performance appraisal and compensation, to lend additional reinforcement to the use and retention of the new skills. For example, skill-based pay is a compensation strategy that can provide effective incentive reinforcement to the successful acquisition and workplace demonstration of new desired skills that lead to increased work productivity.

TRAINING IMPERATIVES FOR THE GLOBAL WORKFORCE

Besides following sound principles and practices for guiding training activities on a global scale, MNCs face critical priorities in particular areas. Key imperatives for global training include building global competencies for international professionals, building global alignment, predeparture and on-site expatriate training, special training considerations for female expatriate assignment success, and HCN training.

BUILDING GLOBAL COMPETENCIES FOR INTERNATIONAL PROFESSIONALS

It is increasingly becoming recognized that to compete in our global marketplace effectively, managers, executives, and other professionals need to develop and hone particular global competencies beyond those that used to suffice in the domestic arena. And because the domestic arena is increasingly being penetrated by international competition, those global competencies are needed by leaders and decision makers both at home and abroad. These professionals require new knowledge, skills, and abilities as they face a new, constantly changing, borderless global marketplace involving a quickening of decision-making requirements, advances in communications technology, and increased demand for prompt data analysis and interpretation.[36] Figure 7.3 features a list of several professional global competencies (often referred to as KSAOs—knowledge, skills, abilities, and other characteristics) identified by various sources that are purported to be critical for meeting the challenges of today's international business environment.[37] There is considerable difference of opinion in the literature on what are the most important forms of knowledge, skills, and competencies for international professionals,[38] yet the literature also tends to commonly highlight many of those competencies listed in Figure 7.3, with some listed as subsets of others.

Figure 7.3 **Global Business Competencies**

Cross-Cultural Awareness/Sensitivity	Emotional Intelligence
Managing Cross-Cultural Conflict	Global Business Savvy
Adaptability to New Situations	Global Organizational Savvy
Cross-Cultural Adjustment	Managing Tensions of Duality (i.e., Think Global, Act Local)
Managing Change	Relationship Skills
Managing Uncertainty	International Negotiation Skills
Managing Paradox	Self-Reliance
Inquisitiveness/Curiosity	People Orientation: Respect and Trust in People
Working in and Managing	Flexibility in Thought and Disposition
International Teams	Open, Nonjudgmental Personality
Language Skills	Self-Maintenance (e.g., Personal Care, Health, Stress Management)

Many of these competencies are interrelated and are often combined to form a general way of thinking about the challenges of the global business environment and responding to those challenges. This general way of thinking and formulating plans for action constitutes a global mind-set, or general global orientation or perspective.[39] Ben Kedia and Ananda Mukherji have proposed the collective international competency of "global perspective," which they consider as a general global mind-set supported by appropriate skills and knowledge to meet performance demands.[40] Stephen Rhinesmith has identified the following four "pillars" of a global mind-set,[41] which can easily been seen as inclusive of many of the global professional competencies identified in Figure 7.3:

- *Business Acumen.* The working understanding of effective principles and practices of functional disciplines as well as broader strategic management knowledge for conducting business in international settings; often involving both external business environment savvy and internal MNC organizational savvy.
- *Paradox Management.* An appreciation and ability to make effective decisions within the uncertainties and complexities of global business, often involving paradoxes and contradictions, such as smaller business entities being able to wield more power than larger entities, or managing the ongoing tensions of thinking on a global scale yet being responsive to local concerns and demands.
- *Self-Management.* The ability to monitor, care for, adapt, and renew oneself to maintain strength and vitality amid the ongoing demands of rapid change, uncertainty, complexity, and otherwise stressful working conditions of international business; often involving planning for achieving balance in intellectual, physical, spiritual, and social realms of life.
- *Cultural Acumen.* An appreciation and interest in other cultures as well as sensitivity to and flexibility in dealing with cross-cultural differences in various settings, including working in and managing multicultural teams in international business.

But how can these international professional competencies be developed effectively? We now examine four major strategies, conveniently labeled the "Four Ts" (for transfer, training, travel, and teams), leading to the development of vital global professional competencies.[42] These strategies involve both a formal, predictable exchange of explicit knowledge and capabilities as well as an informal, less predictable but often extremely powerful exchange of tacit knowledge and capabilities.

Transfer to New Assignment or Job

Although not without its challenges, we are convinced that direct work experience, with its rich combination of demands, tasks, problems, relationships, and uncertainties, provides the greatest opportunity for employee development. Therefore, the most powerful way to develop multiple and deep global competencies is not in a classroom, but through living and working for a significant period in a foreign environment.[43] Many researchers support the ongoing practice of MNCs in using extended international work-assignment transfers as rich experiential training grounds for their future leaders—regardless of nationality and location—in developing a vital global mind-set and orientation to help the MNC meet the global competitive demands of the future.[44]

To be sure, sometimes the MNC's "best and brightest" are already overseas as host country nationals, and their international developmental experience could be in other MNC foreign operations or in the MNC's home country and headquarters.[45] In an extensive field survey of 130 international executives and professionals of various nationalities and functional experiences in fifty firms across Europe, Asia, and North America, 80 percent of those surveyed indicated that living and working in a foreign country was by far the single most influential developmental experience of their life, particularly in terms of developing global competencies useful for their careers.[46] Although some researchers have found evidence that extended international work experience is particularly effective in increasing awareness of global complexities and developing global competencies related to knowledge and skills, they question whether extended international assignments alone are effective in developing more complex and stable personality characteristics, such as openness and curiosity, which also have been found to be critical for international work success.[47] Although some researchers believe that these important personality characteristics are fixed and immutable, other work related to emotional intelligence—which has clear applicability in international work settings—gives strong support for the possibility to change personal attributions underlying personality characteristics.[48] It is highly likely that the international work setting can also serve as a valuable learning laboratory for making useful personality adjustments that better fit the demands of international business; however, these deeper levels of personal learning related to the affective domain may require more carefully structured training activities and experiential learning experiences with follow-up guided analysis and reflection than are typically found in the fairly unstructured, unpredictable nature of the extended international work assignment.

Training

Although in this chapter we generally refer to training as all purposeful learning activities provided for our global workforce—including informal experience sharing and on-the-job training as part of a foreign work assignment—this second strategy of training refers less broadly here to more controlled, structured learning activities with fairly limited topics and specific learning objectives consistent with company goals. Of the "Four T" strategies examined here, training is by far the most formal and has the greatest focus on sharing explicit knowledge. Examples of these more structured training efforts could be a program on global strategy, change management, managing virtual work teams, or international negotiations and conflict management skills, involving as participants middle managers of various nationalities from the MNC's subsidiaries around the world and meeting for one week away from MNC headquarters. Effective programs of this nature include on-site analysis of company problems and development of solutions as well as action-learning assignments for each participant. The latter involve tasks applied in the regular workplace, with possible subsequent follow-up on results and group experience sharing for leveraging learning. Besides the development of valuable global competencies, incidental learning benefits of these kinds of training activities, especially internal programs involving MNC participants from various countries, include the formation of valuable ties and professional networks that encourage future constructive collaboration.

Travel

As part of brief business assignments abroad, even to a foreign site for MNC training, travel in itself can provide a rich source of exposure and experience-based knowledge about foreign cultures and different behavioral norms, diverse economic and political environments, and diverse and often insightful business practices.[49] To gain added exposure from travel experiences, companies often encourage their employees to engage in activities that involve mixing with local cultures, such as shopping in local markets, visiting schools and homes of host country employees, participating in humanitarian service projects, and engaging in other meaningful activities beyond the typically superficial agenda for tourists.

Teams

The global workplace features several different forms of team assignments in multinational and multicultural work teams, including cross-functional task forces or more enduring teams at middle or senior levels, or fairly autonomous and self-managing virtual teams involving quarterly meetings in person. Experiences that involve meaningful interactions with team members of other national and cultural backgrounds and expert behavior modeling can provide a rich exchange of tacit knowledge and capability of many forms, including those related to global leadership competencies. This less explicit and informal form of learning can be particularly effective related to developing the major skill and mind-set of cultural acumen identified earlier.[50] To ensure that these experiences lead to learning that is as productive as possible, they should be preceded, or at least supplemented, by targeted training in cross-cultural awareness, conflict management, and multicultural group dynamics.

Building Global Alignment

MNCs commonly employ various approaches to optimize their control over their foreign work units to achieve goals and performance objectives, including the close supervision by expatriates, rules, and performance-management techniques.[51] These externally provided controls are intended to help align the workforce with the goals and objectives of the organization. As we noted earlier, the systematic acquisition through training of key global competencies and thinking skills among MNC managers and professionals, whether PCNs, HCNs, or TCNs, can lead to greater integration and coordination through a common mind-set. This training can also affect the transfer throughout the MNC's global workforce at all levels of industry-specific critical capabilities linked with success, contributing to a very productive *internal* cognitive alignment.[52] This common mind-set and shared knowledge represent a unifying language that provides alignment in thought and action, facilitating effective interactions and collaborative synergies across the MNC. But beyond commonly held knowledge and thinking skills and capabilities gained through shared experience in activities such as travel, training, teams, and transfers (both short and extended international work assignments) is the potentially valuable development of an MNC culture of common values, identity, beliefs, and priorities that also serves to informally teach, influence, and reinforce desirable behavior within the MNC. There is even strong evidence that the influence of organizational culture can be much more influential and override national culture.[53]

The ongoing learning influenced by an organization's culture pertains not only to the cognitive domain but also to the affective domain in the form of commonly held values, beliefs, attitudes, priorities, and professional identity.[54] Employees' deep identification with the image or identity of their employing organization has been shown to enhance commitment to the organization, job satisfaction and motivation, and organization-related citizenship behavior. The development of this important mechanism of alignment of both "mind and heart" (also referred to as "normative integration" or "cohesion management") takes place naturally through informal learning channels as various parts and members of an MNC develop a history together and gain common work experience.[55] However, it also can be facilitated by purposeful training and communication activities throughout the MNC, as illustrated by Johnson & Johnson's systematic worldwide effort to continually examine, challenge, and embrace its credo, or set of fundamental philosophical guidelines that direct company decision making and behavior. The strengthening of common corporate identity also can be achieved experientially through widespread employee participation in common initiatives in corporate social responsibility, such as DHL achieved among its Asia-Pacific employees through their participation in the company's disaster response to the 2004 tsunami in that region.[56]

Multinational team arrangements and expatriate and inpatriate assignments can serve as effective means of organizational socialization and alignment, resulting in the breaking down of stereotypes and prejudice previously reinforced by impervious national boundary staffing policies and organizational structures. Beyond mere cognitive alignment, this effective socialization through meaningful cross-cultural interaction and collaboration, idea sharing, and open debate can result in the development of commonly held "superordinate" goals and the building up of a common MNC

Global Workforce Challenge 7.2
Training for Appropriate Competencies in Asia

In the face of the cultural variety of Asia and the need to compete in the continent's daunting pace of growth, it appears increasingly difficult to define one leadership style or a set of best practices that will be the most effective. Globalization warrants a new set of business standards combining best practices from Western and Eastern cultures. A "fused" leadership profile will evolve over time. Meanwhile, companies must find creative solutions to nurture expatriates in this challenging environment and prepare them well for their Asian assignments. But what kinds of competencies should we focus on in this vital expatriate preparation and training?

Managers with the highest potential for success in Asia's emerging markets must possess a rare combination of leadership attributes, including a high tolerance for ambiguity, personal flexibility, patience, the ability to look at situations through the eyes of an Asian colleague or employee (i.e., intercultural empathy), as well as stamina, confidence, and a strong drive for results. Where "best in class" leaders from the United States and Europe typically exhibit strong social and participative styles, Chinese executives are decidedly task-focused and hierarchical. Companies should consider not what style is universally better or worse, but what type of leadership roles and styles are the most appropriate for Asia and the specific local market in which they work.

Western managers running businesses in Asia should focus on establishing strong local networks to reflect the current Asian business leadership norms that rely heavily on familial and friendship links. For instance, most Western managers are accustomed to working in countries that have a strong rule of law. But in many parts of Asia, using the legal system to solve business problems is a route of last resort. Learning to solve problems by leveraging personal relationships to create good will with tax and licensing bureaus, customs functions, and other enforcement agencies can be much more effective as well as faster and less damaging. In other words, effective leaders in Asia put the emphasis on nurturing and preserving relationships to get things done rather than using logic and legal arguments.

Source: Adapted from D. Everhart, "Preparing Execs for Asia Assignments," *BusinessWeek. com,* Careers Section, April 1, 2008.

---

identity in a pervasive internal culture characterized by mutual support, trust, and respect. Several MNCs such as Nokia, GE, and IKEA actively work through formal training and informal learning modes of travel and international work assignments to develop this common identity, esprit de corps, or common cultural code that provides a powerful intrinsic form of alignment for the MNC.[57]

EXPATRIATE TRAINING CONSIDERATIONS

There is strong evidence that various forms of training for expatriates can serve as a valuable investment leading to effective performance in international assignments.

For example, one study found that cross-cultural awareness training for Japanese expatriates prior to their international assignment enhanced their ability to relate socially to local host country workforces for achieving strategic control in several foreign subsidiaries.[58] Other studies of U.S. and European MNCs sending expatriates to such countries as South Korea and Saudi Arabia found evidence that training can enhance the speed and effectiveness of expatriate adjustment and performance in the assignment and minimize costly expatriate assignment failure.[59] Despite this evidence favoring expatriate training, most expatriates are sent abroad without any training, often with the rationale that there is inadequate time for the training (which can be true due to poor HR planning), the needs for training are unclear, or that the existing technical skills of the expatriate are adequate to lead to a successful assignment.[60] It is likely that there are considerable benefits to be gained if MNCs more carefully consider and employ cost-effective approaches of expatriate training before and during their assignment. We now will briefly examine important considerations for expatriate training prior to the foreign assignment; later, in Chapter 8, we will consider important issues related to expatriate training during the foreign assignment.

Predeparture Training

The intent of predeparture training is to prepare the expatriate as much as possible prior to actually arriving at the foreign assignment to facilitate adjustment, help avoid costly mistakes, and begin the foreign assignment in as positive and productive a manner as possible. Of particular importance in predeparture training is providing useful information and a sense of personal control in addressing possible challenges, which will help allay concerns or fears that might otherwise raise stress and anxiety to uncomfortable and nonproductive levels prior to the actual start of the foreign assignment. However, painting an unrealistically positive picture of the foreign assignment experience can also lead to very damaging disappointment and disillusionment upon confronting the reality of the foreign assignment. In general, for optimal positive impact the predeparture training should provide positive but realistic expectations regarding the likelihood of success with the foreign experience and include a clear picture of the "good, bad, and ugly" that the expatriate will likely encounter in the course of the assignment.[61]

In firms that offer predeparture training, including for spouses and other family members, the most common form is cross-cultural awareness.[62] This trend is especially true for assignments involving significant cultural distance. Other forms of predeparture training include strategic training, where the expatriate is provided a "big picture" of the assignment and how its goals and objectives relate to overall MNC strategy; and job training, which focuses on the actual knowledge and skills needed for the new assignment.

What is the most cost-effective content and approach for predeparture training? Again, the cardinal rule of contingency that we examined earlier applies—it depends on the situation. Will the expatriate be abroad for three or five years, or for only three months followed by shorter trips thereafter? For the shorter amount of time, intensive language instruction would likely not be necessary, especially when most of the professional interaction is with English-fluent HCNs and PCNs at the foreign site. The actual content and form of appropriate predeparture training depend on various factors such as the following categories of degrees of assignment "toughness":[63]

- *Job Toughness.* The degree to which the work in the new foreign assignment is similar to past work in which the expatriate has been engaged. Does the new job require different working conditions, equipment, or legal or union restrictions?
- *Cultural Toughness.* Also referred to as cultural distance, the degree to which the values, norms, and attitudes of the foreign culture match the expatriate's home culture. For example, a four-year assignment of a German expatriate to the People's Republic of China would involve much greater cultural toughness than would an assignment to Austria. However, cross-cultural awareness training should not be neglected where there is apparently little cultural toughness—often significant culture clashes can occur where they are least expected, and preparation is neglected due to assumed cultural similarity.
- *Communication Toughness.* This third toughness factor relates to the difficulty and amount or frequency of communication involved with HCNs and in the foreign environment. Different conditions related to this factor include differences in norms and rules for written, oral, and interpersonal communication; frequency of foreign communication required; difficulty in learning the predominant foreign language; length of the foreign assignment; and modes of communication used (for example, e-mail, telephone, and face-to-face).

In general, where one or more of the listed factors involve significant toughness, more time and intensity is needed for effective predeparture training (for example, significant practice and high-involvement, application-oriented experiential exercises or assignments in realistic settings). Where the overall toughness is minimal or moderate, appropriate training might be delivered in the form of lectures, cases, role-playing, or assigned readings.

However, it should *not* be assumed that if the parent and host country share the same language, then little rigor and intensity in predeparture cross-culture awareness training is necessary. Even where a common language is shared, significant cross-cultural differences may be expressed in language timing, body language, semantics and vocabulary, style, and other forms of nonverbal and indirect communications that can cause serious misunderstandings for unprepared expatriates. For example, it is often expected that the transition will be easy for English-speaking individuals working and living in English-speaking countries, but simple transition is usually not the case. Rensia Melles highlights the particular cross-cultural challenge between the English-speaking United States and United Kingdom in the following excerpt:

> England . . . is a culture of high-context communication, in which meanings may be implicit, and where relationships and trust precede business transactions. In the United States, however, communication is very low context and is expected to be to the point, factual and often task-oriented.[64] (p. 11)

Despite a common language, there still might be significant cultural differences to overcome. Yet due to the language similarity, these differences might not be expected or anticipated, and when they do surface in various forms of frustration and conflict they can be mistakenly attributed to poor work attitudes, rudeness and insubordination, and personality conflicts. Thus, because of minimal or no local language and cross-cultural awareness training due to assumed similarity with a shared basic language, common language assignments may present the greatest shock, adjustment difficulty, and challenge.

An effective training needs assessment will examine the preceding factors and other conditions to ensure that the actual training is valid and cost-effective. Previous expatriates who worked in the same foreign area often can be a valuable source of input for training. They likely will have had firsthand experience with the stressors and cross-cultural challenges soon to be encountered by the new expatriate. It also has been suggested that inputs from members of a host country workforce—including critical incidents (both positive and negative) from actual interactions with expatriates and events at the foreign workplace—should be part of a comprehensive training needs assessment. Rather than general cross-cultural information and knowledge, these direct experience-based inputs can be very useful for enhancing the validity of expatriate training by identifying what specific behaviors expatriates should avoid and what they should engage in to optimize their success in a given expatriate assignment.[65]

SPECIAL TRAINING CONSIDERATIONS FOR FEMALE EXPATRIATES

As discussed in Chapter 6, female expatriates generally represent a significant but greatly underutilized resource. But special recruitment and selection efforts alone are not enough to help improve the present gender imbalance in expatriate representation. Additional actions in predeparture training and preparation as well as ongoing support during the assignment are warranted to overcome potential obstacles to the success of female expatriates.[66] We will examine appropriate support activities in Chapter 8, dealing with managing international assignments, but here we briefly consider some training ideas for optimizing early and ongoing foreign assignment success.

Local Norms and Values Regarding Women

In providing realistic job expectations as part of predeparture training for women expatriates, information should be provided on local norms, values, and perceptions about expected female role behavior as well as attitudes toward women managers. With this accurate information women can begin to develop effective strategies for coping with possible negative attitudes and perceptions.[67] Strategies that might help offset negative attitudes include working harder than their male peers, developing unique skills and expertise, and developing managerial styles that are more neutral and acceptable to male colleagues, supervisors, and subordinates.[68]

Attitudes and Norms Regarding Expatriate Women versus HCN Women

Successful women expatriates have commented that they are often not held to the same gender role expectations as are women from the local culture.[69] Therefore, a clear picture of the differences in perception about local women and women expatriates could be useful in providing a more accurate picture of the intended work environment.[70]

Behaviors to Avoid

To avoid unnecessary HCN offense with or misinterpretation of their behaviors, women expatriates should receive training on behaviors that should clearly be avoided.[71] For example, one of our American colleagues who had an international teaching assignment in Germany began to complain that as she walked to her apartment each evening she was being followed by male street people who increasingly made lewd and suggestive remarks. Because such behavior by the locals was unusual for the area in which she was living, one of her German colleagues decided to accompany her home one evening. As they walked he noted that the American woman made eye contact and cheerfully greeted each person she passed on the way, including any street people she encountered. The German colleague quickly informed her that generally in Germany such eye contact and greeting with complete strangers is not the cultural norm and might be considered excessively forward and invasive. And coming from women in particular, this behavior might be interpreted as inviting or encouraging a sexual encounter.

Networking with Successful Female Expatriates

Although professional networks in themselves are not forms of knowledge, they can certainly be effective in promoting the sharing of ideas and advice toward performance improvement. Arranging for connections and contacts with female managers who have completed expatriate assignments successfully can provide very helpful channels, both before and during an assignment, through which valuable advice and information can flow for effectively dealing with the unique challenges facing women expatriates.[72]

HCN TRAINING CONSIDERATIONS

HCNs and TCNs represent an important source of success for foreign operations, yet they have been seriously neglected by past research on global training and development, reflecting a significant ethnocentric bias toward PCNs and expatriate training.[73] Although in many cases the predeparture training needs of TCNs and HCN inpatriates mirror those of expatriates,[74] we now examine particular training needs of HCNs that, when filled, can lead to enhanced productivity.

We have presented research based in multiple host country and cross-cultural field settings highlighting productive forms of HCN training and development relevant to both the PCN's expatriate assignment and the foreign operation as a whole.[75] These beneficial forms of training for operative or lower-level host country employees, HCN supervisors and managers, and HCN upper-level managers and executives are listed in Figure 7.4.

Figure 7.4 **Beneficial Forms of HCN Learning for Enhancing Foreign Subsidiary Performance**

HCN Employee Level	HCN Learning
Operative Level	• New employee orientation • Entry job skills • Parent company predominant language • Expatriate and home country cross-cultural awareness training
Supervisory and Middle Management	• Supervision and technical operations management • Home country cross-cultural awareness • Expatriate coaching • Liaison role between parent company expatriates and lower-level HCNs
Upper Management	• Advanced technical system operations • Business-level (subsidiary) strategy • Parent company (MNC) strategy • Parent company (MNC) culture

Operative Level

Four major categories of potentially beneficial forms of training for HCNs at this level include new employee orientation, entry job skills, parent company predominant language (that is, what language is most commonly spoken at MNC headquarters), and cross-cultural awareness training about the parent company's home country culture. These categories relate to forms of HCN learning that would directly contribute to and facilitate both immediate and longer-term job performance.

In addition to basic information as typically offered in new-employee orientation, two messages noted as particularly important by several of the companies are (1) presenting the "big picture" of where the employee fits in and contributes to the global efforts of the MNC and (2) helping the employee develop positive expectations and confidence about how successful performance on the job can contribute to the fulfillment of employee immediate and long-term needs, including career advancement where such is a perceived need. The provision of parent company language instruction for employees at the operative level (often through tuition support for courses offered during off-work hours by external language education providers) can be used to communicate upward mobility and potential opportunity within the parent company, particularly if the employee is willing to put forth the extra effort to do things that would help prepare for promotion. In general, an operative employee who becomes competent in the parent company's predominant language would increase the likelihood of being promoted to higher levels of supervision and management, which may require significantly more communication and interaction with the parent company and its expatriates.

The general host country socioeconomic level has been suggested as a relevant factor in determining the content of HCN training at the operative level.[76] For example, due to their more immediate concern about satisfying basic needs, Mexican lower-level HCNs generally were found to have much less interest in learning about the national culture of their MNC's home country than did their more affluent U.S.

HCN counterparts. The latter employees were much more curious and motivated to learn about the national culture of the parent company as well as the HCN employee's part in the global business enterprise.

Supervisory and Middle Management Level

Forms of beneficial HCN learning-through-training activities at the supervisor and middle management level include supervision and technical operations management, home country cross-cultural awareness, expatriate coaching, and skills related to the often informal liaison role between parent company expatriates and lower-level HCNs. These forms of HCN learning involve close interaction with and support of expatriates in ensuring smooth operations within the foreign subsidiary.

Employees promoted to first-line supervisory positions typically receive training in general supervision and technical operations management. Those in middle management also typically receive technical training, particularly for planning and management of technical system operations. This technical training might be provided primarily on an internal or "in-house" basis through on-the-job training and coaching and occasionally at parent company regional or central headquarters for generally a one- to three-week period. In addition, although seldom offered, it could be very helpful for supervisors and managers who interface with expatriates to receive cross-cultural training related to the parent company and expatriate national culture. In our study, several U.S. managers in Japanese subsidiaries indicated that they basically relied on an unpredictable trial-and-error approach as well as advice from their more experienced HCN peers to try to understand and get along with their expatriate bosses. They indicated that a more formal, systematic training effort would help them better understand and appreciate why their expatriate superiors behaved and made decisions the way they did and thereby help improve work interactions through reduction of waste and inefficiencies incident to miscommunication and misunderstanding. Related to their liaison role, these HCN managers also believed that such enhanced understanding would help them better support and clarify the behavior of the expatriate executives in the eyes of the lower-level HCN operatives.[77]

As discussed in Chapter 8 regarding on-site expatriate training, HCN managers may effectively provide both formal and informal one-on-one ongoing coaching and mentoring to help expatriates avoid costly mistakes and engage in the most productive behavior possible for the host country national operation.[78] This HCN performance of close coaching and mentoring suggests the need for appropriate related competence on the part of HCN managers, and thus where competence does not exist naturally, the need for training to develop such coaching skills. In some countries, particularly those with high power distance characterizing unequal superior-subordinate relationships, additional cross-cultural training might also be in order for HCNs who would otherwise find their responsibility of giving advice and counsel to typically higher-level expatriates very difficult to fulfill, given their cultural background.[79]

In our research we also found several HCN U.S. human resource directors and managers who spent much of their time in a liaison role between expatriates and lower-level HCN operatives, a work performance expectation that they did not anticipate when they were assigned or hired for the job and for which they had received no formal training. One U.S. human resource director within a Japanese bank subsidiary in Los Angeles mentioned that much of her time is spent in addressing destructive rumors within the HCN grapevine and in dealing with other forms of conflict between the lower-level HCNs and Japanese expatriates. She firmly believed that the important liaison role played by herself and other managers in handling inevitable cross-cultural conflict within the foreign subsidiary, often directed toward parent company headquarters, should be clearly recognized. She also felt that ongoing training should be provided to support this important morale-building and maintenance responsibility among the HCNs. The aforementioned coaching skill would fall on the expatriate side of this liaison role, yet the other end represents a critical source of leverage for the MNC among the HCN workforce.

Upper Management Level

Forms of beneficial HCN learning from training efforts directed at the upper-management level include advanced technical system operations, business-level strategy, parent company strategy, and parent company corporate culture. These categories of HCN learning relate to strategic and deep structural factors tied to survival and success at both the local business or subsidiary level and the broader corporate-wide MNC level.

At this level, HCN executives occasionally might receive advanced technical systems operations management and business-level strategy training at parent regional or central company headquarters from periods of one or two weeks to six months. Increasingly HCN managers from foreign subsidiary operations are assigned to parent company central headquarters to work for over two years prior to returning to host country upper-level management responsibility. This "inpatriate" form of longer-term management development experience in the MNC's home country can potentially provide for the HCN manager a helpful exposure to MNC headquarters corporate culture and to the particular style and process of parent company strategic management.[80] When the HCN manager returns to a senior-level assignment within a foreign operation, working closely with or even replacing expatriate management, this manager should now be able to work more effectively within the context of the strategic direction, goals, and culture of the parent company. But this optimal link by HCN executives to the corporate mind-set will likely never be achieved without significant direct work experience and long-term interaction with MNC headquarters. Ultimately, the parent firm will theoretically have more strategic control over this foreign operation than over other operations headed by HCN managers who have not had this in-depth parent company culture/strategy learning experience. The training and leadership development of the HCN at this level is particularly important in helping to achieve a pervasive global orientation for the firm, rather than focusing solely on developing an elite cadre of expatriates originating from the parent country.

SUMMARY

We have examined the strategic role and key contributions of global workforce training and development as well as fundamental concepts and principles for guiding important global training and development activities. Critical imperatives of training and development for the global workforce include building global competencies and workforce alignment. Particular considerations should be made to ensure the effective training of HCNs at all levels and expatriates as well as female expatriates who face unique challenges.

QUESTIONS FOR OPENING SCENARIO ANALYSIS

1. What are major ways in which Motorola University contributes to effective individual and organizational learning for this MNC?
2. How can Motorola's commitment to training contribute to its distinct competitive advantage in the global marketplace?
3. Motorola University is a difficult model to match for smaller firms. However, based on this corporate example and your learning from this chapter, what are particular training activities that smaller and medium-size firms can use to build greater capability for competing in the global marketplace?

CASE 7.1. LEADING THE WAY FOR A NEW CULTURE AT CHRYSLER

Just hours after taking over as CEO of Chrysler Group LLC, Sergio Marchionne settled into a new office at the company's Auburn Hills, Michigan, headquarters, and signaled that he is setting a different tone at the struggling car manufacturer. And, as actions speak louder than words, the priorities reflected by his decisions and behavior are far more powerful in changing organizational culture than a host of formal training programs. Rather than take the top-floor suite that his predecessors occupied in the company's fifteen-floor executive tower, Mr. Marchionne chose a fourth-floor office in its adjoining technical center. To get Chrysler back on its feet quickly after forty-two days in bankruptcy reorganization, Mr. Marchionne felt he should be close to the engineers and managers making day-to-day decisions. "It shows he's going to be very hands-on," said one who meets regularly with senior Chrysler executives.

Mr. Marchionne, who is also CEO of Chrysler's alliance partner, Fiat SpA, faces a herculean task in reviving the smallest of the U.S. Big Three automakers, with slumping postbankruptcy sales, idle plants, work on new models in development ground to a halt, and tarnished image. A big part of Mr. Marchionne's prescription for the company is a rapid flattening out of its management ranks to speed decision making and move top executives closer to the business of making and selling cars and trucks. He also appears determined to instill a new sense of urgency and focus, and demand close cooperation between Chrysler and Fiat. Immediately upon assuming control of Chrysler, Mr. Marchionne announced a broad reorganization that left twenty-three senior managers reporting to him. His immediate predecessor, Robert Nardelli, had only a handful of direct reports. Near his office, an executive conference room has been equipped with twenty-three microphones and videoconferencing gear so the Chrysler team can meet with counterparts in Italy. The two sides hold videoconferences several times a week, and Mr. Marchionne has made clear that all top managers are expected to attend. Since Chrysler's survival isn't yet certain, Mr. Marchionne has also told top executives to expect to work—in the office—most Saturdays and Sundays for the foreseeable future.

Source: Adapted from N.E. Boudette, "Fiat CEO Sets New Tone at Chrysler," *Wall Street Journal,* June 19, 2009: B1.

QUESTIONS FOR CASE ANALYSIS AND DISCUSSION

1. What kinds of values and priorities have been indicated by Mr. Marchionne's early actions as CEO of Chrysler? How is his leadership example important in bringing a new culture to help ensure the survival of Chrysler?
2. What kinds of changes have been made to facilitate the free flow of information and sharing of knowledge to support optimal organizational learning within Chrysler and senior partner Fiat?
3. What activities would you recommend to enhance learning across the heretofore closed boundaries between Chrysler and Fiat that could lead to greater understanding and sharing of mutual strengths between the two organizations?

CASE 7.2. HCN SUPERVISORY TRAINING NEEDS

Annette Dailliez, ATZ Head Plant Manager, was stunned when she returned from an extended vacation and heard that her recently promoted plant manufacturing manager, Aran Trakanthannarong, a Thai national with strong potential at the firm, was planning on leaving the company in two weeks. Several other Thai employees who had worked with the plant for more than four years had already left abruptly. What could possibly have gone wrong over the past seven weeks?

Annette was a French expatriate and had worked for fifteen years in various departments and functional areas at ATZ headquarters in Montanay, France. ATZ is a French manufacturer of chemicals for the leather industry, with products covering the complete range of the leather manufacturing process. From the beginning at ATZ, Annette had expressed a strong interest in gaining international work experience and jumped at the opportunity to take over the head plant manager position at ATZ's five-year-old manufacturing facility in Nonthaburi, Thailand, immediately to the north of Bangkok. Annette had seen a considerable growth of business over the previous three years, with continued projected growth to meet the demand of opening and strengthening markets in Asia. From the beginning of her expatriate assignment, Annette was convinced that Thai workforce training was critical to building needed employee skills and local Thai managerial talent for the future.

Annette had been impressed soon after her arrival by Aran's strong interest as an entry-level employee on the production line in taking advantage of company-sponsored technical training as well as French language instruction offered in the evenings at a local foreign language institute. Aran was an excellent employee, who was responsible and careful in his work and got along well with his fellow Thai employees. Within a year he was promoted to a supervisory position.

During an earlier performance review with Annette, Aran expressed a strong interest in future promotion to a management level when the plant had grown enough to warrant this position. Annette had been pleased a few months earlier when she received the approval from headquarters for a new plant manager position, where Aran would serve a key liaison role between the lower-level Thai operative employees and her and other newly arrived French expatriates. These new French expatriates were assigned to build up the plant's sales, finance, and chemical engineering operations. Annette felt very satisfied with her progress as she headed back to France for a well-deserved seven-week vacation that she had been postponing for far too long.

Upon her return, and hearing of Aran's planned departure, Annette called a quick meeting with the other French expatriates to try to determine what had happened. She then planned to meet with Aran and hopefully succeed in getting him to reconsider his resignation. From what she learned, apparently two of the new French expatriates had unknowingly made a new policy decision that contradicted an existing plant employee work-flexibility benefit, which affected most of the employees. Only recently had they learned that this change created considerable resentment among the employees, who had asked Aran to correct the expatriates. But according to one employee who was a cousin of Aran, he was very hesitant to correct the expatriates, feeling it was not his job or station to criticize them. In addition, in developing their own workforce departmental teams, the more rigid, controlling behaviors of the French expatriates began to bother the Thai employees who were used to a more relaxed team-oriented Thai working style. They didn't understand why these French expatriates behaved differently, and Aran was unable to give them an adequate explanation. Despite their complaints to Aran, he still refrained from sharing this information with the expatriates—even though the expatriates had repeatedly requested that he share any advice on how they could avoid difficulties due to their lack of familiarity with Thai culture. Aran also was feeling stressed out and not sleeping well due to the increasing conflicts he was feeling at work. Finally, six long-time employees who had been friends of Aran accused him of being disloyal to his own people in preference to foreigners and promptly walked off the job, causing a major breakdown in plant operations. After a few days, Aran concluded that he had let down the Thai employees as well as the company and decided that he should resign.

Questions for Case Analysis and Discussion

1. Even though Annette demonstrated a strong commitment to host country workforce training, is there any evidence that Aran was inadequately prepared for his new management position?
2. What kind of preparatory training could have been helpful for Aran to avoid the difficulties he experienced? What kind of training could have been helpful for the general Thai workforce at ATZ? What are some possible ways in which this training for Aran and the other HCN workers could be provided effectively?
3. What recommendations do you have for Annette as she plans for her meeting with Aran?

Recommended Web site Resources

Academy of Human Resource Development (www.ahrd.org). International professional association dedicated to the study and dissemination in practice of human resource development theories, processes, and practices. Also provides opportunities for social interaction among individuals across the globe with scholarly and professional interests in HRD.

ASTD (American Society for Training & Development) (www.astd.org). World's largest association dedicated to workplace learning and performance professionals. ASTD's 70,000 members and associates come from more than one hundred countries and thousands of organizations—multinational corporations, medium-sized and small businesses, government, academia, consulting firms, and product and service suppliers. Provides ongoing educational and information services through conferences, newsletters, journals and other publications, and numerous other resources.

Development Dimensions International (www.ddiworld.com). Global firm with seventy-five offices in twenty-six countries providing a broad range of customized employee training and management development services and resources.

Interchange Institute (www.interchangeinstitute.org). Specializes in training and preparing individuals and families for a transition to a new culture, preparing them to live and work with others who share different cultural values and attitudes, including specially designed training for women, whether they're the employee being sent abroad or the spouse. Conducts research and disseminates information through consulting, workshops, publications, and other resources.

International Federation of Training and Development Organisations (www.iftdo.net). Worldwide network of HR professionals committed to identifying, developing, and transferring knowledge, skills, and technology to enhance personal and organizational growth, human performance, productivity, and sustainable development. Accredited NGO to the United Nations, helping to ensure that members' voices are heard by international policy makers influencing outcomes in human development. Links HR professionals in HR societies, corporations, universities, consultancies, government organizations, and non-profit enterprises. Its 150 member organizations represent more than 500,000 professionals in over fifty countries.

Notes

1. Adapted from "Motorola Adapts Training to Modern Business Demands," *HRM International Digest* 10 (6) (2002): 21–23; for more current detail refer to the Motorola University Web site, http://www.motorola.com/.

2. A.S. Grove, "Why Training Is the Boss's Job," *Fortune* January 23, 1984, 93–96.

3. P. Dvorak, "Theory and Practice: Firms Shift Underused Workers—Employees Gain Skills, Training as Companies Assign Them to New Tasks," *Wall Street Journal,* June 22, 2009; E.M. Norman, "How Multinationals Doing Business in Asia Can Develop Leadership Talent During a Recession," *Workspan* 52 (5) (2009): 34–43.

4. T.N. Garavan, M. Morley, P. Gunnigle, and D. McGuire, "Human Resource Development and Workplace Learning: Emerging Theoretical Perspectives and Organizational Practices," *Journal of European Industrial Training* 26 (2–4) (2002): 60–71; J.N. Streumer and P.A.M. Kommers, "Developments in the Emerging Human Resource Development Discipline," *International Journal of Human Resources Development and Management* 2 (1/2) (2002): 1.

5. M.R. Carrell, N.F. Elbert, and R.D. Hatfield, *Human Resource Management: Strategies for Managing a Diverse and Global Workforce,* 6th ed. (Fort Worth, TX: Dryden Press, 2000): 1254–55.

6. B. Leisen and C.M. Vance, "Cross-National Assessment of Service Quality in the Telecommunications Industry: Evidence from the United States and Germany," *Managing Service Quality* 11 (5)

(2001): 307–17; V.A. Zeithaml, A. Parasuraman, and L. Berry, *Delivering Quality Service: Balancing Customer Perceptions and Expectations* (New York: Free Press, 1990).

7. M. Walton, *The Deming Management Method: The Complete Guide to Quality Management* (New York: Perigee Books, 1986); D. Shipley, "ISO 9000 Makes Integrated Systems User Friendly," *Quality Progress* 36 (7) (2003): 26; B. Wyper and A. Harrison, "Deployment of Six Sigma Methodology in Human Resource Function: A Case Study," *Total Quality Management* 11 (4–6) (2000): S720–S727.

8. R. Dove, "Knowledge Management, Response Ability and the Agile Enterprise," *Journal of Knowledge Management* 3 (1) (1999): 8; G. Perez-Bustamante, "Knowledge Management in Agile Innovative Organizations," *Journal of Knowledge Management* 3 (1) (1999): 6; C.M. Savage, "Agility and the New Business Rules for the Knowledge Economy," *Agility and Global Competitiveness* 1 (4) (1997): 10–13.

9. Zeithaml et al., *Delivering Quality Service: Balancing Customer Perceptions and Expectation.*

10. T. Felin, T.R. Zenger, and J. Tomsik, "The Knowledge Economy: Emerging Organizational Forms, Missing Microfoundations, and Key Considerations for Managing Human Capital," *Human Resource Management* 48 (4) (2009): 555–70; D.R. Briscoe, "Talent Management and the Global Learning Organization," in *Smart Talent Management: Building Knowledge Capital for Competitive Advantage,* ed. Vaiman and Vance (Cheltenham, UK/Northhampton, MA: Edward Elgar Publishing, 2007): 195–216; M.U. Garcia and L.V. Francisco, "Organizational Learning in a Global Market," *Human Systems Management* 21 (3) (2002): 169.

11. H.P. Conn and G.S. Yip, "Global Transfer of Critical Capabilities," *Business Horizons* 40 (1) (1997): 22–31.

12. T.K. Lant, "Organizational Learning: Creating, Retaining, and Transferring Knowledge," *Administrative Science Quarterly* 45 (3) (2000): 622–25; M.W. McElroy, "Integrating Complexity Theory, Knowledge Management and Organizational Learning," *Journal of Knowledge Management* 4 (3) (2000): 195–203; A.L. Nobre, "Learning Organizations and Knowledge Management—People and Technology: The Challenges of the Information Era," *International Journal of Human Resources Development and Management* 2 (1/2) (2002): 113–28; M. Robertson and G.O. Hammersley, "Knowledge Management Practices within a Knowledge-Intensive Firm: The Significance of the People Management Dimension," *Journal of European Industrial Training* 24 (2–4) (2000): 241.

13. I. Berdrow and H.W. Lane, "International Joint Ventures: Creating Value through Successful Knowledge Management," *Journal of World Business* 38 (1) (2003): 15; S. Fernie, S.D. Green, S.J. Weller, and R. Newcombe, "Knowledge Sharing: Context, Confusion and Controversy," *International Journal of Project Management* 21 (3) (2003): 177.

14. G. Labovitz and V. Rosansky, *The Power of Alignment: How Great Companies Stay Centered and Accomplish Extraordinary Things* (New York: John Wiley & Sons, 1997); Anonymous, "Motorola Adapts Training to Modern Business Demands," *Human Resource Management International Digest* 10 (6) (2002): 21–23; A.K. Gupta and V. Govindarajan, "Cultivating a Global Mindset," *Academy of Management Executive* 16 (1) (2002): 116–26; R.W. Rowden, "The Strategic Role of Human Resource Management in Developing a Global Corporate Culture," *International Journal of Management* 19 (2) (2002): 155–200; H. Paul, "Creating a Global Mindset," *Thunderbird International Business Review* 42 (2) (2000): 187–200.

15. D. Mcleod, "Firms Basking in Growth Boom," *Business Insurance* 37 (29) (2003): 10; J. McAllen, "Making Sense of Merger Mania," *Petroleum Economist* (June 2003): 1; "More Equity Deals Could Be on the Way in M&A Uptick," *Euroweek,* April 11, 2003; S. Hume, A. Perlik, M. Sheridan, and L. Yee, "Companies Pursue Growth through Acquisition," *Restaurants & Institutions* 12 (27) (2002): 20; H. Sender, "Foreigners Still Find Korea Takeovers Difficult," *Wall Street Journal,* December 4, 2002; J. Veiga, M. Lubatkin, R. Calori, and P. Very, "Measuring Organizational Culture Clashes: A Two-Nation Post-Hoc Analysis of a Cultural Compatibility Index," *Human Relations* 53 (4) (2000): 539–57.

16. A. Soni and A. Wei, "Developing Global Leaders in India and China," *Benefits & Compensation International* 39 (1) (2009): 17; J.W. Fleenor, "Developing Global Business Leaders: Policies, Processes and Innovations," *Personnel Psychology* 55 (3) (Autumn 2002): 727–30; D.B. Neary and D.A. O'Grady, "The Role of Training in Developing Global Leaders: A Case Study at TRW Inc.," *Human Resource Management* 39 (2/3) (2000): 185.

17. R.A. Noe, *Employee Training & Development* (New York: McGraw-Hill, 2001); R.A. Swanson and E.F. Holton III, *Foundations of Human Resource Development* (San Francisco: Berrett-Koehler, 2001); T. Lapidus, *High Impact Training: Getting Results and Respect* (San Francisco: Jossey-Bass/Pfeifer, 2000); I.L. Goldstein and J.K. Ford, *Training in Organizations: Needs Assessment, Development and Evaluation* (Stamford, CT: Wadsworth, 2000); N.P. Blanchard and J.W. Thacker, *Effective Training: Systems, Strategies and Practices* (Upper Saddle River, NJ: Pearson Education, 1998).

18. D. Bond, R. Cohen, and D. Walker, "Introduction: Understanding Learning from Experience," in *Using Experience for Learning,* ed. D. Bond, R. Cohen, and D. Walker (Buckingham, UK: Society for Research into Higher Education and Open University Press, 1993): 1–17; B.S. Bloom, ed., *Taxonomy of Educational Objectives: The Classification of Educational Goals: Handbook I, Cognitive Domain* (New York: Longmans, Green, 1956).

19. D.R. Krathwohl, B.S. Bloom, and B.B. Masia, *Taxonomy of Educational Objectives: Handbook II: Affective Domain* (New York: David McKay, 1964).

20. J.M. Keller, "Development and Use of the ARCS Model of Motivational Design," *Journal of Instructional Development* 10 (3) (1987): 2–10; J.M. Keller and T.W. Kopp, "Application of the ARCS Model to Motivational Design," in *Instructional Theories in Action: Lessons Illustrating Selected Theories,* ed. C.M. Reigeluth (Mahwah, NJ: Lawrence Erlbaum, 1987): 289–320.

21. E. Simpson, *The Classification of Educational Objectives in the Psychomotor Domain,* Vol. 3 (Washington, DC: Gryphon House, 1972); A. Harrow, *A Taxonomy of the Psychomotor Domain: A Guide for Developing Behavioral Objectives* (New York: McKay, 1972).

22. J.E. Driskell, R.P. Willis, and C. Cooper, "Effects of Over Learning on Retention," *Journal of Applied Psychology* 77 (1992): 615–92; T.T. Baldwin and J.K. Ford, "Transfer of Training: A Review and Directions for Future Research," *Personnel Psychology* 41 (1988): 63–105.

23. Adapted from B.S. Bloom, ed., *Taxonomy of Educational Objectives.*

24. H. Mintzberg and J. Gosling, "Educating Managers beyond Borders," *Academy of Management Learning and Education* 1 (1) (2002): 64–76; A. Bandura, *Social Learning Theory* (Englewood Cliffs, NJ: Prentice-Hall, 1977); C.I. Gragg, "Because Wisdom Can't Be Told," in *The Case Method at the Harvard Business School,* 11th ed., ed. M.P. McNair (New York: McGraw-Hill, 1954).

25. S.B. Merriam and R. Caffarella, *Learning in Adulthood: A Comprehensive Guide,* 2d ed. (San Francisco: Jossey-Bass, 1999); M.S. Knowles, *The Adult Learner: A Neglected Species,* 3d ed. (Houston, TX: Gulf, 1984); K.P. Cross, *Adults as Learners: Increasing Participation and Facilitating Learning* (San Francisco: Jossey-Bass, 1981); M.S. Knowles, *The Modern Practice of Adult Education* (Chicago: Association Press/Follett, 1980).

26. A.D. Wright, "Respect Cultural Differences When Training, Experts Say," *HR Magazine* 54 (12) (2009): 19–20; M.S. Schell, *Managing Across Cultures: The Seven Keys to Doing Business with a Global Mindset* (New York: McGraw-Hill, 2009); C.M. Vance, D. Boje, and H.D. Stage, "An Examination of the Cross-Cultural Transferability of Traditional Training Principles for Optimizing Individual Learning," *Journal of Teaching in International Business* 2 (3/4) (1991): 107–20.

27. C.M. Vance, D.M. Boje, and H.D. Stage, "Convergence or Divergence? A Comparative Analysis of Host Country National Training Design Needs in Five Countries of the Pacific Rim" (paper presented at the Annual Meeting of the Western Academy of Management Big Sky, Montana, March 1988).

28. P.W. Thayer, "Creating, Implementing, and Managing Effective Training and Development: State of the Art Lessons for Practice," *Personnel Psychology* 55 (3) (2002): 748–52; S.M. Sorenson, "Training for the Long Run: Development, Implementation, and Evaluation," *Engineered Systems* 19 (8) (2002): 28; R. Zemke and A. Rossett, "A Hard Look at ISD," *Training* 39 (2) (2002): 26–32; S.E. Hicks, "ISD from the Ground Up: A No-Nonsense Approach to Instructional Design," *Training and Development* 55 (9) (2001): 90; D.C. Wigglesworth, "Using Educational Technology in International Training," *Training and Development* 36 (10) (1982): 14–17.

29. J.H. Harless, *An Ounce of Analysis Is Worth a Pound of Objectives* (Newman, GA: Harless Performance Guild, 1975).

30. I.L. Goldstein, "Training in Work Organizations," in *Handbook of Industrial and Organizational Psychology,* ed. M.D. Dunnette and L.M. Hough (Palo Alto, CA: Consulting Psychologists Press, 1991): 507–619; C. Ostroff, and J.K. Ford, "Assessing Training Needs: Critical Levels of Analysis," in *Training and Development in Organizations,* ed. I.L. Goldstein (San Francisco: Jossey-Bass, 1989): 25–62.

31. C.M. Vance and Y. Paik, "One Size Fits All in Expatriate Pre-Departure Training? Comparing the Host Country Voices of Mexican, Indonesian and US Workers," *Journal of Management Development* 21 (7) (2002): 557–71; C.M. Vance and Y. Paik, "Toward a Taxonomy of Host Country National Learning Process Involvement in Multinational Learning Organizations" (paper presented at the Annual Meeting of the Academy of Management, Washington, DC, August 2001).

32. Vance and Paik, "Toward a Taxonomy of Host Country National Learning Process Involvement in Multinational Learning Organizations."

33. K.N. Wexley and T.T. Baldwin, "Post Training Strategies for Facilitating Positive Transfer: An Empirical Exploration," *Academy of Management Journal* 29 (1986): 503–20; M.L. Broad, and J.W. Newstrom, *Transfer of Training: Action-Packed Strategies to Ensure High Payoff from Training Investments* (Reading, MA: Addison-Wesley, 1992); V.W. Kupritz, "The Relative Impact of Workplace Design on Training Transfer," *Human Resource Development Quarterly* 13 (4) (2002): 427–47; S. Yamnill and G.N. McLean, "Theories Supporting Transfer of Training," *Human Resource Development Quarterly* 12 (2) (2001): 195–208.

34. M. Gold, "8 Lessons about e-Learning from 5 Organizations," *Training and Development* 57 (8) (2003): 54; C. Nolan, "Human Resource Development in the Irish Hotel Industry: The Case of the Small Firm," *Journal of European Industrial Training* 26 (2–4) (2002): 88–99; M. Herron, "Training Alone Is Not Enough," *Training* 39 (2) (2002): 72; R.F. Mager, *What Every Manager Should Know about Training* (Belmont, CA: Lake, 1992).

35. D. Fichter and J. Carroll, "Just-in-Time Training: Creating Viewlets for Intranet Applications," *Online* 26 (2) (2002): 76–78; S. Globerson and A. Korman, "The Use of Just-in-Time Training in a Project Environment," *International Journal of Project Management* 19 (5) (2001): 279–85.

36. M.E. Mendenhall, R.J. Jensen, J.S. Black, and H.B. Gregersen, "Seeing the Elephant: Human Resource Management Challenges in the Age of Globalization," *Organizational Dynamics* 32 (3) (2003): 261–74; M. Harvey and M.M. Novicevic, "The Impact of Hypercompetitive 'Timescapes' on the Development of a Global Mindset," *Management Decision* 39 (5/6) (2001): 448–60.

37. K. Johnson and L. Duxbury, "The View from the Field: A Case Study of the Expatriate Boundary-Spanning Role," *Journal of World Business* 45 (1) (2010): 29–40; M.E. Mendenhall, "Introduction: New Perspectives on Expatriate Adjustment and Its Relationship to Global Leadership Development," in *Developing Global Business Leaders: Policies, Processes, and Innovations,* ed. M.E. Mendenhall, T.M. Kuhlmann, and G.K. Stahl (Westport, CT: Quorum Books, 2001): 1–16; J.S. Black, A. Morrison, and H.B. Gregersen, *Global Explorers: The Next Generation of Leaders* (New York: Routledge, 1999); A. Langley, "Emotional Intelligence: A New Evaluation for Management Development," *Career Development International* 5 (3) (2000): 177–83.

38. V. Suutari, "Global Leader Development: An Emerging Research Agenda," *Career Development International* 7 (4) (2002): 218–33.

39. A.K. Gupta and V. Govindarajan, "Cultivating a Global Mindset," *Academy of Management Executive* 16 (1) (2002): 116–26; H. Paul, "Creating a Global Mindset," 187–200; S.H. Rhinesmith, "Open the Door to a Global Mindset," *Training and Development* 49 (5) (1995): 34–43; also refer to P. Evans, V. Pucik, and J. Barsoux, *The Global Challenge: Frameworks for International Human Resource Management* (New York: McGraw-Hill/Irwin, 2002): 1384–87.

40. B.L. Kedia and A. Mukherji, "Global Managers: Developing a Mindset for Global Competitiveness," *Journal of World Business* 34 (3) (1999): 230–42.

41. S.H. Rhinesmith, "How Can You Manage Global Paradox?" *Journal of Corporate Accounting and Finance* 12 (6) (2001): 3.

42. H.B. Gregersen, A.J. Morrison, and J.S. Black, "Developing Leaders for the Global Frontier," *Sloan Management Review* 40 (1) (1998): 21–32.

43. C.M. Vance, "The Personal Quest for Building Global Competence: A Taxonomy of Self-Initiating Career Path Strategies for Gaining Business Experience Abroad," *Journal of World Business* 40 (4) (2005): 374–85; J. Osland and A. Osland, "Expatriate Paradoxes and Cultural Involvement," *International Studies of Management and Organization* 35 (4) (2005): 91–114.

44. N. Furuya, M. Stevens, A. Bird, G. Oddou, and M. Mendenhall, "Managing the Learning and Transfer of Global Management Competence: Antecedents and Outcomes of Japanese Repatriation Effectiveness," *Journal of International Business Studies* 40 (2) (2009): 200–15; P.M. Caligiuri and S. Colakoglu, "A Strategic Contingency Approach to Expatriate Assignment Management," *Human Resource Management Journal* 17 (4) (2007): 393–410; P. Caligiuri and V. Di Santo, "Global Competence: What Is It, and Can It Be Developed through Global Assignments?" *HR Planning* 24 (3) (2001): 27–35; T.M. Kühlmann, "The German Approach to Developing Global Leaders via Expatriation," in *Developing Global Business Leaders: Policies, Processes and Innovations,* ed. M.E. Mendenhall, T.M. Kühlmann, and G.K. Stahl (Westport, CT: Quorum Books, 2001): 57–71.

45. M.G. Harvey, M.F. Price, C. Speir, and M.M. Novicevic, "The Role of Inpatriates in a Globalization Strategy and Challenges Associated with the Inpatriation Process," *HR Planning* 22 (1) (1999): 38–50; M. Harvey, "Inpatriation Training: The Next Challenge for International Human Resource Management," *International Journal of Intercultural Relations* 21 (3) (1997): 393–428.

46. J.S. Black, A.J. Morrison, and H.B. Gregersen, *Global Explorers: The Next Generation of Leaders* (New York: Routledge, 1999).

47. Caligiuri and Di Santo, "Global Competence: What Is It, and Can It Be Developed through Global Assignments?"; S. Leiba-O'Sullivan, "The Distinction between Stable and Dynamic Cross-Cultural Competencies: Implications for Expatriate Trainability," *Journal of International Business Studies* 30 (4) (1999): 709–25.

48. J.T.F. Poon and I.K.H. Chew, "Emotional Intelligence of Foreign and Local University Students in Singapore: Implications for Managers," *Journal of Business and Psychology* 17 (2003): 345–67; N.M. Ashkanasy and C.S. Daus, "Emotion in the Workplace: The New Challenge for Managers," *Academy of Management Executive* 16 (1) (2002): 76–86; C. Watkin, "Developing Emotional Intelligence," *International Journal of Selection and Assessment* 8 (2) (2000): 89–92; C.D. Fisher and N.M. Ashkanasy, "The Emerging Role of Emotions in Work Life: An Introduction," *Journal of Organizational Behavior* 21 (2000): 123–29; M.E.P. Seligman, *Learned Optimism: How to Change Your Mind and Your Life,* 2d ed. (New York: Pocket Books, 1998).

49. G. Oddou, M. Mendenhall, and J.B. Ritchie, "Leveraging Travel as a Tool for Global Leadership Development," *Human Resource Management* 39 (2/3) (2000): 159–72.

50. M.L. Maznevski and J.J. Di Stefano, "Global Leaders Are Team Players: Developing Global Leaders through Membership on Global Teams," *Human Resource Management* 39 (2/3) (2000): 195–208.

51. J.A. Volkmar, "Context and Control in Foreign Subsidiaries: Making a Case for the Host Country National Manager," *Journal of Leadership & Organizational Studies* 10 (1) (2003): 93–105; S. Beechler, "International Management Control in Multinational Corporations: The Case of Japanese Consumer Electronics Firms in Asia," *ASEAN Economic Bulletin* 9 (2) (1992): 149–68; A. K. Gupta and V. Govindarajan, "Knowledge Flows and the Structure of Control within Multinational Corporations," *Academy of Management Review* 16 (4) (1991): 768–92; C.A. Bartlett and S. Ghoshal, *Managing across Borders: The Transnational Solution* (Boston: Harvard Business School Publishing, 1991); Y. Doz and C.K. Prahalad, "Patterns of Strategic Control within Multinational Corporations," *Journal of International Business Studies* 15 (3) (1984): 55–72.

52. Gupta and Govindarajan, "Cultivating a Global Mindset"; Conn and Yip, "Global Transfer of Critical Capabilities."

53. Mendenhall, Jensen, Black, and Gregersen, "Seeing the Elephant: Human Resource Management Challenges in the Age of Globalization"; R.M. Kanter and T.D. Dretler, "'Global Strategy' and

Its Impact on Local Operations: Lessons from Gillette Singapore," *Academy of Management Executive* 12 (4) (1998): 60–68; G.T. Milkovich and M. Bloom, "Rethinking International Compensation," *Compensation and Benefits Review* 30 (1) (1998): 15–23.

54. J. Nahapiet and S. Ghoshal, "Social Capital, Intellectual Capital, and the Organizational Advantage," *Academy of Management Review* 23 (2) (1998): 242–66; B. Kogut and U. Zander, "What Firms Do? Coordination, Identity and Learning," *Organization Science* 7 (5) (1996): 502–18.

55. A. Stanton, "Cultural Governance," *Public Relations Strategist* 9 (1) (2003): 13–15; E.A. Schein, *Organizational Culture and Leadership,* 2nd ed. (San Francisco: Jossey-Bass, 1997); P. Frost, L.F. Moore, M.R. Louis, C.C. Lundberg, and J. Martin, *Organizational Culture* (Newbury Park, CA: Sage, 1985).

56. M. Chong, "Employee Participation in CSR and Corporate Identity: Insights from a Disaster-Response Program in the Asia-Pacific," *Corporate Reputation Review* 12 (2) (2009): 106–19; P. Lukas, "Johnson & Johnson," *Fortune Small Business* 13 (3) (2003): 91; J. Collins, "The 10 Greatest CEOs of All Time," *Fortune* 148 (2) (2003): 54; K. Walter, "Values Statements That Augment Corporate Success," *HR Magazine* 40 (10) (1995): 87–91.

57. J. Fox, "Nokia's Secret Code," *Fortune,* May 1, 2000: 160–74; N.M. Tichy and E. Cohen, *The Leadership Engine: How Winning Companies Build Leaders at Every Level* (New York: HarperCollins, 1997); Evans, Pucik, and Barsoux, *The Global Challenge: Frameworks for International Human Resource Management,* 105, 112, 115; A. Edstrom and J.R. Galbraith, "Transfer of Managers as a Coordination and Control Strategy in Multinational Organizations," *Administrative Science Quarterly* 22 (1977): 248–63.

58. Y. Paik and J.D. Sohn, "Expatriate Managers and MNC's Ability to Control International Subsidiaries: The Case of Japanese MNCs," *Journal of World Business* 39 (1) (2004): 61–71.

59. J.K. Harrison, "Developing Successful Expatriate Managers: A Framework for Structural Design and Strategic Alignment of Cross-Cultural Training Programs," *HR Planning* 17 (3) (1994): 17–34; J.S. Black and M. Mendenhall, "Cross-Cultural Training Effectiveness: A Review and Theoretical Framework for Future Research," *Academy of Management Review* 15 (1) (1990): 113–36; P.C. Early, "Intercultural Training for Managers: A Comparison of Documentary and Interpersonal Methods," *Academy of Management Journal* 30 (4) (1987): 684–98.

60. PricewaterhouseCoopers, *International Assignments: European Policy and Practice* (Europe: PricewaterhouseCoopers, 1997–98); K. Baumgarten, "Training and Development of International Staff," in *International Human Resource Management,* ed. A. Harzing and J.V. Ruysseveldt (London: Sage, 1995): 205–28.

61. V. Suutari and C. Brewster, "Expatriate Management Practices and Perceived Relevance: Evidence from Finnish Expatriates," *Personnel Review* 30 (5/6) (2001): 554–79; R.L. Tung, "American Expatriates Abroad: From Neophytes to Cosmopolitans," *Journal of World Business* 33 (2) (1998): 125–44; R.L. Tung, "A Contigency Framework of Selection and Training of Expatriates Revisited," *Human Resource Management Review* 8 (1) (1998): 23–37; M. Harvey, "Dual-Career Expatriates: Expectations, Adjustment and Satisfaction with International Relocation," *Journal of International Business Studies* 28 (3) (1997): 627–58.

62. L.N. Littrell, E. Salas, K.P. Hess, M. Paley, and S. Riedel, "Expatriate Preparation: A Critical Analysis of 25 Years of Cross-Cultural Training Research," *Human Resource Development Review* 5 (3) 2006: 355–88.

63. C.D. Fisher, L.F. Schoenfeldt, and J.B. Shaw, *Human Resource Management,* 5th ed. (Boston: Houghton-Mifflin, 2003): 834–35; J.S. Black, H. Gregersen, and M. Mendenhall, *Global Assignments: Successfully Expatriating and Repatriating Global Managers* (San Francisco: Jossey-Bass, 1992); J.S. Black and M. Mendenhall, "Cross-Cultural Training Effectiveness: A Review and a Theoretical Framework for Future Research," *Academy of Management Review* 15 (1) (1990): 113–36; J.S. Black and M. Mendenhall, "A Practical but Theory-Based Framework for Selecting Cross-Cultural Training Methods," *Human Resource Management* 28 (4) (1989): 511–39.

64. R. Melles, "'They Speak English So I'll Be Okay.' Not So Fast," *Canadian HR Reporter* 15 (16) (2002): 11.

65. C.M. Vance and E.A. Ensher, "The Voice of the Host Country Workforce: A Key Source for Improving the Effectiveness of Expatriate Training and Performance," *International Journal of Intercultural Relations* 26 (2002): 447–61.

66. Y. Altman and S. Shortland, "Women and International Assignments: Taking Stock—A 25-Year Review," *Human Resource Management* 47 (2) (2008): 199–216; C.L. Owen and R.F. Scherer, "Doing Business in Latin America: Managing Cultural Differences in Perceptions of Female Expatriates," *S.A.M. Advanced Management Journal* 67 (2) (2002): 37–41.

67. P.M. Caligiuri and W.F. Cascio, "Can We Send Her There? Managing the Success of Western Women on Global Assignments," *Journal of World Business* 33 (4) (1998): 394–416.

68. B.R. Ragins, B. Townsend, and M. Mattis, "Gender Gap in the Executive Suite: CEOs and Female Executives Report on Breaking the Glass Ceiling," *Academy of Management Executive* 12 (1998): 28–42.

69. W. Kirk and R. Maddox, "International Management: The New Frontier for Women," *Personnel* 65 (3) (1988): 46–49.

70. P. M. Caligiuri and R. L. Tung, "Comparing the Success of Male and Female Expatriates from a US-Based Multinational Company," *International Journal of Human Resource Management* 10 (1999): 763–82; N.J. Adler, "Pacific Basin Managers: A Gain, not a Woman," *Human Resource Management* 26 (1987): 169–92.

71. N.J. Adler, L.W. Brody, and J.S. Osland, "The Women's Global Leadership Forum: Enhancing One Company's Global Leadership Capability," *Human Resource Management* 39 (2000): 209–25; Caligiuri and Cascio, "Can We Send Her There? Managing the Success of Western Women on Global Assignments."

72. M.E. Mendenhall and G.K. Stahl, "Expatriate Training and Development: Where Do We Go from Here?" *Human Resource Management* 39 (Summer/Fall 2000): 251–65; A.B. Antal and D.N. Izraeli, "A Global Comparison of Women in Management: Women Managers in Their Homelands and as Expatriates," in *Women in Management,* ed. E.A. Ferguson (Newbury Park, CA: Sage, 1993): 53–102.

73. C.M. Vance and Y. Paik, "Host-Country Workforce Training in Support of the Expatriate Management Assignment," in *Expatriate Management: New Ideas for International Business,* ed. J. Selmer (Westport, CT: Quorum Books, 1995): 157–71; C.M. Vance and P.S. Ring, "Preparing the Host Country Workforce for Expatriate Managers: The Neglected Other Side of the Coin," *Human Resource Development Quarterly* 5 (4) (1994): 337–52.

74. P.J. Dowling, D.E. Welch, and R.S. Schuler, *International Human Resource Management: Managing People in a Multinational Context,* 3rd ed. (New York: South-Western College, 1999); Harvey, "Inpatriation Training: The Next Challenge for International Human Resource Management."

75. C.M. Vance and Y. Paik, "A Field-Based Analysis of Host Country National Learning Needs for Enhancing the Performance of Foreign Subsidiary Operations" (research paper presented at the Annual Meeting of the Western Academy of Management Sun Valley, Idaho, April 2001).

76. C.M. Vance, J.T. Wholihan, and E.S. Paderon, "The Imperative for Host Country Workforce Training and Development as Part of the Expatriate Management Assignment: Toward a New Research Agenda," in *Research in Personnel & Human Resource Management: International Supplement 3,* ed. J.B. Shaw, P. Kirkbride, G. Ferris, and K. Rowland (Greenwich, CT: JAI Press, 1993): 359–73.

77. C.M. Vance, V. Vaiman, and T. Andersen, "The Vital Liaison Role of Host Country Nationals in MNC Knowledge Management," *Human Resource Management* 48 (4) (2009): 649–59.

78. S.M. Carraher, S.E. Sullivan, and M.M. Crocitto, "Mentoring Across Global Boundaries: An Empirical Examination of Home- and Host-Country Mentors on Expatriate Career Outcomes," *Journal of International Business Studies* 39 (8) (2008): 1310–26; M.B. Stanek, "Global Mentoring Programs: Business Relationships beyond Traditional Borders," *Journal of Workplace Learning* 13 (2) (2001): 66–72; D.C. Feldman and M.C. Bolino, "The Impact of On-Site Mentoring on Expatriate Socialization: A Structural Equation Modeling Approach," *International Journal of Human Resource Management* 10 (1999): 54–71.

79. J. Milliman, S. Taylor, and A.J. Czaplewski, "Cross-Cultural Performance Feedback in Multi-

national Enterprises: Opportunity for Organizational Learning," *HR Planning* 25 (3) (2002): 29–43; Y. Paik and J.H.D. Sohn, "Confucius in Mexico: Korean MNCs and the Maquiladoras," *Business Horizons* 41 (6) (1998): 25–33.

80. Personal interview with Thomas Förster, Manager of International Transfer Management, AG Bayer (Leverkusen, Germany, October 22, 2002); Harvey, "Inpatriation Training: The Next Challenge for International Human Resource Management."

8 Managing International Assignments

EXPATRIATE INNOCENCE ABROAD

Carol Williams was excited about the meeting that she just had with the international marketing vice president of her London-based multinational pharmaceutical firm. Since she had joined the firm as a junior sales manager five years earlier, she had been seeking an international assignment—anywhere away from her familiar United Kingdom. She had seen several attractive expatriate assignment opportunities given to male colleagues despite her indications of strong interest, but finally her opportunity had arrived!

She was told that she had been selected to fill an East Asian sales management position in Tokyo that had suddenly become available. From what Carol learned, this position had been filled until recently by Clarence Mitchell, who had moved to Japan with his wife and two children only nine months earlier. Carol didn't know many of the details other than hearing through the grapevine that after some initial struggling, Clarence was finally making some real progress with his international assignment. But apparently his family was still having major difficulty adjusting to their life in Japan, and Clarence actually threatened to leave the firm—after fourteen years of exemplary performance in the United Kingdom before the Japan assignment—if he could not return to the home headquarters.

Although Carol was pleased about this assignment, notwithstanding the unfortunate situation of her predecessor, she was rather surprised that she would need to be ready to relocate in three weeks to avoid missing some critical target business deadlines in Japan. She also was rather surprised that there was no formal predeparture preparation or training to speak of to prepare for her upcoming assignment. She was told to just continue doing the excellent work that she always did and to learn what she could about Japan in the evenings by surfing the Web.

Five months passed, and Carol struggled to cope with her new life and surroundings in Japan. Her first month had seemed like an extended vacation in which she was enthralled by the new sights and sounds—and the many smells of local cuisine. She also was joined for a week by her sister and brother-in-law, who Carol enjoyed hosting as an "experienced" tour guide. She had made real progress in learning basic Japanese through a special class for business professionals. However, for the past two weeks Carol had felt tired and listless. She was also very discouraged about falling short of her six-month performance goals. She seemed to sense that local Japanese businessmen who had long been company clients resented her entering their all-male business circles—no matter how hard she tried to be as polite, nonconfrontational, and "ladylike" as the women working at her office were. In fact, she also seemed to feel real resentment at her office from younger sales representatives, including one who implied that he had hoped to be promoted to the position made available by Clarence Mitchell's unexpected departure.

Carol found that she was spending more and more time alone in her apartment after work and spending time on line looking up familiar places and subjects back home in the United Kingdom. She was feeling despondent—very much alone and unwelcome in this foreign environment. Finally Carol decided to contact Clarence back at company headquarters to get some advice on how to resolve some possible cross-cultural issues that were causing her frustration and to hear his experience-based reaction to some new ideas she had for increasing business. She wondered why she had not thought to contact him before and taken advantage of his experience. However, she was stunned when she called the next day and learned that Clarence had left the firm two weeks earlier and was now working for a major competitor.

Carol was still feeling low and lost the next afternoon when she had a chance meeting at a local market with a Canadian woman who had lived in Japan for four years working for a German engineering software firm. Carol's spirits really seemed to pick up when the woman invited her to attend the next week's meeting of the local Japan chapter of the Alliance of Business Women International, saying, "You'll really like our group—it has made a huge difference to my experience here!"

INTRODUCTION

As new businesses continue to venture beyond their domestic borders and more experienced businesses increase their international activities and global business integration, we continue to see more and more foreign assignments for carrying out international business objectives. These foreign assignments can present significant individual and organizational challenges, as illustrated in the opening scenario of this chapter. Yet these international assignments are not limited to the traditional PCN expatriate assignment. The nature of these assignments is changing dramatically. For example, due to the significant company cost and personal and family disruption of a PCN expatriate assignment, companies might resort to finding more economical and convenient arrangements, such as staffing key management positions in foreign operations with experienced and qualified host country and third country nationals. The effective preparation of an HCN for a critical assignment such as carrying out MNC objectives in the host country can be optimized through a preceding significant inpatriate experience at parent company headquarters,[1] which constitutes an international assignment for the HCN. And new strategies have been developed for the same reasons (avoiding exorbitant costs and personal hardship such as spouse career and family disruption) that take advantage of advancements in technologies, travel, and communications within our increasingly global business environment. Increasingly, international assignments are carried out through frequent use of telecommunications combined with brief visits to foreign operations (for example, "virtual" expatriates); short-term international assignments (that is, three to twelve months in duration) that might even feature commuting; and frequent online and telecommunication-enabled interactions among geographically dispersed members of an international virtual team that occasionally meets in person at a common location.[2]

In this chapter we examine important issues and practices associated with managing traditional long-term international assignments successfully, including predeparture planning and preparation, on-site management for effective adjustment and ongoing support, and repatriation. Besides these important considerations for the traditional PCN expatriate assignment, we will examine issues that might be unique to women expatriates and third country nationals in their expatriate assignments as well as HCN inpatriates who are assigned to work at MNC operations in the MNC home country. We also will briefly examine practices and challenges associated with rapidly increasing forms of short-term international assignments, including working as a "virtual" expatriate with international teams and with global virtual teams, as well as important considerations surrounding frequent travel.

EXPATRIATE PREPARATION, FOREIGN ASSIGNMENT, AND REPATRIATION

An expatriate assignment represents a costly investment—some estimates range from $300,000 to $1 million annually. There is an accompanying risk of assignment failure prompting a premature return (one study found that 10 percent to 20 percent of U.S. expatriates returned prematurely due to dissatisfaction and inability to adjust). A completed assignment duration featuring underperformance or failure to achieve anticipated goals can also be very expensive. This is often reflected indirectly in costs due to early mistakes, lengthy periods of adjustment, loss of market share, and damaged relations with clients, local businesses and vendors, and host country government officials. In addition, expatriate assignment underperformance or failure can have a negative effect on an expatriate's morale and career viability.[3] Even with a successful foreign assignment, there can be significant underutilization and turnover costs when the completion of the expatriate's assignment and transition to the home country are handled poorly. Following the thoughtful selection of an expatriate for an extended foreign assignment, a company must consider the importance of predeparture, foreign experience, and repatriation phases to optimize the company's return on the expatriate assignment investment.

PREDEPARTURE PREPARATION PHASE

As discussed in Chapter 7, effective predeparture training for expatriates and accompanying family members should provide a clear set of expectations about conditions—both positive and negative—that await them in the foreign country. These accurate, realistic expectations provided by a thorough predeparture preview process contribute a form of *anticipatory adjustment* that can greatly facilitate actual adjustment on arrival by reducing uncertainties and increasing predictability in the new setting.[4] In addition, pertinent information on matters unrelated to understanding the upcoming international assignment itself, such as personal details involved in relocation, should be provided prior to the international assignment to help increase confidence and minimize the natural apprehensions and stress involved.[5]

Where possible, adequate time should be allowed between the expatriate decision for accepting the foreign assignment and the actual departure to enable the expatriate and family members to attend to personal arrangements. In addition, this adequate time allows for a more effective appraisal of potential stressors awaiting in the foreign location and the building of helpful cross-cultural skills.[6] In addition to a realistic preview and clarification of expectations about the foreign assignment, there should be clear and honest expectations set about the length of the assignment as well as the uncertainties involved that make sincere long-term intentions about future promotions and activities beyond the foreign assignment difficult to fulfill. If such specific promises about the post-assignment future are given, changes in the organization during the foreign assignment might occur that render the promises unlikely (for example, the manager who made the promise leaves the organization or the unit where the promise applies is closed). This failure to deliver on expectations of future career benefit not only can cause problems upon expatriate repatriation but also can bring significant debilitating disappointment for the expatriate who learns of these unintended changes while still abroad. Rather than making promises about specific arrangements upon completion of the assignment, companies should discuss with the expatriate the value of the international experience as part of his or her long-range career plan and examine in general possible opportunities that could be available when the expatriate returns after a successful international assignment.

Besides formal and specific predeparture training (such as cross-cultural awareness and host country language), more general predeparture preparation might involve informal conversations and exchanges of helpful tips and advice through gatherings and other encouraged interactions between predeparting employees and their families and any available inpatriates and other PCNs having recent experience working and living in the host country. Past and even current expatriates and their families in the same host country can be particularly helpful in identifying relevant areas for final preparation, encouraging the soon-to-depart expatriate and family members to take advantage of what was learned from their own experience. Finally, in this predeparture preparation a mentor or coach from the home workplace could be assigned to keep in regular contact during the assignment via telephone and e-mail, helping the expatriate navigate through the inevitable adjustment and ongoing challenges as well as keeping him or her apprised of company developments back in the home country. Ideally, such a back-home mentor would be experienced in the expatriate's foreign assignment culture (that is, one who successfully served in the same foreign operation), trusted and respected by the expatriate, and truly interested in the expatriate's success.[7]

Global Workforce Professional Profile 8.1
Yvonne McNulty: Breaking the Trailing Spouse Mold

The rather negative term "trailing spouse" conjures up the image of an expatriate on a foreign assignment accompanied by a reluctant spouse (usually female, but increasingly males are accompanying a female expatriate spouse) whose life is miserable and suffers far worse international adjustment anxiety and despondence than the expatriate. This trailing spouse can be a drain on the expatriate's energy and might contribute to a premature end of the assignment. However, we increasingly are meeting spouses who consider their accompaniment on the international assignment as an excellent opportunity to both relocate to a new foreign environment and also gain personal and career developmental experience contributing to their global competence.

Dr. Yvonne McNulty is a great example of this new breed of accompanying spouse. In 1999, she gave up her career at PricewaterhouseCoopers in Sydney, Australia, to relocate with her expatriate husband to Chicago. She and her husband then relocated to Philadelphia, and finally—with a young daughter in tow and another baby on the way—on to Singapore where her husband continues in an international assignment, first with Oracle Corporation and presently with JDA Software. During this time abroad McNulty has certainly been proactive in growing from her international experiences. She completed her PhD on a distance education basis with Monash University in Australia; lectured at numerous American universities; published more than two dozen articles for practitioner magazines, Web sites and journals; and is the founder of the helpful online resource, www.thetrailingspouse.com.

McNulty's new "portable career" emerged after considerable personal reflection resulting from her frustrations as a trailing spouse and her inability to obtain a working visa in the United States. Unlike many trailing spouses, McNulty decided not to remain passive and indifferent but to take charge and look for opportunities that would enrich her life. She decided to complete a master's degree in international human resource management on a distance-learning basis with Southern Cross University in Australia and began to focus on the trailing spouse phenomenon as a world that she was living in that was in great need of study. As a result of her active research, McNulty has found that many spouses come upon this same crossroads experience where they recognize the value of a break in their career to reflect and take stock of their priorities and goals. With this helpful period of personal reflection, spouses often decide to use the time abroad for professional development, as did McNulty, and take coursework, either locally or on a distance basis. Many others decide to engage in volunteer activities with local charities to gain valuable experience in leadership and administration, along with deeper cross-cultural exposure. In their increasingly assertive stance, these spouses also are finding more and more professional advisement firms to assist them in career planning and placement into activities providing valuable work experience, in both meaningful volunteer activity and in actual employment in a growing number of companies in regions such as the European Union, where many countries are now becoming more flexible in providing work permits to spouses.

McNulty's doctoral research focused on expatriate return on investment, the literature review for which yielded a "Best Paper" recognition at the Academy of Management Conference in New Orleans. McNulty is also the author and publisher

(continued)

Global Workforce Professional Profile 8.1 (continued)

of the Trailing Spouse Survey. The survey published the findings of a four-year study of accompanying spouse issues during international assignments, which McNulty conducted as part of her master's degree. The data for the survey were collected on McNulty's Web site between 2001 and 2005 from 264 trailing spouses around the globe. McNulty remains very active with such professional organizations as the Academy of Management, Australian Human Resources Institute, SHRM Global Forum, and Singapore HR Institute.

FOREIGN EXPERIENCE PHASE: INITIAL INTERNATIONAL ADJUSTMENT AND ONGOING SUPPORT

Notwithstanding the importance of careful expatriate predeparture selection, preparation, and training, many believe that it is after arrival in the foreign location that the most important work can be done to secure the success of the expatriate assignment. In regard to this second phase, which begins with arrival at the new location, we will first examine the critical early adjustment period (typically about three months from first arrival)[8] and make suggestions of immediate support for facilitating this adjustment. We then consider important measures for providing helpful ongoing support during an extended international assignment.

Initial International Adjustment

Despite the extent of past international work experience, those beginning a foreign assignment in a new host country inevitably experience a need to make significant adjustments—including conceptual, physical, social, and emotional—to achieve a sense of efficacy and psychological comfort with living and working in the new environment.[9] Some individual adjustments might be primarily cognitive and relatively simple, such as understanding that in Germany the yellow traffic light acts as a warning prior to turning to both red and green, rather than just red as in the United States. Other adjustments are somewhat more challenging and involve psychomotor skills, such as moving from the home country of Italy to Singapore and getting used to driving on the left side of the road. Still other adjustments require major disruptions of a person's comfortable basic routines and even fundamental understanding of how the world should operate, and involve disorientation, significant stress, and a necessary and frequently uncomfortable replotting of one's cognitive map. Effective international adjustment should also be a major concern for a spouse and family members who accompany the expatriate. They often have a more difficult adjustment than the expatriate who is fully occupied at work much of the time. Their lack of effective adjustment can spill over to hinder the expatriate's adjustment, adding an extra strain of concern about family members and impeding work performance and possibly even precipitating a premature termination of the assignment.[10]

International adjustment can be characterized as a five-stage process or cycle (see Figure 8.1) that begins with excitement and euphoria with predeparture anticipation

Figure 8.1   **Five-Stage Process of International Adjustment**

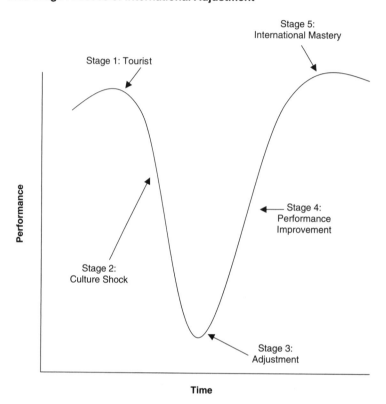

and extends through arrival at the international assignment. In Stage 1, often called the "tourist" or "honeymoon" stage, almost everything about the new international adventure appears positive, and individual performance is augmented by energy and enthusiasm. However, after a few months or only a few weeks in some cases, the euphoria of the first stage wears off and the collective disruption of routine and familiarity in the new environment begins to take its toll, often plummeting the individual into Stage 2, which involves psychological crisis and notable performance debilitation, and is often referred to as *culture shock.*[11] At this point dissatisfaction and homesickness set in, and the individual might experience increasing feelings of irritability and hostility upon regular encounters with unfamiliar and frustrating aspects of everyday realities in the new foreign experience. The daily aggravations may lead the individual to avoidance and withdrawal behaviors, contributing to feelings of isolation, loneliness, and eventual depression. Physical symptoms at this stage can include headaches, chronic fatigue and lack of energy (due to the added effort and stress in coping with the new environment), loss of appetite, upset stomach and colds, and inability to get a good night's sleep.[12] Some individuals never adjust and recover from this debilitating culture shock stage and might even return home early.

During Stage 2 and the accompanying drop in performance the individual struggles with four major adjustment dimensions in the host country: adjustment to work, general adjustment, interaction adjustment, and psychological adjustment.[13] *Adjustment to work* in the new foreign assignment can be facilitated if many company policies and procedures are similar to those back home, especially if a predecessor is still on hand to help the new expatriate get up to speed with the new assignment. At the beginning of the new assignment specific on-site training and coaching, and even assistance provided by a designated HCN mentor, can be very beneficial to the expatriate, relieving stress, building confidence, and improving overall socialization to the new environment.[14] This initial support also can be productively provided by experienced HCNs who have relevant interpersonal skills and insights to facilitate expatriate start-up success.[15] But where job tasks and priorities are initially unclear, such as when an expatriate is assigned to develop or "fix" an errant foreign operation, work adjustment itself may be necessary. In fact, a Mexican HR director who had worked over a period of time with several PCNs assigned to an operation in his country once remarked to us that often the biggest initial challenge that expatriates need to overcome is the inaccurate or unreasonable objectives and expectations given to them prior to departing from company headquarters.

The *general adjustment* dimension involves adapting to the general environment of the host country, including workplace surroundings, housing, transportation, food, shopping, foreign language, and so forth. Besides on-site guidance and support in providing housing and transportation assistance, companies can help minimize this source of shock and facilitate adjustment through effective yet realistic predeparture orientation efforts. The third dimension, *interaction adjustment,* is typically the most difficult, depending on the perceived degree of cultural distance of the foreign assignment, and involves forming a greater understanding and appreciation for the HCNs at work and other local people with whom the expatriate may interact. In general, individuals who are open and inquisitive in their new environment and actively pursue meaningful HCN contact and interactions experience faster and more productive adjustment in this dimension.[16]

The fourth dimension, *psychological adjustment,* involves an overall subjective assessment of well-being, which could pervade and be influenced by the other three dimensions. Whereas the other three dimensions of adjustment involve primarily new knowledge, skills, and behaviors, psychological adjustment deals more with the development and maintenance of new attitudes that assist with adjustment. Psychological adjustment is facilitated when expatriates are able to appraise stressful and perplexing events as challenges and opportunities for personal development. In fact, the negative and initially confusing experiences themselves may prove to be the most productive focal points for reflection and learning that facilitate overall productive international adjustment and learning.[17]

It is important to note that expatriate perceptions about the nature of the initial post-arrival support efforts put forth by the organization—both from back home and at the foreign site—can signal to the expatriate the degree to which the organization is adequately responsive to and cares about his or her well-being and that of any accompanying family members. These perceptions can have a significant influence on adjustment success. Thus, the quality of immediate post-arrival efforts provided, such as cross-cultural training and orientation, assistance in housing relocation, providing membership in home country social clubs in the foreign country, assistance with arranging for schooling for children, and spousal employment, should be carefully addressed to promote effective adjustment.[18]

Attention should be given to alleviating stressors that affect expatriate spouses who typically are less shielded by the workplace and often experience more stress from local pressures, isolation, and a sense of reduced self. Particular attention should be paid to the increasing number of dual-career couple situations, where the international assignment might represent a significant loss of family income and professional challenge and opportunity for the accompanying spouse.[19] Perceived organizational support can be greatly increased by assisting spouses and partners in obtaining appropriate employment opportunities consistent with their qualifications and career goals. To increase their success rate, companies in the host country can join forces to develop and share lists of job and volunteer opportunities, process work permits, and even share the cost of retained professional job placement services. In addition, a consortium of companies can provide a broader network of shared support activities for spouses and partners.

In some cases, such as through the lack of job opportunities or severe work visa restrictions posed by host governments, it will be impossible to find relevant paid employment for spouses and partners. Nevertheless, companies can creatively consider other ways to foster meaningful and rewarding activities to counter the frustration associated with boredom and career interruption, such as encouraging spouse or partner involvement in community volunteer services or direct support activities for other spouses and family members (for example, developing newsletters or organizing educational and social activities). Or companies can facilitate other activities that are meaningful from a career-development perspective, such as providing access to professional development programs and courses and local professional associations.[20] This immediate post-arrival assistance can be especially critical for accompanying male spouses or partners who might feel a greater social stigma with unemployment and not fit in well with established spouse support groups where women predominate.[21]

As indicated in our international adjustment curve in Figure 8.1, the fall in overall performance begins to be arrested through gradual adjustment to the new environment in Stage 3 of our model. Both the extent of performance debilitation and length of time required for effective adjustment can differ from one person to another and from one international assignment to another, often depending on the degree of cultural distance involved in the new assignment as well as local conditions and workforce receptivity and rapport. However, the need for adjustment should be anticipated even where cultural distance is perceived to be low, such as between Canada and the United States.[22]

With effective adjustment, the individual develops and strengthens new skills and perceptions to cope with the new environment (Stage 4), experiencing continued performance improvement in both work and personal life. Unfortunately, however, many simply plateau in this fourth stage, forming personal rules and practices for merely coping and surviving for the duration of the international experience and forming rigid, judgmental stereotypes of the local predominant culture. They also try to associate and gain social support during nonworking hours only with others from the same or similar culture, and minimize meaningful interaction with individuals from the local culture, whom they disdain and try to hold at a distance. They are frequently heard to derogate and put down the local host culture. Thus, due to their lack of desire to learn about the cultural underpinnings that influence the activities and behavior they see around them, these expatriates and family members limit their personal and profes-

Figure 8.2 **Direct and Indirect Activities Promoting International Adjustment**

Direct Activities: Provide	Indirect Activities: Encourage to
• Ongoing consultation with headquarters via regular communications	• Reflect and build self-awareness and understanding, and develop realistic expectations about the foreign experience
• Language and culture training for expatriates and family members	
• Local logistical assistance to handle day-to-day living requirements (for example, grocery shopping, transportation, and schooling arrangements)	• Get involved in international clubs, religious organizations, or other support groups
• New family "adoption" program by experienced expatriate families or host country families that are very familiar with expat's culture, providing social network support	• Develop hobbies (especially recommended for the spouse)
	• Get involved in local school, religious, and/or community activities
• Work and social counseling by PCN peers who have already been in the foreign country for some time	• Keep a journal
	• Plan outings and field trips to better understand the local physical and cultural environment
• Psychological counseling for expatriates and family members experiencing stress and anxiety	
• Job search assistance and career counseling for accompanying spouse to help create a more meaningful life abroad	

sional growth and understanding. Another less common plateau in Stage 4 may develop when individuals "go native" by developing overly positive stereotypes of the local culture and international assignment, assessing everything in the local environment as better than home. In many cases they become more like the host stereotype than the hosts themselves. In terms of personal and professional development, this much more positive plateau is no better than the previous negative one.

In Stage 5, *international mastery,* the individual's performance stabilizes. Here a higher level of personal and professional development in global competence emerges that includes greater ability to appreciate differences and live with and enjoy membership in more than one culture.[23] Through this development, the individual now represents a more valuable asset and resource for the firm.

Organizations should try to avoid serious costs of poor international adjustment and encourage the positive long-term benefits to individuals and firms associated with effective adjustment. Plans should be carefully considered both at MNC headquarters and at the foreign site to fit the unique circumstances facing expatriates, spouses, and other possible accompanying family members. These plans for immediate support also should take into account both direct activities that are formally sponsored and scheduled as well as indirect activities and practices that are strongly encouraged. Several useful examples of these direct and indirect activities are indicated in Figure 8.2.[24] MNCs also can consider using international relocation service firms to provide immediate post-arrival assistance such as language and cross-cultural awareness training, finding homes for expatriates, registering expatriates as resident aliens, and providing general logistical assistance. This option can be particularly appealing to small and mid-size firms that lack the internal staff and experience to provide effective assistance in this critical adjustment phase.[25]

Ongoing Support

Just as perceptions of organizational support in the expatriate assignment are critical for effective adjustment, they also can affect ongoing commitment to assignment success.[26] As with immediate post-arrival assistance, both local and headquarter-based ongoing support efforts signal to the expatriate the degree to which the organization cares for his or her well-being as well as values the expatriate's present and longer-term contributions to the organization.[27] Much of valuable ongoing support can be characterized as providing guidance and mentoring for dealing with local challenges as well as career management activities aimed at combating a possible sense of isolation that may develop even after effective foreign site adjustment.

Beyond initial adjustment assistance, qualified on-site mentors and coaches—from the ranks of both HCNs and PCNs—can be assigned to provide valuable, continued task-related guidance and psychosocial support.[28] These mentors do not have to be older and in higher organizational positions, as we might traditionally consider, but can also be peer PCNs who have useful experience to share as well as lower-level employees whose specialized insights and guidance can be useful for the expatriate. This ongoing support related to job performance can also be productively supplemented, as mentioned earlier, by a back-home mentor who can help provide information resources for ongoing problem solving as well as a broader headquarters-integrative perspective that is more focused on overall global objectives and priorities.[29]

This mentoring activity during the expatriate assignment, especially coming from the parent company, can also be helpful in terms of future career planning and particularly in alleviating a sense of isolation and future repatriation anxiety due to a loss of visibility at the home office.[30] Ongoing communication and contacts with back-home leadership, such as through requests for guidance and receipt of advice, occasional visits to the home office, and visits by executives from the home office, can combat feelings of isolation and keep the expatriate informed about realities at corporate headquarters. The use of advancements in telecommunications such as e-mail, videoconferencing, online information, and shared databases can also greatly facilitate communication and a sense of inclusion with the home office.[31] And specific career planning efforts, such as MNC career path information and job postings, career counseling as part of annual performance reviews, career testing, assessment centers, professional development workshops, and local and online professional network involvement, can be effective in securing an ongoing personal sense of well-being that was critical to the initial psychological adjustment.[32]

REPATRIATION PHASE

The repatriation, or return home, of the expatriate is often the most overlooked phase of the international assignment, yet it is often the most crucial to the expatriate and the MNC. Many expatriates and family members claim that the repatriation shock can be even greater than the initial culture shock of the foreign assignment. Former expatriates often identify the significant loss of decision-making autonomy and status as very difficult aspects of repatriation adjustment. Many firms continue to adopt an ad hoc approach toward both expatriates and their families in the repatriation process, and many expatriate managers continue to experience the repatriation process as falling far short of expectations.[33]

In many cases, due to inadequate HR planning, a manager is selected to be sent abroad with little time for predeparture preparation, let alone the "luxury" of thought about how the expatriate can best be repatriated or what assignment he or she should likely receive upon returning. Then upon the eventual return, with little planning about the effective utilization of the returned expatriate's new skills, he or she is either put on hold until an appropriate position is found or is given an assignment where his or her expertise is greatly underutilized. This underutilization and lack of appreciation for the expatriate's past experience and new skills can be demoralizing and can serve as a prompt for the returned expatriate to leave the company.[34] In one recent study only two of fifty returning expatriates reported high levels of satisfaction with their post-repatriation-related careers, and more than half reported significantly high levels of ambivalence and dissatisfaction after returning home.[35] And due to their dissatisfaction with post-repatriation career options, an estimated 20 percent to 50 percent leave their firms within a year of returning home.[36] Besides losing a talented employee with greater global competencies—after investing a large amount with the expatriate's international experience—the MNC also can lose valuable knowledge and experience as part of its collective knowledge base that could be productively used to address future global business challenges.[37] Furthermore, the negative track record of MNC repatriates is inevitably communicated informally throughout home country operations and can thereby provide a powerful discouragement for talented employees who might otherwise consider accepting an international assignment sometime in the future.

To benefit from their investments on overseas assignments, MNCs should establish high-priority practices that facilitate effective professional and social repatriation, as well as capture and utilize for broader organizational learning the insights and experience gained by returning expatriates.[38] Planning and taking action for successful repatriation should occur well before the actual return and even should be part of predeparture preparation, as was mentioned earlier.[39] Besides sharing ongoing information between the expatriate and company headquarters, the expatriate's periodic performance appraisal information that considers future career planning should also make its way back to HR planning efforts at MNC headquarters. And at least six months before repatriation an internal search should be initiated for a position that suits the expatriate's qualifications following the foreign assignment.[40] More decentralized MNCs that often have less-developed career and succession-planning systems should seriously consider pooling their resources across the MNC to form a more centralized HR function to focus on addressing common repatriate personal career management concerns. In fact, there is evidence that repatriate perceptions of perceived company career support are positively linked with increased productivity and retention.[41] Re-entry training for expatriates and their families also can be beneficial for enhancing adjustment on return from the international assignment. As with the predeparture training discussed earlier, this re-entry training should focus on helping the expatriate and family members align their expectations with what they will face back in the home country culture, both at the job and in nonwork situations.[42]

Global Workforce Challenge 8.1
Repatriation Woes

Recent studies show an alarming trend in the way multinational corporations (MNCs) are managing talent and globally trained managers. On the one hand, MNCs are increasingly relying on managers with experience in running complex operations in foreign locations, and they are spending approximately $2 million per expatriate during a four-year overseas stint. On the other hand, pointing to their dissatisfaction with postrepatriation career options, an estimated 20 percent to 50 percent are leaving firms within a year of returning home. Despite the MNC's heavy investment, the experience and learning with which managers return are largely wasted and not embedded in the organization. According to Dianne Hofner Saphiere, whose company, Nipporica Associates, provides expatriate training, "The return shock is the worst. When you come back, you expect it to be easy, but you've changed, your perspective has changed, and the people around you don't understand." Many expatriates are frustrated that their valuable experience and new knowledge are unappreciated and underutilized. In addition, some expatriates return to downsizing or merging companies and lose their jobs or are demoted in the shuffle. For many returned expats, the exhilaration of their overseas experience is overwhelmed by culture shock when they return.

After seven years in Belgium and five in France with his wife and two children, Steve Murphy was sent back to the United States by his Dutch employer, Royal Packaging Industries Van Leer, which then was acquired by Huhtamaki, a Finnish company. Steve states, "A lot of things struck us when we came back. Everything's bigger here—food portions, cars, roads, people, housing space, land." The faster pace of American life, including less time spent with business contacts and friends over leisurely meals, was one of many readjustments for Steve. After Huhtamaki sold off his division, Steve lost his job, yet building on his experience he later became a founding member of the International Professionals Networking Association, a local Kansas City, Missouri, group of former expatriates looking for jobs or who have become independent consultants. According to Mike Osredker, a former expatriate working in Brazil for Sprint Corp., the changes faced in repatriation require you to "use the mental toughness that you had to use to be successful" abroad. You need "the ability to find solutions within yourself" when returning to reduced responsibilities in the home office.

Linda Allen, director of staffing and international human relations at Black & Veatch in Kansas City, said the company is familiar with the feedback that the amount of change typically experienced with repatriation is difficult for some workers. According to Linda, " . . . we do hear some say that the corporation has changed. We try to keep people current, but if they haven't lived somewhere for two or three years, it's difficult to keep up." Former Black & Veatch engineer Steele Tollison knows this experience well. He was assigned for several years to work in Indonesia, and after an initial struggle, he finally settled in and liked the experience—even meeting and marrying his wife in Jakarta. But as he describes his eventual repatriation to Kansas City, "I found that a majority of the people who were my support system, who'd talked me into going, had died or retired or moved to other positions in other locations. No

(continued)

Global Workforce Challenge 8.1 (continued)

one knew me when I came back. I just showed up and was shown a desk." Steele verbalized the feelings expressed by many expats: "Overseas, you make it happen. Over there, you make decisions that make or break a project. Back at home, you draw significantly less-important assignments."

Sources: Adapted from A. Jassawalla and H. Sashittal, "Thinking Strategically about Integrating Repatriated Managers in MNCs," *Human Resource Management* 48(5), (2009): 769–792; D. Stafford, "For Those Working Abroad, Moving Home Can Be Jarring," *Knight Ridder Tribune Business News,* February 22, 2005: 1.

INTERNATIONAL ASSIGNMENT CONSIDERATIONS FOR SPECIAL EXPATRIATES

Female PCNs, TCNs, and HCNs are increasingly accepting international assignments for a significant duration to meet growing MNC needs for international talent. Although many of the expatriate assignment practices that we have just examined apply to these other groups who also are assigned to work outside of their home country, there are unique aspects that should be considered and addressed for optimizing their international assignment success and the long-term return of MNC investment.

WOMEN EXPATRIATES

As indicated Chapter 6, although women have often been overlooked and neglected as appropriate candidates for international assignment, they are growing in numbers as expatriates and are providing strong indications of their international assignment viability.[43] However, they often face different conditions and challenges than their male counterparts that should be addressed in the predeparture preparation, foreign experience, and repatriation phases of the international assignment to increase the likelihood of international assignment success. Unfortunately, contrary to MNC perceptions of equal treatment, there is evidence that women expatriates perceive less organizational support than do their male counterparts, which can negatively affect the success of the foreign assignment and subsequent repatriation.[44]

As part of predeparture preparation, women should receive training to develop realistic expectations about the work and surrounding cultural context of their international assignment. Depending on where the assignment is made, the local norms, values, and traditions possessed by HCN employees and the surrounding society may underlie and foster negative stereotypes and biases against women in business leadership positions.[45] Knowledge of potentially negative stereotypes and ideas for effectively responding and coping with them can do much to start the foreign assignment on a solid footing. This predeparture training can also help identify ways in which the woman expatriate should behave, including what not to do to avoid misinterpretation and offense and to lessen her likelihood of falling under local behavioral expectations for host country women.

For example, in some countries, adopting local behaviors to fit in with host national women may be something to avoid to minimize conflict with cultural restrictions on local woman. Above all, the female expatriate must establish herself in the eyes of host country nationals first as an effective manager and second as a female.[46]

With effective predeparture preparation, advanced contact with influential HCNs could be made to discuss possible special arrangements or concerns for the upcoming assignment. In some cases it might be beneficial to bring key HCNs to the home country for a planning meeting, which would also emphasize the female expatriate's high status within the company.[47] Finally, arrangements could be made with female managers, within or outside the MNC, who have successfully completed foreign assignments and who could serve during the assignment as mentors and sources of advice periodically via e-mail and telephone contact.[48]

As with male expatriates and their families upon arrival, foreign on-site training and advisement should continue to be provided to promote effective international adjustment. Women face significantly different conditions in their personal and professional lives that should be acknowledged and addressed for providing additional support where possible.[49] For example, fewer expatriate women appear to be married—thus lacking a potentially important source of social support. And when they are married they are much more likely to be faced by a challenging dual-career couple situation and continue to shoulder more of the family's "homemaking" responsibilities.[50] It also should be noted that general local biases against women in managerial positions may be reinforced by the frequently lower position of the expatriate woman held in the hierarchy of the host country operation than her expatriate male counterparts. Therefore, on-site training focusing on productive attitudes and building trust might also be profitably provided for HCN employees with whom the woman expatriate will have significant work interaction.[51]

Women in international assignments tend to be more isolated than their male counterparts, often lacking formal and informal forms of support—such as mentors and professional networks—from their organizations. Because women expatriates may have difficulty finding suitable local mentors, companies might find it useful to provide mentoring programs and encourage the woman expatriate's involvement in local women's professional and global online support networks.[52] In our field research involving American women and international career development, we have been impressed with the number of professional support groups and networks for women located in many cities around the world. Many of these support groups have been organized by expatriate women who didn't wait for an MNC to send them abroad but self-initiated their international assignment and recognized the need for ongoing professional and social support among women facing similar challenges.[53] Other research suggests that MNCs, perhaps supporting their less-positive expectations, might be providing female expatriates with fewer career development activities such as fast-track programs, individual career counseling, and career-planning workshops, which appear to be associated with ongoing effective adjustment and foreign assignment success. Therefore, MNCs should make an extra effort to ensure that their women expatriates are provided with such ongoing professional support activities.[54]

Although mentoring can be important for women in securing and effectively carrying out an international assignment, it appears to be especially critical for successful repatriation. And whereas mentoring is important for the successful repatriation of all expatriates, it can be particularly so for women who often find less ready access to informal networks and mentoring relationships in traditionally male-dominated organizations.[55] According to one field study, the female executives who had mentors while abroad indicated that their mentors provided information, training, advice, and career direction for re-entering their home organizations. In addition, mentors were perceived as important for helping the women keep in touch with developments back home and introducing them, at their return, to important informal networks in their organizations. These female executives suggested that while their international assignment improved their self-confidence and increased their visibility in their organizations, mentors back home provided critical contact and support from the home organization that in turn facilitated re-entry.[56]

INPATRIATES

As discussed earlier, inpatriates, or "inpats," are host country or third country nationals who are invited to MNC headquarters typically for an extended period of time to gain valuable exposure and understanding of company strategy, culture, core competencies, and priorities. They also can serve in a valuable boundary-spanning role by bringing new perspectives and insights about their home. Where the assignment at MNC headquarters is not permanent, a general goal is to eventually give the inpat managerial responsibility either in the home country or a different country operation as a third country national. In both cases inpats have an increased ability to manage the foreign operation in greater alignment with MNC objectives and priorities. In being reassigned to a host country operation where he or she had previously worked as a HCN, the former inpat can be particularly effective in managing the host country operation in line with MNC objectives, yet with a keen awareness of local unique needs and conditions. Thus, as increasingly used by MNCs, inpatriation represents a very important HR investment, with most of the benefit to be gained following this present international assignment to work at MNC headquarters.[57] And while employee retention should be an important objective following any international assignment, long-term retention is particularly critical for realizing the primary increased control and alignment goals of the inpatriate assignment.

Many of the ideas for enhancing the success of the PCN's expatriate assignment also apply to the inpatriate assignment generally. However, several unique issues and conditions must be thoughtfully addressed to ensure the inpatriate's effective initial adjustment, ongoing support, and repatriation to a host country operation management responsibility or transition into a new third country assignment. One of the unique challenges for the inpatriate is the adjustment to and mastery of both internal and external work environments. The PCN expatriate must adjust to the local host country culture and working arrangements but often is shielded to a great degree by the existing MNC home country culture, policies, and support structures at the host country operation. The inpatriate must adjust to the external surrounding culture of the MNC home country as well as the much more established unique organizational culture, written and unwritten rules, and priorities in play at MNC headquarters than are evident in distant host country operations. Especially where they come from developing countries, inpats may face the particularly daunting challenge of adjustment to the complex, mechanistic internal environment of Western postindustrial organizations, which may also involve social stigmatization of "foreignness" and stereotyping, individual aggressiveness and competition, impersonal social interactions, and individual performance-based evaluations.[58]

Some MNCs try to rationalize their minimal investment in predeparture preparation and training of PCN expatriates by thinking that local PCNs presently serving in the foreign operation will naturally provide the ongoing coaching and support needed by the expatriate and accompanying family members. Although such a haphazard approach to expatriate preparation and training has significant problems, there is a natural tendency for well-intentioned tips, suggestions, and warnings to be offered by one's more experienced PCN colleagues in the workplace at the start of an expatriate assignment. But this natural sharing of helpful experience-based information is much less likely for inpatriates who find themselves at MNC headquarters with very few, if any, other inpatriates from their own country who have weathered the trials of international adjustment at the MNC headquarters and in the MNC's home country. In fact, PCN expats and their families from different MNCs are often able to find local PCN same-country expat and family support groups associated with their local embassy or consulate office. Inpats on the other hand, especially those from developing countries, likely are unable to find a similar social support structure to assist with their adjustment. We now consider some important activities and measures that MNCs can use to increase the likelihood of successful inpatriate assignments and subsequent retention for meeting future global strategic staffing needs.[59]

Needs Assessment

To ensure the success of efforts to enhance inpatriate adjustment, a careful needs assessment should be conducted. Factors to consider include cultural distance between the inpat's home culture and that of the new location; whether there will be accompanying family members and what their particular personal needs are (for example, schooling, language instruction, medical care, and banking); and the degree of familiarity with MNC culture and operations (for example, some inpats may have previously had significant exposure to the MNC culture and headquarter operations through long experience with the company and previous short visits to headquarters). This careful needs assessment is essential for anticipating and planning for critical adjustment challenges that the inpatriate will likely face.

Realistic Relocation Preview

Based on the needs assessment, a realistic relocation preview should be planned and conducted before departure with the inpatriate and family members involved in the relocation. As with PCN expats, this preview should be realistic and feature the positives and negatives that can be expected in the future experience. This preview and associated predeparture training also should focus on both accurate expectations and means for successful coping related to the external cultural environment and the internal organizational culture environment.

Training Methods

Methods for conducting predeparture training should fit the experience, background, capabilities, and learning style needs of the inpatriate. In addition, the extensiveness of the training time, experiential exercises, and supportive learning materials should depend on the degree of the learning and adjustment (both internal corporate and external environments) required with the inpatriate assignment. Where possible, customized input and training should be provided by experienced managers from the inpatriate candidate's culture who previously completed a successful inpatriate assignment at MNC headquarters. In addition, as with PCN expatriates, ongoing on-site coaching and mentoring should be made available, especially immediately after arrival at the MNC headquarters, to assist the inpatriate in dealing effectively with cross-cultural adjustment and challenges as they arise. And especially where a primary objective of the inpatriate assignment is developmental for building MNC core competencies and a global mind-set, the inpatriate's ongoing work experience should provide regular opportunity for reflection and insight, facilitated by a coach or mentor responsible for helping the inpatriate maximize learning from this international experience.

Social Support Structures

Besides offering training and clear expectations for managers at MNC headquarters to provide ongoing guidance and support for the newly arrived inpatriate, MNCs should encourage other home country employees with whom the inpatriate may frequently interact to provide informal social support and guidance. This supportive influence of local managers and employees would likely be strengthened if they also received information about the inpatriate and his or her culture to promote cross-cultural awareness and understanding at the inpatriate's worksite.

Besides encouraging social support structures at work, broader social support for the inpatriate outside of the organization can be found, particularly in larger metropolitan areas, through local social groups or business associations designed specifically for immigrants from the inpatriate's home country. For example, for an inpatriate from Vietnam assigned to work at an MNC headquarters in Los Angeles, a cursory search on the Internet of "Vietnamese in Southern California" recently uncovered several Vietnamese organizations, such a Vietnamese-American chamber of commerce, a Vietnamese Baptist church, a Vietnamese radio station, and the Vietnamese Professionals Society of Southern California. All of these resources could yield helpful contacts for social support and guidance, especially to assist in the non-working-hour adjustment of the inpatriate and any family members to the new country culture. Unlike what is probably available at the MNC headquarters, these groups from the inpat's own home country culture can potentially provide very relevant, experience-based guidance promoting external environment cross-cultural adjustment and ongoing support from the inpat's unique cultural perspective.

Career Planning and Compensation Considerations

As with PCN expats, ongoing activities related to career development and planning can be helpful in facilitating inpatriate adjustment and maintaining continued commitment to assignment success. However, career planning efforts for the inpatriate, who as an HCN might be being groomed for an assignment of increased leadership back at a host country operation or in a third country, should be more specific and directed than with a typical expatriate assignment. And ongoing training efforts should be consistent and supportive of these future repatriation career plans.

The design of the inpatriate's compensation package should be considered carefully to ensure its ability to encourage and maintain an ongoing commitment in the inpatriate assignment, yet not lead to subsequent problems following the assignment. For example, to cover local living expenses and avoid feelings of inequity and resentment, the inpatriate should be compensated at a level similar to other peer PCNs at company headquarters. However, especially when the inpatriate comes from a developing country with a much lower average-wage scale, the inpatriate might grow accustomed to a much higher standard of living in the MNC home country and become very hesitant to return back to work at a host country operation under the local wage level. In this case the new compensation package following the inpatriate assignment might need to be adjusted upward and communicated ahead of the repatriation, reflecting new capabilities and leadership responsibilities back at the host country operation and providing an adequate incentive to encourage repatriation and long-term retention.

THIRD COUNTRY NATIONALS

TCNs can be assigned to a host country operation from anywhere besides the MNC's home country and face immediate and ongoing support needs as with the traditional expatriate assignment. However, in cases where the TCN is new to the MNC or has had experience working for the MNC elsewhere with little interaction with and influence by MNC headquarters, beneficial training prior to departure and after arrival could also focus on overall company strategy and priorities to ensure the alignment and coordination of the TCN's new international assignment with MNC objectives.

An attractive feature of having a TCN fill a host country international assignment in the place of a PCN is typically significant cost savings, such as when the TCN is from a location near the target host country and incurs smaller relocation costs compared to those for a PCN, and especially where TCN executive wages are lower than in the MNC home country. In some cases these transfers might be even considered merely "quasi-domestic."[60] With this lower cost and convenience of regional proximity of nearby available TCNs often comes the presumption of advantage in small cultural distance, such as between Hong Kong and mainland China, presenting minimal need for international adjustment on the part of the TCN expatriate. However, field studies have demonstrated that regional and nearby TCN assignments can generate significant stress and challenges to adjustment, and therefore these TCNs also are clearly in need of MNC planning and ongoing support for a successful international assignment.[61] In fact, in one study TCN executives from Hong Kong assigned to work in mainland China in operations owned by Western MNCs reported some of the most difficult experiences found in the literature on international adjustment.[62] In another study, Western expatriates, despite their larger cultural distance, did not have greater difficulty in adjusting to their international assignment in the People's Republic of China than ethnic Chinese expatriates from nearby Hong Kong and, in fact, expressed a greater flexibility and willingness to adjust.[63]

Besides concern for third country nationals' initial adjustment and ongoing assignment success, consideration should be given to support measures that would encourage talented TCN retention by enhancing the effectiveness of their eventual repatriation or even transition into a new country assignment. As mentioned earlier regarding PCN expatriates, TCNs' perceived lack of company support for their future career and personal needs can have a negative effect on their current job performance. For example, TCNs increasingly are opting for "aspatial" careers, or long-term professional assignments in other countries outside of their home country, especially where career options in the home country are fewer and less attractive. Ongoing career guidance and planning support during the TCN's international assignment in anticipation of future career opportunities can enhance current commitment and performance as well as assist in better global manager preparation and utilization.[64] Personal compensation issues also can come into play with TCNs and should be considered and addressed appropriately, such as when TCNs come from a home country with lower average income levels and become accustomed to a higher local or international executive salary scale, making an eventual return assignment home feel like a significant dock in pay. And in the long term, where government pension and retirement measures are not transferable across country borders, the company should consider alternative supportive measures in securing personal needs for future retirement.

NEW AND FLEXIBLE INTERNATIONAL ASSIGNMENTS

As MNCs try to avoid exorbitant costs and challenges associated with international assignments involving the long-term (that is, three to five years or more) relocation of PCNs, HCNs, and TCNs, and as individual employees consider ways to avoid personal hardships often attendant to international relocation (for example, spouse career and family disruption), we have seen the emergence of several new, flexible short-term international assignment arrangements that avoid costly relocation but still enable organizations to achieve their international competitive business goals.[65] These more flexible arrangements, facilitated by ongoing developments in telecommunications technologies and transportation as well as encouraged by disruptions and uncertainties of global conflict, may range from brief regular visits abroad to short-term foreign assignments lasting less than one year. These increasing new, flexible international assignments appear to be received with overall satisfaction among a new class of nonresident expatriates, or "flexpatriates," especially when these employees are allowed significant flexibility and control in balancing work assignment demands with personal needs.[66]

These more flexible international assignments can involve frequent use of e-mail, video, and teleconferencing combined with brief visits to foreign operations (that is, "virtual expatriate assignment") or short-term "bubble" international assignments (for example, one to five months in duration). Or the assignments may be more extended and feature international commuting (for example, one week home per month or living in Paris three days and commuting to work in Brussels four days per week), or involve frequent online and telecommunications interactions among geographically dispersed members of an international virtual team who occasionally meet in person at a common location.[67] The use of these more flexible arrangements is gaining in popularity, as illustrated by the experience of GE, which sends far more employees on short-term international assignments than the more traditional long-term ones.[68] Although companies are finding these shorter international assignments, or secondments, to be very attractive because of the lack of major relocation expenses, investments in predeparture and ongoing training should not be neglected. In fact, employees taking these new assignments actually may have an even greater need for intensive training to learn about and master the challenges of their new location and culture so that they can be productive immediately.[69]

Two features commonly encountered in these new flexible forms of international assignments are significant work in managing and participating within global teams and frequent international travel. We now examine both of these features common to new international assignments.

INTERNATIONAL ASSIGNMENTS INVOLVING GLOBAL TEAMS

The new, flexible international assignments increasingly entail work as a "virtual expatriate" in distantly managing a fairly autonomous team and foreign operation, or multiple autonomous teams of employees located in other countries, with occasional brief visits to foreign operations for direct team interaction. Or the team management assignment may involve organizing and directing on a mostly distance basis the work of team members who are located in different countries and function primarily as a global virtual team. These assignments may also involve work with less direct leadership responsibility as a participating member of a largely self-managing global virtual team, such as a team of product development executives from different MNC operations around the world. We will now examine various measures for enhancing international assignment effectiveness associated with global teams.

Virtual Expatriate Assignments

A critical success factor for the management of a group or team of employees on a distance basis across national boundaries, with occasional visits for direct interactions, is the development of mutual trust. A major source of building this trust is the manager's ability—whether virtually or in person—to provide adequate training for the employees, clearly communicate what is expected, and then empower the employees (with clear individual responsibilities and group roles) to carry out their work. Periodic evaluation of performance progress and provision of support and additional assistance as needed are also important in building an essential rapport of trust and confidence. However, accomplishing this strong team performance on a virtual basis through a potentially very different cultural lens and via communications that are far less rich than interacting in person, can present major challenges.

In establishing clear ground rules, expectations, and mutual trust, it is recommended that longer and frequent contact be made in person at the beginning of the project, with a gradual increase of team management on a distance basis. In addition, besides providing adequate technical training for team members, cross-cultural awareness training can be very beneficial for both the virtual expatriate and international team members to promote understanding and flexibility in working through otherwise frustrating, confusing, and even destructive cross-cultural interactions (both remote and in person). In conjunction with this greater understanding, the manager should take time during foreign site visits to discuss as openly and candidly as possible ways to improve the quality of the distance work processes and interactions, including methods of communications.

According to several international surveys, in most countries employees appear to prefer leaders who are visionary, collaborative and team-oriented, rational and analytic, decisive, and who have integrity. The preparation and ongoing coaching of virtual expatriates should focus on building skills that reflect these general characteristics. In addition, broad national cultural differences suggest the customization of leadership skills, as is the case with longer-term expatriates, to fit the needs and expectations of the assigned workforce.[70] For example, UK workforce teams may expect and prefer a more casual leadership style, whereas French teams may expect more directive and autocratic leadership. German employees may prefer a more formal group work structure or hierarchy, Asian teams may prefer leadership by consensus, and Latin American employees may prefer a more paternalistic approach.[71] A particular challenge might come for virtual expatriates who have employee teams in different countries and need sensitivity and flexibility in managing these different cultural groups—both remotely and in person—according to their different needs and preferences.

Success with Global Virtual Teams

Perhaps a greater challenge than managing a foreign work group and operation largely on a distance basis is the management of a global virtual team, where the manager (if this is not a self-managing group) and team members are from different cultures and countries. As was discussed in Chapter 5, a distinct advantage of global virtual teams, particularly where team members are spread longitudinally across various international worksites, is the ability to perform work asynchronously. This helps global organizations to effectively bridge different time zones and enables teams to be productive over more than one work period. In addition, dispersed members' nearness to different customers, markets, practices, perspectives, and resources in their local contexts can enhance flexibility and innovation capability—thus increasing the ability to balance local awareness with the broader and strategic perspective of the global team. But this geographic and cultural dispersion of all team members—not just the separation of the virtual manager from an intact work group—can greatly magnify the potential for miscommunication and conflict due to lack of in-person interaction.

In addition, group members from high-context cultures might have great difficulty dealing with the dearth of verbal and nonverbal cues associated with the typical low-context telecommunications media of text messaging and telephone. In addition, the asynchronous nature of much of the communication between groups separated by large time zones can interfere with response timeliness that is so important for immediate clarification and feedback.[72]

Again, the development of a high level of trust is key to the productivity and success of global virtual teams. One study of global virtual teams with high levels of trust found three common traits: (1) begin virtual interactions with social messaging (that is, introducing themselves and providing some personal background before getting to the task to be accomplished); (2) set clear roles for each team member within the larger picture of the common group goal—thus, each team is able to identify with one another; (3) demonstrate positive attitudes in all messages, such as through eagerness, helpfulness, action orientation, enthusiasm, providing positive and constructive (not judgmental and critical) feedback, and future orientation with focus on collaborative problem solving rather than fault finding.[73]

Where possible, these priorities for building global virtual team trust should be thoughtfully and thoroughly discussed at an initial meeting convened in person at a common location and reviewed and monitored regularly afterward. This initial discussion should also set clear expectations about group management, including leadership and decision-making style, individual member empowerment and accountability, individual and group performance feedback, and handling conflict and disagreement. Group training to promote common identity and alignment should also be provided at this initial meeting and on an individualized basis afterward—training that focuses on company culture, core values and priorities, and specific goals and objectives of the global team within the larger context of company strategy—again, with clear assignment of individual roles and responsibilities related to team performance objectives.[74] In addition, training should be provided on particular behavioral skills that have been found to enhance a virtual team's ability to function effectively. As shown in Figure 8.3, these important behavioral skills fall into three key areas: virtual-collaborative skills, virtual-socialization skills, and virtual-communication skills.[75]

Cross-cultural awareness training also should be provided to increase each member's awareness of his or her own culture and personal style as well as general cultural characteristics represented by the other team members and how these characteristics might influence or explain individual group member tendencies and behaviors. For example, differing culturally based perspectives about time can yield greatly different attitudes and behaviors among global virtual team members regarding meetings, work schedules and pace, deadlines, urgency, work/personal life timing, and rhythm.[76] Finally, this cultural awareness training should also emphasize the real strengths that different cultural perspectives can bring to a global team that values and manages its diversity effectively. For example, team members reflecting high uncertainty avoidance bring a useful level of order and precision into the team's activities to avoid careless errors, while team members reflecting low uncertainty avoidance bring flexibility and risk taking that promotes creativity and innovation.

Figure 8.3 **Key Skills and Practices for Members of Global Virtual Teams**

Virtual-Collaboration Behaviors
- Exchanging ideas without criticism
- Developing a working document in which team members' ideas are summarized
- Exchanging working documents for editing
- Tracking group member comments in a working document with initials
- Agreeing on activities and priorities
- Meeting individual and interdependent deadlines

Virtual-Socialization Behaviors
- Communicating with other team members immediately, and responding in a timely fashion
- Soliciting team members' feedback on effectiveness of group work processes
- Disclosing appropriate personal information
- Expressing appreciation for ideas, contributions, and completed tasks
- Apologizing for mistakes
- Volunteering for roles
- Acknowledging other group member role assignments

Virtual-Communication Behaviors
- Obtaining local translator assistance when needed
- Rephrasing unclear sentences to ensure understanding by all team members
- Using e-mail typography to effectively communicate emotion, for example, ;-)
- Acknowledging the receipt of messages
- Responding within one business day

TRAVEL CONSIDERATIONS

Regular and frequent travel across international borders is a common feature of the growing number of flexible international work assignments. We were impressed with this reality in a recent visit with MBA students to a maquiladora manufacturing plant in Tijuana, Mexico, where we met an American expatriate plant manager who commuted across the border from his home in nearby San Diego, California. He was scheduled to leave his home early the next morning to catch a flight for an important product division management team meeting that he would lead the following day at a plant in Belgium. This brief trip to Europe would be followed a few days later by a one-day trip to MNC headquarters in Connecticut for additional meetings. This characteristic of frequent travel has important implications for the personal health and safety of those involved with these new flexible international assignments, which should not be overlooked or treated lightly.[77]

SUMMARY

Important issues and practices are associated with successfully managing various assignments for working abroad, including predeparture planning and preparation, on-site management for effective adjustment and ongoing support, and repatriation. Besides these considerations for the traditional PCN expatriate assignment, there are additional issues that may be unique to women expatriates and third country nationals in their expatriate assignments as well as HCN inpatriates who are assigned to work at MNC headquarters.

Global Workforce Challenge 8.2
**Virtual Expatriates and Regular Travelers:
Coping with New Forms of International Assignments**

With the cost of traditional expatriate assignments rising and the greater reluctance of managers in uprooting their personal lives, including family commitments and spouse career complications, MNCs are forced to be more flexible with international assignments. Some executives also feel they can be more effective by remaining close to company headquarters. Scotland-born Ian Hunter, in charge of the Middle East and Pakistan for SmithKline Beecham PLC, isn't based in Istanbul or Dubai but rather at the drugmaker's London headquarters. "My role is to get resources for my team, and being based at headquarters helps me lobby for them." Ian also notes that being a "virtual" expatriate is less expensive for the company, even counting the cost of the sixteen to seventeen weeks a year he travels. Technology has also facilitated this new international assignment. Gerald Lukomski, a Detroit native based in England as Motorola Inc.'s corporate vice president and director of Central Eastern Europe, the Middle East, and Africa, estimates that he spends about 75 percent of his working time traveling. He never leaves home without a laptop and cell phone.

Todd Hoffman, a PricewaterhouseCoopers official in charge of global mobility, once tried to toil in two time zones simultaneously but failed. When he embarked on an eleven-day business trip to six countries in 2002, he barely slept, staying up until 2:30 A.M. every night to handle a key project back in the United States. Then he caught the flu and had to skip Moscow, his last stop. Todd now knows firsthand that you can work at any time and in any place, but "you can't do it all." No matter how talented a global executive you are, it is very difficult to excel amid the strain of such extensive travel associated with these increasing short-term international assignments. The traveler faces ongoing home-office demands plus the grogginess, memory loss, impaired decision-making ability, and indigestion associated with jet lag. To help cope with the challenge of regular travel, global professionals recommend the following:

1. *For nocturnal flights, create a sleep tent.* This trick will insulate you from the distractions about you that will keep you awake. Wear a baseball cap and put the blanket provided by the airline over your head. The cap's bill will create space for breathing and will help shut out the light. Also cover your ears with headphones for more quiet.

2. *Avoid important meetings until the day after you reach your destination.* For the first day, try to schedule less-important tasks that require less challenge and mental concentration.

3. *Don't work past your usual bedtime or schedule business dinners every night.* At your foreign location, focus on your assignment at hand and let go of concerns about the home office. Protect your time for renewal through a good night's sleep. When you go to bed at a decent local time, turn off your cell phone so you will not be disturbed by some work matter at the home office.

4. *Exercise more, preferably in the sunshine.* There is evidence that exercise in the sunshine can help shift the biological clock. Ginny Kamsky, whose firm with

(continued)

Global Workforce Challenge 8.2 (continued)

offices in Beijing and New York helps corporate clients do deals in China, regularly commutes between those distant locales. In Beijing, she regularly runs outside every morning for thirty minutes—longer than normal. She states that her two-mile course "makes me feel like a different person. When you live jet lagged, it's vital that you get yourself adjusted."

Sources: Adapted from S. McKenna and J. Richardson, "The Increasing Complexity of the Internationally Mobile Professional," *Cross Cultural Management* 14(4) (2007): 307–320; J.S. Lublin,"Globe-Trotters' Tips To Boost Performance on Long Business Trips," *Wall Street Journal,* May 31, 2005, B1.

Rapidly changing global conditions and interest in reducing traditional expatriate costs are leading to a considerable increase in various forms of more flexible, short-term international assignments, including work as a "virtual" expatriate with international teams at foreign sites as well as working with global virtual teams where all members are separated by country location and culture. These short-term international assignments present new advantages for conducting business on a global scale as well as new challenges for managing these foreign assignments, including more frequent travel.

QUESTIONS FOR OPENING SCENARIO ANALYSIS

1. How typical would you say are the adjustment experiences of Carol Williams, Clarence Mitchell, and Clarence's family, including repatriation? Critique the effectiveness of Carol Williams's firm in managing its expatriates' overall international assignment.
2. What are particular costs of poor management of international assignments as exemplified by the opening scenario? What changes could be made to improve this company's performance in supporting its expatriates to optimize their international assignment success, including repatriation?
3. What are particular steps that the company could do before and during the assignment to better support Carol as a woman in her international assignment?

CASE 8.1. WORKING IN A SHELTERED ENCLAVE IN SHANGHAI, CHINA

David Smith is an electrical engineer working for an MNC based in Detroit, Michigan. Although U.S. and European companies like David's are more inclined to post their Asian third country nationals on assignments in China, this more economical approach to recruiting managerial talent and deploying expatriates is still limited due to talent scarcity and national laws and regulations inhibiting full mobility. When his company asked him to go to China for an expatriate assignment, David was not really excited about the offer. Although China had achieved remarkable economic growth and frequently made newspaper headlines, he knew very little about the country. He had never studied Mandarin or the history of China. But David's family liked Chinese food and enjoyed watching Chinese movies. For this assignment, David was required to stay at least three years in China until Chinese managers fully learned how to operate the newly opened factory. Furthermore, David's family was faced with two other important family issues that made their decision more difficult: David's wife, Linda, an accountant making a decent income, would have to quit her job. In addition, they would need to find a good private school for their son, Christopher, a second-grader.

David's company insisted that this assignment would provide him with a great opportunity to climb the corporate ladder. After a long deliberation, he decided to take the offer. When David's family arrived at their new house in Shanghai, China, they could not believe their eyes—it was very much like the one they lived in on the outskirts of Detroit. Access to the compound was through a guarded checkpoint. The specially treated water, unlike nearly any other place in China, was pure enough to drink from the tap. Even the garbage was sterilized. David said, "My company is paying $23,000 a month rent for this house."

As a growing number of MNC executives are being brought to China because of their companies' commitment to globalization, more and more are moving to complexes like the one where David's family lives: a recreated American suburbia with rolling lawns, two-car garages, ranch-style homes, and its own school, shopping mall, and golf course—all only ten minutes away from the new international airport. After being in Shanghai for almost two years, David and his family members do not really feel like they are in China. David can totally concentrate on his work at the office, without worrying about his wife at home. On the other hand, he started to worry that living in such an exclusive enclave would only emphasize the division between expatriates and the Chinese community and the markets he was supposed to be learning about. He began to ask to himself, "Am I doing the right thing?"

QUESTIONS FOR CASE ANALYSIS AND DISCUSSION

1. What are potential reasons why David's company would desire to send its own home country expatriate instead of using a local Chinese manager or a third country national.
2. Can you identify the main family issues facing David's family?
3. Do you see any longer-range pitfalls in the approach used by David's company to carry out its HR policy to attract the most qualified expatriates?

CASE 8.2. RE-ENTRY SHOCK: A FAMILY AFFAIR

Hannah Heikkinen looked out the window as she sipped her coffee. As the HR director of Nordic Oils she was taking a quick break from a meeting with the directors from various departments of the company to discuss expatriate assignment issues and, in particular, problems with repatriation. This meeting was prompted by the recent resignation of Pekka Nieminen.

Nordic Oils is a drilling company based in Finland that operates in five countries: Sweden, Norway, France, Canada, and, the newest office, Colombia. Although they had been sending expatriates abroad for more than thirty years, the employees had never been away for more than two years at a time and were often able to visit home during their work terms. But when the Colombian office opened, Pekka Nieminen was sent for a five-year term to train and guide the new office employees. This extended assignment proved very productive for the company, but the repatriation of Pekka and his family fell short. Now as a replacement expatriate was preparing to move to the Colombian office, Hanna and other senior-level colleagues were discussing what improvements should be made to achieve smoother repatriation in the future.

Pekka's extended term to Colombia had been deemed necessary by the Nordic Oils management team due to the extreme cultural and work differences between Finland and Colombia, requiring significant adjustment. The new office start-up also required a major initial time investment in new workforce staffing and training. Pekka had worked with Nordic Oils for ten years before moving to Colombia with his family. He had a wife and two children who were seven and twelve upon departure from Finland. In Colombia, Pekka was the head of a team that included three other Finnish employees who ensured that the Colombian office was run parallel to the Finnish office and that employees were trained according to Finnish standards. Pekka's family experienced culture shock when first introduced to the Colombian culture, but with training and support from the company they worked through it and adjusted.

After the five-year term expired, the family made their way back to Finland to begin reintegration into their home country. This is where major problems began to occur. The children were having difficulties readjusting into their schools. The eldest, who was in his second year of Finnish high school upon return, was facing complications in the company of girls. He was seen as being too forward and aggressive toward his female friends, who were beginning to reject him. The youngest, who was in her last year of primary school, was dealing with the fact that her former friends had changed and had developed new groups of friends. Due to the reserved manner of the Finnish culture, she was finding it harder to meet new people and had quickly acquired the reputation of being overly friendly. These issues were a result of their years in Colombia's very outgoing culture.

Anneli Nieminen, Pekka's wife, worked as a preschool teacher before leaving for Colombia. While away from Finland she didn't work and was not only having a hard time finding work in Finland but was not looking forward to spending days away from her family again. In addition, she was not feeling comfortable with her old friends. During her stay in Colombia she had learned to express herself more openly and developed different values that were more in line with Colombian views. Her friends, however, did not understand her changed mentality. This caused Anneli to perceive them as being slightly cold and aloof.

Pekka was also having some problems, primarily at work. He was not fully aware of changes that had occurred at the Finnish office during his absence and was struggling to settle in. Colleagues who had previously been on par with him had been promoted, which was causing some tension. And while in Colombia Pekka had been in charge of the team overseeing the entire operation and was responsible for many others as well. But back in Finland Pekka was returned to his old position of quality engineer manager and was responsible for far fewer employees and decisions, making his work seem less significant. In addition, before leaving for Colombia, Pekka had been told of the strong likelihood of a promotion at the end his term abroad. Due to the developments and changes within the company during this time, the promised position was no longer available. The lack of increased income with the anticipated promotion made life in Finland very expensive. The family had become accustomed to having an elevated disposable income in Colombia, and moving back to the high cost of living in Finland required them to tighten their budget significantly.

Hannah threw the remaining few sips of her coffee into the staff room sink and began to walk back to the meeting. Based on the company's previous smooth repatriation experiences, Hannah and her colleagues had not been sensitive to the Nieminen family's possible reintegration difficulties. The meeting that afternoon would be the first time this problem had been discussed. Finding solutions would be difficult. It was going to be a long afternoon.

QUESTIONS FOR CASE ANALYSIS AND DISCUSSION

1. What was different about the expatriate assignment to Colombia, compared to the company's previous expatriation experiences, that might have contributed to a more challenging repatriation experience for Pekka and his family?
2. What could Nordic Oils do more effectively before initial departure to Colombia, during the foreign assignment, and after return to improve the family's repatriation adjustment?
3. What could a family like the Nieminens do for themselves to increase the likelihood of a smoother repatriation experience?

RECOMMENDED WEB SITE RESOURCES

Alliance of Business Women International (www.abwi.org). Nonprofit organization founded in 1995 to encourage and support businesswomen involved or interested in international trade opportunities. Supported by women entrepreneurs and corporate executives as well as other profit and nonprofit sectors, a major objective is to form a strong national and international infrastructure for optimal support.

ExpatExchange (www.expatexchange.com). The largest online community for English-speaking expatriates. Free of charge and provides considerable information resource support, including an online newsletter, for all phases of the expatriation and repatriation process. Provides helpful information customized by country as well as helpful general services typically purchased for international employees by HR departments.

Expat Focus (www.expatfocus.com). Free online community providing news and considerable advice for expatriates and family members through posted articles and regular newsletters. Also provides e-mail connection for posting questions and obtaining experienced feedback.

GMAC Global Relocation Services (www.gmacglobalrelocation.com). Provides customized global relocation and assignment management services needs for multinational organizations in more than 110 countries.

Organization of Women in International Trade (www.owit.org). Professional organization addressing the unique needs of women engaged in all forms of international trade by providing networking, information resources, and educational opportunities.

Tales From a Small Planet (www.talesmag.com). Provides a rich assortment of links to resources for expats and their families as well as a global message board for sharing questions and ideas and a special e-list through which expatriate spouses can find mutual support.

Travel.State.Gov (http://travel.state.gov). Considerable travel information for Americans traveling abroad and non-U.S. citizens traveling to the United States, including travel warnings, ideas for travel planning and tips for international travel, general health and safety information, dealing with unexpected emergencies and crises, and information for obtaining passports and visas.

NOTES

1. M. Harvey and M. Buckley, "Managing Inpatriates: Building Global Core Competency," *Journal of World Business* 32 (1) (1997): 35–52.

2. H. Mayerhofer, L.C. Hartmann, and A. Herbert, "Career Management Issues for Flexpatriate International Staff," *Thunderbird International Business Review,* 46 (6) (2004): 647–66; I. St. John-Brooks, "Short-Term Assignments Remain Popular," *Benefits and Compensation International* 33 (8) (2004): 24; S.C. Peppas, "Making the Most of International Assignments: A Training Model for Non-Resident Expatriates," *Journal of American Academy of Business* 5 (1/2) (2004): 41–45; S. Bates, "Study Discovers Patterns in Global Executive Mobility," *HR Magazine* 47 (10) (2002): 14; S. Cummins, "Short-Term Assignments: Combining Employer and Employee Interests," *Benefits and Compensation International* 30 (3) (2000): 8.

3. J. Keogh, "A Win-Win, from Start to Finish," *Workspan* 46 (2) (2003): 36–39; A.W. Andreason, "Expatriate Adjustment to Foreign Assignments," *International Journal of Commerce and Management* 13 (1) (2003): 42–60; J.S. Black and H.B. Gregersen, "The Right Way to Manage Expats," *Harvard Business Review* 77 (2) (1999): 52–63.

4. J.S. Black, M. Mendenhall, and G. Oddou, "Toward a Comprehensive Model of International Adjustment: An Integration of Multiple Theoretical Perspectives," *Academy of Management Review* 16 (2) (1991): 291–317; P. Hom, R.W. Griffeth, L.E. Palich, and J.S. Bracker, "Revisiting Met Expectations as a Reason Why Realistic Job Previews Work," *Personnel Psychology* 52 (1) (1999): 97–112.

5. L.T. Eby and T.D. Allen, "Perceptions of Relocation Services in Relocation Decision Making," *Group and Organization Management* 23 (4): 447–69.

6. J.I. Sanchez, P.E. Spector, and C.L. Cooper, "Adapting to a Boundaryless World: A Developmental Expatriate Model," *Academy of Management Executive,* 14 (2) (2000): 96–106.

7. A.R. Jassawalla, N. Asgary, and H.C. Sashittal, "Managing Expatriates: The Role of Mentors," *International Journal of Commerce & Management* 16 (2) 2006: 130–40; P.H. Siegel, J.B. Mosca, and K.B. Karim, "The Role of Mentoring Professional Accountants: A Global Perspective," *Managerial Finance* 25 (2) (1999): 30–45.

8. S.M. Carraher, S.E. Sullivan, and M.M. Crocitto, "Mentoring Across Global Boundaries: An Empirical Examination of Home- and Host-Country Mentors on Expatriate Career Outcomes," *Journal of International Business Studies* 39 (8) (2008): 1310–26; T. Cavusgil, U. Yavas, and S. Bykowicz, "Preparing Executives for Overseas Assignments," *Management Decision* 30 (1) (1992): 54–58.

9. J. Selmer, "Practice Makes Perfect? International Experience and Expatriate Adjustment," *Management International Review* 42 (1) (2002): 71–87.

10. A. Haslberger and C. Brewster, "The Expatriate Family: An International Perspective," *Journal of Managerial Psychology* 23 (3) (2008): 324–46; A.W. Andreason, "Expatriate Adjustment of Spouses and Expatriate Managers: An Integrative Research Review," *International Journal of Management* 25 (2) (2008): 382–95; H. Lee, "Factors that Influence Expatriate Failure: An Interview Study," *International Journal of Management* 24 (3) (2007): 403–13; V. Suutari and D. Burch, "The Role of On-Site Training

and Support in Expatriation: Existing and Necessary Host-Company Practices," *Career Development International* 6 (6) (2001): 298–311.

11. D.C. Thomas and K. Inkson, *Cultural Intelligence: Living and Working Globally,* 2d ed. (San Francisco: Berrett-Koehler Publishers, 2009); M.A. Shaffer, D.A. Harrison, and K.M. Gilley, "Dimensions, Determinants and Differences in the Expatriate Adjustment Process," *Journal of International Business Studies* 30 (3) (1999): 557–81.

12. R.H. Sims and M. Schraeder, "An Examination of Salient Factors Affecting Expatriate Culture Shock," *Journal of Business and Management* 10 (1) (2004): 73–87; I. Adler, "The Heavy Toll of Culture Shock," *Business Mexico* 13 (3) (2003): 19; I. Varner and L. Beamer, *Intercultural Communication in the Global Workplace* (Chicago: Irwin, 1995).

13. N. Forster, "'The Persistent Myth of High Expatriate Failure Rates': A Reappraisal," *International Journal of Human Resource Management* 8 (4) (1997): 414–33; N. Nicholson and A. Imaizumi, "The Adjustment of Japanese Expatriates to Living and Working in Britain," *British Journal of Management* 4 (1993): 119–34; Black, Mendenhall, and Oddou, "Toward a Comprehensive Model of International Adjustment."

14. Carraher, Sullivan, and Crocitto, "Mentoring Across Global Boundaries," *Journal of International Business Studies* 39 (2008): 1310–26; C.M. Vance and E.A. Ensher, "The Voice of the Host Country Workforce: A Key Source for Improving the Effectiveness of Expatriate Training and Performance," *International Journal of Intercultural Relations* 26 (2002): 447–61; Suutari and Burch, "The Role of On-Site Training and Support in Expatriation," *Career Development International* 6 (6) (2001): 298–311; D.C. Feldman and M.C. Bolino, "The Impact of On-Site Mentoring on Expatriate Socialization: A Structural Equation Modeling Approach," *International Journal of Human Resource Management* 10 (1999): 54–71.

15. C.M. Vance, V. Vaiman, and T. Andersen, "The Vital Liaison Role of Host Country Nationals in MNC Knowledge Management," *Human Resource Management* 48 (4) (2009): 649–59.

16. P.M. Caligiuri, "Selecting Expatriates for Personality Characteristics: A Moderating Effect of Personality on the Relationship between Host National Contact and Cross-Cultural Adjustment," *Management International Review* 40 (1) (2000): 61–80.

17. J. Osland and A. Osland, "Expatriate Paradoxes and Cultural Involvement," *International Studies of Management and Organization* 35 (4) (2005): 91–114. Z. Aycan, "Expatriation: A Critical Step Toward Developing Global Leaders," in *Developing Global Business Leaders: Policies, Processes, and Innovations,* ed. M.E. Mendenhall, T.M. Kuhlmann, and G.K. Stahl (Westport, CT: Quorum Books, 2001): 119–35.

18. M.L. Kraimer, S.J. Wayne, and R.A. Jaworski, "Sources of Support and Expatriate Performance: The Mediating Role of Expatriate Adjustment," *Personnel Psychology* 54 (1) (2001): 71–99; Suutari and Burch, "The Role of On-Site Training and Support in Expatriation: Existing and Necessary Host-Company Practices"; P.M. Caligiuri, A. Joshi, and M. Lazarova, "Factors Influencing the Adjustment of Women on Global Assignments," *International Journal of Human Resource Management* 10 (1999): 163–79; M.A. Shaffer, D.A. Harrison, and K.M. Gilley, "Dimensions, Determinants, and Differences in the Expatriate Adjustment Process," *Journal of International Business Studies* 30 (3) (1999): 557–81; R.A. Guzzo, K.A. Noonan, and E. Elron, "Expatriate Managers and the Psychological Contract," *Journal of Applied Psychology* 79 (1994): 617–26.

19. R.J. Brown, "Dominant Stressors on Expatriate Couples during International Assignments," *International Journal of Human Resource Management* 19 (6) (2008): 1018–34; Andreason, "Expatriate Adjustment of Spouses and Expatriate Managers: An Integrative Research Review."

20. M.J. Moore, "Same Ticket, Different Trip: Support Dual-Career Couples on Global Assignments," *Women in Management Review* 17 (2) (2002): 61–67; M. Harvey, "Dual Career Expatriates: Expectations, Adjustment and Satisfaction with International Relocation," *Journal of International Business Studies* 28 (3) (1997): 627–58.

21. J. Selmer and A. Leung, "Provision and Adequacy of Corporate Support to Male Expatriate Spouses: An Exploratory Study," *Personnel Review* 32 (1) (2003): 9–21; B.J. Punnett, O. Crocker,

and M.A. Stevens, "The Challenge for Women Expatriates and Spouses: Some Empirical Evidence," *International Journal of Human Resource Management* 3 (3) (1992): 585–92.

22. J. Selmer, "Which Is Easier, Adjusting to a Similar or to a Dissimilar Culture? American Business Expatriates in Canada and Germany," *International Journal of Cross Cultural Management* 7 (2) (2007): 185–201; J. Selmer, "Adjustment to Hong Kong: U.S. vs. European Expatriates," *Human Resource Management Journal* 9 (3) (1999): 83–93.

23. Sanchez, Spector, and Cooper, "Adapting to a Boundaryless World: A Developmental Expatriate Model."

24. Adapted from A.W. Andreason, "Direct and Indirect Forms of In-Country Support for Expatriates and Their Families as a Means of Reducing Premature Returns and Improving Job Performance," *International Journal of Management* 20 (4) (2003): 548–55.

25. A.W. Andreason, "Direct and Indirect Forms of In-Country Support for Expatriates and Their Families." For example, refer to Cendant Mobility at https://homepage.cendantmobility.com or GMAC Global Relocation Services at www.gmacglobalrelocation.com.

26. G.W. Florkowski and D.S. Fogel, "Expatriate Adjustment and Commitment: The Role of Host-Unit Treatment," *International Journal of Human Resource Management* 10 (1999): 783–807.

27. Kraimer, Wayne, and Jaworski, "Sources of Support and Expatriate Performance: The Mediating Role of Expatriate Adjustment"; Z. Aycan, "Acculturation of Expatriate Managers: A Process Model of Adjustment and Performance," in *New Approaches to Employee Management,* ed. D.M Saunders and Z. Aycan (Greenwich, CT: JAI Press, 1997): 1–40; R. Eisenberger, R. Huntington, S. Hutchinson, and D. Sowa, "Perceived Organizational Support," *Journal of Applied Psychology* 71 (1986): 500–507.

28. Vance, Vaiman, and Andersen, "The Vital Liaison Role of Host Country Nationals in MNC Knowledge Management."

29. Carraher, Sullivan, and Crocitto, "Mentoring Across Global Boundaries: An Empirical Examination of Home- and Host-Country Mentors on Expatriate Career Outcomes"; Siegel, Mosca, and Karim, "The Role of Mentoring Professional Accountants: A Global Perspective"; Feldman and Bolino, "The Impact of On-Site Mentoring on Expatriate Socialization: A Structural Equation Modeling Approach."

30. Aycan, "Acculturation of Expatriate Managers"; M.H. Ashamalla, "International Human Resource Management Practices: The Challenge of Expatriation," *Competitiveness Review* 8 (2) (1998): 54–65.

31. T. Hippler, "On-Site Adjustment Support for German Expatriates in the Republic of Ireland: An Exploratory Study," *IBAR: Journal of Irish Business and Administrative Research* 21 (2) (2000): 15–37; B. Croft, "Use Technology to Manage Your Expats," *Personnel Journal* 74 (December 1995): 113–17.

32. J. Selmer, "Usage of Corporate Career Development Activities by Expatriate Managers and the Extent of Their International Adjustment," *International Journal of Commerce and Management* 10 (1) (2000): 1–23; also refer to http://www.expatexchange.com for useful online professional information resources.

33. A. Andors, "Happy Returns: The Success of Repatriating Expatriate Employees Requires Forethought and Effective Management," *HR Magazine* 55 (3) (2010): 61–63; U. Wittig-Berman and N.J. Beutell, "International Assignments and the Career Management of Repatriates: The Boundaryless Career Concept," *International Journal of Management* 26 (1) (2009): 77–88; L.K. Stroh, H.B Gregersen, and J.S. Black, "Triumphs and Tragedies: Expectations and Commitments upon Repatriation," *International Journal of Human Resource Management* 11 (4) (2000): 681–97.

34. S. Schneider and K. Asakawa, "American and Japanese Expatriate Adjustment: A Psychoanalytic Perspective," *Human Relations* 48 (10) (1995): 1109–23; J.S. Black et al., *Global Assignments: Successfully Expatriating and Repatriating International Managers* (San Francisco: Jossey-Bass, 1992).

35. A. Jassawalla and H. Sashittal, "Thinking Strategically about Integrating Repatriated Managers in MNCs," *Human Resource Management* 48 (5), (2009): 769–92.

36. D.C. Martin and J.J. Anthony, "The Repatriation and Retention of Employees: Factors Leading to Successful Programs," *International Journal of Management* 3 (2) (2006): 620–31; K. Tyler, "Retraining Repatriates," *HR Magazine* 51 (3) (2006): 97–101.

37. G. Oddou, J.S. Osland, and R.N. Blakeney, "Repatriating Knowledge: Variables Influencing the 'Transfer' Process," *Journal of International Business Studies* 40 (2)(2009): 181–199; J.S. Black and H.B. Gregersen, "The Right Way to Manage Expats," *Harvard Business Review* 77 (2) (1999): 52–63.

38. Jassawalla and Sashittal, "Thinking Strategically about Integrating Repatriated Managers in MNCs."

39. A. Osman-Gani and A.S. Hyder, "Repatriation Readjustment of International Managers: An Empirical Analysis of HRD Interventions," *Career Development International* 13 (5) (2008): 456–75.

40. D.B. Richardson and V. Rullo, "Going Global: Are You Ready for an Overseas Assignment?" *Management Accounting* 73 (1992): 31–39.

41. J. van der Heijden, M. van Engen, and J. Paauwe, "Expatriate Career Support: Predicting Expatriate Turnover and Performance," *International Journal of Human Resource Management* 20 (4) (2009): 831–45; N. Furuya, M. Stevens, A. Bird, G. Oddou, and M. Mendenhall, "Managing the Learning and Transfer of Global Management Competence: Antecedents and Outcomes of Japanese Repatriation Effectiveness," *Journal of International Business Studies* 40 (2) (2009): 200–15; M.B. Lazarova and J. Cerdin, "Revisiting Repatriation Concerns: Organizational Support Versus Career and Contextual Influences," *Journal of International Business Studies* 38 (3) (2007): 404–29.

42. A.M. Osman-Gani and A.S. Hyder, "Repatriation Readjustment of International Managers: An Empirical Analysis of HRD Interventions," *Career* (2008); M.R. Hammer, W. Hart, and R. Rogan, "Can You Go Home Again? An Analysis of the Repatriation of Corporate Managers and Spouses," *Management International Review* 38 (1) (1998): 67–86.

43. G.S. Insch, N. McIntyre, and N.K. Napier, "The Expatriate Glass Ceiling: The Second Layer of Glass," *Journal of Business Ethics* 81 (1) (2008): 19–28; Y. Altman and S. Shortland, "Women and International Assignments: Taking Stock—a 25-Year Review," *Human Resource Management* 47 (2) (2008): 199–216; R.L. Tung, "Female Expatriates: The Model Global Manager?" *Organizational Dynamics* 33 (3) (2004): 243–53; J.P. Guthrie, R.A. Ash, and C.D. Stevens, "Are Women 'Better' than Men? Personality Differences and Expatriate Selection," *Journal of Managerial Psychology* 18 (3) (2003): 229–43.

44. K. Hutchings, E. French, and T. Hatcher, "Lament of the Ignored Expatriate: An Examination of Organisational and Social Network Support for Female Expatriates in China," *Equal Opportunities International* 27 (4) (2008): 372–91.

45. C.L. Owen, R.F. Scherer, M.Z. Sincoff, and M. Cordano, "Perceptions of Women as Managers in Chile and the United States," *Mid-American Journal of Business* 18 (2): 43–50; P.M. Caligiuri and R.L. Tung, "Male and Female Expatriates Success in Masculine and Feminine Countries," *International Journal of Human Resource Management* 10 (5) (1999): 763–82; V.E. Schein, R. Mueller, T. Lituchy, and J. Liu, "Think Manager-Think Male: A Global Phenomenon?" *Journal of Organizational Behavior* 17 (1996): 33–41.

46. Owen, Scherer, Sincoff, and Cordano, "Perceptions of Women as Managers in the United States and Chile"; P.M. Caligiuri and W.F. Cascio, "Can We Send Her There? Maximizing the Success of Western Women on Global Assignments," *Journal of World Business* 33 (1998): 394–416.

47. Caligiuri, Joshi, and Lazarova, "Factors Influencing the Adjustment of Women on Global Assignments."

48. Insch, McIntyre, and Napier, "The Expatriate Glass Ceiling: The Second Layer of Glass"; N.J. Adler, L.W. Brody, and J.S. Osland, "The Women's Global Leadership Forum: Enhancing One Company's Global Leadership Capability," *Human Resource Management* 39 (1/2) (2000): 209–25.

49. J. Selmer and A.S.M. Leung, "Career Management Issues of Female Business Expatriates," *Career Development International* 7(6) (2002): 348–58.

50. J. Selmer and A.S.M. Leung, "Personal Characteristics of Female vs. Male Business Expatriates," *International Journal of Cross Cultural Management* 3 (2) (2003): 195–212; N. Lockwood, "The Glass Ceiling: Domestic and International Perspectives," *HR Magazine* 49 (6) (2004): 2–9; B. Mathur-Helm, "Expatriate Women Managers: At the Crossroads of Success, Challenges and Career Goals," *Women in Management Review* 17 (1) (2002): 18–28.

51. Selmer and Leung, "Personal Characteristics of Female vs. Male Business Expatriates"; Caligiuri and Cascio, "Can We Send Her There? Maximizing the Success of Western Women on Global Assignments."

52. Lockwood, "The Glass Ceiling: Domestic and International Perspectives"; J. Selmer and A.S.M. Leung, "Are Corporate Career Development Activities Less Available to Female than to Male Expatriates?" *Journal of Business Ethics* 34 (1/2) 2003: 125–36.

53. For example, refer to the Federation of American Women's Clubs Overseas at www.fawco.org.

54. Selmer and Leung, "Are Corporate Career Development Activities Less Available to Female than to Male Expatriates?" 125–36.

55. Insch, McIntyre, and Napier, "The Expatriate Glass Ceiling"; H. Harris, "Organizational Influences on Women's Career Opportunities in International Management," *Women in Management Review* 10 (1995): 26–31.

56. M. Linehan and H. Scullion, "Repatriation of Female Executives: Empirical Evidence from Europe," *Women in Management Review* 17 (2) (2002): 80–88.

57. B.S. Reiche, "The Inpatriate Experience in Multinational Corporations: An Exploratory Case Study in Germany," *International Journal of Human Resource Management* 17 (9) (2006): 1572–90; M.G. Harvey, M.M. Novicevic, and C. Speier, "Strategic Global Human Resource Management: The Role of Inpatriate Managers," *Human Resource Management Review* 10 (2) (2000): 153–75.

58. M. Harvey, M.M. Novicevic, M.R. Buckley, and H. Fung, "Reducing Inpatriate Managers' 'Liability of Foreignness' by Addressing Stigmatization and Stereotype Threats," *Journal of World Business* 40 (3) (2005): 267–80.

59. Also refer to C. Lachnit, "Low-Cost Tips for Successful Inpatriatio," *Workforce* 80 (8) (2001): 42–47; M.G. Harvey and H. Fung, "Inpatriate Managers: The Need for Realistic Relocation Reviews," *International Journal of Management* 17 (2) (2000): 151–59; M.G. Harvey, M.M. Novicevic, and C. Speier, "Inpatriate Managers: How to Increase the Probability of Success," *Human Resource Management Review* 9 (1) (1999): 51–81; M. G. Harvey and N. Miceli, "Exploring Inpatriate Issues: An Exploratory Empirical Study," *International Journal of Intercultural Relations* 23 (3) (1999): 339–71; M.G. Harvey, " 'Inpatriation' Training: The Next Challenge for International Human Resource Management," *International Journal of Intercultural Relations* 21 (3) (1997): 393–428.

60. T. Hippler, "European Assignments: International or Quasi-Domestic?" *Journal of European Industrial Training* 24 (9) (2002): 491–504.

61. Hippler, "On-Site Adjustment Support for German Expatriates in the Republic of Ireland: An Exploratory Study"; V. Suutari and C. Brewster, "International Assignments across European Borders: No Problems?" in *International HRM: Contemporary Issues in Europe,* ed. C. Brewster and H. Harris (London: Routledge, 1999); S. O'Grady and H.W. Lane, "The Psychic Distance Paradox," *Journal of International Business Studies* 27 (2) (1996): 309–33.

62. J. Selmer, E. Ling, S.C. Shiu, and C.T. de Leon, "Reciprocal Adjustment? Mainland Chinese Managers in Hong Kong vs. Hong Kong Chinese Managers on the Mainland," *Cross Cultural Management* 10 (3) (2003): 58–79.

63. J. Selmer, "Psychological Barriers to Adjustment and How They Affect Coping Strategies: Western Business Expatriates in China," *International Journal of Human Resource Management* 12 (2) (2001): 151–65.

64. V. Suutari, "Global Managers: Career Orientation, Career Tracks, Life-Style Implications and Career Commitment," *Journal of Managerial Psychology* 18 (3) (2003): 185–207; K. Roberts, E.E. Kossek, and C. Ozeki, "Managing the Global Workforce: Challenges and Strategies," *Academy of Management Executive* 12 (4) (1998): 93–119; C. Reynolds, "Strategic Employment of Third Country Nationals," *HR Planning* 20 (1) (1997): 33–39.

65. Wittig-Berman and Beutell, "International Assignments and the Career Management of Repatriates," 77–88.

66. H. Mayerhofer, L.C. Hartmann, and A. Herbert, "Career Management Issues for Flexpatriate International Staff," *Thunderbird International Business Review* 46 (6) (2004): 647–66; S.C. Peppas,

"Making the Most of International Assignments: A Training Model for Non-Resident Expatriates," *Journal of American Academy of Business* 5 (1/2) (2004): 41–45.

67. D.G. Collings, H. Scullion, and M.J. Morley, "Changing Patterns of Global Staffing in the Multinational Enterprise: Challenges to the Conventional Expatriate Assignment and Emerging Alternatives," *Journal of World Business* 42 (2) (2007): 198–213; S. McKenna and J. Richardson, "The Increasing Complexity of the Internationally Mobile Professional," *Cross Cultural Management* 14 (4) (2007): 307–20.

68. K. Aaron, "Upstate New York Families Accept Challenge of International Relocations," *Knight Ridder Tribune Business News,* April 14, 2003, 1.

69. A. Pinnell, "Managing International HR in a Changing World," *International HR News* (2003), www.oakbridge-global.com/HRNews/June2003.asp.

70. C.M. Vance and Y. Paik, "One Size Fits All in Expatriate Pre-Departure Training? Comparing the Host Country Voices of Mexican, Indonesian and US Workers," *Journal of Management Development* 21 (7) (2002): 557–71.

71. L. Holbeche, "International Teamworking," in *The Global Manager: Creating the Seamless Organization,* ed. P. Joynt and B. Morton (London: IPD House, 1999): 179–206.

72. B. Williamson, "Managing at a Distance," *Business Week,* July 27, 2009.

73. M. LaBrosse, "Managing Virtual Teams," *Employment Relations Today* 35 (2) (2008): 81–86; D. Coutu, "Trust in Virtual Teams," *Harvard Business Review* (May/June 1998): 20–21; also refer to S.L Jarvenpaa, K. Knoll, and D.E. Leidner, "Antecedents of Trust in Global Virtual Teams," *Journal of Management Information Systems* 14 (4) (1998): 29–64.

74. L. Lee-Kelley and T. Sankey, "Global Virtual Teams for Value Creation and Project Success: A Case Study," *International Journal of Project Management* 26 (1) (2008): 51–62; M. Higgs, "Developing International Management Teams through Diversity," in *The Global Manager: Creating the Seamless Organization,* ed. P. Joynt and B. Morton (London: IPD House, 1999): 207–32.

75. K. Knoll and S.L. Jarvenpaa, "Working Together in Global Virtual Teams," in *The Virtual Workplace,* ed. M. Igbarria and M. Tan (Hershey, PA: Idea Group, 1998): 2–23; also see W.F. Cascio, "Managing a Virtual Workplace," *Academy of Management Executive* 14 (3) (2000): 81–90.

76. C. Saunders, C. Van Slyke, and D.R. Vogel, "My Time or Yours? Managing Time Visions in Global Virtual Teams," *Academy of Management Executive* 18 (1) (2004): 19–31.

77. Other useful sources should be consulted for more detailed information and advice, including G.I. Nwanna, *Traveling Abroad Post "9–11" and in the Wake of Terrorism* (Baltimore, MD: Frontline, 2004); C.H. Uber, *Traveling Smart* (Upland, CA: Dragonflyer Press, 1999); R. Dawood, *Travellers' Health: How to Stay Healthy Abroad,* 4th ed. (New York: Oxford University Press, 2002).

Global Workforce Performance Management

PUZZLING PERFORMANCE APPRAISAL

Karl Swenson is the head of a utilities engineering project group in a multinational enterprise based in the United States. With growing opportunities due to globalization, the company has emphasized the need to operate as a truly global organization, not as an MNC with different regions or a U.S.-based company with overseas operations. One implication of this goal is that employees are increasingly working together in different teams, including on a virtual basis, with representatives from all over the world and more frequently have supervisors from different countries. Karl's U.S. group works with software support engineering groups in overseas operations, particularly in Malaysia, on an important new software program in utilities management. Because the team was provided the latest means of technology (for example, teleconferencing and electronic group software) to communicate globally, little training was given to team members on cross-cultural communication. The team is under pressure not only to meet quality standards on the new product but also to get the program to market quickly. To meet these goals Karl sends e-mail messages such as the following to his counterpart team leader, Yusoff, in Malaysia:

We have followed the procedures sufficiently and have done enough retests to reasonably meet our quality standards. Let's now stop the testing of this phase of the program development and immediately move on to the next phase.

These brief e-mail messages were sometimes met with unexpectedly long silences from the counterparts in Malaysia. At other times the responding e-mail messages indicated agreement with Karl's point of view. Regardless of the response, it was clear the Malaysian team appeared to continue doing more testing and looking at the program from different angles and checkpoints.

Toward the end of a particularly important phase of the program-development project, Karl traveled to Malaysia for two weeks to finish the phase. The two weeks stretched to four weeks, but after much hard work the product phase was successfully completed. Just before he was to return to the United States, Karl was reminded of an important task associated with one of the MNC's core values, which is to provide timely "360-degree feedback." As the team leader, Karl was an important source of information in evaluating Yusoff's work performance, and he needed to provide feedback as part of Yusoff's performance appraisal. Using performance evaluation forms provided by the MNC headquarters, Karl met with Yusoff and told him that although he had performed very well on the project overall, there were some areas in which Yusoff could improve. Later Karl documented the feedback in an e-mail to Yusoff and his supervisor in Malaysia. He felt he had carried out the performance appraisal in a transparent, fair manner in full accordance with the standards for feedback set by his company.

Karl was then quite surprised in the week following his return to the United States when he learned that Yusoff had abruptly requested a transfer to another team with a far less important assignment. Thinking back, Karl did recall that Yusoff didn't respond very much to his statements during the meeting evaluating his performance and never offered any direct response to the feedback points. Still, he was puzzled by Yusoff's request for a transfer and wondered why he was not responding to the latest e-mail messages. Yes, there had been some problems, but this is normal with a big project. The most important thing for Yusoff was that they had gotten the job done successfully. Now he had a new product design to work on and he needed the full efforts of Yusoff and the Malaysian office to move quickly to meet the next deadline. Well, maybe it was for the best, Karl decided. If Yusoff couldn't deal with any constructive feedback, then perhaps his team was better off without him. Still, Karl wondered how Yusoff's transfer request was being perceived by other Malaysian team members and whether similar problems might occur with his new counterpart in Malaysia.[1]

INTRODUCTION

The role of managers and supervisors in working closely with individual employees and teams on a regular basis is critical for helping them keep on course and optimizing their contribution to achieving organizational goals. As suggested by our opening scenario, this responsibility for effectively managing individual and team performance across national and cultural boundaries in today's global workplace can present particular challenges and requires important considerations and competencies beyond those appropriate for the domestic workplace. An important approach for managers to take is to become familiar with current research on best practices in human resources and employee performance management,[2] yet maintain a keen sensitivity to local conditions and cultural differences for the actual customized implementation of those practices.[3]

Performance management is a set of regular, ongoing HR activities carried out by managers and supervisors relative to their subordinates to enhance and maintain employee performance toward the achievement of desired performance objectives. These activities, aimed at encouraging optimal employee motivation and development,[4] can be directed toward both individual employees and teams within a given work unit supervised by a manager. Effective performance management provides an important means for aligning individual employee and team working behaviors

Global Workforce Professional Profile 9.1
**Yann Blandy: From Performance
Management to Performance Culture**

"Performance management—or business planning at the individual level—is the HR process where you see the clearest added value from the HR function in achieving business targets," says Yann Blandy, founding partner of MindShift, a consulting firm in Stockholm that specializes in planning and implementing performance management initiatives for several firms in Europe. Blandy was born, raised, and educated in Paris, and at age twenty-four followed his girlfriend (now wife) to her homeland of Sweden. There Blandy developed his career with valuable corporate experiences in sales and human resources and gained a clear picture of the potential impact that attention to the management of individual performance can have on company productivity. "Various studies demonstrate a huge improvement in such measures as productivity, profitability, and customer satisfaction when employees have a clear understanding of how they contribute to the big picture and their managers have appropriate skills to support and facilitate employee performance," Blandy asserts. "Yet many companies neglect attention to vital performance management processes and issues."

With this frequent organizational need in mind, Blandy decided to join his colleagues who had formed their own consulting firm. At MindShift, Blandy works closely with senior HR executives from firms across several different industries and countries to ensure that a true performance culture is available in their organization, where performance management is a top priority held by all. There are three major areas of focus in his work: organization (for example, company culture and the performance management process and its linkage to rewards as well as to management planning); managers (for example, in their development of key skills to coach their individual employees and teams toward higher performance levels); and employees (for example, helping workers develop an understanding of what is expected of them in terms of deliverables and behaviors as well as an understanding of and commitment to company objectives).

Blandy thoroughly enjoys his work in performance management because he sees a direct link between these efforts and company performance. Says Blandy, "The value of an organization is ultimately driven down to the individual level—and that's where performance management comes into the picture!" Although the principles of effective performance management are generally the same around the world, the successful implementation of performance management plans is greatly influenced by local national culture as well as company culture and leadership styles. Blandy greatly enjoys the challenges that he faces on his various company projects with different national and corporate cultural backgrounds. "The variety of challenging opportunities is much greater than when I worked for one corporation," Blandy said. "And my interaction with organizations from various countries, such as the United Kingdom, Finland, Sweden, and France, with different cultural perspectives really adds to my learning."

Figure 9.1 **Performance Management Process**

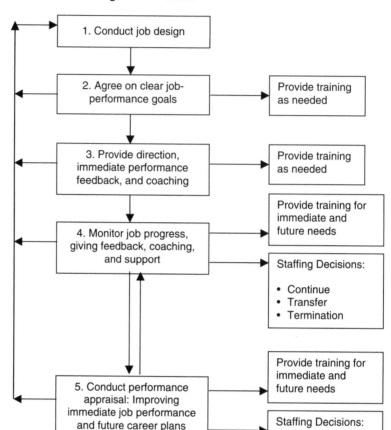

with the organization's goals.[5] Especially in international business, performance management can serve as an effective HR control mechanism for implementing MNC strategy and carrying out important objectives despite significant distance and cultural barriers.[6]

As indicated in Figure 9.1, which depicts the general five-phase performance management process in organizations, performance management comprises such important manager-employee interactions as two-way communication, regular performance feedback, coaching, performance appraisal, and even correctional and disciplinary activities. Notice that although periodic formal evaluations or appraisals of employee performance are an important part of the performance management process, several other important components of performance management should not be neglected. In fact, a major cause of poor performance management is the unbalanced focus on formal performance appraisals at the exclusion of ongoing attention to other important parts of the performance management process.[7] In addition, and consistent with an increasing awareness of the importance of integrating individual HRM activities and functions at home and abroad for optimal impact on organizational productivity,[8] performance management is closely integrated with other major HR management practices including job or work design, training and career planning, staffing, and compensation.

In this chapter we will examine each of the five phases of the performance management process and then consider some essential criteria for effective performance management on a global business scale. We then will examine important principles and practices of performance appraisal for expatriates as well as brief considerations for ensuring the effective appraisal of inpatriates and TCNs. Due to space limitations our primary focus in this chapter is at the individual level. However, systematic approaches for evaluating and managing groups, business processes, and organizational performance are also needed in an effective, comprehensive performance management effort.[9]

PERFORMANCE MANAGEMENT PROCESS

We now take a closer look at each of the five major phases of the performance management process as presented in Figure 9.1. In addition, we briefly examine particularly important points of integration of this process with other HRM functions as well as company strategy.

JOB DESIGN

Performance management is integrated with the broader HR function as well as aligned with company strategy at the first phase, where a specific job or work assignment is carefully designed or *redesigned* (given the tendency of jobs to soon become obsolete in a rapidly changing global business environment) to meet current organization objectives. Although an employee may not yet even be assigned to this job, its thoughtful, careful design, as indicated in Chapter 5 on global HR planning, is essential in contributing to future work performance and success in carrying out MNC performance objectives. The design of the job should not be in the abstract but should include specific tasks, performance expectations, work interactions and reporting relationships, and job qualifications that fit the specific job situation. For example, a computer sales job that covers Western Europe would likely consider multiple-language fluency in English, German, and French as critical job qualifications.

AGREE ON CLEAR JOB-PERFORMANCE GOALS

In this second phase of the performance management process the manager and employee jointly examine the specific tasks, requirements, and expectations of the job within a larger picture of the goals of the organization and obtain a clear understanding and agreement regarding specific job-performance goals and objectives, including

Global Workforce Challenge 9.1
The Worldwide Changing Nature of Work

An essential element in successful performance management is understanding the conditions and situations in which employees work. And the nature of work is definitely changing with ongoing technological advancements. Sheryl Padamonsky spends an average of three days a week away from her company's Austin, Texas, office. But she's not on the road. She spends the time working at home and at the house of her elderly parents in Cleveland, Ohio. Sheryl stays connected with a laptop computer, equipped with built-in wireless technology to tap into the Internet and a webcam for videoconferencing. And she uses a handheld device that makes calls, keeps her calendar, and pulls down her corporate e-mail—all while she's working out on a treadmill at the gym. This forty-year-old administrative assistant seems shocked that anyone would compare her to her always-traveling boss, the head of a high-tech consulting firm, Perficient. "It's really about the ability to balance work life and private life in a way that's good for me, good for my company," Sheryl says.

Once confined to jet-setting CEOs and salespeople who demand day-and-night access to the office, mobile corporate computing is coming to the masses. Super-fast wireless networks, innovative communications software, and a slew of relatively cheap devices from notebook PCs to palmsized handheld devices let practically any worker stay connected to the corporate office, from anywhere he or she may be. Whatever you call it—a productivity breakthrough or a new form of wage slavery—it is clear that work accessibility is becoming an around-the-clock phenomenon. "Work has crept into our lives, and our lives have crept into work in the mobile world," says Tim Woods, director of the research group Internet Home Alliance.

No one has calculated the potential productivity gains, but analysts and businesses providing mobility-support technology, such as Dell, Microsoft, and Cingular Wireless, have no doubt that productivity will continue to rise. Early corporate adopters of mobile technology claim that they win twice: Employees tend to work more for the same pay and the company can cut overhead and office space needs at headquarters. Many employees can now work from home, and managers can do more grunt work for themselves via their high-tech gadgets, meaning fewer administrative employees are needed. "It's really a blue ocean as far as savings," says Michael Howell, a vice president at San Francisco hospital supply manager Broadlane, which is outfitting its salespeople with handheld devices that will let them check on inventories in its 1.5 million-product catalog and submit orders from a client's office.

The tech industry's leaders have been promising ubiquitous computing for more than a decade, but only now is it feasible for tens of millions of people. The rise of the Internet and world standardization on wireless broadband technologies laid the foundation. Then, next-generation cellular networks and the ability to switch to Wi-Fi access on the fly let mobile workers connect anywhere, be it a subway in London, a café in Beijing, or a supermarket in Des Moines, Iowa. To be sure, you can't get wireless signals in a lot of locations, but the build-out support system continues.

(continued)

Global Workforce Challenge 9.1 (continued)

As the line between work and private life blurs, managers and employees will have to develop new discipline and communication etiquette so work and play don't interfere with each other. "With mobile devices, people are going to interchangeably switch from moment to moment, doing e-mail and office tasks but also experiencing pictures, music, and movies," says Scott Horn, Microsoft senior director for mobile and embedded devices.

Sources: Adapted from "Flexible Hours in the Ranks," *HRMagazine: SHRM's 2010 HR Trend Book* (January 2010): 16–17; C. Edwards, "Mobile Computing: Wherever You Go, You're on the Job," *BusinessWeek,* June 20, 2005, 87–90.

special work assignments. In one study across several countries it was found that the clear communication of subsidiary goals and the setting of an employee's job objectives contribute to increased commitment of employees to their organizational and job objectives and subsequently enhances their job satisfaction.[10] This setting and obtaining agreement on work performance goals occurs twice for expatriates at Monsanto, a leading global provider of agricultural products and integrated solutions. The expatriates meet with their corporate manager prior to departure to prepare and agree on work expectations for their predominantly project-based foreign assignments, and then review and refine this understanding and agreement with an assigned host country manager.[11]

In many cases, as indicated by the arrow to the right at this second phase in Figure 9.1, there will be the need for training, concurrently or in the near future, for knowledge or skill development to support desired performance. For example, an otherwise technically qualified Thai employee promoted to a management position with an MNC in Bangkok, and who in the future will require increasing amounts of interaction with French expatriates working for the MNC in that country, may also begin to receive some forms of training to build French language skills and increase the understanding of French and the specific MNC corporate culture. As indicated by the arrow that points back to Phase 1, it is important for two-way communication to occur at this phase to allow for possible input from the employee regarding unanticipated job requirements, or employee needs that might require a slight adjustment or significant revision of the original job design from Phase 1. The clear understanding and agreement on the job expectations at this phase are critical for effective performance management to proceed.

PROVIDE DIRECTION, IMMEDIATE PERFORMANCE FEEDBACK, AND COACHING

The third phase involves the initial work performance of the employee. In many respects, with its ongoing direction and frequent feedback, this phase resembles on-the-job training, the most common form of training in organizations.[12] However, even where the new employee is well qualified for a job, there should still be an arrangement at this work start-up phase for close one-on-one direction and immediate performance feedback, whether provided by the employee's manager or by an assigned experienced peer or other colleague. Coaching here consists of ongoing one-on-one assistance, especially at the early stage of the new job, to provide continued direction, mutual goal setting, feedback, correction, and encouragement as the employee progresses toward optimal performance.[13] In fact, numerous studies across a variety of settings and cultures have demonstrated that frequent feedback sharing and goal setting, particularly within the manager-subordinate coaching relationship and informal context, can be very successful in leading to optimal employee performance.[14] There is always some form of adjustment in the new work assignment, whether the employee is working domestically or abroad, and the close attention provided at this phase can have a very positive effect on work performance adjustment and mastery.[15] It is important for the employee, whether in the home country or abroad, to begin the job on a positive note with positive expectations for success and self-efficacy.[16] The immediate manager as a coach can greatly facilitate the development of these positive expectations through encouragement and ready support as needed,[17] as well as through the development of a trusting and respectful working relationship.[18]

As in the previous phase, there may also appear areas in this start-up phase, once the individual actually begins to perform a job, where more formal training can be provided to help fill in skill and knowledge gaps to support optimal performance. Also, as before, once the actual work has begun, there often are aspects about the predetermined design of the job that are fine in theory but not in practice. Therefore, possible job redesign needs should be considered carefully at this phase, especially with the direct experience-based input of the new employee, which is represented in Figure 9.1 by the arrow cycling back to Phase 1.

MONITOR JOB PROGRESS

In this fourth phase of the performance management process, as the employee over several months becomes more confident and competent in performing work according to expectations, the manager becomes gradually less involved in the close advisement and coaching that we noted in Phase 3. Nevertheless, the manager remains in close contact to provide performance feedback, correction, and coaching as needed to maintain desired performance.

Again, training may be provided at this stage to help reinforce desired performance and fill noted skill gaps that may not have been apparent or mastered earlier. In addition, at this phase where the achievement of immediate work performance has been sufficiently addressed, important but less urgent training may be provided for anticipated future job developments or changes. Also, as performance requirements become even clearer with the additional time and experience gained at this phase, there may be a need to adjust the design of the job to support desired performance. Job design should be considered an ongoing, flexible process to meet the needs of a dynamic global workplace, and managers should continuously consider possible needs for job redesign for optimal influence on work performance. For example, upon review and open discussion with the employee at this phase it may be determined that both the original task requirements for a given job were unrealistic and new work demands have arisen requiring additional critical tasks, prompting a decision to redesign the original job and restructure tasks involving a new assistant's position to provide additional support.

Finally, during this phase, which may transpire over the period of several months to a year, the manager might begin to consider possible new staffing decisions appropriate for the employee. It might become apparent that, despite previous careful selection, close coaching, training, and ongoing efforts to correct performance problems— including actual disciplinary measures—the employee is just not able to perform the work in an acceptable fashion. At this point, therefore, as indicated in Figure 9.1 by the second arrow to the right, a staffing decision may involve continued employment, a transfer to a new job (e.g., for a new developmental experience, promotion, or demotion),[19] or termination. Where it is felt that termination is in order, the manager should be very familiar with the legal requirements and possible consequences, which in some countries can be substantial in the form of significant termination indemnity costs associated with severance and unemployment payments as well as legal costs to deal with growing worldwide litigation in claims about unfair and wrongful termination.[20] In fact, one thorough analysis found that terminating employees in the United States, compared to Europe, Japan, and Canada, involves more work, more time, and higher costs to deal with its associated complex and detailed body of legal rules, uncertainty and threats of litigation, and actual litigation.[21] Given these costs, as well as the significant cost of merely replacing an employee (sometimes as much as three times the employee's annual salary), managers should not follow the common tendency to opt for the quick solution of termination but instead should do all they can to help correct the performance of a problem employee, including asking themselves if they are providing adequate guidance, nurturing, and encouragement in their important work of ongoing performance management.[22]

CONDUCT PERFORMANCE APPRAISAL

At the appropriate time (for example, after six months or a year of work—most formal performance appraisals are conducted annually) and following appropriate preparation, a formal appraisal is conducted concerning the employee's performance for the purpose of enhancing job performance in the future. As will be discussed later in this chapter, the information for evaluating the quality of the employee's performance can come from a number of sources, although the most common source is the employee's direct supervisor.[23] As before, this more formal and official discussion between supervisor and employee regarding past performance and plans for future performance improvement should involve two-way communication, mutual trust and respect, and no surprises for the employee because up until this point there should have been regular, effective feedback regarding the quality of the employee's performance.[24] In addition to this discussion aimed at enhancing job performance in the future, many multinational organizations are finding success in terms of employee satisfaction and retention in using this performance appraisal time as an occasion for also discussing

Figure 9.2   **Major Upstream and Downstream Considerations for Global Performance Management**

Upstream Considerations	Downstream Considerations
• Strategic integration and coordination • Workforce alignment • Organizational learning and knowledge management	• Responsiveness to local conditions • Sensitivity to cross-cultural differences • Establishment of performance management relationship • Comprehensive training

the employee's future career interests and goals.[25] For example, during this planning session the employee could indicate his or her interest in eventually obtaining an international assignment to assist in developing important global leadership competencies that can be beneficial for both the individual and the organization. This potentially productive exchange allows the manager to give advice for useful preparation and developmental opportunities related to these future career plans as well as provide an input, where effective HR information systems are in place, into longer-term HR planning for retaining and utilizing the developing talents of the employee.[26]

At this final phase of the performance management process, results of the formal performance appraisal may point as before to specific training needs for improving future performance in the present job as well as training plans for employee development consistent with the employee's before-mentioned future career plans.[27] In fact, an emphasis on future employee development rather than judgments about past performance has been found to contribute to higher levels of employee productivity, satisfaction, and retention in several different countries.[28] As in the previous phase, this experience can also lead to staffing decisions regarding possible employee continuation in the present job, transfer, termination, and promotion.[29] In addition, the appraisal data are often used as a basis for compensation decisions, especially in organizations that are committed to an effective pay-for-performance approach.[30] Finally, as represented by the return arrow in Figure 9.1 back to Phase 4, following the performance appraisal there should be a continuation of monitoring employee progress, with ongoing manager feedback and support.

IMPORTANT CONSIDERATIONS FOR GLOBAL PERFORMANCE MANAGEMENT

Beyond the particular phases of the performance management process, there are major overarching considerations or priorities for guiding performance management in appropriately addressing, according to the particular MNC strategy, the dual and sometimes conflicting challenges of global integration and control and responsiveness to local needs.[31] As indicated in Figure 9.2, these considerations fall on both the upstream and downstream side. On the upstream side they link with company global competitiveness and strategic management success, and include strategic integration and coordination, workforce alignment, and organizational learning and knowledge management. On the downstream side these considerations involve crucial implementation in carrying out the local performance management process with individuals and teams.[32] These important downstream considerations include responsiveness to local conditions, sensitivity to cross-cultural differences, establishment of the performance management relationship, and training for effective performance management.

UPSTREAM: STRATEGIC INTEGRATION AND COORDINATION

As we have mentioned previously, the expectations for individual and group performance that are established, communicated, and facilitated through the performance management process should be in sync with the strategic objectives of the business unit and company as a whole. For example, where a long-term priority of an MNC is the development throughout its foreign operations of local managerial talent possessing a consistent company mind-set, it would do well to gear its performance management process toward helping identify and prepare high-potential candidates for future advanced managerial training or a possible inpatriation experience at company headquarters.[33]

In addition, where particular functional or geographic business units of an MNC become increasingly interdependent and require greater standardization of processes and performance, a careful coordination of the various relevant performance expectations across these business units should be made.[34] Evans and colleagues illustrate the importance of a tight coordination of performance expectations across geographic business units—leading to consistent forms of work performance—in describing a European client transnational organization. This organization previously had followed a multidomestic strategy requiring little coordination, but was increasingly dealing with customers that desired cross-border product and service availability and thus expected consistent global performance. Thus there was a need for increased coordination of performance expectations among the heads of various business units to achieve greater global performance consistency.[35]

Virtual teams constitute an increasingly common and important coordination and integration mechanism across an MNC's interdependent operations, whose individual members are from different countries or widely dispersed units. Although they may meet occasionally in person, they generally perform a large amount of work on a virtual basis through the use of various information and communication technologies. Their success in coordinating efforts across work units and integrating with company strategy can be greatly influenced by team performance management related to facilitating open communications and cross-cultural understanding, building trust, and overcoming challenges posed by distance separation and time lag. Individual performance management is also critical for ensuring that each member is accountable to the virtual team and develops a sense of team commitment.

UPSTREAM: WORKFORCE ALIGNMENT

In addition to an integration of work expectations with business strategy and goals and coordination of policies, procedures, and structures related to work expectations across business units, another major strategic or upstream consideration for performance management is workforce alignment. This strategic alignment or common direction of performance effected in the minds and hearts (that is, knowledge, skills, and values) of the global workforce at various levels throughout the MNC can provide a powerful contribution to the competitive advantage of the MNC in such areas as worldwide customer responsiveness and service consistency, agility, flexibility, innovation and change management, growth management, and effective knowledge management and internal sharing of best practices.[36] An important step in achieving this common alignment is the development through HR processes (for example, through effective training and development activities, communications, work collaboration assignments, and reward systems) of global leaders throughout the MNC who share common core values, priorities, capabilities, and performance-based expectations. The next step is to implement these congruent performance expectations—with appropriate local adaptation—within their business units.[37] This alignment of leadership throughout the MNC relative to common values, priorities, and performance expectations can also contribute to the development of a common global business culture that can have a unifying influence on individual employee thought, behavior, and performance.[38] When managed effectively, this common MNC culture can even overpower the otherwise divergent effects of greatly differing national cultures represented within the MNC. Finally, as suggested earlier, global workforce alignment can be achieved by having strategic objectives drive the formulation of work expectations throughout the various foreign business units. The role of performance management in supporting this level of global business alignment is especially seen in MNCs with global markets, such as Hitachi, Coca-Cola, Daimler, and Marriott, who employ common worldwide customer satisfaction measures, thus providing comparable measures of business unit performance on a global scale.

UPSTREAM: ORGANIZATIONAL LEARNING AND KNOWLEDGE MANAGEMENT

A third important upstream consideration in performance management is valuable company-wide organization development and change—often discussed in terms of organizational learning,[39] or purposeful changes in company know-how and practices as part of company-wide knowledge management.[40] These changes can eventually take place when those being managed in the performance management process are given the opportunity and are effectively encouraged to provide feedback on performance management systems and input into managerial decision making. Milliman and colleagues make a strong argument for the value of individual and organizational learning from mistakes made in the course of global performance appraisal and management activities, and sharing and implementing this learning company-wide through new policy and practice formulation to improve the overall process of global performance management.[41] To improve MNC organizational learning and knowledge management processes, we recommend the active use and appropriate dissemination of lower-level HCN employee surveys, HCN manager/supervisor experience-based critical incident feedback, and HCN upper manager input to help guide and enhance the validity of MNC expatriate training for those host country operations as well as the accuracy of the host country operation's performance goals and expectations that are formulated at parent company headquarters.[42]

Figure 9.3 **Major External and Internal Conditions Affecting Employee Performance**

External Conditions	Internal Conditions
• Local economic circumstances	• Organization size
• Competition	• Organization resources
• Demographics	• Organization structure
• Supporting infrastructure	• Organizational culture
• Unions	• Management factors
• National/local culture	

DOWNSTREAM: RESPONSIVENESS TO LOCAL CONDITIONS

An ongoing dual and often seemingly irreconcilable challenge of the global corporation is the effective global integration and coordination of business units and processes in carrying out MNC strategy and, at the same time, the implementation of business practices with appropriate awareness of and accommodation to local needs and circumstances.[43] Although performance management represents an important strategic tool for control in implementing company strategy, it too should be implemented in a way that fits and is responsive to local business conditions. These conditions that can greatly influence individual and organizational performance, and should therefore be considered for effective accommodation and implementation of performance management at the local level, are both *external* and *internal* to the firm[44] (refer to Figure 9.3). External conditions affecting local performance include such factors as local economic circumstances, competition, demographics, supporting infrastructure, unions, and national/local culture.

Where local economic conditions are difficult or competition is especially intense, employee performance—especially related to company earnings or overall business-level performance for workforce teams, sales professionals, and top executives—will likely be affected in a negative way and may need extra supportive coaching and encouragement. These external conditions should be considered when comparing the performance of these employees with others at similar levels in other parts of the world that may not have the same level of challenge posed by the local economy or competition. The local demographics, or the characteristics of the local workforce, can also influence the performance management process. For example, where the literacy level and basic skills of the locally available labor force are very poor, much more training and active coaching will be required in the performance management process. Or where a foreign operation is forced to use less than state-of-the-art technology or suffers from poor infrastructure due to the lack of these optimal business supports in a developing country, individual and teamwork performance and productivity expectations would likely be lower than they would under more favorable conditions. And a manager whose work unit has a much higher skill level and more favorable technological and infrastructure support than other managers in other operations might be expected to have higher levels of work unit performance, with his or her managerial performance evaluated accordingly. Unions, especially in countries like Germany where they enjoy large labor representation and significant acceptance and integration in the local economy, can also have a huge impact on work responsibility and performance expectations. Finally, local culture can have a powerful and pervasive influence in many phases of the performance management process. Because of this heavy influence affecting the day-to-day interactions and activities of performance management, we will examine culture later as a separate major downstream consideration in itself.

Internal workplace conditions can affect employee performance and thus should be considered in the performance management process. Such conditions include organization size and resources, organization structure, organizational culture, and management. Larger organizations tend to have more specialized resources and HR management policies and guidelines that can more effectively support the global performance management agenda.[45] Organizational structure, as a major mechanism for implementing strategy, can have a significant impact on performance management and other HR management policies and practices.[46] For example, decentralized MNCs typically will employ differing policies regarding performance management throughout the MNC, likely resulting in inconsistent forms and practices of performance management at the various operations abroad. In some organizational structures, such as matrix organizations or international joint ventures, professional employees and senior managers might have multiple reporting relationships affecting the management of their performance.

Organizational culture consists of the set of values, beliefs, priorities, and assumptions of an organization that guide individual and organizational behavior. Organizational culture develops naturally through the collective experience of organizational members. It also can be shaped and changed through comprehensive, systematic interventions by organizational leadership.[47] Organizational culture is also considered as potentially able to have greater unifying influence on employee behavior and work performance than our more and more pluralistic national cultures.[48] In fact, one study examining the negative effect of culture distance or degree of culture dissimilarity on international joint venture performance found that performance problems originated more from differences in *organizational* culture than from differences in *national* culture.[49]

Large MNCs can also have multiple organizational subcultures in their various operations around the world and even among their operations within the same national boundaries. These differing organizational subcultures at an MNC's local operations can have influence, leading to differing HR practices and behavioral expectations affecting performance management. For example, it was noted by one of the present text authors in his consulting project with a large accounting firm that, contrary to the rather stiff formality and clear expectation at the firm's Chicago headquarters and offices nearby of always dressing in a three-piece suit, the Miami, Florida, office of the firm was much more laid back and casual and allowed professionals to wear a sport jacket and slacks.

MNC management, from top management down through the ranks of line management, can have a powerful effect on global performance management activities; they are essentially the ones who plan and implement performance management practices. The collective backgrounds and experience of top management can certainly influence the range of performance management practices that might be used within an

MNC—a Japanese MNC operating with exclusive Japanese headquarters and foreign operation expatriate management would likely consider and follow a more narrow set of practices than an MNC that has, along with PCNs, significant management representation of inpatriates at headquarters and both HCNs and TCNs in management at foreign operations. The nature of global performance management practices that are adopted and implemented would also likely differ in MNCs where senior management has very little or no experience working abroad compared to those MNCs whose management has significant foreign work experience.[50]

The performance of top managers often speaks louder than words in terms of what really matters in the organization and what gets rewarded, and over time may have an influence on the nature of organization culture.[51] The values, skills, and consistent support of senior management, along with the full contingent of line management, are critical for the effective adoption and implementation of global performance management and other HR management policies and practices.[52] MNCs that desire to follow necessary performance management processes to develop a global business culture of shared values and gain competitive advantage through the transfer of critical business capabilities across global business units will clearly need the ongoing support and commitment of senior and line management.

DOWNSTREAM: SENSITIVITY TO CROSS-CULTURAL DIFFERENCES

One of the biggest areas of concern in this duality challenge is the effective implementation of MNC strategy and goals, yet with appropriate sensitivity to national and especially local cross-cultural differences. The influence of a society's culture can be noted particularly within the context of the performance management process, deeply influencing the various communications inherent in performance management, including even the basic perception of what kind of performance really matters (for example, actual outcomes versus employee obedience and loyalty).[53] Cross-cultural differences pertinent to performance management and appraisal can come into play even within what initially might seem to be homogeneous regional markets and ethnic cultures.[54] For example, in one of our studies we examined management practice preferences related to performance management among national managers in Singapore, Hong Kong, and Taiwan. These three samples reflected a disposition toward a group focus of control rather than individual focus, suggesting that a performance management system designed to primarily measure teamwork rather than individual work performance might be more appropriate. Despite this similarity across these largely ethnic Chinese national cultures, we found significant differences among the three populations, especially between Hong Kong and the other two countries. For example, Hong Kong managers demonstrated less of a disposition toward participative management practices characterized by subordinate involvement in providing input and ideas. Also, Taiwanese managers accepted close supervision more than those in Hong Kong or Singapore. We concluded that MNC managers should be careful to *customize* the design of performance management and appraisal systems as a control mechanism in foreign operations, even within a region where countries are generally considered to be similar to one another culturally.[55] In addition, effective cross-cultural awareness training should be provided—for both expatriates and host country employees where appropriate—to increase the understanding of the complexities of cultural influence in the workplace and to help avoid unnecessary mistakes and conflict that may arise in the course of cross-cultural performance management.[56]

Particular dimensions of national culture that have been found to be very relevant in performance management include power distance, masculinity-femininity, communication context, collectivism-individualism, and orientation toward control.[57] These cultural dimensions should not be considered as independent and mutually exclusive because they frequently operate in concert with complex and surprising forms of influence on workplace behavior. It is also important to keep in mind that due to the increasing pluralism of national societies, national culture can provide only a broad, general picture that requires reexamination and adjustment at the local business unit level. In addition, a company's corporate culture and global management practices can eventually overcome initial local culture resistance, leading to a global standard for company performance management. However, this global alignment in performance management practices requires time and often an initial customization to fit local cultural expectations.[58] We now briefly examine each of these important dimensions as they relate to implementing performance management practices.

Power Distance

As described by Hofstede, the cultural dimension of power distance relates to perceptions that people in a society have about the distribution of power in their organizations and their society as a whole.[59] High power-distance cultures, such as Mexico, South Korea, France, and Malaysia, accept inequality and status differences as appropriate and strongly encourage the showing of respect and deference for superiors—even when superiors are in error. One U.S. executive who was heading up an international joint venture between Corning and Samsung once expressed that he had made an error to his South Korean subordinate manager, to which this subordinate manager replied, "No, you didn't make a mistake. You are the boss."[60] In some U.S. manufacturing plants on the Mexican side of the U.S.–Mexico border (known formerly as maquiladoras), sources of employee dissatisfaction have been described as U.S. expatriates' informal dress and friendly interactions with lower-level employees, who experienced this informal and egalitarian style at work as inappropriate for their cultural expectation of formality in dress and manner based on their difference in power and status. Mexican employees also found it uncomfortable to give upward feedback, even when solicited, to enhance a superior's performance, feeling that to do so would be disrespectful of the rightful elevated station and status of the superior.[61] It has also been found in some high power-distance cultures that managers who encourage high participation and consultation of subordinates in the performance management process, such as in setting performance objectives, may be perceived by their employees as incompetent.[62]

Thus, in high power-distance countries, it should be at least anticipated that there is a prevailing cultural preference for maintaining a respectful distance between manager and subordinate. The performance appraisal session itself would likely not be expected to be very open and interactive, such as in France. In lower power-distance countries, such as Germany, an interest in more interaction and mutual problem solving as part of the appraisal discussion would be expected.[63] And where upward feedback is needed, efforts could be made to encourage the indirect passing of input or corrective feedback to the manager—such as through a third party or by focusing on a concept in the abstract rather than in the context of contradicting or criticizing the superior. At the same time it should be clearly communicated how this upward feedback, provided with constructive intent, is a clear demonstration of loyalty and respect for the superior in supporting his or her performance objectives. Where constructive feedback is given to elders or those with long tenure in a company or other forms of high social status distinction, it is particularly important to show respect in written and oral communication, such as through the use of titles and a marked emphasis on decorum and politeness.[64]

Masculinity-Femininity

As discussed in Chapter 2, a masculine culture is basically a performance-driven society where achievement is recognized and rewarded. In these societies, successful people are expected to be competitive and ambitious and driven by performance goals. On the other hand, in feminine cultures people tend to emphasize the importance of supporting one another, and in providing ongoing nurturing and developmental support.[65] As we might expect, in high masculinity countries such as the United States we often see a strong preference for assessing bottom-line performance, and in holding individuals accountable for achieving their specific performance objectives. Especially in professional and managerial positions we often see versions of a management by objectives (MBO) approach, where employee performance is evaluated against specific goals related to organization objectives. Recognition and bonus rewards, which are often competitive, are clearly tied to desired measurable performance. In contrast, in countries high on the femininity scale we see more qualitative evaluations of individual performance in contributing to the whole job, including quality of interpersonal interaction, supportive and cooperative work relationships, and work climate. In high feminine cultures there also is an emphasis in the appraisal process upon supporting career development and professional progression.[66]

Communication Context

In some cultures, such as that in the United States and Germany, information conveyed in communication is very much limited to the meaning of the written or spoken words used, with little concern for the surrounding context. These low-context cultures can be contrasted with high-context cultures, such as Mexico, China, and Malaysia, where meaning is conveyed by additional nonverbal cues within the context of the communications besides the words themselves, including the status of who is speaking, how words are combined, the timing of the message, inflections used, body language, and past experience.[67] A comical situation often occurs in Mandarin-speaking countries when a foreigner, typically an English-speaking Westerner, is finishing a meal at a restaurant and tries to ask for the bill in Mandarin but, due to a slight difference in tonal inflection, is in reality asking for an egg.

Besides inflection, in some cultures the meaning of a given word depends on the nature of the surrounding context in which it is used. For example, there are many subtle "double meanings" of the Spanish language as spoken in Mexico, and a correct understanding of a message requires attention to the nature of the situation in which the words are used. Meaning that is relatively apparent to a Mexican may appear too subtle or hidden to an individual from the less context-sensitive United States, leading to a possible misunderstanding.[68] Context also comes into play in Mexico in terms of initial "small talk," or opening discussion about family or other personal interests. To the low-context German or American, these conversations seem unrelated to the message or business matter at hand and represent inefficiency. But to the high-context Mexican, they are very much related to the important, broader interpersonal relationship.[69]

Therefore, due to the strong influence of context sensitivity in communications, it should be considered carefully when planning and implementing performance management practices across cultures. For example, employees in a high-context culture, such as many Asian countries, might feel uncomfortable with the many communications of the performance management process when conducted on a low-context virtual basis over e-mail or telephone, where other important cues and sources of information in the larger context of the in-person encounter are unavailable.[70] Or these high-context employees might be particularly sensitive to nonverbal forms of communication and body language and put off by loud, direct oral communication or argumentative voices with exaggerated and excessive hand gestures.[71] Instead of using a manager's office for providing performance feedback for a high-context employee, a private but less formal and more socially comfortable location elsewhere over a cup of coffee or tea—which would reinforce a more personal and supportive relationship with the employee—might work better in terms of constructive impact on the employee.[72] To anticipate possible problems due to cross-cultural differences in sensitivity to context in communications as part of the performance management process, organizations should consider obtaining culturally experienced input to help guide the effective implementation of performance management.[73]

Collectivism-Individualism

This dimension describes how people within a particular culture prefer to relate to one another, from a high level of interdependence on one end of the cultural dimension to significant autonomy on the other.[74] Those in collectivistic societies prefer to be a part of a group or team and to encourage harmony and benefit for all. In the workplace, these individuals prefer to work on team projects and in group arrangements and to not be singled out for individual accomplishment. On the other hand, people in individualistic cultures prefer to work independently where possible and to be held accountable for their individual contributions to performance.[75] Where employees in individualistic cultures may feel comfortable with traditional Western performance appraisal approaches that focus feedback on and reward individual performance, employees in collectivistic cultures will likely prefer feedback on how their work group, with which they identify, performs (for example, team-based appraisals) as well as how they individually relate and contribute to the group and organization overall.

The self-appraisal method, often used as part of performance appraisal in Western countries, would likely not work in collectivistic cultures where self-recognition and praise could be viewed as self-serving, arrogant, and harmful to the harmony of the group.[76] Because of the strong emphasis in collectivist cultures on creating harmony and loyalty among people in the workplace, direct critical feedback on an individual's performance might feel like a personal attack or might seem inappropriate because it threatens group harmony, especially when the feedback is provided by someone perceived as an outsider.[77] And because an individual may strongly identify with a group, any direct criticism of that person might also disturb the harmony and represent a criticism of the person's group. In these situations it could be more productive to provide performance feedback to an employee indirectly through a third party who already has a strong relationship of trust with the employee.[78]

For the longer term, it would be beneficial for the manager to carefully build a personal relationship of trust and respect with the subordinate so that any forthcoming negative performance feedback would be perceived as coming from a member of the team who is interested in the welfare and success of the group.[79] As in many cultures, being polite and showing respect in collectivist cultures (especially in ways that would likely be interpreted as such) are important for gaining respect and trust and building a supportive rapport for effective performance management. Another way to build trust in collectivist cultures is for managers to organize events where they can have friendly and informal discussions with subordinates.[80]

A particular condition known as "vertical collectivism" may exist in cultures that are high in both collectivism and power distance, such as Malaysia, as shown in this chapter's opening scenario, and other Asian countries. In this cultural condition, one perceives him- or herself as part of a group while fully accepting the power and status inequalities within the group.[81] Here it is particularly important to develop a trusting, respectful relationship with those individuals with status in the group (for example, due to age and seniority within the group), which may then yield benefit due to their informal influence in managing the performance of other group members.[82]

Orientation Toward Control

Another important dimension of culture involves the degree to which individuals believe that as human beings they dominate or are in control of or can influence their external environment. On one extreme individuals may believe that they are in total control of their destiny—their future is what they make of it. On the other extreme individuals may regard themselves as dependent on supernatural forces within the universe, and any outcomes that affect them are generally out of their control and are due to predetermined fate or luck. For example, Filipino fatalism is illustrated by the phrase, *bahala na,* which in Tagalog means, "Accept what comes and bear it with hope and patience." And in Thailand, *mai pen rai* means, "Never mind; it is fate and you are not responsible."[83] Another version of this sense of being dominated by the external environment is the belief that nature represents a supernatural force within which we must try to fit harmoniously—greatly different from a traditionally high-control Western perspective that continuously advances technology to harness the powers of nature.[84] Other cultural orientations allow for a combination of these two extremes of who is in control, as illustrated by the German proverb, "Work as if everything depends upon you, then pray as if everything depends upon God." This combination can also be noted where people exert their personal control to optimize their outcomes determined by fate or luck, such as where businesspeople in Turkey often wear a blue-bead amulet for warding off bad luck, or in Hong Kong where feng shui consultants are utilized to show how office furniture can be rearranged to bring more luck to the business.[85]

This dimension is reflected at work in the performance management process in terms of where employees are on the control spectrum, ranging from the belief that they are personally in control of their job performance or that external factors are the major cause of their work performance outcomes. Although the performance management process is based on the fundamental assumption that employees must accept some degree of control and responsibility for their actions and performance outcomes,[86] there should still be an open discussion about what external factors might affect performance outcomes and should be considered in assessing and planning for improving an individual's work performance. In some cases such a discussion can be very enlightening for a manager whose control-oriented actions are repeatedly frustrated, and who would greatly benefit by exploring how his or her efforts can fit more harmoniously within existing intransigent social and institutional systems. Such a discussion can also potentially improve the validity of a performance evaluation by identifying and accounting for extraneous factors beyond the control of the employee that influence employee performance—a significant problem with many high-control Western performance appraisal efforts that create worker dissatisfaction by failing to account for the influence of extraneous factors.[87]

DOWNSTREAM: ESTABLISHMENT OF PERFORMANCE MANAGEMENT RELATIONSHIP

Key in the effective implementation of performance management is the establishment of a viable working relationship with the employee that is based on mutual trust and respect—regardless of differences in nationality, cultural background, age, gender, and other personal characteristics. This trust is developed through clearly setting role and work performance expectations on the part of both employee and supervisor and then following through with those expectations. The role of the supervisor is primarily one of resource provider, supporter, and facilitator of employee performance.

This relationship is also based on the clear recognition that the manager needs the employee and that the manager's success is dependent on the employee's successful performance, both in terms of the manager's ultimate responsibility for work unit performance and the ongoing need of employee feedback to enhance the manager's decision making and overall impact on the work unit.[88] An acknowledgment of this mutual dependence by both manager and employee is essential for the development of a healthy, respectful, and productive performance management relationship.

Finally, the performance management relationship should be based on mutual commitment to achieving performance goals and expectations and a willingness to use two-way communication—in a manner comfortable for both parties and especially to the subordinate to encourage upward feedback—to share perspectives and make inevitable adjustments for eventually achieving performance goals and expectations. Essential here is the manager's willingness to reasonably accommodate personal style and adopt appropriate behaviors that meet the employee's expectations and individual needs for encouraging optimal performance.[89]

DOWNSTREAM: COMPREHENSIVE TRAINING

Training for both manager and employee is essential for the performance management process to function effectively. All involved in the process need information about the purpose and importance of the various performance management activities.[90] Effective skills on assessing employee needs, performance coaching and giving effective feedback, active listening, goal setting, development planning, correction, planning and conducting performance appraisals, and other forms of communications—and often through a diverse cultural lens that can cause misunderstanding and lead to conflict—are not naturally in a manager's repertoire. These critical performance management skills require thoughtful development and refinement.[91] Employees themselves, as active participants and potentially valuable contributors in the process, could also benefit by developing skills in effective feedback solicitation and providing upward feedback, within a context of cultural fit and increased cross-cultural awareness, to minimize confusion and conflict and enhance the overall performance management process.[92]

Many aspects of culture as they affect organizational performance can be very subtle and complex, and we should be ready to adjust and revise our past learning. For example, countering the virtual stereotype of the importance of "saving face" for Asian cultures, field researchers in Vietnam noted that constructive negative feedback could be very effective when provided by a trusted, respected inside group member— whereas an "outsider" would have very different and less favorable reactions to this negative feedback.[93] Therefore, training should be provided with the caveat that we are all continually learning in the global marketplace, especially in the area of cross-cultural relations, and that present training only begins to provide tools and insights for effective application. As part of ongoing professional learning, there should be an individual commitment to continual reflection about international performance management experience to enhance and refine understanding of what contributes to success in various circumstances. And for productive organizational learning, experiences gained—both good and bad—in the course of implementing global performance management should become part of the MNC training agenda and shared throughout the MNC to promote effective global performance management practices.[94]

PLANNING AND IMPLEMENTING GLOBAL PERFORMANCE APPRAISALS

As mentioned earlier in describing the ongoing performance management process, an important phase is the periodic performance appraisal, often conducted in the context of a private interview between a manager and employee. On this more official and special occasion there is an opportunity to review past performance and, with ideally an unrestricted two-way exchange of information, to jointly plan for performance improvement or achieving new performance goals in the future. To enhance the positive motivational impact of the performance appraisal experience, it is critical that it be conducted as fairly and accurately as possible for optimal employee satisfaction.

This performance appraisal exchange also affords the opportunity for considering and planning for the longer-term career progression needs and interests of the employee.[95] Besides this important immediate and longer-term developmental aspect of performance appraisal, its results also often can be used to support administrative decision making that affects the employee's compensation and future staffing arrangements. A performance appraisal's support for administrative decision making can also collectively extend to the broader policy and practice level, such as in identifying common training needs to guide company-wide training plans, input for job redesign, and as a means for evaluating the predictive validity of selection methods (that is, the appraisal can serve to confirm whether a selection approach successfully identifies those who will turn out to be successful employees).[96] Therefore, to support these critical developmental and administrative purposes effectively, performance appraisals should be conducted in a fashion that maximizes both employee motivation and information accuracy.

Although there is evidence that a "best practices" convergence and standardization is taking place in performance appraisal among MNCs based in different countries and facing intense global competition,[97] there are still important points to keep in mind to ensure effective implementation that is responsive to local needs. In addition, pertinent appraisal implementation issues must be considered for particular global employee groups, such as expatriates, inpatriates, and third country nationals. We now examine these important considerations for the global implementation of performance appraisal.

SOURCES OF PERFORMANCE APPRAISAL INPUT

Although most performance appraisals use input primarily from the immediate supervisor for evaluating an employee's work performance, there is strong agreement that additional sources of input with different perspectives can improve the reliability and accuracy of the overall picture of employee performance, especially for developmental purposes.[98] An extreme version of the utilization of additional sources of input is *360-degree feedback* (that is, from multiple angles or perspectives; refer to Figure 9.4), which continues to be an interest among large MNCs for use globally.[99] With 360-degree feedback, those individuals who have relevant interaction with and opportunity to observe the employee in action, including the direct supervisor, subordinates (also called direct reports), fellow workplace peers, internal and external customers, and even the employee him- or herself, can provide input on the quality of his or her performance. Some organizations have reported problems with the use of 360-degree feedback, particularly with the challenge of dealing with so much data and little guidance on how to act on this information for improvement.[100] In fact,

Figure 9.4 **Sources of Performance Appraisal Input in the 360-Degree Feedback Approach**

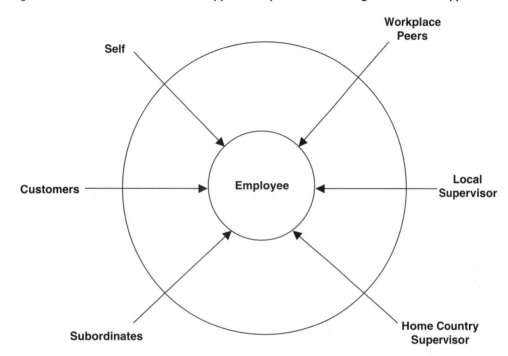

the indiscriminate faddish use of 360-degree feedback has likely led to a finding by the HR consulting firm Towers Watson, in its exhaustive survey of more than 750 MNCs in Europe and North America, that its use actually led to a loss in company productivity.[101] To effectively deal with the large amount of paperwork required by the 360-degree feedback process, several organizations have begun to use the Internet as an efficient means of collecting data from the numerous sources and using special software programs to assist in data analysis, particularly for developmental purposes, in a way that is perceived as meaningful and useful to the employee being appraised.[102] Ultimately, the particular sources used for providing input for performance appraisal should be determined based on the nature of the employee's work and purposes of the appraisal. We will now briefly examine the unique value of each of these input sources identified in Figure 9.4 for contributing to performance appraisal effectiveness.

Supervisor

The direct supervisor to whom the employee reports typically has significant information with which to evaluate the employee's performance. The supervisor is also responsible for the employee's performance and should therefore have a central role in the overall performance management process, including the appraisal. However, in some cases, such as with an expatriate working under a host country manager or an inpatriate working under a manager at company headquarters, there can be misunderstandings and resulting conflict between direct supervisor and employee due to cultural differences. Where the employee has a manager or mentor back at his or her home country who is distantly monitoring the person's performance, it is beneficial for the home country colleague to provide input to both the current direct supervisor and employee that considers and corrects for possible misperceptions.[103] For example, an American direct supervisor for a Panamanian employee working as an inpatriate at company headquarters in Boston might provide performance appraisal input stating that the employee is reluctant to give upward feedback and suggestions for process improvements and, therefore, is apparently not a team player. To help place this input in proper cultural perspective, however, the employee's back-home former direct manager might indicate that this reluctance is due to the employee's respect for the American manager's higher power role (that is, from a high power-distance perspective) and that to give suggestions for improvement would be a sign of disrespect and arrogance. This Panamanian manager might also at this point give suggestions to the American manager about how upward feedback can be effectively obtained within the cultural comfort zone of the Panamanian employee as this employee continues to adjust to the American culture.

Workplace Peers

Companies globally are increasingly using largely self-managing, cross-functional, and virtual team working arrangements where individuals spend much of their work performance outside of the view of a direct supervisor.[104] Therefore, input on the quality of employee performance can be very helpful to compensate for the lack of supervisor information. In addition, the various team members have a potentially useful and differing perspective from the supervisor in terms of their direct experience with the employee's performance and contributions as a team member. An emphasis on this source of input in the performance appraisal process might also be appropriate where employees hold high cultural values in collectivism.[105]

Customers

Both within and beyond our expanding global services sector, organizations increasingly compete for customers through enhanced effectiveness in customer satisfaction and responsiveness. Because this area of performance is being increasingly viewed as essential, many organizations are utilizing inputs from external customers, clients, suppliers, and others to evaluate the quality of the performance of employees who interact with them—especially when the service-providing employee is relatively removed from the supervisor or other employees.[106] The total quality and subsequent ISO 9000 and Six Sigma movements also have brought an interest in examining service quality to *internal* customers, such as those people or departments outside of an employee's work unit that he or she serves and interacts with within an organization.[107] Their inputs might be added and considered by a supervisor in making an overall appraisal of employee performance.

Subordinates

Several organizations have found the upward performance feedback from employees to be useful in evaluating a supervisor's performance, particularly for developmental purposes. Employees hold a unique firsthand perspective on the impact of the supervisor's behavior on their overall interest and ability to perform their job, and their input could be very valuable to a supervisor who is interested in enhancing that impact.[108] A common criticism of performance appraisal is the focus on individual performance at the neglect of attention to more integrated work systems and organizational processes.[109] Upward feedback from subordinates also represents a critical opportunity for the manager to consider other factors above the individual employee level and beyond employee control that can influence performance, such as work design processes or group dynamics. To ensure the quality of upward feedback, measures should be taken to increase employee perceptions that negative upward feedback will be held confidential and safe from retaliatory consequences, and that constructive ideas really can result in managerial and organizational improvements that benefit employees and the organization.[110] In addition, as discussed previously, in high power-distance cultures where employees are not accustomed to and feel uncomfortable with giving upward feedback regarding supervisor performance, less direct and informal means should be utilized to obtain this very important information.

Self

There is strong evidence that employee satisfaction with and perceived value of the performance appraisal experience is optimal when the employee participates in the process by completing a self-appraisal to be considered and used by the supervisor as relevant input. Primarily useful for developmental purposes, this source of input can also be very helpful as a discussion-fostering tool to open up communication between employee and supervisor to avoid misunderstanding.[111] A special caveat in using this source should be held for high collectivist and high power-distance cultures where employees might be especially reluctant to provide input on their outstanding accomplishments, because doing so might give the perception that they are arrogant and raising themselves above the level of the group—thus disrupting group harmony.[112] A gender effect might also apply, obscuring the overall accuracy of this source of input, as one study found that women, unlike men, tend to evaluate their performance lower than do their supervisors.[113]

FREQUENCY OF PERFORMANCE APPRAISAL

Although traditionally performed once a year, research suggests that more frequent performance appraisals tend to lead to enhanced performance, and an increasing number of global companies are conducting formal appraisals at least twice a year and on an informal basis much more frequently.[114] In addition to increased accuracy and timeliness of feedback for improving performance, frequent informal performance feedback sessions have been found to be a significant source of employee satisfaction in several different countries.[115] A cardinal rule regarding performance appraisals, although all too frequently ignored, is that they should feature no "surprises" (usually of the negative, disturbing variety giving the performance appraisal process a very bad image and one of dread among employees). Frequent informal feedback during the ongoing performance management process helps to avoid the destructive, demodulating consequences of these negative surprises.[116] In support of this notion of more frequent performance appraisals and informal feedback-sharing sessions is a study by Hewitt Associates of 437 companies. Its results demonstrated that those with regular, ongoing performance management systems as opposed to the once-a-year formal appraisal (or even less frequent) outperformed competitors without such systems on every productivity and financial measure employed in the study.[117]

CUSTOMIZATION OF PERFORMANCE APPRAISAL

Employee satisfaction and perceptions of fairness tend to be highest when procedures and forms used for performance appraisal are customized to the individuals and work situations involved.[118] There is some evidence that customization often happens naturally as standard performance appraisal methods are implemented locally, and this sensitivity and flexibility in meeting local needs appears to be an important factor in performance appraisal success.[119] A general rule to keep in mind is the more different a host country's environment is from that of the MNC's home country, the greater degree of modification is needed in the home country appraisal procedures and tools for host country application.[120] The meaningfulness and credibility of performance appraisals among employees are greatly enhanced when methods and criteria for evaluating performance are customized to fit the specific working situation. In addition, in some countries legal requirements are in place to ensure that performance appraisals accurately reflect what is required for specific jobs—a "one size fits all" global performance appraisal approach will not work.[121]

PERFORMANCE APPRAISAL FOR EXPATRIATES

As a special international employee, the expatriate often plays a pivotal and unique role in the success of the MNC's global operations. This unique role is often multifaceted and involves distinctive challenges and complexities that merit special considerations when planning and implementing fair and accurate performance appraisals for expatriates.[122] A neglect of these considerations can lead to significant dissatisfaction and perceptions of unfairness, possibly contributing to dissatisfaction, diminished productivity, and even eventual turnover.[123] We will now examine several of these important considerations for effective expatriate performance appraisal.

Awareness and Accuracy of Expatriate Assignment Purposes and Objectives

As discussed in Chapter 6 on global staffing, the expatriate assignment might have multiple purposes, including filling an international assignment that enhances MNC profitability, controlling foreign operations consistent with MNC objectives, developing local host country talent and expertise, contributing to MNC knowledge about foreign markets and global business issues and conditions, and promoting the valuable development of the individual expatriate. Therefore, where multiple roles and purposes of the expatriate are in play, the performance appraisal should also be designed to assess performance in those roles and purposes and not simply measure one convenient, easily measurable aspect such as foreign operation profitability under the expatriate's management. And especially in newer foreign operations where the

MNC has not had much history and experience, the performance objectives for that operation should be fairly tentative and flexible until a clear and accurate picture of reasonable performance expectations are obtained. One Mexican executive we interviewed in Tijuana indicated that by far the biggest reason that expatriates fail to reach performance expectations in Mexico is due not to their inability to adjust but to the faulty and unrealistic performance objectives they receive in the beginning from company headquarters.[124] Holding an expatriate accountable for unrealistic performance objectives can lead to significant frustration and dissatisfaction as well as destructive perceptions of lack of MNC support in the foreign assignment.

Rater Selection

Those who provide input for evaluating the performance of an expatriate should have a clear picture of how the expatriate has performed and the unique conditions involved. A self-assessment by the expatriate is strongly encouraged to provide a useful first-hand perspective and optimal involvement for a productive performance appraisal process.[125] Those working closely with the expatriate, such as subordinates, peers, and local supervisors, can also provide a valuable direct perspective on the expatriate's performance. In addition, those with accurate knowledge of the expatriate assignment (for example, previous expatriates assigned to the foreign operation at hand) as well as others from the expatriate's culture should be considered as raters to ensure that there is adequate input balance from those who are familiar with the unique working conditions and cross-cultural challenges associated with the particular expatriate assignment.[126] For example, an individual who is well familiar with the cross-cultural challenges and differences involved in an expatriate assignment might help provide a more accurate interpretation of an otherwise very negative expatriate performance evaluation from a local host country supervisor or group of subordinates.[127]

Balanced Use of Quantitative and Qualitative Criteria

Quantitative, or "hard," data related to expatriate performance (such as foreign subsidiary measures of productivity and profitability) are frequently used, often to the neglect of other important qualitative criteria. A major problem with the overreliance on financial data is a possible masking effect of rates of exchange and other extraneous influences that may lead to distorted performance interpretations. Other subjective and less readily measurable areas of expatriate performance, such as quality of relationship with host country subordinates and overall local workforce satisfaction, may represent important qualitative, or "soft," criteria to also consider and try to measure as part of an accurate overall appraisal effort.[128]

Sensitivity to Multiple Extraneous Environmental Variables

There can be many possible external environmental variables beyond the control of an expatriate, and these should be taken into consideration when preparing and conducting a fair and accurate appraisal of the expatriate's performance, including when the appraisal involves comparing one expatriate manager's performance with that of another in another foreign operation.[129] For example, an expatriate assigned to head up the operations of a new hotel in Hong Kong should not be held responsible for a huge drop in occupancy and profits following the predominantly East Asian outbreak of the SARS virus, which debilitated the entire regional tourism and travel industry. Nor should French expatriates in the United States be held accountable for any possible loss of business and sales due to U.S. national umbrage and calls by politicians and some of the popular media to boycott French products following that country's lack of support for the U.S.-led actions in Iraq.

Another important variable external to the expatriate assignment and beyond the expatriate's control might actually be brought about by the MNC in the determination of the expatriate assignment. In some cases the MNC might want to penetrate a particular market that faces strong traditional competition or provide a significant threat to a foreign competitor that would tie up its resources and distract its focus from other potentially more fruitful markets that the MNC would like to pursue unfettered by heavy competition. In both of these situations, especially in the short term, the profitability of the expatriate's foreign operation might be unusually low compared to other MNC expatriates, or even negative. However, in these cases the important role of the expatriate in promoting the larger picture of MNC profitability should take precedence.[130]

Local Conditions

Often referred to as "contextual criteria," local conditions typically involve factors in the local working environment of the expatriate assignment that can influence expatriate performance and measures thereof. Such contextual factors include local workforce demographics, worker satisfaction, amount and quality of local MNC resources and support for the expatriate, and cultural distance between expatriate and host country employees. In addition, the local context of the expatriate assignment, such as illustrated earlier with changing exchange rates in or different national policies regarding repatriation of earnings, can significantly influence measures of profitability. As with the many extraneous environmental factors mentioned previously, these local conditions should be considered when devising a fair and accurate expatriate performance appraisal.[131]

Timing and Distance Considerations

An important timing issue for new expatriates is when the performance appraisal takes place in the course of a fairly predictable international adjustment period where the expatriate is typically less productive while working under "culture shock" or adjustment to the new foreign environment and culture. Every new job or assignment, whether at home or abroad, has a "learning curve," where performance improves over time and experience on the job. And this learning curve should be considered when evaluating performance in the first six months or even first year of an expatriate assignment, especially in an assignment involving significant cultural distance or personal change and upheaval with a likely longer adjustment period.[132] Geographic distance also may present a challenge to performance appraisal timeliness and accuracy, where an expatriate's immediate manager is able to meet with the expatriate only on an infrequent basis and without the benefit of frequent informal, in-person coaching interactions. Although e-mail and telephone communications enable frequent interactions, these low-context modern communications technologies are not able to achieve the richness of in-person interviews and interactions. Therefore, where possible, more frequent contacts should be arranged between expatriates and their supervising corporate managers through brief visits to the host country site. In addition, local mentoring and coaching relationships should be established with experienced individuals (HCNs or other experienced expatriates) to provide ongoing feedback and support as part of an effective performance management process.[133]

PERFORMANCE APPRAISAL FOR INPATRIATES AND THIRD COUNTRY NATIONALS

There is a notable lack of research that examines particular needs and considerations for inpatriates and TCNs in planning and conducting effective performance appraisals. However, as has been noted, many of the principles and practices for expatriate selection and training also apply to foreign employees (typically HCNs) for their inpatriation assignments, as well as for the foreign assignments of TCNs.[134] As with expatriates, TCNs and inpatriates experience displacement into a new foreign workplace and culture for a significant period of time. And as with expatriates, there should be input in the overall performance appraisal process for TCNs and inpatriates by individuals who are aware of cross-cultural differences that might interfere with performance as well as influence in a negative way the performance evaluations of individuals from the predominant workplace culture.[135] However, the primary purpose of the inpatriation assignment is developmental—typically far more than for expatriates and TCNs—and to facilitate the development of the HCN in terms of global competencies and a mind-set that is in alignment with MNC strategy and culture. Therefore, the design and conduct of the inpatriate performance appraisal—as well as the entire performance management process—should reflect this priority.[136]

SUMMARY

Performance management at home and abroad is not just an annual or semiannual performance appraisal event but should be considered an ongoing process, beginning with a careful design of work and clear sharing of performance expectations followed by regular feedback. Effective performance management on a global scale involves linking individual employee performance to company priorities and strategies as well as being sensitive to cross-cultural differences and local conditions. It is important to be aware of general principles and practices of effective performance management and appraisal and to adapt these to the unique needs of PCN expatriates, local workforce HCNs, TCNs, and inpatriates to provide optimal support in their differing assignments.

QUESTIONS FOR OPENING SCENARIO ANALYSIS

1. What are some possible cross-cultural challenges associated with the nature of work communications in this scenario?

2. From your reading of this chapter, what are possible explanations for Yusoff's decision to request a transfer?

3. What recommendations do you have for modifying the practice of performance appraisal and ongoing performance management to take account of cross-cultural differences? What other suggestions do you have for improving the overall performance management process for this company that is developing globally?

CASE 9.1. OVERCOMING GENDER STEREOTYPING IN PERFORMANCE MANAGEMENT

Although over the past thirty years or so there has been a dramatic increase of women in the workforce, with more than 50 percent of all managers and professionals being female, women still comprise less than 2 percent of Fortune 1000 CEOs and just 7.9 percent of Fortune 500 top earners. A familiar list of reasons attempts to explain why this is so: Women are reluctant to put in the eighty-hour workweeks and globe-trotting required for a shot at the corner office; they are too concentrated in staff jobs like human resources or marketing, where they never learn crucial profit-and-loss responsibility; they don't have informal mentoring and networking opportunities, such as golfing with male power holders. But these explanations belie the basic truth demonstrated by countless surveys that there is little difference between the leadership styles of successful male and female bosses. A primary problem is that both genders still hold to unwarranted stereotypes. This problem was pointed out in a new study of 296 top executives by Catalyst, the New York research group. To their credit, men said both men and women were roughly equal when it came to team building, mentoring, consulting, and networking. They even gave women higher marks on two qualities: supporting and rewarding. But in a disturbing find, men said they were superior to women on the four critical leadership skills of problem solving, inspiring, delegating, and "influencing upward," or being able to have an impact on the people above you. Yet Catalyst's study found that women are giving up important ground. Women said they are better at supporting and rewarding employees and at the important tasks of problem solving, team building, mentoring, consulting, and inspiring. But they also said men are better at networking, influencing upward, and delegating.

"Women as well as men perceive women leaders as better at *caretaker* behaviors and men as better at *take-charge* behaviors," according to Ilene Lang, president of Catalyst. "These are perceptions, not the reality." But perceptions strongly influence reality. Sex-role stereotypes clearly influence employee performance ratings. After analyzing past reviews of managers, one company found that women who weren't considered "supportive" mentors received negative ratings, while nonsupportive men weren't judged negatively. "Men aren't expected to be supportive, so they're not criticized when they aren't," says Ms. Lang. It isn't surprising that women are rated as more effective leaders when they work in so-called feminine occupations, such as cosmetics or fashion companies, than when they are employed in a traditionally masculine industry such as steel. Respondents in Catalyst's study who had a female boss in a feminine occupation were likely to judge women as better problem solvers than men; but those with a female boss in a masculine occupation expressed profoundly negative views of women leaders. Therefore, simply hiring more women into management positions isn't likely to eliminate stereotyping. Catalyst advises companies to combat stereotyping by making sure men and women are judged equally on performance reviews, and educating managers of both genders about the often unconscious influence of stereotyping.

Adapted from C. Hymowitz, "Too Many Women Fall for Stereotypes of Selves, Study Says," *Wall Street Journal,* October 24, 2005, Eastern Edition: B.1.

QUESTIONS FOR CASE ANALYSIS AND DISCUSSION

1. How are these unfounded gender stereotypes detrimental to an organization's ongoing competitive performance?
2. How can gender stereotypes influence a manager's various performance management activities and decisions?
3. The context of the research examined here is within large Western organizations. What possible additional culturally based challenges might exist for countering such gender stereotypes in developing countries?

CASE 9.2. CUSTOMIZING HCN PERFORMANCE APPRAISAL DESIGN

Mr. Kukka Kaitila is a Finnish senior HR manager for Kalmar, a multinational firm based in Helsinki, Finland. Kalmar is a global provider of heavy-duty materials-handling equipment (such as cranes and forklifts) to ports, terminals, and other industrial customers. Kalmar claims that every fourth container or trailer transfer at terminals around the world is handled by a Kalmar machine. With plans for significant global business growth, the company presently is planning to expand its manufacturing operations to San José, Costa Rica.

In his responsibilities of HR planning to support this particular international business expansion, Kukka is considering the most appropriate work design arrangements for the future Costa Rican employees as well as performance management and appraisal practices that will help implement company local performance objectives. With particular regard to performance appraisal, Kukka realized the importance of local customization, or designing the performance appraisal practices to fit the needs of the HCNs at the future Costa Rican operation. He also knew that no matter how carefully he planned for these appraisal practices and procedures, there would always need to be, after initial implementation, an opportunity for employee feedback and review of effectiveness of the plans he made, followed by appropriate adjustments. But despite an inevitable need to make revisions, the more work in thought and planning he would put in up front would likely mean less revision and refinement after implementation. Once he completed his initial plans, he decided he would contact some HR professionals in Costa Rican companies, through his International Society of Human Resource Management directory, to get their experienced feedback.

In reviewing information that he had found online about the Costa Rican labor force from which Kalmar would recruit to staff much of its new operation, Kukka was impressed by their profile. Approximately 96 percent of the population is literate—one of the highest rates in Latin America—with an ongoing significant investment by the local government in education and technology. Consistent with other Latin American cultures, Costa Ricans are quite high in Hofstede's dimensions of uncertainty avoidance and collectivism (low individualism). But unlike those in other Latin American countries, and particularly Mexico, the Costa Ricans rank high in femininity on Hofstede's masculinity-femininity dimension and low in power distance. Because much of the initial management and supervisory positions of the new Costa Rica plant would be staffed by TCNs from their established facility in Manzanillo, Mexico, Kukka considered this comparison with Mexican culture as potentially an important challenge to remain aware of in plans for ensuring future effective performance management.

QUESTIONS FOR CASE ANALYSIS AND DISCUSSION

1. Based on the information that Kukka was considering, what are some general performance management practices that likely would fit well with Costa Rican HCNs?
2. What particular plans for Costa Rican performance appraisal likely would work well (for example, how appraisal is conducted, who provides performance feedback, team versus individual performance focus, emphasis on development versus achievement, and so on)?
3. What are possible forms of future cross-cultural conflict in the performance management process between Costa Rican HCNs and their Mexican supervisors and managers? What plans should be considered to help minimize this potential for cross-cultural conflict?

RECOMMENDED WEB SITE RESOURCES

ADI (http://aubreydaniels.com/). Provides extensive general training, practical articles and reports, and customized consulting services on a global basis related to performance management and executive coaching.

International Journal of Business Performance Management (www.inderscience.com, use journal locater). Examines both hard and soft perspectives in promoting and coordinating the practice of business performance management in both corporate and public organizations, and with a strong emphasis on international dimensions. Of interest to management practitioners, college faculty, and organization researchers.

International Journal of Productivity and Performance Management (http://juno.emeraldinsight.com, search for journal in publisher products). Addresses new developments and thinking in productivity science and performance management across manufacturing, service, and public sector organizations, including new techniques, approaches and related reflective analysis designed to improve individual, group, and organizational performance.

International Society for Performance Improvement (www.ispi.org). International association dedicated to improving productivity and performance in the workplace, with more than ten thousand international and chapter members throughout the United States, Canada, and forty other countries. Sponsors conferences and educational events, research, and books and periodicals.

McLagan International (www.mclaganint.com). A virtual network of experienced professionals, assembling on a project basis to meet unique client needs in performance and change management as well as general human resource practices.

NOTES

1. Adapted from J. Milliman, S. Taylor, and A.J. Czaplewski, "Cross-Cultural Performance Feedback in Multinational Enterprises: Opportunity for Organizational Learning," *HR Planning* 25 (3) (2002): 29–43.

2. G. Becker and B. Gerhart, "The Impact of Human Resource Management on Organizational Performance: Program and Prospects," *Academy of Management Journal* 39 (4) (1996): 779–801; M. Huselid, "The Impact of Human Resource Management Practices on Turnover, Productivity, and Corporate Financial Performance," *Academy of Management Journal* 38 (3) (1995): 635–72; M. Huselid, S. Jenkins, and R. Schuler, "Technical and Strategic Human Resource Effectiveness as Determinants of Firm Performance," *Academy of Management Journal* 40 (1997): 171–88; P. Sparrow and J.M. Hiltrop, *European Human Resource Management in Transition* (New York: Prentice-Hall, 1994).

3. L. Claus and M.L. Hand, "Customization Decisions Regarding Performance Management Systems of Multinational Companies: An Empirical View of Eastern European Firms," *International Journal of Cross Cultural Management* 9 (2) (2009): 237–58; C.M. Vance, S.R. McClaine, D.M. Boje, and H.D. Stage, "An Examination of the Transferability of Traditional Performance Appraisal Principles across Cultural Boundaries," *Management International Review* 32 (4) (1992): 313–26.

4. D. Waldman and R. Kenett, "Improve Performance by Appraisals," *HR Magazine* (July 1990): 60–69; W.P. Anthony, K.M. Kacmar, and P.L. Perrewé, *Human Resource Management: A Strategic Approach,* 4th ed. (New York: South-Western, 2002).

5. C.D. Fisher, L.F. Schoenfeldt, and J.B. Shaw, *Human Resource Management,* 5th ed. (Boston: Houghton-Mifflin, 2003).

6. L. Claus, "Employee Performance Management in MNCs: Reconciling the Need for Global Integration and Local Responsiveness," *European Journal of International Management* 2 (2) (2008): 132–52; R. Lunnan, J.E. Lervik, L.E. Traavik, S.M. Nilsen, R.P. Amdam, and B.W. Hennestad, "Cultural Counterpoints: Global Transfer of Management Practices across Nations and MNC Subcultures," *Academy of Management Executive* 19 (2) (2005): 77–80; Y. Paik, C.M. Vance, and H.D. Stage, "A Test of Assumed Cluster Homogeneity for Performance Appraisal Management in Four Southeast Asian Countries," *International Journal of Human Resource Management* 11 (4) (2000): 736–50.

7. L. Claus and D. Briscoe, "Employee Performance Management Across Borders: A Review of Relevant Academic Literature," *International Journal of Management Reviews* 11 (2): 175–96; R. Bacal, *Performance Management* (New York: McGraw-Hill, 1999).

8. S. Taylor, S. Beechler, and N. Napier, "Toward an Integrative Model of Strategic International Human Resource Management," *Academy of Management Review* 21 (4) (1996): 959–85; G. Becker and B. Gerhart, "The Impact of Human Resource Management on Organizational Performance: Program and Prospects," *Academy of Management Journal* 39 (4) (1996): 779–801; M. Huselid, S. Jenkins, and R. Schuler, "Technical and Strategic Human Resource Effectiveness as Determinants of Firm Performance," *Academy of Management Journal* 40 (1997): 171–88; D. Welch, "HRM Implications of Globalization," *Journal of General Management* 19 (4) (1994): 52–68.

9. J. Pfeffer, "Low Grades for Performance Reviews," *Business Week,* August 3, 2009.

10. N. Lindholm, "National Culture and Performance Management in MNC Subsidiaries," *International Studies of Management and Organization* 29 (4) (1999/2000): 45–66.

11. C.M. Solomon, "How Does Your Global Talent Measure Up?" *Personnel Journal* 73 (10) (1994): 96–108.

12. M.R. Carrell, N.F. Elbert, and R.D. Hatfield, *Human Resource Management: Strategies for Managing a Diverse and Global Workforce,* 6th ed. (Forth Worth, TX: Dryden Press, 2000); G. Dessler, *Human Resource Management,* 9th ed. (Upper Saddle River, NJ: Prentice-Hall, 2003).

13. F.F. Fournies, *Coaching for Improved Work Performance,* rev. ed. (New York: McGraw-Hill, 2000); Carrell et al., *Human Resource Management.*

14. N. Lindholm, "National Culture and Performance Management in MNC Subsidiaries"; T.D. Ludwig and E.S. Geller, "Assigned versus Participative Goal Setting and Response Generalization: Managing Inquiry Control among Professional Pizza Deliverers," *Journal of Applied Psychology* 82 (2) (1997): 253–61; E.A. Locke and G.P. Latham, *A Theory of Goal Setting and Task Performance* (Englewood Cliffs, NJ: Prentice-Hall, 1990); A.J. Mento, R.P. Steel, and R.J. Karren, "A Meta-Analytic Study of the Effects of Goal Setting on Performance: 1966–1984," *Organizational Behavior and Human Decision Processes* 39 (1987): 52–83.

15. Bacal, *Performance Management.*

16. J. Selmer, "Expatriation: Corporate Policy, Personal Intentions, and International Adjustment," *International Journal of Human Resource Management* 9 (6) (1998): 996–1007; J.J. Martocchio and J. Dulebohn, "Performance Feedback Efforts in Training: The Role of Perceived Controllability," *Personnel Psychology* 47 (2) (1994): 357–73; C.C. Manz and C.P. Neck, "Inner Leadership: Creating Productive Thought Patterns," *Academy of Management Executive* 5 (3) (1991): 87–95.

17. D. Eden and A.B. Shani, "Pygmalion Goes to Boot Camp: Expectancy, Leadership, and Trainee Performance," *Journal of Applied Psychology* 67 (1982): 194–99.

18. H. Levinson, "A Psychologist Looks at Executive Development," *Harvard Business Review* (November/December 1962): 69–75.

19. J.P. Kohl and D.B. Stephens, "Is Demotion a Four-Letter Word?" *Business Horizons* 33 (2) (1990): 74–76; Carrell et al., *Human Resource Management.*

20. T. Shimizu and L. Wozniak, "Termination of Employment in Asia," *Benefits and Compensation International* 32 (4) (2002): 16–22; G.L. Maatman, Jr., ed., *Worldwide Guide to Termination, Employment Discrimination, and Workplace Harassment Laws* (Riverwoods, IL: CCH/Baker and McKenzie, 2000).

21. R.A. Kagan and L. Axelrod, eds., *Regulatory Encounters: Multinational Corporations and American Adversarial Legalism* (Berkeley: University of California Press, 2000).

22. R.C. Nowlin, "Do Managers Mentor Problem Employees?" *Security Management* 47 (1) (2003): 119–20.

23. W.F. Cascio, *Managing Human Resources: Productivity, Quality of Work Life, Profits,* 6th ed. (New York: McGraw-Hill/Irwin, 2003).

24. M.A. Sashkin, *Manager's Guide to Performance Management* (New York: Amacom Book Division, 1986).

25. C.J. Shinkman, "Performance Appraisal: A Positive Approach," *AFP Exchange* 21 (2) (2001): 78–80; D. Davies, R. Taylor, and L. Savery, "The Role of Appraisal, Remuneration and Training in Improving Staff Relations in the Western Australian Accommodation Industry: A Comparative Study," *Journal of European Industrial Training* 25 (6/7) (2001): 366–73; C.F. Fey and I. Bjorkman, "The Effect of Human Resource Management Practices on MNC Subsidiary Performance in Russia," *Journal of International Business Studies* 32 (1) (2001): 59–75; M. Buckingham and C. Coffman, *First, Break All the Rules: What the World's Greatest Managers Do Differently* (New York: Simon & Schuster, 1999).

26. Y. Baruch, "Integrated Career Systems for the 2000s," *International Journal of Manpower* 20 (7) (1999): 432–57.

27. Dessler, *Human Resource Management.*

28. E.A. Grant, "How to Retain Talent in India," *Sloan Management Review* 50 (1) 2008: 6–7; B.S. Reiche, "The Effect of International Staffing Practices on Subsidiary Staff Retention in Multinational Corporations," *International Journal of Human Resource Management* 18 (4) (2007): 523–36; Lindholm, "National Culture and Performance Management in MNC Subsidiaries"; E. Snape, D. Thompson, Y.F. Ka-Ching, and T. Redman, "Performance Appraisal and Culture: Practice and Attitudes in Hong Kong and Britain," *International Journal of Human Resource Management* 9 (5) (1998): 841–61.

29. E. Logger and R. Vinke, "Compensation and Appraisal of International Staff," in *International Human Resource Management,* ed. A. Harzing and J.V. Ruysseveldt (London: Sage, 1995): 252–69; J.N. Cleveland, K.R. Murphy, and R.E. Williams, "Multiple Uses of Performance Appraisal: Prevalence and Correlates," *Journal of Applied Psychology* 74 (1989): 130–35.

30. R.S. Williams, *Managing Employee Performance: Design and Implementation in Organizations* (Stamford, CT: Thomson Learning, 2002); H. Risher, "Pay-for-Performance: The Keys to Making It Work," *Public Personnel Management* 31 (3) (2002): 317–32; Cleveland et al., "Multiple Uses of Performance Appraisal"; C. Mabey and G. Salaman, *Strategic Human Resource Management* (Oxford: Blackwell, 1995); Cascio, *Managing Human Resources: Productivity, Quality of Work Life, Profits,* 436–37.

31. Claus, "Employee Performance Management in MNCs: Reconciling the Need for Global Integration and Local Responsiveness."

32. C.M. Vance, "Strategic Upstream and Downstream Considerations for Effective Global Performance Management," *International Journal of Cross Cultural Management* 6 (1) (2006): 37–56; P. Evans, V. Pucik, and J.-L. Barsoux, *The Global Challenge: Frameworks for International Human Resource Management* (Boston: McGraw-Hill/Irwin, 2002): see especially pages 110–11, 330–35.

33. M.B. Stanek, "The Need for Global Managers: A Business Necessity," *Management Decision* 38 (4) (2000): 232–42; C.M. Vance and Y. Paik, "Toward a Taxonomy of Host Country National Learning Process Involvement in Multinational Learning Organizations" (paper presented at the Annual Meeting of the Academy of Management Washington, DC, August 2001).

34. Claus and Hand, "Customization Decisions Regarding Performance Management Systems of Multinational Companies: An Empirical View of Eastern European Firms"; R. McAdam and D. McCormack, "Integrating Business Processes for Global Alignment and Supply Chain Management," *Business Process Management Journal* 7 (2) (2001): 113–30.

35. P. Evans, V. Pucik, and J.-L. Barsoux, *The Global Challenge: Frameworks for International Human Resource Management* (Boston: McGraw-Hill/Irwin, 2002): 346.

36. H.P. Conn and G.S. Yip, "Global Transfer of Critical Capabilities," *Business Horizons* 40 (1) (1997): 22–31; G. Hamel and C.K. Prahalad, *Competing for the Future* (Boston: Harvard Business School Publishing, 1994); C.K. Prahalad and G. Hamel, "The Core Competence of the Corporation," *Harvard Business Review* (May/June 1990): 79–91; J.A. Petrick, R.F. Scherer, J.D. Brodzinski, J.F. Quinn, and M.F. Ainina, "Global Leadership Skills and Reputational Capital: Intangible Resources for Sustainable Competitive Advantage," *Academy of Management Executive* 13 (1) (1999): 58–69; S. Taylor, S. Beechler, and N. Napier, "Toward an Integrative Model of Strategic International Human Resource Management," *Academy of Management Review* 21 (4) (1996): 959–85.

37. A.K. Gupta and V. Govindarajan, "Cultivating a Global Mindset," *Academy of Management Executive* 16 (1) (2002): 116–26; M.E. Mendenhall, T.M. Kühlmann, and G.K. Stahl, eds., *Developing Global Business Leaders: Policies, Processes, and Innovation* (Westport, CT: Quorum Books, 2001); M.J. Marquard and L. Horvath, *Global Teams* (Palo Alto, CA: Davies-Black, 2001); H.B. Gregersen, A.J. Morrison, and J.S. Black, "Developing Leaders for the Global Frontier," *Sloan Management Review* 40 (1) (1998): 21–32.

38. R.W. Rowden, "The Strategic Role of Human Resource Management in Developing a Global Corporate Culture," *International Journal of Management* 19 (2) (2002): 155–60; K.C. Rallapalli, "A Paradigm for Development and Promulgation of a Global Code of Marketing Ethics," *Journal of Business Ethics* 18 (1) (1999): 125–37.

39. A. Lam, "Organizational Learning in Multinationals: R and D Networks of Japanese and U.S. MNCs in the U.K.," *Journal of Management Studies* 40 (3) (2003): 673–703; K. Uhlenbruck, K.E. Meyer, and M.A. Hitt, "Organizational Transformation in Transition Economies: Resource-Based and Organizational Learning Perspectives," *Journal of Management Studies* 40 (2) (2003): 257–82; M.E. Laiken, "Models of Organizational Learning: Paradoxes and Best Practices in the Post Industrial Workplace," *Organization Development Journal* 12 (1) (2003): 8–19; G. Huber, "Organizational Learning: The Contributing Processes and the Literatures," *Organizational Science* 2 (1) (1991): 88–115.

40. C. Martin-Rios and N.L. Erhardt, "Organisational Knowledge Transfer through Human Resource Management: International Diffusion of Managerial Performance Management," *European Journal of International Management* 2 (2) (2008): 170–91; M. Downes and A.S. Thomas, "Knowledge Transfer through Expatriation: The U-Curve Approach to Overseas Staffing," *Journal of Managerial Issues* 12 (2002): 131–49; R. Bhagat, B. Kedia, P. Harveston, and H. Triandis, "Cultural Variations in the Cross-Border Transfer of Organizational Knowledge: An Integrative Framework," *Academy of Management Review* 27 (2) (2002): 204–21.

41. Milliman et al., "Cross-Cultural Performance Feedback in Multinational Enterprises: Opportunity for Organizational Learning."

42. C.M. Vance, Y. Paik, and E.A. Ensher, "The Voice of the Host Country Workforce: A Key Source for Improving the Effectiveness of Expatriate Training and Performance," *International Journal of Intercultural Relations* 26 (4) (2002): 447–61; Y. Paik, C.M. Vance, J. Gale, and C.A. McGrath, "Improving Global Knowledge Management through Inclusion of Host Country Workforce Input," in *Strategic Knowledge Management in Multinational Organizations,* ed. K.J. O'Sullivan (Hershey, PA: Information Science Reference, 2007): 167–82.

43. Claus, "Employee Performance Management in MNCs"; M. Festing and C. Barzantny, "A Comparative Approach to Performance Management in France and Germany: The Impact of the European and the Country-Specific Environment," *European Journal of International Management* 2 (2) (2008): 208–27; C.A. Bartlett and S. Ghoshal, *Managing across Borders: The Transnational Solution,* 2d ed. (Boston: Harvard Business School Publishing, 2002).

44. B. Kane and I. Palmer, "Strategic HRM or Managing the Employment Relationship?" *International Journal of Manpower* 16 (5/6) (1995): 6–21.

45. D.E. Terpstra and E.J. Rozell, "The Relationship of Staffing Practices to Organizational Level Measures of Performance," *Personnel Psychology* 46 (1) (1993): 27–48; C.D. Fisher and J.B. Shaw, "Establishment Level Correlates of Human Resource Practices," *Asia Pacific Journal of Human Resources* 30 (4) (1992): 30–46.

46. S.E. Jackson, R.S. Schuler, and J.C. Rivero, "Organizational Characteristics as Predictors of Personnel Practices," *Personnel Psychology* 42 (4) (1989): 727–86.

47. J. Martin, *Organizational Culture* (Newbury Park, CA: Sage, 2001); E.H. Schein, *Organizational Culture and Leadership,* 2d ed. (San Francisco: Jossey-Bass, 1992).

48. G.T. Milkovich and M. Bloom, "Rethinking International Compensation," *Compensation and Benefits Review* 30 (1) (1998): 15–23.

49. V. Pothukuchi, F. Damanpour, J. Choi, C.C. Chen, and S.H. Park, "National and Organizational Culture Differences and International Joint Venture Performance," *Journal of International Business Studies* 33 (2) (2002): 243–65.

50. R. Freedman, "Creating Global Leaders," *Chief Executive* 189 (June 2003): 20; M.A. Carpenter, W.G. Sanders, and H.G. Gregersen, "Bundling Human Capital with Organizational Context: The Impact of International Assignment Experience on Multinational Firm Performance and CEO Pay," *Academy of Management Journal* 44 (3) (2001): 493–511; P. Caligiuri, "Global Competence: What Is It, and Can It Be Developed through Global Assignments?" *HR Planning* 24 (3) (2001): 27–35; R.L. Tung, "Strategic Management of Human Resources in the Multinational Enterprise," *Human Resource Management* 23 (2) (1984): 129–42.

51. Schein, *Organizational Culture and Leadership.*

52. R. Kramar, "Strategic Human Resource Management: Are the Promises Fulfilled?" *Asia Pacific Journal of Human Resources* 30 (1) (1992): 1–15; R.D. Lansbury, "Managing Change in a Challenging Environment," *Asia Pacific Journal of Human Resources* 30 (1) (1992): 16–28; P.F. Buller, "Successful Partnerships: HR and Strategic Planning at Eight Top Firms," *Organizational Dynamics* 17 (2) (1988): 27–43; A.S. Tsui and G.T. Milkovich, "Personnel Department Activities: Constituency Perspectives and Preferences," *Personnel Psychology* 40 (3) (1987): 519–37.

53. Milliman et al., "Cross-Cultural Performance Feedback in Multinational Enterprises: Opportunity for Organizational Learning"; M.F.S. De Luque and S.M. Sommer, "The Impact of Culture on

Feedback-Seeking Behavior: An Integrated Model and Propositions," *Academy of Management Review* 25 (4) (2000): 829–49; P.S. Hempel, "Differences Between Chinese and Western Managerial Views of Performance," *Personnel Review* 30 (2) (2001): 203–26.

54. Y. Paik, C.M. Vance, and H.D. Stage, "A Test of Assumed Cluster Homogeneity for Performance Appraisal Management in Four Southeast Asian Countries," *International Journal of Human Resource Management* 11 (4) (2000): 736–50; Y. Paik, C.M. Vance, and H.D. Stage, "The Extent of Divergence in Human Resource Practice across Three Chinese National Cultures: Hong Kong, Taiwan and Singapore," *Human Resource Management Journal* 6 (2) (1996): 20–31.

55. Paik, Vance, and Stage, "The Extent of Divergence in Human Resource Practice."

56. C.M. Vance and Y. Paik, "One Size Fits All in Expatriate Pre-Departure Training? Comparing the Host Country Voices of Mexican, Indonesian and U.S. Workers," *Journal of Management Development* 21 (7) (2002): 557–71; C.M. Vance and Y. Paik, "Toward a Taxonomy of Host Country National Learning Process Involvement in Multinational Learning Organizations" (paper presented at the Annual Meeting of the Academy of Management Washington, DC, August 2001); J.R. Schermerhorn and M.H. Bond, "Cross-Cultural Leadership Dynamics in Collectivism and High Power Distance Settings," *Leadership and Organization Development Journal* 18 (4) (1997): 187–93.

57. Claus and Hand, "Customization Decisions Regarding Performance Management Systems of Multinational Companies"; M. Festing and C. Barzantny, "A Comparative Approach to Performance Management in France and Germany: The Impact of the European and the Country-Specific Environment," *European Journal of International Management,* 2 (2) (2008): 208–27; J. Milliman, S. Nason, E. Gallagher, P. Huo, M.A. Von Glinow, and K.B. Low, "The Impact of National Culture on Human Resource Practices: The Case for Performance Appraisal," *Advances in International Comparative Management* 12 (1998): 157–83.

58. Lunnan et al., "Cultural Counterpoints: Global Transfer of Management Practices across Nations and MNC Subcultures."

59. G. Hofstede, *Culture's Consequences: International Differences in Work-Related Values* (Newbury Park, CA: Sage, 1980); G. Hofstede, "Motivation, Leadership and Organization: Do American Theories Apply Abroad?" *Organizational Dynamics* 9 (1) (1980): 42–63.

60. Noted in *Forging the International Partnership* (Boulder, CO: David Grubin Productions, Inc., 1995).

61. J. Sargent and L. Matthews, "Expatriate Reduction and Mariachi Circle: Trends in MNC Human-Resource Practices in Mexico," *International Studies of Management and Organization* 28 (2) (1998): 74–96.

62. M. Mendonca and R.N. Kanungo, "Managing Human Resources: The Issue of Cultural Fit," *Journal of Management Inquiry* 3 (2) (1994): 189–205.

63. M. Festing and C. Barzantny, "A Comparative Approach to Performance Management in France and Germany."

64. A. Abdullah, "Influence of Ethnic Values at the Malaysian Workplace," in *Understanding the Malaysian Workforce: Guidelines for Managers,* ed. A. Abdullah and A.H.M. Low (Kuala Lumpur: Malaysian Institute of Management, 2001): 1–24; P. Shepard, "Working with Malaysians and Americans: Expatriates and Malaysian Perspectives," in *Understanding the Malaysian Workforce: Guidelines for Managers,* 165–78.

65. G. Hofstede, *Culture's Consequences: International Differences in Work-Related Values* (Beverly Hills, CA: Sage, 1984).

66. Festing and Barzantny, "A Comparative Approach to Performance Management in France and Germany."

67. E.T. Hall and M.R. Hall, *Understanding Cultural Differences: Germans, French, and Americans* (Yarmouth, ME: Intercultural Press, 1990); E.T. Hall, *Beyond Culture* (New York: Doubleday/ Anchor, 1977).

68. C. Greer and G. Stephens, "Employee Relations Issues in U.S. Companies in Mexico," *California Management Review* 38 (3) (1996): 121–37.

69. G. Stephens and C. Greer, "Doing Business in Mexico: Understanding Cultural Differences," *Organizational Dynamics* 24 (1) (1995): 39–55.

70. V. Van Tuan and N. Napier, "Paradoxes in Vietnam and America: 'Lessons earned'—Part II," *HR Planning* 23 (2) (2000): 9–10.

71. A. Abdullah and E. Gallagher, "Managing with Cultural Differences," *Malaysian Management Review* 30 (2) (1995): 1–18.

72. A. Abdullah, F. Elashmawi, and P.R. Harris, *Multicultural Management: New Skills for Global Success* (Houston: Gulf, 2001).

73. C.M. Vance, Y. Paik, and E.A. Ensher, "The Voice of the Host Country Workforce: A Key Source for Improving the Effectiveness of Expatriate Training and Performance," *International Journal of Intercultural Relations* 26 (4) (2002): 447–61.

74. M. J. Gelfand and A. Realo, "Individualism-Collectivism and Accountability in Intergroup Negotiations," *Journal of Applied Psychology* 84 (5) (1999): 721–36; F. Trompenaars and C.Hampden-Turner, *Riding the Waves of Culture: Understanding Cultural Diversity in Business,* 2d ed. (London: Nicholas Brealey, 1997) Hofstede, *Culture's Consequences: International Differences in Work-Related Values.*

75. Milliman et al., "Cross-Cultural Performance Feedback in Multinational Enterprises."

76. S. Singh, "Managing Meetings," in *Understanding the Malaysian Workforce: Guidelines for Managers,* 137–52.

77. Singh, "Managing Meetings"; P. Shepard "Working with Malaysians and Americans: Expatriates and Malaysian Perspectives" (2001): 165–78; V. Van Tuan and N. Napier, "Paradoxes in Vietnam and America: 'Lessons Earned'—Part I," *HR Planning* 23 (1) (2000): 7–8.

78. J. Wallach and G. Metcalf, *Working with Americans* (New York: McGraw-Hill, 1995); Abdullah, "Influence of Ethnic Values at the Malaysian Workplace"; Milliman et al., "Cross-Cultural Performance Feedback in Multinational Enterprises."

79. Singh, "Managing Meetings"; Shepard, "Working with Malaysians and Americans: Expatriates and Malaysian Perspectives."

80. Shepard, "Working with Malaysians and Americans: Expatriates and Malaysian Perspectives"; Abdullah, "Influence of Ethnic Values at the Malaysian Workplace."

81. H.C. Triandis and M.J. Gelfand, "Converging Measurement of Horizontal and Vertical Individualism and Collectivism," *Journal of Personality and Social Psychology* 74 (1) (1998): 118–28; T.M. Singelis, H.C. Triandis, D.S. Bhawuk, and M.J. Gelfand, "Horizontal and Vertical Dimensions of Individualism and Collectivism: a Theoretical and Measurement Refinement," *Cross-Cultural Research* 29 (1995): 240–75.

82. J.R. Schermerhorn and M.H. Bond, "Cross-Cultural Leadership Dynamics in Collectivism and High Power Distance Settings," *Leadership and Organization Development Journal* 18 (4) (1997): 187–93.

83. I. Varner and L. Beamer, *Intercultural Communication in the Global Workplace* (Chicago: Irwin, 1995).

84. G.P. Ferraro, *The Cultural Dimension of International Business,* 3d ed. (Upper Saddle River, NJ: Prentice-Hall, 1998); S. Thiedemann, *Bridging Cultural Barriers for Corporate Success* (Lexington, MA: Lexington Books, 1991).

85. Varner and Beamer, *Intercultural Communication in the Global Workplace.*

86. Fournies, *Coaching for Improved Work Performance.*

87. G.E. Roberts, "Perspectives on Enduring and Emerging Issues in Performance Appraisal," *Public Personnel Management* 27 (3) (1998): 301–20; R. Starcher, "Individual Performance Appraisal Systems," *Production and Inventory Management Journal* 37 (4) (1996): 58–62; D.I. Rosen, "Appraisals Can Make—or Break—Your Court Case," *Personnel Journal* 71 (November 1992): 113–16; H.J. Bernardin and R.W. Beatty, *Performance Appraisal: Assessing Human Behavior at Work* (Boston: Kent, 1984).

88. Fournies, *Coaching for Improved Work Performance.*

89. Vance and Paik, "One Size Fits All in Expatriate Pre-Departure Training?"

90. Anthony et al., *Human Resource Management: A Strategic Approach*; Vance and Paik, "Toward a Taxonomy of Host Country National Learning Process Involvement in Multinational Learning Organizations."

91. "Three Factors Make Performance Management a Success," *Business Wire,* September 8, 2009; http://findarticles.com/p/articles/mi_m0EIN/is_20090908/ai_n35618309/.

92. For example, see Malaysian workforce cross-cultural awareness training found in E. Tamam, "Working with Foreigners," in *Understanding the Malaysian Workforce: Guidelines for Managers,* 179–96; Also refer to De Luque and Sommer, "The Impact of Culture on Feedback-Seeking Behavior: An Integrated Model and Propositions"; J.E. Santora, "How Chrysler Developed and Implemented Its Reverse-Appraisal Program," *Personnel Journal* 71 (May 1992): 42.

93. V. Van Tuan and N. Napier, "Paradoxes in Vietnam and America: 'Lessons Earned'—Part I."

94. Milliman et al., "Cross-Cultural Performance Feedback in Multinational Enterprises: Opportunity for Organizational Learning."

95. K. Dewettinck, "Employee Performance Management Systems in Belgian Organisations: Purpose, Contextual Dependence and Effectiveness," *European Journal of International Management,* 2 (2) (2008): 192–207.

96. Carrell et.al., *Human Resource Management*; Cascio, *Managing Human Resources: Productivity, Quality of Work Life.*

97. Lindholm, "National Culture and Performance Management in MNC Subsidiaries"; Sparrow and Hiltrop, *European Human Resource Management in Transition.*

98. C.D. Fisher, L.F. Schoenfeldt, and J.B. Shaw, *Human Resource Management,* 5th ed. (Boston: Houghton-Mifflin, 2003); W.L. French, *Human Resources Management,* 5th ed. (Boston: Houghton-Mifflin, 2003); H.B. Gregersen, J.M. Hite, and J. S. Black, "Expatriate Performance Appraisal in U.S. Multinational Firms," *Journal of International Business Studies* 27 (4) (1996): 711–38.

99. T. Sweeney, "360° Feedback Leads to Productivity," *Credit Union Management* 25 (8) (2002): 50; L. Atwater and D. Waldman, "Accountability in 360-Degree Feedback," *HR Magazine* 43 (May 1998): 96–104; R. Lepsinger and A.D. Lucia, *The Art and Science of 360° Feedback* (San Francisco: Pfeiffer, 1997); K.W. Luthans and S. Farner, "Expatriate Development: The Use of 360-Degree Feedback," *Journal of Management Development* 21 (9/10) (2002): 780–93; W.P. Anthony, K.M. Kacmar, and P.L. Perrewé, *Human Resource Management: A Strategic Approach,* 4th ed. (New York: South-Western, 2002).

100. M. Pieperl, "Getting 360-Degree Feedback Right," *Harvard Business Review* 79 (1) (2001): 142–47; C. Hymowitz, "Do 360-Degree Job Reviews by Colleagues Promote Honesty or Insults?" *Wall Street Journal,* December 12, 2000; S.J. Wells, "A New Road: Traveling Beyond 360-Degree Evaluations," *HR Magazine* 44 (9) (1999): 82–87.

101. *Human Capital Index: Human Capital as a Lead Indicator of Shareholder Value, 2001/2002 Survey Report* (Washington, DC: Watson Wyatt Worldwide, 2001).

102. E.A. Ensher, T.R. Nielson, and E. Grant-Vallone, "Tales from the Hiring Line: Effects of the Internet and Technology on HR Processes," *Organizational Dynamics* 31 (3) (2002): 224–44; J. Meade, "Visual 360: A Performance Appraisal System That's Fun," *HR Magazine* (July 1999): 118–19; G.D. Huet-Cox, T.M. Nielsen, and E. Sundstrom, "Get the Most from 360-Degree Feedback: Put It on the Internet," *HR Magazine* 44 (5) (1999): 92–103.

103. M.E. Mendenhall and G. Oddou, "Expatriate Performance Appraisal: Problems and Solutions," in *Readings and Cases in International Human Resource Management,* (3d ed.), ed. M. Mendenhall and G. Oddou (Cincinnati, OH: South-Western, 2000): 213–23; M. Harvey, "Focusing the International Performance Appraisal Process," *Human Resource Development Quarterly* 8 (1) (1997): 41–62.

104. S.G. Scott and W.O. Einstein, "Strategic Performance Appraisal in Team-Based Organizations: One Size Does Not Fit All," *Academy of Management Executive* 15 (2) (2001): 107–116; R.L. Cardy, "Performance Appraisal in a Quality Context," in *Performance Appraisal,* ed. J.W Smither (San Francisco: Jossey-Bass, 1998): 132–62; M.E. Hacker and J.D. Lang, "Designing a Performance Measure-

ment System for a High Technology Virtual Engineering Team—A Case Study," *International Journal of Agile Management Systems* 2 (3) (2000): 225–32.

105. Milliman et al., "Cross-Cultural Performance Feedback in Multinational Enterprises."

106. L.L. Berry and A. Parasuraman, *Marketing Services: Competing through Quality* (New York: Free Press, 1991).

107. K.-S. Chin and K.-F. Pun, "A Proposed Framework for Implementing TQM in Chinese Organizations," *The International Journal of Quality and Reliability Management* 19 (2/3) (2002): 272–94; J.C. Poole, W.F. Rathgeber III, and S.W. Silverman, "Paying for Performance in a TQM Environment," *HR Magazine* 38 (October 1993): 68–72; D. Shipley, "ISO 9000 Makes Integrated Systems User Friendly," *Quality Progress* 36 (7) (2003): 26; B. Wyper and A. Harrison, "Deployment of Six Sigma Methodology in Human Resource Function: A Case Study," *Total Quality Management* 11 (4–6) (2000): S720–S727.

108. J.W. Smither, M. London, N.L.Vasilopoulos, R.R.Reilly, R.E. Millsap, and N. Salvemini, "An Examination of the Effects of an Upward Feedback Program Over Time," *Personnel Psychology* 48 (1995): 1–34; J.S. Lubin, "Turning the Tables: Underlings Evaluate Bosses," *Wall Street Journal,* October 4, 1994; K. Ludeman, "Upward Feedback Helps Managers Walk the Talk," *HR Magazine* 38 (May 1993): 85–93.

109. J. Pfeffer, "Low Grades for Performance Reviews," *Business Week,* August 3, 2009.

110. A. Smith and V. Fortunato, "Factors Influencing Employee Intentions to Provide Honest Upward Feedback Ratings," *Journal of Business and Psychology* 22 (3) (2008): 191–207.

111. D.J. Campbell and C. Lee, "Self-Appraisal in Performance Evaluation: Development versus Evaluation," *Academy of Management Review* 13 (1988): 302–14; J.R. Goris et al., "Effects of Communication Direction on Job Performance and Satisfaction," *Journal of Business Communication* 37 (4) (2000): 348–68; Sashkin, *Manager's Guide to Performance Management.*

112. Milliman et al., "Cross-Cultural Performance Feedback in Multinational Enterprises."

113. "Gender Gap," *Wall Street Journal,* July 21, 1992.

114. T.D. Schellhardt, "Annual Agony: It's Time to Evaluate Your Work, and All Involved Are Groaning," *Wall Street Journal,* November 19, 1996; "Labor Letter," *Wall Street Journal,* October 16, 1990.

115. Lindholm, "National Culture and Performance Management in MNC Subsidiaries."

116. Cascio, *Managing Human Resources: Productivity, Quality of Work Life;* Sashkin, *Manager's Guide to Performance Management.*

117. R.B. Campbell and L.M. Garfinkel, "Strategies for Success in Measuring Performance," *HR Magazine* (June 1999): 99–104.

118. J.W. Hedge and M.S. Teachout, "Exploring the Concept of Acceptability as a Criterion for Evaluating Performance Measures," *Group and Organization Management* 25 (1) (2000): 22–44; J.S. Black, H.B. Gregersen, and M.E. Mendenhall, *Global Assignments: Successfully Expatriating and Repatriating International Manage* (San Francisco: Jossey-Bass, 1992); J.S. Black, H.B. Gregersen, and M.E. Mendenhall, "Evaluating the Performance of Global Managers," *Journal of International Compensation and Benefits* 1 (1992): 35–40.

119. Lindholm, "National Culture and Performance Management in MNC Subsidiaries."

120. M. Harvey, "Focusing the International Personnel Performance Appraisal Process," *Human Resource Development Quarterly* 8 (1) (1997): 41–62; C.M. Solomon, "Learning to Manage Host-Country Nationals," *Personnel Journal* 74 (3) (1995): 60–66.

121. Festing and Barzantny, "A Comparative Approach to Performance Management in France and Germany"; T.S. Bland, "Anatomy of an Employment Lawsuit," *HR Magazine* 46 (3) (2001): 145; "Is a Negative Job Evaluation an Adverse Employment Action?" *Bulletin to Management,* September 14, 2000; D.P. Twomey, *Equal Employment Opportunity Law,* 2d ed. (Cincinnati, OH: South-Western, 1990).

122. H.B. Gregersen, J.M. Hite, and J.S. Black, "Expatriate Performance Appraisal in U.S. Multinational Firms," *Journal of International Business Studies* 27 (4) (1996): 711–38.

123. M.E. Mendenhall, and G. Oddou, "Expatriate Performance Appraisal: Problems and Solutions," in *Readings and Cases in International Human Resource Management,* (3d ed.) ed. M. Mendenhall and G. Oddou (Cincinnati, OH: South-Western, 2000): 213–23; J.S. Black, H.B. Gregersen, and M.E. Mendenhall, *Global Assignments: Successfully Expatriating and Repatriating International Managers* (San Francisco: Jossey-Bass, 1992); J.S. Black, "Returning Expatriates Feel Foreign in Their Native Land," *Personnel* 68 (8) (1991): 32–40.

124. Vance and Paik, "One Size Fits All in Expatriate Pre-Departure Training?"

125. M.E. Mendenhall and G. Oddou, "Expatriate Performance Appraisal: Problems and Solutions."

126. Black, Gregersen, and Mendenhall, *Global Assignments*; P.O. Kingstrom and L.E. Mainstone, "An Investigation of the Rater-Ratee Acquaintance and Rater Bias," *Academy of Management Journal* 28 (3) (1985): 641–53.

127. J. Li and L. Karakowsky, "Do We See Eye-to-Eye? Implications of Cultural Differences for Cross-Cultural Management Research and Practice," *Journal of Psychology* 135 (5) (2001): 501–17.

128. A.D. Engle, P.J. Dowling, M. Festing, "State of Origin: Research in Global Performance Management, a Proposed Research Domain and Emerging Implications," *European Journal of International Management* 2 (2) (2008): 153–69; Harvey, "Focusing the International Performance Appraisal Process"; M. Freedland, "Performance Appraisal and Disciplinary Action: The Case for Control of Abuses," *International Labor Review* 132 (4) (1993): 491–507.

129. C. Brewster, "International HRM: Beyond Expatriation," *Human Resource Management Journal* 7 (3) (1997): 31–41; R. Schuler, J. Fulkerson, and P. Dowling, "Strategic Performance Measurement and Management in Multinational Corporations," *Human Resource Management* 30 (3) (1991): 365–92; J. Garland, R.N. Farmer, and M. Taylor, *International Dimensions of Business Policy and Strategy,* 2d ed. (Boston: PWS-Kent, 1990).

130. V. Pucik, "Strategic Human Resource Management in a Multinational Firm," in *Strategic Management of Multinational Corporations: The Essentials,* ed. H.V. Wortzel and L.H. Wortzel (New York: John Wiley, 1985): 429–30.

131. K. Dewettinck, "Employee Performance Management Systems in Belgian Organisations: Purpose, Contextual Dependence and Effectiveness," *European Journal of International Management* 2 (2) (2008): 192–207; Engle, Dowling, and Festing, "State of Origin: Research in Global Performance Management"; C.M. Solomon, "Learning to Manage Host-Country Nationals," *Personnel Journal* 74 (3) (1995): 60–66; Vance et al., "An Examination of the Transferability of Traditional Performance Appraisal Principles across Cultural Boundaries."

132. M.E. Mendenhall and G. Oddou, "The Overseas Assignment: A Practical Look," *Business Horizons* 31 (5) (1988): 78–84.

133. Vance and Paik, "One Size Fits All in Expatriate Pre-Departure Training?"; D.C. Feldman and M.C. Bolino, "The Impact of On-Site Mentoring on Expatriate Socialization: A Structural Equation Modeling Approach," *International Journal of Human Resource Management* 10 (1999): 54–71.

134. M.G. Harvey and N. Miceli, "Exploring Inpatriate Issues: An Exploratory Empirical Study," *International Journal of Intercultural Relations* 23 (3) (1999): 339–71; M.G. Harvey, " 'Inpatriation' Training: The Next Challenge for International Human Resource Management," *International Journal of Intercultural Relations* 21 (3) (1997): 393–428.

135. Li and Karakowsky, "Do We See Eye-to-Eye?"

136. Solomon, "How Does Your Global Talent Measure Up?"

10 Compensation for a Global Workforce

COMPENSATION CONVERGENCE

Designing total compensation packages for expatriates and local host country nationals is often quite complex and, at some companies such as Unilever, always changing. Brian Dive, the head of remuneration at Unilever, an Anglo-Dutch food and household-goods conglomerate, must deal with the problem of how to pay his twenty thousand managers in ninety countries from Bangladesh to Britain. In the past, the boss of a region or a big country determined pay, but now at Unilever, as with many other multinationals, brand managers in different countries are determining pay. Recently, Unilever moved from a narrow grading structure to five global work levels. Managers' pay is still based on the country in which they work, but Brian thinks there will be a regional convergence. In time, he believes, "we will have a pan-European rate."

According to Jonathan Baines of the London executive recruitment firm Baines Gwinner, there is a global converging of compensation. Managers in any of the time zones are increasingly rewarded the same way. But, because their main source of people with technical skills is New York, pay for the moment tends to move to the New York level. As New York pulls up London, so London pulls up Europe. To keep talented people in France, says Marina Eloy, who is in charge of global human resources at Paribas, a French bank, Paribas must pay British prices. "As soon as someone has an international side, you have to give them double the domestic equivalent." In Canada and Mexico, compensation committees routinely look at American boardroom pay in deciding what to offer their chief executives, because they know how easily good managers can move across the border for more money. The market rate for top talent in various industries will continue to converge as more senior executives speak English and gain the increasingly sought-after experience of working in several countries.

Executive compensation often represents a stumbling block in many mergers between American companies and firms from other parts of the world. Whenever a non-American firm buys an American one, stock-related rewards cause problems. A Towers Perrin compensation consultant spent many hours jetting across the Atlantic trying to explain to a French company that had just bought an American company why the American executives needed to retain their stock ownership plans. The consultant explained that the stock incentives are provided because "the Americans are afraid their managers will leave." But the French kept responding, "They'll stay. This is a nice place to work." Senior executives working for British Telecom when it was trying to buy American MCI found it difficult to swallow the idea that some people in their multinational executive teams would be better paid than they were. Almost always, the best way to address these perceived fairness challenges includes new stock incentives (or something similar that fits local legal requirements) to bring a greater sense of equity for MNC executives across business units.[1]

INTRODUCTION

Compensation in its broadest sense—the perspective that managers must take in the global economy—is at the very heart of every organization's performance potential. Compensation provides the point at which organizational and individual priorities and goals meet, encouraging the satisfaction of both parties.[2] It provides the driving force for effectively attracting needed human talent, retaining that talent, and encouraging the talent in ongoing, sustained, desirable, and improved performance. When an individual considers whether his or her ongoing effort in the workplace is really worth it, the "it" refers to our broad sense of compensation in this chapter—the overall picture of rewards (long- and short-term, financial and nonfinancial), incentives, benefits, advantages, even taking into consideration the presence of disincentives or negative aspects of work. Successful nonprofit and start-up organizations, often with very limited financial resources and relying on the work of unpaid volunteers or employees who perceive a personal stake in the organization's future, must operate on this broad view of compensation, clearly understanding that what effectively rewards and motivates employee performance is not limited to direct financial compensation.

Compensation ultimately involves an individual assessment and determination of value or worth in exchange for work effort. Rewards and incentives may be provided based on achieving organizational or team performance goals, but ultimately they must appeal at the individual level and be perceived as having value to have an impact. In addition, as with the maxim, "perception is everything," the individual perception of the total set of rewards, incentives, and disincentives constituting the overall compensation and rewards picture is all that ultimately matters. Regardless of what scientific and technical studies on pay and benefits might conclude about what constitutes reality, it is an employee's perception about what is fair and appropriate in exchange for desired work performance that will finally determine whether he or she will want to continue his or her level and quality of effort. For example, HCN engineers working for Solectron Corp. in Romania were satisfied with their pay rates until they spent some time training in Germany. They then returned dissatisfied and demanded a pay increase to be more in line with their German counterparts.[3] Another perceived inequity problem might arise when global team members with similar MNC job responsibilities work together closely and eventually share their compensation information based on their differing individual home country market rates. This comparison could result in feelings of inequity among group members who learn they are being paid less for doing much of the same kind of work.

Besides perceptions based on relative comparison—because an individual's cultural background can greatly influence perception—the significant cultural differences involved in managing a global workforce greatly augment the challenge facing effective compensation. A general goal for management should be achieving satisfaction and overall positive perceptions regarding total compensation and rewards among the global workforce, which can have a significant impact on workforce performance and productivity. For example, expatriates' perception that their organization is providing adequate financial support appear to be connected to effective international adjustment and commitment.[4]

In this chapter we examine several important and fundamental practices for managing compensation on a global scale. We also look at key compensation considerations for major employee categories within the global workforce, including expatriates, host country nationals, and third country nationals. Although, as one MNC's compensation executive recently asserted to us, compensation is just as much an art as a science and requires creativity and experimentation. It is hoped that this chapter will provide useful information and practical guidelines to help direct and enlighten future decision makers regarding compensation and rewards for the global workforce.

MANAGING COMPENSATION ON A GLOBAL SCALE: FUNDAMENTAL PRACTICES

We now examine critical practices for managing compensation for a global workforce. These critical practices include managing global compensation strategically, paying for performance, anticipating the influence of culture, using a total reward system perspective, and addressing the duality challenge of balancing both global management efficiencies and local responsiveness demands.

MANAGING GLOBAL COMPENSATION STRATEGICALLY

As companies begin to develop business activities involving the transfer to or local staffing of employees in their foreign operations, they typically make ad hoc decisions about compensation arrangements. But as international business activity expands, such an ad hoc, fragmented approach inevitably will lead to costly inefficiencies and missed opportunities without a coordinated, strategic approach to managing global compensation.[5] This approach should be addressed at two primary levels: the link with company strategy and the strategic management of the compensation function itself. At the general company level, compensation should reinforce and encourage compliance with corporate objectives and mandates.[6] The overall system of compensation and rewards plays a huge role in encouraging the effective implementation of an organization's general strategy as well as its multitude of specific business objectives.[7] Beyond the attraction and retention of talented employees—a major source of competitive advantage in itself—compensation can contribute to individual and collective employee commitment to the MNC's purposes and strategic directions.[8] This powerful alignment can set the organization apart in the global marketplace among competitors whose employees have varying levels of commitment and who march in different and even conflicting directions due to a haphazard reward structure. For example, on an individual level, an effective overall compensation "package" with added hardship premiums and incentives (which also considers possible nonfinancial factors that provide additional incentives, such as personal bodyguard protection) can attract qualified internal candidates for a difficult international assignment in a dangerous location (for example, in rebuilding national infrastructures of post-Saddam Iraq). On an organizational level, the reward system can ensure the progress of an MNC toward enhanced global perspectives among its current managers and future leadership. To illustrate, in providing a clear message of intent and attention-grabbing encouragement for its senior leaders to support the development of experience-based global competence among its lower managers and future company leadership, Philips Electronics made 20 percent of each division executive's annual bonus contingent upon achieving the goal of providing ten viable candidates for an expatriate assignment.[9]

For smaller firms, innovation and risk taking often are key strategies for driving future company growth and increasing market competitiveness, especially for new enterprises struggling in developing and transitioning economies. However, these new companies often need to keep their prices down as they try to enter new markets and compete globally, and they typically lack the resources to provide adequate direct financial rewards for their needed human talent. Nevertheless, many of these firms are finding success in attracting and retaining strong talent for the long term to drive innovation and company growth. They are successful by providing, at relatively low cost but with high perceived future value, company share and stock ownership (particularly time-vested and performance-vested restricted stock) with reasonable vesting requirements (for example, working five years with the company before discounted stock can be fully owned and earnings realized with a stock value increase).[10]

On the functional level, effective overall compensation strategy and more specific policies for managing a global workforce should ideally meet the following six objectives:

- Attract and retain employees who are qualified for foreign assignments.
- Facilitate transfers between foreign operations and between home country and foreign locations.
- Establish and maintain reasonable equity in the compensation of employees of all affiliate operations, both at home and abroad.
- Be competitive in relation to the practices of leading competitors (external equity).
- Take cost-saving advantage of economies of scale, and deliver intended rewards in the most cost-efficient manner (including tax consequences).
- Ensure transparency and clear understanding of compensation plans.[11]

Achieving these objectives for administering compensation on a global scale can be challenging given the reality of fluctuating currency exchange rates, inflation rates, differing salary levels across countries for similar jobs (influenced by differences in cost of living), as well as potentially widely differing local government requirements and culturally based social preferences.

The strategic management of global compensation also should be coordinated and integrated with other company HR functions and practices to carry out strategic objectives.[12] For example, to recruit local managerial talent for staffing a new foreign operation, a desirable compensation package should be offered. Or if we want to reward HCNs for effectively following special operational guidelines provided by corporate headquarters leading to standardization and cost savings, we should offer an effective performance management system for measuring and recognizing effective performance as well as providing timely feedback and even discipline (a disincentive to avoid in the future) when correction is necessary. In fact, if an organization's performance appraisal system does not adequately distinguish levels of employee performance effectiveness in a merit-pay plan, pay-increase decisions are likely to be perceived as influenced by irrelevant and even unfair variables such as supervisor bias, thus leading to the reduced effectiveness of merit pay as a motivator of performance.[13]

PAYING FOR PERFORMANCE

The practice of "pay for performance," or making at least part of an employee's compensation contingent on achieving individual, group, or organizational performance objectives, has such a critical link to MNC strategy that it merits special attention in this chapter. This approach represents one of the most significant and rapidly growing trends in compensation practices at all employment levels within individual countries and across globally managed MNCs.[14] Much of this growing trend in pay for performance (often called variable pay) is due to increasing competitive forces that are pushing organizations to use their rewards in as efficient a manner as possible for achieving productivity goals, especially with regard to individual performance. In fact, the Watson Wyatt 2001 Human Capital Index study found that differentiating pay between top-performing and average employees is associated with a significant increase in shareholder value.[15] Thus, there is an increasing concern about avoiding the wasteful practice of rewarding employees who contribute only marginally or completely fail to achieve critical performance objectives, and instead better utilizing rewards to attract and retain employees who actually contribute to organizational effectiveness.[16]

Individual performance-pay approaches tend to emphasize the importance of individual accountability and responsibility, whereas group-based approaches tend to reinforce the essential role of cooperation and helpfulness within work units leading to enhanced unit and organizational productivity. Organization-based approaches, such as profit sharing or gain sharing, tend to emphasize the importance of long-run commitment to the organization, cooperation and sharing of information across organizational units and national borders, and development of common identification with the organization.[17] Profit sharing generally takes place annually and is based on an overall predetermined measure of an organization's profitability. One drawback is that when profits are low, the sharing of these profits can be very meager or nonexistent—thus not providing a very favorable reinforcement for employees. Gain sharing, on the other hand, tends to be rewarded on a regular, more frequent basis according to an established performance measure, such as monthly levels of work unit productivity or cost savings. Especially used as a form of incentive compensation for groups or larger distinct working units, gain sharing tends to provide employees with a clearer sense of how their work is contributing to their rewards, giving them a greater sense of responsibility and control over this reward process.[18]

Besides being dependent on individual, group, or organizational performance goals or criteria, performance-based pay also can be characterized by its relationship to employee-based pay—either accumulating or nonaccumulating.[19] Under an accumulating scheme such as merit pay, which appears to be the most popular approach in Australia, Canada, and the United Kingdom, performance-based payments earned in one evaluation period are added to an employee's base pay, which becomes the new base pay that is used for calculating subsequent pay-related benefits and performance payments.[20] Under a nonaccumulating scheme (such as piece rates, commissions, one-time lump-sum bonuses), the employee is required to re-earn these payments in the future. In general, nonaccumulating schemes are seen to produce a higher average performance at a lower cost to the organization; however, they may also demonstrate a lack of long-term commitment by the organization to its employees.[21]

With the overall increase in the use of targeted performance-dependent or "at risk" pay, organizations based in different countries may differ in the focus of their performance-pay arrangements, often greatly influenced by historical and sociopolitical factors. For example, in an analysis of compensation trends in several countries, Japan, France, and Brazil made the greatest use of performance pay based on organizational performance (for example, employee stock ownership plans, or ESOPs, and profit-sharing plans), whereas the most prevalent form of performance pay in the United States, the United Kingdom, Canada, and Australia was based on individual performance (for example, merit pay, piece rates, commissions, and bonuses).[22] In addition, performance-pay practices within these individual countries have tended to show greater breadth and variety, such as with Australian firms moving toward organizational performance-based rewards and Japanese firms moving toward greater use of individual performance-based rewards.[23]

Recent surveys across several countries suggest that in most cases the individual will become an increasing focus in performance-based pay (for example, individual annual bonus or special merit increase), away from group- and organization-based rewards, despite previous cultural traditions of collectivism, such as those in Asia.[24] In fact, the global HR consulting firm Watson Wyatt has concluded from a survey of top-performing employees across many MNCs that an annual individual cash bonus, based on meeting specific project and work performance targets, has much greater incentive value for motivating strong performance than a base salary increase or stock-based long-term incentives.[25] This finding is likely due to the typical failure of base-salary merit increases to adequately differentiate top performers from average employees, and the employee's lack of direct control over the long-term value of company stock.

Individual performance-based pay in the form of bonuses or even less tangible benefits also can be a vital tool in retaining top talent and keeping employees engaged and focused during tough economic times, as has been seen during the recent global economic downturn. For example, as the world economy plunged into a serious recession and the U.S. housing market crumbled, U.S.-based Home Depot (reportedly the fastest growing retailer in U.S. history with stores in Mexico, Canada, and China) cut jobs in its corporate offices and closed fifteen stores. Amidst this dire economic climate CEO Frank Blake desired to raise morale and set realistic goals within the U.S. operations where the need was greatest. In addition to extending restricted stock grants to assistant store managers, Blake lowered profit and sales targets necessary for hourly employees to receive bonuses. The targets were maintained at levels of meaningful challenge and were designed to meet company performance targets. As a direct result, the highest percentage ever of in-store employees received bonuses. More important was the very positive impact on employee productivity, morale, and retention.[26]

Senior executives, whose individual leadership performance is often associated with organizational performance, will likely continue to have their pay based more on organization performance targets (such as stock price). But increasing public displeasure is driving greater scrutiny and demand for accountability in executive compensation decisions. Considerable outrage erupted in the United States when it came to light that huge multi-million-dollar bonuses were being given to firms who also received federal bailout support. In Germany there was considerable public resentment when former Deutsche Post CEO Klaus Zumwinkel received a lump-sum payment of 20 million euros (26.4 million dollars) in addition to his yearly pension of 970,000 euros. Another case that caused great ire in the United Kingdom when Sir Fred Goodwin retired at the age of fifty with an annual pension worth 700,000 pounds (1 million dollars) after presiding over the near-collapse of the Royal Bank of Scotland. These perceived public inequities have led to an increasing trend toward greater transparency, an emphasis on executives' increased company stock ownership, incentives based on longer-term performance, and much greater shareholder influence at the board decision-making level regarding executive compensation.[27]

In addition, with the increasing focus in many countries on holding individuals responsible for their performance through reward allocations, there needs to be a vigilant eye on possible negative outcomes where work is increasingly designed for individuals when the tasks or the people involved are more appropriate in team arrangements, or where effective workplace cooperation and communication are hindered by compensation practices that focus primarily on rewarding individual performance.[28] And executive pay policies that reward individual executives with exorbitant amounts for meeting organizational performances targets compared to the rest of the employees can contribute to workforce cynicism, lack of motivation and unrest, and turnover, as well as external public reputation damage.[29]

Despite increased interest across the globe in performance-based pay at all employee levels, there also is nearly universal agreement that incentives should constitute a limited portion of the compensation package. In general the lower the employee level, the less the direct financial compensation is at risk with individual, group, and organizational incentives (10 percent for entry-level operative employees, 20 percent for technical and supervisory employees, 40 percent for executives). And according to noted compensation specialist John Shields of the University of Sydney, although

Global Workforce Challenge 10.1
Top Executive Compensation

Public outrage over excessive executive pay unrelated to performance came into heightened global focus with the world's recent economic meltdown and was expected to result in quick and effective regulation of corporate governance structures. The goal of such regulation was to introduce better incentive and accountability structures, aligning executives' interests with the long-term interests of shareholders and companies in the least intrusive way possible. Popular outrage has often been driven by a desire for inequality reduction. Indeed, it has often been noted that MNC CEO pay increased from 140 times the pay of an average worker in 1992 to 500 times the average worker's pay twelve years later. In France, the Fillon decree of March 30, 2009, was approved. The decree regulated the situation until more permanent legislation could be put into place. In a report about reform of the corporate governance structure of financial institutions in the United Kingdom, David Walker called for the enabling of chairmen and nonexecutive directors to challenge chief executives and boards in order to induce better risk-taking incentives. After the bailout of UBS, the Swiss government introduced strict rules regulating performance-based compensation for its managers. Old-fashioned bonus schemes have been replaced with a *bonus-malus* system, in which only one-third of accrued bonuses are actually paid out while the remainder is put in a savings account. If in subsequent years losses are made, bonus-equivalent amounts are subtracted from accumulated bonus payments. Full bonuses become payable only three years after they have initially accrued. A similar system is being discussed by the German government, which would like to institute it for all companies by law.

However, hopes for significant regulatory reforms have not materialized, as could be expected given shifting political focus and the vagueness of existing proposals for change. While direct control by public supervisory bodies may make sense for government-owned companies, such direct control seems to be excessively intrusive for firms under private control. Nevertheless, many boardrooms are getting the message, especially those driven by greatly increased shareholder activism and involvement. Rather than waiting for external regulation, they are taking greater initiative in internal corporate governance related to executive compensation. There is growing acknowledgement in new board policy formation that target ownership plans, in which executives are required to hold a certain amount of equity in the firms they manage, have been shown to produce superior performance compared to option compensation schemes. Also, accountability structures that increase the power of long-term stakeholders (including active shareholder presence on boards) seem to be able to result in more responsible executive compensation decisions without erecting cumbersome new bureaucratic structures.

Source: Adapted from "International: Compensation Reform Loses Momentum," *Oxford Analytica Daily Brief Service* (July 2009): 1.

individually based incentives as a percent of total compensation tend to rise gradually up the organizational hierarchy (for example, 2 percent for assembly employees, 7 percent for technical employees, 15 percent for managers, and 20 percent for executives), executives are especially noted for having a large percent of their total compensation package based on meeting organizational performance objectives (often 20 percent or more).[30] Notwithstanding this greater interest in individual reward and accountability through the incentives provided by performance pay, there remains very strong and virtually universal interest, based on employee expectations and demands, in retaining basic benefits (such as health care, vacation/sick pay, and retirement plans) in the total compensation package.[31]

ANTICIPATING THE INFLUENCE OF CULTURE

National culture can have a significant impact on employee perceptions, preferences, and emotional reactions, including those associated with employee compensation and rewards. An awareness of the local culture and its influence is just as critical as awareness of local laws and regulations in designing effective compensation packages and practices.[32] This awareness presents a particularly complex challenge due to the pervasive and often subtle impact of culture. Even the word *compensation* carries different meanings across cultures. For example, most Europeans would prefer the broader term *remuneration,* encompassing all elements for rewarding work, while considering compensation to be more of a repayment or settlement for injury or damages. The concept of equity or fairness in comparing compensation from one individual to another can also differ across countries, such as in the United States where pay for performance and rewards based on individual merit and contributions generally fit social expectations, whereas in Japan and Korea such an approach seems inappropriate based on historical and culturally reinforced rewards based on education, age, tenure, and social class.[33]

Adding greater complexity to the picture, the varying influences of subcultures can also be noted frequently within countries due to significant internal demographic differences. For example, a study of more than seven hundred managers in large cities in each of China's six major regions suggests that there are at least three distinct subcultures within China: southeast, northeast, and central and western parts of China. The subculture of the southeast region is the most individualistic, whereas the subculture of the central and western areas is the most collectivistic.[34] Because an individual's cultural background can greatly influence perception, in particular personal attitudes about the nature of compensation and rewards in the workplace, there should be sensitivity on the part of managers to the effect of cultural differences when making compensation decisions. In general, there is strong evidence that management practices that reinforce national cultural values are likely to result in greater self-efficacy and higher performance.[35]

As indicated in Figure 10.1, culturally appropriate practices related to compensation may differ greatly based on particular dimensions of country cultures and subcultures, such as power distance, individualism, uncertainty avoidance, and masculinity.[36] In countries and subcultures measuring relatively high in power distance (such as India, Mexico, Panama, Indonesia, and Middle Eastern countries), appropriate compensation practices might employ pay and rewards that reinforce status distinctions with little or no employee participation and involvement in reward determination and distribution decisions, whereas those measuring relatively low in power distance

Figure 10.1 **General Compensation Policies and Practices for Different Cultural Dimensions**

Dimension	Low	High
Power Distance	Employee participation and involvement in reward determination and distribution techniques; profit sharing; gain sharing	No employee participation/involvement; status distinctions reinforced by pay and rewards
Individualism	Group-based contingent rewards; non-economic rewards that satisfy recognition needs with minimal individual distinction	Individual-based contingent rewards; individual praise and recognition
Uncertainty Avoidance	Performance-based (at risk) pay; external equity focus; flexibility; broadbanding (few pay grades)	Limited use of performance-based pay; pay consistency and predictability
Masculinity	Strong emphasis on social benefits; quality of work life; work-life balance; job security; emphasis on sharing versus competing for rewards	Emphasis on performance-based pay; competition in pay, promotion, and recognition

(including Austria, Denmark, Ireland, and New Zealand) might feature employee participation and involvement as well as emphasize profit-sharing and gain-sharing plans. In countries and subcultures that are relatively high in individualism (for example, Sweden, the United States, the United Kingdom, Canada, the Netherlands, France, and Italy), effective practices might emphasize rewards based on individual performance, including individual praise and recognition, whereas those relatively low in individualism (high in collectivism—for example, Ecuador, Colombia, China, Honk Kong, South Korea, and Taiwan) might use practices emphasizing group-based contingent rewards as well as nondirect financial rewards that satisfy recognition needs with minimal individual distinction. Work settings in countries and subcultures that measure high in uncertainty avoidance (including Japan, Germany, Spain, Portugal, Turkey, Belgium, and South Korea) may favor a limited use of performance-based or variable pay to maintain a desired consistency and predictability, while employees in countries low in uncertainty avoidance (for example, the United States, Singapore, Malaysia, the United Kingdom, India, and Denmark) may prefer a higher level of variable performance-based and external market-based pay and flexible pay structural arrangements such as broadbanding, which involves few pay grades. Finally, compensation practices in countries and subcultures registering high in masculinity (such as those of Italy, Switzerland, the United States, the United Kingdom, Mexico, Germany, Austria, and Japan) may emphasize individual and group competition in pay, promotion, and recognition, with a clear emphasis on performance-based pay, while for those low in the masculinity dimension (high in femininity—for example, Denmark, Chile, Finland, Norway, Sweden, the Netherlands, and Thailand), there might be a strong preference in the total compensation package for emphasis on social benefits, quality of work life and work/life balance, and job security, with a clear partiality for sharing over competing for rewards. These are general trends for which managers should be sensitive; however, these trends should not be automatically assumed without careful assessment regarding needs and preferences at a specific workplace under consideration. In addition, as we will examine later, there is increasing evidence that even in countries of often-presumed cultural homogeneity there can be a significant variation in individual preferences.[37]

USING A TOTAL REWARD SYSTEM PERSPECTIVE

Some organizations experience difficulties in their global compensation efforts by using a narrow, fragmented perspective, overlooking the full picture of the reward package by focusing on individual parts. In fact, using a total reward system perspective can be very helpful in developing balanced and comparable compensation packages across national borders by including and estimating other less-direct elements affecting remuneration that make up the total package, including tax and social security contribution, national social benefits, and company benefits.[38] The complete range of possible financial and nonfinancial rewards—total remuneration—should be taken into consideration. Figure 10.2 examines various kinds of rewards that can help attract and retain employees as well as reinforce and encourage desirable work performance. These possible reward factors include direct financial (for example, wage, commission, bonus, and stock ownership), indirect financial (for example, legally required benefits—which may differ from country to country—and voluntary benefits), job-related (for example, challenge, feedback, work meaningfulness, management support, autonomy, and skill development for increased future career security and advancement viability), and internal and external surrounding work environment (such as social environment at work, physical working conditions, policies of workplace flexibility to support work/life balance, nature of commute, and general quality of living conditions during nonwork hours).[39]

Managers and their organizational compensation policies may err in focusing only on the financial forms of rewards and overlooking important nonfinancial considerations. For example, in recruiting internal candidates for an expatriate assignment in a new operation in New Zealand, managers could enhance the attractiveness and perceived reward associated with accepting the foreign assignment by including recruitment information about the high appeal of that part of the world for outdoor recreation—a nonfinancial but potentially enticing reward for some people. As organizations competing globally are feeling more and more pressure to contain costs, they should be aware that some of the most valued rewards for a large percentage of critical skill employees (technical, professional, and managerial) include career development, management team support, flexible schedules (including working from home), and opportunities for advancement—posing very little direct financial cost to the organization.[40] In fact, work flexibility to fit individual employee personal life needs is increasingly recognized as one of the most commonly desirable forms of workplace reward for all levels of employees throughout the world.[41] In addition, particularly in less-industrialized countries, many firms including Johnson & Johnson, ABB, Procter & Gamble, and Siemens have found the key to attracting and retain-

Figure 10.2 **Forms of Employee Rewards**

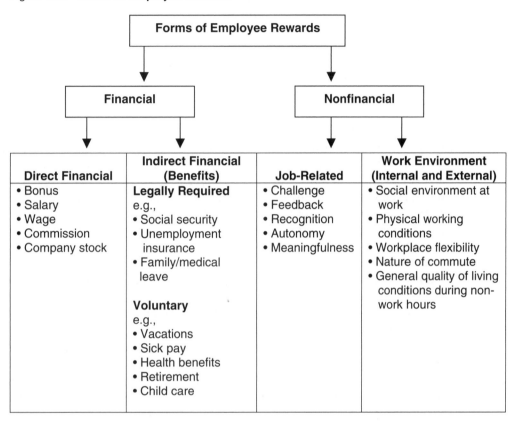

Direct Financial	Indirect Financial (Benefits)	Job-Related	Work Environment (Internal and External)
• Bonus • Salary • Wage • Commission • Company stock	**Legally Required** e.g., • Social security • Unemployment insurance • Family/medical leave **Voluntary** e.g., • Vacations • Sick pay • Health benefits • Retirement • Child care	• Challenge • Feedback • Recognition • Autonomy • Meaningfulness	• Social environment at work • Physical working conditions • Workplace flexibility • Nature of commute • General quality of living conditions during non-work hours

ing local professional talent is providing state-of-the-art training and development programs.[42]

Individual managers often have very little discretion and influence regarding direct and indirect financial forms of compensation, yet they have considerable discretion and control over often highly motivating work-related forms of employee rewards, such as quality and frequency of feedback, recognition, work meaningfulness, challenge, opportunity for professional development, employee autonomy over work, and flexible work schedules and arrangements to support employee work/life balance. Organizations cannot afford to overlook the potentially powerful impact that individual managers have on the overall reward system. Thus, the role of the individual manager is critical in the allocation and management of these highly important job-related rewards for their employees, which should be reflected in manager recruitment, training, appraisal, and incentives.[43]

A total reward system perspective also considers potential negative factors and disincentives. For example, a total compensation package designed for an oil MNC executive to be assigned to Ecuador or Colombia, regions notorious for executive kidnappings, likely would be inadequate if it did not consider and try to make up for the disincentive of the possible personal danger involved. In some cases desirable employee performance may take place initially, only to be punished and discouraged from future occurrence by an informal but strong reward system grounded in social norms or customs.

As a more common illustration, when managers consider significant changes in direction and strategic objectives or even less-momentous operational procedures, employee commitment to the changes should not be assumed automatically. In fact, managers and their organizations would be better off assuming that the existing reward structure will simply reinforce the old direction and procedures, thus pointing to the need for adjusting the reward system to reinforce and support change. In addition, at least two potentially daunting disincentives accompany change: (1) anxiety, based on underlying fear or distrust, about what the change will bring and (2) the effort and sometimes discomfort involved in breaking up an established pattern and pulling oneself out of a comfort zone of familiarity and mastery. These disincentives can block or impede commitment to change and sustained desirable new performance and should be acknowledged. Where possible these and other identified disincentives should be eliminated or reduced, or at least "compensated" or made up for by a new reward structure that takes them into consideration.

Of course, not all disincentives are counterproductive. Some should be formulated and strategically placed by management. For example, besides indicating the expectations of employees in terms of appropriate behavior, organizations should also carefully consider the *unacceptable* forms of employee behavior (for example, dishonesty, theft, fighting, sexual harassment, tardiness—even failure to change and adopt new procedures) and clearly communicate these unacceptable behaviors along with their associated *penalties*. These penalties or prescribed forms of punishment, part of the organization's disciplinary system, can serve as effective disincentives within the overall reward structure of the organization to discourage unacceptable and nonproductive behavior.

Besides potential disincentives in the overall reward structure that block employee performance and commitment, an absence of adequate reward may serve as an impediment of desired performance. As in the old saying, "you get what you pay for," if the reward is virtually nothing or at least nothing of perceived value, the organization can expect a similar level and quality of performance in return. Employee commitment to doing something well "for the good of the cause" without some form of positive reinforcement as perceived by the employee—whether tangible or intangible—tends to last only temporarily until the desired behavior fades away or is extinguished.[44] Another potential problem with the total reward structure can exist when a reward for doing something officially desired by the organization is offset or overpowered by a more attractive reward that encourages an employee to do something else. This problem with competing rewards can exist especially in organizations that have multiple activities, objectives, organizational structures, and priorities. For example, PCNs may experience competing reward pressures when trying to meet differing and sometimes even contradictory expectations between local host country operation managers and managers back at their home country headquarters.

Therefore, when planning compensation, managers should consider within a total reward system the entire spectrum of rewards, incentives, and disincentives—financial

Global Workforce Challenge 10.2
**Quality of Life Attracts Workers to Spain,
Fueling Europe's Nearshore Outsourcing**

Is there any way to attract high-wage earners to low-paying jobs? There is when you understand that the compensation system includes much more than wages. This point is increasingly being illustrated in Spain.

After a slow start, Europe is finally beginning to embrace the offshore/nearshore outsourcing trend. Consulting firm TPI of Woodlands, Texas, figures that European companies awarded $41 billion in outsourcing contracts abroad in 2004, nearly twice the level of two years earlier. One of the most popular destinations for this work is Spain, where thousands of young Europeans flock every year in search of sun and sangria as well as jobs to support this lifestyle. Already about fifty thousand people from all over Europe work in more than two thousand Spanish call centers and shared service centers, which handle functions such as tech support, accounting, and personnel administration. And it is projected that this industry will add thirty thousand jobs in the next two years.

With the benefits of its EU membership and relative nearness, Spain is a convenient location for European firm offshore—or, more precisely due to proximity, *nearshore*—arrangements. However, wages for service-center and other offshore jobs are about 30 percent lower than in northern Europe—representing a significant source of company cost savings. Ordinarily this lower pay might serve as a major obstacle to attracting qualified employees to these jobs—especially from the higher-paid labor markets of northern Europe. Yet in this industry where employee turnover is a big problem, overall quality of life makes a difference in attracting and retaining talent. "Instead of sitting in ten inches of snow in Poland, wouldn't you rather be sitting in ten inches of warm sand in Barcelona?" asks Stephen A. Koutros, a partner of TPI.

Other locales, such as India and Eastern Europe, are also grabbing big call-center business. But Spain retains some potent advantages, especially for European companies looking for nearshore EU advantages. People from anywhere in the European Union can work there without visas or permits. In addition, Spanish operations can handle sensitive banking and medical transactions that aren't allowed to be sent outside the European Union.

Supported by the nonfinancial reward of an enjoyable lifestyle that is successfully attracting qualified labor, Spain's outsourcing trend shows no signs of weakening. French IT services firm Teamlog is expanding its 120-person European help center for Hewlett-Packard outside of Barcelona. Agilent Technologies uses six hundred employees in Barcelona to run outsourced administration, finance, and customer service for firms in Europe, the Middle East, and South America. Citigroup has twelve hundred employees handling customer support and internal services for their Western European business. And Dallas-based Affiliated Computer Services, Inc., has nearly five hundred employees there from thirty-eight countries who speak fourteen languages, mostly providing service to General Motors Europe, including fielding calls from GM's European workers and retirees about paychecks or benefits.

Sources: Adapted from G. Ulloa, and I. Diez, "A Nearshore Thing," *Legal Week* (February 2009): 32–34; A. Reinhardt and C. Vitzthum, "Cafes, Beaches, and Call Centers: Fair-Weather Spain Is the New European Hot Spot for Outsourcing," *BusinessWeek,* September 5, 2005: 51.

and nonfinancial, formal and informal—available to and facing the employee. In addition to the formal compensation package, managers should ask themselves the following questions with regard to the total reward structure facing their employees:[45]

- Are there any disincentives perceived by employees that would discourage the desired performance?
- Are employees actually being punished for the desired performance?
- Are there clear and strong enough disincentives for neglecting or *not* meeting desired performance?
- Are there competing rewards, where employees are rewarded for doing something other than the desired performance?
- Are the overall set of rewards (formal and informal, extrinsic and intrinsic) adequate to sustain desired performance on an ongoing basis?

ADDRESSING THE DUALITY CHALLENGE: GLOBAL MANAGEMENT VERSUS LOCAL RESPONSIVENESS

A major ongoing challenge faced by multinational organizations is the need to manage the enterprise globally while at the same time remaining responsive to local conditions. Compensation for a global workforce is particularly faced with the dynamic tension of this duality challenge. Whereas in the past multinational organizations could succeed by fitting compensation policy to fragmented, multidomestic strategy with a primary focus on local responsiveness, global competition pressures have driven today's organizations to integrate and globalize compensation and benefits programs.[46]

There is an increasingly strong push to manage reward systems *globally* for at least three major reasons: achieving economies of scale, gaining alignment, and building unique firm capability. First, a potential benefit for large multinational organizations is found due to the principle of economies of scale or standardization. When compensation policies and practices are applied in a fairly standard fashion throughout the world, an organization avoids the added expense of managing significantly different compensation arrangements at each international work operation. This standardization results in savings for the organization. Second, especially where international business success calls for significant integration, coordination, and cooperation in internal knowledge sharing, harmonizing manufacturing and distribution, and presenting a consistent company message to customers across international operations and national boundaries, a more centrally managed reward system is needed to encourage workforce alignment.[47] As before, simply *hoping* that those at various international locations will see to the needed integration and cooperation of these company efforts will do so—and with solid commitment—for "the good of the cause" will not make it in the long run. Unless the reward system actually favors and reinforces cooperative and integrative interactive behaviors for alignment of effort in support of MNC strategy, it is folly to expect or hope for anything besides individually motivated, fragmented, and even conflicting efforts across international units.[48] To illustrate this important reinforcement of company-wide behavior, it has been found that an increase in MNC-wide knowledge sharing—increasingly critical to success in a global economy—is associated with global manager bonuses that are based on the MNC's overall performance.[49]

Finally, related to the previously mentioned global integration objective of compensation management, MNCs are increasingly showing interest in developing an international workforce possessing unique global capability. This continuity, which can serve as a distinct competitive advantage, features reliable key competencies as well as a common MNC mind-set that can provide consistency and synergy throughout and across the international business units.[50] This building of unique firm capability through common global competencies and mind-set, as well as common commitment through shared identification with the MNC, can be greatly facilitated through reward structures that support similar international learning experiences (for example, foreign work assignments for building global competencies) as well as MNC-wide forms of compensation and recognition that reinforce the notion of a "global corporate family."

We continually are seeing a significant restructuring of traditional and heretofore seemingly immutable compensation and reward systems among cultures and social systems, such as away from lifetime job security in Japan and very generous social benefits in Germany,[51] and converging to more similar pay and reward-structure models across national boundaries reflecting global "best practices."[52] Yet there still may be local cultural and legal expectations and requirements as well as labor market conditions affecting various practices and components of compensation. In fact, in some cases there can be different regional, national, state, and municipal laws and regulations affecting various kinds of compensation—all of which must be considered and adhered to when making compensation decisions to avoid costly fines and penalties. And these jurisdiction-based laws themselves may even differ in the same areas of compensation, such as differing overtime pay requirements between U.S. federal and California state laws (and where laws about the same subject differ, the law that is more favorable toward the employee is typically the one required).

Sensitivity to local legal, cultural, and labor market expectations and conditions related to various forms of compensation also can be important in competing for local talent. Without sensitivity to these local expectations, even when legal requirements are met, organizations may face serious problems with the recruitment and retention of high-quality employees. For example, across Europe there is strong sentiment in favor of employee social benefits, such as paid maternity and paternity leave, especially compared with those benefits provided (and not provided) in the United States.[53] As discussed earlier related to the impact of local culture, there is strong evidence of the importance of designing HR policies and practices, including those involving compensation, to accommodate deep-seated local prevailing cultural differences. The actual policies and practices for a given location should not be implemented automatically based on inferences from these broad cultural dimensions, but rather carefully assessed and customized to fit specific local cultural preference. Nevertheless, these general prescriptions based on cultural patterns found in countries around the world demonstrate potential culturally driven differences pertinent to compensation to fit local situations.[54]

Based on their extensive field interviews with managers in several countries,

Bloom and colleagues, propose four variable contextual factors for determining the appropriate degree of emphasis on a global versus local perspective in designing compensation systems: heterogeneity, formalization, pervasiveness, and strength.[55] Where there is high cultural diversity or heterogeneity in a particular location, less local cultural sensitivity may be necessary, allowing for greater standardization with a global perspective. Where local laws are highly formalized, pervasive throughout a country (that is, centrally planned), and strongly enforced, a careful local responsiveness would clearly be in order. For example, centralized wage and pay practices in Scandinavian countries present less of an option for an MNC to depart from local regulated compensation practices than in other countries where laws may be much less official or actively enforced or less consistent from region to region within a country. As Bloom and colleagues explain in designing international compensation systems (ICS):

> When variation in factors is greater, MNEs [multinational enterprises] have wider discretion in how to design their international compensation systems, which allows them to pursue global strategic alignment by crafting ICS that more closely reflect their organizational contexts.[56]

With particular regard to sensitivity to local culture, there is evidence that concern about national cultural differences in guiding HR practices has been exaggerated. Some researchers believe that even in countries of relatively low cultural heterogeneity, many organizations might be better off focusing on identifying and clarifying their core priorities and values (part of their unique organizational culture), attracting a workforce that fits these priorities and values, and then clearly communicating and reinforcing these same core priorities and values through the reward system.[57] For example, one MNC was planning on expanding operations into Japan but was very concerned about how its high priority for encouraging employee health and safety, supported by its policy of requiring a smoke-free workplace, would be accepted in a country notorious for heavy smokers. Nevertheless, the MNC's executive team decided that its priority and commitment to employee health was central to its core values and should be applied globally for all its human resources. The MNC therefore moved forward with the business expansion, remaining consistent with its company-wide smoke-free workplace policy. The executive team was pleasantly surprised to note that there were many competent Japanese within the local population who preferred the smoke-free working environment and applied for employment.

To help address this need for flexibility in meeting the constantly changing demands of managing duality in global compensation, Milkovich and Bloom have presented a very helpful three-level model of strategic flexibility.[58] In this model an employee's total compensation is structured into three major sets: core, crafted, and choice (refer to Figure 10.3). The core set of rewards provides clear encouragement for a common company mind-set and support of identified priorities for success (for example, strong flexibility and cooperation for global customer responsiveness), which underlie and reinforce a common MNC global culture. Examples of these rewards include competitive cash rewards, MNC stock arrangements as part of organization-wide profit

Figure 10.3 **Three-level Model for Strategic Flexibility in Global Reward System Design**

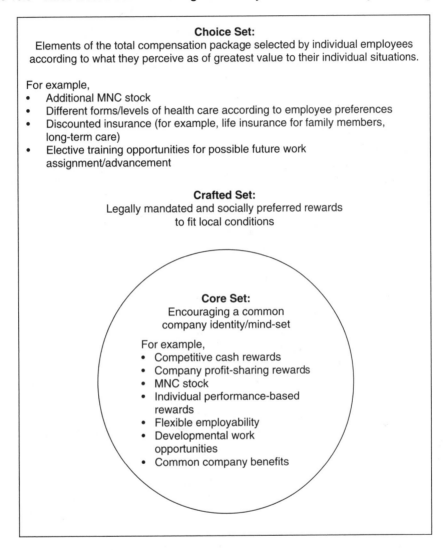

sharing and other rewards serving as a long-term incentive to promote common identity and retention, individual performance-based rewards (for example, a bonus) based on contribution to MNC goals and priorities, flexible employability within the MNC—a form of job security, career-valuable developmental work opportunities abroad or involving international workforce interaction, and common company benefits (where legally feasible) that build a common identity. Such common benefits could include a common retirement annuity contribution to communicate a concern for employees' long-term welfare or even an expense-paid planning meeting and vacation with spouses at an attractive location for high-performing managers from throughout the MNC—an activity of potentially great value for building common identity and culture.

A second set of *crafted* compensation components within the total compensation structure of this strategic flexibility model includes both legally mandated and socially preferred rewards that fit local conditions as well as support and reinforce corporate culture and priorities. For example, although there is no legal minimum standard for paid vacation leave in the United States, in the European Union the legal minimum is four weeks (twenty days), and France requires twenty-five days. Although Germany legally requires twenty vacation days, due to social preference and expectations most employers give six weeks (thirty days).[59] In China a very desirable benefit for general employees is subsidized housing and mortgage loan support, and in the United Kingdom company cars are a popular benefit offered to a relatively large percentage of managers. Besides mandating certain benefits, governments themselves in many countries also provide or guarantee certain benefits, such as retirement pensions and basic health care, and thus remove from MNCs the option and need to consider whether to provide these benefits. One of the most controversial issues that companies face in the United States is the provision of health care—whether or not and to what degree. Yet virtually all countries in Western Europe guarantee universal or near universal health care to residents, who receive these benefits whether or not they are employed.[60]

This second set of crafted reward components assumes that local business unit or regional managers have adequate flexibility to choose those forms of compensation at various employment levels that are important to encourage and sustain desirable performance toward local *and* global objectives *in the particular markets where they operate.* Although corporate goals may be the same, the local rewards and supports necessary for encouraging different workforces to achieve those common goals might be different. For example, a German MNC with manufacturing operations in Mexicali, Mexico, that hires migrant workers from Mexico's poorer hinterlands to the south might have more of an emphasis on hygiene and nutrition (such as providing on-site showers and breakfast and lunch), whereas its operation in South Carolina might emphasize productivity gain sharing or tuition benefits for continuing education. Or an MNC with an operation in a large, congested metropolitan area such as Bangkok, Thailand, might provide different rewards or benefits, such as flexible work schedules or telecommuting arrangements, to support regular and uninterrupted workflow and productivity, whereas these same arrangements may not be needed to achieve the same company objectives in a different workplace location where a small population presents little problem with commuting traffic.

Finally, whereas the previous reward sets are determined primarily *by managers* as they consider supporting both corporate objectives and demands of the local business environment, the *choice* set of compensation components switches to the selection *by employees themselves* of elements of compensation that they perceive of greatest value to their individual situations. Here the individual employee is in charge of customization. Examples of rewards that employees might choose, based on their individual preferences and within a total cost limit, include additional discounted company stock, different kinds and levels of health care (for example, cafeteria-style benefit plans), and training opportunities for possible future work assignment and advancement. In their survey of employees in 431 companies in the United States and Canada, the global HR consulting firm Towers Watson found strong support for this flexible feature of individual employee customization, with some types of rewards being valued differently across various employee demographic classifications, including age, gender, nature of work, tenure with the company, and level of salary.[61] For example, women were more interested in the ability to work at home, while younger employees with less company tenure placed less value on long-term incentives.

Even though this model can be helpful as a general guide for planning and managing compensation and rewards on a global scale—and thus is a tool for global advantage—local responsiveness continues to be an imperative in all three sets of the compensation components. Besides the *crafted* set discussed earlier featuring compensation components that are customized to fit local legal requirements and social expectations, the *core* set of reward components also involves specific practices that may need to vary according to differing market and local conditions while still signaling the MNC's common priorities and desired global mind-set. For example, in particularly high personal tax regions such as Scandinavia, special benefits or perquisites ("perks") that are minimally taxed are often more attractive than an increase in competitive cash payments intended to signal and encourage attention to company priorities. Also, some countries, such as China and Russia, prohibit or place severe restrictions on individual ownership of foreign company securities, thus presenting a significant challenge to MNC stock ownership and stock profit sharing that otherwise provides a common and potentially unifying reward structure.[62] In addition, an MNC's recurring pay-for-performance practice in the form of an extra bonus or benefit to provide adequate individual employee incentive toward common MNC objectives can, in some countries, turn into an entitlement when offered repeatedly over a period of time (for example, two years in Brazil), becoming an "acquired right" that can't be discontinued unilaterally by the employer—thus losing the important "at risk" or contingent feature of the incentive.[63] Even the *choice* set of compensation components that focuses on individual employee selection of particular rewards that best fit the employee's situation is dependent on local legal requirements in terms of what options actually can be offered to employees as well as local social expectations and preferences that would greatly influence individual choice.

KEY COMPENSATION CONSIDERATIONS FOR EXPATRIATES, HCNs, AND TCNs

We now examine key compensation considerations for the major employee categories within the global workforce of expatriates (frequently equated with PCNs), host country nationals (HCNs), and third country nationals (TCNs). Although their compensation issues are often similar and intertwined (for example, TCNs and HCNs who are serving as inpatriates can all be broadly considered expatriates), we will focus on the considerations that are fairly unique to each of these three major international employee categories.

EXPATRIATE COMPENSATION

In the past many companies tended to overcompensate expatriates (PCNs) due in part to the companies' lack of experience and lack of expatriate assignment desirability with many personal and professional uncertainties involved. However, over time and with an increasing number of expatriates, compensation efforts for expatriates tend to be fine-tuned and changed from an ad hoc negotiation process to more accurately reflect global living costs and a more consistent expatriate compensation policy.[64] Nevertheless, as was noted earlier, an expatriate's overall perception of organizational support represented by a compensation package's ability to maintain a standard of living is linked to expatriate adjustment and commitment in the international assignment.[65]

Past approaches to expatriate compensation also have been faulted due to their focus on cost-containment and almost exclusive technical focus on financial rewards, without duly considering other factors such as potential benefit to the expatriate candidate's career and opportunities for valuable experience and global competency development.[66] Especially where these other nonfinancial features appear weak or even potentially punitive, such as with an MNC's poor track record in valuing international experience and retaining former expatriates, the development of an equitable compensation package to attract talented expatriates might be difficult. Evans and colleagues succinctly voice this concern in the following excerpt:

> Nonfinancial rewards such as learning opportunities and expectations of future career gains are also important motivators. When expatriation is a "ticket to nowhere," no amount of effort to fine-tune the compensation package will produce a committed and dedicated expatriate workforce.[67]

Numerous forms of expatriate compensation can be utilized, depending on various international contexts and expatriate work arrangements. Due to the degree of variation across countries in compensation practices and the many complexities involved, MNCs often devote considerable time to internal staff and retain the services of international accounting firms to design and administer the most cost-effective and appropriate rewards for their global workforce. We now examine seven basic approaches to expatriate compensation used by MNCs.[68]

Headquarters-Based Model

Expatriates, regardless of nationality, are paid according to the headquarters' compensation structure. This approach is relatively easy to administer and has few problems with nationality pay discrimination. It is especially common in an MNC's early stages of international business when most or all expatriates are PCNs. This approach is effective in attracting expatriates to the host operation from lower-salary countries (TCNs) but tends to incur high compensation costs with many other nationality expatriates' pay based on the often higher headquarters reference point. This headquarters-based model also may present difficulty in attracting and retaining expatriates from higher-salary countries. In addition, repatriation problems may increase for expatriates (such as TCNs or those brought in as inpatriates from a host country) from lower-salary countries who find that a return to their home country salary structure means a significant decrease in pay.[69]

Home-Based Balance Sheet Model

In this model, expatriates are paid according to their own home country pay and benefits structure. However, this arrangement is *modified* by linking spendable income to a single base-country expenditure pattern, and all nationalities are provided the same host country spendable income to cover local expenses. Purchasing power is preserved at the same level for all expatriates, but with nationality-based differences reflected in home country base pay, tax equalization, incentives, and reserve components (for example, payments for special benefits, pension contributions, and social security taxes).

This is by far the most common model used by U.S. and European MNCs and typically is implemented through some version of what is known as the *balance sheet approach*.[70] The purpose of the balance sheet approach is to help the expatriate avoid personal sacrifice in standard of living or financial loss due to the expatriate assignment as well as provide an attractive incentive or inducement for accepting the assignment.[71] Essentially, the MNC and the prospective expatriate need to determine and agree on what it would take to "balance" and even outweigh the apparent disincentives involved in accepting the foreign assignment, ensuring that the expatriate is left with a feeling of overall equity with the new expatriate experience.

To achieve this balance and even "sweeten the deal" toward acceptance, equalization adjustments may be provided to offset a possibly higher cost of living or dual-tax consequences (home and host country); incentive components may be added in the form of various allowances and premiums for housing, relocation, home leave (for example, one trip per year for the whole family to the expatriate's home country), family private schooling, personal and family displacement, and hardship (that is, assignment to an unfamiliar country or uncomfortable environment where expatriates and family members my be exposed to high levels of crime and political unrest, high levels of pollution, substandard housing, isolation, poor medical facilities, etc.).[72]

Personal income tax rates and practices can differ markedly from country to country, especially when an expatriate moves from a lower-tax country to one with significantly higher taxes, such as an American expatriate being assigned to France. In such a situation a tax adjustment may be in order.[73] In most cases a *tax equalization* method is used in the balance sheet approach where companies deduct income taxes from the expatriate's salary at the rate that would normally be paid in the home country and then pay any additional tax owed due to the higher tax rates in the host country.[74] PCNs from some countries such as the United States must file tax documentation on their foreign earnings with both home and host country and may be faced with a significant dual-tax burden (the U.S. tax code now allows a deduction on foreign-owned income, but income above that deduction is taxable—presenting a dual-tax burden). Tax law for expatriates around the world is quite diverse and complex, and tax consequences should be considered carefully and support provided where appropriate as part of a thorough balance sheet approach. And due to MNCs' efforts to shield an expatriate from excessive tax burdens, the tax expense of an international assignment can be the most costly component of the remuneration package.[75]

The balance sheet approach is commonly used by MNCs due to its overall effectiveness in facilitating expatriate mobility, preserving purchasing power and equity with home country colleagues, and providing some commonality of PNC expatriate pay regardless of assignment location. However, this approach can be quite expensive and complex to administer (for example, keeping track of differing country exchange rates, cost of living, and tax and pension regulations) and may also result in compensation disparities and perceptions of unfairness (due to home-based salary and reserve component differences) between expatriates of differing nationalities and between expatriates and HCNs.[76]

Host Country/Local Market Model

In this approach, which provides simplicity and avoids equity problems, expatriates are paid on the same level as local nationals in the country of the foreign assignment. It is a particularly positive arrangement for expatriates coming from a lower-salary country, such as has been frequently found with Chinese MNC's with operations in the United Kingdom.[77] However, as with the headquarters-based model, higher local pay and benefits in such a host country assignment can render successful repatriation to a lower-salary home country difficult. Often referred to as "localization," this approach works well when transferring a fairly new employee with little international experience primarily for the purpose of international competency development. It also is used when expatriates decide to remain in the foreign location on an indefinite or permanent basis.

Better of Home or Host Model

Here expatriates are paid at a level at least the same or higher than in their home country, depending on the pay structure in the host country. This approach is often used for transfers within regions, most notably within the European Union and Latin America.

International Citizen Model

In this recent alternative to the commonly used Home-Based Balance Sheet Model, an international "basket of goods" (covering expenses for food, clothing, housing, and so forth) is used for all expatriates regardless of country of origin. This approach offers pay adjustments allowing expatriates to purchase comparable local products—but not the same products as in the home country, greatly reducing the costs when following the balance sheet approach. This approach might also be appropriate for international executives who, as international citizens or career diplomats, plan to move from country to country in international assignments. As a global compensation package that typically includes company profit sharing and occasional stock ownership, this approach also might be more effective than others in promoting a global view of the firm's operations.

A scaled-down version of this more global model can be useful for companies that send most or all of their expatriates on assignments within a particular region, such as the European Union. In this case, there is a common compensation package that is tailored to the conditions within the particular economic region rather than relating to a worldwide policy. This regional approach also brings more simplicity to compensation administration and helps to avoid potential perceptions of inequity and subsequent morale problems of expatriates from different counties, such as Portugal and Germany, working closely in similar tasks yet compensated at significantly different levels based on home country standards.

Lump-Sum Model

For short-term assignments, such as those of one to three years, it may be easiest to provide expatriates with simple lump-sum payments to cover additional expenses incurred with the foreign assignment, allowing them to manage their personal finances on their own. This flexible approach avoids unnecessary incentives and inducements as well as intrusion into expatriates' more personal financial matters such as taxes and retirement pensions.

Negotiation Model

This flexible approach is especially appropriate for special or unique assignment situations, or with organizations having few and infrequent expatriate assignments. And as an overall rule, despite recent developments in more standardized models of expatriate compensation, it is recommended that companies maintain flexibility in considering each expatriate's unique needs and situations and fine-tune the actual compensation arrangement through open discussion and negotiation.[78]

HOST COUNTRY NATIONAL COMPENSATION

The bulk of the international management literature, including specifically regarding compensation, has focused on expatriates—especially PCNs—at the neglect of HCNs and TCNs.[79] Yet local HCNs typically make up the majority of the employees in each country of the MNC's foreign operations (collectively often the majority of all MNC employees). They also represent an increasing phenomenon as inpatriates assigned to the MNC's parent country for both individual development and knowledge-sharing benefit for the firm.[80] Because HCNs potentially can have a valuable direct influence on both foreign operation performance as well as future leadership and strategic direction of the MNC, it is imperative that careful attention be given to the design and administration of compensation plans to ensure success in the attraction and retention of talented and committed HCNs in all foreign operations.[81] We now will examine compensation issues and practices for HCNs in their work at both host country locations and in parent-country inpatriate assignments.

HCN Compensation in Host Country

To help build a thorough compensation framework for HCNs staffed in a particular host country, Stephen Perkins recommends that several interrelated factors be carefully considered, including local expectations and regulations regarding compensation package content and administration, local economic and labor market conditions, expectations of management (both local and at global/regional headquarters) and investing partners (that is, joint ventures), the nature and degree of variable rewards (that is, pay for performance), and strategic choices. Important strategic choices typically involve the degree to which compensation should reflect primarily local conditions or also include components promoting common corporate identity worldwide. Another strategic concern relates to possible long-term plans for investment in local employees as human capital for staffing future local, regional, and MNC leadership, where perhaps above-average compensation packages may be offered to those HCNs deemed worth the investment.[82]

To assist in HCN compensation planning, some MNCs now use the concept of *purchasing power parity* (PPP) to compare relative purchasing power between countries. PPP provides indices reflecting differences in both exchange rates and price levels among different nations. When used as a benchmark for equalizing HCN compensation, PPP can be further adjusted to reflect different countries' rates for personal income taxes and mandatory contributions to social benefits programs. Because of its usefulness, in the mid-1990s the International Monetary Fund changed to PPP indices from U.S. dollars to other currencies for economic comparisons across countries. [83]

Local economic and labor market conditions can be very complex and differ markedly across countries, and the quest for accurate information for planning compensation can be very challenging. For example, the determination of pay rates for local employees across different countries must take into consideration differing and changing figures for local cost of living and inflation rates. Different countries also have varied social expectations and legal requirements regarding elements of cash compensation. In Mexico, for example, cash compensation elements also include a Christmas bonus, vacation bonus, and a savings/profit sharing payment. In addition, the provision of noncash benefits must be included in a thorough analysis of local HCN pay arrangements. To illustrate, in India the prevailing salary levels for local managers might appear quite low. However, these managers typically expect and receive other noncash benefits, including a housing subsidy, car allowance, children's education allowance, and so on.[84]

MNCs often consider survey data and other advice provided by international consulting firms to assist in making accurate compensation decisions for attracting and retaining HCNs.[85] Despite the potential value of surveys, however, organizations in many countries may be unwilling to participate in compensation surveys to establish market trends. For example, the idea of sharing details about their employees' pay and positions is offensive to many Russian managers. And in Mexico the public release of such information is legally prohibited. Given these privacy restrictions, some organizations may again use guidance on HCN compensation decisions from consulting firms that can obtain reliable information through their local offices, strategic alliances, and club surveys (that is, more informal surveys conducted among organizations in the same business or industry that convene to share data).[86]

A potential problem with HCN compensation may arise when other nationalities, especially PCNs, are located at the host site operation and work closely together with HCNs and perform similar work yet have a more attractive total remuneration package. Especially where HCNs perceive the foreign employees as colleagues for social comparison, this perceived inequity can lead to dissatisfaction, diminished performance, withdrawal, and ultimately a negative impact on expatriate performance and overall productivity.[87] Stephen Perkins describes an example of this potential inequity dissatisfaction with the following excerpt:

> A multinational energy company had a group of British and Spanish PhD-qualified physicists working alongside one another, at an installation in Madrid, engaged on research into solar panels for electricity generation. The Spaniards were paid 6m pesetas per month, whereas the expatriates, while receiving the same salary of 6m pesetas, in addition received a ten percent cost of living allowance, together with housing provided free of charge in one of the most up-market areas of Madrid, close to the plant, and also close to the international schools. So, the British PhDs being deployed on an expatriate basis in Madrid were receiving, all told, 2½ times as their local colleagues for exactly the same job and contribution. In addition, company cars were provided to the Brits "because they were expatriates," but not the locals. Inevitably, relations were not harmonious.[88]

To help prevent or minimize this potential conflict and drain on productivity due to perceived reward inequity, some organizations look for ways to negotiate with selected expatriates to forego certain benefits and forms of remuneration during the course of the assignment and to be rewarded financially and in other ways on termination of the assignment. Other organizations may attempt to explain compensation disparities to the pertinent HCNs (that is, those likely to make remuneration comparisons) on the grounds of a less desirable tax burden, retirement and health benefits, and so on that the apparently extra compensation is intended to cover. Or they might also try to justify the more favorable reward package by describing the additional knowledge- and experience-sharing, "boundary-spanning" role, and associated key responsibilities and expectations from corporate headquarters, both short- and long-term, that differentiate the expatriate from HCNs.[89] Finally, many organizations avoid the problem by using primarily a localization compensation approach described earlier and reducing the number of experienced expatriates dramatically, employing them in primarily short-term visits.

Inpatriate Compensation

In today's march toward increasing globalization, more and more middle- and upper-level HCN managers and professionals are being transferred for an extended period to parent country headquarters and other parent country locations for developmental purposes, to fill technical positions, to lead project teams, and to learn the corporate culture firsthand.[90] Specific remuneration programs for inpatriate employees tend to be less well defined than for expatriates, most likely as a result of less MNC experience with inpatriates beyond short-term training rotations. Although many of the same compensation issues and practices related to expatriate compensation also apply to HCNs as inpatriates, a well-conceived total compensation and benefits program should be developed for them.[91]

Global Workforce Professional Profile 10.1
**Russ Ringl and the Global
Compensation Challenge**

Russ Ringl is director of global compensation and benefits at International Rectifier, a world leader in providing electronics-enabling and cost-saving power technology to a host of industries. From company headquarters in El Segundo, California, Ringl directs International Rectifier's worldwide compensation, benefits, and expatriate compensation initiatives for more than six thousand employees in sixteen countries. In his role, Ringl serves as a strategic partner to senior management and has participated as a key member of the due diligence teams that recently completed two international acquisitions, one in the United Kingdom and the other in Germany. Ringl received a bachelor's degree in personnel management and a master's in industrial relations, both from the University of Illinois at Urbana-Champaign. He has had many years of experience, both as a generalist and compensation specialist, in human resource executive positions with firms in various industries.

Ringl is addressing an important global workforce challenge by developing a company-wide profit-sharing plan for all employees, contributing to a sense of company unity and common identity. Ringl also recognizes the great importance of adapting compensation and benefits packages to meet local preferences. He travels about 15 percent of the time to company operations in countries such as the United Kingdom, Sweden, Denmark, China, the Philippines, and India to work with local company HR professionals and plan customized packages. In China he recently was involved in strategic HR planning for a new manufacturing plant to be opened in October 2005. Based on local interviews and survey data, he and his assistants put together a compensation and benefits package that included an adjustment to the prevailing local wage program as well as medical and life insurance programs, which would be more competitive in attracting top talent to the plant. In Europe, where considerable social benefits are already provided, Ringl is challenged to look for ways to build on existing benefits to make his firm particularly attractive. Wherever he goes, Ringl is active in getting as much input as possible from company employees through internal interviews and satisfaction surveys to ensure that the company rewards are in line with employee interests. For his work to be effective, Ringl asserts, "I need to stay away from a central corporate mentality and involve local people in compensation package development."

In the ever-changing world of expatriate compensation, Ringl finds he needs to strike a delicate balance between the local employee's pay and benefits practices and the expatriate's pay and benefits demands, while at all times ensuring that the primary purpose of the expatriate's assignment is realized. Ringl finds culture to be his biggest challenge—both the corporate cultures of newly acquired firms and different national cultures where company operations are located. Says Ringl, "I love the international flavor of my work. I'm continually seeing different cultures and mentalities; I'm learning so much and really having fun!"

Unique practices and conditions in the inpatriate's home country should be considered, including differing tax, retirement, and social security regulations as well as social programs and national health care plans. In addition, other factors should be examined such as the duration of the inpatriate assignment, the inpatriate's position and rank in the firm, and the prevailing practices in the particular industry. For example, an inpatriate from a Western European country where medical care is socialized might need to be compensated an extra amount in the foreign assignment to offset higher costs of private medical coverage.[92] Another consideration that may be appropriate when planning inpatriate compensation relates to perceptions of inequity, where, for example, a talented inpatriate from a less-developed country now works side by side with PCNs on the same or similar projects requiring similar skills and duties, yet is paid much less because the expatriate is on a lower home-based remuneration model. Although the resolution to this inequity may be to reward the expatriate at the same rate as PCNs, this approach may lead to the inpatriate not wanting to eventually return home to a lower wage. In our recent conversation with international HR scholar, Jean-Luc Cerdin of Paris, he touched upon this significant challenge to the success of an MNC's inpatriation strategy when he mentioned that inpatriates who come to France from developing countries often, at the close of their inpatriate assignment, simply disappear, not wanting to return to their home country. Thus, overall rewards and incentives related to the inpatriate assignment should also consider what is needed to guarantee effective repatriation and ensure a return on the developmental investment of the inpatriate assignment. These considerations and possible concerns should be addressed carefully and discussed openly with the inpatriate candidate prior to and during the international assignment.[93]

THIRD COUNTRY NATIONAL COMPENSATION

Compensation issues and decisions for third country nationals lie on at least two primary levels: executive and low-level employee. A frequent consideration for TCNs is at the executive level, where they make up a growing contingent of global executives or international cadre who move from extended assignment to extended assignment away from their home country and are paid on a global scale following the international citizen expatriate compensation model. Aside from similar compensation considerations that TCNs at this higher level share with their PCN expatriate counterparts, particular challenges for dealing with these TCNs, due to their long-term cumulative absence from their home country, include providing health, death, and retirement benefits.[94] Within our increasingly mobile society, especially within large economic blocs such as the European Union, TCNs might even arrange to reside on weekends in their home country, such as Brussels, yet work many years at a major foreign company operation in Paris or Amsterdam.

TCNs at lower levels who immigrate into a host country represent a growing source of employees for staffing foreign operations, such as Eastern Europeans flowing (legally or illegally) into European Union countries or Mexicans and Central Americans into the United States. A direct impact that this growing global migration phenomenon has on compensation is holding down or even lowering the prevailing pay scale for lower-level workers, which is causing considerable displeasure and conflict with existing HCNs and their unions who feel increased pressure of competition for lower pay.[95] MNCs that save labor costs by staffing their host operations heavily with these TCN workers—even when they can prove legal documentation—at the neglect of HCNs may be severely criticized and suffer a damaged reputation in the host country.

SUMMARY

Compensation, including the overall system of rewards—formal and informal—provides the driving force for effectively attracting, retaining, and encouraging human talent at home and abroad. Important and fundamental practices for managing compensation on a global scale include managing global compensation strategically, considering performance-based pay where appropriate, anticipating the influence of local culture, using a total rewards system perspective, and addressing the duality challenge of global integration and localization. Careful consideration should be made to effectively address the unique needs, goals, and circumstances of major employee categories within the global workforce, including PCN expatriates, HCNs, and TCNs.

QUESTIONS FOR OPENING SCENARIO ANALYSIS

1. From this scenario and your reading, what are some of the biggest challenges faced by MNCs in their global compensation practices?
2. What are particular global compensation challenges encountered in the process of implementing successful international mergers?
3. What are major areas of convergence in global compensation, and what are forces that are driving this convergence?

CASE 10.1. EUROPE STRAINING UNDER A PENSION SYSTEM BURDEN

Joel Crevecoeur can't wait to turn sixty. "That's the day I stop working," he says, as he lines up a final pool shot and sinks the eight ball. "I'll also get the pension I've been working for my whole life." Like many Europeans, the forty-four-year-old financial analyst for Bank Degroof, a Brussels investment bank, looks forward to a comfortable postcareer life that he believes he deserves. But this bright anticipation has been greatly darkened with the recent global financial crisis that witnessed the drastic drop of stock-based pension values. Nevertheless, the expectation remains. "Americans can work until they're eighty-five," he says. "In Europe, retirement is a sacred right." This sacred right also has become a devilish headache for government leaders. With the population aging quickly, Europe's general social expectation of retirement by sixty—and often even fifty-five—is a big economic liability. Because of the increased spending and the loss of potentially productive working hours through this early retirement, the estimated average increase in European Union GDP—the total value goods and services produced—will be a mere 1.25 percent in the next few decades, according to Kieran McMorrow, a European Commission economist and co-author of the book, *The Economic and Financial Market Consequences of Global Ageing.* Governments across Europe know that pension and retirement changes are greatly needed, and some countries, such as Germany, are beginning to raise the bar for getting state pensions to age sixty-three. But reducing these benefits at either the EU or individual country level risks drawing the ire of voters.

Retirement and pension benefits began with business leaders in the United Kingdom, the United States, and Germany in the late 1890s, when they dreamed up the concept of "retirement" as a way of attracting workers to their companies and weeding out the old and inefficient workers through an enticing retirement package. Before this time, a person worked until he or she died or amassed enough cash for adequate future comfort. Public retirement systems were first devised in the United States in the 1930s with President Franklin Roosevelt's New Deal. In Europe, politicians created retirement, along with other social safety nets, during the decade after World War II. France, Germany, and Italy eagerly used their new prosperity to build a more comfortable social policy.

In various countries in Europe, people who retire by age sixty can collect government-supported pensions that equal as much as 80 percent of their employment income. In Belgium, for example, many people eagerly claim their pensions rather than keep working. Those who want to work often find part-time jobs on the black market to increase their income. Another important but less-discussed part of the problem is cultural. Early retirement has become to French, German, and Italian workers a cultural expectation—not mandated by law but something you are just supposed to do when you get to that age. In the United States, economists say most sixty-year-olds believe they still should be working; Europeans of the same age say they should be painting or gardening.

Source: Adapted from H. Van Meerten, "Pensions Reform in the European Union," *Pensions: An International Journal: Special Issue: Global Pension Perspectives—Part Two* 14 (4) (2009): 259–72; J.W. Miller, "Pension Systems Strain Europe: Early Retirement Culture Has Become a Public-Policy Headache," *Wall Street Journal*, June 16, 2004: A16.

QUESTIONS FOR CASE ANALYSIS AND DISCUSSION

1. Based on this case, how would the mix of company benefits need to be adjusted from what is typical in the United States or other non-European countries to fit the current compensation package needs in Western Europe?
2. What are some possible compensation package incentives that could be used to counter the Western European cultural expectation of early retirement and retain talented employees well into their early and mid-sixties?
3. What are important implications of this case for broader long-term human resource planning, particularly related to the trend of losing experienced workers at an earlier age than in the United States or other non-European countries?

CASE 10.2. EXECUTIVE PAY: INCREASING THE THREAT OF CHINA'S WEALTH GAP

Chinese leaders are trying to resolve two vexing problems: the economy is growing too fast, and most people feel left out of the economic boom. China's bubbling economy, which expanded 9.5 percent in 2004 despite efforts to cool it down, has produced a wealth gap and fueled a surge of social unrest that top leaders worry could undermine Communist rule. Though many issues have been debated for months, officials are gripped by a sense of crisis after several mass riots and thousands of smaller protests over land seizures, corruption, and unpaid wages shook the confidence of the leadership. To address this challenge, Hu Jintao, China's top official, is shifting the country's focus from economic growth to building a "harmonious society" through "scientific development." This ideological campaign emphasizes the need to reduce social conflict, improve social well-being, and share the wealth, replacing the more pro-growth orientation of previous leadership.

Proposals for sharing China's increasing wealth include extending social security to peasants and providing better education and health care in rural areas where many protests have originated. This "sharing of the wealth" emphasis suggests much greater future pressure on MNCs in China to contribute through increased taxes and other measures to help the government address social concerns. There also are direct individual implications for this emphasis toward greater harmony—limiting and reducing the salary gap between executives and lower employees through imposed caps on compensation. China is now considering a cap on executive pay at its state-owned enterprises. Xu Kuangdi, a vice chairman of the Chinese People's Political Consultative Conference, reported that government regulators are formulating a policy that would limit a boss's pay to fourteen times that of the average salary of a company's employees.

The proposed policy underscores the dilemma facing Chinese policy makers as they seek to balance the needs of China's state sector and its overall population. To compete successfully with foreign companies at home and abroad, China's state-owned companies must be able to attract and retain highly qualified managers. In recent years, both foreign companies and private Chinese companies have lured away some of the top Chinese talent with attractive compensation packages. Increasingly, state-run companies are responding by offering competitive salaries. However, at the same time, several corporate scandals and a widening gap between the haves and have-nots in this supposedly egalitarian society have raised complaints and protests among ordinary Chinese workers and sparked fears among leaders of social unrest. Where pressure is being felt toward capping executive compensation among Chinese state-owned enterprises, it is feasible that the pressure could also move across company boundaries to affect non-Chinese executive compensation in joint ventures, acquisitions, and other cross-border alliances with state-owned enterprises—and eventually moving completely into the private sector with government policy-imposed executive compensation restrictions.

Source: Adapted from J. Kahn, "Beijing Tries to Face Unrest over Wealth Gap," *International Herald Tribune,* March 4, 2005: 1, 8.

QUESTIONS FOR CASE ANALYSIS AND DISCUSSION

1. What are major pressures and conflicts faced by the government in this particular case involving rapid industrialization and foreign company involvement through foreign direct investment?
2. What are potential negative outcomes of possible future salary restrictions being placed by China on non-Chinese executives working in China for non-Chinese operations?
3. What are some possible policies and practices that Western firms might consider for addressing rising concerns presented by the growing pay gap described in this case?

RECOMMENDED WEB SITE RESOURCES

GlobalCan (www.goglobalcan.com). Specializes in designing customized local national compensation for MNCs. Combines the resources of the world's largest insurance companies and accountancy/payroll providers, including over eighty firms in some forty countries.

International Benefits Information Services (www.ibisnews.org). Membership-based reporting service about pensions and other employee-benefit programs throughout the world. Sponsors special institute educational programs and conferences.

ORC Worldwide (www.orcinc.com). In addition to providing comprehensive customized compensation consulting services, sponsors and provides seminars, forums, conferences, research reports, local market surveys, and peer networks for all forms of compensation and benefits and levels of employees throughout the world.

The Hay Group (www.haygroup.com). With seventy-four offices in forty-one countries, provides comprehensive customized consulting services in compensation and benefits as well as current information through seminars, conferences, and research reports. Provides an Internet-based platform that enables licensed users worldwide to access and analyze compensation information to support company decision making.

U.S. Department of Labor Bureau of Labor Statistics: Foreign Labor Statistics (www.bls.gov/fls). Provides international comparisons of hourly compensation costs; productivity and unit labor costs; labor force, employment, and unemployment rates; and consumer prices. Comparisons relate primarily to the major industrial countries, but other countries are included in certain measures.

World at Work (www.worldatwork.org). Professional association and useful source for global compensation, benefits, and total rewards information. Provides education and training, news and information, research reports and other resources, and professional networking and advice-sharing opportunities.

NOTES

1. Adapted from "International: Executive Pay Needs Realignment," *Oxford Analytica Daily Brief Service* (April 2009): 1; and "No Man Is an Island: Why Global Rates for Top Talent Are Converging," *Economist,* May 6, 1999.

2. S.J. Perkins and C. Hendry, "International Compensation," in *The Global Manager: Creating the Seamless Organization,* ed. P. Joynt and R. Morton (London: IPD, 1999): 115–43.

3. D. Bilefsky, "High-Tech Moves: European City Wins Jobs—and Looks over Its Shoulder," *Wall Street Journal,* July 8, 2004.

4. G.W. Florkowski and D.S. Fogel, "Expatriate Adjustment and Commitment: The Role of Host-Unit Treatment," *International Journal of Human Resource Management* 10 (1999): 783–807.

5. R. Mattson "Managing the Challenge of Global Compensation," *Employment Relations Today* 35 (2) (2008): 51–57; K.M. Butler, "Out of Touch: Towers Perrin Survey Shows Rewards Seldom Aligned with Business Strategy," *Employee Benefits News,* February 1, 2008: 1; A. Wright, "Don't Settle for Less: Global Compensation Programs Need Global Compensation Tools," *Employee Benefit Plan Review* 58 (9) (2000): 14–18.

6. C.F. Fey and P. Furu, "Top Management Incentive Compensation and Knowledge Sharing in Multinational Corporations," *Strategic Management Journal* 29 (12) (2008): 1301–23; M.E. Mendenhall, R.J. Jensen, J.S. Black, and H.B. Gregersen, "Seeing the Elephant: Human Resource Management Challenges in the Age of Globalization," *Organizational Dynamics* 32 (3) (2003): 261–74; G. Parker, "Establishing Remuneration Practices across Culturally Diverse Environments," *Compensation and Benefits Management* 17 (2) (2001): 23–27.

7. C.R. Greer, *Strategic Human Resource Management: A General Managerial Approach,* 2d ed. (Upper Saddle River, NJ: Prentice-Hall, 2001).

8. Perkins and Hendry, "International Compensation"; G.T. Milkovich and M. Bloom, "Rethinking International Compensation," *Compensation and Benefits Review* 30 (1) (1998): 15–23.

9. P. Evans, E. Lank, and A. Farquhar, "Managing Human Resources in the International Firm: Lessons from Practice," in *Human Resource Management in International Firms: Change, Globalization, Innovation,* ed. P. Evans, Y. Doz, and A. Laurent (London: Macmillan, 1989): 113–43.

10. C. Rosen, "The Employee Ownership Update," National Center for Employee Ownership, July 15, 2005, http://findarticles.com/p/articles/mi_m0EIN/is_20090908/ai_n35618309/; A.V. Zhuplev and C.M. Vance, "Russian Enterprise in an Emerging Market Economy: A Key Insider's View about Management Strategy for a Successful Transition," *Journal of Management Inquiry* 3 (3) (1994): 257–64.

11. W.R. Sheridan and P.T. Hansen, "Linking International Business and Expatriate Compensation Strategies," *ACA Journal* (Spring 1996): 66–79.

12. J. Shen, "Compensation in Chinese Multinationals," *Compensation and Benefits Review* 36 (1) (2004): 15–25; S. Taylor, S. Beechler, and N. Napier, "Toward an Integrative Model of Strategic International Human Resource Management," *Academy of Management Review* 21 (4) (1996): 959–85; D. Welch, "HRM Implications of Globalization," *Journal of General Management* 19 (4) (1994): 52–68.

13. W.L. French, *Human Resources Management,* 5th ed. (Boston: Houghton-Mifflin, 2003).

14. R. Herod, *Global Compensation and Benefits: Developing Policies for Local Nationals* (Alexandria, VA: Society for Human Resource Management, 2008); M. Brown and J.S. Heywood, eds., *Paying for Performance: An International Comparison* (Armonk, NY: M.E. Sharpe, 2002).

15. *Human Capital Index: Human Capital as a Lead Indicator of Shareholder Value* (Washington, DC: Watson Wyatt Worldwide, 2001).

16. J.H. Westover, A.R. Westover, and L.A. Westover, "Enhancing Long-Term Worker Productivity and Performance: The Connection of Key Work Domains to Job Satisfaction and Organizational Commitment," *International Journal of Productivity and Performance Management* 59 (4) (2010): 372–87; J. Du and J. Choi, "Pay for Performance in Emerging Markets: Insights from China," *Journal of International Business Studies* 41(4) (2010): 671–89; Perkins and Hendry, "International Compensation."

17. R.W. Mondy, R.M. Noe, and S.R. Premeaux, *Human Resource Management,* 8th ed. (Upper Saddle River, NJ: Prentice-Hall, 2002).

18. C.D. Fisher, L.F. Schoenfeldt, and J.B. Shaw, *Human Resource Management,* 5th ed. (Boston: Houghton-Mifflin, 2003).

19. G.T. Milkovich, J. Newman, J.M. Newman, and C. Milkovich, *Compensation,* 7th ed. (New York: McGraw-Hill, 2001); G.T. Milkovich and A.K. Wigdor, *Pay for Performance: Evaluating Performance Appraisal and Merit Pay* (Washington, DC: National Academy Press, 1991).

20. M. Brown and J.S. Heywood, "Paying for Performance: What Has Been Learned?" in *Paying for Performance: An International Comparison,* ed. M. Brown and J.S. Heywood (Armonk, NY: M.E. Sharpe, 2002): 261–75.

21. P. LeBlanc and P. Mulvey, "How American Workers See the Rewards of Work," *Compensation and Benefits Review* 30 (1998): 24–31; Milkovich and Wigdor, *Pay for Performance.*

22. Brown and Heywood, "Paying for Performance."

23. J. Shields, "Performance Related Pay in Australia," in *Paying for Performance: An International Comparison,* 179–213; T. Kato, "Financial Participation and Pay for Performance in Japan," in *Paying for Performance: An International Comparison,* 214–35.

24. Herod, *Global Compensation and Benefits;* M.A. Von Glinow, E.A. Drost, and M.B. Teagarden, "Converging on IHRM Best Practices: Lessons Learned from a Globally Distributed Consortium on Theory and Practice," *Human Resource Management* 41 (1) (2002): 123–39.

25. Watson Wyatt Worldwide, *Strategic Rewards: Charting the Course Forward: Maximizing the Value of Reward Programs,* (Survey Report Washington, DC, 2002/2003).

26. J. McGregor, "Keeping Talent in the Fold," *Business Week,* November 3, 2008.

27. "International: Executive Pay Needs Realignment," *Oxford Analytica Daily Brief Service* (April 2009): 1.

28. F. Cairncross, "Survey: Pay: The Politics of Envy," *Economist,* May 8, 1999.

29. A. Blackman, "Putting a Ceiling on Pay," *Wall Street Journal,* April 12, 2004; M. Walker, "Deutsche Bank Trial Tests Bonus Pay," *Wall Street Journal,* January 20, 2004; F. Cairncross, "Survey: Pay: The Politics of Envy," *The Economist*, May 8, 1999.

30. J. Shields, personal communication on July 23, 2003.

31. Von Glinow et al., "Converging on IHRM Best Practices: Lessons Learned from a Globally Distributed Consortium on Theory and Practice."

32. G.S. Marin, "National Differences in Compensation: The Influence of the Institutional and Cultural Context," in *Global Compensation*, ed. L.G. Mejia and S. Werner (London: Routledge, 2008); Herod, *Global Compensation and Benefits*; R.S. Schuler, S.E. Jackson, and Y. Luo, *Managing Human Resources in Cross-Border Alliances* (London: Routledge, 2004); N.M. Firoz, A.S. Maghrabi, and K.H. Kim, "Think Globally, Manage Culturally," *International Journal of Commerce and Management* 12 (3/4) (2002): 32–50; Parker, "Establishing Remuneration Practices across Culturally Diverse Environments."

33. Parker, "Establishing Remuneration Practices across Culturally Diverse Environments."

34. D.A. Ralston, K.C. Yu, X. Wang, R.H. Terpstra, and W. He, "The Cosmopolitan Chinese Manager: Findings of a Study on Managerial Values across the Six Regions of China," *Journal of International Management* 2 (1996): 79–109.

35. M. Muller, "Employee Representation & Pay in Austria, Germany, and Sweden," *International Studies of Management & Organization* 29 (4) (1999/2000): 67–83; K. Newman and S. Hollen, "Culture and Congruence: The Fit between Management Practices and National Culture," *Journal of International Business Studies* (4th Quarter, 1996): 753–79; P. Early, "Self or Group Cultural Effects of Training on Self-Efficacy and Performance," *Advanced Science Quarterly* 39 (1994): 89–117.

36. Adapted from Schuler, Jackson, and Luo, *Managing Human Resources in Cross-Border Alliances*; G. Hofstede, "Cultural Constraints in Management Theories," *Academy of Management Executive* 71 (1) (1997): 81–93.

37. G.T. Milkovich and M. Bloom, "Rethinking International Compensation," *Compensation and Benefits Review* 30 (1) (1998): 15–23.

38. H. Chen and Y. Hsieh, "Key Trends of the Total Reward System in the 21st Century," *Compensation and Benefits Review* 38 (6) (2006): 64–70; G. Parker and E.S. Janush, "Developing Expatriate Remuneration Packages," *Employee Benefits Journal* 26 (2) (2001): 3–5.

39. Adapted from Mondy, Noe, and Premeaux, *Human Resource Management*.

40. E.A. Grant, "How to Retain Talent in India," *Sloan Management Review* 50 (1) 2008: 6–7; *Strategic Rewards: Charting the Course Forward: Maximizing the Value of Reward Programs.*

41. F. Hansen, "Currents in Compensation and Benefits," *Compensation and Benefits Review* 33 (5) (2001): 6–24.

42. Grant, "How to Retain Talent in India"; M. Johnson, "Beyond Pay: What Rewards Work Best when Doing Business in China," *Compensation and Benefits Review* 30 (6) (1998): 51–56.

43. M. Buckingham and C. Coffman, *First, Break All the Rules: What the World's Greatest Managers Do Differently* (New York: Simon & Schuster, 1999).

44. F.F. Fournies, *Coaching for Improved Work Performance,* rev. ed. (New York: McGraw-Hill, 2000).

45. R.F. Mager and P. Pipe, *Analyzing Performance Problems,* 3rd ed. (Atlanta, GA: CEP Press, 1997).

46. Parker et al., "Developing Expatriate Remuneration Packages."

47. Milkovich and Bloom, "Rethinking International Compensation."

48. S. Kerr, "On the Folly of Rewarding A, while Hoping for B," *Academy of Management Executive* 9 (1) (1995): 7–14.

49. Fey and Furu, "Top Management Incentive Compensation and Knowledge Sharing in Multinational Corporations."

50. Mendenhall, Jensen, Black, and Gregersen, "Seeing the Elephant: Human Resource Management Challenges in the Age of Globalization"; H.P. Conn and G.S. Yip, "Global Transfer of Critical Capabilities," *Business Horizons* 40 (1) (1997): 22–31; S.J. Perkins and C. Hendry, "Global Champions: Who's Paying Attention?" *Thunderbird International Review* 43 (1) (2001): 53–75.

51. For examples refer to D. Magee, *How Carlos Ghosn Rescued Nissan* (New York: HarperBusiness, 2003); C. Rhoads and G.T. Sims, "German Wage Reform Gets New Life," *Wall Street Journal,* July 22, 2003.

52. Von Glinow et al., "Converging on IHRM Best Practices: Lessons Learned from a Globally Distributed Consortium on Theory and Practice."

53. L. Claus, "Similarities and Differences in Human Resource Management in the European Union," *Thunderbird International Business Review* 45 (6) (2003): 729–55; A. Joyce, "A World of Difference for Women: One Global Company Had to Change Its Personnel Policy to Fit Local Custom," *Washington Post,* February 2, 2003; M. Budman, "What's Holding Back European Women?" *Across the Board* 39 (4) (2002): 71–72.

54. G. Hofstede, *Culture's Consequences: International Differences in Work-Related Values* (Newbury Park, CA: Sage, 1980); R.S. Schuler and N. Rogovsky, "Understanding Compensation Practice Variations across Firms: The Impact of National Culture," *Journal of International Business Studies* 29 (1) (1998): 159–77.

55. M. Bloom, G.T. Milkovich, and A. Mitra, "International Compensation: Learning from How Managers Respond to Variations in Local Host Contexts," *International Journal of Human Resource Management* 14 (8) (2003): 1350–67.

56. Ibid., 1360.

57. Milkovich and Bloom, "Rethinking International Compensation."

58. Ibid.

59. Article 7 of EU Directive 93/104/European Commission; The Confederation of German Employers' Association (unpublished data, 1999) reported in H. Jorgensen, "Give Me a Break: The Extent of Paid Holidays and Vacation," Center for Economic and Policy Research http://www.cepr.net/give_me_a_break.htm#_ftn3.

60. M.J. Duane, *Policies and Practices in Global Human Resource Systems* (Westport, CT: Quorum Books, 2001); R.K. Chiu et al., "Retaining and Motivating Employees"; Milkovich and Bloom, "Rethinking International Compensation."

61. *Strategic Rewards: Charting the Course Forward: Maximizing the Value of Reward Programs.*

62. C.D. Fisher and A. Yuan, "What Motivates Employees? A Comparison of US and Chinese Responses," *International Journal of Human Resource Management* 9 (3) (1998): 516–28; C. Reynolds, "Global Compensation and Benefits in Transition," *Compensation and Benefits Review* (January–February 2000): 28–38.

63. S.E. Gross and P.L. Wingerup, "Global Pay? Maybe Not Yet!" *Compensation and Benefits Review* (July–August 1999): 25–34.

64. P. Evans, V. Pucik, and J.-L. Barsoux, *The Global Challenge: Frameworks for International Human Resource Management* (Boston: McGraw-Hill/Irwin, 2002); S.P. Nurney, "When to Stop Negotiating Individual Packages for International Assignees," *Compensation and Benefits Review* 33

(4) (2001): 62–67; "KPMG Transferring Abroad: The 50 Most Common Concerns," *International Headquarters* (1998).

65. Florkowski and Fogel, "Expatriate Adjustment and Commitment: The Role of Host-Unit Treatment."

66. Perkins and Hendry, "Global Champions: Who's Paying Attention?"

67. Evans, Pucik, and Barsoux, *The Global Challenge: Frameworks for International Human Resource Management,* 135.

68. See M.L. O'Reilly, "Expatriate Pay: The State of the Art," *Compensation and Benefits Management* (Winter 1996): 54–59; C. Reynolds, *Compensating Globally Mobile Employees* (Scottsdale, AZ: American Compensation Association, 1995); C.M. Gould, "The Impact of Headquarters Location on Expatriate Policy," *HR Magazine* 43 (5) (1998): 8–12; also refer to ORC Worldwide about custom approaches to expatriate compensation at www.orcinc.com.

69. P. Chigbo, "The Inside Scoop on Inpatriates," *CA Magazine* 134 (4) (2001): 14.

70. R. Herod, *Expatriate Compensation: The Balance Sheet Approach* (Alexandria, VA: Society for Human Resource Management, 2008).

71. Reynolds, *Compensating Globally Mobile Employees.*

72. Herod, *Expatriate Compensation.*

73. Gould, "The Impact of Headquarters Location on Expatriate Policy."

74. Herod, *Expatriate Compensation;* G.W. Latta and T.A. Danielsen, "Treatment of Expatriate Tax: A Look at U.S., U.K., and Canadian Practices," *Compensation and Benefits Review* 35 (5) (2003): 54–59.

75. Parker and Janush, "Developing Expatriate Remuneration Packages."

76. K. Leung, Y. Zhu and C. Ge, "Compensation Disparity between Locals and Expatriates: Moderating the Effects of Perceived Injustice in Foreign Multinationals in China," *Journal of World Business* 44 (1) (2009): 85–93; Herod, *Expatriate Compensation.*

77. J. Shen, "Compensation in Chinese Multinationals," *Compensation and Benefits Review* 36 (1) (2004): 15–25.

78. Perkins and Hendry, "Global Champions: Who's Paying Attention?"

79. S.M. Toh and A.S. Denisi, "Host Country National Reactions to Expatriate Pay Policies: A Model and Implications," *Academy of Management Review* 28 (4) (2003): 606–21; V. Suutari, "Global Leader Development: An Emerging Research Agenda," *Career Development International* 7 (4) (2002): 218–33; C.M. Vance and E.S. Paderon, "An Ethical Argument for Host Country Workforce Training and Development in the Expatriate Management Assignment," *Journal of Business Ethics* 12 (8) (1993): 635–41.

80. M. Harvey, T.S. Kiessling, and N. Milorad, "Staffing Marketing Positions during Global Hyper-Competitiveness: A Market-Based Perspective," *International Journal of Human Resource Management* 14 (2) (2003): 223–45; M.G. Harvey and M.M. Novicevic, "Strategic Global Human Resource Management: The Role of Inpatriate Managers," *Human Resource Management Review* 10 (2) (2000): 153–75.

81. C.M. Vance, J.T. Wholihan, and E.S. Paderon, "The Imperative for Host Country Workforce Training and Development as Part of the Expatriate Management Assignment: Toward a New Research Agenda," in *Research in Personnel & Human Resource Management: International Supplement 3,* ed. J.B. Shaw, P. Kirkbride, G. Ferris, and K. Rowland (Greenwich, CT: JAI Press, 1993): 359–73; M.G. Harvey, M.M. Novicevic, and C. Speir, "An Innovative Global Management Staffing System: A Competency-Based Perspective," *Human Resource Management* 39 (4) (2000): 381–94; M.G. Harvey, M.F. Price, C. Speir, and M.M. Novicevic, "The Role of Inpatriates in a Globalization Strategy and Challenges Associated with the Inpatriation Process," *HR Planning* 22 (1) (1999): 38–50.

82. S.J. Perkins, *Internationalization: The People Dimension* (London: Kogan Page, 1997).

83. Harvey et al., "The Role of Inpatriates in a Globalization Strategy."

84. Parker, "Establishing Remuneration Practices across Culturally Diverse Environments."

85. Herod, *Global Compensation and Benefits.*

86. Anonymous, "Towers Perrin & Mercer Examine Pay Levels and Increases in 26 Countries," *IOMA's Report on Salary Surveys* 1 (1) (2001): 2; Perkins and Hendry, "International Compensation."

87. Parker, "Establishing Remuneration Practices across Culturally Diverse Environments."

88. S.J. Perkins, *Internationalization: The People Dimension* (London: Kogan Page, 1997): 110–11.

89. Perkins and Hendry, "International Compensation"; Perkins, *Internationalization: The People Dimension.*

90. C.M. Solomon, "HR's Helping Hand Pulls Global Inpatriates Onboard," *Personnel Journal* 74 (1995): 40–49.

91. M. Harvey and N. Miceli, "Exploring Inpatriate Managers Issues: An Exploratory Empirical Study," *International Journal of Intercultural Relations* 23 (3) (2000): 339–71; M. Harvey and M. Buckley, "Managing Inpatriates: Building Global Core Competency," *Journal of World Business* 32 (1) (1997): 35–52.

92. S.C. Peppas and L. Chang, "The Integration of Inpatriates into Rural Communities," *Management Decision* 36 (6) (1998): 370–77.

93. M.G. Harvey, "Inpatriate Managers: How to Increase the Probability of Success," *Human Resource Management Review* 9 (1) (1999): 51–81; O. Chigbo, "The Inside Scoop on Inpatriates," *CA Magazine* 134 (4) (2001): 14.

94. Perkins and Hendry, *Global Champions*; Parker, "Establishing Remuneration Practices."

95. N. Buckley, "Nation Needs More Migrants," *Financial Times,* April 21, 2006; K.B. Richburg, "Doors Close on EU's New Eastern Front," *Seattle Times,* August 3, 2003; J. Millman and C. Vitzthum, "Changing Tide: Europe Becomes New Destination for Latino Workers," *Wall Street Journal,* September 12, 2003; S.P. Huntington, "The Hispanic Challenge," *Foreign Policy* 141 (March/April 2004): 30–45.

11 Global Employee Relations

WORKPLACE DEMORALIZATION AND DEATH

The body of nineteen-year-old Ma Xiangqian was found at 4:30 A.M. in front of his high-rise company's campus dormitory. The police concluded that he had committed suicide, leaping to his death from a high floor balcony. Ma reportedly hated his work at Foxconn, the world's biggest contract electronics supplier with over four hundred thousand employees in Shenzhen, China, making products for global companies like Apple, Dell, and Hewlett-Packard. Ma's recent pay stub indicated that he worked 286 hours in the month before his death, including 112 hours of overtime, which was about three times the legal limit. He had worked for about three months on an extended overnight shift, seven nights a week, beginning with metal and plastic parts assembly amid dust and fumes, until he was demoted to toilet-cleaning after a conflict with his supervisor.

One suicide is certainly tragic, but what has really grabbed the global spotlight is the twelve additional suicides or attempted suicides over the next four months at the same company—all falling from a campus dormitory—all male and female employees aged 18 to 24, and relatively new to the production facility. Common employee complaints have surfaced about military-style drills, verbal abuse by superiors, "self-criticisms" that employees must read aloud, and occasional pressure to work as many as thirteen consecutive days to complete a big customer order, which often required sleeping on the factory floor. Many workers are migrants from distant rural areas of China seeking an opportunity to support themselves and help family members back home. But the very low wage and dehumanizing working conditions, the lack of purpose and prospects for a better future often render them demoralized and hopeless.

Rather than take their own lives, tens of thousands of other deeply dissatisfied workers at Foxconn have simply quit after only a few months, rejecting the regimented hardships that previous generations endured as the cheap labor army behind China's economic miracle. Many other manufacturers in China also struggle with extremely high turnover. Throughout southern China, the country's industrial heartland, there is an acute labor shortage as a new generation of young employees, better educated and more conscious of their rights, seek more favorable employment conditions and options, including the service sector and jobs closer to home.

Western corporate customers of Foxconn have reported that they are looking into the working conditions there. Steve Jobs, Apple's CEO, said that he was troubled by the suicides, but that Foxconn was "not a sweatshop." Foxconn has defended its operation, saying that it treats workers with respect. Nevertheless, it is very concerned about the spate of suicides, and intends to address worker ills by improving management skills and workplace culture. It also has more than doubled employee wages, and plans to add hotlines and access to counseling, including personal and spiritual advisement by consulting monks.

INTRODUCTION

Employee relations, known simply as "ER" in many organizations, is the broad area of human resources dealing with the nature and quality of the relationship between organizations and their employees.[1] This relationship is characterized by the manner in which employees are treated with regard to their physical, psychological, and economic well-being. This treatment is also influenced by several external factors such as unions and governments, and especially prevailing economic conditions as we recently have felt with the global economic crisis. Thus, the primary focus of employee relations in global workforce management is on the nature in which employees' personal interests and needs are protected and served by MNCs as well as influenced by other external factors.

Besides the MNC, other important external parties have important roles and responsibilities in attending to the interests and welfare of employees, and are often quite influential. Several of these important external parties and influences were discussed in Chapter 1, including social preferences, employee interest organizations (such as unions and NGOs), governments (both individually and collectively through multilateral agreements), and intergovernmental organizations such as the UN, ILO, and WTO. Globally competent firms should be aware of these different external parties and influences in managing a productive employment relationship. Our ER focus in this chapter will be on the roles and influence of the two principal parties of company and employees. In addition, we will examine the influence of unions representing the legal voice of employees.

Commonly—especially in the past—the field encompassing human resources and ER has been referred to more narrowly as industrial relations, labor relations (emphasizing labor unions), or even the combined "industrial and labor relations" (ILR). In this chapter our broad use of ER is inclusive of both union and nonunion workplace arrangements and influences. In addition, our intended scope for global ER reflects the much broader and expanding array of employee work environments beyond industrial and heavy manufacturing. This chapter first examines several current and pressing ER issues in global workforce management. With these major current issues in mind, we consider important practices of MNCs for optimizing their success in globally managing the employment relationship, followed by forms of influence and current issues related to labor unions.

CURRENT ER ISSUES

Ferocious global economic competition has spawned a relentless search by MNCs for the lowest production and operational costs. Their competitive survival often depends on their success in this search. On the supply side, the increasing accessibility of the world's workers has created a huge pool of labor vying to compete for MNCs' low-paying jobs, with little ability to refuse the unsafe working conditions that contribute to low operational costs. And many governments, desperate for increased jobs and national economic strength provided by MNC foreign direct investment, also compete in attracting MNCs for access to cheap and/or skilled labor. Fortunately, market imperatives compete with the tendency to seek the lowest labor costs and help to maintain employment in traditional markets—the advantage of locating business operations near consumers for company recognition and acceptance as well as for logistics savings.

Given this background of global competitive pressure and opportunities for achieving lower labor costs, much of the global labor force is vulnerable to workplace abuse by some shortsighted, unethical organizations—those that seek to maximize their benefits at the expense of workers and their communities. Other organizations with no malicious intent may inadvertently contribute to employee workplace difficulties and abuse due to lack of awareness of the impact of their business activities, such as through their distantly managed operations that are outsourced and contracted to foreign companies and state-owned enterprises. We now will examine current critical global ER issues and challenges related to worker protection that companies should be aware of and consider in their ongoing business planning, including in cooperation with local governments, unions, and other parties concerned with employee protection. These issues include forced labor, harmful child labor, workplace discrimination, health and safety hazards, and job insecurity and displacement.

FORCED LABOR

From an ethical perspective, we believe that the nature of the job in which one is engaged is just as important as whether one is employed. Some jobs are contrary to basic social and human rights and international law and will always be "bad" or unacceptable wherever they are found, regardless of the level of a country's economic development. Many unacceptable jobs are represented by various forms of forced labor, or labor in which the worker is engaged involuntarily and under some form of duress or threat of negative consequence (see Figure 11.1).

The most common form of forced labor is bonded servitude, typically arranged to fulfill a debt or other obligation. Bonded servitude is still common in Southeast Asia, such as when one is forced to enter a working arrangement (essentially slavery) until a debt is paid—or perhaps as a permanent arrangement. A conservative estimate by the ILO (International Labour Organization, a major administrative agency of the United Nations) places the number of victims of forced labor globally at 12.3 million, or at least four victims of forced labor per thousand workers.[2] Certain relatively low-power groups, such as women, ethnic or racial minorities, migrants, children, and the severely economically disadvantaged, are particularly vulnerable to being trapped in various forms of forced labor.

Globally, the majority of cases of forced labor (64 percent) are created by private agents for the purpose of nonsexual economic exploitation. Only 20 percent of all forced labor is perpetrated by governments or armed forces (official or guerrilla),

Figure 11.1 **Forms of Forced Labor**

- Bonded servitude
- Slavery
- Compulsory participation in public works projects
- Forced labor in agriculture and remote rural areas
- Domestic workers in forced labor situations
- Forced labor imposed by the military
- Some aspects of coerced prison labor and rehabilitation through work
- Forced labor imposed by private agents for commercial sexual exploitation

while forced commercial sexual exploitation represents 11 percent of all cases. The category of nonsexual economic exploitation in many cases can be combined with government-imposed forced labor because governments often provide contracted services for MNCs through their state-owned enterprises.[3] According to an ILO global estimate, the greatest number of workers in forced labor conditions for economic exploitation and state-imposed work are in Asian and Pacific countries, followed closely by Latin America and the Caribbean—the primary difference being due to greater state-induced forced labor in Asian and Pacific countries. Other significant locations of economic exploitation through forced labor are in sub-Saharan Africa, followed by the Middle East and North Africa.

Forced labor jobs are typically located in the worker's home country, but also may be found abroad as a result of a growing trend in human trafficking—an illegal global industry estimated at over $14 billion per year. This trend can be noted in cases of transferring workers illegally from poorer countries into developed countries under bonded servitude and in underpaid, dire conditions with the promise, often violated, of future new citizenship and financial prosperity, coupled with the threat of disclosure leading to deportation, local imprisonment, or worse. In many of these cases uncomfortable and unhealthy sweatshop work environments are formed, violating local and global labor standards, through unethical manufacturing and even high-tech "body shop" subcontracted services providers that lie outside of the direct view of large corporations. Unsuspecting organizations, in the interest of securing cheap labor contracts in their own domestic context, often overlook their due diligence responsibilities regarding the documentation details and working conditions of their contracted workers. Due to the above threats, the mistreated workers are afraid to resist and complain to authorities.[4] About 20 percent of all forced labor for economic exploitation is due to human trafficking. Although a relatively small amount of forced labor for economic exploitation is found in industrialized countries and transition countries (for example, former Eastern bloc countries such as the Czech Republic and Romania), approximately 75 percent of forced labor in these countries comes from human trafficking.[5] In one instance, a pickle factory in the United States employed several Indian workers through an international labor-recruitment firm. Upon arrival in the United States the workers' legal travel documents were forcibly taken from them, and they were forced to work twelve to sixteen hours a day, six days a week, at well below the legal minimum wage. Finally, several workers escaped and eventually filed a civil suit against their employer.[6]

HARMFUL CHILD LABOR

An especially heinous form of forced labor for economic exploitation is harmful child labor. Through excessive working hours and under poor conditions, as well as at the neglect of education, the child's personal development can be greatly compromised and permanently damaged, pointing to a lifetime of poverty and misery.[7] This harmful child labor is a pervasive problem throughout the world, especially in developing countries, where work is frequently considered necessary to support family livelihood. Approximately 180 million children between the ages of five and fifteen are engaged in forced labor, or about one in eight children across the world. The Asia/Pacific region has the greatest incidence of child labor at 60 percent of the global total, with sub-Saharan African next at 23 percent.[8] Working children often are the objects of extreme exploitation, where they toil for long hours for minimal pay and under poor working conditions, frequently not provided adequate stimulation and other conditions for proper physical and mental development.

As part of a vicious cycle, child labor is recognized as a cause of poverty because it deprives children of the education, skills, and health they need to find suitable employment at an appropriate age, which could help lift them out of poverty. The absence of national policies actively discouraging child labor, or ensuring effective school attendance of all children up to the specified age, directly and indirectly encourages conditions in which child labor can exist, thereby undermining future skills formation and economic growth. This situation calls for collaborative measures by local governments and businesses to eradicate the need for child labor by improving the employment wage conditions of parents and older children.

Nike announced that it would no longer employ workers younger than eighteen years of age in its shoe factories, putting an end to any fears that it was hiring child labor. Although at first appearing positive, this plan does little for the seventeen-year-old in Indonesia or Vietnam who would rather work for an American multinational than for a domestic employer. Age eighteen is well beyond the end of minimal compulsory education in most Asian countries, the age where the child labor line should be drawn. Nike's solution is partial at best and perhaps even counterproductive, because it ignores the economic reality facing millions of children around the world. The best thing for children, of course, is to stay in school, acquiring skills that will increase their future earning capacity. Several developing countries, including Brazil and Mexico, have launched innovative schemes aimed at providing financial support to poor families so that their children need not leave school to beg or seek work. In some parts of Brazil, for example, school attendance of children from low-income families is encouraged through an income subsidy to mothers conditional upon the children's enrollment and attendance. The positive results of this approach are being closely examined with a view to its wider adoption, both within Brazil and in other countries. There is no guarantee that basic education and effective school attendance will reduce poverty, but lessons from many countries suggest that policies involving investments in present and future labor force education form a major part of a productive response to poverty.[9]

But not all children stay in school, and for them employment in an MNC's manufacturing plant might be better than the next-best legal alternatives: working in domestic industries or begging. An extreme, inflexible policy against all child labor, even part-time, under the age of eighteen could prove more harmful than the child labor itself. For example, in the 1990s, an ethics crusade was launched against major manufacturers of soccer balls, including such brand names as Reebok and Nike. Their balls were made mainly in Pakistan, often by children. Due to the outcry, the companies set up a new manufacturing facility and outlawed the use of child labor. Unfortunately, the community that once made the balls suffered when the companies quit the town due to higher labor costs, leaving the community with fewer job opportunities and no further educational prospects for local workers, especially women and children. Here we see that ethical decision making leading to long-range positive outcomes also must take into account the prevailing relative level of economic development and the potential unintended impact of well-intended decisions.[10]

WORKPLACE DISCRIMINATION

Another major global workforce ER challenge is workplace discrimination, which can have a harmful effect on the economic well-being and livelihood of people from several demographic groups within the global labor force, including racial minorities, members of particular religions, older individuals, women, the disabled, and regional migrants and immigrants.[11] Not only should discrimination be avoided to protect the interests and rights of individuals but efforts also should be made to prevent discriminatory practices where possible to ensure that business decisions are valid and based on relevant job-performance criteria—decisions associated with optimal business performance. For example, although under some conditions nepotism might be a useful recruitment practice to quickly yield an adequate supply of workers, an ongoing recruitment approach that relies primarily on family relationships rather than actual job applicant qualifications and merit will likely lead to a workforce with suboptimal talent and little diversity of background and experience to contribute to company success in a global economy.

In an increasing number of countries, companies can be fined severely for illegal discriminatory practices in the treatment of their employees and potential job candidates, causing an additional burden to their ability to compete. Companies are also finding that they face an "extraterritorial effect," where their legal liability for unfair discrimination can cross national borders to protect their expatriate employees assigned to other countries where antidiscrimination laws may be weak or nonexistent. In addition, despite MNCs' location of home headquarters, they are subject to the local antidiscrimination laws of the host countries, thus protecting HCNs and TCNs. And in some cases equality of treatment requirements can transcend national borders. For example, in a high-profile case, a forty-two-year-old British investment banker who had worked seventeen years for Merrill Lynch in London sued her former U.S.-based employer on British statutes for sex discrimination, unequal pay, and unfair dismissal. She maintained that because she was doing like work and work of equal value as her male colleagues in other countries, she should have been compensated accordingly.[12]

Besides decreased performance capability and increased legal liability due to work-place discrimination, companies can suffer significant damage in image and reputation among consumers and potential employees. Potential customers may boycott or do other damage, even violence, to businesses that are known to discriminate against people like themselves. And where worker shortages exist, including critical high-tech and professional services, regional migrants and immigrants attracted by high work demand may be hesitant to relocate to areas where others like them have experienced discrimination.[13] For example, Britain has significant dependence on foreign nurses, with one in four nurses in some National Health Service (NHS) hospitals having been recruited from abroad, notably South Africa and India. One study found evidence that many of these nurses were being denied promotion due to institutional racism. According to Pippa Gough, who researched the study,

> We have had a huge influx of internationally recruited nurses over the past few years and the NHS is now increasingly dependent on them to plug its staffing problems. But these nurses are finding it very difficult to progress up the career ladder. If we do not do something about this, these foreign nurses are going to be lured to other countries, such as America, and the NHS will be left unable to attract and retain international staff. That could be disastrous. (p. 16)[14]

HEALTH AND SAFETY HAZARDS

The right to a safe and healthful workplace is under threat around the world as the competitive global economy puts tremendous pressure on reducing and minimizing costs associated with occupational health and safety regulations. Worldwide, according to the International Confederation of Free Trade Unions, there are two million fatalities on the job each year (3,300 deaths per day) and 160 million new cases of work-related diseases.[15] Moreover, it is estimated that for each fatality there are 1,200 accidents resulting in three or more days off from work and 5,000 accidents requiring first aid.[16]

In 1984 at the U.S. MNC Union Carbide's plant in Bhopal, India, due to poor training and inadequate safety precautions, a forty-five-ton lethal gas leak killed more than 3,800 people and disabled more than 20,000 in the surrounding community. Workers in Mexico's U.S.-border maquiladoras and in other developing country host operations, like those at Union Carbide's Bhopal plant, often live immediately adjacent to the worksite, in part because wages are so low that they need to be able to walk to work. Not only do workers and the community suffer the catastrophic effects of disasters like that at Bhopal but the employees also regularly receive a "double dose" of toxic exposure—at work and in their homes and communities where the toxicity is also found.[17] Yet the overlap of occupational and community/environmental exposure occurs in both the developed and developing worlds. The lack of updated standards and new rules to address newly recognized hazards, plus the lack of resources (human, financial, and technical) for enforcement activities, clearly indicate that in many cases developed countries face a risk of heading in the same direction as many developing countries.

Direct and indirect company costs due to workplace health and safety neglect leading to debilitating accidents and illness can be considerable, including the following:

- Wages paid for time lost
- Damage to material or equipment
- Higher-paid overtime work by others to fill in for an injured employee
- Disability payments
- Increased company health insurance premiums
- Litigation and possible fines where liability is determined
- Time and expense to recruit and train a replacement to an equal level of performance
- Time spent to investigate an accident

In avoiding these costs, we note that an ethical commitment to meeting employee health and safety needs does not have to detract from a company's competitive viability. Measures aimed at improving occupational safety and health, particularly in the sectors most likely to employ low-skilled labor (such as agriculture, construction, and small-scale manufacturing), can help considerably in raising the sustained performance and productivity of workers and, hence, workers' own motivation and sense of workplace value.[18]

However, if the previously mentioned cost-saving evidence is not enough to redirect company attention and commitment toward improved global workforce health and safety, these firms should understand that liability for health and safety neglect in foreign operations may be decided by their home country's unsympathetic and more globally responsible courts, as U.S. MNCs have found under the Alien Torts Claims Act. U.S. MNCs have witnessed a seemingly unending spate of individual claims litigation supported by this act against Union Carbide due to the Bhopal disaster. The threat from this home country legislation, more than pressure from the governments of developing countries that host foreign operations, has forced firms to tighten safety procedures, upgrade plant safety precautions, and educate workers and communities.[19]

JOB INSECURITY AND DISPLACEMENT

The availability of meaningful employment to protect an individual's ability to earn a decent wage and support personal and family livelihood represents one of the most fundamental global ER concerns. Job insecurity and the threat of worker displacement, which certainly are nothing new and pose a perennial challenge, have increased to a great degree in developing countries due to the pressures and opportunities of globalization as well as technological advancements (for example, through global outsourcing of internal company work and automation).[20] Job loss and worker displacement are major concerns in developing countries, such as China, where entry onto the world business competitive stage places great pressure on increased efficiency of operations and away from inefficient, overstaffed state-owned and subsidized enterprises.[21] Although companies must maintain a primary focus on economic survival and profitability, they still should keep in mind their social responsibility to minimize the negative impact of their business decisions on the well-being of the host countries and communities where their operations are located. As we will examine in more detail later related to handling employee terminations and redundancies, companies should work closely with local governments to lessen the negative impact of operation closures and job loss. And, where possible, MNCs should contribute in the long run to greater skill development within the local labor force, as well as to overall increased socioeconomic stability.

INFLUENCE OF MNCS AND UNIONS ON GLOBAL ER

The practice of ER throughout the world can differ dramatically, and in each business environment context the practice of ER can have several external sources of influence.[22] On the other hand, internal company factors such as company culture, general management philosophy, and prevailing management style also can be very influential in determining ER practices despite heavy government regulation and union presence in the external context, such as the case of McDonald's in Germany.[23] As mentioned earlier, the parties that constitute the primary employment relationship underlying an organization's ER are the company and employees, both individually and collectively, such as when employees are organized in a union. Both the employees and the MNC (including managers and executives representing the MNC who determine and carry out company policy) have a principal influence on the nature and duration of the employment relationship in which ER takes place. Although we now will focus on the part played by MNCs in the employment relationship, we want to emphasize the importance of the active voice and participation of individual employees in determining the nature of this relationship and how they are treated and managed in organizations. And although unions are often considered external to the primary company-employee employment relationship, we also will examine their influence on ER because they often represent the voice of employees. Finally, MNCs should also be familiar with other external forces, as discussed in Chapter 1, such as governments, intergovernmental organizations, and NGOs, which can have a powerful impact on MNC ER decisions and activities. International and local NGOs in particular, compared to the overall waning influence of unions, are increasingly vocal and influential in bringing changes and improvements in employee safety and rights protection.

ROLE OF MNCS IN GLOBAL EMPLOYEE RELATIONS

How should MNCs be involved with the pressing ER issues and challenges presented earlier? Certainly they should expect to follow local regulations of all kinds, including those regarding the treatment of employees. But do MNCs have an ethical responsibility to respect and adhere to the same home country ER practices in their *host country* operations, even though the host country might not have any such standards or regulations, or if they have them, ignore them through virtually nonexistent enforcement? In our competitive global economy, the decisions and actions of MNCs entering new countries can become moral dilemmas. However, as MNC

Global Workforce Challenge 11.1
Model of ER Excellence: Plamex of Tijuana, Mexico

Plamex is a Mexican subsidiary of Plantronics, Inc. (the leading manufacturer of lightweight communications headsets based in Santa Cruz, California) and operates several manufacturing and R&D facilities in the Otay Mesa area of Tijuana, Baja California Norte, Mexico. Innovative in manufacturing and its learning environment, Plamex has won multiple domestic international awards for quality and excellence, workplace safety, and environmental protection.

Fully staffed and managed by Mexican nationals, Plamex is clearly committed to employee involvement, development, and continuous learning. Customized to the local Mexican workforce, local Plamex ER practices include the following:

- Employees are organized in work teams that gather regularly for process and creativity improvement meetings, and are measured both for their efficiencies and their innovation and morale.
- Numerous kiosks are located around the workplace that detail career paths, educational requirements, and opportunities, allowing each employee to form a learning and training plan for advancement opportunities.
- Extensive relationships with local and U.S.-based universities, who offer both certificate and degree programs in general education and engineering on site.
- Each new employee is given a business card, regardless of department or work level, which builds a strong sense of company identity and commitment.
- Each employee is enrolled in a program called "Puntomania" in which she/he can earn points for attendance and performance. The points are redeemed for items carrying Plamex logos (shirts, bags, coffee cups, etc.)
- Children of employees are regularly invited to picnics and festivals at Plamex so they can see where their parents work and to build a sense of connection between the family and the company. Select children are chosen, based on an essay contest, to enroll in special activities and programs at Plamex.
- Plamex hosts an annual group wedding for all employees wishing to get married. This helps couples establish a legal marriage, which is necessary for borrowing and asset development. The cafeteria is converted into a wedding chapel and a wedding is performed each February 14th.
- Numerous employee benefits are provided in addition to base salary, including transportation to and from work, on-site medical care, and subsidized meals in the company cafeteria.

---

operations come under greater scrutiny around the world, consumers, shareholders, communities, and other stakeholders increasingly demand that corporations play a positive role in promoting and upholding high corporate social responsibility.[24] As we indicated in Chapter 1, we believe that for a long-term sustainable strategy of success, companies must adopt as part of their core values common high standards for managing their global human resources, including ER practices, that will meet or surpass individual country standards and regulations. Nike, Walmart, and Reebok are just a few companies that have been under intense pressure to improve their global workforce ER acts, both in their home countries and abroad. And overall, they have responded very favorably to this pressure, raising the expectations for corporate social responsibility.

In its own home country of the United States, the global retail behemoth Walmart was charged, based on its own workplace data patterns, with a huge class-action lawsuit for sex discrimination related to compensation and career advancement.[25] Although companies like Walmart may truthfully deny *conscious* discriminatory practices, their human resource records and data patterns, unless they can be reasonably defended, may still provide sufficient evidence of discrimination and adverse "disparate impact" against a legally protected group, such as women or minorities. Even though business leaders and managers may not intentionally put individuals from one or more groups at a disadvantage, deep cultural influences may still affect human resource decisions leading to systematic unfair discrimination. Disparate or adverse impact, with its focus on actual statistical patterns of ER practice, is a tool to surface unfair discriminatory practice regardless of conscious intention or motive.[26]

Walmart also agreed to pay $11 million to settle a lawsuit accusing it of being complicit in contracting janitorial services for its stores where the contracted employees were illegal aliens. Another lawsuit has sought redress for the undocumented employees, claiming they were underpaid and worked overtime without extra pay. Many of the immigrants from nearly twenty countries, including Mexico, Brazil, the Czech Republic, China, Poland, and Russia, said they generally worked from midnight until 8 A.M. seven nights a week, cleaning and waxing floors.[27] Walmart was held liable despite its claim of not knowing about the illegal status or mistreatment of these contracted workers—they still were held accountable for the quality of ER and treatment of the employees who performed their company-contracted services. Thus, companies must not feel comfortable in merely being unaware of malfeasance and having a clear conscience regarding their ER practices but should actively examine their employment practices on an ongoing basis, including those covering their contracted workers, to ensure that legal and ethical ER practices and standards are followed.

IMPORTANT MNC PRACTICES FOR EFFECTIVE GLOBAL ER

Earlier we examined the issue of employee health and safety in global ER, including both serious costs of the neglect of worker health and safety and benefits to the organization when these needs are addressed. There also can be serious costs to organizations in the form of lowered productivity, fines and legal costs, and damaged image and reputation (potentially affecting both consumer behavior and future recruitment) when companies do not effectively attend to other important and often interrelated ER matters as employee involvement and development, open communications, employee correction and discipline, and employee termination. We now provide recommendations for effective global ER practice that can guide initial planning and future, more detailed study.

Health and Safety

We believe that organizations should have an ethical commitment to protecting employee health and safety and minimizing the risk of work-related harm and injury associated with work assignments wherever they take place around the world. Besides reducing operating costs associated with workplace accidents and injury, attention to health and safety also can point to opportunities for work process improvement and innovation. For example, manufacturing accidents often are caused when employees, whether motivated by incentives or simply an intrinsic desire to improve productivity, find new ways to reduce manufacturing time and may step outside of safety guidelines that were developed for the old, less-efficient process. With an ongoing global commitment and attention to worker safety, managers will work closely with employees to ensure that the employees are appropriately protected as they try out new ideas for company improvement. Alcoa, the world's leading producer of aluminum, is convinced of this link between attention to workplace safety and process innovation, yielding increased productivity. Since 1988, it has made a commitment to safety the company's number one priority and performance measure. With this strong commitment, productivity has soared, as have cost savings due to a dramatic reduction in accidents. Since the start of this strategic focus on safety, Alcoa has reduced lost workday injuries by 90 percent. Seventy-five percent of Alcoa's 487 locations worldwide had zero lost workdays in 2002, ten times better than the average record of its industry peers.[28] We now will examine critical areas to achieve success in planning and dealing with employee health and safety.

Management Support. An effective health and safety effort requires an investment in time and resources (human and financial), which should be budgeted for and allocated appropriately by management. In addition, management commitment to health and safety is critical at all levels, both in active enforcement of program rules and in providing good examples for following those rules.[29] In some cases management must work to counter deep cultural values that discourage the timely reporting of safety threats or violations, or that do not support healthy lifestyles or work behavior. For example, the corporate equivalent of suicide in Japan is known as *karoshi,* or death by overwork. Regular Japanese employees, fearing a shift to temporary staff status, often work extra hours without pay to protect their jobs. Also, hard work and self-sacrifice for the benefit of the group or organization are highly valued. To help reinforce management support at all levels, managers should be held accountable by the organization for their contribution to health and safety.[30] At Alcoa there is an ongoing show of this support from senior management through their attention to safety. Managers of worldwide Alcoa facilities that are underperforming in safety measures and where injuries are reported can expect a telephone call from a member of upper management, with a particular emphasis on discussing possible means for improvement. When safety has improved, managers also are contacted by senior management to provide positive reinforcement.[31]

Ongoing Risk Assessment. Organizations and their workplaces can differ dramatically, and so can the nature of risks to health and safety. Sources of worker harm and injury can vary greatly, for example, between expatriate engineer assignments in Colombia and jobs in meat-processing plants in Portugal. The nature of risk and health hazard can also change with internal changes to work processes and to the surrounding environment. Therefore, management at local operations should analyze work situations carefully on a regular basis to identify and protect against potential risks to health and safety as well as to keep accurate records of work-related accidents or injuries to identify trends and adjust accordingly. Some general trends across diverse industries have found that older employees tend to have fewer accidents. In addition, most accidents occur during the first month of work; the longer an employee has worked for a job, the lower the accident rate.[32] These general trends point to the possible need for special supervisory attention directed toward younger employees and the need for effective communications and training as early as possible to minimize early employment risk.

Regular Audits and Inspections Based on World-Class Standards. Related to the process of ongoing risk assessment, companies should conduct regular inspections and audits, both planned and unannounced, at their operations at home and abroad, including operations where company work has been subcontracted. Such regular assessments, based on high company standards, can help keep safety high in the consciousness of practicing managers and employees alike and is especially important for maintaining company control over safety in distant and outsourced operations. Particularly when such inspections and audits are conducted and reported by impartial groups external to a company, the reports can carry greater credibility, enhancing company reputations and raising standards and expectations in the global business environment.

Baxter International is a global manufacturer of pharmaceutical and biomedical products, with sixty-four manufacturing facilities and about 48,000 employees located throughout the world. In response to a request by a stockholder group wanting increased assurance that data presented to the public is accurate, Baxter now uses external validation with an external consultant to assess and report its performance in environmental protection and employee health and safety. This external consultant, ERM Certification and Verification Services (CVS), Inc., maintains overall quality control of the audit process through verification protocols used by all their auditors assessing Baxter's facilities. These verification protocols build global consistency and help minimize inevitable auditor differences when working in different geographic areas. Mattel uses both internal monitoring and independent audits of safety in its worldwide toy-manufacturing facilities (owned and contracted), mostly found in the Pacific Basin. Its regular public reports of these internal inspections and independent audits include the identification of problems and cases of company safety-code violations as well as action for resolving these situations. This honest public disclosure supports Mattel's commitment and reputation for worker safety and sets a high standard for other companies.[33]

Ongoing Communication and Training. Very early communications and training are especially critical to counter the high risk of accidents during the first month of service. In addition, communication and training should continue on an ongoing basis, particularly as ongoing risk assessment identifies new areas for concern and new rules for prevention. Each safety incident or injury should serve as a learning lesson, not as an occasion for blame and faultfinding. This beneficial learning should be shared through company-wide electronic newsletters, announcements, workshops, and other means both for individual employee awareness and learning and for organizational learning through improved policy and practice. Pacific Northwest National Laboratory credits a weekly article feature, "Lessons Learned/Best Practices," in its internal electronic newsletter with greatly increasing staff awareness and involvement in creating a safer, healthier work environment.[34]

Information sharing and skill training with ongoing skill review in such areas as stress management, managing work/life balance, first aid, crisis management, and general health and wellness training for all employees also can be particularly important in lowering health-related costs as well as in minimizing loss in times of emergency.[35] Beyond their initial thorough training, supervisors in particular should receive ongoing information and training to help support their key role in safety program implementation, including training on new company policies and practices, dealing with possible alcohol and drug abuse, and preventing and dealing with workplace aggression and violence.

Employee Participation. Employees at all levels should have a clear expectation of upholding and contributing to effective company safety and health. Employees at lower levels often are the closest to work processes and have the best vantage point for identifying possible areas for concern in work design and opportunities for improvement. They therefore should be encouraged to provide suggestions for improvement. Effective employee involvement can also be gained through their participation with managers and safety and health specialists on committees that meet regularly to review safety and health concerns and make improvement recommendations to management.[36] At a minimum, employee safety and health concerns about their own work should be considered seriously, and no employee should feel forced into working under unsafe conditions until the concerns can be thoroughly assessed and alleviated.

Employee Feedback and Incentives. A basic step in employee involvement is simply providing employees with regular feedback on their performance—both safety behaviors and outcomes—in promoting a safe and accident-free working environment. Such regular feedback sends a clear message of the importance of safety and that all employees play a crucial role. The one successful Canadian paper mill operation generated feedback by using a questionnaire completed by a broad cross section of employees and based on a model of safety management used by the world's safest companies. This survey produced quantitative data on the state of the organization's safety management, including the effectiveness of safety practices and overall management commitment. Based on this feedback, the company made important changes that drastically improved its safety performance. Before this survey feedback intervention the mill had an average of seven lost-work injuries per year. In the following five years it had no lost-work injuries, and total injuries were reduced by 75 percent.[37]

Financial incentives and other forms of reward (such as recognition and prizes) for exemplary individual, work team, and organizational performance in contributing to lowering accident rates and safety and health care costs also have been found to be effective. In combining employee feedback incentives with high employee involvement, companies may engage in internal cross-departmental or divisional competitions as well as external competitions (both national and international) for awards and recognition—the latter serving as a high source of intangible goodwill image value in local communities. For example, the Bangalore-based electronics division of Bharat Heavy Electricals Ltd. has been awarded the British Safety Council's International Safety Award for the third consecutive year in recognition of its achievements in corporate health and safety. Such internal and external competitions can effectively serve to energize the MNC's global workforce toward improved performance in health and safety. However, management should be very careful to not allow the incentives, competition, and potential negative feedback to discourage honest reporting of accidents.[38]

Employee Assistance Program Support. The concept of an employee assistance program (EAP) centers around providing professional assistance to employees who are experiencing emotional or psychological difficulty that interferes with both employee well-being and overall productivity. Several common situations associated with these personal difficulties include alcohol and drug abuse, marital or family difficulties, stress, financial troubles, depression, and grief. Consistent with the trend of outsourcing many HR services, companies frequently contract with professional EAP services firms that provide counseling and other services to employees who are referred by their companies. These external EAP services also provide a context of anonymity and confidentiality that may be lacking in internal company counseling and advisement services. The purpose of the EAP is to acknowledge that with any large group of employees, at some point a percentage of employees will be debilitated by some difficulty such as those previously listed, and a responsible and ethical organization should assist employees in overcoming these personal challenges with the same human consideration as is given with a physical illness.

In EAP application to the global workforce, many employers begin with their expatriate employees to assist in preventing costly failed assignments and difficult repatriation. However, with a commitment to a truly global workforce, employers should provide consistent benefits and services throughout their employee populations, with EAPs that serve local workforce needs as well as those of expatriates. Because EAPs deal with personal and highly confidential matters, it is essential that, besides meeting global quality standards, they are designed to fit local views regarding counseling, personal relationships, religious preferences, and style. For example, in some countries telephone counseling is preferred, whereas in others a face-to-face approach is essential. Local laws, benefit plans, and confidentiality requirements are also important.

While individual problem solving is an important part of EAP services, employee assistance professionals also may work with managers, union representatives, and HR professionals to solve more challenging problems in the workplace such as alcoholism at work, group conflicts, disruptive employee behavior, and other critical incidents. Beyond ethics and social responsibility, EAPs have demonstrated that companies are far ahead cost-wise when they work to help employees overcome these challenges. Ignoring these problems can lead to much more serious costs, such as dramatically reduced productivity, low morale, and employee replacement and associated training.[39]

Employee Involvement and Development

An important ethical practice of ER that also has important bottom-line benefits includes the design of work, where possible, that is personally satisfying and meaningful beyond just providing a job to support personal and family livelihood. The active involvement of employees in providing input and making decisions related to their work has been found to lead to increased levels of motivation and job satisfaction and is associated with heightened worker productivity and retention and lowered absenteeism and tardiness.[40] Employee involvement is also critical for gaining valuable ideas and information for organizational improvement—often information that is not visible to management. To make the best use of trained and experienced employees, organizations often change their organizational structure, removing multiple layers of management and replacing hierarchy with decentralization of decision making. Employees are encouraged to make decisions on the spot without consulting their supervisors, who often are less directly involved with customer transactions. This premium placed on using the involvement and knowledge of lower-level company employees is voiced by Nerio Alessandri, founder of the Italian multinational Technogym: "The best ideas come from the people in the field or on the production line. The lower the position, the better the idea." Involvement also can contribute to employee understanding of and commitment to new company directions and initiatives. Examples of productive worker involvement include autonomous and semi-autonomous individual and group work designs as well as participation on special task forces, ad hoc committees, and ongoing problem solving and quality enhancement groups leading to improvements at the workplace and in the surrounding community.[41]

The active involvement of employees frequently calls on their utilization of higher-level skills in problem solving and decision making. Such involvement often can result in their development and use of professional and managerial skills and competencies that contribute to their job satisfaction, job advancement within the organization, and career security and marketability outside of the organization should employment be terminated due to layoffs and downsizing. On a larger scale, this commitment to employee development is also aimed at advancing the skill and knowledge level of the local labor force wherever company operations are located.

Open Communications and Grievance Process

Productive and ethical ER practices provide for open communications where employees can be heard and their problems and complaints presented without fear and are genuinely addressed. Because performance appraisal can be a very useful tool

Global Workforce Professional Profile 11.1
Brenda R. Blair and Employee Assistance Programs

Brenda R. Blair is president of Blair Consulting Group of College Station, Texas, where she leads a group of consultants in working with all kinds of organizations in the United States and abroad for the design, development, and enhancement of international EAP and work/life balance services. She works closely with major MNCs and providers of EAP and other ER services in consulting and training. Blair earned a bachelor's degree at Kalamazoo College in Michigan, where she had an early, very influential study-abroad experience in Nigeria. She continued on for her MBA at Northwestern University in Evanston, Illinois, as well as a CEAP (Certified Employee Assistance Professional) from the Employee Assistance Professionals Association. Blair carries with her considerable personal international experience, having lived in Switzerland, Belgium, the Netherlands, and Ghana. Her active international work has included the following:

- Consultation on EAP and work/life services for local host country nationals
- Program review to assure that employer services are consistent across countries yet responsive to local needs
- Program design and implementation
- Identification and evaluation of EAP and work/life vendors in different countries
- For EAP vendors, marketing surveys of opportunities in different countries
- Consultation on mergers, acquisitions, and international strategies for EAP and work/life service delivery
- For international vendors, consultation regarding how to provide services in the U.S. environment
- Escorting international professionals on site visits to U.S. employers and vendors to observe EAP and work/life services
- Consultation on forming alliances with other international EAP and work/life service providers

Blair's work has involved projects in the United States, Canada, France, Japan, South Africa, and the United Kingdom. In addition, an important part of Blair's work involves contributing her expert services and networking at major professional organizations in her field, such as the Employee Assistance Professionals Association, where she has been a member for about twenty years and has served as a local chapter officer; the Association of Work/Life Professionals; and the Society for Human Resource Management, where she is an active participant in SHRM's online Global Forum.

for providing honest feedback aimed at individual employee performance improvement, so too should organizations be open on a regular basis to organizational climate and employee satisfaction surveys. Use of such surveys yields employee input on how to make the workplace more meaningful and rewarding, as well as how to improve company operations. Where more targeted input and feedback are desired from employees, such as when the organization is planning to introduce new work practices or update employee benefits, employee focus groups or special employee task forces can be used. Genuine two-way communication benefits an organization beyond merely surfacing new information and insights, and contributes to a more open and trusting organizational culture. Clear opportunities for employee voice and input also have been linked in studies across many different cultures to individual perceptions of fairness and job satisfaction, which in turn have been linked with such key company performance indicators as productivity, profitability, customer satisfaction, and employee retention.[42]

Of course, cultural differences can affect employee inclination to provide honest input, especially aimed at correction and improvement of superiors and the organization. For some employees, especially those from high power-distance cultures, providing such "constructive" criticism *directly* face-to-face is still criticism, and it may be perceived in a negative light associated with disrespect and lack of loyalty. Managers should therefore be flexible and ready to adjust their methods for accessing employees' candid voice and input. For example, one American manufacturing executive in Los Angeles with a large concentration of immigrant Mexican employees uses a third-party approach for gathering useful corrective input from his workforce *indirectly*—yet still with their clear understanding of the reporting role of this trusted third party.

Whether or not employees are represented by a union in their work environment, they should feel free to bring forth legitimate concerns and complaints without intimidation or fear of retaliation. Many organizations utilize "hot line" or "whistle blower" telephone numbers where employees can report waste, fraud, or abuse by superiors anonymously. Organizations should develop clear procedures, both informal and formal, for airing employee dissatisfaction and complaints. Many organizations strongly encourage employees to first share their concerns on a more informal basis with their direct supervisor, because most problems are due to some form of miscommunication or misunderstanding. Supervisors should be trained in interpersonal communication skills to actively listen and work jointly with employees to resolve concerns at this informal level.

Sometimes problems are not able to be resolved satisfactorily at this initial informal level with the immediate supervisor—especially when a supervisor might be the primary source of the employee concern. Therefore, a more formal grievance procedure for voicing and resolving the employee concern should be used. Although union working environments tend to have more clearly outlined employee grievance procedures for seeking redress, all organizations can benefit by developing and communicating clear, simple, and formal grievance procedures. Such procedures should be adapted to local legal and cultural conditions and especially should be designed with input from all levels of employees to increase credibility and acceptance. These formal step-by-step procedures aimed at eventual grievance and dispute resolution might include such features an internal *ombudsperson,* who can investigate claims or act as an intermediary between employee and management and recommend possible solutions; an *open-door policy,* where an employee can take concerns to levels of management above the immediate supervisor; *peer review panels* composed mostly of an employee's peers to increase perceptions of fairness and ensure that the employee's perspective is heard; and *arbitration,* often the last step, where an agreed-upon unbiased third party examines the evidence and makes a final decision for resolving a grievance dispute.[43] Advantages of such effective formal procedures include the following:

- A mechanism for employee concerns to be handled fairly and quickly within agreed parameters before they develop into major problems and larger disputes
- Explicit recognition of employee's protected right to raise grievances
- A clear step-by-step process to guide employees in raising a grievance, and specific action to be taken if agreement is not reached at each level
- Greater consistency of procedural justice and practice across the organization—especially important for multisite organizations
- Documentation and maintenance of records that are useful in grievance resolution
- The meeting of legal obligations, with grievance procedures that are customized to local governmental statutes[44]

Employee Correction and Discipline

Mistakes happen. Although they should be avoided, there still is nothing more natural in organizations than errors. Ethical and productive ER practices for dealing with employee correction and discipline should be based on this perspective, with the primary focus on performance-problem resolution and improvement and a minimal emphasis on blaming and punishment. If some form of punishment is used in discipline, it should be used only as a means to encourage future desirable performance and discourage undesirable performance, not to mete out some form of just retribution. The most important purpose of employee correction and discipline is performance improvement—there is no room in the enlightened professional organization for managers who seek revenge. Although following an effective disciplinary procedure can even result in employee job termination, the focus is still on work performance improvement.

Employee correction, an important step that should precede discipline, involves providing feedback that the present performance is not satisfactory. Employee correction may also include additional direction and joint problem solving between employee and supervisor to bring about desired performance. Unlike employee discipline, correction should have no punishment or threat of future disciplinary measures if performance is not improved. Misunderstandings and miscommunication of expectations are very common, and usually employee correction will occur simply when employees learn that their performance needs improvement. From their basic needs of self-esteem and self-efficacy, employees generally will desire to perform effectively and have a positive impact and will feel disappointed when they learn that their performance is unacceptable or falls short of expectations. Therefore, at this early correction stage, punishment or even the threat of a future negative consequence brings only unnecessary added anxiety and may even result in resentment.

A primary cause of performance problems leading to the need for often stressful and uncomfortable disciplinary action is failure in performance management. As mentioned previously in Chapter 9 on global workforce performance management, employees should be given performance feedback on a regular basis. However, one of the common weaknesses of supervisors is their reluctance to give negative feedback, hoping that employee performance problems will somehow go away. Unfortunately, this automatic correction without clear feedback is seldom the case, and typically the performance problem only grows and becomes more entrenched, becoming a major employee disciplinary crisis. The effective company-wide practice of performance management should therefore be a high organizational priority and supported and reinforced by ongoing management training and accountability measures.

When initial efforts at employee correction do not bring about a desired change in employee performance, employee discipline should begin. We now will consider useful points to keep in mind in planning and carrying out employee discipline.

Develop, Update, Communicate. A first step to effectively managing employee discipline is to have a disciplinary system in place that is sensitive and adapted to the unique needs, legal regulations, and cultural practices and expectations of the local workplace. For example, some employee behaviors may be very offensive and seriously upsetting to workforce morale in some cultural contexts yet go completely unnoticed and have no disturbing effect in others. This disciplinary system should clearly identify unacceptable employee behaviors and the consequences for employees who engage in them. To ensure relevance and credibility and to avoid accusations of unreasonable treatment and discrimination, discipline should be based on employee behaviors that are pertinent to the company's local operation. In particular and where possible, discipline should be based on critical incidents of past local employee behavior (or behavior experienced by other local companies) that led to negative company consequences. Based on changing social trends and ongoing performance management data and experience, the disciplinary system should be reviewed regularly and updated when appropriate. For example, the relatively recent entry of the Internet and social media technology into the workplace has led to significant employee behavior problems that did not exist before, such as time-wasting Internet personal surfing, texting, and downloading of questionable material, or distractions leading to serious accidents.[45]

Finally, the nature of the disciplinary system, including the behaviors to avoid and their negative consequences if engaged in, should be clearly communicated to employees. Simply burying them in an extensive employee handbook or adding them to the typical information overload of a new employee's first-day orientation is not enough. Separate and ongoing company training and information "refresher sessions" should also be used to ensure that communication is clear for especially common behavioral problems as well as for more serious infractions, such as sexual harassment and other forms of workplace harassment and discrimination.[46] In fact, in some cases regular and reasonable company efforts to inform and train employees regarding inappropriate and illegal discriminatory behaviors can serve to protect or at least limit the company against legal liability in the event of a future lawsuit.[47]

Progressive Discipline. Some first-time infractions may merit immediate termination, such as violence in the workplace, fraud, or stealing. However, such an extreme consequence may be inappropriate and often illegal for other less serious behavior problems

Figure 11.2 **Example of Progressive Discipline: Employee Tardiness**

Order of Occurrence	Negative Consequence
First Time	Discussion with employee to be sure policy is clear—most employees naturally feel bad and sorry at this initial step, which is a sufficiently negative consequence. No threat or external punishment.
Second Time	Warning that if tardiness continues, a note about this performance problem will be placed in employee's personnel file for documentation and available for future review.
Third Time	Note about continuing tardiness problem is signed by supervisor and employee and placed in employee's personnel file. Warning that subsequent tardiness within a given time period may result in one week suspension without pay. Document signed by both parties and placed in employee's personnel file.
Fourth Time	One week suspension without pay. Warning that future tardiness within a given time period may result in immediate termination. Document signed by both parties and placed in employee's personnel file.
Fifth Time	Immediate termination of employee.

at their initial or early occurrence. In addition, given costs for employee replacement and training, companies are usually much better off using a disciplinary system that is aimed at coaching and working with employees for a reasonable period of time to improve performance problems. Also, when disciplinary measures are perceived by other employees as excessively harsh, serious damage may be done to overall employee morale and productivity. Disciplinary systems should therefore reflect a progressive movement of negative consequences, with each consequence appropriate for the particular order of infraction occurrence (for example, first, second, or third occurrence) and intended to be of minimally sufficient strength to effectively discourage future occurrence of the particular performance problem,[48] as illustrated in Figure 11.2.

Hot Stove Analogy. The analogy of a hot stove can be useful in ensuring the effectiveness of a disciplinary system.[49] As a hot stove, a disciplinary system should have the following features:

- *Warning.* As we would naturally want to warn another person unfamiliar with our surroundings against touching a nearby hot stove, so too should inappropriate workplace behaviors and their negative consequences be clearly communicated to employees.
- *Sufficiently Hot.* If a stove is not sufficiently hot, the food will not be cooked in a timely manner. If it is too hot, the food will be burned. In like manner, negative consequences for unacceptable behavior should be minimally strong enough to provide an adequate disincentive against their future occurrence, yet not too strong or extreme so as to cause resentment from the employee and others who are aware of the discipline.
- *Immediate.* As the touch to a hot stove should provide immediate feedback, there should be an immediate response to an employee's performance infraction, with

a clear explanation for why the discipline is being given. A significant delay in discipline may cause the employee to continue the behavior, because he or she concludes erroneously that the infraction is really not a problem.

- *Consistent.* A person who touches a hot stove will consistently feel pain. The lack of consistency in applying discipline can cause perceptions of unfairness or lead to employee notions such as, "Maybe I'll get away with it this time and not get into trouble."
- *Impartial.* It matters not who the person is who touches the hot stove—he or she will still get burned. Likewise, an effective disciplinary system is impartial and does not discriminate or play favorites, treating each employee the same whether she is the daughter of the head janitor or of the company president.

Documentation. Effective documentation is an essential tool in managing discipline. This practice maintains a professional and orderly manner in the process and communicates its seriousness to the employee. Effective documentation also provides clear evidence if needed for review by other parties, such as in a grievance procedure, and is especially important in defending manager and company actions in case of litigation. There have been useful recent human resource information system developments (such as software and Internet applications) to help facilitate a supervisor's effective documentation work for performance management and for managing discipline in particular.[50] When performed effectively, documentation as part of employee discipline should follow these guidelines:

- Describe in behavioral terms the infraction and background in which it took place, including whether this was the first or repeated offense. Be specific, and include all pertinent facts, such as dates, times, witnesses, and other persons involved.
- Describe what must be done to correct the situation and by what date.
- Describe the consequence being applied and the next consequence if the infraction is repeated.

Ongoing Fairness and Support. In minimizing the perceived adversarial nature of employee discipline and to maintain a fair and professional process, disciplinary action should be handled with utmost confidentiality and provide a continuing opportunity for the employee to state and clarify his or her case. Disciplinary action should not be taken without a preceding thorough and impartial investigation of the facts, and employees should be given the right to appeal at each step of the disciplinary process with a clear explanation of procedures to be followed.[51] Above all, employees should sense genuine support and desire on the part of supervisors for the employees to successfully overcome the work performance problem, noted by their ongoing coaching and offer of assistance, joint problem solving for problem resolution, and statements of confidence in the employee to succeed.

Employee Termination and Displacement

Despite their effective efforts in correction and discipline, managers may finally conclude that there is no other recourse than to terminate an employee due to misconduct or inability to perform the work effectively. Or business circumstances may change, leading to the need for termination unrelated to employee performance, such as in the case of a need to downsize the organization due to a merger or acquisition or automation of lower-skill jobs in which employee positions become redundant and unnecessary. On a much broader scale, as we have noted with the severe recent global economic crisis, layoffs might be due to a significant downturn in the economy resulting in loss of business. In any situation that leads to employee termination, pertinent local and country regulations should be examined carefully to avoid costly lawsuits and fines and to be aware of other consequences, such as mandatory severance payments. Employment law in many countries makes it very difficult to terminate an employee, even for just cause, such as serious employee misconduct, and requires significant advance notice and consultation with appropriate regulatory and labor bodies. Regarding statutory severance payments, many countries require that companies, regardless of reason for termination, provide payment to the former employee based on such factors as employee age, years of employment with the company, and last rate of pay. Country severance requirements can differ dramatically, with some employees with twenty years of company service receiving about $50,000 in mandatory severance payment, while in another countries employees with the same length of service receive twice this amount or more.[52]

Where employee termination is deemed necessary on the grounds of redundancy, before approval is granted many countries and regional trade agreements (especially the European Union) have legal requirements for providing detailed information and consultation with individual employees targeted for redundancy, appropriate labor regulatory bodies, and labor interest representatives. Often consultation is required to begin a minimum of thirty to ninety days before the dismissals may take effect. Required consultation and information may cover the following:[53]

- Reasons for the proposed redundancies
- Numbers and descriptions of employees to be made redundant
- Proposed method(s) and criteria for determining employee redundancy
- Proposed methods of implementing dismissals, and period over which dismissals are to take place
- Redundancy payments to be made other than those required by law
- Ways in which the effects of redundancies may be mitigated (such as through outplacement services, which may provide emotional counseling, career counseling and job-search assistance, retraining, retirement and financial management advice)[54]
- Possible means in which redundancies may be reduced or avoided

The last bulleted item requires a thorough analysis of possible alternatives to redundancy that can lessen or even avoid the negative impact of the dismissals. These alternatives may include (1) *natural attrition,* a rather slow and untargeted approach depending on the natural loss of employees through retirement, resignation, and so on; (2) *voluntary early retirement,* often facilitated by a generous incentive offer to employees of a minimum age in targeted departments or areas of redundancy; (3)

transferred redundancy, or "bumping," where an employee in a nonredundant position volunteers and is allowed to trade places with an employee targeted for redundancy; (4) *redeployment,* or relocation of the employee to suitable employment in another place of work within the company, possibly in a different part of the country, and often retaining, unless appropriately compensated by the company, the same level of pay and benefits under an "acquired rights" requirement existing in many countries, particularly in Europe and the European Union; (5) *training,* to hone current workers' quality control and productivity skills when work demand is slow, or for the purpose of facilitating redeployment within the company or placement with a different employer or even self-employment; (6) *work-sharing,* as has traditionally happened in many Asian countries, where all workers' total hours are diminished to fit the reduced work demand and then shared, such as all employees changing to a thirty-five-hour work week; (7) *voluntary part-time,* where individuals voluntarily reduce their total number of working hours, such as in a phased retirement situation where older workers, with an incentive, gradually reduce their working time and responsibilities toward retirement; (8) *coordinated leave or furloughs,* such as with periods of paid and unpaid leave (for example, vacations, maternity, paternity, family care, career breaks, sabbaticals, and professional development) where different workers are still retained, however, in a temporarily inactive status, thus reducing the number of active workers under a diminished work demand; and (9) *job-sharing,* a variation of work-sharing, where two or more individuals share a job for an indefinite period.[55]

A furlough strategy, such as unpaid time off for one day per week or one week per month, often represents the best option in dealing with business demand uncertainty surrounding a major economic downturn, such as with our recent global financial crisis. Smart organizations want to avoid the possibility of long-term damage by laying employees off in the short term and then having to turn around and try to rehire them. For success in a furlough strategy, complete openness and frequent communication, using multiple channels, is essential. Of course, as in other matters that involve managing human resources across national boundaries, local employment laws should first be considered before attempting to implement a furlough strategy across a global workforce. Furloughed employees have recommended the following tips for optimizing the success of a furlough strategy to weather difficult economic times:

- Communicate early and often. As soon as the decision is made to implement a furlough, management should meet with employees face-to-face and follow up with online messages. Don't wait to have all the information to make the announcement, and don't withhold information, such as how to qualify for unemployment benefits.
- Within set parameters, allow flexibility. Some companies permit employees to choose their furlough days as long as their supervisor approves, allowing them to schedule around vacation interests and child-care needs.
- Spread the furlough sacrifice. Companies employing extended time furloughs (e.g., weeklong) should consider spreading the pay loss over several future pay periods.
- Encourage employee involvement. Get employees to share their ideas on how to productively spend time off. This time off can be reinvigorating—from

working on neglected hobbies to spending time with children to starting new business ventures.[56]

Regardless of governmental requirements, organizations are wise to carefully consider possible viable alternatives to layoffs to preserve a positive image and to have a head start against the competition, with a ready workforce, when economic conditions improve. For example, in contrast to their flagging competition at Ford, GM, and Chrysler where workers have been idle and facing an uncertain employment future, workers at Toyota's Princeton, Indiana, manufacturing plant have been busy developing new work process innovations and receiving training to enhance skills in quality control and productivity improvement. This practice is in keeping with the company's pledge to never lay off any of its full-time employees, who are nonunion, and is contributing to a very positive public image as a well-managed organization. According to Jim Lentz, president of Toyota's U.S. Motor Sales, the company believes that keeping employees on the payroll and using the time to improve their skills is very smart in the long run. As Lentz said, "It would have been crazy for us to lose people for ninety days and to rehire and retrain people and hope that we have a smooth ramp-up coming back in."[57]

However, if termination is absolutely necessary, and regardless of the reason, efforts should be made to make the experience as comfortable and supportive as possible. Face saving is important in all cultures, and any forms of humiliation—intentional or unintentional—should be carefully avoided. Efforts also should be made in cooperation with local labor regulatory agencies to minimize the potentially negative impact on local communities of large numbers of dismissals. Attention also should be given in counseling and other support services to other typically neglected victims of downsizing strategies—the survivors of layoffs—who often suffer added stress and anxiety due to increased uncertainty and work overload, resentment toward the company, and even feelings of guilt. In fact, Finnish researchers found evidence that those who survived layoffs were five times more likely to die from heart disease or stroke in the four years after the cuts than employees whose workplaces weren't affected by downsizing.[58] Although an ethical and socially responsible, proactive ER approach to discipline and termination, as well as other major ER practices, might prove more costly in the short term, it can bring many benefits in the long term with improved company morale, better external image and reputation, and minimal costly litigation.

ROLE OF LABOR UNIONS IN GLOBAL EMPLOYEE RELATIONS

The presence and potential influence of labor unions are carefully considered when MNCs are selecting locations for their manufacturing facilities. In a competitive global business market, MNCs carefully consider possible costs and disadvantages associated with unions in a given location. And governments of both developed and developing countries, whose interest is increasing foreign direct investment and maintaining the domestic investment of their own companies, also are concerned about the possible negative impact of unions. As indicated in Global Workforce Challenge 11.2, we note

Global Workforce Professional Profile 11.2
Walmart Accepts Unions In China

Walmart, the world's largest retailer, has earned a strong reputation for avoiding unions—even closing a store in Canada that threatened union certification. Walmart claims that rather than have union representation, it encourages its workers to have "direct communications with the company," where issues of concern are taken seriously and followed up with prompt action. However, in China, where rapid industrialism and capitalism mix with authoritarian communism, Walmart apparently has found a union to its liking. In November 2004, Walmart gave an official statement related to unions unlike any it had ever made before: "Should associates request formation of a union, Walmart China would respect their wishes and honor its obligation under China's Trade Union Law." The company agreed to have its twenty thousand Chinese workers represented, if requested, by the All-China Federation of Trade Unions, a body dominated by the Chinese Communist Party.

Despite the recent global recession, Walmart continues to have ambitious expansion plans for its stores in China (numbering over 145), where it lags behind its global rival, France's Carrefour. Walmart also uses China as a major sourcing center for its U.S. stores. At one stage, according to a credible source, Walmart purchases from China were worth about 10 percent of the country's total exports to the United States.

The All-China Federation of Trade Unions says that all companies, foreign and local, are required to establish a union, using funds from a 2 percent levy on wages. The Federation claims to have 123 million members, a result of the monopoly the government has allowed in the representation of workers' interests. Due to their potential threat to the centralized power of the state, independent unions are banned in China. The Federation unions in China traditionally have been an instrument for the Communist Party to control workers rather than a vehicle for agitation and strikes, which are almost never allowed. And company management has considerable influence on Federation unions through their ability to appoint their choice of individuals to union leadership positions.

China's economic environment has experienced dramatic changes, which has caused a sharp increase in labor unrest. Critics believe that the role of the state-sanctioned Federation unions isn't to channel labor's discontent into achievable gains in worker safety, quality of working life, and standard of living, but rather to contain discontent and make labor compliant to the employer's will, thus supporting a national goal of increased foreign direct investment. Nevertheless, the Federation recently has put pressure on Walmart to reconsider its local restructuring plan, responding to employee objections to the relocation of up to 1,400 Chinese managers to new locations and smaller cities across the country.

Sources: Adapted from K. E. McLaughlin, "Walmart to Shift China Management," *WWD* 197 (86) (2009): 5; H. Meyerson, "Walmart Loves Unions (in China)," *Washington Post*, December 1, 2004: A25.

how Walmart has found the form of union representation in the People's Republic of China, heavily influenced by the Chinese government, to be very favorable to its significant foreign direct investment and expansion plans there.

Labor union structures, priorities, laws, and practices can differ dramatically within countries and from country to country.[59] Some unions are organized on a common industrial basis, such as the United Auto Workers in the United States and Canada. Others are organized on a common occupational basis, such as the National Union of Teachers in the United Kingdom. Some countries require a union presence in the workplace, such as in Germany where the federally legislated principle of *co-determination* dictates union representation on corporate boards and worker councils for lower-level operational decision making. Other countries disallow independent labor union formation, such as in China where independent organizational movements (including religions) that may enter in potential conflict or compete with a communist regime are strongly and forcefully discouraged.[60] In some countries the union focus is restricted to employee personal interests, such as protecting employee wages and safeguarding working conditions, whereas in other countries unions are much more deeply involved in social and political activism. For example, trade unions in Bangladesh, whose behavior is characterized by political activism and features momentous strikes known as *hartals,* have played a crucial role in most political changes in that country.[61]

In several instances unions have formed close working relationships with management and actually lowered company costs through effective contributions in staffing and managing employee discipline. A particular advantage to world labor of having unions in the global economy is that they keep pressure on companies against going for shortsighted profitability at the expense of worker interests and for securing labor rights that could mitigate the negative effects of globalization. This positive pressure role of labor unions in protecting worker interests in company ER was highlighted in a report commissioned by The World Bank, which reviewed more than a thousand studies on the effects of unions and collective bargaining. Based on the report's findings, Ken Georgetti, president of the Canadian Labor Congress, made the following labor union endorsement:

> Workers who belong to unions earn higher wages, work fewer hours, receive more training, and have longer job tenure. Union membership fights discrimination and closes the wage gap between women and men. People join unions because it improves their standard of living and adds to their quality of life. Better pay and working conditions, improved access to benefits like pensions and medical insurance, opportunities to become better workers and better citizens—these are the advantages people have when they come together in solidarity.[62]

Studies of the union effect on workplace health and safety in the United Kingdom, Canada, and the United States have documented that union-supported workplace health and safety committees have had a significant impact on reducing injury rates.[63] Unions also may have indirect influence on company ER policy and practice through their direct influence on local governments to enact legislation and develop regulations favorable to employees. With their advocacy for the personal interests of union employees who also are voting citizens, unions can wield considerable power over local government leaders who desire the support of the electorate.

Union Strengths and Vulnerabilities

Of fundamental concern to MNCs, labor unions may restrict MNC strategic options and flexibility in four primary ways:[64]

1. By influencing local government requirements for wage and benefits levels to the extent that labor costs become noncompetitive. This is the present situation in Germany, where many firms, including German-based ones, are opting to move business facilities elsewhere.
2. By restricting the ability of companies, through union influence on government regulations, to unilaterally change employment levels, such as through layoffs.
3. By limiting the company's ability to utilize active employee participation and involvement initiatives that have demonstrated great effectiveness in quality and process innovation and strategy implementation. This restriction may arise due to a union's claim that such employee group initiatives constitute company-sponsored union activity, and thus interfere with legitimate and protected union activity, even in nonunion organizations.
4. By forcing MNCs to develop parallel operations in different countries to decrease vulnerability to powerful unions, thus hindering the MNCs' increased efficiencies of global integration.

Nevertheless, at the beginning of the twenty-first century, organized labor has diminished economic power and political influence as compared to previous decades. Labor has decreased dramatically in influence as the globalization of production has weakened organized workers' bargaining power to dictate terms to employers. For example, if computer programmers in a developed country like the United States threaten company flexibility and profitability by forming a union, their work can be outsourced to countries such as India and China where more traditional unions are not found. Or if a national union threatens to strike, effectively shutting down MNC operations in one country, the company can increase production in its parallel operations in other countries, thus greatly limiting the negative impact of the strike. And in many developing countries local governments might be reluctant to support the unions for fear of losing potential jobs and capital inflow as well as hard currency from exports.[65] Overall, the global trend has been away from collectivism and trade unionism. Strikes have declined, and the fastest-growing sectors of the economy have been nonunion.[66]

Other factors also can explain the weakening roles of labor unions. Well-educated and trained knowledge workers generally find themselves in one of two circumstances in the global economy. In one circumstance they might be independent contractors who are highly skilled contingent employees, busy investing in their "human capital" as they make themselves consistently employable. These people generally consider themselves to be more akin to sole proprietors than to a collective body of workers. They may network with similarly situated persons, but they will not show solidarity with them. These people usually work on a project-by-project basis. In the past, workers primarily sought job stability and remained with a given company for an average of twenty years. Now, many of these knowledge workers can be "free agents," with an average tenure of only five years or less. Unlike traditional laborers, they may not show significant emotional attachment or organizational loyalty to their current company. In fact, individual independent contractors may not be supportive of the idea of a labor union because they move from one job and one place to another and think of their pay as a price for their service and not as an ongoing wage.[67]

If the knowledge workers are standard rather than contingent employees, they may find that their employers have created such a work-friendly environment that most employees will not consider unions necessary. In fact, in one recent survey of workers in several countries in Europe and the United States, more than 68 percent of workers in every country indicated that unions were not important. In fact, in Germany, where unions are an integral part of the economic fabric, only 29 percent of the respondents said unions were important.[68] As companies recognize the value of human capital over physical capital, employers are very much interested in helping employees achieve personal growth and fulfill personal needs in order to retain the most capable people inside their company.[69] Furthermore, they encourage employees to identify with the company by providing them with benefits such as stock options and profit sharing. These employees would identify the company's success with their own individual career success. Such a spirit of cooperation between management and workers is well known as *kyosei* among Japanese companies, in which individuals and organizations live and work together.[70] Therefore, under these circumstances, employees are unlikely to sympathize with and organize labor unions, whose interests conflict with employers.[71]

Potential Challenge of Union Global Solidarity

Although MNCs are free to merge, consolidate, and grow larger, individual unions themselves cannot easily form solidarity for combined influence across borders for several reasons, including the following.

Regulatory Restrictions. National labor laws typically restrict exercising extraterritorial jurisdiction, and national laws regulating unionization vary substantially from country to country. For example, European firms have tended to deal with labor unions at the industrial level whereas U.S. firms have done so at the firm level.

Reluctance to Yield Autonomy. National union leadership is typically very reluctant to yield power and usually prefers the autonomy to deal with labor practices in a manner that is most familiar. This autonomy is also threatened by fundamental political and philosophical differences, such as between a union in one country committed to a communist form of economy and a union committed to capitalism in another country.[72]

Conflicting National Union and Labor Interests. In their vocal opposition to globalization, national unions from developed countries have been accused of *not* being genuinely concerned about the health and safety of workers in less-developed countries but in reality wanting to protect their own domestic union jobs that contribute to their power base.[73] In addition, labor interests in one country can differ significantly from those in another country, such as with labor in a more affluent Western country being interested in quality of work/life issues, whereas labor in a poorer, developing country being much more motivated by basic livelihood and survival needs. At least for the immediate short term, workers and their representing unions in poorer countries would likely not be very sympathetic to the bargaining demands of their worker and union counterparts in much more affluent countries.[74]

Nevertheless, with greater cross-border collaboration and a consistent shift away from the traditional "IR" of industrial relations to a greater emphasis on international relations, a stronger global union influence in the form of mergers and other alliances may be felt in the future.[75] There are increasing examples of cross-border mobilization of workers represented by different unions. Such was seen when thousands of union members at more than sixty worksites in France, Canada, and the United States joined an International Day of Action to show support and solidarity for the United Auto Worker (UAW) union members' contract negotiation efforts at Norton Abrasives in Worcester, Massachusetts, a subsidiary of the French-based Saint-Gobain Group. According to UAW President Ron Gettelfinger, "International solidarity is the perfect answer to the company's so-called decentralization policy. The well-being of these workers and the community in which they live is not just a local issue. It matters to other Saint-Gobain union members and to workers everywhere."[76]

Another significant development has been the merger of the World Confederation of Labour (WCL), which holds a significant presence in developing countries, with the world's largest labor coalition, the International Confederation of Free Trade Unions (ICFTU). This combined labor coalition represents about 180 million workers in 233 affiliated organizations in more than 154 countries and territories worldwide, with top-priority goals to secure fundamental rights for working people across the world, develop international labor standards, improve gender equality, help end workplace discrimination, and aggressively address instances of exploitation by MNCs. The ICFTU maintains close links with the European Trade Union Confederation (ETUC—which includes all ICFTU European affiliates) and the Global Union Federations, which link together national unions from a particular trade or industry at the international level. As unequivocally expressed by Sharan Burrow, the first woman president of the ICFTU:

> Where governments fail to hold multinational corporations to account for decent labor standards, the international trade union movement will take up these issues and defend the rights of people who are denied fair wages and decent working conditions. Companies that portray themselves as good corporate citizens in developed nations like Australia, the United States, and Europe while exploiting workers in export processing zones and in less developed countries will find themselves the focus of internationally coordinated trade union campaigns.[77]

SUMMARY

The primary focus of employee relations in global workforce management is on the nature in which employees' personal interests, rights, and needs are protected and served by MNCs, which also are influenced by other external factors such as unions and government legislation. Critical challenges for human and worker rights in today's global workplace include forced labor, harmful child labor, workplace discrimination, health and safety hazards, and job insecurity and displacement. As part of their corporate responsibility, organizations should work hard to address and resolve these serious challenges, including cooperating and working closely with government and other nonprofit organizations. Besides encouraging constructive relations where labor unions exist, MNCs also can do much to optimize the effectiveness of their ER policies and practices related to employee health and safety, fair and nondiscriminatory practices, open communications, employee involvement and development, effective management of discipline, and, where necessary, termination.

QUESTIONS FOR OPENING SCENARIO ANALYSIS

1. How does the situation at Foxconn demonstrate that considerations for employee health and safety should go far beyond mere physical concerns?
2. What are important lessons from this tragic case for organizations, both MNCs and their contracted work suppliers, and for the design of healthy working conditions in developing countries? What costs will they inevitably bear if they ignore these lessons?
3. How can governments and other external forces help prevent future demoralization and tragic consequences as occurred at Foxconn?

CASE 11.1. AT DOMINO'S, ER BEGINS WITH MANAGERS

Turnover is a chronic and costly headache for fast-food businesses, which rely on an army of low-paid and frequently part-time workers. A harsh boss, a mean colleague, or a boring day can cause workers who earn the minimum wage to quit for similar pay elsewhere. In the United States, average turnover per year for most large and mid-size companies is about 10 percent to 15 percent. But at fast-food chains, rates as high as 200 percent a year for hourly workers aren't unusual. Some companies are tackling the problem with a higher starting wage. But Domino's Chief Executive Officer David A. Brandon says that although pay is a factor, "you can't overcome a bad culture by paying people a few bucks more." He believes the way to attack turnover is by focusing on store managers—hiring more selectively, coaching them on how to create better workplaces, and motivating them with the promise of stock options and promotions. High turnover hurts the bottom line. It costs money to recruit, hire, and train people and undercuts service when inexperienced employees don't work as efficiently. Mr. Brandon commissioned research that showed the most important factor in a store's success wasn't neighborhood demographics, packaging, or marketing but the quality of its store manager. "When that position is turning over at a high rate, the ripple effect of that is enormous," he says. His strategy seems to be working. By last year, the company's overall turnover had declined to 107 percent.

Domino's is trying to hire and train people like manager George Escobar. To give the store a friendlier feeling for employees, George says he bought boxes of tea bags and put them on a small folding table in the back with hot water and sugar. He discovered that his assistant manager brightened up when talking about his pets. So George bought a pet fish for the store. Seeking a way to discipline employees without alienating them, he bought a pair of dopey-looking, oversized black-framed glasses. They're called the "mistake glasses," and workers have to wear them when they make errors. The joke is that if you couldn't see what an obvious mistake you were making, you need glasses. "You want to make it like a fun environment but at the same time, you get your point across," George says. He says no one has ever refused to wear the glasses. He also avoids correcting employee mistakes in public.

Regional manager Rob Cecere coaches his managers constantly. His stores are now averaging sales of about $20,000 each week, up from $8,500 four years ago. Often he gives common-sense advice: treat employees respectfully, be polite and patient. He hammers home that it's not the pay that makes employees stick around, it's their relationship with their manager. "You've got to make sure they are happy to come to work for you." Dileep Kumar Kalludi, a Domino's manager in New Jersey, picked up a tip sheet at one of the company's management meetings, which he later tacked on his office wall. "Management is communicating, communicating, communicating," it reads.

Source: Adapted from E. White, "New Recipe: To Keep Employees, Domino's Decides It's Not All about Pay; Pizza Chain Attacks Turnover by Focusing on Managers," *Wall Street Journal,* February 17, 2005: A1.

QUESTIONS FOR CASE ANALYSIS AND DISCUSSION

1. Why should ER also be considered part of the overall picture of employee compensation and rewards to motivate employee productivity and retention?
2. Why is the direct supervisor and manager role so critical for effective ER in organizations?
3. What are important managerial practices for effective ER as exemplified in the Domino's case?

CASE 11.2. AGE DISCRIMINATION IN THE WORKPLACE

The graying of the workforce, with fewer younger replacements in the pipeline, is drawing more and more concern from governments in developing countries. A growing number of retired workers drawing state social benefits and not contributing to national productivity and tax revenues represent an increasing drag on national economies. One measure that countries are using to slow this effect is through changed personal tax measures, such as in the United States, which allows workers to continue working full-time and also draw social security payments without the previous daunting tax penalty against drawing a full salary. Age discrimination in the workplace also is recognized as a strong work disincentive for older employees, and countries also are moving to pass and enforce stronger regulations to fight this discouraging workplace malady. In the United Kingdom, stronger laws banning age discrimination are going into force, and it's not a moment too soon, according to the Employers' Forum on Age. By the time the new regulations take effect, it is predicted that British workers aged between forty-five and fifty-nine will be the single largest group in the labor force.

But for too many, reaching fifty still means being thrown on the scrapheap. A report by the United Kingdom's National Audit Office found that 2.7 million people between fifty and pension age were out of work. Of those, 700,000 to 1 million said they would like to work, whereas 200,000 were actively seeking work. The reasons why the workforce is aging are clear. The baby boomer generation of the sixties is reaching retirement age, medical advances mean that people are healthier for longer, and the pensions crisis in Britain is forcing people to work into old age. These factors all create difficulties for employers, who often believe that older workers will take more sick time off, cost more to retire, and will not accept taking orders from younger managers. "There's a fear about how to manage someone as old as your parents, so firms must invest in people-management skills," says Sam Mercer of the Employers' Forum on Age. The reality is that older workers are often hugely committed and motivated, may have better communication skills, and, as retailers such as B&Q have found, can be a hit with the public. They also have fewer accidents in the workplace, representing a lower risk to workers' compensation costs.

The problem of finding a job in later years is well illustrated by Dave Evans, an engineer with British Gas. As he turned fifty, he was made redundant. Though able to work as a freelance contractor, he found his age a barrier to landing a permanent job. "When I applied for a job, I didn't mention my age, but they would still say they were looking for someone younger," he says. "It was quite a low time." Yet Dave, now fifty-eight, is proof of how employers are waking up to the reality of an aging workforce. He was rehired in 1999 by British Gas to cope with a drastic shortage of engineers. And two years ago he joined a scheme to encourage older engineers to stay with the business. Those prepared to do irregular shifts or more physical work are paid more, whereas others have the guarantee of regular hours and lighter duties.

Source: Adapted from N. Paton, "British Bosses Face New Laws Banning Age Discrimination," Knight Ridder Tribune Business News, November 28, 2006: 1.

QUESTIONS FOR CASE ANALYSIS AND DISCUSSION

1. Besides their commitment to ethics and social responsibility, why should companies be motivated to eliminate age discrimination in the workplace?
2. Why does age discrimination pose a threat to the economic health of developing countries?
3. What measures can companies take to reduce discriminatory treatment and other negative workplace features to provide a more positive working environment and encourage the retention of older workers?

RECOMMENDED WEB SITE RESOURCES

Employee Assistance Professionals Association (www.eapassn.org). World's oldest and largest membership organization for employee assistance professionals, with approximately 5,000 members in the United States and more than thirty other countries. Hosts an annual conference, publishes the *Journal of Employee Assistance,* and offers training and other resources to enhance the skills and success of its members and the stature of the employee assistance profession.

European Agency for Safety and Health at Work http://europe.osha.eu.int/legislation). Presents information on several EU directives, standards, and guidelines for protecting the health and safety of Europe's workers.

Human Rights Watch (http://hrw.org). Independent NGO with headquarters in New York and offices throughout the world, dedicated to exposing abuses and protecting human rights around the world, including in work situations. For current international initiatives related to worker rights, health, and safety click Global Issues, then Labor & Human Rights.

International Confederation of Free Trade Unions (www.icftu.org). Provides current worldwide news and information on global trade union concerns and activities related to worker and trade union rights, labor standards, child labor, and health and safety at work. Provides detailed information to assist local union organization and development across industries and trade sectors, as well as to facilitate multi-union collaboration across national boundaries in support of worker issues and to counter the influence of MNCs.

International Industrial Relations Association (www.ilo.org/public/english/iira). Sponsored by the ILO, promotes the study of industrial and employee relations throughout the world through conferences, publications, member online networking, and study groups.

International Labour Organization (www.ilo.org/public/english/standards/norm). Answers five basic questions about the ILO's original function since 1919 on developing and promoting globally a system of international labor standards: what are they, how are they enforced, why are they needed, where do they come from, how are they used. Click "sitemap" to find specific information related to such areas as child and forced labor, industrial relations, worker safety and health, and protection of women workers.

Labor and Industrial Relations Networks (www.orcinc.com). ORC's labor and industrial relations network offer member companies the chance to share best practices, discuss on-going issues of labor and industrial relations, and focus on common concerns. These groups are multi-industry.

NOTES

1. P. Lewis, A. Thornhill, and M. Saunders, *Employee Relations: Understanding the Employment Relationship* (New York: Prentice-Hall/Financial Times, 2003).

2. "A Global Alliance against Forced Labor: Global Report under the Follow-up to the ILO Declaration on Fundamental Principles and Rights at Work," ILO Report I (B) (International Labour Conference, 93rd Session, International Labour Office, Geneva, 2005).

3. Ibid.

4. S. Hamm and M. Herbst, "America's High-Tech Sweatshops," *BusinessWeek,* October 12, 2009.

5. Ibid.

6. M. Chooki, "300 South Asian Workers among 10,000 in Forced Labor in U.S.," *News India-Times* 35 (42) (2004): 12.

7. K. Beegle, R. Dehejia, and R. Gatti, "Why Should We Care About Child Labor? The Education, Labor Market, and Health Consequences of Child Labor," *Journal of Human Resources* 44 (4) (2009): 871–89.

8. "A Future without Child Labour: Global Report under the Follow-up to the ILO Declaration on Fundamental Principles and Rights at Work," ILO Report I (B) (International Labour Conference, 90th Session, International Labour Office Geneva, 2002).

9. G. Melloan, "Workers of the World Are Shedding Their Chains," *Wall Street Journal*, September 3, 2002.

10. S. Chakrabarty and U. Grote, "Child Labor in Carpet Weaving: Impact of Social Labeling in India and Nepal," *World Development* 37 (10) (2009): 1683–93. T. Donaldson, "Values in Tension: Ethics away from Home," *Harvard Business Review* (September/October 1996): 48–62; T. Donaldson, *Ethics of International Business* (New York: Oxford University Press, 1989).

11. For example, refer to J. Arcand and B. D'hombres, "Racial Discrimination in the Brazilian Labour Market: Wage, Employment and Segregation Effects," *Journal of International Development* 16 (8) (2004): 1053–67; O. Omar and V. Ogenyi, "A Qualitative Evaluation of Women as Managers in the Nigerian Civil Service," *International Journal of Public Sector Management* 17 (4/5) (2004): 360–73; M. Tataryn, "Attitudes That Don't Work," *Women & Environments International Magazine* (66/67) (2005): 21–24; K. Gomm, "EU Ageism Law Could Put an End to 'Milk Round' Campus Recruitment," *Computer Weekly*, February 1, 2005.

12. Anonymous, "Sex Discrimination Goes Cross-Border," *Lawyer* 28 (June 2004): 4.

13. H.C. Jain, P.J. Sloane, and F.M Horwitz, *Employment Equity and Affirmative Action: An International Comparison* (Armonk, NY: M.E. Sharpe, 2003); C. Selvarajah, "Equal Employment Opportunity: Acculturation Experience of Immigrant Medical Professionals in New Zealand in the Period 1995 to 2000," *Equal Opportunities International* 23 (6) (2004): 50–73; S. Sudeshna, "Nepal: Indian Teachers Protest Alleged Discrimination," *News India-Times* 35 (51) (2004): 18.

14. S. Prasun, "Racism Hampering Foreign Nurses' Promotion: British Study," *News India-Times* 35 (31) (2004): 16.

15. International Confederation of Free Trade Unions 2002 Statement on "World Health Day," http://www.icftu.org.

16. J. Takala, "Life and Health Are Fundamental Rights for Workers," http://www.ilo.org/public/english/region/eurpro/moscow/areas/safety/docs/takala.pdf.

17. S. Baldauf, "Bhopal Gas Tragedy Lives on, 20 Years Later: Evidence of Contaminated Water in Indian City Mounts," *Christian Science Monitor*, May 4, 2004; G.D. Brown, "The Global Threats to Workers' Health and Safety on the Job," *Social Justice* 29 (3) (2002): 12–25.

18. B. Champ, "The Safety Culture Revolution: Making It Happen," *Canadian Chemical News* 49 (1997): 12.

19. Anonymous, "One CEO's Nightmare: Bhopal Ghosts (still) Haunt Union Carbide," *Fortune*, April 3, 2000: 44–46.

20. J. Evans, "Jobs and Globalization: Promise or Threat," *OECD Observer* 249 (2005): 23.

21. Y. Zhu and M. Warner, "Changing Chinese Employment Relations since WTO Accession," *Personnel Review* 34 (3) (2005): 354–70.

22. I.H. Chow, "The Impact of Institutional Context on Human Resource Management in Three Chinese Societies," *Employee Relations* 26 (6) (2004): 626–42.

23. T. Royle, "Multinational Corporations, Employers' Associations and Trade Union Exclusion Strategies in the German Fast-Food Industry," *Employee Relations* 4 (24) (2002): 437–60.

24. R. Welfrod, "Corporate Social Responsibility in Europe, North America and Asia: 2004 Survey Results," *Journal of Corporate Citizenship* 17 (2005): 33–52; B.W. Fraser, "Corporate Social Responsibility," *Internal Auditor* 62 (1) (2005): 42–47.

25. J. Birchall, "Walmart Case Set to Go to Trial," *Financial Times*, April 27, 2010; L. Featherstone, *Selling Women Short: The Landmark Battle for Workers' Rights at Wal-Mart* (New York: Basic Books, 2004).

26. A.K. Baumle, "Statistical Discrimination in Employment: Its Practice, Conceptualization, and Implications for Public Policy," *American Behavioral Scientist* 48 (9) (2005): 1250–74.

27. S. Greenhouse, "Wal-Mart to Pay U.S. $11 Million in Lawsuit on Immigrant Workers," *New York Times*, March 19, 2005.

28. I.A. Jackson, and J. Nelson, "Values-Driven Performance: Seven Strategies for Delivering Profits with Principles," *Ivey Business Journal Online* (November 1, 2004): http://www.allbusiness.com/company-activities-management/company-structures/13481497–1.html; S.J. Spear, "Workplace

Safety at Alcoa (B)," Harvard Business School Case No. 9–600–068 (Boston: Harvard Business School Publishing, 2000).

29. L. Hope and K. Mearns, "Managing Health Risks in the Offshore Workplace: Impact on Health Climate, Safety Climate and Risk Identification," *International Journal of Risk Assessment and Management* 7 (2) (2007): 152–164.

30. D.A. Hofmann and F.P. Morgenson, "Safety-Related Behavior as a Social Exchange: The Role of Perceived Organizational Support and Leader-Member Exchange," *Journal of Applied Psychology* 84 (1999): 286–96.

31. S. Smith, "America's Safest Companies: Alcoa: Finding True North," *Occupational Hazards* 64 (10) (2002): 53.

32. H. Liao, R.D. Arvey, and R.J. Butler, "Correlates of Work Injury Frequency and Duration among Firefighters," *Journal of Occupational Health Psychology* 6 (3) (2001): 229–42; S. Graham, "Debunk the Myths about Older Workers," *Safety & Health* (January 1996): 38–41; F. Siskind, "Another Look at the Link between Work Injuries and Job Experience," *Monthly Labor Review* 105 (2) (1982): 38–40.

33. B.W. Fraser, "Corporate Social Responsibility," *Internal Auditor* 62 (1) (2005): 42–47; A.I. Goldman, "Mattel to Report on Factory Conditions: The Firm Today Will Offer New Details on Overseas Plant Problems and How It's Addressing Them," *Los Angeles Times*, October 12, 2004.

34. E. Hood, "Lessons Learned? Chemical Plant Safety Since Bhopal," *Environmental Health Perspectives* 112 (6) (2004): 352–9; B. Mohler, "Sharing Lessons Learned," *Occupational Hazards* 66 (9) (2004): 57–59.

35. Hope and Mearns, "Managing Health Risks in the Offshore Workplace: Impact on Health Climate, Safety Climate and Risk Identification"; D. Smith, "For Whom the Bell Tolls: Imagining Accidents and the Development of Crisis Simulation in Organizations," *Simulation & Gaming* 35 (3) (2004): 347–62; J. Pulling, "Companies Find Success through Wellness Programs," *State Journal* 21 (23) (2005): 5.

36. D. Cadrain, "Workplace Safety's Ergonomic Twist," *HR Magazine* (October 2002): 43–47.

37. J.M. Stewart, "The Turnaround in Safety at the Kenora Pulp & Paper Mill," *Professional Safety* 46 (12) (2001): 34–44.

38. C. McGuire, "Hidden Tragedies: Are Workplace Injuries and Illnesses Being Underreported? *Safety Compliance Letter* (2493) (September 8, 2008): 1–4,6,13; D. Zohar, "Modifying Supervisory Practices to Improve Subunit Safety: A Leadership-Based Intervention Model," *Journal of Applied Psychology* 87 (2002): 156–63; R.M. Yandrick, "Behavioral Safety Helps Shipbuilder Cut Accident Rates," *HR News* (February 1996): 3, 11; W.G. Pardy, *Safety Incentives: The Pros and Cons of Award and Recognition Systems* (Jacksonville, FL: Moran Associates, 1999); E.S. Geller, "The Truth about Safety Incentives," *Professional Safety* (October 1996): 34–39; Anonymous, "Safety Award for BHEL," *Businessline*, June 8, 2005: 1.

39. A. Blyth, "Support Pays Off," *Personnel Today*, July 5, 2005; G. Gonzalez, "Canadian EAPs Making a Comeback," *Business Insurance* 39 (25) (2005): 26; K.M. Quinley, "EAPs: A Benefit That Can Trim Your Disability and Absenteeism Costs," *Compensation & Benefits Report* 17 (2) (2003): 6–7.

40. E.A. Grant, "How to Retain Talent in India," *Sloan Management Review* 50 (1) 2008: 6–7; B.S. Reiche, "The Effect of International Staffing Practices on Subsidiary Staff Retention in Multinational Corporations," *International Journal of Human Resource Management* 18 (4) (2007): 523–36.

41. R. Levering and M. Moskowitz, "10 Great Companies to Work For," *Fortune* European Edition 151 (1) (2005): 28; P. Lewis, A. Thornhill, and M. Saunders, *Employee Relations: Understanding the Employment Relationship* (New York: Prentice-Hall/Financial Times, 2003).

42. T. Dundon, A. Wilkinson, M. Marchington, and P. Ackers, "The Management of Voice in Non-Union Organizations: Managers' Perspectives," *Employee Relations* 27 (3) (2005): 307–19; L.Soupata, "Engaging Employees in Company Success: The UPS Approach to a Winning Team," *Human Resource Management* 44 (1) (2005): 95–98; R. Cropanzano, H. Aguinis, M. Schminke, and D.L. Denham, "Disputant Reactions to Managerial Conflict Resolution Tactics: A Comparison among Argentina, the Dominican Republic, Mexico, and the United States," *Group and Organization Management* 24 (1999): 124–54; M. Buckingham and C. Coffman, *First, Break All the Rules: What the World's Greatest Managers Do Differently* (New York: Simon & Schuster, 1999).

43. J.W. Budd, *Labor Relations: Striking a Balance* (Burr Ridge, IL: McGraw-Hill/Irwin, 2005); H. Katz and T.A. Kochan, *An Introduction to Collective Bargaining and Industrial Relations*, 3d ed. (Burr Ridge, IL: McGraw-Hill/Irwin, 2004); A.J.S. Colvin, "Institutional Pressures, Human Resource Strategies, and the Rise of Nonunion Dispute Resolution Procedures," *Industrial and Labor Relations Review* 56 (2003): 375–92.

44. M. Marchington and A. Wilkinson, *People Management and Development: Human Resource Management at Work*, 2d ed. (Wimbledon, UK: Chartered Institute of Personnel and Development, 2002).

45. J.T. Arnold, "Twittering and Facebooking While They Work," *HR Magazine* 54 (12) (2009): 53–55; R. Connell, "Another Red-Light Probe for Metrolink," *Los Angeles Times*, December 2, 2009; C. Borchert, "Killing Time Electronically," *Canadian Underwriter* 75 (6) (2008): 66–67; M. Segalla, "An International Study of Dysfunctional E-Mail Usage and Attitudes Among Managers," *International Journal of Human Resources Development and Management* 5 (4) (2005): 425–36.

46. Arnold, "Twittering and Facebooking While They Work"; J. Sample, "The Compelling Argument for Harassment Prevention Training: Implications for Instructional Designers," *Performance Improvement* 46 (7) (2007): 18–26.

47. W.F. Casio, *Managing Human Resources: Productivity, Quality of Work Life, Profits*, 7th ed. (Boston: McGraw-Hill/Irwin, 2006); A.N. Jacobs, "An Instant Message from the Supreme Court: Are You Listening?" *Employment Source Newsletter*, July 27, 2004, http://www.epexperts.com.

48. P. Anderson and M. Pulich, "A Positive Look at Progressive Discipline," *Health Care Manager* 20 (1) (2001): 1–8; P. Falcone, "A Blueprint for Progressive Discipline and Terminations," *Human Resources Focus* 77 (8) (2000): 3–5.

49. H.L. Moore, "Discipline + Help = Motivation," *Credit Union Management* 21 (8) (1998): 33–35.

50. For current developments and recommendations, refer to the HR Technology Exchange Forum of the Society for Human Resource Management available at www.shrm.org/hrtx.

51. *Advisory, Conciliation, and Arbitration Services, Code of Practice No. 1: Disciplinary and Grievance Procedures* (London: ACAS, 2000).

52. D.R. Briscoe and R.S. Schuler, *International Human Resource Management: Policy and Practice for the Global Enterprise*, 2d ed. (London: Routledge, 2004).

53. Lewis et al., *Employee Relations: Understanding the Employment Relationship*.

54. N. Doherty, "The Role of Outplacement in Redundancy Management," *Personnel Review* 27 (4) (1998): 343–53.

55. P. Dvorak, "Theory & Practice: Firms Shift Underused Workers—Employees Gain Skills, Training as Companies Assign Them to New Tasks," *Wall Street Journal*, June 22, 2009; C. Zatzick, M. Marks, and R. Iverson, R., "Which Way Should You Downsize in a Crisis?" *MIT Sloan Management Review* 51 (1) (2009): 79–86; A. Fox, "Avoiding Furlough Fallout," *HR Magazine* 54 (9) (2009): 37–40; H. De Witte, J. Vandoorne, R. Verlinden, and N. De Cyyper, "Outplacement and Re-Employment Measures during Organizational Restructuring in Belgium: Overview of the Literature and Results of Qualitative Research," *Journal of European Industrial Training* 29 (2/3) (2005): 148–66; Lewis et al., *Employee Relations: Understanding the Employment Relationship*.

56. Fox, "Avoiding Furlough Fallout."

57. N. Shirouzu and K. Linebaugh, "Toyota Keeps Idled Workers Busy Honing Their Skills," *Wall Street Journal*, October 13, 2008.

58. N. Paulsen, V.J. Callan, T.A. Grice, D. Rooney, C. Gallois, E. Jones, N.L. Jimmieson, and P. Bordia, "Job Uncertainty and Personal Control during Downsizing: A Comparison of Survivors and Victims," *Human Relations* 58 (4) (2005): 463–96; W.M. Glenn, "Downsizing or Wrongsizing?" *OH & S Canada* 21 (2) (2005): 84–85; A. Mantica, "New Workplace Hazard: Survivor Syndrome," *Prevention* 56 (9) (2004): 52; K. Sahdev, "Revisiting the Survivor Syndrome: The Role of Leadership in Implementing Downsizing," *European Journal of Work and Organizational Psychology* 13 (2): 165–96.

59. C. Reade and M.R. McKenna, "Seeding the Clouds for Industrial Relations Climate Change in Emerging Economies," *Thunderbird International Business Review* 51 (2) (2009): 125–41; M.

Rothman, D. Briscoe, and R. Nacamulli, eds., *Industrial Relations around the World* (Berlin: Walter de Gruyter, 1993).

60. M. Nham, "The Right to Strike or the Freedom to Strike: Can Either Interpretation Improve Working Conditions in China?" *The George Washington International Law Review* 39 (4) (2007): 919–45; B. Baugh, "Respecting Chinese Workers' Rights Makes Moral and Economic Sense," *World Trade* 17 (6) (2004): 10–11.

61. J.P. Azam and C. Salmon, "Strikes and Political Activism of Trade Unions: Theory and Application to Bangladesh," *Public Choice Leiden* 119 (3/4) (2004): 311–34; H.N. Wheeler, *The Future of the American Labor Movement* (New York: Cambridge University Press, 2002); G.J. Bamber and R.D. Lansbury, eds., *International and Comparative Employment Relations*, 3d ed. (London: Sage, 1998).

62. T. Aidt and Z. Tzannatos, *Unions and Collective Bargaining: Economic Effects in a Global Environment* (Washington, DC: World Bank, 2002).

63. Rory O'Neill, "When It Comes to Health and Safety, Your Life Should Be in Union Hands," http://www.hazards.org/unioneffect/unioneffect.pdf.

64. S.L. Thomas and J. Best, "Work Teams and Unions: Keeping Employee Involvement Legal," *Business* 26 (3/4) (2003): 4–13; H. Movassaghi, "The Workers of Nations: Industrial Relations in a Global Economy," *Compensation and Benefits Management* 12 (2) (1996): 75–77.

65. D. Bacon, "Globalization: Two Faces, Both Ugly," *Dollars and Sense* (March/April 2000): 18–20.

66. "Research in the Sociology of Work," in *Labor Revitalization: Global Perspectives and New Initiatives* 11, ed. D.B. Cornfield and H.J. McCammon (Stamford, CT: JAI Press, 2003); S. Kuruvilla, S. Das, H. Kwon, and S. Kwon, "Trade Union Growth and Decline in Asia," *British Journal of Industrial Relations* 40 (3) (2002): 431–61.

67. M.D. Yates, "The 'New' Economy and the Labor Movement," *Monthly Review* 52 (11) (2001): 28–42.

68. J. Chazyn, "Workers 'Satisfied' in the U.S. and Europe," *International Herald Tribune*, October 5, 2007: 2.

69. R. Levering and M. Moskowitz, "The 100 Best Companies to Work for," *Fortune* 147 (1) (2003): 127–52; E. May, "Are People Your Priority? How to Engage Your Workforce," *Healthcare Executive* 19 (4) (2004): 8–15.

70. R. Kaku, "The Path of Kyosei," *Harvard Business Review* (July/August 1997): 55–63.

71. G. Gall, "Organizing Non-Union Workers as Trade Unionists in the 'New Economy' in Britain," *Economic and Industrial Democracy* 26 (1) (2005): 41–63; R.J. Flanagan, "Has Management Strangled US Unions?" *Journal of Labor Research* 24 (1) (2005): 33–64.

72. K. Scipes, "Labor Imperialism Redux? The AFL-CIO's Foreign Policy since 1995," *Monthly Review* 57 (1) (2005): 23–36.

73. G. Melloan, "Workers of the World are Shedding Their Chains," *Wall Street Journal*, September 3, 2002.

74. C. Welz and T. Kauppinen, "Industrial Action and Conflict Resolution in the New Member States," *European Journal of Industrial Relations* 11 (1) (2005): 91–105; P. Fairbrother and G. Griffin, eds., *Changing Prospects for Trade Unionism: Comparisons between Six Countries (London: Continuum, 2002).*

75. J. Gennard, "A New Emerging Trend? Cross Border Trade Union Mergers," *Employee Relations* 31 (1) 2009: 5–8; J. Harrod and R. O'Brien, *Global Unions? Theory and Strategies of Organized Labour in the Global Political Economy* (London: Routledge, 2002).

76. "French, US, and Canadian Workers to Hold Common Day of Action at Saint-Gobain Worksites," *UAW News*, June 9, 2003, http://www.uaw.com/news/newsarticle.cfm?ArtId=199.

77. K. Carr, "Workers Face Same Challenge the World Over," New South Wales Teachers Confederation, http://www.nswtf.org.au/edu_online/68/samest.html; Anonymous, "Worldwide Union Set to Fight for Staff Rights," *Personnel Today*, December 14, 2004.

Name Index

Italic page references indicate boxed text, charts, and graphs.

Subject Index

About the Authors

Charles M. Vance is a professor of management and human resources at Loyola Marymount University in Los Angeles, and has considerable experience in the United States and abroad teaching at executive, MBA, and undergraduate levels. He has a PhD from Syracuse University, and has considerable experience as a consultant in training design and curriculum development and broader human resource development applications for many corporations and nonprofit organizations in Asia, North and South America, and Europe. His clients have included Boeing, FedEx, Mattel, Northrop Grumman, Texaco, China-Europe International Business School, *Los Angeles Times,* American Management Association, U.S. Department of Labor, Akademie für Internationale Bildung, Fresenius Kabi, and Catholic University of Uruguay. In 2005 and 2006 Vance held double Fulbright teaching and research appointments in Austria and China. He has two other books, *Mastering Management Education* (Sage) and *Smart Talent Management* (Edward Elgar), and recent publications in such journals as *Journal of World Business, Academy of Management Learning and Education, Human Resource Management, International Journal of Human Resource Management, Thunderbird International Business Review, International Journal of Cross Cultural Management, Journal of Small Business Management, Journal of Managerial Psychology,* and *Journal of Business Ethics.*

Yongsun Paik is a professor of international business and management at Loyola Marymount University in Los Angeles. He holds a PhD in International Business from the University of Washington and a Master's in Latin American Studies from the University of Texas, Austin. He served as country economist at the Export-Import Bank of Korea between 1979 and 1984. He was awarded a Fulbright grant for his appointment at Yonsei University in Korea during spring 2005. His primary research interests focus on international human resource management, global strategic alliances, and Asian Pacific business studies. He has published a book, *The Changing Face of Korean Management* (co-edited with Chris Rowley), and over forty articles in major international business and management journals such as *Journal of International Business Studies, Journal of World Business, Academy of Management Executive, Academy of Management Learning and Education, Journal of Business Ethics, Management International Review, Journal of International Management, Business Horizons, International Journal of Human Resource Management,* and *Journal of Management Inquiry.* He is currently an editorial board member of *Journal of World Business, Thunderbird International Business Review,* and other journals.